"Standing athwart the tide of st                             lon
confidence in the truthfulness a                            ıme
constitute a defense of historic                           ıre.
Mercifully, however, they are not mere regurgitations of pa         are
informed, competent, and sometimes creative contributions that urgently deserve the
widest circulation. In months and years to come, I shall repeatedly refer students and
pastors to this collection."

**D. A. Carson,** Research Professor of New Testament,
Trinity Evangelical Divinity School

"Few Christian convictions are of as pervasive importance as the absolute perfection of
Scripture—and few convictions fall under more perennial criticism. Hence the need for
this volume, which seeks to defend the evangelical doctrine of biblical inerrancy against
scholars who argue that in accommodating his truth to human understanding, God has
made his Word susceptible to error. Here James Hoffmeier, Dennis Magary, and a broad
range of learned colleagues take seriously the self-witness of Scripture and respond to
some of the latest, hardest objections to inerrancy by providing clear, comprehensive,
persuasive, and charitable answers. *Do Historical Matters Matter to Faith?* is an invalu-
able resource for any student of Scripture who doubts the doctrine of inerrancy or has
serious questions about the historical reliability of the Bible."

**Philip G. Ryken,** President, Wheaton College

"Whether in a university open forum or in the church, I am consistently asked about the
trustworthiness and authority of Scripture. I am therefore delighted that the authors
have engaged the critics' challenge as well as the Bible afresh and met the arguments
head-on with insightful scholarship and the historicity of Scripture. I commend this
unique and timely volume and believe it will be an important work for decades to come."

**Ravi Zacharias,** Founder and President, Ravi Zacharias International Ministries;
author, *Jesus Among Other Gods*

"To scholars unconvinced of the classical Christian doctrine of Holy Scripture, *Do
Historical Matters Matter to Faith?* offers a challenge both substantive in its argumentation and respectful in its tone. To scholars convinced of this doctrine, this volume
models how to advance the argument on a multidisciplinary, evidentialist basis. We owe
the editors and authors a debt of gratitude."

**Ray Ortlund,** Lead Pastor, Immanuel Church, Nashville, Tennessee

"The debate over biblical inerrancy is a crucial issue for evangelicals. *Do Historical
Matters Matter to Faith?* is an important response to this challenge, and its essays,
written by leading evangelical scholars, present a robust defense of the reliability of the
historical narratives of the Bible. The book makes a compelling case that holding to
inerrancy does not mean one must avoid examining the issues raised by critical scholarship, but rather the accuracy of Scripture can itself be the conclusion of a reasoned and
critical examination of the evidence."

**Michelle Lee-Barnewall,** Associate Professor of Biblical and Theological Studies,
Biola University; author, *Paul, the Stoics, and the Body of Christ*

"This is a book that has been sorely needed. The Bible has long been under attack from those outside evangelical faith, and now more recently from those supposedly inside. Here in one volume the questions are addressed in a comprehensive way, including theological, historical-critical, and archaeological issues. Written with an irenic tone—and yet confronting the questions directly—this book will surely take a prominent place on the shelves of all those who love the Bible and look for solid answers to give to its detractors. The editors are to be commended for bringing the book to fruition and for their breadth of vision in organizing it."

**John Oswalt,** Distinguished Professor of Old Testament,
Asbury Theological Seminary

"James Hoffmeier and Dennis Magary have assembled a first-rate team of evangelical writers to join them in exploring the historical issues related to the interpretation of Holy Scripture and the formation of Christian theology. Each chapter makes a significant contribution to this comprehensive and focused volume—which both affirms and defends the complete truthfulness and full authority of the Bible while fully engaging the questions and challenges raised by modern and postmodern approaches to biblical interpretation. Informative and winsome, this impressive work will be immensely helpful for a generation of students, pastors, and scholars alike."

**David S. Dockery,** President, Union University

"How evangelicals view the Bible has been, and continues to be, under attack. This volume effectively defends the Bible's historicity and adeptly explains why it matters. Any pastor or person teaching and defending the Bible will be greatly helped by this book."

**Alistair Begg,** Senior Pastor, Parkside Church, Cleveland, Ohio

"Today, some so-called evangelicals have questioned and outright denied the full extent of the inerrancy, authority, and trustworthiness of God's Word, claiming it may apply to faith and practice but not to history and science. As disturbing as these claims are against the Scriptures, I give thanks to God that they have prompted an excellent response, so that we now have a much stronger foundation for affirming the inerrancy of God's Word, including matters of history. *Do Historical Matters Matter to Faith?* is one of the best and most thorough treatments in defense of the Bible as completely true and trustworthy in the realm of history. It is a much-needed antidote to some so-called evangelicals' unhealthy (and inaccurate) view of inerrancy. In matters relating to the doctrine of the Scriptures, this will be the book I recommend to pastors and leaders. It will serve them and the church well, and deserves the highest of commendations!"

**Gregory C. Strand,** Director of Biblical Theology and Credentialing,
Evangelical Free Church of America

"Here is a collection of first-rate essays written by an international team of scholars, each affirming what must be called the historic Christian view of Holy Scripture—that the Bible, God's Word written, is trustworthy and totally true in all that it affirms. Rather than simply rehearsing platitudes of the past, this volume advances the argument in the light of current debate and recent challenges. A magisterial undertaking to be reckoned with."

**Timothy George,** Founding Dean, Beeson Divinity School;
General Editor, *Reformation Commentary on Scripture*

"In recent decades evangelicals have felt increasing pressure to abandon their high views of Scripture—a pressure that comes not only from scholars outside their circles, but also from some inside. This volume represents a welcome response to both, but especially to the latter. The contributors represent evangelical scholarship at its best as they address critical challenges with clarity and conviction, even while keeping their tone civil and charitable. This book will serve as a handy reference tool for students, pastors, and scholars who need a fair and responsible treatment of the evidence and clear declaration of their conclusions."

**Daniel I. Block,** Gunther H. Knoedler Professor of Old Testament, Wheaton College; author, *The Gospel according to Moses: Theological and Ethical Reflections on the Book of Deuteronomy*

"Twenty-first-century hubris insists on immediate answers from a Book of great antiquity that is fundamentally about God's intervention in human history. Yet even with advances in scientific archaeological method and modern scholarship, there is still much to learn about the Bible's ancient setting, language, history, and sociopolitical context. This book engages honestly with a number of thorny issues concerning the history and evidence for key biblical narratives. Its propositions are robustly defended in a clear yet scholarly fashion, making it accessible to informed lay and academic readers alike. I commend it to anyone seeking an orthodox evangelical perspective on the flash points in current debates about the historicity of the Scriptures."

**Karin Sowada,** CEO, Anglican Deaconess Ministries Ltd.; Hon. Research Associate, Macquarie University

"Singapore Bible College was founded in 1952 to uphold the authority of God's Word when the Scriptures were under severe attack from the liberals of that era. Today, we are a living testimony to the effectiveness and authority of God's Word as we expound a Bible-based theological education. The mocking of the Word of God did not liberate people from what the liberals claimed to be superstition or outdated scholarship. But it did destroy the faith of many poorly grounded believers, confused the church concerning her mission and purpose, created tension in the mission field, and set the church backward on many fronts in Asia and elsewhere. James Hoffmeier and Dennis Magary have assembled an able team of evangelical scholars to address and defend the issues of the authority of God's Word from theological, biblical, and archaeological perspectives. They are not afraid to face the issues head-on in a comprehensive and thorough manner, yet with the right spirit. I hope this book will help many students of the Scriptures to have a deeper conviction of the authoritative and inerrant Word of God."

**Albert Ting,** Principal, Singapore Bible College

"This volume well documents the analysis and evidence integral to understanding the role of historical data in biblical understanding. The authors are to be congratulated for writing a book that would withstand rigorous cross-examination!"

**Mark Lanier,** President, Christian Trial Lawyers Association; author of numerous legal books and articles; owner, Lanier Theological Library

"To the credit of its editors and authors, this book is not so much a *reaction* to the recent statements of Peter Enns and Kenton Sparks on biblical inerrancy, which called it forth, but an *apologetic response* to their works. To that effect, it is not a monument to the doctrine, but rather an advancement of its method and intent."

C. Hassell Bullock, Pastor, Warren Park Presbyterian Church, Cicero, Illinois;
Franklin S. Dyrness Professor of Biblical Studies Emeritus, Wheaton College

"This is a timely work, both in the sense that it addresses an emerging issue—a loss of confidence in the historicity of the Bible—and in the sense that its authors are conversant in the current state of the debate. The topics discussed include all the essentials: the foundational theological issues, the major source-critical and historical-critical questions, and matters arising from archaeology. This book will be a valuable resource for both scholars and students."

Duane A. Garrett, Professor of Old Testament,
The Southern Baptist Theological Seminary;
author, *A Modern Grammar for Biblical Hebrew* and *Amos:
A Handbook on the Hebrew Text*

"This is a brilliant response to evangelical skeptics such as Peter Enns and Kenton Sparks, and, in a broader sense, also to mainstream skeptics such as Philip Davies, Keith Whitelam, or Robert Coote. The list of contributors is a stellar lineup of first-rate scholars in their disciplines who defend the traditional, orthodox view of Scripture as historically reliable in sophisticated and convincing ways. Even those who might remain unconvinced of the book's main argument will have to rethink their positions. I highly recommend this work."

David M. Howard Jr., Professor of Old Testament,
Bethel University, St. Paul, Minnesota

"This book takes us to the front lines of many of the contemporary confrontations in critical scholarship, addressing the skeptics head-on. A host of able defenders contend for the trustworthiness of the Bible in the face of critical challenges and fairly criticize some of the 'assured results' of biblical criticism—opening the way for a more confident faith. Only the Holy Spirit himself can fully confirm the truth of God's Word, but he can use books like this to confound the doubter and affirm the faithful."

Bill Kynes, Senior Pastor, Cornerstone Evangelical Free Church, Annandale, Virginia;
author, *A Christology of Solidarity*

"This is a thoughtful and heartening response to Sparks and other progressive evangelicals who believe the time has come to move beyond what they perceive to be an outdated view of Scripture's inerrancy. Those seeking to rightly handle the word of truth (2 Tim. 2:15) will find here methodological, philosophical, theological, archaeological, and geographical resources for navigating the historical context of Scripture that call attention to its divine origins. Hoffmeier and Magary have provided a great service to the academy and church in this scholarly compilation of evangelical writers who conserve the tradition of the plenary inspiration and inerrancy of the Old and New Testament Scriptures. *Soli Deo gloria*."

Laura C. Miguélez, Adjunct Professor of Theology, Wheaton College

# DO HISTORICAL MATTERS MATTER TO FAITH?

## A CRITICAL APPRAISAL OF MODERN AND POSTMODERN APPROACHES TO SCRIPTURE

EDITED BY

### JAMES K. HOFFMEIER AND DENNIS R. MAGARY

FOREWORD BY

### JOHN D. WOODBRIDGE

::: CROSSWAY

WHEATON, ILLINOIS

*Do Historical Matters Matter to Faith?*
*A Critical Appraisal of Modern and Postmodern Approaches to Scripture*

Copyright © 2012 by James K. Hoffmeier and Dennis R. Magary
Published by Crossway
        1300 Crescent Street
        Wheaton, Illinois 60187

Cover design: Tobias' Outerwear for Books
Cover image: Getty Images
Interior design and typesetting: Lakeside Design Plus

First printing 2012
Printed in the United States of America

Unless otherwise indicated, Scripture quotations are from the ESV® Bible (*The Holy Bible, English Standard Version*®), copyright © 2001 by Crossway. Used by permission. All rights reserved.

Scripture quotations marked KJV are from the King James Version of the Bible.

Scripture quotations marked NASB are from *The New American Standard Bible*®. Copyright © The Lockman Foundation 1960, 1962, 1963, 1968, 1971, 1972, 1973, 1975, 1977, 1995. Used by permission.

Scripture quotations marked NIV are from the *Holy Bible, New International Version*®. Copyright © 1973, 1978, 1984 Biblica. Used by permission of Zondervan. All rights reserved. The "NIV" and "New International Version" trademarks are registered in the United States Patent and Trademark Office by Biblica. Use of either trademark requires the permission of Biblica.

Scripture quotations marked NRSV are from *The New Revised Standard Version*. Copyright © 1989 by the Division of Christian Education of the National Council of the Churches of Christ in the U.S.A. Published by Thomas Nelson, Inc. Used by permission of the National Council of the Churches of Christ in the U.S.A.

Scripture quotations marked TNIV are taken from the Holy Bible, *Today's New International Version*. TNIV®. Copyright © 2001, 2005 by International Bible Society. Used by permission of Zondervan. All rights reserved.

All emphases in Scripture quotations have been added by the authors.

| | |
|---|---|
| Trade paperback ISBN: | 978-1-4335-2571-1 |
| ePub ISBN: | 978-1-4335-2574-2 |
| PDF ISBN: | 978-1-4335-2572-8 |
| Mobipocket ISBN: | 978-1-4335-2573-5 |

**Library of Congress Cataloging-in-Publication Data**
      Do historical matters matter to faith? : a critical appraisal of modern and postmodern approaches to
   Scripture / edited by James K. Hoffmeier and Dennis R. Magary ; foreword by John D. Woodbridge.
         p. cm.
      Includes bibliographical references and index.
      ISBN 978-1-4335-2571-1 (tp)
        1. Bible—History of biblical events. 2. Bible—Evidences, authority, etc. I. Hoffmeier, James Karl, 1951–
   II. Magary, Dennis Robert, 1951–
   BS635.D56 2012
   220.6—dc23

                                        2011037802

Crossway is a publishing ministry of Good News Publishers.

| SH | 24 | 23 | 22 | 21 | 20 | 19 | 18 | 17 | 16 | 15 | 14 | 13 | 12 |
|----|----|----|----|----|----|----|----|----|----|----|----|----|----|
| 14 | 13 | 12 | 11 | 10 | 9 | 8 | 7 | 6 | 5 | 4 | 3 | 2 | 1 |

*In Memory of Donald J. Wiseman*
*October 1918–February 2010*

# CONTENTS

# FOREWORD

## JOHN D. WOODBRIDGE

Most of us like invitations to consider fresh opportunities. The present book constitutes a winsome invitation for its readers to consider a very significant claim: the Bible's historical narratives are trustworthy. The narratives correspond to what happened in real time and in real places.

The opportunity is "fresh" especially for those readers who doubt the reliability of Scripture's historical accounts. The invitation suggests that they should take a second look at the claim that the Bible's historical narratives are indeed trustworthy. This assertion has significant entailments for Christianity itself. Christians believe the bodily resurrection of Jesus Christ is at the heart of their faith. If the resurrection did not take place in real history, then as the apostle Paul wrote, our faith is groundless, and we are still in our sins: "If Christ has not been raised, then our preaching is in vain and your faith is in vain" (1 Cor. 15:14).

Within the last thirty or forty years, skepticism about the accuracy of the biblical documents has affected the ways scholars have pursued the academic study of the Israelite religion, Old Testament theology, and biblical theology.

To address this skepticism, Professors James Hoffmeier and Dennis Magary have assembled a group of distinguished scholars to tackle a good number of the "hard case" questions contributing to the prevalent skepticism in certain circles. Not only do these scholars take the questions seriously, but they also avoid offering contrived or beside-the-point responses to the queries. Readers are invited to assess for themselves whether the responses satisfactorily engage the matters under consideration.

The publication of Kenton Sparks's work *God's Word in Human Words* created the immediate occasion for the writing of *Do Historical Matters Matter to Faith?* In his book Professor Sparks, an accomplished scholar in his own right, offers a sustained critique of the doctrine of biblical inerrancy, particularly as it relates to the historical reliability of Scripture. Whereas some "higher critics" of Scripture never espoused the doctrine of biblical inerrancy, Sparks once upheld the belief. Now, with missionary zeal he hopes to persuade evangelical Christians who are inerrantists that they should follow his lead, adopt his thoughtful appropriation of higher criticism, and acknowledge that the Bible contains historical errors. From Sparks's point of view, these moves neither compromise a person's good standing as an evangelical Christian nor by implication undermine essential evangelical doctrines. Evangelical Christians should recognize, he insists, that reputable scholarship sustains his view that the biblical narratives are errant.

By contrast, the authors of the present book, a number of whom are world-class archaeologists, calmly extend the invitation by implication to Professor Sparks, and others, to reconsider the validity of his errancy proposal. There is a simple reason to do so. These scholars demonstrate that Sparks's arguments do not possess the persuasive power he attributes to them.

I would add that the witness of many Christians in the past indicates that Sparks's proposal is not as heuristic for evangelical theology as he imagines. He is not the first to defend the errancy position. In earlier ages Christian scholars often rejected equivalent versions of Sparks's proposal as perilous doctrinal innovations. These varieties of the errancy view departed from the Augustinian teaching about the Bible's complete infallibility (for faith and practice and history and science), which constituted the central church doctrine of the Western churches. For his part, Augustine did not countenance the idea of errors in Scripture. His viewpoint constituted standard church teaching for centuries. The Roman Catholic theologian Hans Küng observed, "St. Augustine's influence in regard to inspiration and inerrancy prevailed throughout the Middle Ages and right into the modern age."[1]

As late as the nineteenth century, the Roman Catholic Church formally defended the inerrancy of Scripture. In *Providentissimus Deus Encyclical of Pope Leo XIII on the Study of Holy Scripture* (Nov. 18, 1893), Leo XIII sharply criticized those who limited the inerrancy of Scripture to matters of faith and morals.

> But it is absolutely wrong and forbidden either to narrow inspiration to certain parts only of Holy Scripture, or to admit that the sacred writer has erred. For the system of those who, in order to rid themselves of these difficulties, do not hesitate to concede that divine inspiration regards the things of faith and morals, and nothing beyond, because (as they wrongly think) in a question of the truth or falsehood of a passage, we should consider not so much what God has said as the reason and purpose which He had in mind in saying it—this system cannot be tolerated.[2]

---

[1]Hans Küng, *Infallible? An Enquiry* (London: Collins, 1971), 174.
[2]Pope Leo XIII, *Providentissimus Deus*, sec. 18.

Later in the encyclical, he wrote, "It follows that those who maintain that an error is possible in any genuine passage of the sacred writings, either pervert the Catholic notion of inspiration, or make God the author of such error."[3] He cited passages from Augustine as Patristic warrants for his teaching.

Whereas Professor Sparks indicates that Scripture contains errors, in a letter (AD 405) to Faustus the Manichean, Augustine indicated that Scripture is "free from error."

> I confess to your Charity that I have learned to yield this respect and honor only to the canonical books of Scripture: of these alone do I most firmly believe that the authors were completely free from error. And if in these writings I am perplexed by anything which appears to me opposed to truth, I do not hesitate to suppose that either the manuscript is faulty, or the translator has not caught the meaning of what was said, or I myself have failed to understand.

Whereas Sparks believes there are no negative entailments for acknowledging the existence of errors in Scripture, Augustine proffered quite the contrary sentiment:

> It seems to me that the most disastrous consequences must follow upon our believing that anything false is found in the sacred books; that is to say that the men by whom the Scripture has been given to us and committed to writing, did put down in these books anything false. . . . If you once admit into such a high sanctuary of authority one false statement . . . , there will not be left a single sentence of those books, which, if appearing to any one difficult in practice or hard to believe, may not by the same fatal rule be explained away as a statement, in which intentionally, . . . the author declared what was not true.[4]

Whereas Sparks believed that it is not necessarily important to seek the careful harmonization of biblical texts, Augustine indicated that unbelievers used "contradictions" in an attempt to overthrow the Christian religion. In discussing the harmony of the Gospel accounts, Augustine averred:

> And in order to carry out this design to a successful conclusion, we must prove that the writers in question do not stand in any antagonism to each other. For those adversaries are in the habit of adducing this as the primary allegation in all their vain objections, namely that the evangelists are not in harmony with each other.[5]

---

[3] Ibid., sec. 25.
[4] Augustine, *Letters of St. Augustine* 28.3.
[5] Augustine, *Harmony of the Gospels* 1.7.10.

Like Professors Jack Rogers, Donald McKim, and Peter Enns, Professor Sparks mistakenly thinks that God accommodated Scripture to the faulty worldviews and perspectival human limitations of the biblical writers. Given the "human authorship" of Scripture, it necessarily contains errors. Sparks writes, "To attribute error to God is surely heresy, but to deny the errant human elements in Scripture may verge on a kind of docetism."[6] He advocates a form of "accommodation" but unwittingly identifies it with what Richard Muller and Glen Sunshine have labeled a Socinian doctrine. Socinian accommodation is quite a distinct teaching from the Augustinian doctrine of accommodation. For Augustine and those who followed his lead, such as John Calvin, God accommodated Scripture to the weakness of our understanding, not to the potentially errant cosmologies of the biblical writers. Thus Scripture is written in the language of appearance—the way we see things. Scripture often presents things simply so we can understand it. But Scripture remains truthful in its simplicity. The Holy Spirit's inspiration of Scripture guarantees that the biblical authors, despite their sinfulness and humanness, wrote without error.

Sparks mistakenly states that evangelicals who affirm the doctrine of biblical inerrancy have no room in their theology for the doctrine of biblical accommodation: "Where evangelicals adhere strictly to certain conceptions of inerrancy, which disallow even the slightest human errors in the biblical text, this will oblige them in principle (or so it would seem) to reject the conceptual validity of accommodation altogether."[7] Perhaps some evangelicals do reject the teaching, but many others, such as J. I. Packer, heartily embrace the Augustinian definition of accommodation.

By contrast, most evangelicals agree in rejecting categorically the Socinian version of the doctrine. In an earlier day, for example, the Methodist John Wesley used especially strong language in criticizing a similar proposal to Sparks's contention that the Bible's history contains errors owing to its accommodated character. In his *View of the Internal Evidences of the Christian Religion*, Soame Jenyns, one of Wesley's contemporaries, had adopted a Socinian definition of accommodation. Jenyns claimed that the biblical writers had recounted stories "accommodated to the ignorance and superstition of the times and countries in which they had been written." He continued, "In the sciences of history, geography, astronomy and philosophy, they appear to have been no better instructed than others, and therefore were not less liable to be mis-lead by the errors and prejudices of the times and countries in which they lived." Wesley would have none of this proposal and countered:

---

[6]Kenton L. Sparks, *God's Word in Human Words: An Evangelical Appropriation of Critical Biblical Scholarship* (Grand Rapids: Baker Academic, 2008), 256.
[7]Ibid., 247.

He [Jenyns] is undoubtedly a fine writer; but whether he is a Christian, Deist, or Atheist I cannot tell. If he is a Christian, he betrays his own cause by averring, that "all Scripture is given by inspiration of God; but the writers of it were sometimes left to themselves, and consequently made some mistakes." Nay, if there be any mistakes in the Bible, there may be as well a thousand. If there be one falsehood in that book, it did not come from the God of Truth.[8]

Charles Hodge lamented that a similar Socinian understanding of accommodation informed the writings of Johann Salomo Semler, often touted as the "Father of German higher criticism." Semler proposed that scholars should engage in the "free search" for a canon within a canon of Scripture in order to identify the "authentic" word of God. In this quest, scholars should dismiss the cultural dross of biblical writings as error laden. Hodge argued that Semler's approach to studying Scripture had subverted much of German theology in the late eighteenth century.

Sparks's proposal and similar positions have been frequently weighed and found wanting in the history of the Christian churches. Not only does his viewpoint depart from a traditional Christian understanding of Scripture's truthfulness, but it likewise does not accord with Scripture's self-attestation about its truthfulness or trustworthiness.

Sparks may dismiss these comments as misguided. But he has the burden of explaining why in fact they are such. Certainly, my comments are not intended to raise any questions about Professor Sparks's personal faith. Rather they constitute an invitation for him to reconsider his account of the history of biblical authority and hermeneutics—an account that seriously misconstrues the history of accommodation.[9]

Sparks might respond that when all is said and done, the basic thrust of his argument does not focus on the accuracy of his history of biblical interpretation but centers upon the reliability of the historical narratives. In this context, the present volume assumes its undoubted significance. The authors of *Do Historical Matters Matter to Faith?* address in a straightforward manner the challenges Sparks offers to the trustworthiness of the Bible's historical narratives. They honor Professor Sparks's scholarship by taking his proposal seriously.

After all, is *Do Historical Matters Matter to Faith?* not a fresh invitation for those who doubt the reliability of the historical narratives in Scripture? By portraying the import of this volume in this fashion, I am assuming that

---

[8] John Wesley, *Journal*, July 24, 1776.
[9] See Glenn Sunshine, "Accommodation Historically Considered," in *"But My Words Will Never Pass Away": The Enduring Authority of the Christian Scriptures*, ed. D. A. Carson (Grand Rapids: Eerdmans, 2012).

people of good faith are open to changing their viewpoints on the basis of the evidence. Certainly, Sparks envisioned wooing inerrantists to adopt his position through the arguments he posited. But errantists sometimes become inerrantists after further research and reflection. Robert Yarbrough recounts the story of Eta Linnemann, a renowned Bultmannian higher critic who late in her career embraced the doctrine of Scripture's full trustworthiness.

It is my hope not only that this volume will strengthen the convictions of evangelical Christians who believe that the Bible is the inerrant Word of God (including its historical narratives), but also that it will serve as an attractive invitation to those readers who have dismissed this stance to reconsider their commitment to biblical errancy. Should they affirm the doctrine of biblical inerrancy, their new doctrinal commitment would accord with the central doctrine of Scripture among Western churches and with Scripture's own teaching about its truthfulness. They will be able to teach the full counsel of the Word of God without having first to discriminate between what is authentic Scripture and what is inauthentic, error-prone cultural or mythic dross. Engaging the well-informed and lucid arguments of this book is a fresh opportunity not to be missed.

# PREFACE

❈

During the past thirty years biblical and theological scholarship has had to cope with many serious challenges to orthodox and evangelical understanding of Scripture. In addition to the Enlightenment positivist readings of the Bible (which continue with us after more than two centuries), we can now add postmodern literary approaches that treat the biblical narratives solely as literature that should be read as fiction. One of the consequences of this development has been the minimalist-maximalist historiography debate. The generally skeptical mood toward much of the history of the Bible (e.g., the Genesis ancestors of ancient Israel, the Egyptian sojourn, the exodus, the wilderness wanderings, the conquest of Canaan, and the united monarchy) has naturally taken its toll on the academic study of Israelite religion, Old Testament theology, and biblical theology, as these disciplines are intimately connected to history.

These two radically distinct paradigms for analyzing the Old Testament, despite the methodological differences, come to similar conclusions regarding the historical trustworthiness of the Hebrew narratives from Genesis to 1 Kings. J. Maxwell Miller and John H. Hayes well represent the "modern" (yet two-centuries-old!) approach when they opine:

> We hold that the main story line of Genesis–Joshua—creation, pre-Flood patriarchs, great Flood, second patriarchal age, entrance into Egypt, twelve tribes descended from the twelve brothers, escape from Egypt, complete collections of laws and religious instructions handed down at Mt. Sinai, forty years of wandering in the wilderness, miraculous conquests of Canaan, . . .—is an artificial and theologically influenced literary construct.[1]

Adherents of the postmodern hermeneutic arrive at nearly the same conclusion. Thomas Thompson serves as a representative for this model: "Biblical Israel, as an element of tradition and story, such as the murmuring stories in the wilderness, . . . is a theological and literary creation."[2] Similarly, Philip

---

[1] J. Maxwell Miller and John H. Hayes, *A History of Ancient Israel and Judah* (Philadelphia: Westminster, 1986), 78.
[2] Thomas L. Thompson, *The Mythic Past: Biblical Archaeology and the Myth of Israel* (London: Basic Books, 1999).

Davies seemingly offers an obituary on the age of Moses, declaring, "Most biblical scholars accept that there was no historical counterpart to this epoch, and most intelligent biblical archaeologists accept this too."[3] Traditional critical scholars are dismayed by these extreme positions, as is evidenced in the title of a recent article by Siegfried Herrmann, "The Devaluation of the Old Testament as a Historical Source."[4]

New Testament studies has not been immune to scholarship that has challenged traditional readings of the Bible. There were the quest for the historical Jesus that began a century ago with Albert Schweitzer and Rudolf Bultmann's demythologizing approach to the Gospels, both of which treated the New Testament as a suspect document historically. Just as Old Testament scholars have been dominated by the radical stances of the historical minimalists in recent decades, the field of New Testament studies has had do deal with the Jesus Seminar and its dismissive claims of the Gospels with respect to the birth, life, and death of Jesus.

Evangelical biblical scholars have rightly rejected the extreme positions of historical minimalism, whether in Old Testament or New Testament studies. The rise of postmodern approaches, despite the many negative aspects, has detracted from the ascendancy of traditional higher criticism as practiced in the academy since the nineteenth century. One consequence of these competing approaches to biblical studies is that there is no longer a consensus among critical scholars; rather, a plurality of approaches is in vogue. Given the loss of a consensus on the academic study of the Bible, it is surprising that some evangelicals would challenge their colleagues to embrace the findings of critical scholarship, to dismiss the historicity of many events in both Testaments, and then to insist that intellectual honesty requires an admission that the Bible contains many errors and inconsistencies. It goes without saying, in the view of some, that the doctrine of inerrancy should be radically revised, if not laid to rest. "Progressive evangelicals," as they have identified themselves, are raising some important questions regarding recent academic trends and traditional evangelical views of Scripture. They advocate looking to Scripture purely for theology while setting aside questions of history in the name of bending the knee to the latest conclusions of critical biblical scholarship—a new manifestation of an old neoorthodoxy.

---

[3]Philip Davies, "The Intellectual, the Archaeologists and the Bible," in *The Land I Will Show You: Essays on the History and Archaeology of the Ancient Near East in Honour of J. Maxwell Miller*, ed. J. A. Dearman and M. P. Graham (Sheffield: JSOT, 2001), 247.
[4]Siegfried Herrmann, "The Devaluation of the Old Testament as a Historical Source," in *Israel's Past in Present Research: Essays on Ancient Israelite Historiography*, ed. V. Philips Long (Winona Lake, IN: Eisenbrauns, 1993).

Peter Enns's book *Inspiration and Incarnation*[5] has raised some good questions about the relationship between ancient Near Eastern literature and the Bible and inspiration. It was, however, Kenton Sparks's more recent book *God's Word in Human Words*[6] that turned out to be the catalyst for this collection of essays. While both books focus largely on the Old Testament, and both of these scholars are Old Testament scholars, they do treat New Testament and theological issues. Sparks's book is the more provocative, as he feels that the way around the "contradictions" and "errors" in the Bible is to accept source-critical theories that the Bible preserves multiple traditions within a narrative or among different books (e.g., Kings and Chronicles, or the Synoptic Gospels and John).

This collaborative book is an outgrowth of a panel discussion by faculty members of the Department of Old Testament and Semitic Languages at Trinity Evangelical Divinity School in February 2009. The noon colloquium organized by the Old Testament department was attended by almost eighty students. Dennis Magary, chair of the department, moderated the meeting, and Willem VanGemeren, Richard Averbeck, and James Hoffmeier offered appraisals, followed by a period of questions and answers. Students indicated much appreciation that we were addressing some of these issues, and many expressed the hope that we would publish our thoughts and critique. Not only were Old Testament students present, but a broad range of students from other departments and programs participated, and the questions raised during the seminar and subsequent to it reflected the breadth of Sparks's book, which treats problems with the Old and New Testaments, but also theology and church history.

The questions our students were asking regarding critical issues and the Bible, especially issues identified by Enns and Sparks, prompted Drs. Magary and Hoffmeier to organize this book and to expand the list of contributors to include a broad range of scholars who represent the fields of Old and New Testament studies, archaeology, theology, and church history, using their respective specializations to address these issues head on. Our desire is to offer thoughtful, substantive responses to questions raised by critical scholars, regardless of their theological orientation, rather than *ad hominem* retorts. While this book will place a great deal of emphasis on the Old Testament and archaeology, there will also be chapters on the New Testament (especially touching on synoptic problems and the New Testament view of

---

[5]Enns, *Inspiration and Incarnation: Evangelicals and the Problem of the Old Testament* (Grand Rapids: Baker Academic, 2005).
[6]Sparks, *God's Word in Human Words: An Evangelical Appropriation of Critical Biblical Scholarship* (Grand Rapids: Baker Academic, 2008).

the Old Testament) and what happens to biblical and systematic theology
when history is dismissed.

Sparks's book *God's Word in Human Words* reads like a reprise of James
Barr's *Fundamentalism*,[7] especially his attack on evangelical/conservative
biblical scholars (see esp. chap. 5). Sparks resuscitates Barr's caricature of
evangelical scholars, which was outdated and inaccurate in the 1970s, a caricature that portrayed evangelicals as not really understanding critical scholarly
methods because they were trained in theologically conservative institutions,
or as taking the easy path of archaeology and Near Eastern studies in order to
avoid dealing with critical issues raised by critical scholarship. Barr asserted,
"Probably none of the writers of conservative evangelical literature on the
Bible *who are actual professional biblical scholars* can be found to be so completely negative towards the main trend in biblical scholarship as are those
like Kitchen who look on the subject from the outside."[8] This elitist view is
clearly a broadside against scholars who are looking at the Old Testament
(in particular) from the perspective of Near Eastern studies. It is as if only
when one agrees with the "assured results" of critical scholarship can one be
treated as a "professional biblical scholar."

Equally condescending is Sparks's recent pronouncement that "many
fundamentalists avoided these difficulties by majoring in 'safe' disciplines
(text criticism, Greek classics, and Near Eastern studies) or by studying in
institutions where critical issues could be avoided (especially in conservative
Jewish Schools and in British universities)."[9] (The contributors of this book
who did their doctoral work in British universities—Aberdeen, Oxford, and
Cambridge—would hardly agree with this assessment!) The readers need only
to review the list of contributors to see where they completed their PhDs,
and it will be abundantly clear that the vast majority worked in secular and
critical contexts and had to deal directly with critical issues. In fact, even in the
context of Near Eastern studies, the critical approaches of *Altstestamentlers*
were a part of the curriculum.

The writers in this volume who use archaeological materials as a vehicle
for understanding the context of a passage of Scripture and treat them as
tools for interpreting biblical texts are all *practicing* field archaeologists who
work with both the biblical and many cognate languages as well. Three of
the authors were students of William G. Dever, the dean of North American
Syro-Palestinian archaeology, who in the 1970s and 1980s chastised conservative biblical scholars for being "armchair" archaeologists who lacked field

---

[7]Barr, *Fundamentalism* (Philadelphia: Westminster, 1977).
[8]Ibid., 131, his emphasis.
[9]Sparks, *God's Word in Human Words*, 145.

training and, therefore, the requisite tools for having the proper conversation between archaeology and texts. Thomas Davis, Steven Ortiz, and Michael Hasel studied with Dever because they were eager to become professional archaeologists in order to work alongside biblical studies in a responsible way.

Many of the great biblical and Near Eastern scholars of the past fifty years (e.g., William F. Albright, Cyrus Gordon, Donald Wiseman, William Hallo, and Kenneth Kitchen) considered the contextual materials to be vital tools for interpreting the Old Testament, a position taken by many of the contributors to this volume. It is hardly an easy and safe approach as, in addition to working with the Hebrew of the Old Testament and the various literary approaches used in biblical studies, there are the demands of knowing cognate languages and ancient Near Eastern history, religion, and culture. Having a working knowledge of all these fields is no easy task (and raises other questions and challenges to faith and theology), but it is an extremely rewarding and valuable way of reading the Bible. Furthermore, the scholars mentioned above saw the ancient Near Eastern contextual approach to offer an external method for evaluating critical theories that were formulated about the Bible in Western universities rather than in the Semitic world where the biblical text originated. What is curious about Barr's and Sparks's view on those who come at the Bible "from the outside" is that they seem so certain about the conclusions of (objective) critical scholarship (despite its constant shifting of positions and ever-increasing number of newer critical approaches) that they do not welcome an analytical evaluation of their own guild's cherished "critical" scholarship. This is hardly a scientific or intellectually honest position when exculpatory evidence is produced against their charges. It seems, rather, that there is a special pleading for methodologies that have been seriously challenged in recent years (as some of the essays in this volume show) from *within* the guild itself. Postmodern critical scholars of the past twenty to thirty years have done more damage to the assured results of Enlightenment critical theories than all the evangelical scholars of the last century.

We offer this book to help address some of the questions raised about the historicity, accuracy, and inerrancy of the Bible by colleagues within our faith community, as well as those outside it. There will be a special emphasis placed on matters of history and the historicity of biblical narratives, both Old and New Testaments, as this seems presently to be a burning issue for theology and faith. Hence, we begin with a group of essays that deal with theological matters before moving on to topics in the Old Testament, the New Testament, and archaeology.

It is always difficult when individuals attack something or someone near and dear. When the stakes are as high as they are in the present dialogue, language can become strident. Motives can all too easily be misunderstood or misconstrued. We seek not to impugn but to inspire. It is our hope that the essays in this volume will engage the issues and their proponents with the grace and Christian character with which the late Donald J. Wiseman, the scholar in whose memory we dedicate this book, went about his work. Just about two years ago, Donald passed away, leaving a wonderful legacy as a biblical and Near Eastern scholar (a key figure in the NIV translation committee, a founder of Tyndale House in Cambridge, a writer of Old Testament commentaries, and a contributing Assyriologist) and as a churchman and academic mentor. He was a gracious and kind gentleman whose irenic spirit we should all emulate.

# ABBREVIATIONS

✳

| | |
|---|---|
| AASOR | Annual of the American Schools of Oriental Research |
| AB | Anchor Bible |
| *AION* | *Annali dell'Istituto Orientale di Napoli* |
| *AJA* | *American Journal of Archaeology* |
| AnBib | Analecta biblica |
| *ANET* | *Ancient Near Eastern Texts Relating to the Bible.* 3rd ed. Edited by James B. Pritchard. Princeton: Princeton University Press, 1969 |
| AnOr | Analecta orientalia |
| *ANRW* | *Aufstieg und Niedergang der römischen Welt: Geschichte und Kultur Roms im Spiegel der neueren Forschung.* Edited by H. Temporini and W. Haase. Berlin, 1972– |
| ANTF | Arbeiten zur neutestamentlichen Textforschung |
| AOAT | Alter Orient und Altes Testament |
| *ARE* | *Ancient Records of Egypt.* Edited by J. H. Breasted. 5 vols. Chicago, 1905–1907. Reprint, New York, 1962 |
| ARM | Archives royales de Mari |
| *AUSS* | *Andrews University Seminary Studies* |
| *BA* | *Biblical Archaeologist* |
| *Bapt.* | *Baptism* (Tertullian) |
| *BAR* | *Biblical Archaeology Review* |
| *BASOR* | *Bulletin of the American Schools of Oriental Research* |
| BBET | Beiträge zur biblischen Exegese und Theologie |
| *BBR* | *Bulletin for Biblical Research* |
| BBRSup | Bulletin for Biblical Research Supplement |
| BDAG | Bauer, W., F. W. Danker, W. F. Arndt, and F. W. Gingrich. *Greek-English Lexicon of the New Testament and Other Early Christian Literature.* 3rd ed. Chicago, 1999 |
| BECNT | Baker Exegetical Commentary on the New Testament |
| *BibInt* | *Biblical Interpretation* |
| *BurH* | *Buried History* |
| BWANT | Beiträge zur Wissenschaft vom Alten und Neuen Testament |
| BZAW | Beihefte zur Zeitschrift für die alttestamentliche Wissenschaft |

| | |
|---|---|
| BZNW | Beihefte zur Zeitschrift für die neutestamentliche Wissenschaft |
| CAH | Cambridge Ancient History |
| CANE | *Civilizations of the Ancient Near East*. Edited by J. Sasson. 4 vols. New York, 1995 |
| CBQ | *Catholic Biblical Quarterly* |
| CBQMS | Catholic Biblical Quarterly Monograph Series |
| CBS | critical biblical scholarship |
| CHANE | Culture and History of the Ancient Near East |
| *Civ.* | *The City of God* (Augustine) |
| COS | *The Context of Scripture*. Edited by W. W. Hallo. 3 vols. Leiden, 1997– |
| CT | *Cuneiform Texts from Babylonian Tablets in the British Museum* |
| CTJ | *Calvin Theological Journal* |
| Dtr | Deuteronomist |
| EKK | Evangelisch-katholischer Kommentar zum Neuen Testament |
| *Ep. Afric.* | *Epistle to Africanus* (Origen) |
| *Ep. Orig.* | *Epistle to Origen* (Julius Africanus) |
| ErIsr | *Eretz-Israel* |
| EvQ | *Evangelical Quarterly* |
| EvT | *Evangelische Theologie* |
| ExAud | *Ex auditu* |
| ExpTim | *Expository Times* |
| FLP | Tablets in the collections of the Free Library of Pennsylvania |
| FOTL | Forms of the Old Testament Literature |
| FRLANT | Forschungen zur Religion und Literatur des Alten und Neuen Testaments |
| *Hist. eccl.* | *Ecclesiastical History* (Eusebius) |
| HKAT | Handkommentar zum Alten Testament |
| HS | *Hebrew Studies* |
| HSS | Harvard Semitic Studies |
| HUT | Hermeneutische Untersuchungen zur Theologie |
| ICC | International Critical Commentary |
| IEJ | *Israel Exploration Journal* |
| ITQ | *Irish Theological Quarterly* |
| JAOS | *Journal of the American Oriental Society* |
| JBL | *Journal of Biblical Literature* |
| JCS | *Journal of Cuneiform Studies* |
| JEA | *Journal of Egyptian Archaeology* |

| | |
|---|---|
| JEOL | *Jaarbericht van het Vooraziatisch-Egyptisch Gezelschap (Genootschap) Ex oriente lux* |
| JESHO | *Journal of the Economic and Social History of the Orient* |
| JETh | *Jahrbuch für evangelikale Theologie* |
| JETS | *Journal of the Evangelical Theological Society* |
| JHS | *Journal of Hebrew Scriptures* |
| JNES | *Journal of Near Eastern Studies* |
| JSJSup | Supplements to the Journal for the Study of Judaism |
| JSNTSup | Journal for the Study of the New Testament: Supplement Series |
| JSOT | *Journal for the Study of the Old Testament* |
| JSOTSup | Journal for the Study of the Old Testament: Supplement Series |
| JSS | *Journal of Semitic Studies* |
| JTS | *Journal of Theological Studies* |
| LÄ | *Lexikon der Ägyptologie.* Edited by W. Helck, E. Otto, and W. Westendorf. Wiesbaden, 1972 |
| LXX | Septuagint |
| Mari | *Mari: Annales de recherches interdisciplinaires* |
| MDOG | Mitteilungen der Deutschen Orient-Gesellschaft |
| MT | Masoretic Text |
| NAC | New American Commentary |
| NCB | New Century Bible |
| NICNT | New International Commentary on the New Testament |
| NICOT | New International Commentary on the Old Testament |
| NIDOTTE | *New International Dictionary of Old Testament Theology and Exegesis.* Edited by W. A. VanGemeren. 5 vols. Grand Rapids, 1997 |
| NIGTC | New International Greek Testament Commentary |
| NIVAC | NIV Application Commentary |
| NovT | *Novum Testamentum* |
| NPNF[1] | *Nicene and Post-Nicene Fathers*, Series 1 |
| NPNF[2] | *Nicene and Post-Nicene Fathers*, Series 2 |
| NRTh | *La nouvelle revue théologique* |
| NTL | New Testament Library |
| NTOA | Novum Testamentum et Orbis Antiquus |
| NTS | *New Testament Studies* |
| NTTS | New Testament Tools and Studies |
| OBO | Orbis biblicus et orientalis |
| OLA | Orientalia lovaniensia analecta |

| | |
|---|---|
| OTE | *Old Testament Essays* |
| OTG | Old Testament Guides |
| OTL | Old Testament Library |
| OTS | Old Testament Studies |
| OTT | Old Testament theology |
| PEQ | *Palestine Exploration Quarterly* |
| Prol. Sal. | *Prologue to Sapientia Salomonis (Wisdom of Solomon)* (Jerome) |
| PSB | *Princeton Seminary Bulletin* |
| RÄR | *Reallexikon der ägyptischen Religionsgeschichte.* H. Bonnet. Berlin, 1952 |
| RB | *Revue biblique* |
| RBén | *Revue bénédictine* |
| RBL | *Review of Biblical Literature* |
| RelSRev | *Religious Studies Review* |
| RevQ | *Revue de Qumran* |
| RHR | *Revue de l'histoire des religions* |
| RlA | *Reallexikon der Assyriologie.* Edited by Erich Ebeling et al. Berlin, 1928– |
| RIMA | The Royal Inscriptions of Mesopotamia, Assyrian Periods |
| RNT | Regensburger Neues Testament |
| RS | Ras Shamra |
| RTR | *Reformed Theological Review* |
| SAA | State Archives of Assyria |
| SAAS | State Archives of Assyria Studies |
| SBLABS | Society of Biblical Literature Archaeology and Biblical Studies |
| SBLDS | Society of Biblical Literature Dissertation Series |
| SBLSymS | Society of Biblical Literature Symposium Series |
| SBLWAW | Society of Biblical Literature Writings from the Ancient World |
| SBS | Stuttgarter Bibelstudien |
| SC | Sources chrétiennes. Paris: Cerf, 1943– |
| SEÅ | *Svensk exegetisk årsbok* |
| SecCent | *Second Century* |
| SHANE | Studies in the History of the Ancient Near East |
| SJOT | *Scandinavian Journal of the Old Testament* |
| SNTSMS | Society for New Testament Studies Monograph Series |
| SVTQ | *St Vladimir's Theological Quarterly* |
| TA | *Tel Aviv* |
| TJ | *Trinity Journal* |
| TLZ | *Theologische Literaturzeitung* |

| | |
|---|---|
| *TRE* | *Theologische Realenzyklopädie.* Edited by G. Krause and G. Müller. Berlin, 1977– |
| *TRev* | *Theologische Revue* |
| *TS* | *Theological Studies* |
| *TynBul* | *Tyndale Bulletin* |
| UF | *Ugarit-Forschungen* |
| *VE* | *Vox evangelica* |
| *VT* | *Vetus Testamentum* |
| VTSup | Supplements to Vetus Testamentum |
| WBC | Word Biblical Commentary |
| WdF | Wege der Forschung |
| WMANT | Wissenschaftliche Monographien zum Alten und Neuen Testament |
| *WTJ* | *Westminster Theological Journal* |
| WUNT | Wissenschaftliche Untersuchungen zum Neuen Testament |
| WVDOG | Wissenschaftliche Veröffentlichungen der deutschen Orientgesellschaft |
| YOSR | Yale Oriental Series, Researches |
| *ZÄS* | *Zeitschrift für ägyptische Sprache und Altertumskunde* |
| *ZDPV* | *Zeitschrift des deutschen Palästina-Vereins* |
| *ZNW* | *Zeitschrift für die neutestamentliche Wissenschaft und die Kunde der älteren Kirche* |
| *ZTK* | *Zeitschrift für Theologie und Kirche* |

# Part 1

# BIBLICAL, SYSTEMATIC, AND HISTORICAL THEOLOGY

# 1

# RELIGIOUS EPISTEMOLOGY, THEOLOGICAL INTERPRETATION OF SCRIPTURE, AND CRITICAL BIBLICAL SCHOLARSHIP

*A Theologian's Reflections*

## THOMAS H. MCCALL

✵

## Introduction

*"Do you want us to listen to you?"*[1] Peter van Inwagen puts this question to contemporary mainstream New Testament scholarship. He makes clear just who he means by "you": those who engage in historical-critical study of the New Testament, those who presuppose either a denial of "or neutrality about its authority, to investigate such matters as the authorship, dates, histories of composition, historical reliability and mutual dependency of the various books of the New Testament," those who study the Bible by such methods as "source criticism, form criticism, and redaction criticism."[2] He also specifies just who he means by "us": believing Christians who are not trained New Testament scholars but who regard the New Testament as historically reliable; "we" are "ordinary churchgoers" and "pastors who minister to the ordinary

---

[1]Peter van Inwagen, "Do You Want Us to Listen to You?," in *"Behind" the Text: History and Biblical Interpretation*, ed. Craig G. Bartholomew et al. (Grand Rapids: Zondervan, 2003), 101. An earlier version of this essay appeared as "Critical Studies of the New Testament and the User of the New Testament," in *Hermes and Athena: Biblical Exegesis and Philosophical Theology*, ed. Eleonore Stump and Thomas P. Flint (Notre Dame, IN: University of Notre Dame, 1993), 159–90.

[2]Van Inwagen, "Do You Want Us to Listen to You?," 101, 105.

33

churchgoers," as well as "theologians who regard the New Testament as an authoritative divine revelation."[3]

*Do you want us to listen to you?* Van Inwagen asks this as a serious question, and he follows it with an equally serious argument for some surprising conclusions.

> First, "ordinary" Christians (Christians not trained in New Testament scholarship) have grounds for believing that the gospel stories are (essentially) historical—grounds independent of the claims of historical scholarship. Secondly, New Testament scholars have established nothing that tells against the thesis that ordinary Christians have grounds independent of historical studies for believing in the essential historicity of the gospel stories. Thirdly, ordinary Christians may therefore ignore any skeptical historical claims made by New Testament scholars with a clear intellectual conscience.[4]

What van Inwagen says about New Testament studies may just as easily be extended to critical biblical scholarship (hereafter CBS) more generally.[5] Many proponents of CBS may be surprised and puzzled by van Inwagen's question, and may reply, "*Of course we want you to listen to us. We expect you to listen to us, and any honest seeker of truth naturally will look to the experts in the field for information. If you want to know the sober truth of the important issues at stake, then of course you will listen to us. Indeed, failure to listen to us is evidence of noetic laziness (at best) or intellectual dishonesty (at worst).*"

But what *would* prompt a question such as that of van Inwagen? What is it that drives arguments such as his? A well-respected analytic philosopher, van Inwagen is not known for intellectual laziness, and to dismiss his claims out of hand as "dishonest" would itself be both lazy and judgmental. Furthermore, he speaks for many honest Christians; his concerns are more representative of many Christians who think long and hard about these matters than they are idiosyncratic.

In this essay, I first offer a sketch of some important recent work in religious epistemology, work that has direct bearing upon the efforts of CBS—but work that is often not given sufficient consideration by the proponents of CBS. I then relate that work in religious epistemology to some relevant issues in CBS, and I briefly engage with the work of some representative proponents of it. I

---

[3]Ibid., 101, 104.
[4]Ibid., 103.
[5]Indeed it has been extended more broadly, e.g., Alvin Plantinga, *Warranted Christian Belief* (Oxford: Oxford University Press, 2000), 374–421. Plantinga says that he concurs "for the most part" with van Inwagen (375 n. 2).

conclude, not with any kind of slam-dunk argument, but with some serious epistemological and theological reflections.

## Important Work in Religious Epistemology: A Brief Overview of Some Recent Contributions

The last few decades have been particularly fruitful in discussions of religious epistemology. While the vast majority of what has taken place is beyond the scope of this discussion, several particularly important elements deserve mention. So while I make no pretense that what follows is anything more than the barest sketch of some of these developments, even such a brief overview will serve to highlight some of the most important of these aspects.

### Justification in Religious Epistemology

The position often known as "classical foundationalism" (or, alternatively, "strong foundationalism") has been prominent in many quarters. Often pictured as a pyramid of knowledge, this view (or family of views) holds that claims to knowledge that could count as truly justified are of two classes: either those that are properly foundational (or "basic") or those that are appropriately structured upon the properly foundational beliefs. Beliefs that could count as genuinely foundational or properly basic are only those that are either self-evident (e.g., laws of logic and mathematics) or evident to the senses.[6] So if a belief is really justified, it is so by virtue of being either self-evident or evident to the senses (if foundational), or appropriately built upon such beliefs. Any justified belief would meet one of these two conditions: it will either satisfy

(CF1) being either self-evident or evident to the senses;

or

(CF2) being appropriately structured upon such (CF1) beliefs.

Classical foundationalism has attracted much criticism, and, while it is not without contemporary defenders, it is safe to say that it is on the defensive. One of the main areas of criticism is that classical foundationalism's criteria for justified belief simply cannot account for a great deal of what we (safely) take to be true. Is the world more than five minutes old? Are there other minds? Critics of classical foundationalism (Alvin Plantinga being among the most

---

[6]Sometimes the category of "incorrigible" is included here as well.

important and distinguished of these critics) argue that it is notoriously hard to account for such important—one might even wish to say *basic*—beliefs as these: surely the world is more than five minutes old, and surely solipsism is false, but it is hard to rule out such obviously erroneous beliefs on classical foundationalism. Classical foundationalism is also commonly charged with being self-referentially incoherent. Is classical foundationalism itself properly basic? If it is, then it must either be self-evident or evident to the senses. So is it self-evident? Not at all. Is it evident to the senses? Not at all. Well, then, is it appropriately built up from something that is self-evident or evident to the senses? Not obviously. But if it cannot satisfy its own stated conditions for justified belief, then it is self-referentially incoherent. Being self-referentially incoherent is not a virtue, and the continuing defenders of classical foundationalism generally recognize that they have work before them. Nicholas Wolterstorff goes so far as to conclude that "on all fronts foundationalism is in bad shape. It seems to me that there is nothing to do but give it up for mortally ill and learn to live in its absence."[7]

If the future of classical foundationalism is less than bright, what other options are there? One of the main alternatives is *coherentism*.[8] Coherentism eschews the picture of the pyramid of knowledge, and instead conceives of knowledge as more akin to a *web* or a *raft*.[9] There are various versions of coherentism, but what they share in common is the notion that a belief *B* is justified if and only if it coheres with the other beliefs in the system or web of beliefs. Some of the beliefs in the web will be more central than others and vital to the strength or integrity of the raft or web, while others will be on the periphery and of less importance. These beliefs can be adjusted "on the move"; just as one might be able to replace a piece of a raft while floating on it (as long as it is not too large or central), so also beliefs may be added or dropped as their coherence with the rest of the system is tested. Is a belief *B* justified for someone? Well, there is a way to check: is it consistent with the other beliefs in the epistemic web?[10] If the belief in question is not consistent, then it is not justified. If it is consistent, then it can count as a

---

[7]Nicholas Wolterstorff, *Reason within the Bounds of Religion*, 2nd ed. (Grand Rapids: Eerdmans, 1984), 56.

[8]This is not to be confused with a coherence theory of truth; it is possible to hold both to a coherence theory of epistemic justification and to a correspondence theory of truth.

[9]See Ernest Sosa, "The Raft and the Pyramid: Coherence versus Foundations in the Theory of Knowledge," in *Epistemology: The Big Questions*, ed. Linda Alcoff (Oxford: Oxford University Press, 1998), esp. 192–93.

[10]The exact pattern or criteria will vary between coherence theories (e.g., positive or negative coherentism, or linear or holistic). For further discussion, see John C. Pollock, *Contemporary Theories of Knowledge* (Totowa, NJ: Rowan and Littlefield, 1986).

justified belief (and, of course, if it is a justified *true* belief, then it counts as genuine knowledge).[11]

Coherentism has also, however, come in for its share of powerful criticism.[12] There are some common and powerful philosophical objections to coherentist theories of justification: as Plantinga argues (via his example of the "Epistemically Inflexible Climber"), coherence is not sufficient for justification. As engagement with any real "true believer" in a conspiracy theory shows, it is possible to have a very coherent set of beliefs while many of those beliefs are completely out of touch with reality. Nor is it clear that coherence is necessary for justification. Many people will admit that there are times in their lives when it is hard to make *everything* "add up," yet we seem to have good reason to hold to all of these beliefs. While tight coherence might be desirable, to conclude that it is necessary for justification would threaten to rule out many beliefs that really belong. At any rate, coherentism makes it tough to choose between competing "webs" or traditions. As William P. Alston puts it, "Coherentism continues to be faced with the stubborn fact that, however the notion of coherence is spelled out, it seems clear that there is an indefinitely large multiplicity of equally coherent systems of belief, with no way provided by coherence theory for choosing between them."[13]

So if classical foundationalism and coherentism are both in trouble, what other options are there? Some of the most interesting proposals on the contemporary scene are those of the *modest foundationalists*, the most interesting and influential of which is Plantinga's "Reformed Epistemology."[14] Plantinga is among the most insightful and powerful critics of both classical foundationalism and coherentism,[15] but he thinks that the basic foundationalist structure is not itself problematical. The problems with classical foundationalism come from a foundation that simply is too narrow; the problems come when too little is allowed as properly basic. Taking suggestions from "reliabilism," Plantinga proposes that "a belief is warranted if it is produced by our properly

---

[11]For the sake of continuity with the major discussions, I am assuming that knowledge is "justified true belief" (or something closely akin to it). But see the *locus classicus* of objections to this way of thinking about knowledge, Edmund L. Gettier, "Is Justified True Belief Knowledge?" *Analysis* 23 (1963): 121–23.

[12]E.g., Alvin Plantinga, *Warrant: The Current Debate* (Oxford: Oxford University Press, 1993), 66–161.

[13]William P. Alston, *Epistemic Justification: Essays in the Theory of Knowledge* (Ithaca, NY: Cornell University Press, 1989), 13.

[14]Other "founding fathers" of "Reformed Epistemology" would include Nicholas Wolterstorff and William P. Alston. I once heard Alston say that he was still holding out for "Episcopalian Epistemology," but that he didn't think it was going to catch on.

[15]Among other options criticized by Plantinga.

functioning cognitive faculties working in accord with their design plan."[16] Belief in God, he argues, itself is (or can be) properly basic. In other words, if it is produced by our cognitive faculties working according to their "design plan" (the *sensus divinitatis*, before the fall, or the "internal instigation of the Holy Spirit," in the postlapsarian state), belief in God need not be built upon beliefs that are more basic. So although the traditional arguments for the existence of God may have a useful place, they are not necessary for genuine or *warranted* belief. Moreover, the full panoply of Christian belief—the "great things of the gospel": Trinity, incarnation, resurrection, atonement, salvation, eternal life, etc.—is also (or can be) "properly basic" for believers (on the "Extended Aquinas/Calvin Model"). So whatever value there might be in the arguments of evidentialist apologetics for, say, the historicity of something reported in the Bible, such arguments themselves are not necessary for robust and warranted Christian belief.[17]

Acceptance of the "Extended A/C" proposal does not mean that there is no place at all for apologetics, for Christian belief is not insulated from challenges and potential "defeaters" (some of which are recognized to come from CBS). It means only that apologetics will be focused (at least primarily) on "negative apologetics" (the task of responding to such challenges). Plantinga's proposal continues to engender much debate, and we shall return to some relevant aspects of that controversy shortly. But even from this sketch it should become obvious that the proposal of "Reformed Epistemology"—as well as the state of play within religious epistemology more generally—has important implications for Christian engagement with CBS.

### Internalism, Externalism, and Epistemic Virtues

The debates between internalists and externalists in epistemology are also interesting and important for our discussion. W. Jay Wood locates the "crux of the debate between internalists and externalists" in "the nature and extent of the personal access, or oversight, each of us must have to the factors contributing to our justified beliefs."[18] Internalists, whose ranks are composed of both foundationalists and coherentists, insist that the grounds of any truly justified beliefs must be something to which we have access (or could get such access in fairly short order if we were to turn our attention there). The grounds for

---

[16]Kelly James Clark, Richard Lints, and James K. A. Smith, *101 Key Terms in Philosophy and Their Importance for Theology* (Louisville: Westminster John Knox, 2004), 20.

[17]See William Lane Craig's distinction between "knowing" and "showing" the truthfulness of Christianity, e.g., *Reasonable Faith: Christian Truth and Apologetics*, 3rd ed. (Wheaton, IL: Crossway, 2008), 43–60.

[18]W. Jay Wood, *Epistemology: Becoming Intellectually Virtuous* (Downers Grove, IL: InterVarsity, 1998), 138.

our beliefs are *internal* to us, and we can get at them (if we know how and where to look). Stouter versions of internalism will insist upon quicker and more immediate access, and correspondingly will maintain that we exercise a sizable degree of control over our beliefs; weaker or more modest versions will insist only that we be able to gain the prerequisite access. But what they have in common is this conviction: for our beliefs to be truly justified, we must have access to—and corresponding responsibility for and control over—the grounds for those beliefs.

Externalists, not surprisingly, deny that the grounds for our justified beliefs must be internal to us or within our cognitive reach. Tending to emphasize "reliabilism" more than "responsibilism," they

> deny, however, that individual cognitive agents must have personal access to all the elements contributing to a belief's being justified. The agent is not responsible for personally overseeing that the right sort of connection between belief and the world obtains; either it does or it does not, but this is not a fact of which the agent need be aware in order for her beliefs to be justified.[19]

We do not *earn* epistemic justification by our efforts; "justification is something that happens to us."[20] Where many classical foundationalists and coherentists alike are internalists, many modest foundationalists incline toward or endorse externalism. Thus Plantinga prefers "warrant" to "justification"; since we do not earn or merit epistemic justification, we should get rid of deontological notions and instead talk about "warranted" belief in terms of "proper function."[21]

Many epistemologists are convinced that the choice between internalism and externalism is not best conceived in terms of polar opposites and all-or-nothing categories.[22] Rather than think of only the extremes of internalism and externalism, they say, we should think of these matters in terms of a continuum. Perhaps we do not exercise *complete* or *direct* access to or control over our beliefs, but maybe we do have *some* access and control (even if that access is limited and the control is indirect). It is at this point that "virtue epistemology" often makes an entrance into the conversations between internalists and externalists.[23] Virtue epistemologists are concerned to recover

---

[19]Ibid., 141.
[20]Ibid.
[21]Cf. Alvin Plantinga, *Warrant and Proper Function* (Oxford: Oxford University Press, 1993).
[22]Thus Linda Zagzebski notes that William P. Alston favored "internalist externalism," "Religious Knowledge and the Virtues," in *Rational Faith: Catholic Responses to Reformed Epistemology*, ed. Linda Zagzebski (Notre Dame, IN: University of Notre Dame Press, 1993), 201.
[23]See especially Linda Zagzebski, *Virtues of the Mind* (Cambridge: Cambridge University Press, 1996).

the place of such characteristics as wisdom, prudence, discernment, honesty in the pursuit of truth, perseverance, and willingness to suffer for the truth. They are equally concerned to avoid the opposing vices of "folly, obtuseness, gullibility, dishonesty, naivete, and vicious curiosity."[24] These virtue theorists work hard to remind us that intellectual and moral concerns cannot be neatly separated, and without the prerequisite moral virtues we will not likely be the kind of people who know what we can and should know. Epistemic equipment involves much more than mere IQ levels and adequate neurological health; it also involves commitment to the truth—and to being the kind of persons who can gain access to it.

The relationship of discussions in virtue epistemology to the internalism-externalism debates is complex, but the basic point made by the virtue theorist may be summarized this way: Even if we cannot directly access or control the grounds for (all) our beliefs, we surely can exercise some control over the kinds of activities and commitments that put us in places where we can—or cannot—gain true beliefs. Even if the grounds to all beliefs are not directly within our grip, we do have some level of access (and responsibility) through the belief-forming ("doxastic") practices in which we engage. For it is through these doxastic practices that we can gain the tools and positions that are needed for knowledge. As Wood concludes, both internalism and externalism

> capture important intuitions about justification. One requires that our justified beliefs be strongly tied to the truth, and the other requires that we bear some responsibility for overseeing our interior intellectual lives. . . . A virtuous intellectual agent believes justifiably and tracks the truth without necessarily being cognizant at the time of the grounds of the belief.[25]

### Religious Epistemology and Critical Biblical Scholarship

This brief survey, sketchy as it is, is relevant background for an evaluation of the claims of CBS. With this in mind, just what are we to make of the claims of CBS, on one hand, and, on the other hand, those of van Inwagen and company?

#### Some Observations

Even those practitioners of CBS who are (apparently) committed to classical orthodoxy often insist upon the utter necessity of CBS. N. T. Wright denounces "pre-critical" readings because such interpretations make it all too

---

[24]Wood, *Epistemology*, 16.
[25]Ibid., 144, 147.

easy for the theologically motivated reader to "inflict his or her own point of view onto unwilling material,"[26] and he insists that he agrees "completely with the [Jesus] Seminar that the search for Jesus in his historical context is possible, vital, and urgent. I am as convinced as they are that if the church ignores such a search it is living in a fool's paradise."[27] Kenton Sparks says that many evangelical biblical scholars are "poorly trained" (owing, in part, to their work in British or Jewish universities), and he makes the assertion that "fideism, specious arguments, misconstruing evidence, strained harmonizations, leaving out evidence, special pleading, and various kinds of obscurantism" are "par for the course."[28] The average Christian, on his view, is "in most cases" completely out of the loop and "in no position to evaluate, let alone criticize, the results of critical scholarship."[29] On the other hand, as we have seen, van Inwagen argues that "ordinary Christians" (laity, pastors, and theologians alike) have grounds for believing in the historical veracity of the biblical claims—grounds that are independent of CBS. He also argues that CBS does nothing to undercut those grounds, and he concludes that such Christians "may therefore ignore any skeptical historical claims" made by the practitioners of CBS.

Facing this impasse, I suggest that we think in terms of the major epistemological options. Consider Rick, an interpreter who thinks that—to choose as an example an issue that is deeply traditional but not exactly part of the creedal faith—the exodus from Egypt was a historical event. Rick is confronted with the claims of CBS that the exodus did *not* happen, and he finds those claims impressive (if also a bit strident). Suppose that Rick is a classical foundationalist; he is committed to the view that his belief in a historical exodus must be supported by the appropriate evidence (evidence that is more basic) to count as justified. Suppose further that Rick is an internalist; he thinks that he must have access to the grounds of his belief for the belief to be justified (whether or not Rick is philosophically sophisticated or even aware of the

---

[26]N. T. Wright, *Jesus and the Victory of God,* vol. 2 of *Christian Origins and the Question of God* (Minneapolis: Fortress, 1996), 117.

[27]N. Thomas Wright, "Five Gospels but No Gospel: Jesus and the Seminar," in *Authenticating the Activities of Jesus,* ed. Bruce Chilton and Craig Evans, NTTS 28/2 (Leiden: Brill, 1999), 119. Wright goes on to say, "My own study of Jesus leads me to believe that 'conservative' and 'orthodox' Christianity, in the twentieth century at least, has often, indeed quite regularly, missed the point of Jesus' sayings and deeds almost entirely." Wright says further that traditionally minded Christians are "capable of all kinds of fantasies and anachronisms in reading the Gospels, and to pull the blanket of canon over our heads and pretend that we are safe in our private, fideistic world is sheer self-delusion." "Jesus and the Identity of God," *ExAud* 14 (1998): 49.

[28]Kenton L. Sparks, *God's Word in Human Words: An Evangelical Appropriation of Critical Biblical Scholarship* (Grand Rapids: Baker Academic, 2008), 168–69.

[29]Ibid., 70.

epistemological debates is not at issue, as it is possible to be committed to a position while untutored in matters epistemological). Suppose further still that Rick is convinced that the methods of CBS are the best (or only) way to discover the truth about the purported exodus event. If he becomes convinced that CBS undercuts the evidence for belief in a historical exodus, then he is in epistemic trouble. In this case, Rick likely will conclude that his (prior) belief in a historical exodus is not justified.

Of course this route is not inevitable for Rick. Suppose that when faced with the challenges of CBS, he reviews the classical theistic arguments and the arguments from religious experience, and again he concludes that they (or at least some of them) provide justification for belief in the existence of God. He also revisits evidential arguments for distinctly Christian claims, and again he concludes that belief in the incarnation and resurrection of Jesus Christ is justified. Beyond this, he thinks that the New Testament and the basic Christian account of salvation require a historical exodus, and he concludes that there is yet warrant for belief in a historical exodus. Or Rick's investigations into the matter introduce him to the work of Old Testament scholars and Egyptologists who make a strong case for the historicity of the exodus.[30] Either way, Rick is—despite the challenges from some proponents of CBS—convinced that belief in Mosaic authorship enjoys epistemic justification. So while it *may* be the case that Rick's classical foundationalism leaves him vulnerable to the claims of CBS, it does not follow that such claims will inevitably be decisive for him.

Consider Rick's brother Corey. Corey is a coherentist. He is also a convinced internalist (whether or not he has been burdened with a philosophical education and is an informed coherentist or internalist) who thinks that the methods of CBS are generally above reproach. Corey has thought that there was a historical exodus, but he becomes aware of the "consensus" of CBS that there was *not* a historical exodus. He cannot square his belief in a historical exodus with the web of beliefs that include the conviction that CBS offers the best methods *and* that CBS will not allow belief in a historical exodus. Corey's internalism demands that he have direct access to the grounds for his beliefs, and since he cannot access adequate grounds for belief in the historicity of the exodus, the conclusion becomes clear: intellectual honesty demands that he reject the view that there was a historical exodus.

Now consider further their cousin Bill. Bill holds to "Reformed Epistemology"; he is a modest foundationalist who also eschews internal-

---

[30]Good places to begin are James K. Hoffmeier, *Israel in Egypt: The Evidence for the Authenticity of the Exodus Tradition* (Oxford: Oxford University Press, 1996); and Kenneth A. Kitchen, *On the Reliability of the Old Testament* (Grand Rapids: Eerdmans, 2003).

ism for (some version of) externalism. His belief in the truthfulness of the Bible is warranted because it is triggered by the "internal instigation of the Holy Spirit," and, as part of the "great things of the gospel" it is part of the fulsome package of "warranted Christian belief" and thus part of the set of beliefs that is "properly basic." In this case Bill would have van Inwagen's "grounds" for these beliefs—grounds that are completely independent of CBS. Furthermore, since CBS has "established nothing" against the "thesis that ordinary Christians have grounds independent" of CBS for believing in the essential historicity of the biblical accounts, CBS does nothing whatsoever to undermine or overturn "Reformed Epistemology" or what it delivers. Suppose Bill is confronted by the claims of CBS that belief in a historical exodus is deeply mistaken and embarrassingly naive. He is not able, by the tools of CBS, to make a compelling case for a historical exodus. But he has a properly basic belief in the "great things of the gospel," and he is convinced that the biblical account of the gospel is deeply intertwined with an actual Passover and exodus. Upon reflection, he realizes that CBS does nothing to undercut or overturn his "warranted Christian belief," and he concludes therefore that it does nothing to destroy his belief that what the Bible says about the matter is warranted. He concludes with van Inwagen, therefore, that he "may therefore ignore any skeptical historical claims . . . with a clear conscience." This does not mean that he *must* or *should* ignore such claims. On the contrary, Bill is intrigued by them and continues to wrestle with the claims of CBS on the matter. Many of his friends (some of whom know the methods and conclusions of CBS much better than he does) see things very differently than he does, and he is genuinely interested in conversation. But as he engages them, he takes the scorn of the guild of CBS for what it is. While honestly admitting that he does not have a complete answer to their arguments (on strictly critical grounds), he nonetheless holds fast to his belief in the truthfulness of the claims of Christ and Scripture.

Even from this brief reflection, we are in a position to see that epistemological commitments make a major difference in engagement with the claims of CBS. This is true whether those epistemological commitments are informed and sophisticated or inchoate and ill-formed. The believer who holds to Reformed Epistemology is in a position to conclude that while the declarations of CBS might be important and interesting, they do nothing to touch grounds for beliefs that are not reliant upon such methodology. Such a believer may—though he need not—ignore the conclusions of CBS. The classical foundationalist (or the coherentist), on the other hand, may be in a very different situation. To be clear, he *may be* in a difficult epistemic place, but he is not necessarily in that place. The classical foundationalist who takes

CBS to be finally authoritative on the matters in question will likely face a dilemma, as will the coherentist. But those coherentists and classical foundationalists who take a critical look at CBS itself and then conclude that it is not above reproach might be in a position to maintain a healthy distance from it as well. Indeed, some philosophers have looked at crucial aspects of CBS and concluded just that: CBS itself, at least as commonly practiced, is not above reproach. Interestingly, it is supported by, and sometimes seems to be motivated by, distinctly *philosophical* underpinnings. And, as we shall see, this philosophical support itself is not entirely stable.

### CBS and the Shadow of Naturalism

As we have seen, philosophical reflection on the deliverances of CBS sometimes shows that critical conclusions about the nature, meaning, and authority of the Bible may not have the last word. But sometimes further reflection probes the very foundations of the enterprise.[31] Central to much contemporary CBS is commitment to the principles of *correlation*, *analogy*, and *criticism*. From their formulation by Ernst Troeltsch forward, these principles (or their siblings and progeny) have exercised great influence on biblical scholarship.[32] The principle of correlation can be roughly stated as the belief that explanations for historical events should be found with reference to their immediate and natural historical contexts. The principle of analogy maintains that records of alleged historical occurrences should be understood by comparison to what happens (or might happen) today. The principle of criticism is basically the view that the historian stands as judge over the record of the historical incident. The discussions of these principles have a long history, and the debates are not yet done. While this is not the place to rehearse the history of such debates, it is worth noting that the principles themselves have drawn criticism on distinctly *philosophical* grounds. C. Stephen Evans has pointed out that these principles usually come loaded up with strongly internalist (and foundationalist-evidentialist) baggage—but as we have seen, there is good reason to think that such epistemologies themselves are somewhat less than compelling.[33] Evans has pointed out further that the principles are ambiguous; the principles of correlation and analogy, for instance, seem to be potentially problematic only when (metaphysical) naturalism is smuggled into them.[34] But

[31]These are not, alas, always happy encounters. See the introduction to Stump and Flint, *Hermes and Athena*, xiii–xvi.
[32]One of the most forceful and rigorous of the contemporary advocates is Van Harvey, e.g., *The Historian and the Believer* (New York: Macmillan, 1966).
[33]C. Stephen Evans, *The Historical Christ and the Jesus of Faith: The Incarnational Narrative as History* (Oxford: Oxford University Press, 1996), 186.
[34]Ibid., 198–99.

this very smuggling operation is what often happens. And when naturalistic assumptions serve to control "real history," we should not be surprised to see the proponents of historical criticism either struggle to maintain belief in the historical reliability of the biblical accounts or give up on that reliability entirely (or, in some cases, almost entirely). But the claims of metaphysical naturalism should have no hold on historians who are Christian believers (or other theists). Moreover, as Plantinga's famous "evolutionary argument against naturalism" shows, metaphysical naturalism itself is not without some stiff challenges (some of which are epistemological in nature).[35] As Evans points out:

> It is not clear, therefore, why a historian who did not share Harvey's philosophical bases would be disqualified as a "critical historian." Harvey's procedure is in effect a commitment to a kind of "methodological naturalism" in history, but if I am right in claiming that it is Harvey's dubious metaphysical naturalism, or equally dubious epistemological assumptions about miracles, that underlie this methodological naturalism, then there seems no reason at all to think that a responsible, critical historian must follow Harvey.[36]

Evans speaks here both of "metaphysical naturalism" and "methodological naturalism." What about "methodological naturalism" (hereafter MN)? Should a Christian who denies metaphysical naturalism (naturally enough) also engage in historical scholarship that proceeds pretty much *as if* naturalism were true? *Can* a Christian historian do so? *Must* he or she do so? Evans engages the thought of N. T. Wright on this question.

Evans argues that Wright should be interpreted as a kind of methodological naturalist with respect to historical studies.

> The historical method generally followed by Wright (with some important exceptions to be noted) is essentially similar to that defended by Ernst Troeltsch and Van A. Harvey, and this method is the dominant method employed by historical biblical scholars [and] this historical method incorporates a commitment to what is usually termed "methodological naturalism."[37]

Evans helpfully analyzes the category of "methodological naturalism," and he draws a distinction between what he calls Type-1 MN and Type-2 MN.

---

[35]See, e.g., Plantinga, *Warranted Christian Belief*, 199–240. See also Michael C. Rea, *World without Design: The Ontological Consequences of Naturalism* (Oxford: Oxford University Press, 2002).
[36]Evans, *Historical Christ*, 197.
[37]C. Stephen Evans, "Methodological Naturalism in Historical Biblical Scholarship," in *Jesus and the Restoration of Israel: A Critical Assessment of N. T. Wright's* Jesus and the Victory of God, ed. Carey C. Newman (Downers Grove, IL: InterVarsity, 1999), 182, see also 188–95.

Type-1 MN holds that the rules of MN are "somehow binding or obligatory on historians, such that one who does not follow them is not practicing good history."[38] Type-2 MN, on the other hand, maintains only that "these rules simply prescribe a method that can be followed and may be valuable to follow, without regarding that method as obligatory for historians."[39] Evans argues that Type-2 MN is a route that is open to believing historians, and I think that the conclusions of Evans are sane and sensible. We soon will return to these issues, but for now these basic points should be clear: first, the dominant principles of (much) CBS are often freighted with hidden—but dubious— epistemological and metaphysical commitments; second, Christian scholars would be well advised to understand these entanglements and to stand firm in their own epistemological and metaphysical commitments (where those are defensible). Beyond this, Evans's conclusion that there might be a proper place for CBS brings us to another interesting question: What are we to make of "believing" biblical criticism?[40]

### What about "Believing CBS"?

Evans's reflections regarding "methodological naturalism" raise some inter- esting questions about the future of the involvement of biblical scholars who are committed to classical orthodoxy in the work of CBS. The proposals of Sparks are particularly intriguing here, both because he actually begins with attention to "epistemology" and because he is a bright and knowledgeable Old Testament scholar who has wrestled at length with these issues. His book *God's Word in Human Words: An Evangelical Appropriation of Critical Biblical Scholarship* actually begins with a chapter titled "Epistemology and Hermeneutics." Unfortunately, there is not a lot here in the way of devel- oped hermeneutics, and there is even less in the way of careful epistemology.[41] Instead, we are presented with a kind of general "intellectual history," one that proceeds by way of a surface discussion of the "pre-modern," "modern," and "postmodern" periods (Kant is dealt with in two paragraphs; Hegel's influential contributions get one). The main lessons to be learned from this history seem to be these: Descartes was very important, and "Cartesianism" is very bad—"faulty Cartesian philosophy" is the root of many evils and is "fundamentally flawed," while Carl F. H. Henry's "arguments are thoroughly

---

[38]Ibid., 184.

[39]Ibid.

[40]See, e.g., Sparks, *God's Word in Human Words*, 133.

[41]Sparks states that some friends who read earlier drafts suggested that the book would be stronger without this chapter (ibid., 25). I am in firm agreement with these friends. Sparks's considerable knowledge of CBS is not matched by his grasp of epistemology (or historical and systematic theology).

Cartesian, of course."[42] It is not at all clear how Sparks conceives of the relations between hermeneutics and epistemology or between epistemology and revelation. The closest we get to a concrete epistemological proposal is his advocacy of something called "practical realism." Thankfully, we learn that Sparks insists that humans are finite knowers (though I must confess that I did not know that such was in question) and that he thinks that genuine knowledge is available. But we are left to wonder what "practical realism" means (with respect to epistemic justification, etc.). Meanwhile, he brings an impressive volley of arguments from CBS to the conclusion(s) that many traditional beliefs about the nature and claims of Scripture are simply untenable, and he concludes by heaping scathing criticism upon evangelical biblical scholarship: evangelical scholars are akin to those who would deny the Copernican revolution and have a "well-deserved reputation for not playing fair."[43]

Sparks's full-throated advocacy of CBS raises some important questions about just what is meant by "criticism." He explicitly endorses the principles of correlation, analogy, and criticism (two of them with their Troeltschian labels unpeeled).[44] He thinks that the need for this critical approach is "obvious," but he denies that employment of it must go down the way of naturalism.[45] He insists that he is completely open to the possibility of the supernatural in history, but he also insists that where the tools of CBS do not uncover what should be unmistakable, telltale signs of the supernatural, we should conclude that there was no such supernatural activity. This leads Sparks to conclude that while there is decent historical evidence that Jesus Christ was raised from death, there is no such comparable historical evidence that, say, Jericho was razed to death: honest Christians should conclude not only that such events as the Passover and exodus either never occurred or were "much less significant historically than the Bible now remembers"[46] but also that "the Pentateuch's narrative is more often story than history, and that its five books were composed by several different authors living in contexts at some remove from the early history of Israel."[47] The story continues with a standard laundry list of critical issues: the historical records of early Israel are contradictory and not trustworthy as historical sources; a "serious and sober reading of Isaiah will easily suggest to readers that large portions of this prophetic collection

---

[42]Ibid., 258, 138.
[43]Ibid., 373. While he says it would be "too strong and unfair" to describe evangelical biblical scholarship as "flat-earth" scholarship (373), Sparks does describe the work of Kenneth A. Kitchen as an argument "that the earth was flat" (12).
[44]Ibid., 57.
[45]Ibid.
[46]Ibid., 157.
[47]Ibid., 100.

were not written by an eighth century prophet whose name was Isaiah"; the Synoptic Gospels are partly history but partly fictive; and overall there are a great deal of mistaken historical claims, fabrications, and propaganda within the Bible.[48] It is hard to avoid the conclusion that while there is openness to the supernatural *in principle*, in actual practice most claims of CBS are taken fully on board. Maybe Sparks is not sufficiently critical of the common employment of the principle of criticism. Perhaps he is not sufficiently critical of the principle itself.

Sparks's advocacy of CBS also raises questions about what he means by the claim that it is "*believing* criticism." His discussion of the views of Jesus (and the writers of the New Testament) is telling indeed.

> Most modern biblical scholars believe that Moses, Isaiah, and Daniel were not the authors of the books traditionally attributed to them. The difficulty this seems to raise is that Jesus and the New Testament writers clearly identified Moses as the author of the Pentateuch, Isaiah as the author of the second half of Isaiah, and Daniel as the author of the Daniel apocalypses.[49]

Sparks is undoubtedly correct in pointing out that Jesus and Paul believed in Mosaic authorship of the Pentateuch (e.g., John 5:46–47; 7:19; Acts 3:22; Rom. 10:5). It seems to me that Sparks lays this out as an all-or-nothing proposition (or something very close to it): either affirm Mosaic authorship or deny any compositional or redactional activity. It also seems to me that this approach is overly simplistic—surely it is possible to affirm Mosaic authorship *and* allow for what seem to be obvious threads and layers of later activity. But *Sparks* is convinced that there indeed *is* a dilemma, and he paints the options with utter starkness: Jesus believed in and taught Mosaic authorship of the Pentateuch, but CBS insists that Moses did not write the Pentateuch. Supposing the dilemma is really this grim, what is to be done?[50]

Sparks's response is clear. There is only one responsible way forward: honesty demands that we go with CBS over Jesus and deny that Moses had anything to do with the authorship of the Pentateuch. For although Christians "will want to consider seriously what Jesus and the New Testament writers said about the Old Testament," this does nothing to outweigh the conclusions of CBS.[51]

---

[48]Ibid., 108 (73–132).

[49]Ibid., 164.

[50]Such a supposition helps us see the epistemological and theological issues more clearly, and at any rate it helps us engage directly with the proposals of scholars such as Sparks.

[51]Sparks, *God's Word in Human Words*, 164.

If the critical evidence against the traditional authorial attributions in the Old Testament is as strong as it seems to be, then it is perhaps evangelical Christology—and not critical scholarship—that needs to be carefully reconsidered. . . . So the putative testimony of Jesus and the Bible, while important, cannot be adduced as foolproof evidence for our judgment about who wrote the books of the Old Testament. There are good reasons to suspect that Jesus' words about these matters are not historical-critical testimonies so much as the everyday assumptions of a pious, first-century Jew. Precritical orthodoxy makes it possible, and modern critical research makes it likely, that Jesus has not told us who really wrote the Pentateuch, Isaiah, or Daniel.[52]

So for Sparks it comes to this: either the views of Jesus or the assured conclusions of CBS. At least we know what the choice is. What we do not yet know is what good reasons there might be for preferring CBS over the views of Jesus. Sparks points out that the statements of Jesus probably were not "historical-critical testimonies." Surely Sparks is right; I am tempted to say, "*Of course* Jesus was not engaged in historical-critical research." But how is this even relevant? If—and only if—historical-critical research were the only way that Jesus might learn about the authorship of the Pentateuch (or other matters), then we might have good reason to dismiss the claims of Jesus. But why think that Jesus would have had to do historical-critical research to know such things?[53] I can readily think of other possible ways of knowing—for starters, being the omniscient incarnate Son might be relevant.

Perhaps this is too quick, for Sparks says that we may need to reevaluate our commitment to classical christology. Exactly what he is proposing is something less than pellucid, but one option is this: because Jesus was fully human, he was necessarily mistaken about some matters.[54] Sparks elsewhere often conflates finitude and error, as if to be human *qua human* is to be mistaken.[55] So Jesus "would have erred in the usual way that other people err because of their finite perspectives."[56] If Jesus was fully human (as Scripture teaches and the

---

[52]Ibid., 164–65.

[53]Although this is not the place to explore such matters, I register my concern that Sparks has routinely misunderstood patristic (and Reformation) views of the nature and authority of Scripture. Notably, Sparks fails to engage such important work as that of John D. Woodbridge or Richard A. Muller.

[54]Or perhaps Sparks thinks that Jesus's problems come with his *fallen* human nature; on which see Sparks, *God's Word in Human Words*, 252 n. 67. To this possibility I will make only these brief observations: first, Sparks gets the traditional view exactly backward (his reference to Aquinas shows that Aquinas takes the opposite view); second, there are very good theological reasons to hold to the traditional view and *reject* the (oft-confused) notion that the humanity of Christ was "fallen." To the latter, see Oliver D. Crisp, *Divinity and Humanity: The Incarnation Reconsidered* (Cambridge: Cambridge University Press, 2007), 90–117.

[55]E.g., Sparks, *God's Word in Human Words*, 55, 171, 225–26, 252–54, 298–99.

[56]Ibid., 252.

creeds affirm), then Jesus necessarily was mistaken about some things. And, of course, if CBS says that his views on the authorship of the Pentateuch (or other matters) could not be right, then his views on these matters would be in the "mistaken" category. Several observations are important here. First, and fundamentally, on this reading, Sparks is committed to the view that the property *being said or authored by a human* entails the property *being mistaken*. But he gives us no reason to think that this entailment holds. Nor *are* there good reasons to think that this entailment holds.[57] There are, on the other hand, good reasons to think that such a claim is manifestly false (as accurate statements on all sorts of matters are available).

The second and more important set of observations concerns the christology itself. On standard medieval christologies (either part-whole or subject-accident models), the human soul of Christ enjoys the beatific vision and its privileges.[58] I cannot see how Sparks's mistaken Jesus could be consistent with such models. Major alternative pro-Chalcedonian approaches do not seem much more promising for Sparks's view. Thomas V. Morris's "Two Minds" christology posits a divine mind that is (naturally enough) omniscient as well as a human mind that is limited and finite (as human minds are).[59] But his account has an "asymmetrical accessing relationship" between the two minds, and the divine mind (as omniscient) knows all things and informs the human mind of what it needs to know. On this model the human mind is limited, but that does not mean that it is committed to false beliefs. It is one thing to say, "I don't know" (cf. Mark 13:32); it is another thing entirely to make something up or even mistakenly to repeat a falsehood. Some versions of kenotic christology might be more hospitable to Sparks's proposal, but even there we see what is at best an awkward fit.[60] Suppose that Jesus empties himself of the standard access and use of the essential divine-knowledge attribute (omniscient-unless-kenotically-and-redemptively-incarnate) and

---

[57] At least none that I can think of—which admittedly isn't very impressive.

[58] On these proposals, see Richard Cross, *The Metaphysics of the Incarnation: Thomas Aquinas to Duns Scotus* (Oxford: Oxford University Press, 2002); Marilyn McCord Adams, *Christ and Horrors: The Coherence of Christology* (Cambridge: Cambridge University Press, 2006), 108–43.

[59] Thomas V. Morris, *The Logic of God Incarnate* (Ithaca, NY: Cornell University Press, 1986); "The Metaphysics of God Incarnate," in *Trinity, Incarnation, and Atonement: Philosophical and Theological Essays*, ed. Ronald J. Feenstra and Cornelius Plantinga Jr. (Notre Dame, IN: University of Notre Dame Press, 1989), 110–127.

[60] Some of the more radical kenotic christologies probably *would* fit well with Sparks's proposal, but these are *alternatives* to the Chalcedonian faith rather than versions of it. See the illuminating essay of Thomas R. Thompson, "Nineteenth-Century Kenotic Christology: The Waxing, Waning, and Weighing of a Quest for a Coherent Orthodoxy," in *Exploring Kenotic Christology: The Self-Emptying of God*, ed. C. Stephen Evans (Oxford: Oxford University Press, 2006), 74–11.

simply does *not* know "the day or the hour."[61] Would this mean that he was mistaken about Moses? Not at all; even on kenotic accounts, the incarnate Son is led and nourished by the Holy Spirit, who protects him and who gives him divine knowledge. Even on kenotic models of the incarnation, it does not follow that Jesus was mistaken about Moses. To the contrary, there still might be good reason to believe that he would have been *right* about such things.

Sparks offers yet another possibility. He says that "even if Jesus knew the critical fact that Moses did not pen the Pentateuch, it is hardly reasonable to assume that he would have revealed this information to his ancient audience."[62] Note that this move assumes the very issue in question and so begs the question. But note further the very important theological claim that is being made here: if Jesus knows that Moses had nothing to do with the writing of the Pentateuch but nonetheless *says* that it was written by Moses, then it is clear that Jesus is not merely mistaken—he is actively and intentionally bearing false witness. What else is there to conclude from such a suggestion? Would not Jesus be stating as true something that he knows to be false? Does not this make the christological situation worse: instead of a mistaken Jesus who knows far less about his Scriptures than modern critical scholars know, would we not now have a Jesus who intentionally misleads?

So what Sparks offers is this choice: the claims of Jesus or the assured conclusions of CBS—and with the latter a rejection of commitment to classical, orthodox christology.[63] At least we know what the stakes are. As for me and my house, in such a dilemma we will go with orthodox christology and with the teachings of Jesus over the pronouncements of CBS. And we think that there is good epistemic *warrant* for doing so—warrant that CBS does not undercut or override.

## Some Concluding Reflections

*Do you want us to listen to you?* As a theologian (and preacher) who wants to foster good interpretation of the Bible, I highly respect and deeply value rigorous biblical scholarship. I want "us" to listen to "you"—but I also want "you" to have something truly valuable to say to "us." I don't wish to discourage good biblical scholarship, but I do dare to hope for some improvements.

---

[61] See Ronald J. Feenstra, "Reconsidering Kenotic Christology," in Feenstra and Plantinga, *Trinity, Incarnation, and Atonement,* 128–52.

[62] Sparks, *God's Word in Human Words,* 165.

[63] Note that this is not the same as saying that Sparks pushes us to *reject* orthodox christology (or that he does so himself). But what is clear is this: Sparks expects us to be more committed to CBS than to the beliefs and claims of Jesus himself.

In this essay I have, following the barest sketch of some important issues in religious epistemology, tried to show that while some epistemological positions might leave the scholar critically vulnerable to whatever the latest "consensus" of CBS dictates to us, there are other approaches that do not depend upon the pronouncements of CBS for robust belief and confidence. Indeed, there are some epistemological positions that do not depend upon CBS, are not undercut by CBS, and thus make it possible for the believer (with van Inwagen) to "ignore" the skeptical claims of CBS with a "clear intellectual conscience." I have also suggested that CBS is (at least partially, perhaps mostly) operating upon distinctly philosophical scaffolding, but that there is reason to suspect that this very scaffolding is itself unstable.[64] I conclude that there is good reason to think that, say, *believing what Jesus says is authoritative* enjoys warrant. Sparks says that the views of Jesus are not "foolproof evidence" against the pronouncements of CBS.[65] There is a sense in which Sparks is undoubtedly correct; we do not have to look far to see that this kind of evidence does not penetrate certain forms of foolishness. But how does that observation count as an objection against taking the statements of Jesus as authoritative?

I suggest that there is a better way for "believing CBS" to proceed. Recall Evans's distinction between different versions of methodological naturalism: Type-1 MN holds that the rules of CBS are "binding and obligatory"; Type-2 MN holds only that the methods of CBS "can be followed and may be valuable for historians" but do not give the only or final word on all matters (historical or otherwise).[66] While Type-1 MN is overly restrictive and itself without warrant, Type-2 MN might be very valuable for a whole range of reasons. As Evans explains, it has parallels.[67]

Suppose that Kelly, a Christian bioethicist, wishes to convince her colleagues that a particular research program *P* is morally problematic. Kelly's orthodox Christianity may give her distinctly religious or theological reasons and motivation to oppose *P*, but she knows that these reasons will not be persuasive to her Buddhist and secular colleagues. She does, however, find common ground with these colleagues, and she argues accordingly. She should not, of course, be duplicitous; she should not pretend to be something (a secularist) that she is not. But nor should she ignore or reject her Christian beliefs. She may know that she has *additional* reason to reject *P*, and she

---

[64]Philosophers also sometimes criticize the actual *practices* (as well as the principles) of various sectors of the CBS world. See, e.g., William P. Alston on the criterion of "double dissimilarity." "Historical Criticism of the Synoptic Gospels," in *"Behind" the Text*, 151–79.

[65]Sparks, *God's Word in Human Words*, 165.

[66]Evans, "Methodological Naturalism," 184.

[67]Ibid., 199–200.

may wish that her colleagues shared that basis with her. In fact, she might think that getting them to embrace the right view about P might give them reason seriously to consider the Christian faith. In the case that her "common ground" arguments are less than fully convincing, she can readily admit that fact while still not capitulating on the issue or ignoring her own convictions. She may use all the "common ground" arguments available to her, and she can admit that sometimes they are sufficient for the task but that sometimes they may not be. But they are not the only—or even the strongest—reasons for her to take a position on P. She can do her best work, honestly admit its strengths and weaknesses, and at the end of the day's labors rest with a "clear intellectual conscience."

To use a different illustration, Max the Mountaineer may know of several routes to the top of a challenging peak. He joins a party of climbers who insist that the route up the Liberty Ridge is the *only* route to ascend, and he agrees to help them. Part way up, however, they realize that they simply cannot make it. Perhaps they could summit with better tools or more training, but they come to the conclusion that they simply cannot reach the summit in current conditions. Max is disappointed, for he sincerely wants his fellow climbers to succeed. But the fact that they do not make it via the Liberty Ridge does not mean that the summit *cannot* be reached, and the fact that his fellow climbers refuse to try any route other than the Liberty Ridge does not mean that there are no other routes. If Max knows of other routes and has climbed via them—if he has seen the view from the top—then he will continue to believe that there is a summit and that it in fact is within reach. He may be disappointed that he cannot either help his fellow climbers make it via the Liberty Ridge or convince them to try another route, but he may rest from his labors with his belief that the mountain can be climbed yet intact. And he may do so "with a clear intellectual conscience."

I suggest that pursuing CBS in the Type-2 MN sense (especially when done from an externalist epistemology) might be helpful for believing Christians.[68] Accordingly, the Christian who engages in CBS might weigh evidence and make arguments with all the rigor that he can muster. He has good reason to hope that these arguments will be successful and persuasive to other scholars. But he will not be tempted (or at least *as* tempted) to overestimate either the importance of the views with which he engages or his own work. He will see that his engagement with CBS is a valid exercise, one that might be helpful and salutary. For pragmatic and apologetic reasons, his work may be very

---

[68]I do not mean to suggest that this should be the course of action for *all* Christians (or all *honest* Christians).

valuable. But in the event that he faces a critical argument that he cannot answer, he does not feel pressure to capitulate immediately. If, after all, he has grounds for belief that are independent of CBS and that are not undercut by CBS, he has no reason to despair when faced with difficult arguments from CBS. Given his epistemic virtues, he will not wish to stretch or mash the evidence (the evidence available from CBS) in dubious ways. In the event that his arguments fail to convince other critical scholars, he can readily admit that as well—and again without feeling pressure (from epistemological internalism) to give up a belief simply because he cannot show exactly how it is justified for him.[69] If pursued in this way, perhaps critical biblical scholarship can be "appropriated" in a way that is both intellectually and spiritually healthy. For the sake of us all, I hope so.

[69]What I suggest here is in some respects parallel to the proposal of "skeptical theism" (with respect to the problem of evil). For an excellent introduction to this discussion, see Michael Bergmann, "Skeptical Theism and the Problem of Evil," in *The Oxford Handbook of Philosophical Theology*, ed. Thomas P. Flint and Michael C. Rea (Oxford: Oxford University Press, 2009), 374–99.

# 2

# THE PERIL OF A "HISTORYLESS" SYSTEMATIC THEOLOGY

## GRAHAM A. COLE

❖

## Introduction

I was in my second year as an undergraduate at the University of Sydney when a special meeting on campus was advertised by the Christian student organization. A classicist from nearby Macquarie University was coming to speak on the subject of the Christ of myth and legend. I was very new to the faith, so I did not know anything of the lecturer. I was expecting a polemic against the Christianity I had only recently embraced. Instead I found a careful argument about second-century Gnostic gospels and literature as presenting a Christ of religious imagination. At the very end Professor E. A. Judge said, almost as a throw-away line, that if anyone wanted a contrast, he should read Matthew, Mark, Luke, and John, the canonical Gospels.[1] He said that in those writings you have the testimony of authors who thought they were writing of things that had actually happened—in other words, history.

Historian Mark A. Noll sums up why history ought to matter to Christians.

> The Christian stake in history is immense. Every aspect of lived Christianity—worship, sacraments, daily godliness, private devotion, religiously inspired benevolence, preaching—every major theme of Christian theology—the nature of God in relation to the world, the meaning of Christ, the character of salvation, the fate of the universe—directly or indirectly involves questions about how the present relates to the past.[2]

---

[1] Professor E. A. Judge was in his first year as professor and went on to become a renowned classicist. See James R. Harrison's introduction to E. A. Judge, *The First Christians in the Roman World* (Tübingen: Mohr Siebeck, 2008), 1–32.
[2] Mark A. Noll, "History," in *Dictionary for the Theological Interpretation of the Bible*, ed. Kevin J. Vanhoozer (Grand Rapids: Baker Academic, 2005), 295. The whole article is worth reading.

But Noll's excellent point raises an important question: What is meant by the term *history*?

*History* as a term is, of course, ambiguous. It may refer to what actually happened (words spoken, deeds done, circumstances leading up to, consequences arising from). Or it may refer to our account of what actually happened (an interpretation of words spoken, deeds done, circumstances leading up to, consequences arising from). In this essay *history* refers to the former rather than the latter. As for that strange term *historyless*, I stipulatively mean theological articulations of the Christian faith that are more interested in the ideas of the faith than in the events that I believe are at its core.

To start, we consider the question of why history matters. And the history in mind is biblical history (e.g., the call of Abraham, the exodus, the incarnation and resurrection, and so forth).[3] Next, we consider the peril of doing systematic theology in a way that forgets the great deed at the center of the gospel. Even so, the value of systematic theology must not be neglected in reaction. Systematic theology has great value as a discipline. It asks normative questions (more anon). However, systematic theology needs to stay tethered to the historicity of biblically narrated events, lest it drift off to an alien place. The historically given needs full appreciation. Then we consider the idea of accommodation. The idea of accommodation (as in Calvin) as opposed to that of the accommodated sense (as in Kenton Sparks) helps preserve that appreciation. Finally, before drawing the discussion to a close, we look at the relation between systematic theology, history, and our worship.

## Why History Matters

History matters because of who God is in biblical presentation.[4] Noll, though writing in the first instance about the study of church history, captures the point well that the Christian faith has an "irreducibly historical character."

> The Bible itself is rife with explicit statements of that great truth. For instance, God gave the Ten Commandments to the children of Israel in direct consequence of his action-in-history on their behalf: "I am the Lord your God, who brought you out of Egypt, out of the land of slavery. You shall have no other

---

[3] Another sort of history also ought to matter to the systematician; namely, the history of Christian thought over the last two millennia. However, that important element in doing theology is not in purview here.

[4] This claim does not entail that every biblical book is a narrative. Proverbs for example, isn't. Nor does it entail that God from a literary point of view has only one way of disclosing his will and ways. A Gospel has a narrative structure but may contain genealogy, proverb, parable, song, and so forth. The Gospel of Luke is an example. Scripture exhibits a diversity of genres, but within the framework of an overarching narrative that stretches from creation through fall through redemption to consummation.

gods before me" (Exod. 20:2–3). The vision of the New Testament is just as fully taken up with historical realities. The narrative heart of Christian faith, as well as its central dogma, is the truth that the Word became flesh (John 1:14). The apostle John spoke further of the Christian faith in concrete terms of that "which we have heard, which we have seen with our eyes, which we have looked at and our hands have touched" (1 John 1:1). Luke wrote at the beginning of his Gospel that the Christian message depended on "the things that have been fulfilled among us, just as they were handed down to us by those who from the first were eyewitnesses and servants of the word" (Luke 1:1–2). The apostles spoke of events in Jewish history that provided "examples" for believers in the first century (1 Cor. 10:6, 11).[5]

God is rendered in Scripture not as some kind of explanatory principle cited to make sense of the natural world. The God of the Bible is not like the idea of water in Thales, the ancient Greek philosopher. For Thales, water was the key to understanding nature.[6] Rather the God of Scripture is the living God who creates, speaks, saves, and judges. Broadly speaking, sensitivity to the historical dimension of Scripture is not an option. It is inescapable if justice is to be done to the Bible's own content. Daniel L. Migliore is right to argue:

> Historical study of the Bible also reminds us that the narrative of the Bible refers to realities outside the text. The central narrative is not to be construed as a mere construct of the imagination of the community of faith. If the Gospels refer to the living God acting and suffering in Christ for our salvation, if the story they tell is not simply pious fiction, then historical study can never be *irrelevant* for Christian faith.[7]

Migliore draws our attention to "the central narrative." In fact, the Christian gospel may be construed as "an interpretation of history." E. A. Judge expresses this angle of vision in fine fashion: "There is one avowedly educational work in the New Testament corpus. [The Gospel of Luke is on view.] It is a history." He explains further: "It is aimed not simply at the inculcation of a set of ideas, but more particularly at the interpretation of a series of occurrences, the tradition of which is certified by the gospel writer. The apostolic catechesis is a reappraisal of history."[8] Lesslie Newbigin may be added to

---

[5] Mark A. Noll, *Turning Points: Decisive Moments in the History of Christianity*, 2nd ed. (Grand Rapids: Baker Academic, 2008), 15.

[6] A. P. Cavendish, "Early Greek Philosophy," in *A Critical History of Western Philosophy*, ed. D. J. O'Connor (New York: Free Press, 1964), 3.

[7] Daniel L. Migliore, *Faith Seeking Understanding: An Introduction to Christian Theology*, 2nd ed. (Grand Rapids: Eerdmans, 2004), 53, his emphasis.

[8] E. A. Judge, "The Times of This Ignorance: Christian Education as a Reappraisal of History, 1. History in the Apostolic Catechesis," *Journal of Christian Education* 1, no. 2 (June 1958): 81–82.

this chorus: "At the heart of the Christian message was a new fact: God had acted—and let us remember that the original meaning of 'fact' is the Latin factum, 'something done.'"[9]

## The Peril of Systematic Theology

Systematics can be great fun for the conceptually inclined. Exploring the propositional content of Scripture and the work of theologians reflecting on Scripture is an exercise full of possibilities.[10] For example, assuming that Christ took a perfect human nature in the incarnation, does that have any implications for the doctrine of Scripture? Christ is the Word of God; Scripture is the Word of God. There is an apparent nexus between christology and bibliology. If Christ is perfect, must it not follow that Scripture is perfect in some sense (in the autographs)? But what if Christ assumed fallen human nature? Would that mean that our understanding of perfection would need revision? And if there is a nexus between christology and bibliology, does it follow that the servant form of God's revelation in Christ and the servant form of God's revelation as Scripture mean that our understanding of the perfection of Scripture needs to be rethought? Thought experiments like this are part of the work of the systematician. As Bernard Ramm argues, theologians are trying to uncover the widest implications of the biblical text. This task is theological exegesis, and the great theologians were the masters of it (e.g., Calvin).[11] In this process of thinking theologically one can forget that the object of inquiry is ultimately God in self-disclosure: the God who has spoken and acted in time and space.[12] British theologian J. S. Whale was aware of the danger. He wrote with reference to the event of Good Friday:

> We have to get somehow from *mandata Dei* ["the commandments of God"] to *Deus mandans* ["the commanding God"] if our study of Christian doctrine is to mean anything vital. We want a living synthesis where those very facts,

---

[9]Lesslie Newbigin, *Proper Confidence: Faith, Doubt, and Certainty in Christian Discipleship* (Grand Rapids: Eerdmans, 1995), 4.

[10]There is more to Scripture than propositions. Scripture, in fact, contains a diversity of speech acts. To look no further than the Ten Commandments of Ex. 20:1–17, "I am the Lord your God who brought you up out of the land of Egypt" is a propositional claim (v. 1). However, "Honor your father and mother" is an imperative (v. 12). See the helpful essay by Nicholas Wolterstorff, "True Words," in *But Is It True? The Bible and the Question of Truth*, ed. Alan G. Padgett and Patrick R. Keifert (Grand Rapids: Eerdmans, 2006), 34–43.

[11]Bernard L. Ramm, "Biblical Interpretation," in Bernard Ramm et al., *Hermeneutics* (Grand Rapids: Baker, 1974), 28–29.

[12]Much in systematics depends upon whether in the first instance, logically speaking, the object of inquiry is God in self-revelation (e.g., B. B. Warfield), or the Christian consciousness (e.g., Friedrich Schleiermacher), or Christian praxis (e.g., Gustavo Gutiérrez).

which the intellect dissects and coldly examines, are given back to us with the wholeness which belongs to life. . . . Instead off putting off our shoes from our feet because the place whereon we stand is holy ground, we are taking nice photographs of the burning Bush, from suitable angles: we are chatting about theories of Atonement with our feet on the mantelpiece, instead of kneeling down before the wounds of Christ.[13]

Such awareness may keep the theologian from a perennial temptation: namely, to turn Scripture into a mere resource of ideas or a field in which to search for "logical cohesions" between concepts.[14]

It is no accident then that the great creeds of the early church such as the Apostles' and Nicene Creeds preserve the biblical narrative structure: the Father as Creator, the Son as incarnate, and the Spirit as life giver. These early Christians believed that God had spoken and acted not in some suprahistorical realm but in the here and now. For Gnostics like the Basilidians the idea of a real flesh-and-blood incarnation was an indigestible surd. There had to be another, more acceptable way to tell the Christ story. In this story—and a fantastic, complex story it is—Christ is the Father's first-begotten mind sent to deliver those who believe. He only appears to be human. But what of the cross? "Basilides" explains what happened this way:

Wherefore he did not himself suffer death, but a certain Simon of Cyrene, being compelled, bore the cross in his stead; Simon was transfigured by him, that he might be thought to be Jesus, and was crucified, through ignorance and error, while Jesus himself received the form of Simon, and, standing by, laughed at them. For since he was an incorporeal power [a spirit] . . . he transfigured himself as he pleased.[15]

The narrative structure of Scripture and creed should remind Christians, especially in liturgical churches every time they are rehearsed, that the God of Scripture and creed is no phantom.

---

[13] J. S. Whale, *Christian Doctrine* (London: Fontana, 1957), 146.

[14] D. A. Carson observes, "The danger is that sometimes a systematic reading of Scripture that tends to be atemporal—it's looking for the logical cohesions—may start overlooking the historical groundings of [biblical] texts." "Why Can't We Just Read the Bible?," *Modern Reformation* 19, no. 4 (July/August 2010): 34.

[15] This is Irenaeus's presentation of the second-century Basilides's position. There is some debate as to whether it was Basilides's own position or that of later Basilidians. Hence I have put *Basilides* in scare quotes. See, for the fuller quotation and discussion, J. Stevenson, ed., *A New Eusebius: Documents Illustrative of the History of the Church to A.D. 337* (London: SPCK, 1970), 81–83. Also see John Anthony McGuckin, *The Westminster Handbook to Patristic Theology* (Louisville: Westminster John Knox, 2004), 45, for a brief treatment. This Basilidian christology is docetic in that Christ only appears to be human (Gr. *dokein*, "to appear").

## The Point of Systematic Theology

In my view there are orders of Christian discourse. First in importance is gospel. (I will use *kerygma* as a synonym.) This is the news of what God has said and done in Christ to reconcile his alienated images to himself. There are a number of summaries of the gospel to be found in New Testament literature. For example, in Johannine literature we read most famously, "For God so loved the world that he gave his one and only Son, that whoever believes in him shall not perish but have eternal life" (John 3:16).[16] Paul also contributes examples. He reminds the Thessalonians:

> The Lord's message rang out from you not only in Macedonia and Achaia—your faith in God has become known everywhere. Therefore we do not need to say anything about it, for they themselves report what kind of reception you gave us. They tell how you turned to God from idols to serve the living and true God, and to wait for his Son from heaven, whom he raised from the dead—Jesus, who rescues us from the coming wrath. (1 Thess. 1:8–10)

His first letter to the Corinthians contains another important summary statement of the gospel: "For what I received I passed on to you as of first importance: that Christ died for our sins according to the Scriptures, that he was buried, that he was raised on the third day according to the Scriptures" (1 Cor. 15:3–4).

Indeed this news is what sets the Scriptures apart from other literature. The Bible is the Holy Bible in this set-apart sense. In Romans 1:1–4 Paul describes himself as an apostle set apart for the work of the gospel (Rom. 1:1). So too are the Scriptures (*graphais hagiais*, Rom. 1:2). Paul then writes that these Scriptures speak of Christ's descent from David and his resurrection from the dead (Rom. 1:2–4). In 2 Timothy 3:14–17 Paul reminds Timothy of how Timothy had been acquainted with Scripture from his infancy (2 Tim. 3:15). These Scriptures he describes as "holy Scriptures" (*hiera grammata*). They are able to make Timothy "wise for salvation through faith in Jesus Christ" (2 Tim. 3:15). As in Romans 1:1–4, in view is a body of writing set apart for the gospel task.

Next in logical order there is apology: the defense of truth claims. The news of Christ raises questions. This gospel holds out a great hope, but why believe it? The New Testament is plain. Believing the gospel is a faith venture, but not a blind faith venture. Jesus tells his disciples that if they do not believe him for what he says, they should believe him for what he does (John 14:11). The book of Acts speaks of "many convincing proofs" of the

---

[16]Scripture quotations in this chapter are from the New International Version, 1984 edition.

resurrection (Acts 1:3). Apology is at times addressed to the outsider, as in the case of Paul before King Agrippa: "So Paul motioned with his hand and began his defense: 'King Agrippa, I consider myself fortunate to stand before you today as I make my defense against all the accusations of the Jews, and especially so because you are well acquainted with all the Jewish customs and controversies'" (Acts 26:1–3). At other times apology may be addressed to the insider, as Paul's defense of the reality of Christ's resurrection in his first Corinthian letter shows (1 Cor. 15:1–20). Apology is not the province of only a few gifted Christian communicators though. Peter counsels every reader: "Always be prepared to give an answer to everyone who asks you to give the reason for the hope that you have" (1 Pet. 3:15). The great antithesis in the New Testament is not between faith and reason, but between faith and fear (Mark 4:40), as well as between faith and sight (2 Cor. 5:7).[17]

Systematic theology comes third and presupposes both the gospel and its apology. This discipline searches out the widest implications of the scriptural presentation. It asks normative questions in the light of what God has self-disclosed: What ought we to believe? What ought we to value? How ought we to live? Who ought we to worship? It is not content therefore with mere description: what Paul thought, what John thought, and so forth. It asks these questions in a logical order and organized way. However, if it loses touch with the kerygma, it is adrift. Indeed systematic theology has a further role of protecting the kerygma. For example, the Gospels tell of Christ who prayed to God the Father in the garden of Gethsemane (Luke 22:39–46). How can this be? Is not Christ God (as well as human)? Does this event not raise such a question? Drawing out the widest implications of the biblical testimony, in the context of early church debate, leads ultimately to the doctrine of the Trinity: one divine substance in three persons.

Last in logical order is Christian worldview building (*Weltanschauung*).[18] In this discourse, Christian thinkers in the light of the biblical given ask exploratory questions of every other discipline, from science to philosophy. However, when it comes to value, first things need to be first. This came home to me in a dramatic way when years ago I gave a talk on Marx and Christianity at a major state university. After the presentation I was in discussion with a Marxist law professor. A young Christian undergraduate inserted himself

---

[17]By "reason" I mean the human ability to recognize presuppositions and entailments, marshal evidence, and mount and refute arguments, in contradistinction to "Reason" with a capital *R* which situates the opinionated self as the arbiter of all claims to truth.

[18]The order is a logical one, not necessarily the existential one. The *ordo essendi* ("order of being") and *ordo cognoscendi* ("order of knowing") need not match. In life a Christian academic working in the field of psychology may focus first of all on Christian worldview building. See my "Do Christians Have a Worldview?," http://www.thegospelcoalition.org/pdf-articles/Cole.pdf.

into the conversation and began to challenge the Marxist on the lack of explanatory power of his worldview in comparison with the Christian one. The Marxist listened quietly and then said, "Tell me what your Christian worldview says about the role of economic forces in shaping human institutions." There was silence and the young man slipped away. It made me think. Did this young person's faith reside in the explanatory force of the Christian worldview or in the cross and the deed done there? Did he slip away with his Christian faith in tatters?

## Appreciating History: Doctrines and Divine Deeds

The great benefit held out in the New Testament testimony is the forgiveness of sins. This is particularly clear in Luke-Acts. In the Lukan Great Commission the risen Christ points out to his disciples that the forgiveness of sins is to be proclaimed in his name to all nations, with Jerusalem as the starting point (Luke 24:45–47). In Luke's second volume, Acts, whether to Jews or God-fearers, or more generally to Gentiles, the forgiveness of sins is the thematized blessing of the gospel (cf. Acts 2:38; 10:43; 13:38; 26:15–18). What is patent is that the forgiveness of sins is tied to a real Christ who came, and to a real deed done, the atonement. In other words, there is a vital nexus between key doctrines such as the forgiveness of sins and divine action in history.

A theologian of the past who appreciated the nexus between the forgiveness of sins and divine action was P. T. Forsyth, who wrote:

> The centre of Christ is where the centre of our salvation is. He is Christ, He is God, to us in that He saves us. And He is God by that in Him which saves us. He is Christ and Lord by His cross. Christian faith is our life-experience of complete forgiveness and final redemption in Christ. It does not *include* forgiveness; it *is* forgiveness. Its centre is the centre of forgiveness. . . . And we have it where the evangelical experience has always found forgiveness—in the cross. . . . Our faith begins with the historic Christ.[19]

In his day Forsyth was particularly concerned about those for whom "the centre of gravity has been transferred from the cross to the parable of the prodigal."[20]

Forsyth's concern remains relevant. I recall some years ago at a university listening to a lecture from a prominent liberal Christian. He argued that Christianity had nothing to do with this shed-blood-of-Christ business. Instead the Christian faith is summed up in the parable of the prodigal son. The son

---

[19]P. T. Forsyth, *The Cruciality of the Cross* (London: Hodder and Stoughton, 1909), 25–26, his emphasis.
[20]Ibid., 46.

repented of his behavior and returned home to the waiting father. The key to his change of mind was not the cross but self-moral awareness: "he came to his senses" (Luke 15:17). So must we, he contended. In so doing we too will be forgiven and accepted by God just as the father in the parable accepted and forgave his son. This was an example of the worse kind of proof texting. The parable was abstracted from the whole narrative flow of Luke-Acts with its Passion Narrative and the Christ who referred to his coming death in terms of the new covenant in his blood (Luke 22:20).

Helmut Thielicke usefully distinguishes two kinds of theology.[21] Cartesian theology starts from the ego, following Descartes's celebrated starting point for philosophical reflection (*cogito ergo sum*, "I think therefore I am"). This way of doing theology seeks relevance to the cultured despisers of Christianity. Schleiermacher, the father of modern liberal theology, is the classic example of this style of theologizing, as is Rudolf Bultmann and his demythologizing program in more recent times. Non-Cartesian or kerygmatic theology has a different starting point. There is a given. God has spoken. God has acted. There is consequently a message to be proclaimed. There is a given embraced by faith. This was P. T. Forsyth's position and Thielicke's own preference.

## Systematic Theology, Accommodation, and History

The history of Christian thought reveals a great richness in discussing Scripture and remains instructive. One of the most fertile ideas generated in such discussion is the idea of divine accommodation. It is found in Origen, Chrysostom, Augustine, Calvin, and others right up to the present day. Origen described accommodation in these terms: "God condescends and comes down to us, accommodating to our weaknesses, like a schoolmaster talking a 'little language' to his children, or like a father caring for his own children and adopting their ways."[22] Calvin also provides a case in point. For Calvin, God is like a great rhetorician who accommodates his discourse to the context of his hearers such that his communicative action is understood. Biblical anthropomorphisms provide illustrations for Calvin. God represents himself in Scripture as though he has a mouth, fingers, hands, arms, and feet. Yet, as Calvin well knows, God is Spirit and therefore bodiless.[23]

---

[21]Helmut Thielicke, *The Evangelical Faith*, vol. 1, *Prolegomena: The Relation of Theology to Modern Thought-Forms*, trans. Geoffrey W. Bromiley (Grand Rapids: Eerdmans, 1974), 212–18. Thielicke articulates the distinction in terms of Cartesian versus non-Cartesian theology or theology A versus theology B.
[22]Quoted in Alister E. McGrath, *Christian Theology: An Introduction*, 4th ed. (Malden, MA: Blackwell, 2007), 198.
[23]See the discussion of Calvin's view in ibid., 198–200.

Indeed, that they dared abuse certain testimonies of Scripture was due to base ignorance; just as the error itself sprang from execrable madness. The Anthropomorphites, also, who imagined a corporeal God from the fact that Scripture often ascribes to him a mouth, ears, eyes, hands, and feet, are easily refuted. For who even of slight intelligence does not understand that, as nurses commonly do with infants, God is wont in a measure to "lisp" in speaking to us? Thus such forms of speaking do not so much express clearly what God is like as *accommodate* the knowledge of him to our slight capacity. To do this he must descend far beneath his loftiness.[24]

As a teacher and preacher, I know this principle well. The difference in degrees of difficulty in a talk on the Trinity that I may give to a Sunday school class versus a doctoral seminar is considerable. The good teacher strives to start where the student is and then move on from there. So too with God, according to the accommodation thesis.

A recent controversial work on Scripture that appeals to the accommodation idea is that of Kenton Sparks. On the one hand, Sparks wants to affirm the Scriptures as God's Word, and, on the other hand, he alleges that Scripture is an errant-in-places human word.[25] The idea of accommodation provides him a conceptual tool to do so. His definition of accommodation is pivotal: "Accommodation is God's adoption in inscripturation of the human audience's finite and fallen perspective. Its underlying conceptual assumption is that in many cases God does not correct our mistaken human viewpoints but merely assumes them in order to communicate with us."[26]

This idea of accommodation constitutes the heart of Sparks's proposal that evangelicals need to be progressive in appropriating modern criticism in reading Scripture. Intellectual honesty and academic authenticity require no less. Sparks aggressively dismisses evangelicals who remain conservative in

---

[24]John Calvin, *Institutes of the Christian Religion*, ed. John T. McNeill, trans. Ford Lewis Battles (Philadelphia: Westminster, 1960), 1.13.1, my emphasis; in *The Comprehensive John Calvin Collection*, CD-ROM version (Rio, WI: Ages Software, 2002). The anthropomorphites were "[a] sect of Christians that arose in the fourth century in Syria and extended into Scythia, sometimes called Audians, from their founder, Audius. Taking the text of Genesis, i, 27, literally, Audius held that God has a human form." *The Catholic Encyclopedia*, vol. 1 (New York: Robert Appleton, 1907); in *New Advent: Featuring the Catholic Encyclopedia*, CD-ROM version, 2nd ed. (Pennsauken, NJ: Disc Makers, 2007).
[25]A much more modest proposal for rethinking an evangelical doctrine of inspiration is found in Peter Enns, *Inspiration and Incarnation: Evangelicals and the Problem of the Old Testament* (Grand Rapids: Baker Academic, 2005). Unlike Sparks, Enns affirms an analogy between christology and bibliology (cf. Enns, 17–18, and Kenton L. Sparks, *God's Word in Human Words: An Evangelical Appropriation of Critical Biblical Scholarship* (Grand Rapids: Baker Academic, 2008), 252–53). And unlike Sparks, Enns affirms the inerrancy of Scripture. See his "Response to G. K. Beale's Review Article of *Inspiration and Incarnation*," *JETS* 49 (2006): 323. However, Enns's own position carries its own raft of problems. Not the least of which is the way in which he affirms "myth" in Scripture—albeit qualified.
[26]Sparks, *God's Word in Human Words*, 230–31.

approach.[27] For example, on his view, the Pentateuch exhibits real contradictions and contains myths and legends.[28] He contends, "Accommodation does not introduce errors into Scripture; it is instead a theological explanation for the presence of human errors in Scripture."[29] In methodological terms, Sparks is comfortable with practicing *Sachkritik* ("content criticism" of a text). *Sachkritik* may lead the exegete to contend that there are errors in the text, as it has led Sparks. Ironically, the willingness to practice *Sachkritik*, according to Stephen Sykes, is one of the distinguishing characteristics of liberal theology. Sykes explains:

> Liberalism in theology is that mood or cast of mind which is prepared to accept that some discovery of reason may count against the authority of a traditional affirmation in the body of Christian theology. . . . For many Protestant Christians the most momentous step of theological liberalism is taken when they deny the traditionally accepted belief in the inerrancy of Scripture.[30]

Sparks has clearly taken that step, but wants to retain his identification as an evangelical. How stable this position is remains to be seen.[31]

Importantly, different kinds of accommodation have been described in theological literature. One is the Calvinian kind, which speaks of the divine stooping in communication in such a way that the truth-value of Scripture is not compromised. As Richard A. Muller describes this kind of accommodation:

> The Reformers and their scholastic followers all recognized that God must in some way condescend or accommodate himself to human ways of knowing in order to reveal himself. This *accommodatio* occurs in the use of human words and concepts for the communication of the law and gospel, but it in no way implies the loss of truth or the lessening of scriptural authority.[32]

Another kind is Socinian.[33] Here the divine stooping is content to use the erroneous conceptions of humankind as vehicles for communication. Again

---

[27]See ibid., 144–68, for Sparks's analysis of "the poverty of evangelical scholarship."

[28]Ibid., 218–20.

[29]Ibid., 256. Paradoxically, Sparks posits a God who speaks inerrantly and yet has left his people an errant Bible, 357.

[30]Stephen Sykes, *Christian Theology Today*, rev. ed. (London: Mowbray, 1983), 12. Sykes writes as a professed theological liberal.

[31]Jewish scholar James L. Kugel writes perceptively of the uncomfortable position of those scholars "wanting to have their Bible and criticize it too." Kugel, *How to Read the Bible: A Guide to Scripture, Then and Now* (New York: Free Press, 2007), 676–77.

[32]Richard A. Muller, *Dictionary of Latin and Greek Theological Terms: Drawn Principally from Protestant Scholastic Theology* (Grand Rapids: Baker, 1986), 19.

[33]For this useful distinction, see Glenn Sunshine, "Accommodation in Calvin and Socinus: A Study in Contrasts" (master's thesis, Trinity International University Library, Deerfield, IL, 1985), 78: "In all

Muller: "*The accommodated sense* [*sensus accommodatitius*] i.e. the sense
of a text of Scripture is interpreted, not literally, but with a view toward rec-
onciliation of problematic statements with historical-critical discoveries."[34]
Muller points out that this strategy was "denied by all the Protestant orthodox as applicable to Scripture" and further that this approach reflected "the
impact of rationalistic exegesis."[35] (This is where those slippery words *myth*
and *legend* come into play.) An implication of this view is that the systematician must carefully sift Scripture to find the kernels of truth amid the husks
of error. Aware of it or not, Sparks appears to be in step with this tradition.

History—what happened—is vital for any systematic theology that has a
high estimate of Scripture's value. That value is threefold: value as a source of
ancient cultural expressions (e.g., measuring weight in shekels), value as a witness
to God's words and deeds (e.g., rescuing Israel from Egypt, raising Jesus from
the dead), and value chiefly as God's inspired Word (as in the *theopneustos* of
2 Tim. 3:14–17, esp. v. 16).[36] There is a way of viewing divine accommodation
that does not dissolve that history. Augustine practiced it, as did Calvin. But
there is a way of viewing divine accommodation that is acidic. The doubts that
Sparks raises concerning the historicity of Israel's exodus from Egypt may serve
as an example.[37] Only the academic guild—or should I say a section of it—can
broker the differences between kernel and husk. Is this a way of doing theology
that ultimately will take the Bible out of the hands of the poor?[38]

To distinguish the two kinds of accommodation, perhaps it would be a
way forward to speak of accommodated *form*, on the one hand, and accommodated *sense*, on the other.

## Systematic Theology, History, and Worship

The last book in the biblical canon includes a vision of heavenly worship.
John the seer views God enthroned, and around him twenty-four elders on

---

this we see a great difference in the use of accommodation between Calvin and Socinus. While Calvin
appealed to accommodation to reconcile apparent contradictions in Scripture, Socinus accepted the
contradictions and used accommodation to explain why and how they happened." Socinus's view
and that of Sparks are strikingly similar at this point (see n. 28 above).

[34] Muller, *Dictionary of Latin and Greek Theological Terms*, 278, his emphases.

[35] Ibid.

[36] I take a different approach to Scripture's value as a source than does Brevard S. Childs, *Biblical
Theology of the Old and New Testaments: Theological Reflection on the Christian Bible* (Minneapolis:
Fortress, 1993), 98. The problem that Childs addresses occurs if Scripture is naturalized to be only
valuable as a source for ancient cultural expressions and nothing more.

[37] Sparks, *God's Word in Human Words*, 155–57.

[38] Ibid., 358–62; here Sparks recognizes the issues his position raises for instructing the laity who
are outside the guild of critical scholars. It would be interesting to know what he thinks folk in the
majority world should be taught, many of whom live in poverty.

their thrones. Four exotic creatures—one lion-like, another ox-like, a third human-like, and the last eagle-like—unceasingly declare the holiness of God.

> Holy, holy, holy
> is the Lord God Almighty,
> who was, and is, and is to come. (Rev. 4:8)

The twenty-four elders, in response to the creatures glorifying, honoring, and thanking God, fall down before the divine throne and declare,

> You are worthy, our Lord and God,
> to receive glory and honor and power,
> for you created all things,
> and by your will they were created
> and have their being. (Rev. 4:11)

Their praise has a narrative base. God is the Creator without whom creatures would cease to be. Their worship is not directed to an abstraction.

In the very next chapter, with the appearance of Jesus in the throne room as the Lamb of God, the four living creatures and the elders sing a new song. Creation this time is not the reason for praise, but redemption is. Hence, the accent is on newness.

> You are worthy to take the scroll
> and to open its seals,
> because you were slain,
> and with your blood you purchased men for God
> from every tribe and language and people and nation.
> You have made them to be a kingdom and priests to serve our God,
> and they will reign on the earth. (Rev. 5:9–10)

Here too is worship informed by a narrative structure, this time focusing on the historical story of Christ and his cross. The chorus swells: "Then I looked and heard the voice of many angels, numbering thousands upon thousands, and ten thousand times ten thousand. They encircled the throne and the living creatures and the elders" (Rev. 5:11). Redemption once more is the accent.

> Worthy is the Lamb, who was slain,
> to receive power and wealth and wisdom and strength
> and honor and glory and praise! (Rev. 5:12)

The chorus swells still further.

Then I heard every creature in heaven and on earth and under the earth and
on the sea, and all that is in them, singing:

> "To him who sits on the throne and to the Lamb be praise and honor
> and glory and power, for ever and ever!" (Rev. 5:13)

The only fitting response to the rehearsal of the story of redemption is universal creaturely praise. Thus, "the four living creatures said, 'Amen,' and the
elders fell down and worshiped" (Rev. 5:14).

On earth the irreducibly historical nature of the Christian faith can especially be seen when the people of God gather to celebrate the Lord's Supper.
As Paul reminds the Corinthians who were experiencing their own form of
"supper strife":[39]

> I received from the Lord what I also passed on to you: The Lord Jesus, on the
> night he was betrayed, took bread, and when he had given thanks, he broke it
> and said, "This is my body, which is for you; do this in remembrance of me."
> In the same way, after supper he took the cup, saying, "This cup is the new
> covenant in my blood; do this, whenever you drink it, in remembrance of me."
> For whenever you eat this bread and drink this cup, you proclaim the Lord's
> death until he comes. (1 Cor. 11:23–26)

When a church celebrates the Lord's Supper as an important part of its regular
assembly, it has a safeguard in place against historical amnesia. The systematic
theologian needs to be a member of a worshipping community mindful of
redemptive history.

## Conclusion

The God of the Bible is no mere organizing idea to help us find our way about.
Instead, the God to whom we pray is the one who creates, speaks, redeems,
and judges—the living God! God's redemptive entrance into our history has
created news. A deed has been done. This gospel (news) is an interpretation
of history. At its core is an interpreted event: Christ died (event) for our sins
(interpretation). Systematic theology done without sufficient sensitivity to
this news is full of peril.

It has been said that most academics want to know everything about something but theologians want to know something about everything.[40] In the quest

---

[39]Historically speaking, "supper strife" refers to the famous contretemps between Luther and Zwingli
at the time of the Reformation on the question of Christ's presence at the celebration of the Lord's
Supper. See my "Lord's Supper," in Vanhoozer, *Dictionary for the Theological Interpretation*, 464–65.
[40]It was Nicholas Lash of Cambridge, I believe.

to satisfy that curiosity, the theologian may forget that his or her work is done *coram deo* (before God), to use Calvin's phrase. Participation in the corporate worship of God's people helps us guard against that loss of memory. In particular the Lord's Supper has an inescapably historical referent. Here in the gathering of God's people the mighty words and deeds of God in Christ are recalled and confessed. Prayer and praise, reflective of the prayer and praise of heaven, issue on that basis. Theological reflection and piety need to comport. Once more J. S. Whale has it right: "The need is obvious. Is it met anywhere? The answer is that it is met in the worship of the Church, where the Christian religion is given to us in all its living meaning."[41]

---

[41] Whale, *Christian Doctrine*, 146.

# 3

# THE DIVINE INVESTMENT IN TRUTH

*Toward a Theological Account of Biblical Inerrancy*

## MARK D. THOMPSON

The doctrine of biblical inerrancy, long an emphatic affirmation of the Christian theological tradition in both its Protestant and Catholic branches, is looked upon with considerable suspicion in the first decades of the twenty-first century.[1] Much of that suspicion, it should be admitted, stems from the way some have used assent to this doctrine as a shibboleth. Individuals and institutions have been black-listed for raising doubts about the way the doctrine has been constructed in the past.[2] Only those who are able to affirm biblical inerrancy without qualification are to be trusted. Others have insisted that the doctrine is ill-conceived, insufficiently taking account of the simple fact that not every literary genre is susceptible to a judgment of truth or error.[3] They argue that the genuine humanity of the Bible, arising from the conscious contribution of its human authors (who were undeniably men and women of their time, with all the limitations this implies), is fatally compromised by a

[1]The concept of biblical inerrancy and even the term *inerrant* can be found in Catholic conciliar documents, the writings of the Reformers, and highly influential treatises from the patristic period. A number of important studies have gathered the evidence, chief among which must remain John D. Woodbridge, *Biblical Authority* (Grand Rapids: Zondervan, 1982); John D. Hannah, *Inerrancy and the Church* (Chicago: Moody, 1984); and the two volumes edited by D. A. Carson and John D. Woodbridge, *Scripture and Truth* (Grand Rapids: Zondervan, 1983), and *Hermeneutics, Authority, and Canon* (Grand Rapids: Zondervan, 1986).

[2]One of the most conspicuous examples remains Harold Lindsell, *The Battle for the Bible* (Grand Rapids: Zondervan, 1976). See also Craig D. Allert, *A High View of Scripture: The Authority of the Bible and the Formation of the New Testament Canon* (Grand Rapids: Baker, 2007), 165–71.

[3]"The best of inerrantists take into account the genres of Scripture but many do not. In these latter cases, everything tends to be flattened and reduced to a set of propositions that are then deemed to be inerrant." A. T. B. McGowan, *The Divine Spiration of Scripture: Challenging Evangelical Perspectives* (Nottingham: Inter-Varsity, 2007), 117.

preoccupation with Scripture's "perfections."[4] Most serious of all, though, is the way still others, reared on the strictest form of the doctrine of biblical inerrancy, have abandoned the faith under the intense questioning of biblical criticism.[5] Forced to choose between a perfect, unblemished text and seemingly incontrovertible evidence of error in Scripture, such people begin to lose confidence in the gospel proclaimed throughout Scripture. In the light of such cases, the doctrine of biblical inerrancy might even be deemed dangerous.

However, the doctrine should not be judged by the abuse of it or by inadequate explanations. An examination of each case may well demonstrate that the shipwreck of faith was not due entirely or even primarily to tension between an ideal Scripture such people were taught to trust and the reality of the Scripture they had in their hands. Strong convictions about the inerrancy of Scripture need not mean that this aspect of the doctrine of Scripture is elevated above all others in importance.[6] Biblical inerrancy need not entail literalism and a failure to take seriously the various literary forms in which God's words come to us, nor need it repudiate genuine human authorship in a Docetic fashion.[7] Precisely because a great deal of static has made it difficult for some to hear what is in fact being affirmed by the doctrine of biblical inerrancy, and passions continue to run high on both sides of the debates, careful attention must be given to a theological account of the doctrine. Such an account must be theological in at least two senses: it must argue from the nature and character of God as revealed in the teaching, life, death, and resurrection of Jesus Christ—that is, it must be a christological and evangelical

---

[4]This objection is forcefully made by Karl Barth, *Church Dogmatics*, 1.2, *The Doctrine of the Word of God*, ed. G. W. Bromiley and T. F. Torrance, trans. G. T. Thomson and H. Knight (Edinburgh: T&T Clark, 1956), 528: "We must not compromise either directly or indirectly the humanity of its form and the possibility of the offence which can be taken at it." Similar concerns are raised by John Webster in connection with what he calls the genuine "creatureliness" of the text. John Webster, *Holy Scripture: A Dogmatic Sketch* (Cambridge: Cambridge University Press, 2003), 20.
[5]"Too often it [the evangelical tradition] has equipped its students with a view of Scripture that could never endure rigorous academic scrutiny." Kenton L. Sparks, *God's Word in Human Words: An Evangelical Appropriation of Critical Biblical Scholarship* (Grand Rapids: Baker, 2008), 374.
[6]One contemporary account of inerrancy that seeks to keep a sense of biblical proportion is that of Timothy Ward, *Words of Life: Scripture as the Living and Active Word of God* (Nottingham: Inter-Varsity, 2009), 132–42.
[7]To this end, it is instructive that alongside the Chicago Statement on Biblical Inerrancy (1978) stands the Chicago Statement on Biblical Hermeneutics (1982) and the Chicago Statement on Biblical Application (1986). So too Don Carson's sage observation: "For it is one thing to find an example of a sentence in Scripture to which some such term as 'inerrant' does not easily apply, and another to infer that the Bible is errant. What believers mean when they say that the entire Bible is inerrant is that wherever the category (and in the theological arena it is a sophisticated category!) is applicable in the Bible, it prevails. To find some places where it is not directly applicable is not the same thing as finding places where it is applicable but is falsified." D. A. Carson, *The Gagging of God: Christianity Confronts Pluralism* (Leicester: Inter-Varsity, 1996), 165.

account; and it must attend to the self-attestation and the phenomena of the Scripture we have in fact been given.

It is sometimes suggested that the absence of such an account prior to the nineteenth century is evidence of the novelty of the doctrine.[8] Passing references to the utter truthfulness of Scripture are certainly made in earlier centuries, and these include such extended comments as those made by Augustine in the fourth century and Martin Luther in the sixteenth.[9] It is evident that both the concept and the terminology of inerrancy were known and endorsed by the early church fathers, by the medieval scholastic theologians, and by the Reformers and their heirs. Nevertheless, it must be acknowledged that, among all else that is attributed to Scripture, the doctrine of biblical inerrancy is singled out for special and detailed attention only in the wake of rather concerted attempts to discredit the veracity and historical reliability of the Bible in the eighteenth and nineteenth centuries. This evidence, though, allows another interpretation. There was no detailed exposition of biblical inerrancy prior to the nineteenth century because on all sides the truthfulness of Scripture as the word of God was assumed. There was no serious challenge to primary divine authorship (alongside a clear recognition of a genuine and substantial human contribution to the text) and consequently no serious doubt that what is taught in Scripture is true. As so often happens in the history of Christian theological reflection, the need for a detailed treatment of a specific theological topic became obvious only in the light of challenges and efforts to recast a long-standing theological consensus.

What follows is an attempt to provide a theological account of the doctrine of biblical inerrancy. While not wanting to cast any doubt on the validity of other approaches, and without minimizing the genuine humanity of the biblical text, I will give sustained attention to a critical element of what is involved in locating the doctrine of Scripture within the Christian doctrine of God.[10] All that follows could be supplemented by an exploration of precisely what view of Scripture is entailed in the way Scripture is cited or used by Scripture (especially in the light of Craig Allert's insistence that this is not distinctive

---

[8]E.g., Jack B. Rogers and Donald K. McKim, *The Authority and Interpretation of Scripture: An Historical Approach* (San Francisco: Harper & Row, 1979).

[9]Augustine, *Epistle* 82 (to Jerome); Martin Luther, *Genesisvorlesung* (1535–1545), *Luther's Works*, 2:239 (= WA 42:431.40–41).

[10]Webster, *Holy Scripture*, 39. Such a dogmatic location enables us to take Scripture seriously as "an operative factor in God's plan of salvation." Robert Preus, *The Inspiration of Scripture: A Study of the Theology of the Seventeenth Century Lutheran Dogmaticians* (Edinburgh: Oliver & Boyd, 1957), 170. It also provides a safeguard against all attempts to present too sharp a distinction between the biblical texts and God's self-revelation. As we will see, while these texts refer beyond themselves to the living and personal reality of God himself, there is an ineradicably verbal element to God's dealings with his creatures, of which the Scriptures are an integral part.

and that extracanonical texts are cited in identical ways);[11] a detailed exegetical investigation of key biblical texts such as 2 Timothy 3:14–17, 2 Peter 1:16–21, John 10:34–38, and John 17:14–19; a historical survey of how the term *inerrancy* and the concept have been used throughout the last two thousand years; a careful analysis of the notions of truth and error that are involved in any affirmation of inerrancy; and some attention to the impact of the fall on human reason and communicative ability. However, much of this work has already been done, not least in the volumes produced between 1977 and 1987 by the International Council on Biblical Inerrancy.[12] So, in keeping with a growing conviction that the true subject of Christian theology is the God who has made himself known in his Son and through his Spirit, what is offered here is a more tightly focused *theology* of biblical inerrancy.

## A Doctrine Both Theologically Robust and Exegetically Defensible

A persistent criticism of the doctrine of biblical inerrancy is that this doctrine, though presented as evidence of a high view of Scripture, has in fact an inadequate evidential base in the teaching of Scripture itself. Hans Küng famously remarked that "there is not a passage in Scripture that speaks of its inerrancy."[13] James Dunn and John Goldingay have expressed similar sentiments, insisting that it is not a biblical doctrine.[14] An initial response might be that there are many other important doctrines that have no single proof text but are instead built from, and demanded by, a series of related biblical affirmations. The doctrine of the Trinity is the most obvious example. Yet we might just as well cite the doctrine of providence, which brings together biblical affirmations about creation, the fall, the nature and purpose of evil, the reality of both divine sovereignty and genuine human agency, and the goal toward which everything is heading. Another example would be the doctrine of the last things. Systematic theology is not simply analytical but also synthetic. It is occupied with the coherence of biblical teaching, the connection between

---

[11] Allert, *High View of Scripture*, 70–73.

[12] E.g., John D. Hannah, *Inerrancy and the Church*, ed. Norman L. Geisler (Grand Rapids: Zondervan, 1980). See also *God's Inerrant Word: An International Symposium on the Trustworthiness of Scripture*, ed. John W. Montgomery (Minneapolis: Bethany, 1974), the two volumes already cited by Carson and Woodbridge, and Vern S. Poythress, *In the Beginning Was the Word: Language—A God-Centered Approach* (Wheaton, IL: Crossway, 2009).

[13] Hans Küng, *Infallible? An Enquiry*, trans. Eric Mosbacher (London: Collins, 1971), 181.

[14] James D. G. Dunn, "The Authority of Scripture according to Scripture," *Churchman* 96 (1982): 107; John Goldingay, *Models for Scripture* (Grand Rapids: Eerdmans, 1994), 273. See also Dennis E. Nineham, "Wherein Lies the Authority of the Bible?," in *On the Authority of the Bible*, ed. Leonard Hodgson (London: SPCK, 1960), 88; and James Barr, *Fundamentalism* (London: SCM, 1977), 277.

biblical ideas and the consequences that flow from particular affirmations, especially when they are affirmed alongside others.

At another level entirely, we should also say that the evidential base of the doctrine of inerrancy in Scripture is far broader and deeper than it might at first appear. It relies upon the biblical portrait of God, his character, his purpose, and the pattern of his dealings with the human race from the very beginning. Our understanding of the nature of Scripture is not isolated as a part of prolegomena but takes its shape within an appreciation of God's loving activity in creation and redemption. It does not assume how God must act on the basis of some *a priori* definition of divine causation determined elsewhere, subsequently imposing such assumptions upon the phenomenon of Scripture. Rather, the chief determinant is the teaching of Scripture itself. There are certainly specific biblical affirmations that provide the building blocks of the doctrine, and it is not at all difficult to demonstrate that an assumption of utter truthfulness is necessary in order to explain the use of earlier Scripture by later Scripture (including Peter's appeal to the writing of Paul in 2 Pet. 3:14–16). However, larger biblical-theological themes, attested throughout the Old Testament and the New, provide the proper context for considering the nature of this gift we have been given.

It quickly becomes clear that the doctrine of Scripture raises acutely the question of theological method. How is Christian doctrine constructed? How are we to avoid claiming too much or indeed claiming too little? A great deal of attention has been given to this subject in recent years, but it is not merely a contemporary concern. Francis Turretin asked whether Christian doctrine was to be legitimately proved "only by the express word of God" or also from "consequences drawn from Scripture." He observed that "a thing may be said to be in Scripture in two ways: either *kata lexin* (expressly and in so many words); or *kata dianoian* (implicitly and as to the sense)."[15] It is unnecessarily reductionist to suggest that a doctrine is biblical only if a proof text can be adduced. Turretin drew attention to Basil's response to the Arians in which he argued that their demand for a proof text to establish the *homoousion* rendered them "syllable-catchers," and to Gregory of Nazianzus's description of one who denied the divinity of the Spirit because no single text explicitly affirmed it as "an A.B.C. Sophist and a pettifogger of words."[16]

---

[15]Francis Turretin, *Institutes of Elenctic Theology*, trans. George Musgrave Giger, ed. James T. Dennison Jr., 3 vols. (Phillipsburg, NJ: P&R, 1992–1997), 1:37.

[16]Ibid., 1:39. "The petty exactitude of these men about syllables and words is not, as might be supposed, simple and straightforward; nor is the mischief to which it tends a small one" (Basil, *De*

With specific reference to the doctrine of biblical inerrancy, questions of method have been addressed at length by R. C. Sproul and Paul D. Feinberg.[17] Feinberg begins with Dewey Beegle's observation of two broad approaches to reasoning, and so to establishing doctrine: deduction and induction.[18] Deduction begins with general premises (e.g., "it is the nature of the divine to be perfect") and moves toward particular conclusions (e.g., "therefore this text must be perfect"), while induction moves from particular premises (e.g., collecting specific biblical affirmations or observations about the phenomena of Scripture) toward generalized conclusions (e.g., "therefore this is what we can say about the nature of Scripture").[19] However, Feinberg will not accept that these are the only options, nor does he accept Beegle's categorization of the defenders of biblical inerrancy as "deductivists pure and simple."[20] Instead he explores a third path, one that operates in scientific theory formulation and justification and might be labeled *retroduction*:

> A paradigm, or conceptual model, is formulated through an informed and creative thinking process, generally involving the data to be explained, and is then brought back, adduced, or tested against the data for "fit," or accuracy. . . . The theory is not created strictly by induction from data or phenomena nor by deduction from first principles. Yet both induction and deduction operate in the imagination of the scientist so that a theory is born.[21]

---

*Spiritu sancto*, 4 [*NPNF*², 8:3]). "Neither, if I found something else either not at all or not clearly expressed in the Words of Scripture to be included in the meaning, should I avoid giving it utterance, out of fear of your sophistical trick about terms." Gregory of Nazianzus, *Oration* 31, "On the Holy Spirit," 24 (*NPNF*², 7:325).

[17]R. C. Sproul, "The Case for Inerrancy: A Methodological Analysis," in Montgomery, *God's Inerrant Word*, 242–61; Paul Feinberg, "The Meaning of Inerrancy," in *Inerrancy*, ed. Norman L. Geisler (Grand Rapids: Zondervan, 1980), 267–304, esp. 269–76.

[18]Dewey M. Beegle, *Scripture, Tradition, and Infallibility* (Grand Rapids: Eerdmans, 1973), 16.

[19]Some accounts tend to privilege observations about the phenomena of Scripture as basic to an inductive approach and fail to recognize that the explicit statements of Scripture are themselves indispensable "phenomena." So Kenton Sparks, critiquing Carl Henry, presents an appeal to Scripture's explicit teaching about itself as "deductivist": "Henry argues that our doctrine of Scripture *cannot* be inductively derived from what Scripture does and how it works; we must begin instead by deductively learning what the Bible explicitly teaches about itself. . . . He used deductivist theories about the Bible as a shield to exclude inductive insights based on the Bible's actual content" (Sparks, *God's Word in Human Words*, 139). But why is attending to the explicit statements of Scripture about itself necessarily "deductivist" in this strict sense?

[20]Feinberg, "Meaning of Inerrancy," 271; Beegle, *Scripture, Tradition, and Infallibility*, 218.

[21]This term is John W. Montgomery's, though he also uses the expression "abduction" and Arthur Holmes uses "adduction" for basically the same procedure. Feinberg, "Meaning of Inerrancy," 273. John W. Montgomery, "The Theologian's Craft: A Discussion of Theory Formation and Theory Testing in Theology," *The Suicide of Christian Theology* (Minneapolis: Bethany, 1970), 267–313; Arthur F. Holmes, "Ordinary Language Analysis and Theological Method," *Bulletin of the Evangelical Theological Society* 11 (1968): 131–38.

When such an approach is taken to the construction and explanation of a doctrine of biblical inerrancy, a broader evidential base is possible, the distinction between Scripture and theologizing on it is preserved (it is Scripture that is inerrant but better formulations of the doctrine of Scripture are possible), and a rationale is provided for holding to the doctrine in spite of problems with some of the phenomena.[22] Anomalies "do not necessarily disconfirm the theory if that theory fits most of the data. Rather, they show that the phenomena are not fully understood or that the theory needs further amplification. . . . The theologian works both with phenomena and doctrine to resolve the conflict."[23] The biblical shape of the doctrine emerges in this interaction between explicit biblical affirmations together with the phenomena of Scripture, on the one hand, and theological concepts derived from Scripture, on the other.[24] Yet room remains for variety in the details of the approach taken in any particular instance. This variety can be observed in contemporary treatments of the doctrine of biblical inerrancy.

A brief glance at three classic definitions of the doctrine and one very recent alternative demonstrates the basic coherence within the variety of approaches taken by those who defend and expound it. The name most associated with the doctrine today is that of Benjamin Breckinridge Warfield, professor of didactic and polemic theology at Princeton Seminary from 1887 until 1921. His article "The Inerrancy of the Original Autographs" begins in this fashion:

> Our Lord and his apostles looked upon the entire truthfulness and utter trustworthiness of that body of writings which they called "Scripture," as so fully guaranteed by the inspiration of God, that they could appeal to them confidently in all their statements of whatever kind as absolutely true; adduce their deliverances on whatever subject with a simple "it is written" as the end of all strife; and treat them generally in a manner which clearly exhibits that in their view "Scripture says" was equivalent to "God says."[25]

---

[22] These are simply three of seven advantages Feinberg identifies. Feinberg, "Meaning of Inerrancy," 275–76.

[23] Ibid., 276.

[24] One of the most profound and stimulating accounts of the process of doctrinal formulation, presented in the context of a contemporary account of biblical Trinitarianism, is found in Thomas F. Torrance, *The Christian Doctrine of God: One Being, Three Persons* (Edinburgh: T&T Clark, 1996), 83–92. See also his *Reality and Evangelical Theology: The Realism of Christian Revelation* (repr., Downers Grove, IL: InterVarsity, 1999). Torrance's approach is helpfully augmented by an account of how doctrine functions in the life of the believer and in the church, such as that found in Kevin J. Vanhoozer, *The Drama of Doctrine: A Canonical-Linguistic Approach to Christian Theology* (Louisville: Westminster John Knox, 2005).

[25] Benjamin B. Warfield, "The Inerrancy of the Original Autographs," *The Independent*, March 23, 1893; reprinted in *Selected Shorter Writings of Benjamin B. Warfield*, ed. John E. Meeter, 2 vols. (Nutley, NJ: Presbyterian and Reformed, 1970–1973), 2:580.

It is instructive, and often unnoticed, that Warfield begins his treatment of this subject with the attitude of Jesus toward the Scripture of his own time, our Old Testament.[26] Although Warfield was undoubtedly influenced by Scottish common sense realism (as were many of his colleagues and indeed his opponents in the debates over Scripture), it is not this or any other epistemology that is the launching pad for his most direct treatment of the doctrine of biblical inerrancy. Warfield, in keeping with the classical Calvinist tradition, operates with an assumption of the basically reliable and trustworthy nature of the biblical testimony to Jesus.[27] More recent studies confirm that Warfield had good grounds for taking seriously the eyewitness character of the Gospel records and the general historical reliability of the New Testament.[28] It is, then, on the basis of this reliable record of Jesus's teaching that Warfield is able to appeal to Jesus's attitude toward Scripture as critically determinative for that of his disciples.

Warfield ties the confidence of Jesus and the apostles in the truthfulness and trustworthiness of Scripture to the guarantee provided by its inspiration. It is evident from his other essays that he is concerned to avoid a conception of inspiration that denies the genuine human authorship of Scripture with all that this implies about the particularities of each text.[29] However, genuine human authorship is something that Scripture has in common with all other literature. Warfield was drawing attention to the most important distinguishing feature of these texts, namely, the concursive activity of both the human authors and the ultimate divine author. Precisely because this is an inspired text in this sense, where "Scripture says" equates not only to "David says" or "Moses says," for example, but also to "God says," what is being taught at each point can be relied upon as both truthful and trustworthy.

Later in this same article, Warfield addresses one of the most enduring criticisms of the doctrine: that it is in reality an affirmation about a text we do not have. Strictly speaking, inerrancy is affirmed of the original autographs

[26]It is also often unnoticed that one of the most important of the books produced by the International Council on Biblical Inerrancy, the volume of essays edited by Norman Geisler, opens in a similar fashion: John W. Wenham, "Christ's View of Scripture," in Geisler, *Inerrancy*, 3–36.

[27]See Sproul's outline of the logic of the classical method of treating this doctrine. Sproul, "The Case for Inerrancy," 248–49.

[28]Paul W. Barnett, *Is the New Testament History?* (Carlisle: Paternoster, 1998); Richard Bauckham, *Jesus and the Eyewitnesses: The Gospels as Eyewitness Testimony* (Grand Rapids: Eerdmans, 2006).

[29]"In the first place, we may be sure that they [divine and human elements in the Bible] are not properly conceived when one factor or element is so exaggeratingly emphasized as to exclude the other altogether. . . . According to this conception, therefore, the whole Bible is recognized as human, the free product of human effort, in every part and word. And at the same time, the whole Bible is recognized as divine, the Word of God, his utterances, of which he is in the truest sense the Author." Benjamin B. Warfield, "The Divine and Human in the Bible," *The Presbyterian Journal*, May 3, 1894; reprinted in Meeter, *Selected Shorter Writings of Benjamin B. Warfield*, 2:543, 547.

rather than of copies or translations. This is or should be unexceptional. No one has ever seriously defended the proposition that all who translated, copied, or printed the Bible over the centuries have been inspired or preserved from error. Nevertheless, even in Warfield's time the doctrine of inerrancy was pilloried as the doctrine of the lost perfect text that says nothing about the text we actually have in our hands. Warfield's response is to distinguish between the autographic *codex* and the autographic *text*.[30] We may not have the manuscript with Paul's own large letters (Gal. 6:11), but along with the Westminster divines Warfield affirms that the genuine text of Scripture has been preserved to us "by the singular care and providence of God."[31] He points his readers to examples in history of a thoroughly orthodox and appropriate use of what we might label *textual criticism* to identify that text.

In more recent times the standard definition and exposition of biblical inerrancy is often taken to be that presented in the Chicago Statement on Biblical Inerrancy (1978). It is worth recognizing that the "Articles of Affirmation and Denial," the central section of this statement, begin with affirmations of the identity and authority of Scripture as the word of God, the larger context of God's revelatory activity, and the doctrine of inspiration.[32] Only then do we arrive at articles specifically dealing with the doctrine of inerrancy.

XI. We *affirm* that Scripture, having been given by divine inspiration, is infallible, so that, far from misleading us, it is true and reliable in all matters it addresses. We *deny* that it is possible for Scripture to be at the same time infallible and errant in its assertions. Infallibility and inerrancy must be distinguished, but not separated.

XII. We *affirm* that Scripture in its entirety is inerrant, being free from all falsehood, fraud, or deceit. We *deny* that Biblical infallibility and inerrancy are limited to spiritual, religious, or redemptive themes, exclusive of assertions in the fields of history and science. We *further deny* that scientific hypotheses about earth history may properly be used to overturn the teaching of Scripture on creation and the flood.

---

[30] "It is another curiosity of the controversial use of a phrase, to find the Church's careful definition of the complete truth and trustworthiness of the Scriptures as belonging, as a matter of course, only to the genuine text of Scripture, represented as an autograph—as if it were the autographic *codex* and not the autographic *text* that is in question." Warfield, "Inerrancy of the Original Autographs," 583.

[31] Ibid., 586.

[32] Strictly speaking the statement has three parts: a summary statement (five brief paragraphs), nineteen "Articles of Affirmation and Denial," and an exposition of the preceding parts under the headings "Creation, Revelation and Inspiration," "Authority: Christ and the Bible," "Infallibility, Inerrancy, Interpretation," "Skepticism and Criticism," "Transmission and Translation," and "Inerrancy and Authority."

XIII. We *affirm* the propriety of using inerrancy as a theological term with reference to the complete truthfulness of Scripture. We *deny* that it is proper to evaluate Scripture according to the standards of truth and error that are alien to its usage or purpose. We *further deny* that inerrancy is negated by Biblical phenomena such as a lack of modern technical precision, irregularities of grammar or spelling, observational descriptions of nature, the reporting of falsehoods [e.g., the lies of Satan], the use of hyperbole and round numbers, the topical arrangement of material, variant selections of material in parallel accounts, or the use of free citations.[33]

Among the distinctive contributions of this statement is a careful distinction-without-separation of the contested terms *inerrant* and *infallible*, two words that have been virtually synonymous in theological discourse for most of the past two thousand years. The biblical idea of inspiration—that these human texts, products of the conscious and creative activity of uniquely commissioned human authors, are at the same time and without prejudice to their genuine humanity the God-breathed written Word of God—carries with it the idea that Scripture will unfailingly fulfill God's purpose for it and will do that by speaking truthfully. Scripture will infallibly convey the truth about God, the world he has made, how human beings have perverted themselves and the world given to them as the appropriate context for life with God, and what God has done in Jesus Christ to restore men and women to himself and to secure "new heavens and a new earth in which righteousness dwells" (2 Pet. 3:13). Yet such theological material cannot be neatly disentangled, separated, or quarantined from statements about history and matters we might describe as scientific. Our faith is useless, Paul conceded, if the bodily resurrection of Jesus Christ from the tomb did not actually take place in space and time (1 Cor. 15:14). Biblical theology is deeply embedded in biblical history and so in the real world in which we all live. The historical particularities of Israel's history, and especially those associated with the life and work of Israel's Christ, cannot be dismissed without doing violence to the understanding of God and his purposes that they express. Furthermore, while the central concern of Scripture is to speak of Jesus the Christ, the incarnate, crucified, risen and glorious Son of the Father, Scripture does nonetheless also speak of other things. Questions of reliability and truthfulness are not easily restricted to purely religious or theological matters.

Of particular importance is the attention given in the statement to appropriate standards of truth and error. Far too often in the discussion of bibli-

[33]Chicago Statement on Biblical Inerrancy (1978) reprinted in Carl F. H. Henry, *God, Revelation and Authority*, vol. 4, *God Who Speaks and Shows. Fifteen Theses, Part Three* (Waco, TX: Word, 1979), 211–19.

cal phenomena in this context, anachronistic expectations have been placed upon the texts, and little attention has been given to the difference between the conventions of the first and the twenty-first centuries in a range of areas.[34] Greater sensitivity to the variety of literary devices used in Scripture (e.g., metaphor, hyperbole, phenomenological description) and the extent to which our "rules" are in fact conventions (e.g., standardized spelling, grammar, verbatim quotation) removes a great many difficulties at a single stroke. In addition, the provisionality of the historical and scientific consensus is too often overlooked in the rush either to vindicate particular biblical affirmations or else to conclude that they are genuine errors.[35] Care must be taken in the way the language of "truth" and "error" is used in the discussion about Scripture.[36]

The third classic definition, and the one most often quoted by friend and foe alike, is that penned by Paul Feinberg as part of his contribution to the International Council on Biblical Inerrancy held in Chicago during October 1978. At the time, he was associate professor of biblical and systematic theology at Trinity Evangelical Divinity School, and his definition highlights three important elements of the doctrine: "Inerrancy means that when all facts are known, the Scriptures in their original autographs and properly interpreted will be shown to be wholly true in everything they affirm, whether that has to do with doctrine or morality or with the social, physical, or life sciences."[37] With the expression "when all the facts are known," Feinberg adds

---

[34]"There is a vast difference between exactness of statement, which includes an exhaustive rendering of details, an absolute literalness, which the Scriptures never profess, and accuracy, on the other hand, which secures a correct statement of facts or principles intended to be affirmed. It is this accuracy, and this alone, as distinct from exactness, which the Church doctrine maintains of every affirmation in the original text of Scripture without exception. Every statement accurately corresponds to truth just as far forth as affirmed" (Archibald A. Hodge and Benjamin B. Warfield, *Inspiration* [repr., Grand Rapids: Baker, 1979], 28–29). In this connection, John Frame distinguishes truth and maximal precision. John M. Frame, *The Doctrine of the Word of God* (Phillipsburg, NJ: P&R, 2010), 173.

[35]Carl Henry famously illustrated the premature conclusion of historical error with reference to the existence of "ancient Hittites in the Fertile Crescent, of camels in Egypt in Abraham's time, of writing in Moses' time, and of Sargon and Belshazzar in much later centuries." Each of these judgments has been revised in the light of new evidence. Carl F. H. Henry, "The Inerrancy of Scripture," *God, Revelation and Authority*, 4:174.

[36]For fuller discussion of these issues, see Thomas F. Torrance, "Truth and Authority: Theses on Truth," *ITQ* 39, no. 3 (1972): 215–42; Roger Nicole, "The Biblical Concept of Truth," in Carson and Woodbridge, *Scripture and Truth*, 287–98; D. Groothuis, "Truth Defined and Defended," in *Reclaiming the Center: Confronting Evangelical Accommodation in Postmodern Times*, ed. Millard J. Erickson et al. (Wheaton, IL: Crossway, 2004), 59–79; Andreas Köstenberger, *Whatever Happened to Truth?* (Wheaton, IL: Crossway, 2005); and Michael C. Rea, "Authority and Truth," in *The Scripture Project: The Bible and Biblical Authority in the New Millennium*, ed. D. A. Carson (Grand Rapids: Eerdmans, forthcoming). In particular, Rea distinguishes between realist and antirealist conceptions of truth, between epistemic and nonepistemic conceptions of truth, as well as between correspondence theories of truth and all the rest.

[37]Feinberg, "Meaning of Inerrancy," 294.

an eschatological note to the doctrine of biblical inerrancy. The doctrine does not require all difficulties to be settled immediately. It is just conceivable that in any particular case of difficulty all the relevant facts are not yet known. Once again, the warning is not to declare the question settled too quickly—in one direction or another. However, this eschatological perspective takes us further. Scripture plays a role in the larger purposes of God, which reach their fulfillment only in the eschaton. It is possible to become myopic, to lose all sense of proportion and give the impression that everything depends upon the resolution of all biblical difficulties in the present. This has never been a part of classic expositions of the doctrine. The early church fathers, the Reformers, and later staunch defenders of inerrancy such as B. B. Warfield all recognized difficulties that were resistant to an easy solution.

Second, Feinberg's definition affirms a place for a proper and responsible hermeneutics. Error can arise from misinterpretation as well as from mistakes occurring in the process of translation, copying, or printing. Failure to attend to context, literary style, genre, and canonical and biblical-theological location can result in affirmations that not only are erroneous but conflict with others found elsewhere in Scripture. Once again it is important to note that the Chicago Statement on Biblical Inerrancy (1978) sits alongside the Chicago Statement on Biblical Hermeneutics (1982). The doctrine of biblical inerrancy should not be misused as a way of shielding any particular interpretation of a biblical text from evaluation. Precisely because it is Scripture that is affirmed as inerrant and not our interpretations of Scripture, all biblical exposition and theological construction must be tested. Even if contemporary hermeneutical theory has become so overladen that it threatens to be self-defeating—would we be better to abandon the language of "interpretation" for "responsible (or attentive) reading"?—the point remains that not every reading of Scripture is appropriate, and the truthfulness and trustworthiness of what is taught depends upon a prior submission to what the text actually says on its own terms and in its own context.[38]

Third, Feinberg stresses that Scripture is wholly true *in what it affirms*. A similar point is made when the Chicago Statement speaks of biblical "assertions." This is not a matter of reducing Scripture to an anthology of theological propositions. Rather, it is a recognition that in the course of its teaching, Scripture includes records of perspectives that it does *not* endorse. The lies of the Satan in Genesis 3 and the erroneous advice of Job's friends are conspicuous examples. So too, and more notoriously, is the record of the

---

[38]On the "heavy weather" contemporary hermeneutics makes of reading, see Peter F. Jensen, *The Revelation of God* (Leicester: Inter-Varsity, 2002), 205–29. Jensen shares with John Webster a preference for the term *reading*. Webster, *Holy Scripture*, 86–87.

lying prophet in 2 Kings 22 and 2 Chronicles 18.[39] Furthermore, the stress on biblical affirmations also guards against a flattening of the biblical texts in which incidental details are confused with what is actually being taught at each point. On one level this might simply be a specific instance of sensitivity to genre and the type of language being used. So, the parable of the rich man and Lazarus (Luke 16:19–31) makes its point about the sufficiency of (Old Testament) Scripture to establish our ultimate accountability to God for how we live now, without requiring us to establish whether such a rich man did in fact live or whether there is a physical chasm dividing those who after death enjoy fellowship with Abraham and those who endure torment in hades. Similarly, Paul's statement that "every knee should bow, in heaven and on earth and under the earth" (Phil. 2:10) need not imply a biblical endorsement of tripartite cosmology. Paul is speaking of the final and universal vindication of the One who took the form of a servant and suffered death on the cross for us. At each point it is important to recognize what is being affirmed and the purpose of the affirmation, to the extent that this can be discerned from the text itself.[40] Timothy Ward takes this point further when he insists that it is not simply isolated words or expressions that are inerrant but the "speech acts" of God.[41]

More recently, Michael Horton has proposed a summary statement that is explicitly theological: "Whatever the holy, unerring, and faithful Father speaks is—simply by virtue of having come from him—holy, unerring, and faithful."[42] Horton's summary is anchored in the character of the God who speaks in Scripture. Critically he identifies God as Father, with all the connotations of benevolence associated with that name in the New Testament (Matt. 7:11; 2 Thess. 2:16; James 1:17). The divine decision to address his creatures with words is itself an act of self-giving and love. His speech is a form of his self-expression, and as such his words bear his character even if, in order for them to be intelligible to us, they must also be, in an important sense, "human words."[43] As he is holy, unerring, and faithful, so are the words that come from him. Scripture constitutes that "pattern of sound words" (2 Tim. 1:13), the God-breathed "sacred writings, which are able to make you wise for

---

[39]This incident raises other issues as well. See P. J. Williams, "Lying Spirits Sent by God? The Case of Micaiah's Prophecy," in *The Trustworthiness of God: Perspectives on the Nature of Scripture*, ed. Paul Helm and Carl R. Trueman (Grand Rapids: Eerdmans, 2002), 58–66.

[40]Frame, *Word of God*, 174, makes this point in his succinct definition: "When we say that the Bible is inerrant, we mean that the Bible makes good on its claims."

[41]Ward, *Words of Life*, 137.

[42]Michael S. Horton, "The Truthfulness of Scripture: Inerrancy," *Modern Reformation* 19, no. 2 (2010): 26.

[43]Mark D. Thompson, *A Clear and Present Word: The Clarity of Scripture* (Nottingham: Inter-Varsity, 2006), 65–66; Poythress, *In the Beginning*, 37–38; Frame, *Word of God*, 82–84.

salvation through faith in Christ Jesus" (2 Tim. 3:14–17). Horton's emphasis on the character of the God who is the ultimate source of Scripture is not absent from the classic expositions. This is why he, with them, denies that inerrancy should be treated as "the foundation of our doctrine of Scripture, much less of the Christian faith." Instead he insists that the proper starting point is "the content and claims of Scripture, centering on Christ."[44] The more substantial and rigorous accounts of the doctrine have always recognized that the nature of Scripture must be understood in deep relation to this central content. Truthfulness and trustworthiness are defined by and realized in the God who has made himself known in Jesus Christ.[45]

Despite differences of emphasis and approach, there is a basic coherence to the classic expositions of the doctrine, which extends to influential contemporary accounts. This variety suggests a breadth of biblical warrant and a depth of theological reflection that is seldom recognized by its critics, who too often operate with prejudice and caricature. Facile dismissals of biblical inerrancy as the product of evangelical insecurity in the face of the "assured results" of biblical criticism, as captive to a modernist epistemology (alternatively a Platonic one), or as simply "unbiblical" or "Docetic" betray a lack of familiarity with the classic and best contemporary expositions of the doctrine.

## The Five Theological Pillars of the Doctrine of Biblical Inerrancy

A theological account of biblical inerrancy unfolds the simple observation of R. C. Sproul: "The infallibility of Scripture does not rest on the infallibility of the human writers but on the integrity of God."[46] This is much more than a simple syllogism: (1) God is perfect; (2) Scripture is ultimately from God; therefore (3) Scripture is perfect. It takes into account God's character and the nature of his dealings with human beings in the world, at each stage recognizing that the proper point of reference for understanding these is the life, words, and work of the incarnate Son. The scope of what is involved becomes apparent when the five theological pillars of the doctrine are identified.

### God's Personal Veracity

The testimony to God's truthfulness is consistent throughout Scripture. As the Creator of all, God knows all things as they truly are. He is neither ignorant nor deceived. His word can be relied upon. So, faced with the attempts

---

[44]Horton, "Truthfulness of Scripture," 28.

[45]Colin E. Gunton, "Trinity and Trustworthiness," in Helm and Trueman, *The Trustworthiness of God*, 284.

[46]Sproul, "The Case for Inerrancy," 257.

of Balak and the princes of Moab to influence the words that come from the Lord, Balaam declares:

> God is not man, that he should lie,
>     or a son of man that he should change his mind.
> Has he said, and will he not do it?
>     Or has he spoken, and will he not fulfil it? (Num. 23:19; cf. 1 Sam. 15:29)

This testimony to God's veracity, we are told, is a word put in Balaam's mouth by God himself (v. 16). The emphasis at this point of the narrative is certainly on the infallibility of God's word. He will not fail to do what he has said he will do. His promise to Abraham and his descendants will stand. However, this infallibility stands in stark contrast with the lies of human beings. God's words are unfailingly true, while men and women are prone to lie. Similarly, Agur the son of Jakeh insisted,

> Every word of God proves true;
>     he is a shield to those who take refuge in him. (Prov. 30:5)

The psalmist also testifies,

> The sum of your word is truth,
>     and every one of your righteous rules endures forever. (Ps. 119:160)

Throughout the Old Testament God's truth and faithfulness are brought into the closest possible relation.

The New Testament repeats and amplifies this same testimony to God's personal investment in truth. The hope of eternal life is guaranteed by the promise of God, "who never lies" (Titus 1:1–3; Heb. 6:17–18). "Let God be true though every one were a liar," Paul declares (Rom. 3:4). Affirmations of the truthfulness of God operate almost as a refrain throughout the book of Revelation (6:10; 15:3; 16:7; 19:2, 11). However, the incarnation of the Word gives a sharper focus to these affirmations. In Jesus Christ we are confronted by one who is "full of grace and truth" (John 1:14, 17). Jesus stands in the midst of creation as the one who uniquely embodies the truth that has been on view from the beginning. Like the prophets before him, he speaks the truth (John 8:44) and bears witness to the truth (John 18:37); but unlike any other, he is himself the truth (John 14:6). Here is the exposition of God as he really is, his purposes as they really are. Precisely because Jesus Christ is the Word become flesh, he is able truly to make the Father known (John 1:18) and to share with his disciples the true words of the Father (John 8:40). It is

Jesus, self-designated as the way, the *truth*, and the life, who is able to testify to the truth of God's word (John 17:17). He insists that "Scripture cannot be broken" (John 10:35). He promises that after his departure he will send the Spirit of truth to his disciples (John 15:26), and just as *he* speaks the word given to him by his Father, so too, he says, the Spirit will "take what is mine and declare it to you" (John 16:14).

All truth converges in the God who has made himself known in Jesus Christ. As Colin Gunton once put it, "God's trustworthiness in the economy is a function of the ontological security of his being."[47] Yet the extent of God's trustworthiness in the economy and the nature of the eternal relations that constitute this ontological security are manifest only in Jesus Christ. The Son's self-emptying and obedience to death are the ultimate demonstrations of God's faithfulness and love (Phil. 2:5–11; 1 John 4:9–10). Just so, it is his eternal sonship that explicates the fatherhood of God and why the Spirit of truth (John 14:17) is also the Spirit of adoption (Rom. 8:15). The truth of what God says is fully grounded in the truth that God is.[48] Truth and trustworthiness are not abstract principles but personal and indeed Trinitarian realities.

In this way it becomes clear why we must insist that God's power is not exercised independently of his veracity, his faithfulness, and his necessary infallibility.[49] It is sometimes suggested that God's unfettered sovereignty is compromised by the insistence that his involvement in the production of the biblical text necessarily ensures an infallible and inerrant product. Isn't God able to make himself known effectively through an errant text? Aren't the advocates of biblical inerrancy in fact limiting God's power with an unwarranted assumption that "given the nature and character of God, the only kind of Scripture he could 'breathe out' was Scripture that is textually inerrant?"[50] After all, God uses fallible, broken instruments to effect his purposes all the time (consider Abraham, Moses, David, and Peter—not to mention modern-day preachers, missionaries, and theologians!). However, God's sovereign freedom with respect to his creation is *God's* sovereign freedom. Certainly nothing is able to hinder or frustrate his purposes, not even the finitude and fallenness of his creatures, but this does not mean that all options are open to him. When God acts and speaks, he always acts and speaks according to his nature. He cannot lie (Heb. 6:18) and he cannot deny himself (2 Tim. 2:13). Truth and faithfulness are eternal and essential attributes of God. In

---

[47]Gunton, "Trinity and Trustworthiness," 280.
[48]John Frame observes that the Bible speaks of metaphysical truth, propositional truth, and ethical truth, and he concludes that God is truth in all these senses. Frame, *Word of God*, 170.
[49]Paul Helm, "B. B. Warfield's Path to Inerrancy: An Attempt to Correct Some Serious Misunderstandings," *WTJ* 72 (2010): 32.
[50]McGowan, *Divine Spiration of Scripture*, 113, 118.

Johannine terms God *is* light and God *is* love (1 John 1:5; 4:8). This has pro-found consequences for "God-breathed" (inspired) Scripture. As Paul Helm has written, summarizing the argument of Warfield:

> God not only has not failed in any respect, he could not fail. And being essen-tially veracious, he could not fail to be veracious. Hence, his word has not and cannot fail. Hence, the Bible is not only true, as some merely human documents are true, but if it is divinely inspired then it is infallibly true.[51]

### God's Concursive Involvement in the Created Order

We have already begun to consider the way God operates within the world he has made. The distinction between the Creator and his creation is no bar-rier to God's genuine involvement in the created order. God's transcendence ought not to be misunderstood in terms of remoteness. Nor is it the opposite of immanence. This is a point made clearly and forcefully by Karl Barth.

> The biblical witness to God sees His transcendence of all that is distinct from Himself, not only in the distinction as such, which is supremely and decisively characterised as His freedom from all conditioning by that which is distinct from Himself, but furthermore and supremely in the fact that without sacrific-ing His distinction and freedom, but in the exercise of them, He enters into and faithfully maintains communion with this reality other than Himself in His activity as Creator, Reconciler and Redeemer.[52]

One consequence of this perspective is that God's activity in the world is not only recognized in moments of miraculous intervention, though there is ample testimony to such intervention throughout Scripture. God is also involved in and alongside the "ordinary" processes of everyday life, even directing the decisions of men and women in a way that does not compromise genuine human agency.[53] The decisions that they make, whether for good or for evil, remain entirely their own, made for their own reasons, while in and through those decisions God is at work. The classic biblical instances of this *concursus* (or, as it is sometimes described, "compatibilism," since divine sovereignty and genuine human agency are presented as ultimately compat-

---

[51] Helm is explicitly engaging McGowan's criticism of Warfield at this point. Helm, "B. B. Warfield's Path to Inerrancy," 32.

[52] Karl Barth, *Church Dogmatics*, 2.1, *The Doctrine of God*, ed. G. W. Bromiley and T. F. Torrance, trans. T. H. L. Parker et al. (Edinburgh: T&T Clark, 1957), 303.

[53] Barth's impressive treatment of the topic draws toward a close with the observation, "The uncon-ditioned and irresistible lordship of God means not only that the freedom of creaturely activity is neither jeopardized nor suppressed, but rather that it is confirmed in all its particularity and variety." Karl Barth, *Church Dogmatics*, 3.3, *The Doctrine of Creation*, ed. G. W. Bromiley and T. F. Torrance, trans. G. W. Bromiley and R. J. Ehrlich (Edinburgh: T&T Clark, 1960), 146.

ible) remain the sale of Joseph by his brothers to Midianite traders who just happen to be passing by on their way to Egypt (Gen. 45:4–5; 50:20) and the politico-religious execution of Jesus (Acts 2:23). In both cases decisions are freely made, with motives that are transparent to the readers of the narrative, and yet in the final analysis it is God's purposes that are accomplished through the resulting action. What is critical in each incident, and elsewhere in Scripture (e.g., Job 1–2), is the way God's personal integrity is not in question for a moment. The malice of the human agents in each of these instances is never attributed to God. God's involvement in a contingent world never entails the surrender of his sovereignty. His involvement in a fallen world never entails the compromise of his holiness and truthfulness. Indeed, so far from implicating God in the myriad of injustices associated with the act, the fact that God "put forward" Christ Jesus "as a propitiation by his blood" serves to "show his righteousness at the present time, so that he might be just and the justifier of the one who has faith in Jesus" (Rom. 3:21–26). God's sovereign involvement in the created order need not be seen as jeopardizing genuine human agency, nor need it be taken as ensnaring God in the real limitations and moral failures of the human agents.

Warfield makes much of this idea of God's concursive involvement in the created order as he strives to explain a doctrine of the verbal inspiration of Scripture that does not necessarily degenerate into a doctrine of mechanical dictation.

> Nevertheless, God did not give us these books, as he gave Moses the Ten Words, written without human intermediation, by his own finger, on the tablets of stone. He gave them not only by, but through men. They are the Oracles of God, and every word of them is a word of God. But they are also the writings of men, and every word of them is a word of man. By a perfect confluence of the divine and human, the one word is at once all divine and all human. So then, for their proper and complete understanding, we must approach each book not only as the Word of God, but also as the words of Peter, or of Paul, or of John.[54]

> Justice is done to neither factor of inspiration and to neither element in the Bible, the human or the divine, by any other conception of the mode of inspiration except that of *concursus*. . . . The fundamental principle of this conception is that the whole of Scripture is the product of divine activities which enter it, however, not by superseding the activities of the human authors, but confluently

with them; so that the Scriptures are the joint product of divine and human activities, both of which penetrate them at every point.[55]

God's engagement with the biblical text is not somehow subsequent to its production. He does not merely appropriate an already existing creaturely artifact for his purposes. The God-breathed text is the product of his providential ordering, in which God remains God and acts in ways consistent with his character while sustaining genuine human agency. As Warfield concludes, "It is only when we forget that God's providence is over all that we can fancy that the human factor may introduce into the Bible aught that would mar its designed perfection as the Word of God."[56]

### God's Willingness to Accommodate Himself for Our Sake

God's involvement with human beings amid the realities of their existence in the world is an expression of his love. As such it is accommodated to the capacity of its recipients. The use of human language to express God's purposes and describe his activity is one critical example of such an accommodation. Calvin drew attention to the anthropomorphic expressions in the biblical portrayal of God as a clear instance of divine accommodation. It is in this context that he spoke memorably of God being "wont in a measure to lisp" to us.[57] However, neither Calvin nor those who used the concept before him were suggesting that the process of accommodation involved distortion or error. The truth about God is expressed in language that is clearly figurative at points and based on our experience of human agency at other points, and yet its proper reference is accessible to the skilled and the unskilled alike. The use of such expressions aids understanding of the truth rather than diverting it.

However, without a doubt the most significant example of divine accommodation is the incarnation of the Son and his death for sinners. Ultimately it is Jesus Christ who must determine for us the extent and limitation of this concept. The eternal Son took the form of a servant and assumed our humanity at the deepest possible level in order to make God known to us and effect our salvation. The human nature he took to himself, as the Spirit overshadowed the virgin, was real and not illusory. He was and remains genuinely one of

---

[55]Warfield, "The Divine and Human in the Bible," 546, 547.

[56]B. B. Warfield, "God's Providence over All," in Meeter, *Selected Shorter Writings of Benjamin B. Warfield*, 1:113.

[57]John Calvin, *Institutes of the Christian Religion*, ed. John T. McNeill, trans. Ford Lewis Battles (Philadelphia: Westminster, 1960), 1.13.1. The image was in fact not novel. Chrysostom illustrated the principle behind the use of anthropomorphisms and other expressions in Scripture with reference to a father talking "'lispingly' to his children." John Chrysostom, "Homilies on Titus," 3 (on Titus 1:12), in *NPNF¹*, 13:529.

us without ceasing to be the Son of the Father. The earliest Christians recognized even the slightest dilution of his humanity as a departure from the testimony of Scripture every bit as serious as a denial of his divinity because of its implication for our salvation. As Gregory of Nazianzus insisted, "That which He has not assumed He has not healed."[58]

Yet the consistent testimony of the New Testament is that he was also entirely without sin. The writer to the Hebrews is emphatic: "Therefore he had to be made like his brothers in every respect"; he is able to sympathize with our weaknesses since in every respect he has been tempted as we are, "yet without sin" (Heb. 2:17; 4:15). The righteousness of Christ is a critical factor in the atonement: he who knew no sin was made sin for us (2 Cor. 5:21); he "suffered once for sins, the righteous for the unrighteous" (1 Pet. 3:18). While we may still speak about his assumption of *fallen* humanity in the sense that Jesus lived his earthly life under conditions of mortality that are the ever-present consequences of the fall, and both the temptation he faced in the wilderness (Matt. 4:1–11) and the terror he experienced in the garden (Luke 22:39) were real, nevertheless, such language needs careful qualification in order to preserve this biblical testimony to his sinlessness.[59] The Son was sent, writes Paul, "in the likeness of sinful flesh" (Rom. 8:3), and every word in that pregnant expression is carefully chosen. It is, after all, the incarnate Son who testifies without qualification, "I am the way, and the truth, and the life" (John 14:6). His is a real accommodation at far more than the level of appearance, yet it does not entail the corruption of his genuinely human heart and mind and will. In him we are reminded that it is not sin or error or failure that makes us genuinely human.

The application of the doctrine of accommodation to the language and conceptualities of Scripture has an impressive lineage, as we have seen. Furthermore, those who first used it did not intend to suggest error or distortion in the biblical texts. However, Faustus Socinus proposed a different understanding of accommodation in the very early seventeenth century that would prove popular in rationalist circles later that century and throughout the next.[60]

---

[58] Gregory of Nazianzus, "Epistle 101 (to Cledonius the Priest against Apollinarius)," $NPNF^2$, 7:440.
[59] The debate on this particular issue has produced a massive amount of literature in recent years. Among those most insistent upon the assumption of our *fallen* humanity has been Karl Barth (*Church Dogmatics*, 1.2.147–59; 2.1.397–98). On the other side of the debate, Oliver Crisp has raised a series of philosophical and theological problems with speaking of Christ's humanity as fallen. Oliver Crisp, "Did Christ Have a *Fallen* Human Nature?," *International Journal for Systematic Theology* 6, no. 3 (2004): 270–88.
[60] Martin I. Klauber and Glenn S. Sunshine, "Jean-Alphonse Turrettini on Biblical Accommodation: Calvinist or Socinian?," *CTJ* 25, no. 1 (1990): 12–14. John Woodbridge suggests that this critical attitude toward Scripture is carried into more mainstream European scholarship by Richard Simon, Jean

Accommodation, on this understanding, involves an accommodation to the erroneous worldviews of the human authors and their contemporaries. Rather than challenge the prevailing consensus that Moses was the author of the Pentateuch or that there will be a general resurrection of both the righteous and the wicked to judgment at the end of time, Jesus simply adopted the language and conceptual framework of his contemporaries. Writing about the idea of a general resurrection, Socinus and the others with him at the Rakow Colloquium in 1601 suggested:

> One should deal cautiously with this matter, just even as Christ himself and the Apostles accommodated themselves to the level of the people as the parable of Lazarus [Luke 16:20ff.] and the rich man teaches. This was not the time to perturb the Jews, as even now is not the time, although Jesus sometimes speaks thus in order that it be sufficiently clear that he will resuscitate only the faithful. . . . Thus, in the meantime, certain things may be said that even indicate this thing [general resurrection] to men, until at length age matures and men are able to accustom themselves to these ways of talking [about the state and destiny of the unrighteous dead].[61]

This second view of accommodation was advanced by Jack Rogers and Donald McKim as a major plank in their argument that the Christian tradition has always had the resources to deal with a variety of genuine errors in Scripture without compromising its essential infallibility (understood functionally as its unfailing fulfillment of the purpose for which it was intended).[62] More recently Kenton Sparks has reiterated this claim, charging those who deny the influence of flawed human perspectives on the teaching of Scripture with Docetism, perhaps borne of a faulty Cartesian epistemology.[63] He insists that "God does not err when he accommodates the errant views of Scripture's human audiences."[64]

There is, however, plenty of evidence in the Gospels of Jesus's refusing to accommodate himself to mistaken views and practices. He does not simply echo the consensus of those around him. One of the repeated refrains of the Sermon on the Mount is, "You have heard that it was said . . . but I say to

---

Le Clerc, and most importantly Hermann Samuel Reimarus and Johann S. Semler. John D. Woodbridge, "Pietism and Scriptural Authority: The Question of Biblical Inerrancy" in *The Scripture Project*.

[61]Faustus Socinus et al., "Epitome of a Colloquium Held in Rakow in the Year 1601," in *The Polish Brethren: Documentation of the History and Thought of Unitarianism in the Polish-Lithuanian Commonwealth and in the Diaspora, 1601–1685*, 2 vols., ed. George H. Williams (Missoula, MT: Scholars Press, 1980), 121–22.

[62]Rogers and McKim, *Authority and Interpretation of Scripture*, 10–12, 18–20, 27–30, 77–79, 98–100, 152–54, 169–71, 431–33, 461.

[63]Sparks, *God's Word in Human Words*, 256, 258–59.

[64]Ibid., 256.

you" (Matt. 5:21–22, 27–28, 31–32, 33–34, 38–39, 43–44). Jesus challenges the Pharisees' ceremonial understanding of what confers defilement or sanctity (Matt. 15:10–20; 23:16–22), and he challenges the prevailing consensus on divorce with an appeal to God's creational intention (Matt. 19:3–12). Jesus certainly speaks in order to be understood, using the language and ideas of those with whom he is speaking; the parables alone are ample testimony to that. However, he is certainly capable of standing outside of the consensus of his time and saying new things. Accommodation in the second sense is an imposition upon rather than explication of the biblical phenomena. God is able to make himself and his purposes known effectively and truthfully. It is this prior and proper sense of accommodation that has been an integral part of the Christian theological tradition and provides an important part of the theological context in which affirmations of biblical inerrancy can be made.

### God's Creation and Use of Human Speech and Writing

Human language is not simply a human achievement. It is a divine gift. God created the first man and woman as speech partners not simply for each other but for himself. Indeed, in the biblical narrative, the first to use language is God himself, who addresses the man and woman in the garden, presumably in a fashion that is intelligible to them (Gen. 1:28–30; 2:16–17). The words God uses are, apparently, deemed by him appropriate to convey his purposes in a way consistent with his character. Human language would later be used to converse with God—a use that affirms its value as a vehicle for the divine-human relationship—and then to speak to others about God. The theological significance of the place given to language in the opening chapters of Genesis ought not to be understated. The One who speaks the universe into being uses words to address human beings. As J. I. Packer suggests:

> Both a sense of God and a language in which to converse with Him were given to men as ingredients in, or perhaps preconditions of, the divine image from the start. By depicting God as the first language user (1:3, 6ff.), Genesis shows us that human thought and speech have their counterparts and archetypes in Him.[65]

Of course the biblical narrative does not proceed very far before we have examples of language being misused. Instead of speaking truth and bringing blessing, the words of the Satan are lies and misrepresentations, which result

---

[65]James I. Packer, "The Adequacy of Human Language," in Geisler, *Inerrancy*, 214. Packer then went on to opine, long before postmodernism had become vogue in theological circles, that "the biblical position that God's speaking and God's image in man imply a human capacity to grasp and respond to His verbal address shows up the arbitrariness, and indeed, the provincialism, of the post-Christian, positivistic theory of language on which the skepticism of linguistic philosophers rests."

in the arrival of the curse (Genesis 3). However, this is not a defect in language as such, but rather a result of an abuse of language. After all, true and faithful things are still said after the fall. Language is not inherently distorting, even when used by fallen human beings.[66] The emphasis of some on the fragility of human language and consequently a natural expectation of some echo of this in the text of Scripture fails at precisely this point.[67]

God continues to use human language to address men and women after the fall and, indeed, after the multiplication of languages following the Babel incident (Gen. 11:1–9). In an important sense, God's use of words provides the crucial momentum for the entire biblical meganarrative. Abram hears the words of God (Gen. 12:1–3), as do the other patriarchs. Moses hears God's voice from the bush, which does not burn (Ex. 3:1–4:17). Samuel is called in the night (1 Samuel 3). David is identified as God's chosen king when Samuel hears the voice of the Lord in Bethlehem (1 Samuel 16). In the New Testament a voice from heaven is heard at Jesus's baptism (Mark 1:9–11) and again when he is transfigured on the mountain (Mark 9:2–8). Most significant of all, Jesus himself makes extensive use of words as he preaches the kingdom of God and teaches his disciples—he is never simply a mute-but-radiant divine presence. Finally, the book of Revelation ends with a voice from the throne (Rev. 22:16). God is the preeminent speaker throughout Scripture, and he uses words that can be heard and understood by men and women—in that sense, genuinely human words.

In the course of this unfolding biblical narrative, God also gives words to appointed spokesmen, who take his words to others. The paradigmatic case is that of Moses and Aaron. "You shall speak to him and put the words in his mouth," the Lord tells Moses, "and I will be with your mouth and with his mouth and will teach you both what to do. He shall speak for you to the people, and he shall be your mouth and you shall be as God to him" (Ex. 4:15–16). Later the prophets are the spokesmen of God, and in the New Testament, Jesus's commission is given to the apostles to take his words to the ends of the earth until the end of the age (Matt. 28:18–19). There is not the slightest suggestion in the Old Testament or the New that God's words are *necessarily* distorted as they are spoken from one human being to another.

---

[66]Richard Gaffin, "Speech and the Image of God: Biblical Reflections on Language and Its Uses," in *The Pattern of Sound Doctrine: Systematic Theology at the Westminster Seminaries: Essays in Honor of Robert B. Strimple*, ed. D. VanDrunen (Phillipsburg: P&R, 2004), 191.

[67]Karl Barth's description of the form of God's Word as "not a suitable but an unsuitable medium for God's self-presentation" has been influential on many. Karl Barth, *Church Dogmatics*, 1.1, *The Doctrine of the Word of God*, ed. G. W. Bromiley and T. F. Torrance, trans. G. W. Bromiley (Edinburgh: T&T Clark, 1975), 166. For a full-length treatment of the issues surrounding God and language, see Poythress, *In the Beginning*, 17–81.

Once again, God's words *may* be misrepresented, as they were by Satan in the garden and in the wilderness, but this need not be so, and especially when God's superintendence of the words he conveys to others is taken into account. The writer to the Hebrews sums up God's dealings with humanity by saying, in effect, "God having spoken . . . spoke" (Heb. 1:1–3).

It is God himself who effects the transition from oral word to written word in the life of Israel. We are repeatedly told that the Ten Words are written by the finger of God; the note struck at this point of the narrative is one of immediacy (Ex. 24:12; 31:18; 32:16). Though earlier Moses is instructed to write a record of God's promise to destroy the Amalekites (Ex. 17:14), the command for Moses to write on a larger scale comes only afterward (Ex. 34:17). There is no loss of authority, no sense of distortion as this transition from speaking to writing is made. Indeed, speaking and writing exist side by side, most strikingly when Moses's successor, Joshua, hears God's voice instructing him to meditate on the book of the law day and night, even though he has God's promise that he will be with him as he has been with Moses (Josh. 1:1–9).

Speech, words, and even writing are not foreign to God. They are an essential part of the currency of divine-human relationships from the beginning. At no point do the historical, cultural, or linguistic particularities present obstacles to an effective communication of God's character and purposes. The human authors are most certainly people of their own time, sharing the worldview of their contemporaries. Yet the limitations of the authors do not automatically transfer to the biblical text, precisely because they are not the only ones involved in its production. We return again to Sproul's observation: "The infallibility of Scripture does not rest on the infallibility of the human writers but on the integrity of God." Even the necessity for translation is taken in stride as the New Testament appears freely to make use of the Septuagint, while Hebrew and Aramaic terms are explained in the Greek New Testament (Matt. 1:23; 27:33; Mark 5:41; 15:22, 34; John 1:41; 9:7; 20:16), and, most strikingly of all, on the day of Pentecost an assortment of people present in Jerusalem hear the earliest Christians testifying to "the mighty works of God" in their own languages (Acts 2:1–13). There is no reason why genuinely human language or a genuinely human text *must* be fallible or contain errors. The capacity of language to carry truth about the true God is amply demonstrated from Scripture itself.

### God's Gift of Scripture

The Scriptures do not spontaneously arise out of the piety of the ancient Hebrews or the first followers of the crucified and risen Christ. The final of these five theological pillars of biblical inerrancy is the direct connection between the living God and this particular set of writings. It is here that the crucial piece of biblical self-testimony—that "all Scripture is breathed out by God [*theopneustos*] and profitable for teaching, for reproof, for correction, and for training in righteousness, that the man of God may be complete, equipped for every good work" (2 Tim. 3:16–17)—comes most clearly into play. God is not just involved in human language generally, as its Creator and as one who addresses men and women personally in human words. His relation to this particular body of writing marks it out from all other literature.[68] This distinctive character and status is recognized, not only in the Old Testament texts to which Jesus and his apostles regularly appeal, but also in the apostolic writings themselves (witness Peter's association of Paul's letters with "the other Scriptures" in 2 Pet. 3:15–16). Scripture bears a unique authority because of its unique relation to the God who is Lord of all.

The doctrine of inspiration is routinely misunderstood either as the elimination of all human involvement in the production of Scripture (as in the label *mechanical dictation*) or as an affirmation about the uniqueness of the biblical writers. Enough has already been said in response to the first misunderstanding. As for the second, it is Karl Barth who is most famous for insisting that inspiration is not a general, uniform, and permanent quality of a text (the imposition of the adjectives is instructive) but a dynamic process of God's gracious self-revelation to the biblical authors.[69] Yet the critical biblical affirmation of inspiration is of the inspiration *of the text*. The Spirit was undoubtedly at work in the prophetic writers of the Old Testament (2 Pet. 1:20–21), but it is the resulting text that is described as "God-breathed." Barth may label this "inspiredness" (as opposed to "inspiration") and consider it a fabrication of the Protestant orthodox if he wishes, but the point being made in 2 Timothy 3 is that God is directly, not just indirectly, involved in the production of Scripture, and this is the reason why Scripture is the proper basis for faithful thinking, living, and service.

However, does such direct involvement lead us inexorably to an affirmation of biblical inerrancy? Might not Hans Küng be right when he quips that "God, quite unlike Shakespeare, writes straight even on crooked lines"?[70] More tellingly, does the doctrine of biblical inerrancy ignore the miracle of grace in God's use of fallible and, at points, errant words to make himself known

---

[68]This most definitely raises questions about the formation, nature, and function of the biblical canon, which are not our immediate concern.

[69]Barth, *Church Dogmatics*, 1.1.112, 114; 1.2.518–19. See also Mark D. Thompson, "Witness to the Word: On Barth's Doctrine of Scripture," in *Engaging with Barth: Contemporary Evangelical Critiques*, ed. David Gibson and Daniel Strange (Nottingham: Inter-Varsity, 2008), 188.

[70]Küng, *Infallible?*, 180.

to us?[71] In response we might ask why the miracle of God using fallible and faulty human words as his own word is preferable to the miracle of the Spirit so superintending the entire process of a human writer's development, experience, and literary expression that he or she freely writes the words that God intended.[72] We are brought back here to our earlier observation that God acts, not just in terms of what is possible, but in ways that are at every point in keeping with his character. *Inspiration* and *inerrancy* are not synonyms, that is true. Nevertheless, it is the unfailing veracity of God that gives a particular character to the texts, which are God-breathed. Inspiration and inerrancy are inseparable in this case because of the identity and character of the One who gives us "the sacred writings, which are able to make [us] wise for salvation through faith in Christ Jesus" (2 Tim. 3:15).

## A Perspective on the Difficulties

As we acknowledged at the beginning, there is much more that could be said. However, it is evident that the theological anchorage of the doctrine of biblical inerrancy is both broad and deep. Our understanding of Scripture cannot be isolated from the person and character of the God who gave it to us, just as it may not bypass the genuine freedom and conscious involvement of the human authors of each particular text. What it means for this collection of texts to be the written word of God and what it means for it to be "genuinely human" must be determined first and foremost with reference to God's self-revelation in Jesus Christ. Yet what is involved is much more than a theological syllogism or a hasty and unqualified appeal to the hypostatic union of divine and human natures in Christ. Larger theological themes are integrated with Scripture's self-attestation and with a sensitivity to the textures of what we have in fact been given in Scripture.

Biblical inerrancy has more often been critiqued in caricature than with serious attention to the best and most serious expositions of the doctrine. Contemporary assessments of the phenomena of Scripture have too often been given priority over the express biblical affirmations or the broader theological framework sketched above. On the one hand, a preoccupation with incidental details has not often been disciplined by sustained attention to the purposes for which Scripture has been given, while, on the other, too little attention has been given to the way in which the central message of Scripture is inextricably bound to matters of history and observations about the world in which we live. *A priori* judgments have colored arguments on both sides

---

[71]Barth, *Church Dogmatics*, 1.2.529.
[72]Thompson, "Witness to the Word," 195.

of the debates. One recent attack on the doctrine of inerrancy chided advocates for presupposing rather than investigating what God has actually done in Scripture, while proceeding to set out what a text insulated from human fallenness should look like if we had one.[73]

However, the doctrine of biblical inerrancy almost inevitably becomes distorted when it becomes the most important thing we want to say about Scripture. Timothy Ward's assessment that inerrancy is "a true statement to make about the Bible but is not in the top rank of significant things to assert about the Bible" is timely.[74] More than this, the larger context of our engagement with Scripture needs to be recognized in order to keep a sense of proportion. Herman Ridderbos once wrote, "God did not inspire the Bible to give us a holy book, but in order to bring us into fellowship with him, in order to give us to Christ."[75] That is another way of saying that the Christian concern for biblical inerrancy is relational and soteriological.

So how does the Christian respond to unresolved difficulties in the biblical text? It has long been recognized that no doctrine of biblical inerrancy requires all such difficulties to be resolved. Certainly, we need to take difficulties seriously without imposing a predetermined solution, insisting on harmonization, or expecting that all answers will be known in the present. Difficulties are an opportunity to return again to Scripture to see if we have indeed rightly understood what we've read. They are an invitation to sustained serious engagement with the Scripture given to us by the God who is unfailingly true and always speaks and acts in accordance with his nature. So, rather than suspending judgment, we trust as we wrestle with the difficulties.[76]

---

[73]Sparks, *God's Word in Human Words*, 226.

[74]Ward, *Words of Life*, 132. See also Feinberg, "Meaning of Inerrancy," 304: "Inerrancy is not the only quality of the Bible that needs to be affirmed."

[75]Herman N. Ridderbos, "An Attempt at the Theological Definition of Inerrancy, Infallibility and Authority," *International Reformed Bulletin* 32/33 (1968): 31.

[76]Frame, *Word of God*, 179–80.

# 4

# "THESE THINGS HAPPENED"

## Why a Historical Exodus Is Essential for Theology

### JAMES K. HOFFMEIER

### Biblical Theology: Past and Present

Biblical theology and biblical history are intricately woven together, forming a tightly spun tapestry. In modern academic study, *biblical theology* has been so identified since 1787, when Johann Philipp Gabler gave his inaugural (and seminal) lecture at the University of Altdorf as professor of theology; the English lecture title from the original Latin was "On the proper distinction between biblical and dogmatic theology and the specific objectives of each."[1] He distinguished between two branches of theology by saying,

> There is truly a biblical theology, of historical origin, conveying what the holy writers felt about divine matters; on the other hand there is a dogmatic theology of didactic origin, teaching what each theologian philosophises rationally about divine things, according to the measure of his ability or the times, age, place, sect, school, and other factors.[2]

One distinguishing element of biblical theology is its concern for history, whether it is in the Old Testament or the New. Old Testament theology (hereafter OTT) in much of the Western Christian academic world has normally been closely tied to the New Testament, so much so that Jewish Bible scholars have had little interest in OTT. Jon Levenson, as recently as 1985, labeled OTT "an almost exclusively Gentile affair."[3] The reality is that most evangelical academics, especially those teaching in seminaries, use a "biblical theology

---

[1] Johann P. Gabler, "On Biblical Theology," in *Old Testament Theology: Flowering and Future*, ed. Ben Ollenburger (Winona Lake, IN: Eisenbrauns, 2004), 498–506.
[2] Ibid., 501.
[3] Jon Levenson, *Sinai and Zion: An Entry into the Jewish Bible* (San Francisco: Harper & Row, 1985), 1.

of the OT" approach. The thematic and theological connection between the Testaments (hence "biblical theology") has also been the focus of biblical scholars and theologians from mainline traditions. John Bright (1908–1995) put it this way: "The two Testaments have to do with one and the same God, one history, one heritage, one people. Since this is so, the Christian must claim the Old Testament, as the New Testament did. . . . The unity of the Testaments within a single redemptive history must at all times be affirmed."[4] No evangelical would disagree with Bright's affirmation of the unity of the Testaments and a "single redemptive history." In his confession we see again the centrality of history to biblical theology. It is not surprising, therefore, that in addition to writing books on Old Testament/biblical theology,[5] Bright also wrote his enduring *History of Israel*, now in its fourth, and posthumous, edition.[6]

William Foxwell Albright (1891–1971), the Johns Hopkins University archaeologist, linguist, and biblical scholar, exerted considerable influence on key players in what Brevard Childs called "the Biblical Theology Movement," a largely North American phenomenon that, he maintains, sprang up after World War I and ended in the 1960s.[7] While Albright himself did not write books on biblical theology per se, his students certainly did. Interestingly, John Bright dedicated his *Kingdom of God* "to my teacher, William Foxwell Albright," and his *History of Israel* (2nd ed.) was inscribed "to the Memory of William Foxwell Albright."

No student of Albright's better exemplified the priority of history and archaeology to OTT than G. Ernest Wright (1909–1974), who taught at Harvard Divinity School. Like Albright, Wright was a field archaeologist and was the founding editor of the periodical *Biblical Archaeologist*. His classic theological work *The God Who Acts* has as its operating assumption that

> Biblical theology is first and foremost a theology of recital, in which Biblical man confesses his faith by reciting the formative events of his history as the redemptive handiwork of God. The realism of the Bible consists in its close attention to the facts of history and of tradition because these facts are the facts of God.[8]

---

[4]*The Authority of the Old Testament* (Nashville: Abingdon, 1967), 199–200.
[5]In addition to his *The Authority of the Old Testament*, see his earlier work, *The Kingdom of God* (Nashville: Abingdon, 1953).
[6]The first edition was John Bright, *A History of Israel* (Philadelphia: Westminster, 1959). The fourth edition was published in 2000 by Westminster John Knox Press.
[7]Brevard Childs, *Biblical Theology in Crisis* (Philadelphia: Westminster, 1970).
[8]G. Ernest Wright, *God Who Acts: Biblical Theology as Recital* (Naperville, IL: Allenson, 1952), 38.

He argued that one of the distinguishing features of Israel's religion, when compared with the religious traditions of her neighbors, "is the peculiar Israelite attention to historical traditions."[9] "In Biblical Faith," Wright believed, "everything depends upon whether the central events actually occurred."[10] Wright walked his talk. Trained in the field by Albright,[11] he spent many years in the archaeology of Israel seeking that illusive evidence at Beitin/Bethel, Shechem, and Gezer. He was a key figure in advancing scientific methods into biblical archaeology at Shechem and Gezer.[12] Late in his career, when the archaeological data did not meet his theoretical expectations, Wright became somewhat disillusioned.[13]

He no doubt, like many others, had placed too great a burden on archaeology, as if it could confirm any and every biblical event. As a field archaeologist myself, I am keenly aware of how little has actually survived from the ancient past, owing to natural forces, such as moisture in many forms, deflation, and earthquakes, as well as human impact in the form of later occupation (in ancient times), reusing earlier building materials, human destruction (war and burning), and modern development (urban and agricultural). Realistic expectations about what archaeology can and cannot do for biblical studies must always be kept in mind.

It is generally agreed that the biblical theology movement, with its interest in biblical history and archaeology, emerged as a more objective approach than the dominant Old Testament higher-critical approaches and sought a middle ground in early twentieth-century debates between modernists and fundamentalists (the former dismissing or minimizing the Bible and the latter taking a literalistic stance).[14] Childs correctly summarized the role of archaeology in the "American form" of "biblical theology as having great interest in the study of the background of the Bible. For Old Testament studies this meant a concentration on the Ancient Near Eastern setting with a particular focus on the role of archaeology."[15] Childs, however, saw cracks developing in this movement in the 1960s, and its subsequent demise late in that decade. For Childs, two blows were responsible for this downfall. First was an essay by

[9]Ibid., 39.

[10]Ibid., 126.

[11]Wright was on the 1934 staff at the initial season of work at Beitin/Bethel; see William F. Albright and James L. Kelso, *The Excavation of Bethel (1934–1960)*, AASOR 39 (Cambridge, MA: American Schools of Oriental Research, 1968), 4.

[12]Thomas Davis, *Shifting Sands: The Rise and Fall of Biblical Archaeology* (New York: Oxford University Press, 2004), chap. 3.

[13]See Thomas W. Davis's assessment of Wright's uncertainty late in his career in "Faith and Archaeology: A Brief History to the Present," *BAR* 19, no. 2 (1993): 54ff.

[14]Childs, *Biblical Theology in Crisis*, 17–31; Davis, *Shifting Sands*, 23–89.

[15]Childs, *Biblical Theology in Crisis*, 47.

Langdon Gilkey, who critiqued Wright and others for using orthodox language to describe God's action in history but then attributing natural causes to the events.[16] Gilkey's critique actually reflects an Enlightenment-based scientific worldview that bifurcates natural and supernatural, which is antithetical to ancient worldviews in which no such dichotomy existed.

Essays by James Barr in the early 1960s Childs described as the "final blow."[17] I am not at all convinced that Childs was correct because Barr was not attacking a historical approach to theology per se. Rather he questioned those who claimed that "'history' is the absolutely supreme *milieu* of God's revelation."[18]

One gets the impression that the reason Childs was so quick to bury the biblical theology movement is that it afforded him the opportunity to advance his alternative, "canonical" approach.[19] No doubt Childs's canonical method has been one of the major positive methodological developments of the past forty years. In a sense, his canonical approach is biblical theology in which history is marginalized. I maintain that both approaches can work synergistically.

Despite the developments of the early 1960s and Childs's obituary for a historically based OTT, not everyone saw the demise of historically based biblical archaeology. Roland de Vaux, the Dominican archaeologist, historian, and theologian, made the historicity of Old Testament events a matter of personal faith when he confessed in 1965, "If the historical faith of Israel is not in a certain way founded in history, this faith is erroneous and cannot command my assent."[20] In 1976 Gordon Wenham declared that "Biblical theology may be crudely described as a theology of history. This is even clearer in the Old Testament than the New. But both Testaments are primarily concerned with telling us what God has done, is doing and will do in history."[21] It is fair to say that evangelicals would side with de Vaux and Wenham, and disagree with Childs that historical approaches to OTT are passé on philosophical or theological grounds.

It is obvious, however, that since the early 1970s, when Wright passed away, historically based Old Testament theologies, except among evangelicals, have given way to more centered or canonical approaches. Nevertheless,

---

[16]Ibid., 65.

[17]Ibid., 65–66.

[18]James Barr, "Revelation through History in the Old Testament and in Modern Theology," *PSB* 56 (1963): 4–14.

[19]Childs, *Biblical Theology in Crisis.* Part 3 is subtitled "Testing a Method."

[20]"Method in the Study of Early Hebrew History," in *The Bible in Modern Scholarship*, ed. J. P. Hyatt (Nashville: Abingdon, 1965), 16.

[21]In *History, Criticism, and Faith: Four Exploratory Studies*, ed. Colin Brown (Leicester: Inter-Varsity, 1976).

some advocates of thematic approaches still recognize the importance of the "central events."

Walther Eichrodt's classic *Theology of the Old Testament*, the first German edition of which appeared in 1933, uses covenant as the unifying theme. In later editions he critiqued Wright, and even von Rad, for an "over emphasis" on history.[22] I would agree that an OTT that relies *solely* on historical events as the main vehicle of revelation is incomplete because it minimizes or overlooks large sections of the canon, above all, creation (conspicuous by its absence in Wright's work). Eichrodt nevertheless recognized the importance of ancient contextual data to the study of the Old Testament, opining, "No presentation of OT theology can properly be made without constant reference to its connections with the whole world of Near Eastern religions."[23] "OT theology," he acknowledged, "presupposes the history of Israel."[24] And he spoke of the need *"to have the historical principle operating side by side with the systematic in a complementary role."*[25] Eichrodt rightly understood that the events of Bible history must be viewed through a theological lens, but they could not be marginalized.

More damaging than Childs's critique to historically based approaches, however, was the challenge posed to traditional understandings about historiography and the historical accuracy of the Old Testament, which began in the mid-1970s.[26] First, the historicity of the patriarchal narratives of Genesis were questioned and dismissed by Thomas Thompson and John Van Seters in two separate but nearly contemporary studies.[27] Here began the slide toward historical minimalism that rejected the authenticity of the Joseph story, the sojourn and exodus narratives, the conquest of Canaan (a broadside on the Albright-Wright conquest model), the early monarchy, and most recently the kingships of David and Solomon.[28] The historical conclusions of Maxwell

---

[22]Walther Eichrodt, *Theology of the Old Testament*, vol. 1 (Philadelphia: Westminster, 1961), 14.

[23]Ibid., 25.

[24]Ibid., 32.

[25]Ibid., his emphasis.

[26]In response to the reevaluation of historiography in the Old Testament, I organized a conference at Wheaton College in November 1990 as part of the McManis Lecture Series that was tied to the annual Archaeology Conference. The papers were published as *Faith, Tradition, and History: Old Testament Historiography in Its Near Eastern Context*, ed. A. R. Millard, J. K. Hoffmeier, and D. W. Baker (Winona Lake, IL: Eisenbrauns, 1994).

[27]Thomas Thompson, *Historicity of the Patriarchal Narratives: The Quest for the Historical Abraham*, BZAW 133 (Berlin: de Gruyter, 1974). John Van Seters, *Abraham in History and Tradition* (New Haven: Yale University Press, 1975).

[28]Some of the works include Gösta W. Ahlström, *Who Were the Israelites?* (Winona Lake, IN: Eisenbrauns, 1986); Thomas Thompson, *The Origin Tradition of Ancient Israel: The Literary Formation of Genesis and Exodus 1–23* (Sheffield: JSOT, 1987), and Thompson, *The Mythic Past: Biblical Archaeology and the Myth of Israel* (London: Basic Books, 1999); Robert Coote, *Early Israel: A New*

Miller and John Hayes in 1986 well reflect the growing skepticism toward
the historical value of the Old Testament. They considered that the biblical
narrative regarding early Israel—including the

> entrance into Egypt, twelve tribes descended from the twelve brothers, escape
> from Egypt, complete collections of laws and religious instructions handed down
> at Mt. Sinai, forty years of wandering in the wilderness, miraculous conquests
> of Canaan, . . .—is *an artificial and theologically influenced literary construct.*[29]

In other words, the biblical narrative was too ideologically and theologically
motivated for use in reconstructing real history. Bernard Batto came to a
similar conclusion: "The biblical narrative in the books of Genesis through
Joshua owes more to the folkloristic tradition of the ancient Near East than
the historical genre."[30]

Regarding the origin of Israel in the land of Canaan, the recent sentiment
has been that the Israelites were indigenous to the land and were never in Egypt,
and there was no exodus, Sinai wilderness experience, or militaristic entry
into Canaan.[31] Regarding the sojourn and exodus, it is not as though some
new compelling archaeological discoveries were made that led to dismissing
the history of these crucial (at least to the religion of Israel and OTT) events.
Rather it is the consequence of changing views of historiography, that is, the
collapse of Enlightenment/scientific methods in the humanities and the rise
of postmodern hermeneutics. The latter tends to view all texts, the Bible
included, as purely literature and certainly not history. The titles of some recent
articles well reflect the current climate, for example, Siegfried Herrmann's
"The Devaluation of the Old Testament as a Source for History"[32] and Baruch
Halpern's "Erasing History: The Minimalist Assault on Ancient Israel."[33]

---

*Horizon* (Minneapolis: Fortress, 1992); Philip Davies, *In Search of "Ancient Israel"* (Sheffield: JSOT,
1992); Israel Finkelstein and Neil Asher Silberman, *The Bible Unearthed: Archaeology's New Vision of
Ancient Israel and the Origin of Its Sacred Texts* (New York: Free Press, 2001); Thomas L. Thompson,
*The Messiah Myth: The Near Eastern Roots of Jesus and David* (New York: Basic Books, 2005);
Israel Finkelstein and Neil Silberman, *David and Solomon: In Search of the Bible's Sacred Kings and
the Roots of the Western Tradition* (New York: Free Press, 2006); John Van Seters, *The Biblical Saga
of King David* (Winona Lake, IN: Eisenbrauns, 2009).

[29] J. Maxwell Miller and John H. Hayes, *A History of Ancient Israel and Judah* (Philadelphia: Westminster, 1986), 78, my emphasis.

[30] Bernard Batto, *Slaying the Dragon: Myth-making in the Biblical Tradition* (Louisville: Westminster
John Knox, 1992), 102.

[31] For a summary of the theories of Israel's origins, see James K. Hoffmeier, *Israel in Egypt* (New
York: Oxford University Press, 1999), chaps. 1–2; William G. Dever, *Who Were the Early Israelites
and Where Did They Come From?* (Grand Rapids: Eerdmans, 2003).

[32] In *Israel's Past in Present Research: Essays on Ancient Israelite Historiography*, ed. V. Philips Long
(Winona Lake, IN: Eisenbrauns, 1993), 346–55.

[33] *Bible Review* 11, no. 6 (1995): 26–35, 47.

This devaluation had immediate (and not illogical) consequences in the study of Israelite religion and OTT. Susan Niditch's 1997 book on the religion of Israel, for example, proposes that "there is, however, a way to explore the Israelite story without using the Hebrew Bible"[34] by solely using archaeological data. Without the Bible, not surprisingly, the Egyptian and Sinai traditions are passed over in her study, as they are in most works on Israel's religion over the past fifteen years.

Similarly a number of recent Old Testament theologies have employed alternative approaches that ignore history. Leo Perdue's 1994 OTT book *The Collapse of History* expresses the state of affairs. While Perdue is not prepared to abandon history (and historical-critical methods) altogether, he believes that "new methods for studying the Bible" are necessary, those "nurtured within a newly emerging sociopolitical ethos in the contemporary world," which would essentially make the older methods obsolete.[35] Consequently, pluralism, feminism, liberation, and third-world theologies now set the agenda, and the events of the Old Testament can now be reinterpreted from the reader-response hermeneutic offered by postmodernism. When the exodus, for example, figures into Old Testament theologies in recent years, it is paradigmatic and can be applied to various forms of liberation theology.[36]

To be sure, not everyone in the past twenty years has dismissed the biblical-sojourn and exodus traditions in developing their OTT. Elmer Martens utilizes Exodus 5:22–6:8 as the focus of his Old Testament theology *God's Design*, but broadens his scope to include treating creation and wisdom literature within his scheme.[37] Within the mainline protestant tradition, Bernhard Anderson (1916–2007) in *Contours of Old Testament Theology* (1999),[38] while embracing the concerns of Childs's canonical approach and being sensitive to contemporary issues as identified by Perdue, nevertheless follows the historical sequence of the covenants: Noachic, Abrahamic, Sinaitic, and Davidic. Interestingly, Anderson was the annual professor at the American Schools of Oriental Research in Jerusalem (1963–1964) and dedicated his OTT book to G. Ernest Wright. In the same year that this book was published, he gave a lecture for the Biblical Archaeology Society entitled "The Relevance of Archaeology

[34]Susan Niditch, *Ancient Israelite Religion* (New York: Oxford University Press, 1997), 9.
[35]Leo Perdue, *The Collapse of History: Reconstructing Old Testament Theology* (Minneapolis: Fortress, 1994), 4–5.
[36]See Perdue's sequel for a summary of these newer theologies: Leo G. Perdue, *Reconstructing Old Testament Theology: After the Collapse of History* (Minneapolis: Fortress, 2005).
[37]Elmer Martens, *God's Design: A Focus on Old Testament Theology*, 2nd ed. (Grand Rapids: Baker, 1994).
[38]Minneapolis: Fortress, 1999.

to Biblical Theology."[39] These factors attest to his interest in studying OTT within its historical and Near Eastern setting.

I began this essay looking at the place of history in OTT,[40] but as it has progressed, I have intentionally narrowed the historical focus to the sojourn and exodus from Egypt because these events, along with the Sinai legislation, are recognized as the most important events in Old Testament salvation history. Gerhard von Rad, even if he regarded them as "the theology of Israel's historical traditions" rather than genuine history, as Wright maintained,[41] nevertheless held that the sojourn and exodus traditions stood at the center of Israel's creedal confessions. He described Deuteronomy 26:5–11 as an "old Credo,"[42] the opening part of which affirms:

> And you shall make response before the LORD your God, "A wandering Aramean was my father. And he went down into Egypt and sojourned there, few in number, and there he became a nation, great, mighty, and populous. And the Egyptians treated us harshly and humiliated us and laid on us hard labor. Then we cried to the LORD, the God of our fathers, and the LORD heard our voice and saw our affliction, our toil, and our oppression. And the LORD brought us out of Egypt with a mighty hand and an outstretched arm, with great deeds of terror, with signs and wonders. And he brought us into this place and gave us this land, a land flowing with milk and honey."

It is the contention of this paper, in agreement with von Rad, Wright, and others, that the exodus and wilderness narratives are central to OTT, and that without them, the tapestry of Israel's faith and the foundational fabric of Christianity unravels.

## The Exodus and Theology

The past thirty years has seen radical shifts in how the Old Testament books from Genesis to 1 and 2 Samuel have been viewed as sources for Israel's history, but hardest hit has been the Egypt and Sinai reports. Many in the Jewish community in North America were surprised to read that the eminent Israeli archaeologist Israel Finkelstein was questioning the biblical exodus and wilderness tradition in *The Bible Unearthed*. He and coauthor Neil Silberman claim that "the historical saga contained in the Bible—from Abraham's encounter

---

[39]Biblical Archaeology Society video, 1999.
[40]For a helpful overview of various Old Testament theologians and the place of history within their systems, see Elmer Martens, "The Oscillation Fortunes of 'History' within Old Testament Theology," in Millard, Hoffmeier, and Baker, *Faith, Tradition, and History*, 313–40.
[41]This is the subtitle of volume 1 of his *Old Testament Theology* (New York: Harper & Row, 1962).
[42]Ibid., 176.

with God and his journey to Canaan, to Moses' deliverance of the children of Israel from bondage . . . [is] a brilliant product of the human imagination."[43] That same year, many Jews were dismayed[44] when Rabbi David Wolpe, from a Conservative Movement synagogue in Los Angeles, during Passover services stated, "Virtually every modern archaeologist who has investigated the story of the Exodus, with very few exceptions, agrees that the way the Bible describes the Exodus is not the way it happened, if it happened at all."[45]

What is disturbing about this trend is that some who identify themselves as a "new generation of evangelicals" and embrace the label "progressive evangelical" are accepting this revisionist agenda.[46] Kenton Sparks points to the lack of evidence in Egypt for the exodus as reason to embrace the conclusions of critical scholarship that the exodus was not a major event at all. Sparks assails scholars like Kenneth Kitchen and me for being fideistic obscurantists because of our rejection of most of the methodology and conclusions of biblical criticism.[47] There are good and objective reasons for being wary of, if not critical toward, "critical" biblical scholarship or "biblical criticism." Perhaps most significantly, rather than being the "scientific" (*wissenschaftliche*) method nineteenth-century European biblical scholarship claimed it to be, it was theoretically based and often quite subjective, influenced by evolutionary theory, and lacked external checks that ancient Near Eastern sources could offer. Furthermore, there is a well-documented and unacceptable anti-Semitic element to much of nineteenth- and early twentieth-century critical biblical scholarship.[48]

One would think that a "scientific approach" to biblical literature would result in unchanging conclusions. True enough, for decades Wellhausen's developmental and dating scheme for the Pentateuch dominated the academe, but his source-critical scheme was at odds with the tradition-history approach of

---

[43]Finkelstein and Silberman, *The Bible Unearthed*, 7–8.
[44]Because of the stir Rabbi Wolpe caused, I was invited later that year (Nov. 5, 2001) to lecture about the exodus as an Egyptologist at the University of Judaism in Los Angeles (now the American Jewish University of Los Angeles) and met some people from that congregation. They expressed appreciation for my lecture and my book *Israel in Egypt*.
[45]This story was reported in the *Los Angeles Times* and other newspapers. The quote cited here is from an article entitled "L.A. Rabbi Creates Furor by Questioning Exodus Story," by Tom Tugend, *Jewish Telegraphic Agency* (May 4, 2001).
[46]Kenton Sparks, *God's Word in Human Words: An Evangelical Appropriation of Critical Biblical Scholarship* (Grand Rapids: Baker Academic, 2008), 11–14.
[47]Ibid., 136–57.
[48]For a recent comprehensive study of this subject, see Anders Gerdmar, *The Roots of Theological Anti-Semitism: German Biblical Interpretation and the Jews, from Herder to Kittel and Bultmann* (Leiden: Brill, 2009).

Gunkel, von Rad, Noth, and others.[49] The nineteenth-century source-critical consensus has completely collapsed in the past thirty years, and today there is little agreement about anything.[50] Consequently Rolf Rendtorff could recently write, "The Wellhausen paradigm no longer functions as a commonly accepted presupposition for Old Testament exegesis."[51]

Enlightenment-based critical methods of the nineteenth century and most of the twentieth century have been replaced in many cases by equally skeptical postmodern hermeneutics. Today biblical criticism is not a monolithic system, but includes a variety of approaches. Nevertheless, Sparks chides evangelical scholars for not bending the knee to critical biblical scholarship. He apparently has faith in these ever-evolving approaches to the Old Testament.

Concerning the exodus, Sparks asserts that the "silence of the Egyptian evidence on these matters [i.e., the Passover and exodus] is therefore an important argument against the historicity of these miracle reports."[52] In the end, for Sparks, the gap between historical or archaeological evidence and the claims of the Bible leads him to opine that "original events were much less significant historically than the Bible now remembers."[53]

My intention in this essay is not to review the historical and archaeological data I have already amassed to show the authenticity of the Egypt-Sinai narratives in two monographs, *Israel in Egypt: The Evidence for the Authenticity of the Exodus Tradition* (New York: Oxford University Press, 1996/1999) and *Ancient Israel in Sinai: The Evidence for the Authenticity of the Wilderness Tradition* (New York: Oxford University Press, 2005), the latter of which Sparks has completely ignored. Here is not the place for a detailed critique of Sparks's limited grasp of Egyptian archaeology, but a few comments are in order.[54]

First, the delta of Egypt, within which was the land of Goshen, where the Hebrews resided, is the least excavated area of Egypt. Second, because of the moist environment of northern Egypt from millennia of annual Nile inundations, objects made from perishable materials do not survive. In fact, not a single scrap of a papyrus document has survived from the delta from pharaonic times. Only a few Roman-era papyri have been found in Tanis,

---

[49]See the insightful discussion on this subject by Rolf Rendtorff, "The Paradigm Is Changing: Hopes—and Fears," *BibInt* 1 (1993): 34–53.
[50]For a summary of developments in biblical criticism of the Old Testament, see Hoffmeier, *Israel in Egypt*, 7–10.
[51]Rendtorff, "The Paradigm Is Changing," 44.
[52]Sparks, *God's Word in Human Words*, 157.
[53]Ibid.
[54]The ideas recited here were previously advanced in James K. Hoffmeier, *BAR* 33, no. 1 (2007): 20–41, 77.

thanks to the carbonized condition of some that were kept in clay jars (à la the Dead Sea Scrolls).[55] Third, those who excavate at delta sites are normally limited in accessing lower levels from earlier history, owing to high water tables. Archaeologists who employ a costly pumping system, such as at Tell el-Dab'a and Buto, have been able to reach earlier strata. I have seen this system at work at Dab'a during an April 2002 visit. The scriptorium of the fifteenth-century palace was being excavated. Only clay bullae with seal impressions that once sealed papyrus documents were found, but no papyrus survived! The same was true in my own excavations at Tell el-Borg, where we discovered several mud bullae,[56] and even though it is a desert setting, because of rain this area experiences, no papyrus was extant. Thus, when a biblical scholar points out that there is no Egyptian evidence to support the presence of the Hebrews in Egypt, or for the exodus, it is rash to conclude that this absence of evidence is evidence of absence.

Sparks's willingness to make a historical declaration based on the lack of evidence is a patently obvious fallacy, the fallacy of "negative proof." Historian David Hackett Fischer describes this approach as "an attempt to sustain a factual proposition merely by negative evidence."[57] He cogently observes, "Evidence must always be affirmative. Negative evidence is a contradiction in terms—it is no evidence at all."[58] Sparks and other revisionists are simply wrong to draw historical conclusions about the accuracy of the sojourn and exodus narratives through the fallacy of negative proof.

The reality is that historians of the ancient Near East have often accepted the witness of written documents without corroborating archaeological data. During the fall of 2010, I participated in a conference in Germany on the exodus and conquest. In a panel discussion, a distinguished German colleague repeated the mantra that there is no Egyptian evidence for the exodus, which raises questions about the historicity of the biblical tradition. I asked if he believed that Thutmose III invaded Canaan in the mid-fifteenth century BC, besieging and taking the city of Megiddo. He responded, "Of course." Then I pointed out that this military campaign is one of the best documented reports from the ancient Near East as it is recorded both in royal sources (e.g., Annals of Thutmose III, Gebel Barkal Stela, Armant Stela, Buhen Temple

[55]Francis Ll. Griffiths and W. M. F. Petrie, *Two Hieroglyphic Papyri from Tanis* (London: Egypt Exploration Fund, 1889), 1–4.
[56]Two bullae with the cartouche of Horemheb (1323–1295 BC) were discovered. See James K. Hoffmeier and Jacobus van Dijk, "New Light on the Amarna Period from North Sinai," *JEA* 96 (2010).
[57]David Hackett Fischer, *Historians' Fallacies: Toward a Logic of Historical Thought* (New York: Harper & Row, 1970), 47.
[58]Ibid., 62.

Text, Karnak Seventh Pylon Text, Karnak Toponym lists)[59] and in private documents and biographies of officers who accompanied the king.[60] Despite all this textual evidence (from a variety of genres of literature) for the battle of Megiddo in 1457 BC and a seven-month siege of the city (according to the Barkal Stela), I reminded him, there is still no archaeological evidence from Megiddo for the Egyptian attack! Megiddo, as it turns out, is probably the most excavated site in ancient Israel, having been investigated with regularity since 1903, and work is ongoing. This scholar was prepared to accept the claims of various Egyptian texts, although they were shaped by religious, ideological, and propagandistic agendas, despite the absence of any clear archaeological evidence to support the written claims. I concluded my observation by saying that as historians were willing to give Thutmose III's written claims the benefit of the doubt, I was prepared to do the same for the exodus narratives.

I have long advocated treating ancient texts, biblical or from elsewhere in the Near East, as "innocent until proven guilty," rather than "guilty until proven innocent."[61] In other words, if a text, be it Egyptian, Assyrian, or Hebrew, makes a claim that X happened at location Y, or King A built a temple at site B, I accept that statement unless there is compelling evidence to the contrary. William Dever has recently commented on the blatant bias against the Bible: "How is it that the biblical texts are always approached with postmodernism's typical 'hermeneutic of suspicion,' but the non-biblical texts are taken at face value? It seems to be that the Bible is automatically held guilty unless proven innocent."[62]

Postmodern hermeneutics, the recent rage in many circles, and equally problematic for orthodox readings of Scripture, has had its share of detractors. Jonathan Chaves, of George Washington University, recently offered a devastating critique of postmodern hermeneutics entitled "Soul and Reason in Literary Criticism: Deconstructing the Deconstructionists."[63] This is an intriguing "no holds barred" critique of postmodern hermeneutics that cuts to the heart of the deconstructionists' agenda. Chaves argues that their approach to language is "profoundly anti-Christian"[64] and that deconstructionists are Marxists "who are no longer satisfied to apply their leftist analysis to the actual

---

[59]For a treatment of all Thutmose III's texts related to this campaign, see Donald B. Redford, *The Wars of Syria and Palestine of Thutmose III* (Leiden: Brill, 2003).
[60]Ibid., 165–84.
[61]For the gist of my approach to texts and a critique of minimalists, see *Israel in Egypt*, chaps. 1–2 and *Ancient Israel in Sinai*, 20–22.
[62]William Dever, *What Did the Biblical Writers Know and When Did They Know It? What Archaeology Can Tell Us About the Reality of Ancient Israel* (Grand Rapids: Eerdmans, 2002), 128.
[63]Chaves, "Soul and Reason in Literary Criticism: Deconstructing the Deconstructionists," *JAOS* 122 (2002): 828–35.
[64]Ibid., 830.

world, with its emphasis on the sphere of politics. They now apply this same worldview to literature, art, and thought itself."[65] He goes on to observe that their agenda is to attack religion and social mores, and to deny that language can communicate truth and the transcendent. In the end, Chaves believes that postmodernism's hermeneutics reflects a "deep, underlying spiritual crisis" and that "only a return to God will allow a return to sanity in literary criticism, as in everything else."[66] From my engagement over the past two decades with professional Old Testament scholarship through participating in the Society of Biblical Literature, hearing papers, and reading books and articles by postmodern critics, I resonate with Chaves's conclusions. Why should evangelicals, whether scholars or lay people, want to embrace a "profoundly anti-Christian" approach to reading the Bible?

Recent biblical criticism has needlessly driven a wedge between Scripture's historical claims and theology. Readers of the Bible must decide whether such a bifurcation is consistent with Christian orthodoxy in general and evangelicalism in particular. The neoorthodox alternative is not particularly helpful. While Sparks claims to have "reservations" about this option, when it comes to history and theology, that seems to be the direction he wants to take us. Reducing the exodus story to a minor event (if it occurred at all) leaves one with only the option of extracting theological or ethical lessons from the story even if it is not historical (a tenet of neoorthodoxy). Colin Brown lays bare the deficiency of this approach: "If an event such as the Exodus is seen as a paradigm of God's care for his people, the comfort and hope that the believer is exhorted to draw from it are surely ill founded if there is no corresponding historical base."[67] This is clearly the argument made in Psalm 78, the focus of which are the "deeds" and "the wonders that he has done" (v. 4) in the exodus from Egypt, so that future generations

should set their hope in God
and not forget the works of God. (v. 7)

The Old Testament Scriptures do not treat the sojourn-exodus-wilderness events as trivial matters. Rather, these events stand at the heart of Israel's religious life, as evidenced by the fact that these themes are ubiquitous throughout the Old Testament itself. Clearly the biblical writers throughout the Old Testament believed that the exodus occurred as presented in the Pentateuch, for they repeatedly affirm their faith in Yahweh, who brought them out of

---

[65]Ibid., 831.
[66]Ibid., 835.
[67]Brown, *History and Faith: A Personal Exploration* (Grand Rapids: Zondervan, 1987), 76.

Egypt, through the Sinai wilderness, and into the land, as God had promised Abraham and his offspring. Eichrodt acknowledges such an understanding.

> How deeply this attitude to history was rooted in the fundamental events of the Mosaic era is shown by the part which the deliverance from Egypt and the occupation of the Holy Land play as a sort of paradigm of the divine succour, not only in the historical books, but also in the prophets and the law.[68]

Similarly, the theologian Wolfhart Pannenberg noted that Yahweh was "revealed in his acts in history. At first, this idea was linked most vividly with the exodus from Egypt, which ancient Israel took as Jahweh's primal act of salvation."[69] In the New Testament, Paul was able to make a theological point and application for the Corinthians from the Israelite sea crossing because "these things happened to them" (1 Cor. 10:11). Simply put, if these things did not happen, there is no theological lesson!  *Or Truth*

## Sojourn, Exodus, and Wilderness Themes in the Old Testament

Archaeology has, to date, not been able to "prove" the historicity of the book of Exodus, though the authenticity of many of its claims has been shown to be credible. As a historian and archaeologist, I accept its historicity because of the way these narratives are used throughout the Bible in so many different ways. What follows, though not an exhaustive list, is an overview of some of the ways the exodus and wilderness narratives shape the religion of later Israel. Most of the references within the Torah itself are not cited, but only those that connect a particular religious institution, law, or event. Each category introduced here could be expounded in detail and expanded to article- or monograph-length studies.

### Divine Self-Disclosure

"I am the LORD your God who brought you out of the land of Egypt" is a formula used frequently when God discloses himself to his people (Ex. 20:2; Lev. 19:36; 25:34, 55[70]; 26:23; Num. 15:41; Deut. 5:6; Ps. 81:10; Hos. 12:9; 13:4[71]). It has been shown that this introductory formula was used in the ancient Near East as a way for kings to publicize their accomplishments.[72] God appears to Abraham saying, "I am the LORD who brought you out from Ur

[68]Eichrodt, *Theology of the Old Testament*, 42.
[69]Wolfhart Pannenberg, *Revelation as History* (New York: MacMillan, 1968), 125.
[70]V. 55 offers a slight variation on the order of the formula.
[71]The Hosea references do not employ the clause "who brought you out," and hence are a variation on the longer form.
[72]Umberto Cassuto, *A Commentary on the Book of Exodus* (Jerusalem: Magness, 1967), 76.

of the Chaldeans" (Gen. 15:7). Before the exodus, God introduces himself to Moses: "I am the LORD. I appeared to Abraham, to Isaac, and to Jacob..." (Ex. 6:2–3). A few verses later he says, "I am the LORD, and I will bring you out from under the burdens of the Egyptians" (6:6). In the first part, the introduction, as in the first occurrence of the formula in Genesis 15:6, God associates himself with what he has previously done. Exodus 6 uses an interesting variation, speaking of what Yahweh *will* do (*waw* + 1st com. sing. hiphil perf.). After the exodus, not surprisingly, the deliverance is typically spoken of in the past tense (1st com. sing. hiphil perf.).

The corollary of this expression is that Moses describes the Israelites as "your people, whom you brought up out of the land of Egypt" (Ex. 32:7, 11). When King Balak of Moab sent messengers to procure the services of Balaam the prophet, the Israelites were described by the clause "a people has come out of Egypt" (Num. 22:5, 11).

The phenomenon of identifying an ethnic group and their bond with their deity (or deities) in terms of a particular event is not attested among Israel's neighbors. The link between Israel and the exodus is unique and is recognized by religionists and theologians. Rainer Albertz maintains that "the liberation from Egypt" resulted in more than just "the relationship with God as such but the special tie to the god Yahweh."[73] Rendtorff takes this connection a step further, believing that the expression "I will be your God and you shall be my people" is "the covenant formula," which expresses God's relationship and solidarity with Israel as his covenant people.[74] It is noteworthy that the first occurrence of the expression is found in Exodus 6:7 in anticipation of the departure from Egypt: "I will take you to be my people, and I will be your God, and you shall know that I am the LORD your God, who has brought you out from under the burdens of the Egyptians." In a sense, every time "my people" occurs in the Old Testament, it is a reminder to Israel that they are God's people, liberated by him from slavery in Egypt, and now bound to him by the Sinaitic covenant, to which we turn next.

### The Historical Prologue to the Sinaitic Covenant

In 1931 the Orientalist Viktor Korošec studied a group of Hittite treaties, offering some analysis of their structure. He was the first to recognize their six-part structure. In 1955 George Mendenhall discovered the structural par-

---

[73]Rainer Albertz, *A History of Israelite Religion in the Old Testament Period* (Louisville: Westminster John Knox, 1994), 49.

[74]Rolf Rendtorff, "The Concept of Revelation in Ancient Israel," in Pannenberg, *Revelation as History*, 23–53; and Rendtorff, *The Covenant Formula: An Exegetical and Theological Investigation* (Edinburgh: T&T Clark, 1998).

allel between the ancient treaty formula on the Hittite tablets, which date to
the fourteenth and thirteenth centuries, and Exodus 20–24, leading him to
write, "It is very difficult to escape the conclusion that this narrative rests
upon traditions which go back to the period when the treaty form was still
alive."[75] These treaties begin with the preamble in which the maker of the
treaty, the lord or suzerain, introduced himself by name, followed by the
second point, the historical prologue. The importance of this prologue was
that it provided the historical rationale for the treaty, namely, what the great
king had done for his vassal or servant. Here is an example from the first two
sections of a treaty between Suppiluliuma of Hatti (i.e., the Hittite) and his
subject Sharrupshi of Nuhashshi (Aleppo):

*Preamble/Title*
Thus says My Majesty Suppiluliuma, Great King, King of Hatti, Hero.[76]

*Historical Prologue*
When the king of the land of Mittanni sought to kill Sharrupshi, and the
king of the land of Mittanni entered the land of Nuhashshi together with his
infantry levies and his chariotry, and when he oppressed (?) him, Sharrupshi
sent his messenger to the King of Hatti, saying: "I am the subject of the King
of Hatti, Save me!" And I, My Majesty, sent infantry and chariotry to his aid,
and they drove the king of the land of Mittanni, together with his troops and
his chariotry out of the land of Nuhashshi.[77]

Here we see the circumstances that prompted Sharrupshi to call on his
superpower neighbor to aid him against the invasion of his territory by
Mittanni in northern Mesopotamia. Suppiluliuma summarizes the forego-
ing by saying "and I, [the] Great King, was not silent in regard to that matter,
but I went to the aid of Sharrupshi."[78] Because the Hittite king had delivered
Nuhashshi of the Mittannian invasion, Sharrupshi was obliged to become
the subject or servant of Suppiluliuma, and the treaty was the legal means
by which the relationship was formalized.

Exodus 20:1–2b follows the same pattern, albeit in much briefer form.

*Preamble/Title*
And God spoke all these words saying, I am the LORD your God (20:1–2a)

[75]George Mendenhall, "Covenant Forms in Israelite Tradition," *BA* 17, no. 3 (1954): 32.
[76]Gary Beckman, *Hittite Diplomatic Texts* (Atlanta: Scholars Press, 1999), 54.
[77]This is from the treaty between Suppiluliuma I the Hittite and Tette of Nuhashshi. Translation in
Beckman, *Hittite Diplomatic Texts*, 54–55.
[78]Ibid.

*Historical Prologue*
who brought you out of the land of Egypt, out of the house of slavery. (20:2b)

Just as the people of Nuhashshi were bound to Suppiluliuma, and a list of treaty stipulations or laws (the third part of the covenant formula) followed to govern the relationship, so too because God delivered Israel from its servitude in Egypt, Israel would now become Yahweh's people by the Sinaitic covenant (treaty), which carried with it laws or stipulations. Notice that after the brief historical prologue in Exodus 20:2b, the laws begin immediately.

Because the historical prologue plays such a vitally important role in establishing the basis for the treaty, one might logically conclude that an actual historical event (or events) is reflected in the prologue. Consequently, Delbert Hillers, in his study of biblical treaties or covenants, argues that historical prologues were not stereotypical, because each treaty had its own set of circumstances; inasmuch as it provided the rationale for the obligation, "it had to be substantially accurate."[79] If not, there was no reason to be bound to the treaty obligations.

The book of Deuteronomy, in the minds of some scholars, rather than being a pious forgery of the period of Josiah (à la the "orthodox" view of critical scholarship), is the record of a covenant-renewal ceremony at the end of the wilderness period, before the death of Moses and the entry into Canaan.[80] Deuteronomy's historical prologue (Deut. 1:6–3:29) traces the history of God's dealings with Israel from the departure from Mount Sinai to the arrival in Moab. Because of this particular focus, the exodus is assumed from the previous Sinaitic covenant. The historical prologue of the renewal ceremony at the end of Joshua's life, on the other hand, does reflect back on the exodus and wilderness period.

> Jacob and his children went down to Egypt. And I sent Moses and Aaron, and I plagued Egypt with what I did in the midst of it, and afterward I brought you out. Then I brought your fathers out of Egypt, and you came to the sea. And the Egyptians pursued your fathers with chariots and horsemen to the Red Sea. And when they cried to the LORD, he put darkness between you and the Egyptians and made the sea come upon them and cover them; and your eyes saw what I did in Egypt. And you lived in the wilderness a long time. Then I

---

[79]Delbert Hillers, *Covenant: The History of a Biblical Idea* (Baltimore: Johns Hopkins University Press), 31.
[80]Meredith G. Kline, *Treaty of the Great King: The Covenant Structure of Deuteronomy* (Grand Rapids: Eerdmans, 1963); Kenneth Kitchen, *On The Reliability of the Old Testament* (Grand Rapids: Eerdmans, 2003), 283–94.

brought you to the land of the Amorites, who lived on the other side of the Jordan. (Josh. 24:4b–8a)

The sojourn-exodus-wilderness story stands at the heart of Israel's covenant with the Lord and her creeds. Then, too, some of Israel's laws find their roots in the Egypt experience.

### Legal Matters

Law codes from Mesopotamia have long been studied as parallel legal material with biblical law. While many interesting parallels exist, one feature of Hebrew law not encountered in the Mesopotamian laws is that some biblical statutes include the specific historical event that created the precedent, for example, the sojourn and exodus. The following are other examples in which the sojourn and exodus are offered as the rationale for particular laws.

In ancient Israel, a family member, out of a sense of familial obligation, was encouraged to redeem a relative who was in debt (Lev. 25:46–54). But the ultimate reason for redeeming a family member was the divine precedent set by God, who redeemed Israel from Egypt, as Leviticus 25:55 notes: "For it is to me that the people of Israel are servants. They are my servants whom I brought out of the land of Egypt: I am the LORD your God." In dealing with the release of slaves after their maximum six-year term of service was completed, the Israelites were encouraged to provide generously for the liberated individuals, for "You shall remember that you were a slave in the land of Egypt, and the LORD your God redeemed you; therefore I command you this today" (Deut. 15:15).

Israelites were not to mistreat or oppress sojourners or aliens (gērîm), "for you were sojourners in the land of Egypt" (Ex. 22:21), and "you know the heart of a sojourner, for you were sojourners in the land of Egypt" (Ex. 23:9). Not only should the alien not be wronged, but "you shall love him as yourself, for you were strangers in the land of Egypt" (Lev. 19:34; similarly see Lev. 25:42; Deut. 24:17–18).

Military laws are recorded in Deuteronomy 20:1–20. The passage begins with the reminder, "When you go out to war against your enemies, and see horses and chariots and an army larger than your own, you shall not be afraid of them, for the LORD your God is with you, who brought you up out of the land of Egypt" (Deut. 20:1). The point seems to be that Israel has experienced God's strong arm defeating Pharaoh's powerful army and chariotry; therefore, when going to war, they need only trust God and follow his directives.

### Religious Festivals, Observances, and Rites

Religious rituals are reenactments or repetitions of sacred moments or events, behind which stands an archetype;[81] and, as Mircea Eliade observes, "reality is acquired solely through repetition or participation; everything which lacks an exemplary model is 'meaningless,' i.e., lacks reality."[82] According to Eliade's phenomenological method, each religious holy day or festival "represents the reactualization of a sacred event that took place in a mythical past, 'in the beginning.'"[83] For Israel the two principal archetypes are creation and God's salvific deliverance from Egypt.

Passover (*pesaḥ*) and unleavened bread (*maṣṣôt*) are the ultimate "reactualization of a sacred event." While they are connected festivals in later times, they may have originated as separate observances, the former being pastoral and the latter being connected to agriculture.[84] Passover is associated with the tenth and final plague, in which a lamb or kid is sacrificed, and blood is painted on the doorposts of the homes of the Hebrews to avoid divine judgment (Ex. 12:1–13). Immediately after the Passover ritual meal is introduced, the text continues, "And you shall observe the Feast of Unleavened Bread, for on this very day I brought your hosts out of the land of Egypt" (12:17). Moses then instructs the people, "Remember this day in which you came out of Egypt, out of the house of slavery" (Ex. 13:3), and he continues:

> You shall tell your son on that day, "It is because of what the Lord did for me when I came out of Egypt." And it shall be to you as a sign on your hand and as a memorial between your eyes, that the law of the Lord may be in your mouth. For with a strong hand the Lord has brought you out of Egypt. You shall therefore keep this statute at its appointed time from year to year. (13:8–10)

*Pesaḥ* and *maṣṣôt* have no other explanation for their origin than the exodus from Egypt (cf. Ex. 23:15; 34:18; Deut. 16:1–6). The feast of booths (*sukkôt*) is related to the feast of ingathering (*qāṣîr*). Leviticus 23:42–43, however, connects this otherwise agricultural occasion to the exodus because the people lived in temporary dwellings after leaving Egypt: "You shall dwell in booths for seven days. All native Israelites shall dwell in booths, that your generations may know that I made the people of Israel dwell in booths *when I brought them out of the land of Egypt*: I am the Lord your God." Presenting the first

---

[81] Mircea Eliade, *Cosmos and History: The Myth of the Eternal Return* (New York: Harper & Row, 1954), 21.

[82] Ibid., 34.

[83] Mircea Eliade, *The Sacred and the Profane* (New York: Harcourt Brace Jovanovich, 1959), 68–69.

[84] Roland de Vaux, *Ancient Israel*, vol. 2, *Religious Institutions* (New York: McGraw Hill, 1965), 484–93.

fruits was a part of the harvest celebrations. When the instructions are given
in Deuteronomy 26:1–5, Moses introduces the words of the above-mentioned
"old credo" of von Rad: "A wandering Aramean . . . ." Once again, the sojourn
and exodus are linked to an agricultural festival. It is unclear on what other
occasions this confession was recited.

The Sabbath arises from creation as an observance of the seventh day,
when God's work was completed (Gen. 2:1–3). In the covenant stipulations of
Exodus 20, the fourth commandment, "Remember the Sabbath day" (20:8),
includes mention of its association with creation (20:11). In covenant renewal
in the plains of Moab in Deuteronomy 5, resting on the seventh day is again
commanded, as in Exodus 20. Missing in the Deuteronomy passage, however,
is any reference to creation; rather the salvation from Egypt is cited: "You
shall remember that you were a slave in the land of Egypt, and the LORD your
God brought you out from there with a mighty hand and an outstretched arm.
Therefore the LORD your God commanded you to keep the Sabbath day" (5:15).

Consecration of the firstborn of all Israel is mentioned in Numbers 8:17–18
and is tied to the slaying of the firstborn of Egypt in the Passover event.
Likewise, the Levites are set aside for service in the sanctuary: "For all the firstborn among the people of Israel are mine, both of man and of beast. On the
day that I struck down all the firstborn in the land of Egypt I consecrated them
for myself, and I have taken the Levites instead of all the firstborn among the
people of Israel" (8:17–18). The status of the Levites is treated in more detail
in Numbers 3, and again the connection to the Passover serves as the basis.

> And the LORD spoke to Moses, saying, "Behold, I have taken the Levites from
> among the people of Israel instead of every firstborn who opens the womb
> among the people of Israel. The Levites shall be mine, for all the firstborn are
> mine. On the day that I struck down all the firstborn in the land of Egypt, I
> consecrated for my own all the firstborn in Israel, both of man and of beast.
> They shall be mine: I am the LORD." (Num. 3:11–13)

The consecration (or redemption) of the firstborn is actually first encountered
in Exodus 13:1, 11–16. Moses explains for future generations this practice
(and the consecration of firstborn livestock).

> And when in time to come your son asks you, "What does this mean?" you
> shall say to him, "By a strong hand the LORD brought us out of Egypt, from the
> house of slavery. For when Pharaoh stubbornly refused to let us go, the LORD
> killed all the firstborn in the land of Egypt, both the firstborn of man and the
> firstborn of animals. Therefore I sacrifice to the LORD all the males that first
> open the womb, but all the firstborn of my sons I redeem." It shall be as a mark

on your hand or frontlets between your eyes, for by a strong hand the LORD brought us out of Egypt. (13:14–16)

Israel's sanctuary, first the tabernacle and then the Jerusalem temple, was to contain memorials of the exodus-wilderness period. First, the stone copies with the laws of Sinai were to be placed in the ark of the covenant (Ex. 25:16), in keeping with the "Deposition" or fourth part of the previously introduced "covenant formula," in which the copies of treaty texts were placed in the sanctuary of the recipient of a treaty.[85] When the "Book of the Law" (i.e., Deuteronomy) was completed by Moses, it too was placed in the ark of the covenant: "Take this Book of the Law and put it by the side of the ark of the covenant of the LORD your God, that it may be there for a witness against you" (Deut. 31:26). Centuries later, when Solomon's temple was dedicated, the ark of the covenant was transferred to the new sanctuary (1 Kings 8:4). The ark is described as having in it the "two tablets that Moses put there at Horeb, where the LORD made a covenant with the people of Israel, *when they came out of the land of Egypt*" (8:9).[86]

Manna was a mysterious food provision for the Hebrews in Sinai. When it first appeared, Moses passed on the divine instruction that some manna be set aside and placed in the sanctuary.

> "Let an omer of it be kept throughout your generations, so that they may see the bread with which I fed you in the wilderness, *when I brought you out of the land of Egypt*." And Moses said to Aaron, "Take a jar, and put an omer of manna in it, and place it before the LORD to be kept throughout your generations." (Ex. 16:32b–33)

Apostasy in Israel was turning to other deities and spurning Yahweh, who brought the people out of Egypt. This theme, which will be dealt with more in the prophets section below, is first encountered in Deuteronomy 13:1–5. This passage anticipates false prophets who would lead the people to worship other gods, and it spells out the severe punishment to be meted out on such a provocateur: "That prophet or that dreamer of dreams shall be put to death, because he has taught rebellion against the LORD your God, *who brought you out of the land of Egypt* and redeemed you out of the house of slavery,

---

[85]The following is written in the treaty between Suppiluliuma of Hatti and Sattiwaza of Mittanni and records that copies of the treaty are deposited in the sanctuaries of both parties, lord and subject: "A duplicate of this tablet is deposited before the Sun-goddess of Arinna . . . and in the land of Mittanni a duplicate is deposited before the Storm-god. . . ." Beckman, *Hittite Diplomatic Texts*, 46.
[86]Emphasis mine. The absence of the "Books of the Law" and bowl with manna in 1 Kings 8:9 might be explained by it being "empty" when the Philistines captured it in Eli's day (cf. 1 Sam. 6:3–5); i.e., these items had been removed and not redeposited after the ark was returned to Israel.

to make you leave the way in which the LORD your God commanded you to walk" (13:5). Similarly at the dedication of the temple, God appeared again to Solomon and warned that departure from his commandments (i.e., Sinai covenant stipulations) would lead to the desolation of the temple (1 Kings 9:1–8). When the ruined temple was seen by passersby, they would explain the calamity by stating that the Israelites "abandoned the LORD their God *who brought their fathers out of the land of Egypt* and laid hold on other gods and worshiped them and served them" (9:9).

The earliest example of apostasy was the golden-calf incident at Mount Sinai. Aaron introduced the image, saying, "These are your gods, O Israel, who brought you out of the land of Egypt" (Ex. 32:4). Throughout this episode Moses was regularly denounced by the disgruntled people as "this Moses, the man who brought us up out of the land Egypt" (32:1, 23). This classic story of apostasy, which is called a "great sin" (32:21, 30, 31), becomes the tragic prototype for the golden-calf sanctuaries of King Jeroboam I at Bethel and Dan. At their dedication Jeroboam declared to the people: "You have gone up to Jerusalem long enough. Behold your gods, O Israel, who brought you up out of the land of Egypt" (1 Kings 12:28). Here the use of the expression "who brought you up out of the land of Egypt" indicates that so deeply ingrained in the northern Israelites was the belief that Yahweh had brought the Hebrews out of Egypt, that this new cult (be it Yahwistic or otherwise) was associated with the exodus event in order to gain legitimacy.

Lastly, when David proposed to the prophet Nathan that he build a temple for Yahweh, the prophet received a "word" from Yahweh (2 Sam. 7:2–4).

> Go and tell my servant David, "Thus says the LORD: Would you build me a house to dwell in? I have not lived in a house *since the day I brought up the people of Israel from Egypt to this day,* but I have been moving about in a tent for my dwelling. In all places where I have moved with all the people of Israel, did I speak a word with any of the judges of Israel, whom I commanded to shepherd my people Israel, saying, 'Why have you not built me a house of cedar?' " (7:5–7)

Not only is the departure from Egypt mentioned, but here it is specifically used as a chronological benchmark (*limîyôm*) (see below). The point is that God's glory accompanied the Hebrews when they left Egypt (Ex. 14:17–20) and dwelt with his people in the desert sanctuary (Ex. 40:34–38), and then through the period of the Judges to the present day, making a fixed sanctuary unnecessary. As with the various religious feasts, observances, and practices reviewed in this section, the exodus and wilderness theophanies played an important role in Israelite hymnody in Israel's sanctuaries.

*Hymnody*

In the previous section, we saw that at the heart of many of Israel's religious institutions is the exodus-wilderness tradition. So it is fitting that Israel's hymnody and liturgy refer frequently to these foundational events. Sometimes the references are overt, while in other cases, echoes suffice for the hearer to know to what a given hymn was referring.

The Song of Moses (or Song of the Sea) (Ex. 15:1–18) and the Song of Miriam (15:21) are placed in the exodus narrative immediately following the crossing of the sea and the triumph over the Egyptian army and chariotry. While there has been much scholarly discussion about the relationship between the former song and the shorter one, which borrows the opening lines of the former, Frank Moore Cross and David Noel Freedman (among others) have argued persuasively that these songs, along with the Song of Deborah (Judges 5), are "genuinely archaic" in their poetic structure and orthography, dating as early as the twelfth century BC, based on comparative study with Ugaritic poetry.[87] Exodus 15:4 celebrates the casting of Pharaoh's chariots into the sea: "His chosen officers were sunk in the Red Sea."

The setting of the Song of Deborah is the aftermath of Israel's victory over the Canaanite oppressors under the leadership of Barak the judge and Deborah the prophetess. Israel's victory in the narrative passage in Judges 4 is likened to God's leading Israel, after the Sinai theophany, through Edom in order to take the Promised Land:

> Lord, when you went out from Seir,
>     when you marched from the region of Edom,
> the earth trembled
>     and the heavens dropped,
>     yes, the clouds dropped water.
> The mountains quaked before the Lord,
>     even Sinai before the Lord, the God of Israel. (Judg. 5:4–5)

The same theme of Yahweh's coming from Sinai also occurs in the blessings of Moses in Deuteronomy 33:2. The literary analysis and comparative study by Cross and Freeman lead them to offer a date before the eleventh century BC for this song.[88] These three early songs each refer to aspects of the exodus

---

[87]Frank Moore Cross Jr. and David Noel Freedman, "The Song of Miriam," *JNES* 14 (1955): 237–50, and *Studies in Ancient Yahwistic Poetry* (Missoula: SBLDS, 1975; repr., Grand Rapids: Eerdmans, 1995), 1–45.

[88]Cross and Freedman, *Studies in Ancient Yahwistic Poetry*, 4. Previously published as Frank Moore Cross Jr. and David Noel Freedman, "The Blessings of Moses," *JBL* 67 (1948): 191–210.

or wilderness tradition, indicating that these foundational events were not some late inventions from the imagination of biblical poets.

The songs in the Psalter likewise deal with exodus and wilderness themes. They are framed in terms of God's "deeds" and "works." Several psalms are lengthy and detailed, rehearsing many aspects of the exodus and wilderness episodes of God's salvific acts as evidence of Yahweh's sovereign protection and guidance for the people throughout its history. Psalms 78, 105, and 106 belong to this category, with the first two even reciting most of the ten plagues. These are sufficiently known and require no further comment. Shorter references to the exodus and wilderness motifs are tucked into various psalms. Here are some examples.

> Come and see what God has done:
>     he is awesome in his deeds . . . .
> He turned the sea into dry land;
>     they passed through the river on foot. (Ps. 66:5–6)

Another allusion to the events of Exodus 14[89] appears in Psalm 74.

> God my King is from of old,
>     working salvation in the midst of the earth.
> You divided the seas by your might. (vv. 12–13)

Along the same line, Psalm 76:6 hints at the victory over the Egyptian chariotry.

> At your rebuke, O God of Jacob,
>     both rider and horse lay stunned."[90]

Psalm 77 remembers the deeds and works of Yahweh. "When the waters saw you, O God," verse 16 proclaims, "they were afraid." The hymn ends with these words:

> Your way was through the sea,
>     your path through the great waters;
>     yet your footprints were unseen.
> You led your people like a flock
>     by the hand of Moses and Aaron. (77:19–20)

---

[89]This psalm appears to associate the *Chaoskampf* motif with God's controlling the Sea of Reeds for the Israelites to flee Egypt. See Marvin Tate, *Psalms 51–100* (Dallas: Word, 1990), 254.
[90]The language alludes to the Songs of Moses and Miriam.

Psalm 81 begins by referring to the celebration of religious festivals that were decreed "when [God] went out over the land of Egypt" (v. 5), an allusion to the Passover. "I tested you at Meribah" is a reference to the people's rebellion at Meribah and Massah in the wilderness (Ex. 17:7; Num. 20:2, 13). And Psalm 81:10 recites the well-known formula,

> I am the LORD your God,
>> who brought you up out of the land of Egypt.

The Massah and Meribah rebellion is mentioned again in Psalm 95:8, as well as the "forty years" in the wilderness (v. 10). Moses and Aaron are referred to as God's priests in Psalm 99:6, and the following verse mentions the "pillar of the cloud" through which God spoke to the people.

Psalm 114 opens with the words,

> When Israel went out from Egypt,
>> the house of Jacob from a people of strange language . . . .
> The sea looked and fled;
>> Jordan turned back. (vv. 1, 3)

It ends by describing Yahweh as the one "who turns the rock into a pool of water" (114:8). The latter harks back to the wilderness episodes in which divinely produced water flowed from the rock, and it explains the origins of the names Massah and Meribah (Ex. 17:1–8; Num. 20:2–13).

Psalm 68:8 recalls God's presence with his people in Sinai and the awesome theophany.

> The earth quaked, the heavens poured down rain,
>> before God, the One of Sinai.

Israel is likened to a vine that God brought out of Egypt and planted (in Canaan) in Psalm 80:8.

Finally, exodus themes are found in Psalms 135 and 136. The former refers to the death of the firstborn of Egypt (135:8), as does the latter (136:10). Psalm 136 also proclaims God's covenant loyalty (hesed), as evidenced by his overthrowing "Pharaoh and his host in the Red Sea" (v. 15) and leading his people through the wilderness (v. 16).

The preponderance of exodus and wilderness allusions in these psalms demonstrates that these saving acts were focal points of Israelite worship. These data clearly complement the religious festivals reviewed above, and in some cases may have been sung in conjunction with holy days.

*Prophetic Literature*

The prophets of ancient Israel are generally considered covenant enforcers who are often portrayed as bringing a lawsuit (*rîb*)[91] against God's recidivist covenant violator Israel. Servant, son, and wife motifs are often used to symbolize this relationship. Because the covenant was made with Israel after its departure from Egypt in Sinai, the exodus and wilderness episodes are regularly mentioned.

We begin with some examples in Judges and Samuel of prophets speaking. An unnamed prophet proclaims God's word after the people call out for deliverance from the invasion of the Midianites in Judges 6.

> The LORD sent a prophet to the people of Israel. And he said to them, "Thus says the LORD, the God of Israel: I led you up from Egypt and brought you out of the house of slavery. And I delivered you from the hand of the Egyptians and from the hand of all who oppressed you, and drove them out before you and gave you their land. And I said to you, 'I am the LORD your God; you shall not fear the gods of the Amorites in whose land you dwell.' But you have not obeyed my voice." (6:8–10)

Another anonymous "man of God" prophesies to Eli the priest, reminding him that his priestly authority came from divine appointment in Egypt: "Did I indeed reveal myself to the house of your father when they were in Egypt subject to the house of Pharaoh? Did I choose him out of all the tribes of Israel to be my priest, to go up to my altar, to burn incense?" (1 Sam. 2:27–28). These rhetorical questions require an emphatic *yes* answer.

Citations of exodus- and wilderness-related events abound in the literary prophets. Only a selection is offered here. In Hosea we read,

> When Israel was a child, I loved him,
>     and out of Egypt I called my son. (Hos. 11:1)

Later on, God speaks again: "I am the LORD your God from the land of Egypt" (12:9), an expression repeated in 13:4. This introduction is followed by,

> It was I who knew you in the wilderness,
>     in a land of drought. (13:5)

The leadership of Moses in the exodus is implied in the statement, "By a prophet the LORD brought Israel up from Egypt" (12:13).

---

[91]For uses of *rîb* in this manner, see Isa. 3:13; 12:1; 49:25; 57:16; Hos. 4:1, 4; 12:3; Mic. 6:1–2.

Amos, Hosea's eighth-century colleague, uses similar language, speaking of Israel as "the whole family that I brought up out of the land of Egypt" (Amos 3:1). Israel's origin is likened to that of two of her neighbors.

> Did not I bring up Israel from the land of Egypt,
>     and the Philistines from Caphtor and the Syrians from Kir? (9:7)

Jeremiah also mentions the Philistines as originating in Caphtor (Jer. 47:4), which is identified with Crete.[92] It would be inexplicable for the prophet (and his audience) to know the origins of the Philistines and Arameans but be wrong about Israel's origin!

Another contemporary, Micah, encapsulates the entire exodus-wilderness story in a short pericope that is a part of the so-called *rîb* formula or covenant lawsuit.[93]

> For I brought you up from the land of Egypt
>     and redeemed you from the house of slavery,
> and I sent before you Moses,
>     Aaron, and Miriam.
> O my people, remember what Balak king of Moab devised,
>     and what Balaam the son of Beor answered him,
> and what happened from Shittim to Gilgal,
>     that you may know the righteous acts of the LORD. (Mic. 6:4–5)

Commenting on this passage, Gerhard Maier observes that history

> runs very briefly through the Exodus from Egypt, Moses, Aaron, Miriam, Balak, Balaam, Shittim, and Gilgal—in the chronological sequence found in the Pentateuch, incidentally—and speaks of God's actions encountered by Israel at each of these stages in its history, without needing to clarify any elements of this history.[94]

Isaiah also employs exodus motifs in his preaching. In Isaiah 10:5 Assyria is likened to the "rod of my anger," and the staff is associated with Yahweh's rod that "struck Midian at the rock of Oreb" (i.e., killed the Midianite chief

---

[92] Cyprus has also been suggested, but Crete remains a more likely location. Cf. Richard Hess, "Caphtor," *Anchor Bible Dictionary*, ed. D. N. Freedman, vol. 1 (New York: Doubleday, 1992), 869–70.

[93] Francis Anderson and David Noel Freedman, *Micah* (New York: Doubleday, 2000), 510–11.

[94] Gerhard Maier, "Truth and Reality in the Historical Understanding of the Old Testament," in *Israel's Past in Present Research: Essays on Ancient Israelite Historiography*, ed. V. Philips Long (Winona Lake, IN: Eisenbrauns, 1999), 204.

Oreb by Gideon in Judg. 7:25), the same staff that would be stretched over the sea, "as he did in Egypt" (Isa. 10:26).

One of the developing themes in the prophets is to use the exodus from Egypt as the archetype for the return of Israelites from Assyrian captivity or Judeans from Babylonian exile. Isaiah employs this when he anticipates the day in which

> there will be a highway from Assyria
>    for the remnant that remains of his people,
> as there was for Israel
>    when they came up from the land of Egypt. (11:16)

Jeremiah likens the Judeans who survive the fall of Jerusalem or the exile to those who "found grace in the wilderness" (Jer. 31:2). "Grace" (ḥēn) is applied to the survivors of the golden-calf episode (Ex. 33:12–13, 16–17).

One could easily write a monograph of Jeremiah's use of the exodus and wilderness themes in his messages. A few examples will suffice. Jeremiah contrasts Israel's faithfulness as a bride in the wilderness (2:2b) with the present situation where the people do not say,

> Where is the LORD
>    who brought us up from the land of Egypt, who led us in the wilder-
>       ness . . . ? (2:6)

In his celebrated temple sermon, the prophet stresses the principle of obedience rather than sacrifice by announcing, "In the day that I brought them out of Egypt, I did not speak to your fathers or command them concerning burnt offerings and sacrifices" (7:22). And he reminds his audience that he has sent prophets to drive home this point: "From the day that your fathers came out of the land of Egypt to this day, I have persistently sent all my servants the prophets to them, day after day" (7:25).

When the prophet speaks of violating the covenant and its commandments, he reminds his people that this occurred when "I commanded your fathers when I brought them out of the land of Egypt" (11:4; see also 11:7). The oath formula apparently used by the people, when evoking the name of their deity was "as the LORD lives who brought up the people of Israel out of the land of Egypt" (16:14). This historical memory, the prophet anticipates, will be replaced with a new oath formula to reflect God's rescue of the Jews from Mesopotamia: "As the LORD lives who brought up the people of Israel out of the north country and out of all the countries where he had driven them" (16:15).

Jeremiah's "new covenant" will not be like the covenant made with their ancestors when they came out of Egypt (31:31–32; see also 34:13). In the prophet's prayer in the "Book of Consolation" he recalls "signs and wonders in the land of Egypt" (32:20–21).

Exilic and postexilic prophets also appeal to the exodus tradition. Ezekiel uses the marriage motif to describe the relationship between Yahweh and Israel that was legalized with the covenant (cf. Ezekiel 16). Yahweh made himself "known" to them in bringing them out of Egypt and into the wilderness, where he gave his laws (20:5–10), but his bride violated his laws and went "whoring" after other gods (20:22–31). Israel's bent toward idolatry (spiritual infidelity) is even traced back to "the land of Egypt" (23:19, 27).

Daniel's prayer in Babylon mentions not obeying the commandments "written in the Law of Moses" (Dan. 9:13); the people had failed the "Lord our God, who brought [his] people out of the land of Egypt" (9:15). Haggai in the Persian period mentions the "covenant that I made with you when you came out of Egypt" (Hag. 2:5).

From the earliest prophets, to those from the end of the Old Testament period, the exodus and wilderness history, and especially the Sinaitic covenant, are constant themes. And it was the violation of that ancient treaty with God that accounted for the calamities they were encountering from the Assyrian through Persian periods.

### Statements of Non-Israelites

It might be unexpected to find that non-Israelites confess their faith in the God of Israel because of the exodus from Egypt. The first in this category is Jethro, the Midianite priest and father-in-law of Moses. When he meets up with Moses and the Israelites by Mount Sinai and learns of the deliverance of the Hebrews (Ex. 18:5–9), he affirms, "Blessed be the Lord, who has delivered you out of the hand of the Egyptians and out of the hand of Pharaoh and has delivered the people from under the hand of the Egyptians. Now I know that the Lord is greater than all gods, because in this affair they dealt arrogantly with the people" (18:10–11). As mentioned previously, King Balak of Moab sent messengers to Balaam (of Amaw in Syria) who referred to the Israelites as a people new to the area: "A people has come out of Egypt" (Num. 22:5, 11). In one of his discourses, Balaam confesses,

> God brings them out of Egypt
> and is for them like the horns of the wild ox. (Num. 23:22)

This same statement about Israel is repeated in the third discourse (Num. 24:8).

A third case of faith by a foreigner is that of Rahab of Jericho. Upon receiving the Hebrew spies, she admits that she and the people of the land have heard of the wonders of the exodus: "I know that the LORD has given you the land, and that the fear of you has fallen upon us, and that all the inhabitants of the land melt away before you. For we have heard how the LORD dried up the water of the Red Sea before you when you came out of Egypt" (Josh. 2:9–10).

Another example is slightly different, but quite revealing. In the battle of Ebenezer, the Philistines panic when they hear the cheering and shouting of the Israelite armies as the ark of the covenant is carried into their camp. First Samuel 4:6–8 reports:

> And when they learned that the ark of the LORD had come to the camp, the Philistines were afraid, for they said, "A god has come into the camp." And they said, "Woe to us! For nothing like this has happened before. Woe to us! Who can deliver us from the power of these mighty gods? These are the gods who struck the Egyptians with every sort of plague in the wilderness."

This reading suggests that while the Philistines were familiar with the exodus story, they had a garbled version of the events, as the "plagues" did not strike the Egyptians in the wilderness. Alternatively, the LXX reading "and in the wilderness" may better preserve the original reading.[95]

This fear notwithstanding, the Philistines rally, defeat Israel, and seize the ark in a battle near Aphek (1 Sam. 4:9–11). But the Philistines' war trophy backfires as the cult image of Dagon at Ashdod topples over in the presence of the ark of Yahweh (5:1–4), and the men are hit with a plague of tumors (5:9). This embarrassment prompts the Philistines to return the ark. Their "priests and diviners" (6:2) advise that the political leaders include gold images of tumors and mice—still an obscure act—to give glory to the God of Israel (6:5). The advisors then ask: "Why should you harden your hearts as the Egyptians and Pharaoh hardened their hearts?" (6:6).

Thus we have two cases of the Philistines recalling details from the exodus story. Such knowledge may have been transmitted by Israelites in the Shephelah, where they recounted their national story to their Philistine neighbors.

### Chronological Benchmark

The exodus from Egypt, because it was a founding national event, served as a chronological benchmark or anchoring point in subsequent periods. First

---

[95]David Tsumara, *The First Book of Samuel* (Grand Rapids: Eerdmans, 2007), 194, offers a good review of different interpretations and readings of this text.

of all, the exodus event, memorialized by Passover, served as the beginning of the religious calendar (cf. Ex. 12:1–2). Especially in the Torah, noteworthy events are dated from the departure from Egypt.

In the wilderness itinerary, two early stops are dated. In the first, "they set out from Elim, and all the congregation of the people of Israel came to the wilderness of Sin, which is between Elim and Sinai, on the fifteenth day of the second month after they had departed from the land of Egypt" (Ex. 16:1); then, "On the third new moon after the people of Israel had gone out of the land of Egypt, on that day they came into the wilderness of Sinai" (Ex. 19:1). The book of Numbers begins with a chronological datum: "The LORD spoke to Moses in the wilderness of Sinai, in the tent of meeting, on the first day of the second month, in the second year after they had come out of the land of Egypt (Num. 1:1). This is followed by the dating of an oracle reminding the people of the proper date to celebrate Passover: "And the LORD spoke to Moses in the wilderness of Sinai, in the first month of the second year after they had come out of the land of Egypt, saying, 'Let the people of Israel keep the Passover at its appointed time'" (Num. 9:1–2). Aaron the priest is reported to have died "in the fortieth year after the people of Israel had come out of the land of Egypt, on the first day of the fifth month" (Num. 33:38). Then Deuteronomy 1 dates the arrival of the Israelites in the land of Moab to the "fortieth year, on the first day of the eleventh month" (1:3); the departure from Egypt is understood.

The ghastly rape, murder, and dismemberment of a Levite's concubine is viewed as an unparalleled shocking occurrence. People respond by saying, "Such a thing has never happened or been seen from the day that the people of Israel came up out of the land of Egypt until this day" (Judg. 19:30). Put another way, for the entirety of the nation's history, "such a thing has never happened."

A similar usage occurs in 1 Samuel 8:8, where the propensity of the people to rebel against God is described as spanning their entire history: "According to all the deeds that they have done, from the day I [God] brought them up out of Egypt even to this day, forsaking me and serving other gods, so they are also doing to you [Samuel]."

The beginning of the construction of Solomon's temple is dated to "the four hundred and eightieth year after the people of Israel came out of the land of Egypt, in the fourth year of Solomon's reign" (1 Kings 6:1). This reference is unique. We see that the regnal dating system was introduced with the monarchy (i.e., dating events to the year of a king's reign), while the exodus event remained a meaningful benchmark. Biblical scholars have long debated how the 480-year figure should be interpreted, whether literally or symbolically (i.e., 12 × 40, thus 12 generations).[96] I have recently suggested that the figure might be a *Distanzangaben*.[97] This literary phenomenon is used in Assyrian texts, where large blocks of time are mentioned (e.g., 720 or 760 years) to connect a current temple building or renovation with the original construction. Regardless of which of these three interpretations is correct, all assume the exodus as the foundational event that serves as the chronological anchor for present dating purposes.

### Historical Retrospective

Historical retrospectives are a recognized genre in which a figure, often a king late in his reign, recalls his earlier achievements, usually in the form of a speech recorded on a stela or temple, typically with a political (or religious) agenda in mind.[98]

As the Israelites approach Mount Sinai, they are attacked by the Amalekites, a nomadic desert people, and a battle ensues (Ex. 17:8–16). The end of the narrative anticipates transgenerational war with Amalek. This bitter memory is appealed to in Deuteronomy 25:17–19.

> Remember what Amalek did to you on the way as you came out of Egypt, how he attacked you on the way when you were faint and weary, and cut off your tail, those who were lagging behind you, and he did not fear God. Therefore . . . you shall blot out the memory of Amalek from under heaven; you shall not forget.

During the reign of Israel's first king, Saul (ca. 1030–1010 BC), Samuel speaks a prophetic word giving license for the armies of Israel to wipe out Amalek: "Thus says the LORD of hosts, 'I have noted what Amalek did to Israel in opposing them on the way when they came up out of Egypt'" (1 Sam. 15:2). Saul warns another nomadic people, the Kenites (i.e., the Midianite relatives of Moses) to separate themselves from the vile Amalekites so as not to be harmed, since "you showed kindness to all the people of Israel when they came up out of Egypt" (15:6).

Moses uses a retrospective in his communication to the king of Edom when asking for permission to transit through his territory. He recalls the

---

[96]For a recent discussion of various views, see James K. Hoffmeier, "What Is the Biblical Date for the Exodus?," *JETS* 50 (2007): 225–47.

[97]Ibid., 237–39.

[98]I am following Redford's understanding of "retrospective" (Redford, *Wars of Syria and Palestine of Thutmose III*, 158, 242). This is similar to Van Seters's category of "political use of the past," which is well documented in Hittite texts (see John Van Seters, *In Search of History* [New Haven, CT: Yale University Press, 1983], 114–18).

sojourn in Egypt, the oppressive treatment the Hebrews experienced, and God's deliverance.

> You know all the hardship that we have met: how our fathers went down to Egypt, and we lived in Egypt a long time. And the Egyptians dealt harshly with us and our fathers. And when we cried to the LORD, he heard our voice and sent an angel and brought us out of Egypt. And here we are in Kadesh, a city on the edge of your territory. Please let us pass through your land. (Num. 20:14–17)

The reason the Moabites and Ammonites are not welcome in Israel's sanctuary is "because they did not meet you with bread and with water on the way, when you came out of Egypt" (Deut. 23:4).

Within the covenant curses of Deuteronomy, violators can expect to be struck with boils ($s^e\hat{h}\hat{\imath}n$), which of course are the same malady mentioned in the sixth Egyptian plague (Ex. 9:9–10). Another curse mentions "all the diseases of Egypt" (Deut. 28:60). Curses are a part of all ancient treaty texts in all periods, but only in the Hebrew Bible are curses connected to specific earlier events.[99] In addition to the exodus plagues, the fate of covenant violators includes an overthrow "like that of Sodom and Gomorrah" (Deut. 29:23), another allusion to an earlier biblical event (Gen. 19:24–28).

A number of retrospectives are found in the Judges cycle. When Gideon is called to save his people from the Midianites, he expresses his hope that God will display "his wonderful deeds that our fathers recounted to us, saying, 'Did not the LORD bring us up from Egypt?'" (Judg. 6:13). The subject of Israel's arrival in the Transjordan arises when Judge Jephthah tries to settle a territorial dispute with the Ammonites (11:13–16). The local king begins this retrospective, saying, "Because Israel on coming up from Egypt took away my land, from the Arnon to the Jabbok and to the Jordan; now therefore restore it peaceably" (11:13). Jephthah in the following verses recounts the travel from Egypt to Moab: "Israel did not take away the land of Moab or the land of the Ammonites, but when they came up from Egypt, Israel went through the wilderness to the Red Sea and came to Kadesh" (11:15–16).

When Saul is acclaimed the king at Mizpah, Samuel offers a historical retrospective to place this event in its proper context. He begins by proclaiming, "I brought up Israel out of Egypt, and I delivered you from the hand of the Egyptians and from the hand of all the kingdoms that were oppressing you"

---

[99] A review of ten treaties in Beckman's volume (*Hittite Diplomatic Texts*, 29, 33, 40, 48, 52, 64, 69, 86, 92, 112) shows none to be connected to some past plague or calamity.

(1 Sam. 10:18). After Saul defeats the Ammonites, who attacked Jabesh-Gilead, Samuel rallies the people at Gilgal to "renew the kingdom" (11:14). Here too he brings historical perspective to his speech to the nation.

> The LORD is witness, who appointed Moses and Aaron and brought your fathers up out of the land of Egypt. Now therefore stand still that I may plead with you before the LORD concerning all the righteous deeds of the LORD that he performed for you and for your fathers. When Jacob went into Egypt, and the Egyptians oppressed them, then your fathers cried out to the LORD and the LORD sent Moses and Aaron, who brought your fathers out of Egypt and made them dwell in this place. (12:6–8)

In each of the examples cited here, the retrospective of the nation's history typically begins with the exodus from Egypt, which may include references to the wilderness experience.

## Conclusion

Biblical theology has employed history as the foundation to its theological task for over two centuries in Western academe. Indeed there have been important corrective measures taken by biblical theologians who have rightly recognized that history should not be used as the *exclusive* means of revelation and divine activity for their theology. Here Barr was right. For those who today wish to minimize history in relationship to faith and theology because some critics of the Bible question the historicity of certain Old Testament events, the exodus in particular, it is worth noting what Barr said in the same 1962 essay.

> There really is a *Heilsgeschichte*, a series of events set within the place of human life and in historical sequence, through which God has especially revealed himself. I would not doubt that we have been generally right in saying that this can be taken as the central theme[100] of the Bible, that it forms the main link between Old and New Testaments, and that its presence and importance marks biblical faith off clearly from other religions.[101]

I have focused here on the exodus and wilderness episodes since they have been foundational to theology and faith, and because biblical minimalists now reject the historical worth of the Bible's claim regarding these events. Indeed, archaeological evidence does not exist that "proves" the historicity

---

[100]He distinguishes between theme and organizing principle.
[101]Barr, "Revelation through History," 10.

of the exodus and wilderness narratives, but the absence of evidence cannot disprove their historicity. Indirect evidence from Egypt demonstrates that these foundational events are plausible, and the Egyptian background to the narratives is unquestionable. The biblical evidence for the exodus and wilderness periods reviewed above so overwhelmingly supports the historicity of these events that the priests, prophets, psalmists, people of Israel, and foreigners believed these events occurred, and consequently they celebrated festivals, sang songs, dated events, and observed laws that assumed that Yahweh's salvation from Egypt was authentic.

If orthodox Christian faith based on the Bible does not require its foundational events to be real and historical, one must ask, Why have anti-Christian polemicists for nearly two thousand years—from the second-century Gnostics and philosophers to Enlightenment philosophers, as well as their followers in German and other continental higher critics and recent postmodern hermeneuts[102]—been so obsessed with undermining the Bible's historicity and accuracy, along with ridiculing the supernatural? Obviously they think historicity matters, and in their mind if the Bible is shown to be inaccurate and filled with errors, its message is invalidated. There is no better illustration of the deleterious effect of "critical" scholarship on Christianity than the shrinking church in Europe and North America.[103]

Meanwhile, the church in the Southern Hemisphere is exploding and vibrant.[104] Philip Jenkins, in his penetrating book *The Next Christendom: The Coming of Global Christianity* (2002), offers some extremely cogent observations about the direction of the Southern (Hemisphere) church as compared with her older sister in the North that progressive evangelicals should consider before insisting that we bow at the altar of Wellhausen and his successors in Western academe. The impact of secular Enlightenment thought birthed in the eighteenth century is still with us. It has attacked Scripture and its central doctrines: "The Trinity, the divinity of Christ, the existence of hell, all fell into disfavor, while critical Bible scholarship undermined the familiar bases of faith."[105] The questions that have so troubled

---

[102]For a historical treatment of some of the key figures in the history of criticism, see R. K. Harrison, *Introduction to the Old Testament* (Grand Rapids: Eerdmans, 1969), 3–62; and Baruch Halpern, *The First Historians: The Hebrew Bible and History* (San Francisco: Harper & Row, 1988), chap. 2.
[103]Conveniently reviewed in Philip Jenkins, *The Next Christendom: The Coming of Global Christianity* (New York: Oxford, 2002), 6–10.
[104]See David Barrett, George Kurian, and Todd Johnson, *World Christian Encyclopedia*, 2nd ed. (New York: Oxford University Press, 2001); Philip Jenkins, *The New Faces of Christianity: Believing the Bible in the Global South* (New York: Oxford University Press, 2006); and Jenkins, *The Next Christendom*.
[105]Jenkins, *The Next Christendom*, 9–10.

Western Christendom (and dragged it down!) are irrelevant to the dynamic and exploding Southern Hemisphere. "From this point of view," Jenkins concludes, "the churches that are doing best in the world as a whole are the ones that stand farthest from Western liberal orthodoxies, and we should learn from their success."[106]

---

[106]Ibid., 14.

# 5

# *FUNDAMENTUM ET COLUMNAM FIDEI NOSTRAE*

## *Irenaeus on the Perfect and Saving Nature of the Scriptures*

## MICHAEL A. G. HAYKIN[1]

The discovery of a cache of fifty or so Gnostic texts at Nag Hammadi in 1945 proved to be the major catalyst in the emergence of the twentieth-century study of Gnosticism as a significant academic discipline. And as that discipline has matured over the years, these texts have confirmed in the minds of some scholars that the earliest communities of professing Christians were truly diverse bodies.[2] Yet, while an attentive reading of these texts does reveal some clear differences between the various Gnostic communities, such a reading also makes evident that they shared a number of commonalities over against their opponents in the ancient catholic church. The majority of the Gnostics were essentially committed to a radical dualism of immateriality and matter. The former was divine and wholly good, while the latter was irredeemably evil. They were essentially hostile to monotheism, since they postulated the existence of a variety of divine beings. Through an upheaval within the supreme divine being, which the various Gnostic systems explained by means of an atemporal myth, elements of the divine became trapped within material bodies. These material bodies and

[1] I am grateful to Joe Harrod and Dwayne Ewers, both of Louisville, Kentucky, for help received during the writing of this essay.
[2] See, for example, David Brakke, *The Gnostics: Myth, Ritual, and Diversity in Early Christianity* (Cambridge, MA: Harvard University Press, 2010).

the entire material realm were the work of a lesser divinity (the demiurge), understood as either the God of the Old Testament or even Satan. Since awareness of the divine elements' entrapment in the human body was not immediately known, knowledge of one's true state was needed, which, for most Gnostic systems, involved Jesus as the revealer, and hence his role as Savior. Central to this entire quest was an eschatology that entailed escape from all materiality and temporality.[3]

Combating Gnosticism involved the finest of the earliest Christian thinkers, from Justin Martyr (ca. 100/110–ca. 165) to the great Alexandrian exegete Origen (ca. 185–254). But it is intriguing that probably the most significant reply to the leading heresiarchs of the second century, Valentinus (fl. 138–166)[4] and Marcion (fl. 150s–160s),[5] came from a missionary theologian who complained about his ability to write theology. Although Greek was his mother tongue, he reckoned that he had spent far too much time among the Celts of Gaul speaking Gaulish, a Celtic language now extinct, and thus he believed he had lost any real facility he had had with his own language.[6] Moreover, he claimed that he had never formally studied rhetoric and that he had neither the literary skills nor the "beauty of language" necessary for the task of a theologian.[7] And yet many later students of his thought rightly believe

---

[3]For this mini-morphology of Gnosticism, I am indebted to Christoph Markschies, *Gnosis: An Introduction*, trans. John Bowden (London: T&T Clark, 2003), 16–17; Robert A. Segal, "Religion: Karen L. King, *What Is Gnosticism?*," *Times Literary Supplement* (November 21, 2003), 31. For a selection of Gnostic texts, see Werner Foerster, ed., *Gnosis: A Selection of Gnostic Texts*, trans. R. McL. Wilson, 2 vols. (Oxford: Clarendon, 1972, 1974).

[4]According to Irenaeus, *Against Heresies* 3.4.3, Valentinus came to Rome during the episcopate of Hyginus (ca. 138–ca. 142) and was there till that of Anicetus (ca. 155–ca. 166). For Valentinus and his followers, see especially Markschies, *Gnosis*, 89–94; Einar Thomassen, *The Spiritual Seed: The Church of the "Valentinians"* (Leiden: Brill, 2006); Ismo Dunderberg, *Beyond Gnosticism: Myth, Lifestyle, and Society in the School of Valentinus* (New York: Columbia University Press, 2008). In an interesting venture into virtual history, Dunderberg has also written an article about what "Christianity" would have looked like if Valentinus's heresy had been successful in subverting orthodoxy. As with all virtual history, the further away in time Dunderberg's speculations are from Valentinus's actual lifetime, the more "sci-fi-ish" they get. See his "Valentinus and His School: What Might Have Been," *The Fourth R* 22, no. 6 (Nov.–Dec. 2009): 3–10.

[5]According to Irenaeus, *Against Heresies* 3.4.3, Marcion was principally active in Rome during the episcopate of Anicetus. For two recent overviews of Marcion's life and teaching, see Markschies, *Gnosis*, 86–89; Paul Foster, "Marcion: His Life, Works, Beliefs, and Impact," *ExpTim* 121 (March 2010): 269–80. There were significant differences between Marcion and the Gnostics, and in many ways Marcion should not be classified as a Gnostic. On this, see the brief summary by Markschies, *Gnosis*, 88–89.

[6]Irenaeus, *Against Heresies* 1.pref.3. For discussion of Irenaeus and Gaulish, see also C. Philip Slate, "Two Features of Irenaeus' Missiology," *Missiology* 23, no. 4 (October 1995): 433–35.

[7]Irenaeus, *Against Heresies* 1.pref.3. All translations from *Against Heresies* are mine unless otherwise indicated. For the Greek and Latin text of *Against Heresies*, I have used Adelin Rousseau et al., eds., *Irénée de Lyon: Contre les heresies*, 5 vols., SC 100/1–2, 152–53, 210–11, 263–64, 293–94 (Paris: Les Éditions du Cerf, 1965 [vol. 4], 1969 [vol. 5], 1974 [vol. 3], 1979 [vol. 1], 1982 [vol. 2]).

him to be a truly gifted expositor of what would become the core of ortho-dox Christianity.[8] The person in question is, of course, Irenaeus of Lyons (ca. 130/140–ca. 200), and there is a vigor and winsomeness about him that makes many students of his extant works wish that far more was known about his life than is available.[9]

## Sparse Details of a Significant Life

There seems to be no consensus in patristic scholarship about the place of Irenaeus's birth. Very likely it was Smyrna (the modern Turkish city of Izmir), since he heard Polycarp of Smyrna (69/70–155/156) preach there when he was young, and Polycarp appears to have been something of a Christian mentor to him.[10] Irenaeus's date of birth is also obscure, with suggestions ranging from 98 to 147.[11] Most likely he was born between 130 and 140.[12] It is also quite possible that Irenaeus studied under Justin Martyr, either in Ephesus or later at Rome.[13] By the mid-150s, the time of Polycarp's martyrdom, Irenaeus was residing in Rome,[14] where he may have come with Polycarp on the latter's visit to Rome in 153 or 154, two years prior to his death.[15] It was during this time

---

On Irenaeus's claim to have no knowledge of rhetoric, see Robert M. Grant, *Irenaeus of Lyons* (London: Routledge, 1997), 46–53; M. A. Donovan, *One Right Reading? A Guide to Irenaeus* (Collegeville, MN: Liturgical, 1997), 10–11; Eric Osborn, *Irenaeus of Lyons* (Cambridge: Cambridge University Press, 2001), 3–4.

[8] W. Brian Shelton, "Irenaeus" in Bradley G. Green, ed., *Shapers of Christian Orthodoxy: Engaging with Early and Medieval Theologians* (Downers Grove, IL: InterVarsity, 2010), 15–16.

[9] F. R. Montgomery Hitchcock, "Irenaeus of Lugdunum," *ExpTim* 44 (1932–1933): 167. Cyril C. Richardson was surely right when he stated, "The significance of Irenaeus cannot be overestimated" ("Introduction to Early Christian Literature and Its Setting," in *Early Christian Fathers*, trans. and ed. Cyril C. Richardson, The Library of Christian Classics 1 [Philadelphia: Westminster, 1953], 18). It needs noting that there are some, however, who "find Irenaeus and what he stood for to be truly and genuinely unappealing" (C. E. Hill, *Who Chose the Gospels? Probing the Great Gospel Conspiracy* [Oxford: Oxford University Press, 2010], 52). Hill details the dislike of certain contemporary scholars for Irenaeus and his thinking (*Who Chose the Gospels?*, 52–68).

For what follows in terms of a biographical sketch of Irenaeus, I have found the following sketches of his life helpful: Denis Minns, *Irenaeus* (Washington, DC: Georgetown University Press, 1997), 1–9; Grant, *Irenaeus of Lyons*, 1–10; Donovan, *One Right Reading?*, 7–10; Osborn, *Irenaeus of Lyons*, 1–7; Shelton, "Irenaeus," 17–24; D. Jeffrey Bingham, "Irenaeus of Lyons," in *The Routledge Companion to Early Christian Thought*, ed. D. Jeffrey Bingham (London: Routledge, 2010), 137–39; Michael Todd Wilson, "Preaching Irenaeus: A Second-Century Pastor Speaks to a Twenty-First Century Church" (DMin thesis, Knox Theological Seminary, 2011), 60–76.

[10] *The Martyrdom of Polycarp* 22.2 and "The Ending according to the Moscow Manuscript" 2; Irenaeus, Letter to Florinus, in Eusebius, *Ecclesiastical History* 5.20.4–8; Irenaeus, *Against Heresies* 3.3.4.

[11] Osborn, *Irenaeus of Lyons*, 2.

[12] Ibid.

[13] See Michael Slusser, "How Much Did Irenaeus Learn from Justin?," in *Studia Patristica*, ed. F. Young, M. Edwards, and P. Parvis (Leuven: Peeters, 2006), 40:515–20.

[14] *The Martyrdom of Polycarp*, "The Ending according to the Moscow Manuscript" 2.

[15] Irenaeus, Letter to Victor of Rome, in Eusebius, *Ecclesiastical History* 5.24.11–18.

in Rome that Irenaeus had significant contact with the followers of Valentinus and Marcion, whose ideas Irenaeus would seek to refute in his magnum opus, *The Detection and Refutation of the Pseudo-Knowledge* (ca. 180), known today more simply as *Against Heresies*.[16]

From Rome, Irenaeus traveled to Lyons (Latin, Lugdunum) in southern Gaul as a missionary. This move would have taken place before the mid-160s, when Justin Martyr was put to death in Rome for his faith in Christ.[17] Situated at the confluence of the Rhône and Saône Rivers, second-century Lyons was a miniature Rome in many ways. A bustling cosmopolitan center of some seventy thousand or so in Irenaeus's day, it was the key port on the trade routes up and down the Rhône River. It was also a provincial capital, the heart of the Roman road system for Gaul, and the seat of an important military garrison. Similar to Rome, its population contained a large Greek-speaking element, and it was among this element that Christianity had become firmly established in the city.[18] For example, in an account of the martyrdom of a large number of believers from Lyons and nearby Vienne in 177, two individuals were identified as coming from Asia Minor and would therefore have been Greek-speaking: Attalus, whose family came from Pergamum, and a certain Alexander of Phrygia.[19]

Irenaeus was away in Rome during this brutal outburst of persecution. When he returned to the Rhône valley, he found the leadership in the churches of Lyons and Vienne decimated. He was subsequently appointed bishop of Lyons, as the previous bishop, Pothinus (ca. 87–177), had succumbed in prison after being beaten during the persecution.[20] Within a couple of years after his return to Lyons, Irenaeus was hard at work writing *Against Heresies*.[21] The final sight we catch of Irenaeus on the scene of history is a letter that he wrote to Victor I, bishop of Rome (189–198), seeking to defuse the Quartodeciman controversy. Differences between the church at Rome and various churches in Asia Minor regarding the dating of Easter had led the former to threaten excommunication of the latter if the Eastern churches

---

[16]The title of the treatise is based on the wording of 1 Tim. 6:20. On Irenaeus's encounter with disciples of Valentinus, see *Against Heresies* 1.pref.2. Irenaeus also had a collection of Gnostic works that he studied so as to better respond to his theological opponents. See *Against Heresies* 1.31.2.
[17]Hitchcock, "Irenaeus of Lugdunum," 168.
[18]For this overview about the city of Roman Lyons, I am indebted to Edward Rochie Hardy's introduction to "Selections from the Work *Against Heresies* by Irenaeus, Bishop of Lyons," in Richardson, *Early Christian Fathers*, 347–48.
[19]Eusebius, *Ecclesiastical History* 5.1.17, 49.
[20]Eusebius, *Ecclesiastical History* 5.1.29.
[21]For the date of *Against Heresies*, see Robert M. Grant, *Greek Apologists of the Second Century* (Philadelphia: Westminster, 1988), 182–83; Donovan, *One Right Reading?*, 9–10.

did not get into line with Roman practice. Irenaeus pled for tolerance and diversity of practice.[22]

This display of irenicism appears to have been typical of the second-century theologian. When it came to the Gnostics and their thinking, though, Irenaeus was fiercely antagonistic of what he saw as sheer error.[23] At the heart of this antagonism was Irenaeus's deeply held conviction about the perfection of the Scriptures and the fact that this perfection provided solid ground for saving belief in the metanarrative of the Bible.

## Scripturae Perfectae

Norbert Brox has rightly noted that in "Irenaeus this principle stands at the beginning [of his thought]: that the Bible is in every respect perfect and sufficient."[24] Irenaeus's stress upon the perfection and sufficiency of the Scriptures was due in part to the strident affirmation by the Gnostics of the errancy of the Bible. When confronted with biblical arguments against their views, the Gnostics, according to Irenaeus, maintained that the Scriptures could not be trusted. They rejected key aspects of the Old Testament out of hand, while they were adamant that the apostolic documents of the New Testament were penned by men who could be mistaken and who thus introduced contradictions into their writings. What alone could be trusted was the teaching from the apostles that had been passed down to them by word of mouth (*per vivam vocem*). And for support of this secret oral tradition, they adduced Paul's words in 1 Corinthians 2:6 ("among the mature we do impart wisdom").[25]

Over against the Gnostic distortion of the Scriptures, Irenaeus revealed himself to be, as Reinhold Seeberg aptly put it, "the first great representative of biblicism."[26] The Scriptures are to be the normative source for the teaching of the Christian community. As Ellen Flesseman-van Leer noted,

---

[22]Eusebius, *Ecclesiastical History* 5.23–25. On Irenaeus's role in this controversy, see also Roch Kereszty, "The Unity of the Church in the Theology of Irenaeus," *SecCent* 4 (1984): 215–16; Osborn, *Irenaeus of Lyons*, 5–6. According to a late and unreliable tradition, first mentioned by Gregory of Tours (d. 594), Irenaeus died as a martyr (*The Glory of the Martyrs,* 49). For a discussion of the claim that Irenaeus was martyred, see J. van der Straeten, "Saint Irénée fut-il martyr?," in *Les martyrs de Lyon (177)* (Paris: Éditions du Centre national de la Recherche scientifique, 1978), 145–53.

[23]It was Eusebius of Caesarea who first described Irenaeus as a peacemaker, making a play on the meaning of his name. See Eusebius, *Ecclesiastical History* 5.24.18.

[24]Norbert Brox, "Irenaeus and the Bible: A Special Contribution," in *Handbook of Patristic Exegesis: The Bible in Ancient Christianity*, ed. Charles Kannengiesser (Leiden: Brill, 2004), 486. On Irenaeus's bibliology, see also D. Farkasfalvy, "Theology of Scripture in St. Irenaeus," *RBén* 68 (1968): 319–33.

[25]*Against Heresies* 3.2.1–2.

[26]"Irenäus . . . ist der erste große Vertreter des Biblizismus" (*Lehrbuch der Dogmengeschichte*, 2nd ed. [Leipzig: A. Deichert'sche, 1908], 290). Note the caution by Osborn, *Irenaeus of Lyons*, 172.

when "Irenaeus wants to prove the truth of a doctrine materially, he turns to Scripture."[27] Its words are the "Scriptures of the Lord" (*dominicis Scripturis*), and it would be absolute folly to abandon the words of the Lord, Moses, and the other prophets, which set forth the truth, for the foolish opinions of Irenaeus's opponents.[28] Given the Gnostic argument that the Scriptures had been falsified and the Gnostic propensity to pass off their writings as genuine revelation, Irenaeus rightly discerned that a discussion of the nature of Scripture was vital.

Scholars disagree over the exact boundaries of Irenaeus's New Testament,[29] with some even asserting that he was the creative genius behind the formation of the New Testament canon.[30] And there is also no essential agreement as to how Scripture relates to tradition in Irenaeus's thought.[31] But what is not disputable is his view of Scripture. The bishop of Lyons was confident that the "Scriptures are indeed perfect [*perfectae*]" texts because they were spoken by the word of God and his Spirit.[32] Referring specifically to the human authors of various books of the New Testament, Irenaeus asserted that they were given perfect knowledge by the Holy Spirit and thus were incapable of proclaiming error.[33] "Our Lord Jesus Christ," Irenaeus argued,

> is the Truth and there is no falsehood in him, even as David also said when he prophesied about his birth from a virgin and the resurrection from the dead, "Truth has sprung from the earth" (Ps 85:11). And the Apostles, being disciples

[27] *Tradition and Scripture in the Early Church* (Assen: Van Gorcum, 1953), 144.
[28] *Against Heresies* 2.30.6. For the translation of the phrase *dominicis Scripturis*, see John Lawson, *The Biblical Theology of Saint Irenaeus* (London: Epworth, 1948), 23–24 n. 4.
[29] For differing perspectives on Irenaeus's canon, see, for example, G. Nathanael Bonwetsch, *Die Theologie des Irenäus* (Gütersloh: C. Bertelsmann, 1925), 40; Osborn, *Irenaeus of Lyons*, 180–82; Brox, "Irenaeus and the Bible," 484; M. C. Steenberg, "Irenaeus, *Graphe*, and the Status of *Hermas*," *SVTQ* 53 (2009): 29–66; Andreas Köstenberger and Michael J. Kruger, *The Heresy of Orthodoxy: How Contemporary Culture's Fascination with Diversity Has Reshaped Our Understanding of Early Christianity* (Wheaton, IL: Crossway, 2010), 151–75.
[30] For example, see Elaine Pagels, *Beyond Belief: The Secret Gospel of Thomas* (New York: Random House, 2003), 74–142; Arthur Bellinzoni, "The Gospel of Luke in the Apostolic Fathers," in Andrew F. Gregory and Christopher M. Tuckett, eds., *Trajectories through the New Testament and the Apostolic Fathers* (Oxford: Oxford University Press, 2005), 49 n. 17. According to Bellinzoni in this footnote: "Irenaeus . . . essentially created the core of the New Testament canon of Holy Scripture." But see the convincing riposte by Hill, *Who Chose the Gospels?*, 34–68.
[31] See, for instance, Juan Ochagavía, *Visibile Patris Filius: A Study of Irenaeus' Teaching on Revelation and Tradition* (Rome: Pont. Institutum Orientalium Studiorum, 1964), esp. 174–205; Dominic J. Unger and John J. Dillon, introduction to *St. Irenaeus of Lyons: Against the Heresies*, trans. Dominic J. Unger, rev. John J. Dillon (New York: Newman, 1992), 8–10. Also critical to note—though I do not have space to deal with it in this essay—is Irenaeus's emphasis on the role of the church in the interpretation of Scripture. For this emphasis, see the helpful remarks of Brox, "Irenaeus and the Bible," 495–99.
[32] *Against Heresies* 2.28.2. See also 4.33.8.
[33] *Against Heresies* 3.1.1.

of the Truth, are free from all falsehood, for falsehood has no fellowship with the truth, just as darkness has no fellowship with the light, but the presence of the one drives away the other.[34]

Here Irenaeus based the fidelity of the apostolic writings upon the absolute truthfulness of the Lord Jesus Christ and the conviction that truth and falsehood are polar opposites. From Irenaeus's standpoint, if Christ is the embodiment of truth, it is impossible to conceive of him ever uttering falsehood. By extension, the writings of Christ's authorized representatives are also incapable of error. This quality of absolute truthfulness can also be predicated of the authors of the books of the Old Testament, since the Spirit who spoke through the apostles also spoke through the Old Testament writers.[35] Thus the Scriptures form a harmonious whole: "All Scripture, which has been given to us by God, shall be found to be perfectly consistent . . . and through the many diversified utterances (of Scripture) there shall be heard one harmonious melody in us, praising in hymns that God who created all things."[36]

A second major emphasis in Irenaeus's bibliology is the unity of the Testaments and, by extension, the unity of the history of God's salvific work. Marcion's denial of the revelatory value of the Old Testament led Irenaeus to affirm that the God who gave the law and the God who revealed the gospel is "one and the same." One piece of proof lay in the fact that in both the Old and New Testaments, the first and greatest commandment is to love God with the entirety of one's being and then to love one's neighbor as oneself.[37] Another line of evidence was the similar revelation of the holiness of God in both Testaments.[38] Irenaeus also urged his readers—which he hoped would include his Gnostic opponents—to "carefully read [*legite diligentius*]" both the Old Testament prophets and the apostolic writings of the New Testament, and they would find that the leading contours of Christ's ministry were predicted by the prophets of ancient Israel.[39] There is therefore a common theme that informs both Old Testament prophets and the New Testament apostles: Christ. He is that which binds together

---

[34] *Against Heresies* 3.5.1.

[35] *Against Heresies* 3.6.1, 5; 3.21.4; 4.20.8; *Demonstration of the Apostolic Preaching* 49. See also Bernard Sesboüé, "La preuve par les Ecritures chez S. Irénée; à propos d'un texte difficile du Livre III de l'*Adversus Haereses*," *NRTh* 103 (1981): 872–87.

[36] *Against Heresies* 2.28.3. Elsewhere, Irenaeus speaks of the "order [τάξις] and continuity [εἱρμός] of the Scriptures" (*Against Heresies* 1.8.1).

[37] *Against Heresies* 4.12.3.

[38] *Against Heresies* 4.27.4–28.1.

[39] *Against Heresies* 4.34.1; see also 4.7.1; 4.9.1; 4.11.4; 4.36.5.

the covenants.[40] And this commonality speaks of one God behind both portions of Scripture. To reject the Old Testament is therefore tantamount to a failure to discern this christological center of the entirety of the Bible and to show oneself as not truly spiritual, a strong indictment of the Gnostics and their exegesis.[41]

## Fundamentum et Columnam Fidei Nostrae

Help in elucidating this unified history of salvation was especially found in the words of the apostle Paul, particularly those Pauline texts that had to do with the unity of the church.[42] Irenaeus viewed the Old Testament prophets as having an essential unity with the New Testament since, in his mind, they were actually members of the body of Christ. As Irenaeus explained:

> Certainly the prophets, along with other things that they predicted, also foretold this, that on whomever the Spirit of God would rest, and who would obey the word of the Father, and serve him according to their strength, should suffer persecution, and be stoned and killed. For the prophets prefigured in themselves all these things, because of their love for God and because of his word. For since they themselves were members of Christ, each one of them in so far as he was a member . . . revealed the prophecy [assigned him]. All of them, although many, prefigured one, and proclaimed the things that belong to one. For just as the working of the whole body is disclosed by means of our [physical] members, yet the shape of the total man is not displayed by one member, but by all; so also did all the prophets prefigure the one [Christ], while every one of them, in so far as he was a member, did, in accordance with this, complete the [established] dispensation, and prefigured that work of Christ assigned to him as a member.[43]

---

[40]*Against Heresies* 4.9.1; 4.26.1. See in this regard Iain M. MacKenzie, *Irenaeus's Demonstration of the Apostolic Preaching: A Theological Commentary and Translation* (Burlington, VT: Ashgate, 2002), 60–62.

[41]*Against Heresies* 4.33.15. Irenaeus had been asked—possibly by a Gnostic—if the ministry of Christ had been announced and typified in the Old Testament, what then was truly new about his coming? Well, Irenaeus explained, the difference was this: what had been a matter of types and predictions was now reality, the Lord himself had come among them and filled his servants with joy and freedom. See *Against Heresies* 4.34.1.

[42]John S. Coolidge, *The Pauline Basis of the Concept of Scriptural Form in Irenaeus*, Protocol of the Colloquy of the Center for Hermeneutical Studies in Hellenistic and Modern Culture 8 (Berkeley, CA: The Center for Hermeneutical Studies in Hellenistic and Modern Culture, 1975), 1–3; Richard A. Norris, "Irenaeus' Use of Paul in His Polemic Against the Gnostics," in *Paul and the Legacies of Paul*, ed. William S. Babcock (Dallas: Southern Methodist University Press, 1990), 91–92.

[43]*Against Heresies* 4.33.10, trans. Alexander Roberts and W. H. Rambaut, in A. Cleveland Coxe, *The Apostolic Fathers with Justin Martyr and Irenaeus*, Ante-Nicene Fathers 1 (1885; repr., New York: Charles Scribner's Sons, 1903), 509, altered.

The diverse predictive ministries of the Old Testament prophets were essentially part of the unity of the revelation of Christ. Irenaeus went on to borrow Pauline passages that spoke of the unity of the universal church in Ephesians 4 to describe the attentive reader's perception of the unity between the prophetic texts of the Old Testament and the texts that contain their New Testament fulfillment. In his words:

> If any one believes in the one God, who also made all things by the Word, just as both Moses says, "God said, 'Let there be light,' and there was light" [Gen. 1:3], and as we read in the Gospel, "All things were made by him, and nothing was made without him" [John 1:3], and similarly the Apostle Paul [says], "There is one Lord, one faith, one baptism, one God and Father, who is over all, and through all, and in us all" [Eph. 4:5–6]—this man will first of all "hold the head, from which the whole body is firmly joined and united together, and which, through every joint according to the measure of the supply of each several part, causes the body to grow so that it builds itself up in love" [Eph. 4:16]. Then afterwards shall every word also seem consistent to him, if he will carefully read the Scriptures among those who are presbyters in the Church, among whom is the apostolic doctrine, as I have shown.[44]

In another instance, Irenaeus applied 1 Corinthians 12:4–7, a passage that speaks of the diversity of the gifts in the body of Christ as being essential to the unity of the church, to the unity between the different prophetic ministries in the Old Testament and the saving work of Christ in the new covenant.[45] As John Coolidge has rightly pointed out, it appears that, for Irenaeus, perception of the unity between the Testaments is concomitant to participation in the communal unity of the church.[46]

It is surely this use of Pauline statements about ecclesial unity to affirm the unity of the Scriptures that explains Irenaeus's curious treatment of a phrase from 1 Timothy 3:15. The church, the Pauline verse declares, is the "pillar and ground of the truth" (KJV). This striking statement becomes for Irenaeus an affirmation about the Scriptures. At the outset of book 3 of *Against Heresies*, where Irenaeus explicitly rejected the claim by some of the Gnostics that the apostles compromised the truth in their transmission of it, the missionary theologian defended the integrity of the "plan of salvation [*dispositionem salutis*]" as it had come down to him in the written text of the Bible. The oral message of the apostles was identical to what was enshrined

---

[44] *Against Heresies* 4.32.1. On Irenaeus's conviction of the vital importance of reading the Scriptures within the context of the church catholic, see also 3.24.1; 5.20.2.
[45] *Against Heresies* 4.20.6.
[46] Coolidge, *Pauline Basis of the Concept of Scriptural Form*, 3.

in the Scriptures, and thus the latter could serve as "the ground and pillar [*fundamentum et columnam*] of our faith."[47] Again, when Irenaeus insisted that there had to be four Gospels, and only four, because of the four corners of the earth and the earth's four winds—there being an aesthetic harmony between the four Gospels and creation[48]—he again stated that "the pillar and ground of the Church is the Gospel and the Spirit of life [στύλος δὲ καὶ στήριγμα ἐκκλησίας τὸ εὐαγγέλιον καὶ πνεῦμα ζωῆς]."[49] The inclusion of the Holy Spirit here was not accidental, for if Christ is the common theme of all of the Scriptures, the Spirit is the one who inspired all of the authors of the Bible to speak of the one Savior.

## Immortalitas Panis

In Irenaeus's mind what was at stake in this battle between the ancient church and her Gnostic opponents was nothing less than eternal salvation. The myth making of the Gnostics subverted the biblical narrative of creation, fall, redemption, and consummation. It attributed creation to the ignorant Demiurge and thus was constrained to find life's meaning outside of the created realm and history. The Gnostic denial of the biblical account of the fall of Adam and Eve into disobedience[50] had profound implications for understanding the enslavement of their progeny to the Devil,[51] their progeny's enmity to God,[52] and the reign of death on the earth.[53] The Gnostics further rejected the corporal nature of the incarnation and death of Christ, and thus undermined the core of biblical salvation, the main lineaments of which had been predicted by the Old Testament writers, and which was accomplished by Christ.[54] Finally, their failure to appreciate Christ's salvific work as it relates to the whole human being also meant that they distorted the biblical understanding of the consummation.[55]

An excellent prism through which Irenaeus's conception of this metanarrative of Christianity can be seen is his teaching regarding the work of the

---

[47] *Against Heresies* 3.1.1.
[48] Hill, *Who Chose the Gospels?*, 34–38.
[49] *Against Heresies* 3.11.8.
[50] *Against Heresies* 3.22.4; 3.23.1. On the creation of Adam, see 3.23.2; 4.14.1.
[51] *Against Heresies* 3.23.2.
[52] *Against Heresies* 5.17.1.
[53] *Against Heresies* 5.23.1–2.
[54] *Against Heresies* 1.10.1; 3.18.7; 5.1.1; 5.14.1–3. Irenaeus is the first to formulate explicitly what would become a cardinal tenet of Christianity, namely, in the words of Henry Chadwick, "Any part of human nature, body, soul, or spirit, which the Redeemer did not make his own is not saved." *The Church in Ancient Society: From Galilee to Gregory the Great* (Oxford: Oxford University Press, 2001), 102.
[55] *Against Heresies* 1.10.1; 5.8–7. For a helpful overview of Irenaeus's understanding of the entire Christian metanarrative, see Shelton, "Irenaeus," 44–50.

Holy Spirit.[56] The Spirit was intimately involved in the work of creation, for he and the Son are "the hands [*manus*]" of God the Father. By his Word and by his Spirit, the Father "makes, disposes, and governs all things, and gives existence to everything."[57] Thus, Irenaeus understood God's statement in Genesis 1:26, "let us make man," to be a discussion between the Father and his "hands," the Son and the Holy Spirit. In Irenaeus's words:

> The Scripture says, "And God formed man, taking dirt of the earth, and breathed into his face the breath of life" [Gen. 2:7]. Angels, therefore, did not make us nor did they form us, for angels were not able to make the image of God [*imaginem . . . Dei*], nor any other but the true God, nor any power far away from the Father of all things. For God did not need these [beings] to make what he had himself predetermined to make, as if he did not have his own hands. For always present with him were the Word and Wisdom, the Son and the Spirit, by whom and in whom, freely and independently, he made all things, to whom also he speaks, saying, "Let us make man according to our image and likeness" [Gen. 1:26].[58]

Far from being an image that subordinates the Spirit, this idea of the Spirit as being one of the Father's hands gives expression to a rich Trinitarian view of God and his creative work.[59]

The Spirit not only created the first man and woman, Adam and Eve, but also rested on them in the garden, providing them with a "robe of sanctity [*sanctitatis stolam*]," which was lost at the fall, as was the Spirit himself.[60] And without the Spirit of God, there was only death.[61] One of the great purposes, then, of the coming of Christ was the restoration of the Spirit to humanity. The Spirit descended on Christ so that he could give the Spirit

---

[56]J. N. D. Kelly rightly observed that "Irenaeus's vision of the Godhead [is] the most complete and . . . most explicitly Trinitarian" of all the authors of the second century except for the Latin-speaking North African Tertullian (fl. 190–215) (*Early Christian Doctrines*, 4th ed. [London: Adam & Charles Black, 1968], 107). Similarly Hitchcock, "Irenaeus of Lugdunum," 170. See also MacKenzie, *Irenaeus's Demonstration of the Apostolic Preaching*, 83, and the nuanced discussion of M. C. Steenberg, *Irenaeus on Creation: The Cosmic Christ and the Saga of Redemption* (Leiden: Brill, 2008), 62–64. *Pace* Brakke, *Gnostics*, 124, who argues that "Irenaeus did not simply believe in one God. Rather, he distinguished between the ultimate God, the Father, . . . and two clearly lower manifestations of God: the Word or Son . . . and the Spirit." *St Irenaeus: The Demonstration of the Apostolic Preaching*, trans. J. Armitage Robinson (London: Society for Promoting Christian Knowledge, 1920), 24–68, is still a helpful summary of Irenaean pneumatology.
[57]*Against Heresies* 1.22.1.
[58]*Against Heresies* 4.20.1. See also 2.2.5; 4.pref.4; 5.1.3; 5.15.4; 5.28.4. On these texts, see Steenberg, *Irenaeus on Creation*, 62–84.
[59]Lawson, *Biblical Theology of Saint Irenaeus*, 119–39; Steenberg, *Irenaeus on Creation*, 62–84.
[60]*Against Heresies* 3.23.5. For discussions on how to understand Irenaean anthropology, see Lawson, *Biblical Theology of Saint Irenaeus*, 199–251 passim; Mary Ann Donovan, "Alive to the Glory of God: A Key Insight in St. Irenaeus," *TS* 49 (1988): 283–97; Steenberg, *Irenaeus on Creation*, 101–93.
[61]*Against Heresies* 5.9.3.

to fallen human beings and lead them to communion with the Father, thus making them spiritually fruitful in their lives.[62] By indwelling the human heart, the Spirit prepares men and women for the beatific vision, since he is "the bread of immortality [τὸν τῆς ἀθανασίας ἄρτον/*immortalitas panis*]."[63] And thus, in the end, "the fruit of the Spirit's work is the salvation of the flesh."[64]

## An Irenaean Prayer

Irenaeus was confident that a humble listening to and reading of the Word of God would produce a faith that was "firm, not fictitious, but solely true."[65] And one of his manifest goals in *Against Heresies* was to produce such a faith among his Gnostic opponents. Irenaeus's fierce opposition to Gnosticism did not arise from a hunger for power, as some recent scholars have argued, but out of a genuine love for truth and a sincere desire for the spiritual well-being of his fellow believers and their theological opponents.[66] This pastoral heart is well revealed in his prayer for the latter at the close of his third book of *Against Heresies*.

> And now we pray that these men may not remain in the pit that they have dug for themselves, but . . . being converted to the church of God, they may be legitimately begotten, and that Christ be formed in them, and that they may know the framer and maker of this universe, the only true God and Lord of all. This we pray for them, for we love them better than they think they love themselves. For our love, as it is true, is saving to them, if they will receive it. It is like a severe remedy, taking away the excessive and superfluous flesh that forms on a wound; for it puts an end to their exaltation and haughtiness. Therefore we shall not tire in endeavoring with all our might to stretch out [our] hand to them.[67]

## A Personal Addendum

Twenty-nine years ago, at the outset of my academic career, I wrote a small piece on the subject of this essay in an extremely popular format for a

---

[62]*Against Heresies* 3.9.3; 3.17.1–3; 5.1.1–2.
[63]*Against Heresies* 4.38.1. See also *Against Heresies* 5.8.1; 5.12.1–4.
[64]*Against Heresies* 5.12.4.
[65]*Against Heresies* 3.21.3. On humility as an interpretative principle, see *Against Heresies* 2.28.2–3.
[66]*Against Heresies* 3.2.3; 3.6.4; 3.25.7. See also Marian Balwierz, *The Holy Spirit and the Church as a Subject of Evangelization According to St. Irenaeus* (Warsaw: Akademia Teologii Katolickiej, 1985), 50–57; Osborn, *Irenaeus of Lyons*, 5; Bingham, "Irenaeus of Lyons," 145.
[67]*Against Heresies* 3.25.7, trans. Roberts and Rambaut, in Coxe, *The Apostolic Fathers with Justin Martyr and Irenaeus*, 460.

Canadian Baptist magazine: "Irenaeus and the Inerrancy of Scripture."[68] In large part that foray into this subject arose because of the battles among North American evangelicals over inerrancy in the 1970s and early 1980s. Now, it is personally rewarding in this essay to return to Irenaeus and his view of the Bible in order to deal with it in a much more rigorous academic fashion. What is disturbing, though, is that the current scene is witnessing a renewal of those battles from twenty-five to thirty years ago.[69] Albeit there are some new emphases, the end result is the same: a diminution of the authority of the Scriptures. It was helpful to listen to Irenaeus in the so-called Battle for the Bible thirty years ago, and, in the midst of these new challenges, it is still wisdom to heed, among other voices from the past, this second-century missionary theologian.

---

[68] *The Evangelical Baptist* 29, no. 11 (October, 1982): 8–9.

[69] See, for example, Greg Beale, *The Erosion of Inerrancy in Evangelicalism: Responding to New Challenges to Biblical Authority* (Wheaton, IL: Crossway, 2008).

# Part 2

# THE OLD TESTAMENT AND ISSUES OF HISTORY, AUTHENTICITY, AND AUTHORITY

# 6

# PENTATEUCHAL CRITICISM AND THE PRIESTLY TORAH

## RICHARD E. AVERBECK

At the beginning of the second decade of the twenty-first century the scholarly study of the Old Testament is in a confused state of methodological pluralism. This is not all bad. At times during the twentieth century the field was dominated by one method or another and closed to other legitimate ways of handling the Hebrew Bible. In broad strokes it went something like this:

The century opened under the influence of the end of the nineteenth century and, therefore, with source criticism. Other diachronic methods such as form, tradition, and redaction criticism, respectively, were added to it in the early twentieth century in various combinations. All of them focused on a kind of archaeology of the text in terms of its literary, historical, and theological strata. Out of this came what is often referred to as the historical-critical method and its "scholarly consensus."

The middle section of the twentieth century brought with it a shift to another kind of archaeology—the so-called "biblical archaeology" movement—and along with it an increased emphasis on ancient Near Eastern comparative resources overall. It concerned itself largely with archaeological rather than textual strata and the light that this, along with artifacts, texts, and other kinds of cultural information, might shed on the text and its interpretation. Today large segments of Old Testament scholarship remain devoted to one or the other of these methods as their primary concern, although they have both been chastised along the way. These two sets of methods can either challenge or complement each other, but neither of them dominates the field any longer.

In the last third of the twentieth century a third trend developed. The focus shifted to various synchronic approaches: rhetorical criticism, canonical criticism, the Bible as literature, new literary criticisms of various sorts, and more sophisticated linguistic discourse approaches have been applied to the analysis of the Hebrew text as it stands. Again, this shift did not eliminate the practice of the previous methods, but added to the mix. It gained a sort of dominance for a short time and then settled in as another accepted part of the methodological pluralism that currently characterizes the field. The diachronic historical-critical methods tend to fragment the text and explain it in terms of its various stages of composition through time; archaeological and comparative contextual methods attempt to explain it in light of the ancient world from which it comes; and synchronic methods tend toward treating it as a unified literary or theological composition or both. None of these ways of approaching the Bible has been eliminated, and none dominates. Some scholars attempt to combine them in creative ways, but at other times they clash and compete.

## Foundations of the Historical-Critical Method

The Jewish secularist Old Testament scholar Jacques Berlinerblau, for example, argues that Old Testament scholarship has shown that the text is a hopelessly confused and, in fact, a meaningless "aggregate" of combined sources that is not worthy of being called "literature" and should not inspire any kind of faith or confidence in the god who ostensibly reveals himself through it.[1] He argues this by accepting the "assured results" of historical-critical diachronic analysis of the text and forcing them to their natural conclusions. This is Berlinerblau's strategy for promoting secularism in biblical scholarship and freedom from the Bible in modern-day society, politics, and public policy.[2]

Actually, this is nothing new. Back in the 1870s and '80s, in his *Prolegomenon to the History of Israel*, Julius Wellhausen referred to Baruch Spinoza (1632–1677) as one of the founders of the historical-critical method to which he was

---

[1] Jacques Berlinerblau, *The Secular Bible: Why Nonbelievers Must Take Religion Seriously* (Cambridge: Cambridge University Press, 2005).

[2] His modern political and public policy concerns come through in *The Secular Bible*, but he develops these further in his more recent book *Thumpin' It: The Use and Abuse of the Bible in Today's Presidential Politics* (Louisville: Westminster John Knox, 2008). In this latter book he points out that the Bible is "raw power" when it comes to politics in the United States. In his view, the Bible is most often irrelevant to the actual issues facing us today, and when this is not the case, it is vulnerable to contradictory interpretations. It should never be used for making public policy. Nevertheless, its use in the political arena is a force to be reckoned with by all involved, liberal or conservative. It is interesting that, as Seymour Feldman put it in his introduction to the recent reprinting of Spinoza's treatise, like Berlinerblau, Spinoza was deeply concerned about the use of the Bible in politics in his own day: "To defend both political and intellectual freedom Spinoza argued for the secularization of politics and the emancipation of philosophy from political and religious supervision and influence." Baruch Spinoza, *Theological-Political Treatise*, 2nd ed., trans. Samuel Shirley (Indianapolis: Hackett, 1991), xvi.

heir.[3] There were even earlier precursors than Spinoza, of course. Wellhausen was aware of that,[4] and others also contributed to the method in substantial ways,[5] but Spinoza stands out as a leading secularist in the field. He had written his *Theological Political Treatise* two centuries earlier as part of the movement toward the so-called Enlightenment.[6] It is actually a fascinating work. He drew together all sorts of observations within the text and about it, some of which are still basic to the whole historical-critical enterprise. This is not the place for a detailed discussion, but, for example, he highlighted post-Mosaic elements in the Pentateuch and concluded that "the book of the Law of God which Moses wrote was not the Pentateuch, but a quite different book which the author of the Pentateuch inserted in proper order in his own work."[7] So he allowed for a historical Moses, but not as the author of the Pentateuch in anything like its current form. The elaborate theories of compositional history that developed over the next three centuries (see the brief summary above) had not yet developed, of course, but Spinoza was fully aware of the implications of his work. He wrote,

> Those who look upon the Bible, in its present form, as a message for mankind sent down by God from heaven, will doubtless cry out that I have committed the sin against the Holy Spirit in maintaining that the Word of God is faulty, mutilated, adulterated and inconsistent, that we possess it only in fragmentary form, and that the original of God's covenant with the Jews has perished.[8]

Spinoza set a trend in biblical studies that endures to the present day in various forms. Berlinerblau's work is a most recent example. He cites Franz Delitzsch, a contemporary of Wellhausen, who wrote about him, "If his conclusions be true, the Old Testament cannot in any distinctive sense be the word of God." Berlinerblau responds: "Franz Delitzsch was correct. Higher criticism, as well as other modern approaches, teems with heretical potential. Scratch its surface, and all sorts of destabilizing implications for Jewish and Christian dogma come swarming forth."[9] He uses the more recent literary-

---

[3] Julius Wellhausen, *Prolegomena to the History of Israel*, ed. D. A. Knight (1885; repr., Atlanta: Scholars Press, 1994), 6.

[4] See, e.g., his reference to the medieval Jewish scholar Abraham Ibn Ezra (ibid., 9).

[5] See the recent helpful analysis and explanation in John Barton, *The Nature of Biblical Criticism* (Louisville: Westminster John Knox, 2007), 117–36.

[6] Spinoza, *Theological-Political Treatise*. Note especially chaps. 8–10, pp. 105–37. See also the helpful summary of Spinoza's work in John H. Hayes and Frederick Prussner, *Old Testament Theology: Its History and Development* (Atlanta: John Knox, 1985), 26–34.

[7] Spinoza, *Theological-Political Treatise*, 110.

[8] Ibid., 145.

[9] Berlinerblau, *The Secular Bible*, 40.

critical methodology of "deconstruction" to pursue his task and applies it
not only to the Hebrew Bible (arguing that it undermines itself), but also to
believing historical-critical scholarship, contending that such scholarship
thoroughly undermines belief in God. Thus, he argues that it is absurd to
believe in a God whose supposed revelation of himself is composed in such
a haphazard manner with such self-contradictory results. So, according to
Berlinerblau, the historical-critical enterprise has turned back against itself.
The Bible itself has come to a dead end. Historical critics have done their
work of chopping up the text into traditions, documents, redactions, editorial
revisions, and so forth—and they have done their job well. He agrees with
their analysis and conclusions. As far as Berlinerblau is concerned, he is only
drawing out the real implications of their critical results. They have killed the
Bible. Those scholars who are still believers just haven't buried the corpse yet.

At the end of the day, according to Berlinerblau, the kind of historical-
critical scholarship that Spinoza, Wellhausen, their compatriots, and their
heirs have practiced leads us to a kind of nihilism of the divine in Scripture.
The fact that the Scripture is what it is according to the historical-critical
view of the matter is so incredible that the Bible is not credible. It cannot be
a guide to truth in any meaningful sense. The serious study of it leads the
scholar into a tangled-up morass from which he cannot extricate himself.
Intellectual and religious honesty requires that he reject anything that one
could call meaningful faith in the Lord supposedly revealed in this kind of a
Bible. The approach chops the Scriptures into so many pieces that it kills not
only the Bible, but faith in the God of the Bible. In other words, historical-
critical biblical scholars have become their own undoing, whether they know
it or not, and whether they are willing to admit it or not. This is Berlinerblau's
point. As for me, I think he is right!

Of course, Berlinerblau has even less good to say about conservative evangelical scholars like me, who do not believe in this kind of aggregate view
of the composition of the Hebrew Bible and the contradictory nature of the
text. Nor has he room for nonconservative literary scholars such as Robert
Alter, who sees less breakage in the text than the standard historical-critical
method allows.[10] Berlinerblau will not allow for a coherent Bible, and he
will not allow for belief in the God of the Bible unless the Bible is coherent.
Again, this is Berlinerblau's strategy for promoting secularism in biblical
scholarship and in society at large, although he knows that the implications
he draws from the work of historical-critical scholars are not followed by all
or even most of them.

---

[10] Jacques Berlinerblau, "The Bible as Literature?," *HS* 45 (2004): 9–26.

## Believing Scholarship That Is Both Evangelical and Critical

Over the past thirty-five years of doing research, writing, and teaching in the field of Hebrew Bible and ancient Near Eastern studies, I have worked mainly in the Torah—"the five books of Moses"—and the history and literature of the world in which it was composed. This ongoing work has included heavy involvement in the larger academy of historical-critical scholarship and the other methods outlined above, as a way of staying on the cutting edge of the field as a conservative evangelical scholar. The fact of the matter is that, as far as I can tell, many if not most scholars in the academy of biblical scholarship hold to some level or kind of belief in the God of the Bible in spite of the implications of their critical work as Berlinerblau sees them. They do not follow him to the precipice and leap into the abyss of unbelief with him, even if they do indeed accept the historical-critical method and its "assured results" in some form. Recently, in fact, there have been a number of volumes published by believers of one stripe or the other (some of them relatively conservative or even "evangelical," some not; some Christian, some Jewish), describing and prescribing the historical-critical method and its results not just for the academy but in some cases also for their broader communities of faith.[11]

The problem is that the "assured results" of the method are not so "assured." And the scholarly application of the method is seriously flawed. It has far overstretched its textual foundation. Conservative evangelical biblical scholars are not anticritical; that is, depending on how you define *critical*. The term actually refers to "the art of objective evaluation."[12] As for the term *evangelical*, it comes from the Greek word commonly rendered "gospel" (i.e., "good news") in the New Testament and, in general, refers to those who put their faith in the person and work of Jesus Christ for life now and forever. Defining *evangelical scholarship*, however, is a very slippery matter these days. As far as I am concerned, I reserve this term for those who are "critical" in the proper sense of the term. As John Barton put it, "Skepticism about the

[11]See, for example, Marc Zvi Brettler, *How to Read the Bible* (Philadelphia: The Jewish Publication Society, 2005); Barton, *The Nature of Biblical Criticism*; James L. Kugel, *How to Read the Bible: A Guide to Scripture, Then and Now* (New York: Free Press, 2007); Joseph A Fitzmyer, SJ, *The Interpretation of Scripture: In Defense of the Historical-Critical Method* (New York: Paulist, 2008); Kenton L. Sparks, *God's Word in Human Words: An Evangelical Appropriation of Critical Biblical Scholarship* (Grand Rapids: Baker Academic, 2008); Peter Enns, *Inspiration and Incarnation: Evangelicals and the Problem of the Old Testament* (Grand Rapids: Baker Academic, 2005). Jean-Louis Ska, *Introduction to the Reading of the Pentateuch*, trans. Sr. Pascale Dominique (Winona Lake, IN: Eisenbrauns, 2006), is a fully historical-critical summary of the results of Pentateuchal scholarship from the point of view of a believing Catholic scholar (cf. also Fitzmyer above).
[12]Barton, *The Nature of Biblical Criticism*, 120, citing Reinhart Kosellek, *Critique and Crisis: Enlightenment and the Pathogenesis of Modern Society* (Oxford: Berg, 1988), 105. Kosellek notes that critics who were nonbelievers in the days of the Enlightenment were called "criticasters."

truth of Scripture is by no means built into the critical impulse."[13] Yes, it is true that conservative evangelical scholars naturally give the text the benefit of the doubt in terms of historical, theological, and compositional integrity. Guilty as charged! But evangelicals do not see this as an intellectual or methodological weakness. No, it is a strength and, in fact, a critical procedural advantage because we patiently stay with the text, allowing the (re)working of our understanding as we do our research.

On the one hand, our approach does not make the scholar prone to escape the plain meaning of the text by assigning diverse elements within it to different sources or whatever, and then going his merry way on a revisionist historical-critical trail. These trails either tend to go nowhere, or end up back where they started, so to speak. The confused diversity of historical-critical opinion within the "scholarly consensus" is telling. There are so many different revisionist trails and trends to follow, and so little agreement between them, that there is virtually no solid ground here. The trick for conservative evangelical scholars, on the other hand, is to be willing and able to follow the text wherever it takes us, even if we have trouble fitting it into what we have been taught or currently believe based on our current level of understanding. We need to know the difference between what we believe to be true and what we can actually show to be so under intellectually honest "critical" examination, properly understood.

## The Mosaic Origin of the Pentateuch

Yes, there are legitimate historical-critical issues that simply arise in the text for all to see without some kind of elaborate underlying destructive theory or scheme lurking there. Good conservative evangelical scholars do not shy away from this kind of data or its implications. There is nothing to fear in facing real data, biblical or extrabiblical. The theoretical constructions sometimes built on the basis of such data, whether conservative or liberal, however, are often open to question. We need to clearly distinguish between data and theories about the data. Some of the confusion in the field arises out of scholars treating their theories as if they are data or, conversely, ignoring actual data as if it were not there. This is not the place to enter into all the details, but let's take for example the question of Mosaic authorship of the Pentateuch, a perennial topic of discussion and debate through the ages, especially since the rise of the historical-critical method. In fact, historical-critical scholars often begin with this question.

---

[13]Barton, *The Nature of Biblical Criticism*, 124.

Clearly, there are post-Mosaic elements in the Torah, indicating that there was further compositional development of the Pentateuch after Moses.[14] For instance, the book of Deuteronomy begins, "These are the words that Moses spoke to all Israel across the Jordan" (Deut. 1:1), referring to Moses in the Transjordan region before his death. This is written from the perspective of the later writer, who looked back at events from his location on the Canaan side of the Jordan River. Likewise, consider Deuteronomy 2:12b: ". . . Esau drove them out. They destroyed the Horites from before them and settled in their place, just as Israel did in the land the LORD gave them as their possession" (NIV). The past tense "did" here is from the perspective of the conquest of the land already accomplished, after the death of Moses. Of course, the death-notice of Moses in Deuteronomy 34:5–9 is not from his own hand, and neither is verse 10: "Since then, no prophet has risen in Israel like Moses, whom the LORD knew face to face" (NIV).

Genesis 36:31 says, "These are the kings who reigned in the land of Edom before any king reigned over the Israelites." We know that there were no kings in Israel until long after Moses was off the scene. So it appears that this was written into the book of Genesis by a post-Mosaic author, probably drawing from the virtually identical passage in 1 Chronicles 1:43–50 or a source common to both. Apparently, at a later time the scribal author inserted the expanded genealogy of Esau here in order to bring it up to date, perhaps indicating the importance of the Edomites in the history of Judah. We know that the writers of Scripture used sources in the composition of the text because some of them are cited. See, for example, "The Book of the Wars of the LORD" in Numbers 21:14. Incidentally, there is also the intriguing reference in Genesis 5:1: "This is the book [lit. "scroll"] of the generations of Adam." This passage refers to a written source perhaps used in composing this section of Genesis, whether by Moses or another writer.

Some conservatives may squabble with some or all of these observations, but by and large we take these points into consideration when we refer to the "essentially" Mosaic authorship or origin of the Pentateuch. On the one hand, we should not argue that Moses himself wrote every word of the Pentateuch as we now have it. On the other hand, however, there are places where the text clearly states that Moses wrote at least certain parts of the text (see, e.g., Ex. 17:14; 24:4; Deut. 31:9, 22), and there are innumerable places where it is written that God spoke to or through Moses, or that Moses himself spoke.

---

[14]See, e.g., the lists and remarks in Kugel, *How to Read the Bible*, 30–31; and Sparks, *God's Word in Human Words*, 78–79. For a helpful treatment of these and other issues regarding the Pentateuch from an evangelical point of view, see Michael A. Grisanti, "Inspiration, Inerrancy, and the OT Canon: The Place of Textual Updating in an Inerrant View of Scripture," *JETS* 44 (2001): 577–98.

There is no good reason to deny this the status of data. It is simply what the text says and means.

We should not exclude the possibility that Joshua or someone else served as Moses's amanuensis in some instances, like Baruch with Jeremiah (Jeremiah 36). In this case, Moses would not be the author who actually wrote the original text, but it originated from him, or from God through him. We know that, according to the text itself, Joshua had no problem with adding to "the book of the Law of God" after Moses's death (Josh. 24:26). Moreover, the repeated copying of the scrolls that made up the canon of Scripture even through the Old Testament period alone allowed for scribal updating and shaping of passages, books, and the canon through the Old Testament period and beyond. This and much more is part of the process of composition and transmission of the Hebrew text. This is how we got our Bible. We could and should nuance the matter further, but this will have to suffice for the time being.

Of course, by and large, nonconservative historical-critical scholars past and present would not take seriously the notion that Moses actually wrote any part of the current Pentateuch, and they certainly would not take seriously the references cited in the paragraph above as evidence that he did. Some of them do not even believe that there ever was such a person as Moses. Nevertheless, much of their work I find helpful, and it fascinates me just in terms of intellectual history, if nothing else. More importantly, however, I take God's existence, character, and direct (sometimes miraculous) involvement and guidance in history and biblical revelation to be historical realities. To leave God and his work out of the historical-critical enterprise, therefore, is to compromise the very nature and validity of such scholarship. Yes, scholars with whom I disagree, and their work, are worthy of respect and fair treatment, but the same is also due to the ancient writers and their writings, and above all the Lord himself.

There are serious problems with many of the ways the historical-critical method is applied to the Bible. The method carries a marked negative bias against historical, compositional, thematic, and theological integrity in the Bible.[15] And when you get right down to it, the arguments are often circular: "We conclude this because of this other thing, but we derive the other thing from what we have concluded." I will illustrate this below in the discussion of Exodus 19–24 as a window into the historical-critical treatment of the Pentateuch and its results. To be sure, there are problems in the Hebrew text. That is no excuse, however, for multiplying the problems with a method that finds problems where there are none.

---

[15] J. Maxwell Miller, "Israelite History," in *The Hebrew Bible and Its Modern Interpreters*, ed. D. A. Knight and G. M. Tucker (Decatur, GA: Scholars Press, 1985) 2.

## The Exodus 19:1–24:11 Narrative: A Window into the Historical-Critical Method

The narrative framework in Exodus 19–24 (more specifically through 24:11) has been the subject of unceasing scholarly debate since before Wellhausen.[16] In a recent highly regarded introduction to the reading of the Pentateuch, where Jean-Louis Ska summarizes the issues mainly from a European historical-critical point of view, he writes, "The Sinai pericope is one of the most complicated passages in the entire Pentateuch." He explains:

> The Sinai theophany is a text that has been revised primarily because it contains the experience on which Israel based its existence as a people; as a result, it bears the marks of this people's complex history. The text, in its present form, is certainly Postexilic, post-Priestly, and post-Deuteronomistic. It will always be extremely difficult to find a suitable method for identifying with substantial certainty the oldest elements and—even more difficult—for determining their origin.[17]

I cannot attempt a thorough treatment of the whole passage in this short essay, of course. That will have to wait for another time and place.[18] The remainder of this essay will focus on certain sections and features of this passage. It will serve not only as a window into the practice of the historical-critical method, but also as a key to the priestly heart and heartbeat of the Torah. I will use Ska as a source for the "state of the question" among Old Testament historical-critical scholars, but will also consider the work of others.

In order to accomplish our purpose we need to get into some of the details of the passage and the history of historical-critical research as it is applied to it. For some readers this will already be familiar territory. For others it will be completely new and perplexing. I will make every effort to make it as understandable as possible to beginners, but such readers will also need some patience and perseverance. Still others will stand somewhere in between these two extremes.

The unit begins in Exodus 19 with the theophany at Sinai, "the mountain of God" (see Ex. 18:5; 24:13; cf. 3:1; 4:27), by which God initiates the covenant that will be ratified in Exodus 24:1–11, where the unit ends. Chapter 20 describes what happened at Sinai with the Ten Commandments (lit. ten "words"; cf. Ex. 34:28; Deut. 4:13; 10:4) that the Lord pronounced there in

---

[16]See the extensive summary of the debate in Brevard S. Childs, *The Book of Exodus*, OTL (Louisville: Westminster, 1974), 344–64, 499–502.

[17]Ska, *Introduction to the Reading of the Pentateuch*, 213–14.

[18]See Richard E. Averbeck, *Priest, People, and Ritual: A Priestly Theology of the Old Testament* (forthcoming).

the hearing of the people (Ex. 20:1–17; cf. Deut. 4:9–14; 5:4–5 for clarification); the chapter continues with the story of how Moses actually became the mediator between the Lord and the people (Ex. 20:18–21); and it ends with Moses as the mediator passing on to the people the regulations about idols and altars (20:22–26). Exodus 21–23 continues Moses's mediation with a major section of legal ordinances (lit. "judgments," 21:1; 24:3) designated as "the book [lit. "scroll"] of the covenant" in Exodus 24:7.

As for the rudiments of the historical-critical method, the most adamant supporter of the source-critical Documentary Hypothesis these days is Richard Elliott Friedman. According to Friedman's version of the theory, the main sources are as follows: (1) J, the Yahwist document (the German J is pronounced Y), used the name Yahweh (cf. Ex. 3:14–15) right from its beginning in Genesis 2:4 and gave an account of history written in the southern kingdom during the ninth and eighth centuries BC. (2) E, the Elohist document, used the name El or Elohim until the name Yahweh was revealed to Moses (cf. Ex. 6:2–3), and provided a parallel account written in the northern kingdom during the same period as J. (3) RJE is the Redactor who used both the J and E accounts to compose a unified history soon after the destruction of the northern kingdom in 722 BC. (4) P refers to the priestly account that, according to Friedman, was composed shortly after J and E were combined (thus the JEPD theory), but is dated as the latest source to the sixth or fifth centuries by many or perhaps most scholars (thus the JEDP theory). (It should be noted that some scholars do not see P as an independent document at all, but as a late redaction of the other documents.) (5) D takes up most of the book of Deuteronomy and was the law book that was both composed and found in the temple in the days of Josiah (ca. 622 BC, late seventh century; 2 Kings 22:8–13). (6) Finally, R is the Redactor who put all these sources together into the five-book combination that we know as the Pentateuch.[19]

With regard to Exodus 19–24:11 specifically, similar to most other scholars, Friedman assigns only 19:1 to P (the priestly writer) and nothing else.[20] Take special note of this because it will become important in the discussion below. According to Friedman verse 2a belongs to R (the redactor), 19:2b–9 belongs to E (the Elohist), the remainder of chapter 19 is a mixture of E and J (the Yahwist), with only a small redaction R or RJE in verse 24 ("you and Aaron with you"; there are complications with Aaron in the account); 20:1

[19]Richard Elliott Friedman, *The Bible with Sources Revealed* (San Francisco: HarperCollins, 2003), 3–5.
[20]The exception is John Van Seters, *The Life of Moses: The Yahwist as Historian in Exodus–Numbers* (Louisville: Westminster John Knox, 1994), 278; Van Seters, "'Comparing Scripture with Scripture': Some Observations on the Sinai Pericope of Exodus 19–24," in *Canon, Theology, and Old Testament Interpretation: Essays in Honor of Brevard S. Childs*, ed. Gene M. Tucker et al. (Philadelphia: Fortress, 1988), 113–14. See more on this below.

also belongs to R, the Ten Commandments in 20:2–17 is an independent text, except for verse 11, which is another redaction, and all the rest from 20:18–24:11 belongs to E.[21]

Of course, the historical-critical method is not limited to the source-critical Documentary Hypothesis outlined above. In particular, there is another school that comes at the whole matter very differently, sometimes referred to as the tradition-history approach.[22] These scholars begin with form-critical analysis, which seeks to isolate the original oral tradition(s) that either lie behind the source-critical documents referred to above, or have nothing at all to do with them. In the latter case, this approach in some sense essentially and intentionally rejects the Documentary Hypothesis. Along with the form-critical foundation comes tradition criticism, which concerns the history of Israel's traditions, not the history of Israel itself. It traces how the various form-critical units grew and were combined into cycles of tradition. Redaction criticism deals with the processes and strategies of written composition that shaped these received traditions into their literary form to yield, for example, the text of the Pentateuch. This approach will sometimes come into view in the analysis of Exodus 19–24 by Brevard Childs and others (see below).

As a test case, T. D. Alexander has already written a very helpful summary and critique of the historical-critical method as it has been applied to this passage, showing how the text actually hangs together quite well as it stands, contrary to documentary or tradition-historical analysis.[23] Kent Sparks has criticized Alexander for selecting this passage as his test case because historical-critical scholars have already admitted the failure of their method in this unit.[24] Nevertheless, I have chosen the same unit to be the focus here, not because the critical method is supposedly more vulnerable to critique here than in most other places, but because it is such a key passage. The way scholars handle this unit can determine a great deal about how they handle the rest of the Sinai revelation. Alexander's positive analysis of literary unity in Exodus 19–24,

---

[21]Friedman, *The Bible with Sources Revealed*, 151, 160–61.

[22]For a good introduction to how the other school operates and its critique of the Documentary Hypothesis, see Rolf Rendtorff, *The Old Testament: An Introduction* (Philadelphia: Fortress, 1986), 157–63. See pp. 14–17 for a general discussion of the Sinai narrative from this point of view.

[23]T. D. Alexander, *From Paradise to Promised Land: An Introduction to the Pentateuch* (Grand Rapids: Baker Academic, 2002), 62–79.

[24]Sparks, *God's Word in Human Words*, 157–58. Because he is so committed to the need for evangelicals to appropriate the critical method and its standard results, he tries to discount Alexander's work by treating it as a "red herring"—a ploy to distract us from the real issues. Unfortunately, his counterarguments on this passage are rather pathetic, as we shall see below. I consider Kent Sparks a friend, and I mean no disrespect here. He is a good scholar, colleague, and conversation partner. But it saddens me that some evangelical scholars today are so uncritical in their acceptance of historical-critical positions and, in fact, defensive about criticisms of it.

combined with further research, suggests a very different way forward than is afforded by the standard documentary, form-critical, tradition-historical, and redaction-critical methods. Failure of method in this primary unit is no small matter to be simply excused away as if it really does not matter. And it is not enough just to criticize the work of others, as some are wont to do, conservative or nonconservative. When all is said and done, we need to try to set forth positive proposals that can stand the test of time and scrutiny.

One of the goals in the remainder of this essay, therefore, is to isolate and clarify standard practices in the historical-critical method that are open to serious question. There are a number of them. Lest I be misunderstood, let me emphasize that this is a critique of how the historical-critical method is commonly practiced by those who follow the nonconservative scholarly consensus. By and large, I do not take the consensus or the varied and often contradictory results of this scholarship to be valid. The chaos here is precisely because of the way it is practiced. It is often incredible to me that scholars find the kinds of arguments used to be convincing. These are very intelligent, well-trained, and well-read people. At least part of the problem seems to be that they are so caught up in their particular scholarly method and its consensus that they cannot accept or recognize a more straightforward reading even when it is staring them in the face. They have their own dogma. This gives me pause in my own work too, however, for it is possible for me to miss something that is staring me in the face when coming at the whole thing from a different direction.

I consider myself an evangelical historical-critical scholar who tries to deal fairly and critically ("criticism" = "the art of objective evaluation," see above) with the literary and historical context, references, and accounts in the text, the factors involved in its composition and transmission, and the variegated theology that arises within it. It seems to me there are whole new sets of actual data that need to be brought together judiciously today to do good critical scholarship. This material should be welcomed into the discussion by both conservatives and nonconservatives, and can be taken fully into consideration only if there is a thoroughly critical "rethinking" of the older methods and theories, again, both conservative and nonconservative. The tendency is to selectively absorb this material into one's own position without actually rethinking the position. True, data can be evaluated in different ways and from different perspectives in terms of its meaning and implications. But we need to be careful about putting so much "spin" on it that real data is actually discounted in the end.

Here are two prime examples of the kind of important data that I have in mind. First, a great deal of archaeological, historical, and textual data from the ancient Near Eastern world of the Old Testament is readily available to us today that was not known to scholars, or not so accessible to them, during the two centuries or more when the historical-critical approach initially developed. There is a need to rethink the critical method and its results in light of what is extant today. K. A. Kitchen, for example, has brought together much of this material and has made an argument for the reliability of the Old Testament based on it.[25] No matter what one may think of his arguments and conclusions, the data he presents so well really must be taken seriously.

Second, there has been some relatively new work done on empirical data for the study of the processes of composition and transmission of the Hebrew Bible. Jeffrey Tigay has led the way here in his work on the Gilgamesh Epic,[26] and others have joined him.[27] In this case, we are talking about documents for which there is extant textual material for studying the various stages in the development of a composition, not just hypothetical reconstructed documents such as are proposed for the Documentary Hypothesis (i.e., JEDP). Tigay concludes that, to some degree at least, this data supports some elements of the theories of composition of the Hebrew Bible forwarded in the historical-critical method. But he also notes that trying to reconstruct the sources and processes without the actual preexisting materials in hand is by no means assured of success.[28] Be that as it may, scholars need to look carefully at the results of this kind of work and take it seriously when trying to discern the sources and the compositional and scribal processes used, for example, in the formation of the Pentateuch (see above).

The second goal in what follows is to work out some of the historical-critical and exegetical issues in Exodus 19–24 in a way that not only clarifies what is going on in the passage itself, but also has substantial implications for the overall analysis and interpretation of the priestly Levitical material in Exodus through Numbers. We have noted above and will say more below about the fact that the standard historical-critical consensus assigns only

---

[25]See especially K. A. Kitchen, *On the Reliability of the Old Testament* (Grand Rapids: Eerdmans, 2003). Sparks, for example, is very critical of Kitchen's criticisms of the historical-critical method and its results based on the factual data Kitchen marshals (Sparks, *God's Word in Human Words*, 11–12, 144–51, 156–59). The fact is that, no matter what kind of "spin" this or that scholar puts on it, the data itself needs to be reckoned with in an intellectually honest and responsible way. Kitchen's grasp of the data is impressive.

[26]Jeffrey H. Tigay, *The Evolution of the Gilgamesh Epic* (Philadelphia: University of Pennsylvania Press, 1982).

[27]See, for example, the other authors in *Empirical Models for Biblical Criticism*, ed. Jeffrey H. Tigay (Philadelphia: University of Pennsylvania Press, 1985); and most recently the further work on the development of the Gilgamesh Epic, for example, in Daniel E. Fleming and Sara J. Milstein, *The Buried Foundation of the Gilgamesh Epic: The Akkadian Huwawa Narrative* (Leiden: Brill, 2010).

[28]See, e.g., Tigay, *Empirical Models for Biblical Criticism*, 51, 240–41.

Exodus 19:1 or 1–2a to P (the priestly writer). There is virtually no P in all of Exodus 19:1–24:11. In my opinion, this is a major error caused by the method and the way it is applied to this and other texts.

### Covenant Ratification in Exodus 24:1–11 and Source-Critical Literary Method

Since what we have in our hands is the text, a literary text, it is best to start with how one reads it. As noted above, the literary method of the historical-critical method, sometimes called "old literary criticism," has certain peculiarities that cause it to have a fragmentary bias. This is not to say that it always fragments texts—just that it has a bias in that direction. Exodus 24:1–11 is a good passage for illustrating this. In his analysis, for example, Ska notes that "the command in 24:1 is not carried out until 24:9," so "verses 3–8 quite clearly interrupt the narrative line of vv. 1–2, 9–11." In fact, he draws a general redaction-critical principle from this passage and his earlier treatment of Exodus 14:11–12: "There are many examples of this kind of procedure in the Pentateuch. However, they are not all as obvious as in the two cases presented above. Consequently, it is not always easy to prove the existence of a redactional addition with decisive, irrefutable arguments."[29] Thus, it is clear that he considers his analysis of literary disunity in Exodus 24:1–11 to be irrefutable. There are really two original and unconnected stories here, not just one, and they have been brought together by a later redactor.

Generally speaking, this has been a consensus among historical-critical scholars.[30] The scholarly discussion here is somewhat bound up with the analysis of Exodus 19:3–8 in relation to 24:1–11, so our discussion will reflect that. In 1974 Brevard Childs wrote that "it has been generally recognized" that verses 3b–8 of Exodus 19 "have a compositional integrity of their own," although there is no general agreement on the actual date and authorship of the passage. He concludes that, "although the passage contains old covenant traditions, probably reflected through the E source, its present form bears the stamp of the Deuteronomic redactor" because in its present position the passage appears to be "summarizing the whole Sinai pericope."[31] Moreover, some kind of close correspondence between the introduction to the Sinai covenant in 19:3b–8 (esp. vv. 4–6) and its ratification in 24:3–8 is a commonly agreed-upon conclusion among historical-critical scholars.[32] Ernest

---

[29]Ska, *Introduction to the Reading of the Pentateuch*, 77.

[30]It is interesting that Friedman disregards this consensus by assigning all of Ex. 24:1–11 to E. See above and Friedman, *The Bible with Sources Revealed*, 160, and his rather extensive source-critical explanation there.

[31]Childs, *The Book of Exodus*, 360–61.

[32]See the recent brief summary of all this in Ska, *Introduction to the Reading of the Pentateuch*, 92.

Nicholson treated 19:3b–8 as a later Deuteronomic addition that explains the significance of the rite in 24:3–8, which is pre-Deuteronomic.[33] John Van Seters critiqued Nicholson's view and assigned both 19:3b–8 and 24:3–8 to his late post-Deuteronomic Yahwist.[34] For our purposes here there are two main points of interest: (1) most scholars today see a close correspondence between Exodus 19:3b–8 and 24:3–8 so that they tend to put them together in date and authorship in one way or the other, and (2) no one assigns these two passages to the priestly source.

So much for Exodus 19:3b–8 and 24:3–8. What about the rest of Exodus 24:1–11? Historical-critical analysis of Exodus 24:1–2 and 9–11 as related to verses 3–8 yields even more mixed and contradictory results so that, in Childs's opinion, the "arbitrariness" of much of the reasoning regarding it "does not increase confidence in the suggested source analysis."[35] Childs himself suggests that, on the oral preliterary level, verses 3–8 "reflect both in form and content a covenant renewal ceremony." Similarly, verses 1–2 and 9–11 "reflect an old tradition of a covenant meal following a theophany," but he insists that the meal "was originally unconnected to the Mosaic office of mediator." Although he readily admits that the tradition of a meal with the Lord has a firm parallel in the near canonical context (Ex. 18:12), he concludes that "these verses [i.e., 24:1–2, 9–11] remain a foreign body which the chapter has difficulty absorbing."[36] From the viewpoint of method, therefore, for this kind of literary-critical analysis, "the major literary problem of the chapter has to do with the lack of apparent unity" between the account in Exodus 24:1–2, 9–11 as opposed to that in verses 3–8.[37] They seem to tell two different kinds of stories, neither of which shows any connection to the other.

Similar to Ska and Childs, Nicholson argues for a lack of unity between these units because, as the text now stands, "Verses 3–8 abruptly interrupt the obvious connection between vv. 1–2 and 9–11."[38] It is especially telling that a key part of Nicholson's argument for viewing the inclusion of verses 9–11 (along with vv. 1–2) as redactional rather than original is that "a covenant rite has already been described in vv. 3–8, so that *prima facie* one does not expect it to be followed immediately by yet another description of a rite."[39] The fact of the matter, however, is that the combination of an oath like in

---

[33]Ernest W. Nicholson, *God and His People: Covenant and Theology in the Old Testament* (Oxford: Clarendon, 1986), 169–71.
[34]John Van Seters, *The Life of Moses*, 247–89.
[35]Childs, *The Book of Exodus*, 500.
[36]Ibid., 500–502. See the brief review in Alexander, *From Paradise to Promised Land*, 66–68.
[37]Childs, *The Book of Exodus*, 500.
[38]Nicholson, *God and His People*, 121.
[39]Ibid., 127.

verses 3–8 with a meal like in verses 9–11 for ratifying a covenant is a natural part of covenant-making narratives elsewhere in the Torah (see, e.g., Gen. 26:26–31; 31:43–54, esp. vv. 53–54), which Nicholson himself makes special note of just a page earlier.[40] He makes no effort to excise one from the other in those passages, so why is it so *prima facie* in Exodus 24? Nicholson goes on to insist that the meal in Exodus 24:11, however, was not a covenant meal,[41] but this argument *prima facie* has little to commend it.

Alexander confirms that this is the majority opinion, the scholarly consensus on this passage. From his summary of several historical-critical treatments of this passage, including that of Childs, he concludes, "While diverging over the precise identity of the sources in Exodus 24:1–11, critical scholars generally agree that verses 1–2, 9–11 differ in origin from verses 3–8."[42] He rejects this critical opinion based on the similar pattern found in the account in Deuteronomy 27:1–8: building a stone altar, sacrificing burnt and peace offerings, and eating in the presence of the Lord. It should be noted, however, that the blood oath ritual in Exodus 24:3–8 does not find a clear parallel in Deuteronomy 27, so the level of correspondence between Exodus 24 and Deuteronomy 27 does not really confirm the unity of Exodus 24:1–11.

There is, however, an apparent link between the two (i.e., between 24:1–2, 9–11 and 24:3–8) that has largely been overlooked by those who follow this method. The food and drink for the meal on the mountain in verse 11 should most likely be understood to be portions from the peace offerings sacrificed in verse 5, as Sarna has suggested.[43] Where else would it have come from in the context? The peace offerings in verse 5 undoubtedly supplied a covenant communion feast for the whole congregation at the foot of the mountain. That is by nature what happened with the meat of peace offerings. They became a banquet. When Moses, his two sons, and the seventy elders came up on the mountain (v. 9) as they had been instructed (vv. 1–2), they simply brought some of the provisions with them for the purpose of supplying the covenant feast there on the mountain in the immediate presence of God. They knew what was going on the whole time, and the ancient authors and readers would have easily understood it too.

From a historical, cultural, literary, and ritual point of view, therefore, the whole passage makes perfectly good sense as it stands. It all hangs together very well as one unified original narrative account. The source- or redaction-

[40]Ibid., 125–26.
[41]Ibid., 127, 130–32.
[42]Alexander, *From Paradise to Promised Land*, 67–68.
[43]Nahum M. Sarna, *The JPS Torah Commentary: Exodus* (Philadelphia: The Jewish Publication Society, 1991), 153.

critical literary analysis that reads disunity here is wrongheaded to begin with. And this is repeated over and over again in the application of the method. As noted above, Ska presents this historical-critical literary analysis of Exodus 24:1–11 as one of the parade exemplars among "many examples of this kind of [redactional addition] procedure in the Pentateuch." If this is so, then it is not much of a parade.

When Sparks criticizes Alexander for using Exodus 19–24 as a test case, he misses the fact that, for example, within the historical-critical scholarly consensus there has been little disagreement over this piece of it (i.e., the disunity of 24:1–11). But clearly the consensus in this piece of the passage is just as confused as the admitted confusion in the other units. Furthermore, Sparks criticizes Alexander for not continuing his analysis into 24:12–18 because, if he had, Alexander "would have needed to explain why Moses was called up to the mountain of God in verse 12 when he was already there in verse 11."[44]

Are we really supposed to take such arguments seriously? Are we really going to require the ancient writer to make a point of saying that they came down from the mountain after they ate and drank in verse 11? The following verses make it clear that only Moses and Joshua were supposed to go up on that occasion, and the elders were supposed to wait at the foot of the mountain with the people. Could not a writer assume that a reader had the intelligence to know that they came down off the mountain between verses 11 and 12? Writers necessarily assume that readers (or hearers) of their texts bring something to the reading (or hearing), at least something this obvious. Writers both ancient and modern commonly leave such things to their readers. Totally explicit writing is not possible anyway, and it would not be good writing even if it were possible. This brings us back to the narrative framework at the beginning of the unit in Exodus 19–20.

### Covenant Initiation in Exodus 19–20 and Tradition-Critical Literary Method

Instead of distinguishing divergent preexisting documents behind the current text, tradition criticism looks for an ancient core in the passage (usually oral in origin) and tries to reconstruct how the current text has been built up around that core progressively through time, in multiple stages. This involves attending to the oral form-critical core tradition along with the buildup of traditions around it (i.e., the tradition-critical history of the passage), including the redactions that shaped the written text. Sometimes scholars will combine this analysis with the documentary approach to one degree or another

---

[44]Sparks, *God's Word in Human Words*, 158.

by assigning at least certain parts of the current text to one or more of the documents (J, E, D, or P) and viewing other portions as either independent documents or redactions that arose in putting it all into its current form. It is not uncommon for the "redactor(s)" to be called the author(s) of the text.

The narrative in Exodus 19–20 (see also 24:1–11) is one of those genuinely confusing passages in the Hebrew Bible. It is one of the classic cases. Recall Ska's evaluation (cited in full above) of the narrative framework in Exodus 19:1–20:1, 18–22; 21:1; 24:1–11: "It bears the marks of this people's complex history. . . . It will always be extremely difficult to find a suitable method for identifying with substantial certainty the oldest elements and—even more difficult—for determining their origin."[45] In another place he observes that, for example, "It is not easy to follow all of Moses' 'ups and downs'" in chapter 19. There is actually one place in the text where it appears that Moses himself is confused by all the going up and down the mountain. The Lord has descended to the top of Sinai and called Moses up to him (v. 20), but then the Lord tells him to "go down" in order to warn the people not to follow him up the mountain. Well, the boundary around the mountain to keep the people back has already been established (vv. 12–13), so Moses objects: "The people cannot come up . . ." (v. 23). This confusion on Moses's part suggests that perhaps our confusion is justified, and that the historical scene itself really was confusing to begin with. This is simply recognized in the account, not created by confused redactors. We shall come back to this point later.

Many have sought to relieve the difficulties by applying diachronic historical-critical methods that assign the seemingly divergent materials, on the one hand, to different documentary sources or, on the other hand, to a sequence of traditio-historical redactions.[46] Others have recently argued that the problems can be resolved by careful synchronic literary analysis of the text as it stands.[47] The proposed solution as Ska articulates it, for example, is to argue that 19:3–8 is a "redactional insertion" or addition. In his estimation, "Here

---

[45]Ska, *Introduction to the Reading of the Pentateuch*, 213–14.

[46]For the details of this approach to the unit up through 1974 see Childs, *The Book of Exodus*, 337–64. In addition to what he refers to there, consider more recently, for example: Van Seters, "Comparing Scripture with Scripture," 111–30, and Van Seters, *The Life of Moses*, 247–89; Thomas B. Dozeman, *God on the Mountain: A Study of Redaction, Theology, and Canon in Exodus 19–24* (Atlanta: Scholars Press, 1989).

[47]See, e.g., G. C. Chirichigno, "The Narrative Structure of Exod 19–24," *Biblica* 68 (1987): 457–79; Joe M. Sprinkle, *"The Book of the Covenant": A Literary Approach*, JSOTSup 174 (Sheffield: JSOT, 1994), 16–34; J. H. Sailhamer, *The Pentateuch as Narrative: A Biblical-Theological Commentary* (Grand Rapids: Zondervan, 1992), 47–59; Sailhamer, *Introduction to Old Testament Theology: A Canonical Approach* (Grand Rapids: Zondervan, 1995), 277–87; and recently Sailhamer, *The Meaning of the Pentateuch: Revelation, Composition and Interpretation* (Downers Grove, IL: InterVarsity, 2009), 374–98.

the indications are clear."[48] His argument is reminiscent of what Sparks set forth for Exodus 24:11–12 (see the end of the previous section), having to do with Moses's going up and down the mountain. The critique offered there applies here too, but the discussion is more complicated.

First, "In Exod 19:3a Moses goes up the mountain to God, while in 19:3b YHWH calls to him from [Heb. preposition *min*] the mountain to give him a message to be communicated to Israel."[49] According to Ska, these are "two incompatible movements." The immediate question that comes to mind, however, is whether they are really incompatible in Hebrew, especially in light of the fact that, for example, when Moses approached the bush in Exodus 3:4, "the LORD called to him from [Heb. preposition *min*] the midst of the bush." Are Moses's going up the mountain and God's calling to him "from" the mountain really contradictory? A more generous reading would recognize that this could well be a way of saying that Moses went up to some place on the mountain and God spoke to him from the mountain while he was standing there at that place.

Ska's second point is largely dependent on the first. On the basis of the supposed contradiction between Exodus 19:3a and b, he proposes that "the text becomes clear when we separate 19:3b–8, 9 from the preceding and following passages"; that is, from verses 3a, 10–14. There are two different original narrative traditions here that the redactor has put together as one. In verses 3b–9 "all the action happens in the plain at the foot of Mount Sinai." As for the other story in verses 3a, 10–13, there "he climbs the mountain, where he receives the instructions given in 19:10–13, then he goes back down in 19:14." The remainder of chapter 19, with 20:18–21 and 24:1–11, follows on this later account. Thus, verses 3b–9 constitute a redactional insertion.[50]

The real problem with Ska's explanation is this. In the mind of the redactor, what would have been gained by placing verse 3a where it is, so far removed from verse 10? Why did he not simply insert what is now verses 3b–9 at the end of verse 2, so that what is now verse 3a would stand at the front of verse 10, where it belongs according to Ska. There does not seem to be any reason that Moses could not have been with the people at the foot of the mountain in 19:3–9, like in 20:18–20. Is this just an awkward mistake by the redactor? I do not think so.

Again, on a more generous reading of the passage one could wonder why the ancient writer would need to recount every movement of Moses up and down the mountain. Could he not assume that the ancient readers would

---

[48]Ska, *Introduction to the Reading of the Pentateuch*, 92.
[49]Ibid.
[50]Ibid.

naturally understand that if Moses was up on the mountain and the people
were not, he would need to come down off the mountain to address them?
Could it not be that the reason Moses's coming down from the mountain
is recorded in 19:14 is that here his going up and down begins to become a
key complicating factor in the telling of the account and in what actually
happened on this occasion? He needed to go down in verse 14 to prepare
the people for the terrifying theophany on the third day, at which time they
would come out to meet God at the foot of the mountain with Moses (see
v. 17). As noted above, when the theophany becomes more and more intense
and terrifying, the going up and down becomes confusing even to Moses
(vv. 20–24).

According to the text as it stands, the theophany in the narration of Exodus
19:9–20:21 was calculated to so impress the ancient Israelites with their God
that they would take their covenant commitment to him seriously (Ex. 19:9;
cf. esp. Deut. 5:28–33, and also more generally Exodus 32–34; Leviticus 10;
24:10–23; Num. 15:32–41; etc.). And the narrative is largely sequential, as
some scholars have argued from certain literary features of the story and the
parallel passages in Deuteronomy 4:10–14, 33; 5:4–5, 22–31.[51] In addition, a
key grammatical pattern unifies the passage and clarifies the movements in
it: namely, the consistent alternation of the Hebrew prepositions for going up
"in/at/on" (Heb. *b*) the mountain, used for what the people do, as opposed
to "to/into/unto" (Heb *'el*) the mountain, for what Moses does. See the comprehensive list of occurrences below:

Moses        Exodus 19:3—went up "*to* [*'el*] God."
The People   19:12a—must *not* go up "*in* [*b*] the mountain or touch *in* (*b*)
             its edge" during the three-day preparation period.
             19:12b—"all who touch *in* [*b*] the mountain" during the three-
             day preparation period "shall surely be put to death."
             19:13—"they shall go up *in* [*b*] the mountain" only when the
             ram's horn sounds on the third day.
             19:17—"and they stood *in* [*b*] the foot [i.e., lower part] of the
             mountain" on the third day—note the qualification: *in* "the
             lower part" of the mountain.
Moses        19:20—the Lord called Moses "*to* [*'el*] the top [head] of the
             mountain"—note the qualification: *to* the "top of" the moun-

[51]See, e.g., the simple outline in S. M. Paul, *Studies in the Book of the Covenant in the Light of Cuneiform and Biblical Law*, VTSup 18 (Leiden: Brill, 1970), 29, and the careful analysis in Alexander, *From Paradise to the Promised Land*, 73–78.

|            | tain (cf. vv. 3, 23, 24), and the obvious contrast to the people in verse 17 above, "*in* the lower part." |
|------------|---------------------------------------------------------------------------------------|
| The People | 19:23—must *not* go up "*to* ['*el*] mount Sinai" because of the boundary established in verses 12–13 above. |
|            | 19:24—do *not* allow the priests and the people to "come up *to* ['*el*] the Lord" on the mountain. |
| Moses      | 20:21—the people stood at a distance, but Moses "drew near *to* ['*el*] the dark cloud" where God was. |
| Moses      | 24:1a—the Lord told Moses to "come up *to* ['*el*] the Lord" with the priests and elders—but note the qualification in verse 2a below. |
| Moses      | 24:2a—Moses alone, however, shall draw near "*to* ['*el*] the Lord." |

Even though, on the surface of things, the narrative story line is confusing, this syntactic analysis of the consistency of prepositions does not bode well for analyses that propose disunity here. It is unlikely that multiple sources, redactors, or redacted sources would have produced this. If it is a redactional unity, then the redactors have done their work so well that they have indeed "disappeared" from our view, which naturally raises the question of whether they were ever there in the first place.[52] The fact of the matter is that, according to the account itself, the scene was even confusing to Moses and the people, but here is what a close reading of the text suggests. Moses *descended* the mountain (Ex. 19:14) to consecrate the people. Although they trembled at the sound and appearance of the divine theophany on the ominous third day (19:16), Moses brought the people out to meet God "at the foot of the mountain" (19:17; i.e., at the lowest edge of the mountain outside the boundary referred to in 19:12–13), the top of which was ablaze with God's theophany (19:18, 20; cf. Ex. 3:1–12).

As the people stood there at the foot of the mountain, "Moses was speaking and God was answering him in thunder" (19:19b). Then Moses *ascended* to the *top* of the mountain (19:20) only to be told by God that he should *descend* (19:21) once more to make sure that the people obey his boundary restrictions and, in addition, to fetch Aaron up with him (19:21–24). It seems that the reason for the Lord's concern was that he himself was going to *descend* further down the mountain in a cloud of thick darkness (20:21; cf. 19:16) in order to speak "face to face" with not only Moses but also the people (Deut.

---

[52] John Barton, *Reading the Old Testament: Method in Biblical Study*, rev. ed. (Louisville: Westminster John Knox, 1996), 57.

5:4). If the people were too far up the mountain (i.e., beyond the designated border), the Lord would "break out against them" as he descended (Ex. 19:22).

After Moses had descended to the people at the foot of the mountain to follow the Lord's most recent instructions (19:25), the Lord God descended toward the people in the cloud to meet with Moses and the people and pronounced the Ten Commandments to them "face to face" (20:1–17; cf. 19:25 with 20:1 and Deut. 4:10–13; 5:22; 9:10b). After speaking the commandments, God paused (Deut. 5:22). As he had been speaking, the fear of the people grew so overwhelming that they moved back away from Moses, who was at the foot of the mountain with them, and "stayed at a distance" (Ex. 20:18), thus putting Moses in a position of standing between the people and the Lord (see Deut. 5:4–5).[53]

When the Lord paused, the people approached Moses (who was therefore apparently within the reach of the people and standing outside the boundary) to request that he be their mediator (Ex. 20:19–20; cf. Deut. 5:23–27). God responded positively to their request (Deut. 5:28–29; cf. Ex. 20:20) and told Moses to have them return to their tents (Deut. 5:30) while Moses himself was to approach and stand there by the Lord (i.e., in the cloud of "thick darkness where God was," Ex. 20:21) to hear the remainder of the revelation. Consequently, as their mediator, Moses received from the Lord "all the commands, decrees and laws" (i.e., Ex. 20:22–23:33), which he would then be responsible to "teach" them to live by in the land (Deut. 5:31; cf. 4:14). This series of events in Exodus 19–20 created the temporal and literary division between the Ten Commandments and "the book of the covenant" (Exodus 21–23).

According to Exodus 19:24, the Lord intended that Moses bring only Aaron back up with him on the mountain the next time he came up. But the next reference to Aaron is not until Exodus 24:1, where the Lord commanded Moses to bring "Aaron, Nadab and Abihu, and seventy of the elders of Israel" up with him. The backing away of the people in Exodus 20:18–20 appears to have changed the situation so that there was no longer any point in Moses's bringing Aaron back up on the mountain with him. By their request, Moses alone now became the mediator (20:21), as was the intention of the Lord from the beginning of the theophany: "I am going to come to you in a dense

[53]Deut. 5:5 implies that, amid all the thunder and trumpets, etc., when the people moved to stand at a distance away from the foot of the mountain (Ex. 20:18–19), they also lost the ability to understand what the Lord was saying when he pronounced the Ten Commandments (Ex. 20:1–17; Deut. 5:6–21). Moses, therefore, had to "declare" to them even "the word of the Lord" (Deut. 5:5) in the Ten Commandments, which follow immediately in Deut. 5:6–21. See Sprinkle, *The Book of the Covenant*, 23–24, and Chirichigno, "The Narrative Structure of Exod 19–24," 470. For a good summary of the problems scholars have had with Deut. 5:5 see M. Weinfeld, *Deuteronomy 1–11*, AB 5 (New York: Doubleday, 1991), 240–41.

cloud, so that the people will hear me speaking with you and will always put their trust in you" (19:9, NIV).

I have not been able to deal with all the details here in this discussion. In general, the point is that yes, the account seems confusing, but that is because it is describing a scene that was complex to begin with, even for the people who were there in the day. Upon a closer reading, however, the narrative framework of Exodus 19–24 is unified and largely sequential.

### The Kingdom of Priests in Exodus 19:6 and the Diachronic Fallacy
This final section cannot be developed in any real depth, first, because this essay is already too long and, second, because the topic is simply too large. It has major implications for the study of the priestly material in the Pentateuch overall.[54] Again, there are many variations among historical-critical scholars, but one constant stands out: no one who follows the standard historical-critical method classifies Exodus 19:5–6 as priestly (i.e., P), although the priestly nature of the passage is abundantly clear: "Now if you obey me fully and keep my covenant, then out of all nations you will be my *treasured possession*. Although the whole earth is mine, you will be for me a *kingdom of priests* and a *holy nation*." It is my contention that the reason for this blunder in classifying the passage can be seen in the argumentation that characterizes the method.

For example, John Van Seters argues that the Yahwist (J) in Exodus 19:6 sees "no need for a special priesthood" because the whole nation is a kingdom of priests, but the priestly writer (P) in 19:12–13a, 20–24 revises J because, among other things, the passage regards the "priests as distinct from the rest of the people."[55] This kind of thinking has been pervasive since before Wellhausen and is a staple of the method. It is as if ancient writers could not hold two related concepts together. The assumption is that such a tension must be explained diachronically; that is, two different writers or schools of writers at different times must have written these verses, and a redactor must have put them together later when "the time was right," so to speak, or perhaps one of the writers was the redactor, or whatever. This is a "diachronic fallacy." Yes, there is diachronic development in the composition and transmission of the Hebrew Bible as noted, for example, in the discussion of the authorship of the Pentateuch above. But to completely rewrite the history of Israel and its religion on the basis of such thinking is ill-advised at best, and at worst, perverse.

---

[54] For a thorough treatment of the whole topic, see my forthcoming volume entitled *Priest, People, and Ritual*.
[55] Van Seters, *The Life of Moses*, 278; Van Seters, "Comparing Scripture with Scripture," 113–14.

I myself am not convinced that we should try to isolate a "P source" in the first place, but that is not in any way to deny that there are certain primary priestly themes and sections of material in the Pentateuch. The point is that Exodus 19:5–6 initiates one of those major priestly themes that permeate the remainder of Exodus all the way through Numbers. In fact, even Deuteronomy recalls some of the same essential terms and expressions found in Exodus 19:5–6, especially at the very end of the law section, thus creating a distant echo of the beginning of the law at the end: "Today the LORD has obtained your agreement: to be his *treasured* people as he promised you, and to keep his commandments; for him to set you high above all nations that he has made, in praise and in fame and in honor; and for you to be a people *holy* to the LORD your God, as he promised" (Deut. 26:18–19, NRSV). The command to keep the covenant is also present there (vv. 16–17). In Moab as at Sinai the people declared once again their commitment to the covenant, and the Lord in turn declared his commitment to them as his "treasured possession" and his "holy nation" (vv. 18–19; cf. also Deut. 7:6 and 14:2). The phrase "kingdom of priests," however, occurs only in Exodus 19:6, not in Deuteronomy 26, and carries with it special implications for Israel as a "holy nation" in Exodus 19–24 and beyond.

First, there have been those who have recognized the connection between the promise of Israel's becoming a "kingdom of priests" in Exodus 19:6 and the covenant ratification ritual in Exodus 24:6–8, where the blood is splashed first on the altar and then on the people, as a kind of general consecration and ordination rite for the "kingdom of priests."[56] The manipulation of blood both before and after the oath, of course, made it a blood-oath commitment by the people to live according to the covenant stipulations in the book of the covenant, which Moses recited to them there. But why was the oath enacted in this particular and peculiar manner? The answer, it seems, is in the direct connection that the blood of the ritual established between the people as a whole and God himself, represented by the altar.

Through this ritual they not only swore a covenant oath but were essentially ordained and consecrated as the kingdom of priests who had access to the presence of God at Sinai, the mountain of God. Later this access to God extended from the solitary altar at the foot of Mount Sinai to the tabernacle presence of God as well, which is the subject of the following chapters in Exodus. The tabernacle, after all, was essentially a moveable Sinai. Sinai was the mountain of God. The tabernacle was the tent of God. His glory-cloud presence was visible over and upon both. He made his glory cloud visible to

---

[56]See Nicholson, *God and His People*, 172–74, and the literature cited there.

the Israelites in leading them to Sinai, then at Sinai itself, and then in leading them away from Sinai. He traveled with them through the wilderness to guide them to the Promised Land. They had their tents and he had his tent, and they met with him there at this "tent of meeting" (see, e.g., the interchange of the terms *tabernacle* and *tent of meeting* in Ex. 40:34 and Lev. 1:1).[57]

Second, John Davies has shown convincingly how the Exodus 24:6–8 ritual is comparable to the ordination of the Aaronic priests in Leviticus 8:22–24.[58] Moses "daubed" (8:23) the blood on the right earlobe, right thumb, and right big toe of Aaron and his sons (vv. 23–24), and "splashed" (v. 24b) the rest of the blood all around on the altar. The "daubing" of the blood here matches the daubing of the blood of the sin offering on the horns of the altar earlier in the procedure (8:15a). In fact, the extremities of Aaron and his sons seem to match the extremities (i.e., horns) of the altar. The earlobe, thumb, and big toe are like "horns" of a man in relation to the "horns" of the altar.[59] In other words, the ordination-offering blood consecrated the priests in a way that matches the consecration of the altar by means of the blood of the sin offering. The priests were "de-sinned" just as the altar had been (see 8:15 and the remarks above). Both were thereby made fit to function in making atonement for the children of Israel. Aaron and his sons had now become the priests for the kingdom of priests.

The remainder of the ordination-offering blood was "splashed" around on the altar (8:24b) like that of the burnt-offering blood (8:19). These were the normal procedures for the blood in the performance of burnt and peace offerings, the ordination offering belonging to the main category of peace offerings. The same action with the blood was used in Exodus 24:6–8, where the blood was splashed on the altar and then on the people, making them the kingdom of priests. Combine that with the "daubing" of the blood on the horns of the altar and the "horns" of the priests, and one can see a close correspondence between the procedures in Exodus 24 and in Leviticus 8.

The main goal in Exodus 24 was to consecrate the people as a kingdom of priests and holy nation. The main goal in Leviticus 8 was to consecrate Aaron and his sons as the priests for the kingdom of priests. In both instances the binding of the people and priests to the altar is vivid and filled with implications. The blood manipulation was individual and more precise in Leviticus 8 probably for two reasons. First, the Aaronic priesthood stood between the

---

[57]For more on the centrality and critical importance of the tabernacle presence of God, see Richard E. Averbeck, "Tabernacle," in *Dictionary of the Old Testament: Pentateuch*, ed. T. Desmond Alexander and David W. Baker (Downers Grove, IL: InterVarsity, 2003), 822–25.

[58]John A. Davies, *A Royal Priesthood: Literary and Intertextual Perspectives on an Image of Israel in Exodus 19:6* (London: T&T Clark, 2004), 119–24.

[59]See the remarks in Jacob Milgrom, *Leviticus 1–16*, AB 3 (New York: Doubleday, 1991), 528–29.

altar and the kingdom of priests. Non-priests could never approach the altar
to place blood or anything else upon it. The Aaronites did that for them. They
came closer. Second, it would be difficult to perform the daubing action on
all the people in Exodus 24. There were just too many of them, and it was a
collective oath-commitment rite in any case, so the ritual action needed to
be collective.

Third, it is essential that we extend this line of argument further to include
the continuity with the blood manipulation of the guilt-offering ritual for
the cleansing of the skin-diseased person in Leviticus 14:12–18. There the
blood is applied to the common person's right earlobe, thumb, and big toe
in the same way as the priests' in Leviticus 8. This tells us clearly that the
priestly link between the covenant people and the Lord was not compromised
by the kingdom of priests' having priests of the kingdom. As noted earlier,
the people as a kingdom of priests and the Aaronic priests of the kingdom
complemented rather than competed with each other. Exodus 24, Leviticus 8
(cf. Exodus 29), and Leviticus 14 are the only three instances where the blood
of a sacrificial offering is ritually applied to the body of a person or group
of persons in the Hebrew Bible.[60] The line of connection from Exodus 19:6a,
where the Lord designates all Israel to be his "kingdom of priests," leads
through the covenant ratification and the consecration and ordination ritual
for that kingdom of priests in Exodus 24, to the consecration and ordination
of the Aaronic "priests of the kingdom" in Leviticus 8, and from there back
again to the reconsecration of common individuals belonging to the "kingdom
of priests" in Leviticus 14.

This carries major historical-critical and theological implications. The
question becomes, Are we really talking about diachronic developmental
historical and compositional factors, or is a synchronic sociological explanation better? The fact of the matter is that the basic theology of the Exodus
19:6 "kingdom of priests and holy people" and its ritual initiation in Exodus
24:3–8 penetrates deeply into the priestly core of the Torah. The basic idea
remains the same and works its way into and through the theology of the
tabernacle priesthood and its sacrificial practices. There are two sides to the
matter—two sides of the same coin, so to speak.

On the one hand, the combination of Exodus 19:6 with the blood ritual in
Exodus 24 views Israel's covenant relationship with the Lord from the larger
perspective of the nation overall as a "kingdom of priests." The guilt-offering
ritual for the cleansing of the skin-diseased person displays the effects of the

---

[60]Gordon Wenham briefly anticipated certain elements of this line of argument in his Leviticus
commentary, but no one has worked out the details. See Gordon J. Wenham, *The Book of Leviticus*,
NICOT (Grand Rapids: Eerdmans, 1979), 143, 209–11.

Exodus 19:6 "kingdom of priests" and "holy nation" theology as it works its way into the fabric of the priestly ritual system. This "kingdom of priests" theology views the matter from a standpoint in the community, outside the tabernacle looking in. On the other hand, Leviticus 8 views the Aaronites as the designated priests for this kingdom of priests. They look out at the larger community from inside the tabernacle, from the perspective of their position as priests for the kingdom of priests. The two belong together in time and place.

A guilt offering rather than an ordination/peace offering was required in Leviticus 14 because the skin-diseased person, who belonged to the "kingdom of priests," had become desecrated away from the "holy nation" (cf. Ex. 19:6) and the tabernacle, having to live outside the camp as required in Leviticus 13:46: "As long as he has the infection he remains unclean. He must live alone; he must live outside the camp." The general purpose of the guilt offering was to make atonement for desecration of sancta (holy persons, places, or things), as Jacob Milgrom and others have argued. The skin-diseased person was "sancta," since he was a member of the kingdom of priests and *holy* nation.

Second, there is no way the priest himself would have missed the many correspondences between his own ordination and consecration, and the rituals he performed for the healed common person. It would be hard for either the priest or the person healed to miss the fact that the people were priests too, a kingdom of priests. The people were holy too, a holy nation. They were sacred. The priest would also have noticed, however, that there were certain differences between these rites and those by which he was consecrated as a priest. One of the main differences was that no blood or oil was taken off the altar and "sprinkled" on the healed person, as was done in the consecration of the priests (Lev. 8:30). So the healed person was not consecrated to function as a priest at the altar. The Aaronic priests of the kingdom of priests did that for him or her. Moreover, there was no eating of the guilt-offering meat by the healed person that corresponded to the priests when they ate the meat of the ordination offering (8:31–32). No common person would eat the meat of a guilt offering. It was brought for their atonement, so the meat was eaten by the priests who made the atonement (Lev. 7:6), not the one who brought the offering. The priest would have understood that he was functioning as a priest for the person who belonged to the kingdom of priests.

## Conclusion

Of the two main sections of this essay, the first is largely reflective and programmatic; the second is a combination of theory and method along with its selective, illustrative, and evaluative application to the Sinai covenant-making narrative in Exodus 19–24. With regard to the latter, the literary reading of the text as it is applied from within the historical-critical "scholarly consensus," if there is such a thing, leaves a great deal to be desired. Thus, the results of the method are open to serious challenge. The literary, theological, and ritual linkage from Exodus 19:6 through 24:6–8 to Leviticus 8 and then Leviticus 14 crosses over source-critical boundaries in a way that undermines the proposed divisions between them. In reality, the theology of Exodus 19:6, with the ritual expression of it in 24:6–8, works its way from the supposed J, E, or D world (depending on the particular scholar's source-critical assignment of these texts) directly into the theology, ritual procedures, and sociology of the supposedly distinct and contradictory world of what is called P. One of the main lines of argument for insisting that Exodus 19:5–6 and 24:3–8 are not part of P is that the notion of Israel as a whole kingdom of priests stands in competition with the Aaronites serving as the priests of the kingdom. The way these theological themes interpenetrate each other in the set of texts discussed, however, weighs against this notion.

The sociology is especially important here. The same theology is being applied in ways that are appropriate for the needs of different kinds of specific situations in the lives of both priests and commoners during the same period of time and at the same place. The explanation is sociological and synchronic, not diachronic and developmental. Some may say this is a redactional or supplementary coherence imposed later, if they so desire. But the coherence is there, nevertheless, and enough of this kind of coherence will eventually erode the foundations of imposed theories that depend on the lack of coherence to provide the necessary fodder for their theories to arise and survive in the first place. In the meantime, we can simply follow the Bible's self-consciousness about its own compositional process. Contrary to Berlinerblau, the Bible actually speaks explicitly about and openly reflects on the processes through which it came into being.

This brings us back to the first major part of this essay. Conservative scholars need to think critically too. We need to identify and take fully into account the verifiable data that applies to the text in part and in whole, and evaluate the scholarly theories about the data objectively, whether the theories are conservative or nonconservative. Simplistic harmonizations and such get no one anywhere. But the secularist biblical scholar Jacques Berlinerblau is wrong. He has adopted wholesale an approach and its "assured results" that is neither methodologically unbiased nor productive in terms of results that are truly assured. Yes, there are certainly problems in the Hebrew text as we have it, but the approach taken in the various forms of the standard historical-critical method often multiplies the problems far beyond those that are actually there. Some say that this is the only way to read the text because it just does not make sense as it stands. My own work has assured me that, allowing for problems of textual corruption, it is methodologically wise to take a more generous stance toward the reliability of the text and argue that the problem is with the scholar's misunderstanding of the text, sometimes my own included, but not the text itself.

# 7

# OLD TESTAMENT SOURCE CRITICISM

*Some Methodological Miscues*

## ROBERT B. CHISHOLM JR.

Old Testament source criticism seeks to identify literary sources within the biblical text as a basis for reconstructing the text's evolution into its final form. Of course, it would take an entire volume, or set of volumes, to offer a thorough critique of this method in all of its many facets. Because of space limitations this brief essay will not address the matter of doublets, whether actual (for example, Genesis 1 and 2) or alleged (for example, 1 Samuel 13 and 15). Instead our focus will be two passages where critics see sources interwoven in a single story. To avoid the charge of using "misleading test cases," I have chosen two of source criticism's parade examples of texts where sources allegedly have been woven together to produce an incoherent and contradictory account—the stories of the Genesis flood and of David's introduction to Saul's court.[1] In both cases I concede that one can make a case for the presence of sources, but, contrary to the claims of source critics, I argue that this does not undermine literary unity and coherence. In the process I identify some of the methodological flaws of source criticism.

---

[1] Kenton Sparks, in his critique of Desmond Alexander's use of Exodus 19–24 as a test case of the legitimacy of source criticism, writes, "There is, in principle, nothing wrong with using test cases to point out the weaknesses of a theory, but when this is done, the test obviously needs to examine actual evidence for the theory to be criticized" (Kenton L. Sparks, *God's Word in Human Words: An Evangelical Appropriation of Critical Biblical Scholarship* [Grand Rapids: Baker Academic, 2008], 158). I have chosen two prime examples of the theory, both of which Sparks cites in support of his thesis that source critics are often correct about the biblical text (see pp. 83–85, 102). In each case I present the source-critical arguments and attempt to show that they are unconvincing.

## The Genesis Account of the Flood

Source critics regard the flood account as a parade example of how two sources (J and P) have been woven together, albeit sloppily. For example, Alexander Rofé confidently asserts that "there are blatant problems of continuity in the story of the flood" and that the story is "rife with duplication and contradiction."[2]

Source critics typically point to the following evidence to support their position:

### Variation in Divine Names
- Yahweh: 6:3, 5–8; 7:1, 5, 16b; 8:20–21.
- Elohim: 6:9, 11–13, 22; 7:9, 16a; 8:1, 15; 9:1, 6, 8, 12, 16–17.

### Doublets[3]
- Yahweh/Elohim sees the wickedness of the earth: 6:5 (J), 11–12 (P).
- Yahweh/Elohim decides to judge the earth: 6:7 (J), 13 (P).
- Command to load the ark: 6:18–21 (P); 7:1–3 (J).
- Noah, family, and animals enter the ark: 7:7–9 (J, redactor), 13–16a (P).
- The flood arrives: 7:10 (J), 11 (P).
- Water rises, and the ark floats: 7:17b (J), 18 (P).
- Total destruction: 7:21 (P), 22–23 (J).
- The flood comes to an end: 8:2b–3a (J), 3b–5 (P).
- Yahweh/Elohim promises no future flood: 8:20–22 (J); 9:11–17 (P).

### Contradictions
- In P Noah brings two of each animal into the ark (6:19–20; 7:15; cf. 7:8–9, attributed to a redactor), while J mentions seven (pairs) of each clean animal (7:2–3).
- Noah and his family enter the ark seven days before the flood in J (7:4, 7, 10), but on the very day the flood begins in P (7:11, 13).
- According to J the flood lasted forty days (7:4, 12), while P suggests it lasted 150 days (7:24).
- According to P the fountains of the deep and the windows of the heavens were the sources of the flood (7:11), while J simply mentions rain as the source (7:4, 12).

---

[2] Alexander Rofé, *Introduction to the Composition of the Pentateuch* (Sheffield: Sheffield Academic, 1999), 19.
[3] For convenience, see the summary in Gordon J. Wenham, *Genesis 1–15*, WBC 1 (Waco, TX: Word, 1987), 167–68.

Table 1 shows the division of the sources, and the attached notes provide a brief explanation for the division in each case.[4]

### Table 1. The division of sources

| J | | P |
|---|---|---|
| 6:1–8 | | 6:9–22[1] |
| 7:1–5[2] | | 7:6[3] |
| 7:7[4] | 7:8–9 (redactor) | |
| 7:10[5] | | 7:11[6] |
| 7:12[7] | | 7:13–16a[8] |
| 7:16b[9] | | 7:17a[10] |
| 7:17a (40 days), 17b[11] | | 7:18–21[12] |
| 7:22–23[13] | | 7:24–8:2a[14] |
| 8:2b–3a[15] | | 8:3b–5[16] |
| 8:6–12[17] | | 8:13a[18] |
| 8:13b[19] | | 8:14–19[20] |
| 8:20–22[21] | | 9:1–17[22] |

[1]Note the use of *Elohim* and the presence of doublets (cf. 6:11–13 with 6:5, 7, J).

[2]Note the use of *Yahweh*, a doublet (cf. 7:1–3 with 6:18–21, P), and a different tradition pertaining to the number of animals (cf. 7:2–3 with 6:19–20, P).

[3]Note the chronology in relation to Noah's age, which links the account to P's chronology in chapter 5.

[4]Note the doublet (cf. 7:13, P).

[5]The reference to seven days links the statement to 7:4 (J).

[6]Note the chronology in relation to Noah's age, and the doublet (cf. 7:10, J).

[7]The reference to the rain falling for forty days links the statement to 7:4 (J).

[8]"On that very day" links the statement with 7:11 (P). Note also the doublet (cf. 7:13–16a with 7:7–9, J/redactor), the use of *Elohim* (7:16a), and the naming of Noah's sons (cf. 7:13 with 5:32 and 6:10, P).

[9]Note the use of *Yahweh*.

[10]Note verbal parallels with 6:17; 7:6b (both P).

[11]Note the reference to forty days (cf. 7:4, 12, J) and the doublet (cf. 7:17b with 7:18, P).

[12]Note doublets (cf. 7:18 with 7:17b, and 7:21 with 7:22–23, J) and verbal links between 7:21 and 6:17 (P).

[13]Note the doublet (cf. 7:22–23 with 7:21, P) and verbal links with 6:7 (J).

[14]Note the alternate chronological scheme (7:24, P), the use of *Elohim* (8:1), and verbal parallels between 8:2 and 7:11 (P).

[15]Note the reference to rain (cf. 8:2b with 7:12, J) and the doublet (cf. 8:2b–3a with 8:1b–2a, P).

[16]Note the alternate chronological scheme (cf. 7:24, P).

[17]Note the return to the earlier chronological scheme emphasizing the numbers seven and forty.

[18]Note the chronology in relation to Noah's age.

[19]Noah's action is the logical conclusion to the action described in 8:12 (J).

[20]Note P's chronological scheme (8:14) and the use of *Elohim* (8:15).

[21]Note the use of *Yahweh*.

[22]Note the use of *Elohim* and the doublet (cf. 9:11–17 with 8:20–22, J).

---

[4]For this division of sources, see E. A. Speiser, *Genesis*, AB (Garden City, NY: Doubleday, 1964), 47–50, 57–58; and Claus Westermann, *Genesis 1–11: A Commentary*, trans. J. J. Scullion (Minneapolis: Augsburg, 1984), 395–96. Westermann (p. 431) sees a redactor's hand in Gen. 7:8–9 (and in portions of 7:3, 23); Speiser (*Genesis*, 48) sees "two of each" as a gloss in 7:9. For a convenient summary of the typical division of sources, see Wenham, *Genesis 1–15*, 167.

In addition to this evidence for sources, critics contend that each individual source is self-contained and coherent, with its own "distinctive beginning, chronology, and ending."[5] To critics the combined version looks suspiciously conflated because it disturbs the supposed coherence of the individual accounts and lacks literary coherence.

The case for the source-critical consensus is overstated. First, when one examines the sources closely, it is apparent that the division is not as neat and clean as critics assume and affirm.

1. 7:7 (J) has P terminology (cf. 6:18).
2. 7:8–9 has J terminology (note the reference to clean and unclean animals; cf. 7:2), but it sounds like P (note the use of *Elohim*) and is a doublet of a later P (!) section (cf. 7:13–16a). Perhaps this is why some attribute it to a redactor. This may seem like a convenient and reasonable safety valve for those committed to the theory, but for those who are not, it rightly generates skepticism about the method being employed.
3. 7:10 (J) has P terminology (cf. 6:17; 7:6).
4. The splicing of 7:16–17 seems rather intricate and complex.
5. 7:18–20 contains a good deal of verbal repetition, but is nevertheless attributed to P in its entirety. Contrast with this the separation of 7:17b from 7:18 on the basis of repetition.

Second, the stories are not as continuous and coherent as claimed.

1. In the J version there is a major gap between the general announcement of judgment in 6:1–8 and the reference to the ark (cf. 7:1). There is no prior reference to either the ark or the flood. Without the P material, the J account appears elliptical.
2. The reference to the Lord shutting in Noah (7:16) is out of order and belongs after verse 7 or 10.[6]
3. The reference to forty days in 7:17 is repetitious and fragmented.
4. Though source critics typically speak of the flood lasting forty days in J, this cannot be, for, as it stands, 8:6 refers not to the end of the flood, but to the receding of the waters (v. 3).[7]
5. The chronology of P does not make sense in 7:6–8:4: The flood prevails for 150 days (7:24), and then the waters abate at the end of 150 days (8:3), but P's timetable puts all this within 150 days (cf. 7:11; 8:3–4). How did the flood prevail for 150 days and the waters abate at the end of that same 150 days?

---

[5]Sparks, *God's Word in Human Words*, 83.
[6]To solve the problem, Westermann, *Genesis 1–11*, 431, 437, moves v. 10 before v. 7 and places v. 16b with v. 7.
[7]For this reason Westermann, *Genesis 1–11*, 447, moves v. 6a before v. 2. While this solves the problem, it is an admission that the J story, as it stands, lacks coherence.

Did the abating of the waters occur on the 150th day? In fact, the chrono-logical problem in P can be reconciled only when the material attributed to P is joined with the forty-day scheme present in J, which makes it clear that a flashback is involved. When the "sources" are combined, the text displays a coherent and masterful literary design at the discourse level (see below).

Having offered a critique of the traditional source-critical approach to the flood story, now I will demonstrate the literary design and coherence of the canonical version of the story. I offer a structural outline accompanied by observations regarding key literary features.

*6:1–8 (Yahweh Section)*
- 6:1–5. Description of human wickedness
- 6:6–7. Yahweh's response
- 6:8. Yahweh's favor to Noah

*6:9–22 (Elohim Section)*
- 6:9–10. Heading and introduction (Noah's character and family)
- 6:11–13. Announcement of divine judgment upon the sinful earth
- 6:14–16. Instructions to build the ark
- 6:17. Announcement of divine judgment upon the earth through a flood
- 6:18. Promise to Noah (covenant)
- 6:19–21. Instructions to bring animals into the ark in pairs
- 6:22. Conclusion (obedience formula)

*Observations*
1. The heading and the shift in divine name mark out this new section formally. The appearance of the name Elohim coupled with the theme of Noah's godly character form an inclusio for the unit 6:9, 22). The use of the name Elohim here may indicate the presence of sources, but it may simply be a structuring device, helping to mark out this unit from the ones that precede and follow it.

2. The narrator uses a technique here that he employs throughout the flood story. He repeats information, but also supplements it with the addition of new details.[8]

a. Human wickedness is described in both 6:5 (J) and 6:11–12 (P), but the latter emphasizes the point through repetition (note the repetition of כל־בשר,

---

[8]This is a form of narrative parallelism that is exactly what one might expect to see in oral litera-ture, where paneling is common. On structuring in oral literature, see H. van Dyke Parunak, "Oral Typesetting: Some Uses of Biblical Structure," *Biblica* 62 (1981): 153–68. See as well Duane Garrett's discussion of repetition in narrative in *Rethinking Genesis* (Grand Rapids: Baker, 1991), 23–25.

חמם, and שחת). Rhetorically, there is a growing sense of human evil, as the already emphatic description of 6:5 is expanded.

b. Both units (6:1–8 and 6:9–22) speak of divine awareness of evil (6:5, 12) and both describe Yahweh/Elohim as speaking (6:7, 13), but in the latter unit he speaks to Noah, whereas in the former unit the speech is internal. This makes sense literarily since Noah was mentioned after the initial reference to seeing and speaking (6:8). The repetition contributes to the theme of the Lord's special favor to Noah—he allows him to be privy to his plan.

c. The first unit simply informs us that Noah found favor in the eyes of Yahweh (6:8), but the second elaborates upon this and provides the basis for this divine response (6:9).

d. *Within* the second unit (P), this same literary technique appears. In 6:13 Elohim announces judgment upon all flesh; in 6:17 he expands this by announcing that the means of judgment will be a flood. In 6:14–16 he makes immediate provision for Noah by instructing him to build an ark; in 6:18 he places this provision within a covenantal framework.

### 7:1–5 (Yahweh section)
- 7:1. Instructions to enter the ark
- 7:2–3. Instructions to bring seven (pairs?) of every clean animal and two of every unclean animal into the ark
- 7:4. Announcement of judgment upon the earth through a flood
- 7:5. Conclusion (obedience formula)

### Observations
1. This new section is formally marked out by a shift in divine name. The appearance of the name Yahweh coupled with the theme of Noah's godly character form an inclusio for the unit (7:1, 5). The use of the name Yahweh here may indicate the presence of sources, but it may simply be a structuring device, helping to mark out this unit from the one that precedes it.

2. The narrator again uses the repeat-and-supplement technique.

a. In 6:7 Yahweh announced he would destroy every creature; here he announces he will accomplish this by sending rain for forty days. In relation to 6:17–18, he now adds a timetable for the flood.

b. In 6:19 Noah was told to bring the animals into the ark in pairs. Here Yahweh specifies that seven (pairs?) of clean animals be brought aboard.

### 7:6–24 (Mixed Section)
- 7:6. Introduction (Noah's age at the time of the flood).
- 7:7. Noah enters the ark (cf. 7:1).

- 7:8–9. Noah brings the animals into the ark in pairs in obedience to Elohim's command (cf. 6:19–21).
- 7:10–12. The flood arrives just as Yahweh predicted (cf. 7:4).
- 7:13. Noah enters the ark on the day the flood begins (cf. 7:7).
- 7:14–16a. Noah brings the animals into the ark in pairs in obedience to Elohim's command (cf. 6:19–21).
- 7:16b. Yahweh shuts Noah into the ark (cf. 7:1, 13).
- 7:17–24. Flood is described in detail (cf. 7:10–12).

*Observations*

1. This new section is formally marked out by an offline, subject-fronted clause (7:6). The appearance of the phrase "waters upon the earth" (מים על־הארץ) in verses 6 and 24 forms an inclusio for the section. (This expression occurs only three times in the Old Testament—in these two verses and in 6:17.)

2. This literary unit exhibits parallelism in the form of corresponding panels: 7:7//7:13; 7:8–9//7:14–16; 7:10–12//7:17–24. The narrator again uses the repeat-and-supplement technique.

a. In 7:7 Noah and his family enter the ark; in 7:13 the number and names of Noah's sons (given earlier; cf. 6:10) are included in the description of entry into the ark. The point is made that they entered the ark on the very day the flood began. It is important to note that Noah did not enter the ark a week before the flood began; 7:13 specifically states otherwise. The command of 7:1 was actually carried out seven days later. The statement in 7:10 does not mean that the flood came seven days after Noah entered the ark (cf. 7:7), but rather that the flood came seven days after Yahweh predicted its arrival (cf. 7:4). Verse 10 is not in sequence with verse 7. It is introduced by ויהי, indicating that it begins a new subunit; it relates back to the statement of verse 4, where "seven days" is last mentioned.

b. The two descriptions of the animals (7:8–9, 14–16) are similar, but the second one is longer (forty-three words in the Hebrew text, compared with twenty-eight words in vv. 8–9). Emphasis is placed on the all-inclusiveness of the animals gathered. The word כל appears just once in 7:8–9, but eight times in verses 14–16. The second section also ends with the observation that Yahweh shut Noah into the ark.

c. The first phase of the flood is the focus of 7:10–12, while 7:17–24, after mentioning the first phase, continues the account of what happened and reports the death of all life.

*8:1–22 (Elohim Section with Yahweh Conclusion)*
- 8:1. Elohim remembers Noah and causes the water to cease.
- 8:2–5. Account of how the waters abated.

- 8:6–12. Noah sends out birds.
- 8:13–14. Account of how the waters dried up.
- 8:15–19. Noah leaves the ark as instructed by Elohim.
- 8:20. Noah offers a sacrifice to Yahweh.
- 8:21–22. Yahweh promises not to destroy the earth again.

### Observations

1. A shift in divine name and a change in theme (from judgment to deliverance) mark the switch to this new unit. References to Noah and the animals being in/leaving the ark form an inclusio for the main narrative (8:1, 19), which tells how the flood ended.

2. There is a flashback at 8:1 with the observation that Elohim remembered Noah.[9] Verses 2–4 record what happened between days 40 and 150. There are actually two perspectives juxtaposed in 7:17–8:14, mirroring 7:10–16. Judgment is the focus of 7:10–12 and 17–24, while provision/deliverance is the theme of 7:13–16 and 8:1–14. The structure of 7:17–8:14 may be outlined as follows:

Judgment (7:17–24)
- Waters increase (רבה) and lift up the ark (v. 17).
- Waters prevail (גבר) and increase greatly (רבה מאד) upon the earth (v. 18).
- Waters prevail greatly (גבר מאד מאד) upon the earth and cover (כסה) the high mountains (vv. 19–20).
- Waters prevail (גבר) upon the earth for 150 days (v. 24).

It is noteworthy how the repetition of the verbs and the use of מאד mirror the reality of the water increasing and covering the earth.[10] Verse 24 is a summary statement for the entire period of judgment.

Provision (8:1–14)
Verse 1 is a summary statement, which tells us that God remembered Noah and sent a wind to remove the water from the earth.[11] The verb

---

[9]Though *wayyiqtol* clauses are most often sequential, sometimes in parallel or supplemental accounts they flash back chronologically to a point prior to where the immediately preceding account ends (see Judg. 2:6; 8:4; 12:1).

[10]B. W. Anderson, "From Analysis to Synthesis: The Interpretation of Genesis 1–11," *JBL* 97 (1978): 35–36.

[11]On the pivotal place of Gen. 8:1 in the structure of the story, see Wenham, *Genesis 1–15*, 156–57. See as well G. J. Wenham, "The Coherence of the Flood Narrative," *VT* 28 (1978): 336–48; and Anderson, "The Interpretation of Genesis 1–11," 36–38. Wenham's case for an intricate chiastic structure for the entire flood story has been challenged by J. A. Emerton, "An Examination of Some Attempts to Defend the Unity of the Flood Narrative: Part Two," *VT* 38 (1988): 6–10. For an insightful critique of Emerton's arguments, see Garrett, *Rethinking Genesis*, 28–29.

שכך describes the cessation of the waters.[12] It assumes the whole process outlined in verses 2–13 and jumps to its culmination in verse 14. Verse 2 begins a detailed account of how the waters abated and disappeared.[13] The events described in verse 1b (the disappearance of the waters as a result of a wind blowing) cannot have occurred prior to what is described in verse 2 (the cessation of the flooding and of the rain).[14]

The process of the waters abating is described as follows:

- Sources of the flood were closed (סכר) (v. 2a) (after forty days, cf. 7:17a).
- Rain was restrained (כלא) (8:2b).
- Waters returned (שוב) from upon the earth (v. 3a).
- Waters abated (חסר) after 150 days (v. 3b), and the ark rested on a mountain (v. 4).
- Waters continued to abate (הלוך וחסור), and the tops of the mountains became visible (v. 5).
- Waters had subsided (קלל) from upon the earth (v. 11).
- Waters were dried up (חרב) (v. 13a); the surface of the ground was dry (חרב) (v. 13b).
- The earth was finally completely dry (יבש) (v. 14).[15]

The progression of various verbs and the repetition of חסר mirror the gradual abating of the floodwaters. The perspective here differs from that of 7:17–24. The floodwaters prevailed for 150 days (from the perspective of judgment outlined in 7:17–24), but they abated from day 40 to day 150 (from the perspective of deliverance outlined in 8:1–14).[16]

## 9:1–17 (Two Elohim Sections, vv. 1–7, 8–17)
- 9:1–7. Elohim gives the mandate to populate the earth.
- 9:8–17. Elohim establishes a covenant with all creatures through Noah.

---

[12]This rare verb occurs only in Est. 2:1; 7:10; and (in the *hiphil* stem) in Num. 17:20 (= English v. 5). Its precise meaning in the Esther passages is difficult to discern (it could mean "lessen, diminish" or "cease entirely, end"). However, usage in Num. 17:20 indicates the latter meaning (note the use of the *piel* of כלה "make an end," as a synonym in v. 25 [= English v. 10]).

[13]This focusing or specifying function of a *wayyiqtol* form after a summary statement is fairly common. Prime examples can be seen in Ruth 1:7, which begins a detailed account of Naomi's return following the summary statement in v. 6 (note the repetition of "returned" in vv. 6, 22), and Ruth 2:3b, which begins a more detailed account of how Ruth came to glean (cf. v. 3a).

[14]Recognizing v. 1 as a summary statement adequately counters the attack against the text's unity made by J. A. Emerton, "An Examination of Some Attempts to Defend the Unity of the Flood Narrative: Part One," *VT* 37 (1987): 403–5.

[15]Anderson, "The Interpretation of Genesis 1–11," 36, points out that dual perspectives are at work in vv. 13–14; v. 13 reflects "Noah's perception," while v. 14 describes it as "objective fact."

[16]See Wenham, *Genesis 1–15*, 183–84.

*Observations*

1. The switch back to Elohim (cf. 8:20–22) marks the beginning of this new unit. The two subunits are delineated by inclusio. Both begin with references to Elohim speaking (vv. 1, 8). The first is bracketed by references to being fruitful and multiplying (vv. 1, 7), while the second begins and ends with references to establishing a covenant (vv. 8, 17).

2. The narrator again uses the repeat-and-supplement technique: In 8:20–22 Yahweh says to himself that he will never again strike (נכה) all living creatures. In 9:8–17 Elohim announces to Noah and his sons that he will never again destroy (שחת) all flesh and formalizes the promise with a covenant.

## David's Introduction to Saul's Court

In 1 Samuel 17–18 the Old Greek version (cf. Codex Vaticanus) differs significantly from the Hebrew text. Entire verses or portions of verses are missing, including 17:12–31, 41, 48b, 50, 55–58; 18:1–6a, 10–11, 12b, 17–19, 21b, 29b–30. In addition to these more substantive differences, there are less significant variations involving just a few words. There are even a few cases where the LXX adds material.[17] The evidence has been interpreted in different ways. Some suggest that the Greek version is the result of deliberate shortening in an attempt to produce a more consistent story that eliminates tensions and doublets. Others argue that the Hebrew text is the product of fusing alternative traditions and doublets.[18] In either case, the assumption is that the Hebrew text is incoherent and that sources have been fused, but not well. The text's own editorial attempts to harmonize the sources (cf. 17:12, 15, 23; 18:2, 21) are dismissed as unconvincing.[19] Sparks, who prefers the view that the Septuagint is deliberately shortened, attributes the fusion of sources to the so-called Deuteronomistic historian, whose "uncritical use of sources" has "produced something well shy of a perfectly accurate account of Israel's past."[20]

---

[17]For a thorough text-critical analysis of 1 Samuel 16–18, see Emanuel Tov, "The Composition of 1 Samuel 16–18 in the Light of the Septuagint Version," in *Empirical Models for Biblical Criticism*, ed. J. H. Tigay (Philadelphia: University of Pennsylvania Press, 1985), 97–130.

[18]For a survey of viewpoints, see Ronald Hendel, "Plural Texts and Literary Criticism: For Instance, 1 Samuel 17," *Text* 23 (2007): 100. For a defense of the view that the LXX represents a distinct source, see Tov, "Composition of 1 Samuel 16–18," 100; and Hendel, 100–101. For a defense of the view that the LXX deliberately abridged the story, see Alexander Rofé, "The Battle of David and Goliath: Folklore, Theology, Eschatology," in *Judaic Perspectives on Ancient Israel*, ed. J. Neusner, B. A. Levine, and E. S. Frerichs (Philadelphia: Fortress, 1987), 119–21.

[19]See, for example, Rofé, "The Battle of David and Goliath," 121–22.

[20]Sparks, *God's Word in Human Words*, 102.

Given the fact that two versions of the story actually do exist, we could conclude that sources were indeed fused and that the Septuagint version represents one such source. The Septuagint does seem to provide a seamless, well-constructed story. Furthermore, the introduction of 17:12–31 seems to intrude (albeit in a pivotal location) into a chiastic structure that encompasses verses 4–11 and 32–40.[21] As noted above, there are also signs of editorial work (17:12, 15, 23 [cf. 8–10]; 18:2, 21).

However, the claim that the story does not cohere is wrong. The main problem is the so-called double introduction of David to Saul. Assuming that 16:14–23 and 17:55–58 cannot be harmonized, critics then find other evidence of incoherence in the longer, Hebrew version of the story. I will now state the critical arguments and respond to each one:[22]

1. *Critical Argument.* David is introduced to Saul for the first time on two occasions: 16:17–23 and 17:55–58 (the latter is not in the LXX). After making the point that the Deuteronomistic historian "seems to have used older sources that sometimes contradicted one another," Sparks states the critical position as follows:

> A good example is found in 2 [*sic*] Samuel 16–17. According to this text, David appears to meet Saul *twice* for the *first* time. In the first instance (2 [*sic*] Sam. 16), David was a warrior-musician who soothed Saul's evil spirit with harp music and subsequently became the king's armor bearer. In the following chapter, however, David appears on the scene again, this time as a shepherd boy unaccustomed to war. When he unexpectedly defeats Goliath in mortal combat, Saul inquired of David, "Whose son are you, young man?" Now how is it that, in this second instance, Saul failed to recognize his favorite musician and chief armor bearer? Is it our modern and critical imagination, or does Saul really meet David twice for the first time? One thing that is certain is that this is not our modern imagination.

After asserting that the LXX "deftly corrected the problem by deleting" the problematic verses, he states, "So, unless Saul was suffering from a serious case of amnesia or senility, it seems that both of these stories cannot be historical."[23]

---

[21] See Johan Lust, "The Story of David and Goliath in Hebrew and in Greek," in Dominique Barthélemy et al., *The Story of David and Goliath: Textual and Literary Criticism*, OBO, 73 (Göttingen: Vandenhoeck & Ruprecht, 1986), 11.

[22] For the critical arguments given below, see Tov, "Composition of 1 Samuel 16–18," 122; Lust, "The Story of David and Goliath," 14; and Antony F. Campbell, *1 Samuel*, FOTL 7 (Grand Rapids: Eerdmans, 2003), 173–74.

[23] Sparks, *God's Word in Human Words*, 102.

*Response.* The critical argument misunderstands the syntax and purpose of Saul's question. In 17:55–58 Saul does not ask for David's name, as if he does not know it. He asks for the identity of David's father, since he promised to grant the family of the father of Goliath's slayer tax-exempt status and to give his daughter in marriage to the victor (17:25).[24] The question בן־מי, "the son of whom?" occurs only in this context (vv. 55–56, 58). The closest syntactical parallel to Saul's question is found in Genesis 24:23–24, where the question בת־מי, "the daughter of whom?" appears (this is the only context in which this question appears). In the story of the servant's quest for a bride for Isaac, the servant's primary concern was the identity of *the father* of Isaac's future bride (24:4). His question to Rebekah means exactly what it says: "Who is your father?" Her answer is exactly what we expect: "I am the daughter of Bethuel" (24:24). In the same way, Saul's question means, "Who is your father?" David's answer is exactly what we expect: "I am the son of your servant Jesse" (1 Sam. 17:58). In neither case is the question equivalent to, "What is *your* name?" or "Who are *you?*" If this had been Saul's intent, he would likely have said מה־שמך (cf. Gen. 32:27; note Jacob's straightforward answer) or מי אתה.[25] If Saul had been merely asking for David's identity, David would have replied, "I am David." Instead, like Rebekah, he identified his father's name because that was what the question asked for, and with good reason in both contexts.[26]

Of course, recognizing the import of the question does not entirely solve the problem. Saul and Abner had heard Jesse's name before (1 Sam. 16:18–22), and one might expect them to have known it. But it is possible they had forgotten it with the passing of time, especially when one realizes that David was only a part-time lyre player (cf. 17:15). More importantly, their ignorance has a literary function in the story. It suggests that David's family, as he himself confessed, was insignificant (18:18, 23). However, at the same time, their ignorance contributes to the narrator's characterization of Saul by depicting him (and his right hand man) as out of touch with God's purposes, in contrast to Samuel (16:1–13), the servant who initially mentioned David to Saul (16:14–23), Jonathan (18:1–5), and the people (18:7). Furthermore, the mention of Jesse's name is ironic literarily, "for it is the house of Jesse

---

[24]See David W. Gooding, "An Approach to the Literary and Textual Problems in the David-Goliath Story: 1 Sam 16–18," in Dominique Barthélemy et al., *The Story of David and Goliath*, 79.
[25]See Gen. 27:18–19 (note Jacob's syntactically straightforward, albeit deceptive, reply "I am Esau"), 32 (note the straightforward reply, "I am your firstborn son, Esau"); and 2 Sam. 1:8. See as well 2 Kings 10:13, where the plural pronoun is used in the question, which receives a straightforward answer of personal identity, and Ruth 3:9, where the question is addressed to Ruth, who answers, "I am Ruth."
[26]One might think that Saul, if seeking Jesse's name, could have simply asked מי אביך, "Who is your father?," or מה שם אביך, "What is your father's name?" But neither question ever appears in the Old Testament.

that has at this moment eclipsed the house of Saul in military prowess, and is destined to supplant it as the reigning house."[27]

Depicting Saul as seeking Jesse's name has yet another literary function. When he sought Jesse's name, the king seemed ready to follow through on his offer to the victor and his family (cf. 17:25), but he quickly backed away from this as he sensed David's growing popularity and he eventually made David risk his life for what rightfully should have been his (18:17–21). When placed in this larger literary context, Saul's inquiry concerning Jesse contributes to the narrator's depiction of Saul as duplicitous.

A further complication is that Saul referred to David as "(this) young man" (נער, 18:55, 58) and "this boy" (עלם, v. 56), such descriptive terms perhaps suggesting that he did not know his name. But Saul's words need not imply this. Earlier he had called David a "young man" (נער) in contrast to the seasoned warrior Goliath, who had been fighting since his youth (מנעוריו, 17:33). His description of David after the battle continues that vein of thought, emphasizing the contrast in age between the victor and his defeated foe and thereby the remarkable nature of David's deed. Some even think that Saul intentionally denigrated David by referring to him in this condescending way and was already showing signs of jealousy and suspicion.[28]

2. *Critical Argument.* Saul offered one of his daughters to David on two occasions: 18:17–19 (not in LXX) and 18:20–27.

*Response:* The text itself (cf. 18:21b, "second time") harmonizes 18:17–19 and 18:20–27. There is nothing inherently improbable about Saul trying this ploy a second time.

3. *Critical Argument:* The first account of Saul's attempt to kill David (18:10–11 [not in LXX]) is misplaced and is virtually repeated in 19:9–10. In the LXX (shorter) version Saul's hatred of and hostility toward David develop gradually; the outburst described in 18:10–11 is premature.

*Response:* Does 18:10–11 really interrupt the narrative, or does it heighten the suspense and drama? (Will such an outburst occur again?) Given Saul's condition, such erratic behavior is not surprising.

4. *Critical Argument:* David and his father, Jesse, are introduced in 17:12 (not in LXX), even though chapter 16 has already identified them.

---

[27] Gooding, "The David-Goliath Story," 80.
[28] See Diana Viklander Edelman, *King Saul in the Historiography of Judah*, JSOTSup 121 (Sheffield: Sheffield Academic, 1991), 133, and Keith Bodner, *1 Samuel: A Narrative Commentary* (Sheffield: Sheffield Phoenix, 2009), 189–90.

*Response:* 17:12 *formally* introduces David and his family, for it is only at this point that he becomes the focal point of the narrative. Samuel is the central character in 16:1–13, while Saul dominates 16:14–23. Indeed David does not speak for the first time in the story until 17:26.

5. *Critical Argument:* David is an armor-bearer and mighty warrior in 16:14–23, but appears as a shepherd in 17:12–31, 55–58 (not in LXX).

*Response:* 17:15 provides an explanation for why David, though an armor bearer, warrior, and court musician, was not at the battle site. Saul's description of David in 17:33 does not necessarily conflict with 16:18. In comparison to Goliath, David was relatively inexperienced. The label "warrior" in 16:18 may reflect David's potential, not reality, but it is certainly justified in light of his accomplishments as a shepherd (cf. 17:34–37, where David reasons that his ability to kill wild animals makes him capable of defeating the Philistine). First Chronicles 12:28, 38 calls Zadok a נער, "young man" (cf. 1 Sam. 17:33) and a גבור חיל, "mighty man of strength" (cf. 1 Sam. 16:18), and includes him among the "men of war" (cf. 1 Sam. 16:18).

6. *Critical Argument:* David is twice made an officer in Saul's army: 18:5 (not in LXX) and 18:13.

*Response:* 18:5, 13 probably refer to different positions in Saul's army. In 18:5 David is promoted from armor bearer (cf. 16:21), while in 18:13 he is elevated to an even higher rank.

7. *Critical Argument:* Saul's dealings with David (as described in 18:20–27) and David's statement of his unworthiness (18:23) are inconsistent with the stated policy of 17:25.

*Response:* Saul's failure to follow through on his promise contributes to the narrator's negative portrayal of him (see above). David's hesitancy (18:18, 23) is certainly understandable in light of 18:10–11. Did David suspect Saul's intentions?

8. *Critical Argument:* Eliab's reaction to David in 17:28 seems inconsistent with 16:13, where he and his brothers witnessed the anointing of David.

*Response:* Should we underestimate the power of human jealousy, especially among siblings (cf. 16:6–7)?

9. *Critical Argument:* Twice we are told that David "killed" the Philistine— once with a sling (and no sword in his hand; cf. 17:50, which is omitted in LXX) and once with the giant's own sword (17:51).

*Response:* The alleged "double killing" of the Philistine in 17:50–51 can be explained reasonably when one takes a closer look at the Hebrew text. In verse 50 a *hiphil* form of מות, "die," is collocated with "he struck down," while in verse 51 a *polel* form of מות is used to describe how David killed the Philistine with the sword. The collocation of verbs in verse 50 has the nuance "dealt a mortal blow." The *polel* of מות (v. 51) is used in eight other passages in the Old Testament. In three poetic texts, it appears to mean, simply, "kill, put to death" (Pss. 34:21; 109:16; Jer. 20:17). But in narrative (all in Judges–Samuel) it appears to have a specialized shade of meaning, referring to finishing off someone who is already mortally wounded (Judg. 9:54; 1 Sam. 14:13; 2 Sam. 1:9–10, 16). Abimelech's statement (Judg. 9:54) is particularly instructive—he asked the armor bearer to kill him (*polel*) because otherwise people would say that a woman killed him (the verb is הרג, "kill"). So who killed Abimelech? Two answers are possible and both are correct—the woman (she delivered a mortal blow that made death certain) and the armor bearer (he delivered the death blow in the technical sense = *polel*). How did David kill the Philistine? Again two answers are possible and both are correct—with a sling stone (David delivered a mortal blow with the sling that made death certain) and with the Philistine's sword, which he used to deliver the deathblow in a technical sense (= *polel*).[29]

Another possible explanation for the "double killing" emerges when one considers the discourse structure of 1 Samuel 17:49–51. Verse 49 uses six *wayyiqtol* clauses to describe how David struck down the Philistine with a sling stone. He reached into the bag, took a stone, and slung it. The stone struck the Philistine and penetrated deep into his forehead, causing him to topple to the ground. The three *wayyiqtol* clauses in verse 50a summarize David's victory: he triumphed over the Philistine with just a sling and a stone, struck him down, and killed him. However, there is more to the story than this. Verses 50b–51 provide a more detailed account of how David actually finished off the Philistine, who was probably unconscious from the blow on his head. The offline, subject-fronted clause in verse 50b takes us back to where verse 49 left off; it reminds us that David had no sword in his hand at the point when the giant fell. Verse 51, using a series of *wayyiqtol* clauses, then tells us that David ran and stood over the Philistine, took the giant's sword, and finished him off by decapitating him. In this case the summary statement of verse 50a looks both backward and forward. The statements "So David triumphed over the Philistine with a sling and a stone" and "he struck

---

[29] Joe Arthur, "Giving David His Due" (PhD diss., Dallas Theological Seminary, 2005), 83–85. See also Gooding, "The David-Goliath Story," 77.

down the Philistine" summarize verse 49, while the phrase "and killed him" is filled out in detail in verses 50b–51.

10. *Critical Argument:* The conflict with the Philistines is introduced twice to the reader (17:1–3, 19 [not in LXX]).

*Response:* There is repetition, but verse 19 may be in discourse; if so, the narrative frame does not repeat itself. Even if verse 19 is part of the narrative frame and is evidence of sources being used, it is simply repetitive and does not result in incoherence.

11. *Critical Argument:* The Philistine champion is introduced twice by name and town (17:4, 23 [not in LXX]).

*Response:* This may be evidence of the merging of sources, but if so, it is simply repetitive and does not produce incoherence. On the other hand, the repetition may be a linking device designed to take us back to the terrifying description of 17:4–7, sort of the narrator's way of saying, "The champion was coming up, Goliath the Philistine was his name, from Gath (and you remember the rest!), from the ranks of the Philistines. . . ."

12. *Critical Argument:* According to 17:54, David took Goliath's head to Jerusalem, but in 17:57 (not in LXX) he still has it in his hand.

*Response:* This is an obvious example of temporal overlay; note the offline construction at 17:55.

13. *Critical Argument:* David is portrayed in a double light as being both faith-filled and ambitious (17:26–27).

*Response:* The ambiguity surrounding David's character persists through-out the story![30]

Some alleged inconsistencies occur within 17:12–31:

14. *Critical Argument:* Jesse had eight sons, according to 17:12 (cf. 16:1–13), but Eliab's statement in 17:28 suggests only four sons (cf. 17:13).

*Response:* Was Eliab really implying that there was no one left at home to care for the sheep or was he exaggerating? Furthermore, in 16:11 David was the only one shepherding. In 17:20 he left the sheep with a keeper. Perhaps the brothers had other duties.

---

[30]See Robert B. Chisholm Jr., "Cracks in the Foundation: Ominous Signs in the David Narrative" (paper presented at the annual meeting for the Evangelical Theological Society, 2008).

15. *Critical Argument:* According to 17:16, Goliath challenged the Israelites to single combat twice a day for forty days after his initial challenge (17:8–11). If a stalemate had developed, why would the Israelites present themselves for battle (17:20)? Why would the Israelites all of a sudden run from Goliath in fear (17:24), if this were just the same routine they had seen on a daily basis?

*Response:* First, when Israel took their battle positions and shouted a war cry (17:20), this would have been a signal to the Philistines that they had rejected the offer of single combat and intended to fight army against army (cf. Isa. 42:13). Second, Goliath's actions, as described in 1 Samuel 17:23, were different from his usual routine. According to 17:3, the armies were on hills with a valley in between. Goliath challenged an Israelite to come down (ירד) to fight him (17:8), indicating that when Israel set their battle lines, they remained on the hill, while he stood in the valley. His usual procedure is described in 17:16: he approached and took his stand. But in 17:23 the narrator grabs our attention (note והנה) and describes him as coming up (עלה). This was a new, more threatening movement.[31] It was this more aggressive movement that frightened the Israelites when they saw it (17:24; notice that they referred to him "coming up" in 17:25). There is a progression in the verbs used of his movements: he came out (v. 4) and stood (v. 8), then later approached and took his position (v. 16), and finally came up as he issued his earlier challenge (v. 23, cf. vv. 8–10). The verbs in verses 4, 8, 16 are *wayyiqtol*s that simply describe what he did, but in verse 23 a participle is used to depict movement and heighten the drama. Goliath was not just standing (vv. 8, 16) and shouting now; if they refused to send somebody down to him (v. 8), he would come up (v. 23)! There is also a change in Israel's response: earlier they were dismayed (חתת) and afraid at his words; now they fled (נוס) and were afraid at the mere sight of him. Of course, literarily their intensifying fear at the intensified aggression of Goliath serves as a foil for David's courage and faith.

## Concluding Reflections

Source critics certainly look closely at textual details, but unfortunately their vision is slanted. Their approach degenerates into a tendentious attack upon the text's unity that is seriously flawed at several levels.

Their analysis of the flood story is hampered by an insensitivity to discourse features.[32] Source critics misinterpret the text's use of repetition, perhaps

---

[31] See David T. Tsumura, *The First Book of Samuel*, NICOT (Grand Rapids: Eerdmans, 2007), 452.

[32] In this regard it is instructive to read Meir Sternberg's scathing critique of the typical source-critical handling of Judg. 4:11, where he argues that its "scissors-happy" approach fails to discern "the laws of discourse." See his *The Poetics of Biblical Narrative* (Bloomington, IN: Indiana University Press, 1985), 280.

because they are programmed to see a simple A-to-Z plotline, instead of a cyclical, repeat-and-supplement style conducive to oral literature. There seems to be little, if any, awareness of fundamental Hebrew narrative techniques such as flashback/temporal overlay, juxtaposed points of view, the strategic use of discourse markers, or the detailed expansion of an initial summary statement. To make matters worse, as they delineate alleged sources, they tend to downplay (by appealing to a redactor) flaws in their own system. Their division of the story into sources actually creates two truncated accounts that need to be combined to attain literary coherence.

The typical critical approach to 1 Samuel 16–18 proves to be even more problematic. A glaring exegetical mistake (the misinterpretation of Saul's question regarding the identity of David's father) becomes a foundation of sand, upon which several weak arguments are then constructed into a house of cards. Once the assumption is made that David was introduced to Saul twice, critics assume the stories cannot be harmonized and point to several textual details that supposedly corroborate this conclusion. On the surface, the list looks imposing, but a closer look reveals a chain made of paper links. A chain made entirely of weak links is no chain at all. The arguments for textual incoherence are superficial and sometimes exegetically flawed. Worse yet, their flawed presupposition causes critics to dismiss the text's own harmonizing statements, all of which are plausible, and to miss discourse features that attest to the story's coherence.

However, beyond these methodological miscues, there is a more fundamental flaw that is particularly alarming. Source criticism, as illustrated by some of the quotations included in this essay, too often approaches the text with an arrogant attitude that essentially says, "If the text does not fit my idea of what literature should look like, then it must be flawed. If it seems incoherent to me, then it must be!" In reality the interpreter's vision is clouded, and his method circular. As we approach these ancient texts, we would do well to listen to Robert Alter, who, in interacting with the typical approach to Numbers 16, admits there seems to be some "confusion" within the story, but then reminds us that there is also "evidence of some careful aesthetic and thematic structuring." Alter concludes with this tongue-in-cheek remark: "All this leads one to suspect that the Hebrew writer may have known what he was doing but that we do not."[33]

In the two texts we have examined, both parade examples for source critics, there may indeed be evidence that the narrators used sources in constructing their stories. But one must not assume that this means the text as it stands is

---

[33]Robert Alter, *The Art of Biblical Narrative* (New York: Basic Books, 1981), 136.

incoherent. While a superficial reading of the stories from the vantage point of one's modern bias might at first suggest this, in reality the ancient narrators, if they did utilize sources, blended them together in a masterful manner. Our job is not to analyze their work from our biased perspective, as if the text is guilty until proven innocent, but to give them the benefit of the doubt and humbly seek to discover the techniques they in fact used to construct the text, whether we are comfortable with them or not.

# 8

# WORD DISTRIBUTION AS AN INDICATOR OF AUTHORIAL INTENTION

## A Study of Genesis 1:1–2:3

### ROBERT D. BERGEN

❈

Summary: Authors of biblical narratives implicitly revealed their communicational intentions by controlling the distribution of lexical items within stories. The intentional placement of lexical items throughout a narrative serves to draw the readers' attention to author-selected thematically central points. This study demonstrates that not only are lexical items and word types unevenly distributed within the semantic subdivisions of Genesis 1:1–2:3, but also lexical items signifying actions, beings, and objects of high value within the writer's community in ancient Israel were present in significantly greater numbers in the thematically central episode, 1:24–31 (the sixth day of creation). These results provide strong evidence that objective, retrievable indicators of an author's communicative intentions are embedded into narrative texts, and that lexical-distribution analysis provides a means to view them.

## Introduction

### General introductory comments

Textual interpretation is a dance involving both an author and a reader. The question in this partnership is, who should lead? Proponents of various postmodern hermeneutical methods suggest that the reader should lead; as a result they have de-emphasized efforts to discern authorial intent. Proponents from the historic Christian evangelical tradition, who have understood God as the Bible's ultimate author and humans as proximate authors, have consistently advocated deferring to the authors. And with good reason: a text is the consciously crafted work of another person, not a limp lump of unworked clay; and interpreters are more visitors touring a museum than studio artists. The current study attempts to examine the text of Genesis 1:1–2:3 as a consciously and purposefully shaped narrative and to use analytic techniques to discern aspects of its communicative intentions.

From a historic Christian evangelical perspective, the Bible is a reliably accurate historical record of the lives of persons mentioned in its narrative passages. Can discourse-level linguistic studies, such as this one, provide proof of a narrative's complete historical veracity? Of course not. What then, if anything, can a study of this nature do to buttress the claim for the historical accuracy of the text? Simply this: discourse-linguistic analyses of biblical Hebrew narrative texts can demonstrate to a reasonable degree that the biblical authors were intentional and precise communicators who produced literature containing recoverable clues that allow for the successful transfer of information to competent readers/auditors. One may plausibly infer from this that the biblical authors maintained a corresponding level of concern for precision and accuracy with respect to historical details included in the narratives.

### Introduction to the essay proper

Theme is classically defined as "the central or dominating idea in a literary work."[1] Underlying this definition is the assumption that an author intentionally highlights some information more than the rest in a literary work. The definition also invites the conclusion that the physical, grammatical, and semantic dimensions of the text contain author-placed hints to assist the audience in identifying the concepts the author deemed most significant. But what sort of clues might authors bake into their literary bread for later readers to find? What mechanisms are employed within biblical Hebrew narrative—and human language systems generally—to assist audiences in reconstructing authorial intention?

Identifying these signals, if indeed they exist, is a relevant task for persons concerned to understand and appreciate the message of the biblical text. The present article, written from a perspective informed by discourse linguistics,[2]

---

[1]Hugh Holman, *A Handbook to Literature*, 3rd ed. (Indianapolis: Odyssey, 1972), s.v. "Theme."

[2]Three publications in the field of discourse linguistics that can serve as introductions to the discipline are Robert E. Longacre, *Joseph: A Story of Divine Providence* (Winona Lake, IN: Eisenbrauns, 1989); John Beekman et al., *The Semantic Structure of Written Communication* (Dallas: Summer Institute of Linguistics, 1981); and Robert D. Bergen, ed., *Biblical Hebrew and Discourse Linguistics* (Dallas: SIL, 1995). Discourse criticism is a form of synchronic biblical text investigation that draws heavily upon language insights gained from the area of discourse linguistics. An introductory article detailing essential aspects of the theory underlying discourse criticism is located in Robert D. Bergen,

seeks to provide evidence detailing one subtle yet significant mechanism involved in the production and transference of meaning in biblical Hebrew narrative from writer to reader.

## Key Linguistic Presuppositions Underlying the Research

Before we proceed with a discussion of the evidence and conclusions, it is appropriate to present some of the most pertinent assumptions about language related to the present topic. These assumptions are drawn from the field of discourse linguistics.

### Narrative texts are composed of both linguistic objects and semantic features; meaningful conclusions about a text's theme can be drawn by analyzing either of these dimensions

Just as a product sitting on a store shelf consists of both packaging and contents, so stories are made up of linguistic objects (e.g., words, clauses, and sentences) and semantic features (e.g., descriptions, ideas, word meanings). As with boxed-up products in a store, a text's linguistic packaging is closely tied to the nature of the semantic product contained in it. Analogous to the fact that a customer can accurately predict the number and approximate size of the items contained in an egg carton by examining the carton's shape and size, a careful analyst can draw useful conclusions regarding a text by paying careful attention to the linguistic objects used to package the story.

### The linguistic objects and semantic structures within a well-formed narrative text are hierarchically organized

Though a shallow reading of canonical Hebrew stories might suggest that they are merely a collection of words or the presentation of a sequence of events and statements, in fact the narratives are far more sophisticated than that. Biblical narratives consist of a dazzlingly complex hierarchy of successively higher levels of organizational features. At the lowest level are letters; letters form syllables, which form words, which form phrases, which are constituents of clauses; clauses constitute sentences, which form paragraphs. Higher aggregate forms include episodes, stories, story collections, and even collections of story collections. Evangelical Christians are also comfortable recognizing

---

"Text as a Guide to Authorial Intention: An Introduction to Discourse Criticism," *JETS* 30 (1987): 327–36. Further information is available in the *Encyclopedia of Hebrew Language and Linguistics*, s.v. "Discourse Linguistics Biblical Hebrew," also by Bergen.

even higher levels of organization, including Testament and Bible.[3] Each successively higher level of textual organization consists of organized groupings of lower-level features, just as a human body is composed of systems that are made up of organs composed of cells, which are themselves composed of subcellular structures formed out of molecules, which are composed of atoms, which are in turn composed of subatomic particles.

The lowest organizational levels of language are solidly grammatical; above the sentence level, however, the distinctive organizational features are usually treated as semantic entities owing to the sheer number of components in them, along with the resulting array of possible combinatory options.

Authors create narrative features such as episodes and stories in part by isolating one series of events from another. Semantically, these divisions within a story are created by manipulating the variables of location, time, and cast. Episodes are created literarily by having sets of events to occur at different locations and/or times, and often through the use of different sets of characters.

### Higher levels of textual organization impose constraints on the size, form, and content of all lower-level features contained within them

Every hierarchical text is shaped by what may be termed *vertical pressure*; higher levels of textual organization play a determinative role in shaping each successively lower order of a text. At the highest level of a narrative, for example, the overarching theme of a story determines the size, order, and content of the episodes. The theme of each episode determines the type and number of events contained in it. The author-determined importance of each event determines the amount of detail provided for it. These paragraph-level considerations in turn affect the number, order, length, and content of constituent sentences; in turn, sentences delimit clause-level features; clause-level considerations affect phrase- and word-level details. Finally, word-level considerations affect syllabic and letter-level issues.

But the level of influence of the higher levels goes further than just influencing the organizational level below it. Each successively lower level is affected by all successively higher levels of a text. Thus, word choice at any point in a well-formed text is an expression of clause-, sentence-, paragraph-, episode-, and story-level considerations.[4]

---

[3] Within Judaism, one might think of a given text as being fixed in the framework of the Law, Former Prophets, Latter Prophets, or the Writings, and, at a higher level, as being part of the Hebrew Bible as a whole.

[4] As an illustration of the ability of a high-level textual feature to dictate a low-level feature, consider the presence of a one-letter prefix added to one word in Gen. 1:31. While each of the accounts of the first six days in the story of the seven days of creation ends with the formula "And there was evening and there was morning, day . . . ," only the formula at the conclusion of day six, the thematically

*Authors mark the relative importance of each portion of a well-formed text using semantic, grammatical, and structural means, and the variables of information amount, type, and order*

Narrative texts are not semantically "flat." Skillful authors construct literary creations so as to make certain sections of their work more attention-grabbing than others. Writers use deliberate semantic inequality in a text to make an audience focus their conscious thought processes on some sections of text more than on others, and thus to consider these author-highlighted portions of a text to be the most important. What's more, good writers drop multiple hints at many different levels of textual organization to make it easier for readers to identify the most important portion of a narrative. This multiplicity of clues will predictably consist of both linguistic objects and semantic content.

Semantically within a narrative these markers almost always take the form of extra details—e.g., notations regarding time, location, weather, sounds, seemingly inconsequential actions, or personal details such as references to emotion, specific body parts, or equipment. The inclusion of these details causes the textual division's word count—a structural feature—to increase, which further increases its prominence.

Predictably, an author-designated key moment in a narrative will also have the most important character or characters present in the action, have abnormal activities take place at a culturally important location and time, and make mention of culturally significant objects. Structurally, these semantic tasks may be marked by the employment of statistically rare vocabulary or abnormal sentence structures. Making explicit references to divine beings (e.g., God, the Angel of the Lord), socially powerful people (e.g., kings, generals, prophets, priests), locations of strategic importance to a society (e.g., Jerusalem, Bethel, Yahweh's temple), and culturally significant times (e.g., famines, times of war, religious festivals, times of sacrifice) automatically gives added importance to the words and events in that textual unit.

Within narrative passages where writers want ideas to be more highlighted than actions, biblical Hebrew authors commonly insert speech events—relatively (or extremely) long quotations spoken by important characters (e.g., Deut. 5:1b–26:19)—into the event line. They may also temporarily abandon the story line to insert an extended narrator comment (e.g., 2 Kings 17:7–23). The interruption of a narrative with nonnarrative material such as descriptions or lists (e.g., Ex. 38:24–31) creates another type of natural highlighting. Nonnarrative passages will be structurally identifiable through

---

central episode, includes the one-letter definite article prefix on the number—i.e., "the-sixth." This prefix sets that otherwise perfunctory episode-ending formula apart from all the others and thereby helps to mark the sixth day as the climactic day of creation.

the employment of clusters of clauses centered on something other than *wayyiqtol* verb forms.

In addition to semantic hints, skilled writers provide grammatical and structural clues designed to mark significant points within a text. These structural indicators can be found at all levels of textual organization. At the word level within biblical Hebrew narrative one may expect to encounter a larger number of words with prepositional and pronominal affixes within the author-designated most prominent section (e.g., Gen. 1:24–31). Also within biblical Hebrew narrative passages where the writer marked the action as especially significant, a higher number of non-Qal stem verbs can be expected (e.g., Gen. 24:18–19). Key passages can also be marked by increased numbers of subordinate clauses (Gen. 31:18–19) and sentences of unusual length (Gen. 19:4) within them. The employment of statistically rare lexical features in a text also has the effect of drawing the reader's attention to the textual zone in which they appear, thus increasing its thematic prominence.

The most freewheeling variable within the language code is that of vocabulary. While any literary genre within a given language may have a dozen standard clause typologies, it will possess thousands of different lexical items. Within a given text, greater diversity and complexity will be present with respect to this variable than any of the others. Not all the words of a given language are considered by its speakers to be of equal semantic significance. Words that describe activities, concepts, or objects that are highly valued by a particular culture elicit a higher interest and response level both for the creator of a text and the text's intended audience than do words that describe culturally mundane items, concepts, and events. For example, the word *gold* possesses a higher interest value in American culture as a whole than does the word *paper*, the verb *win* likewise more than the verb *do*, the word *Dallas* more than the word *Lufkin*. Biblical communicators controlled the employment of lexical features as a means of governing the interest levels within a text. By tracking the distribution of each of the lexical items among the various textual divisions, an analyst can compile evidence for making adequately objective identifications of the author-highlighted information units of a text. Such clarifications can serve as a substantial foundation for making credible decisions regarding textual theme.

Just as location plays a role in the perceived value of a piece of real estate, so information's location within a text plays a role in indicating its relative importance. Within typical narratives authors put their most important episode within the final twenty percent of the episodic units, and the last half (by word count) of the overall text. Thus, a reader can predict that the most important, tense, or exciting portions of a story will be those found in its last several pages. Similarly, in a typical scholarly article, the most important presentation of information is found in its summary and conclusion at the end of the work. However, not every communication task places the most important information last. In the presentation of the divine law code at Mount Sinai the most important laws—the Ten Commandments—are presented first, in much the same way that a newspaper places the most important information in an article at the beginning.

## Collection of Data

### Division of the text into subunits

An essential first step in analyzing a document is identifying the smaller units of material the author created within a text. Depending on the complexity of the ideas or actions presented in the overall text, there will be multiple levels of divisions, and they will be hierarchical in nature. It is as though the writer was composing a document from an outline possessing roman numerals, capital letters, arabic numerals, lowercase letters, and perhaps subpoints below that. These subdivisions—at whatever level—will predictably be of different sizes and possess different content. Thus, in analyzing a document discourse critically it is essential to determine the number and extent of each of the organizational levels the writer built into a text.[5]

Because textual units above the sentence level are most usefully understood as semantic structures, it should come as no surprise that the criteria used for determining the beginning and ending points of these units are also semantic in nature. In nonnarrative materials, the main criterion is similarity of topic. Of course, a meaning-based criterion like "similarity of topic" is by its very nature subjective. As a result, different analysts may subdivide the same text differently.[6] When this occurs, this means that two discourse-linguistic analysts performing word-count based studies and investigating the same text will arrive at conclusions at variance with one another. Needless to say, inconsistency at the point of drawing semantically determined boundaries can prove frustrating and has motivated past analysts to attempt to formulate a universally recognized set of rules for establishing textual margins.[7]

---

[5]If one were analyzing an automobile according to its parts, it would be useful to know how many bolts are present in the overall car, but if one's goal were to determine the most mechanically complex component in the car, it would be even more useful to know how many bolts are in each of the car's components.

[6]This is frustratingly apparent when one compares different commentaries' outlines of the same biblical book or passage.

[7]Such an attempt was made in 1981 by the Summer Institute of Linguistics with the publication of *Semantic Structure of Written Communication*.

To circumvent the subjectivity problem as much as possible, the current study analyzes a passage that has minimally ambiguous unit boundaries. Genesis 1:1–2:3, the story of the seven days of creation, contains clearly defined boundaries at three different hierarchical levels. At the story level, the beginning point is 1:1, which is also the beginning point of the Bible. The story's ending point is 2:3, an unambiguous point since 2:4 begins a "toledoth" section.

A second level of textual organization is apparent just below the story level. Evidence for this is found in an apparent inclusio marked by the statements found in 1:1 and 2:1: "In the beginning God created the heavens and the earth. . . . Thus the heavens and the earth were finished, and all the host of them." Thus, the story of the seven days of creation is composed of two separate units: 1:1–2:1, consisting of the first six days of creation, and 2:2–3, consisting of the seventh day.

A third sharply defined level of textual organization consists of eight sub-divisions. The first is a "stage" (1:2), which functions to identify and position the key participants for the action that follows. The seven "day" episodes (1:3–5, 6–8, 9–13, 14–19, 20–23, 24–31; 2:2–3) embody the narrative's actions. Each of these is unmistakably separated from one another through the sixfold employment of the phrase "And there was evening and there was morning, day . . . ." Listed in table 2 are the partitions utilized in the present analysis of the passage.

A fourth level of textual organization—one that could be termed the "para-graphic" level—is also listed in this chart. However, the criteria for determining paragraphic division points are semantic and highly subjective in nature; the textual breaks were made on the basis of reader-perceived connectedness of activities. Even so, because the same criteria were used in making each para-graphic determination, the divisions should be internally valid. Because of spatial limitations in this chapter, however, only limited analysis is performed on paragraph-level features, and then only in the final part of this presentation.

### Determining word distribution throughout the subunits

The number and location of the various words and word features in Genesis 1:1–2:3 were determined in a multistep process. After the text was divided into its hierarchy of features, each unit was checked for the total number of words present within it. The lexical variety was also investigated for each textual division. Next, the count of different word types was determined: nouns, verbs, conjunctions, and prepositions were all identified and counted within the bounds of each textual subunit. For the purposes of this study it is assumed that the structural dimension of a word consists of its lemma

**Table 2. Textual divisions and word-related data of Genesis 1:1–2:3**

| | 1 | 2 | 3 | 4 | 5 | 6 | 7 | 8 | 9 | 10 | 11 | 12 | 13 | 14 | 15 | 16 | 17 | 18 | 19 |
|---|---|---|---|---|---|---|---|---|---|---|---|---|---|---|---|---|---|---|---|
| Story level | 1:1–2:3 | | | | | | | | | | | | | | | | | | |
| Sublevel 1 "Inclusio" | 1 / 1:1–2:1 | | | | | | | | | | | | | | | | | | 2 / 2:2–3 |
| Sublevel 2 "Episode" | 1 Bracket (I) 1:1 | 2 Stage 1:2 | 3 Ep. 1 1:3–5 | | 4 Ep. 2 1:6–8 | | 5 Ep. 3 1:9–13 | | | 6 Ep. 4 1:14–19 | | 7 Ep. 5 1:20–23 | | 8 Ep. 6 1:24–31 | | | | 9 Bracket (F) 2:1 | 10 Ep. 7 2:2–3 |
| Sublevel 3 "Paragraph" | 1:1 | 1:2 | 1:3–5a | 1:5b | 1:6–8a | 1:8b | 1:9–10 | 1:11–12 | 1:13 | 1:14–18 | 1:19 | 1:20–22 | 1:23 | 1:24–25 | 1:26–31a | 1:31a | 1:31b | 2:1 | 2:2–3 |
| Word count | 7 | 14 | 25 | 6 | 32 | 6 | 25 | 38 | 6 | 63 | 6 | 51 | 6 | 32 | 102 | 9 | 6 | 5 | 30 |
| Lexical variety | 9 | 14 | 17 | 6 | 21 | 6 | 23 | 25 | 6 | 36 | 6 | 37 | 6 | 23 | 53 | 10 | 6 | 8 | 22 |
| Word count | 7 | 14 | 31 | | 38 | | 69 | | | 69 | | 57 | | 149 | | | | 5 | 30 |
| Noun count | 4 | 10 | 16 | | 18 | | 36 | | | 35 | | 26 | | 70 | | | | 3 | 9 |
| Nouns with both a prepositional and pronominal affix | 0 | 0 | 0 | | 0 | | 3 | | | 0 | | 2 | | 10 | | | | 0 | 0 |
| Conjunction count | 1 | 4 | 10 | | 11 | | 17 | | | 20 | | 14 | | 39 | | | | 3 | 8 |
| Preposition count | 1 | 2 | 4 | | 11 | | 11 | | | 22 | | 6 | | 31 | | | | 0 | 6 |
| Adverb count | 0 | 0 | 0 | | 1 | | 2 | | | 1 | | 0 | | 3 | | | | 1 | 1 |
| Verb count | 1 | 2 | 10 | | 10 | | 20 | | | 16 | | 14 | | 30 | | | | 1 | 9 |
| Wayyiqtol verbs | 0 | 0 | 7 | | 8 | | 10 | | | 7 | | 6 | | 13 | | | | 1 | 4 |
| Yiqtol verbs | 0 | 0 | 1 | | 2 | | 3 | | | 3 | | 3 | | 4 | | | | 0 | 0 |
| Qatal verbs | 1 | 1 | 2 | | 0 | | 3 | | | 1 | | 2 | | 6 | | | | 0 | 4 |
| Imperative verbs | 0 | 0 | 0 | | 0 | | 0 | | | 0 | | 0 | | 5 | | | | 0 | 0 |
| Participle verbs | 0 | 1 | 0 | | 0 | | 0 | | | 0 | | 0 | | 2 | | | | 0 | 0 |
| Infinitives | 0 | 0 | 0 | | 0 | | 0 | | | 5 | | 0 | | 0 | | | | 0 | 1 |
| Lexical variety | 9 | 14 | 21 | | 26 | | 43 | | | 40 | | 45 | | 66 | | | | 8 | 22 |
| Lexical concentration | 1 | 6 | 2 | | 4 | | 13 | | | 16 | | 7 | | 38 | | | | 1 | 4 |
| Deity nouns | 1 | 1 | 4 | | 3 | | 5 | | | 4 | | 4 | | 10 | | | | 0 | 3 |
| Non-verb domination words | 0 | 0 | 0 | | 1 | | 1 | | | 7 | | 4 | | 8 | | | | 0 | 0 |
| Extremity words | 0 | 0 | 0 | | 0 | | 0 | | | 0 | | 0 | | 0 | | | | 0 | 0 |
| Fertility, sexuality, and creativity words | 1 | 0 | 0 | | 1 | | 15 | | | 1 | | 6 | | 21 | | | | 0 | 4 |
| Benedictory verbs | 0 | 0 | 0 | | 0 | | 0 | | | 0 | | 1 | | 1 | | | | 0 | 1 |
| Negative words | 0 | 4 | 5 | | 6 | | 2 | | | 9 | | 1 | | 0 | | | | 0 | 2 |
| Termination verbs | 0 | 0 | 0 | | 0 | | 0 | | | 0 | | 0 | | 0 | | | | 1 | 3 |

(i.e., the dictionary entry of the word's core element) and any affixes (i.e., prefixes or suffixes) attached to it. Because in biblical Hebrew certain prefixes (i.e., conjunctive, prepositional, and articular) and suffixes (i.e., object pronoun) are lemmatic in nature—that is, they are treated as separate dictionary entries—these affixes are treated as lemmas and are included in the study.

Verbs received additional scrutiny, since six different structural types were present among the words in the story: *wayyiqtol*, *yiqtol*, *qatal*, imperative, participle, and infinitive verbs were all identified and tallied. The *wayyiqtol* verbs were distinguished from other *yiqtol* (otherwise known as imperfect) verbs, because their function within narrative-genre material is critical; more than any other verb type, they convey the semantic content that moves a narrative's story line forward.[8]

Each of the textual divisions was also checked for the presence of words that fit into certain semantic categories. Categories being investigated included "deity nouns," "domination nouns," "fertility, sexuality, and creativity nouns," "superior-degree nouns," and "negative or subordinative words."

## Presentation and Interpretation of the Results

Written words can be understood to possess four different dimensions: physical,[9] phonetic,[10] structural, and semantic. The current study examines only the structural and semantic aspects of the words in the story of the seven days of creation.

As used in this study the term *structural* refers to the words themselves—the bundled set of letters but not their meaning—and their grammatical features. Included in this dimension of the analysis are the quantity and types of words (e.g., nouns, verbs), as well as the quantity and type of prefixes, lemmas, and suffixes associated with each word.

The semantic dimension of a biblical Hebrew word is the set of meanings assigned to it by those who originally used it. For the purposes of this study it is assumed that the definitions assigned to the lemmas in standard biblical Hebrew lexicons correspond to those assigned to them by the original users of the words. Many words possess different meanings, so that the specific mean-

---

[8]See the writings of Robert E. Longacre, the discourse linguist most responsible for applying discourse-linguistic theory to biblical Hebrew texts, for extensive discussion of this matter; in particular, *Joseph*, 64–82.

[9]The physical includes the means by which the word is recorded. Aspects of this dimension include the size, shape, number, and color of the ink marks that record the word.

[10]The sounds associated with a word and its componential phonemes make up the phonetic dimension, which is also structural in nature. This feature of the words in the text is ignored in the present investigation.

ing of a given instance of a word depends on the context in which it appears. Thus, in many instances it is up to the reader to determine the appropriate meaning for a given word. Obviously, this adds yet another subjectivity component to a textual analysis, though for the purposes of this type of analysis this additional subjectivity is usually inconsequential. The assignment of a word to a particular semantic category (e.g., "extremity") obviously contains a subjective aspect to it as well. Readers are free to decide for themselves if the words were properly categorized for the purposes of this study.

## Analysis of structural aspects of the text
### Word count

Obviously, written narratives and their constituent episodes are made of words. Because an increased word count is a usual side effect of an author's semantic efforts to make one part of a story stand out more than the rest, it follows that comparing the number of words in each textual subdivision will provide evidence for determining the author-designated point of central significance in a story.

The data table provides a division-by-division presentation of the word-count data for the story of the seven days of creation. At the "inclusio" level of textual organization it is clear that the initial portion of the story contains the bulk, almost 94 percent (439 words), of the words in the story. This supplies a clear indicator that the writer intended the readers to find the most important ideas in the opening section of the story.

Within the inclusio itself (Gen. 1:1–2:1), a study of the subdivisions easily reveals that division 8 (1:24–31), the episode detailing the events of day six, significantly outsizes all the others. With 149 words—about 32 percent of the story's overall word count—the day six account is more than twice as large as the next largest episode.

### Lexical variety

Among the 469 words present in Genesis 1:1–2:3, a total of 117 different lemmas, or lexical items, were identified. These items were distributed irregularly throughout divisions of the text. The table above lists the number of different lexical items that occurred within each of the sections of the story. The reader will note that division 8 (1:24–31) is clearly dominant in the story, containing 66 different lexical items. This number exceeds by 21 the total for any other division and represents more than 55 percent of the total number of lemmas present in the story as a whole.

Though these statistics are not decisive in themselves, they nevertheless provide evidence that the creator of the story encoded this division as the most significant one among them all. It can be argued that, by employing such a large portion of the total number of lexical items at least once within division 8, he was attempting to create a heightened interest level in this textual zone. The sheer variety of vocabulary would naturally (though probably subconsciously) have increased the audience's attention and perceived significance level at that point.

*Lexical concentration*
Further evidence of the special degree of highlighting given to Genesis 1:24–31 is provided by the fact that division 8 not only contains the largest proportion of the total lexicon, but it also utilizes more of these words more frequently than any other section of text. A total of 55 of the 66 lemmas present in division 8 were found as frequently in this portion of the text as anywhere else in the story. In 38 instances they occur more frequently here than elsewhere. This latter figure is more than twice as great as the corresponding statistic for any other division. Thus, this division of the text dominates both in the matter of lexical breadth (lexical variety) and in the matter of lexical depth (lexical concentration).

Once again, the clear implication is that the creator of the text was deliberately dropping word-level hints suggesting that the sixth day of creation was to be taken as the primary interest point within the story.

*Verb concentration*
One means of identifying points of author-designated special interest is to locate the textual regions that contain the largest number of verbs. As a rule, the higher the verb count, the more dynamically prominent the section is. It comes as no surprise that division 8, the textual region with the greatest number of words, also has the most verbs. Its 30 verbs are 50 percent more than in any other section. As indicated in the data table, the division with the second highest verb count is division 5, which contains 20 verbs.

To discover further aspects of the verbal dimension of a text, it is instructive to examine the distribution of the six different verb types throughout the text. Because in biblical Hebrew narrative the *wayyiqtol* verbs are the primary carriers of the event-line, it can safely be assumed that the textual zone with the greatest number of third-person *wayyiqtol* verbs is the portion of a story containing the greatest number of events. Authors of stories highlight episodes they consider to be most important by including more events in them. As the data table indicates, division 8 has 13 of these—30 percent more than the second-place division (division 5).

Imperative verbs are also of interest, because they are the least ambiguous verb form utilized for the conveyance of hortatory discourse.[11] Within biblical Hebrew narrative, true imperative verbs are found only in direct speech. Thus, identifying the location of imperative verbs within a narrative text simultaneously identifies zones in which a member of the narrative cast is expressing behavioral guidelines. Because imperative verbs also express an elevated level of urgency, their presence in a textual zone can also be an indicator of that zone's intentionally elevated significance. Within the ten divisions of Genesis 1:1–2:3, only two contain imperatives, divisions 7 and 8. Not surprisingly division 8 contains the majority of these—5, versus 3 for division 7.

Perhaps of significance is the fact that no infinitives are present in division 8. As nonfinite verbs, infinitive constructs might be considered more static in nature. Thus, their absence from the most important textual division might have resulted from the writer's desire to maintain a higher level of "dynamicity" for this stretch of text.

*Noun concentration*
The single most commonly occurring word type in biblical Hebrew narrative is the noun. A total of 54 different noun lemmas are present in Genesis 1:1–2:3. These are distributed unevenly throughout its ten textual divisions. These lexical items are used varying numbers of times, ranging from 1 (e.g., *rēʾšît*) to 35 (*ʾĕlōhîm*) times.

In keeping with the word-distribution pattern noted in all the data to this point, division 8 also contains the largest number of noun words. A total of 70 nouns are present in this textual unit. This number represents 47 percent of the division's 149 words. While this figure is a substantial percentage of the overall words, the noun/word-count ratio is smaller in division 8 than in seven other divisions (1 [57 percent], 2 [71 percent], 3 [52 percent], 4 [47.4 percent], 5 [52 percent], 6 [51 percent], 9 [60 percent]). The three highest ratios are found in the least dynamic portions of the story: the initial and final brackets, and the stage. The data reinforces the conviction that at some level of consciousness the Hebrew writer manipulated the distribution of word types to make certain portions of a story feel more static and others more vivid.

Biblical Hebrew nouns are capable of having prepositional and pronominal affixes added to them. Depending on one's criteria, the most complex and semantically laden noun words in Genesis 1:1–2:3 are those that contain both a prepositional prefix and a pronominal suffix, since they are also necessarily "definite" and in the construct state.[12] Identifying the zones with the highest

---

[11]See Longacre, *Joseph*, 121.
[12]A hyper-literal translation of one such word, *leminâh*, would be "to the species of her."

number of these types of words provides evidence of an author's attempt to create a highlighted region. This is so because complex words require additional mental processing, necessarily resulting in readers paying greater attention to textual zones where "difficult" words are present. As the data table reveals, only 3 textual divisions have any words of this variety. Division 8 contains 10 such words—more than 3 times the number present in division 5, the zone with the next highest count. The dominating presence of this comparatively sophisticated noun form in division 8 simply adds one more type of author-created distinction to an already highly marked textual zone.

*Conjunction, preposition, and adverb concentration*
Conjunctions occur in biblical Hebrew either as prefixes or as individual words. Because of this, the number of conjunctions in a textual unit is indirectly tied to the number of words in a text. A total of 127 conjunction features are present in Genesis 1:1–2:3; they occur either as prefixes (*w-* or *wa-*) or as independent words (*ʾašer, kî*). As with all other word categories discussed to this point, conjunctions are not evenly distributed throughout the ten divisions. As one might expect at this point in the investigation, division 8 contains the greatest number of this category of feature; its 39 conjunctions almost double those of division 6, which has 20. Furthermore, all three types of conjunctions are present in this section of text, a distinction shared with only one other division, division 5 (1:9–13).

Prepositions, like conjunctions, are present in biblical Hebrew both in the form of prefixes and as separate words. Assuming *kᵉ-* is treated in its traditional way as a preposition, and *mi-* and *min* are treated as separate prepositions, 9 different prepositions are represented in the textual corpus of Genesis 1:1–2:3 (*ʾel, bᵉ-, bên, k-, lᵉ-, mi-, min, ʿal, taḥat*). The presence of prepositions—and therefore prepositional phrases—in a unit of material suggests the presence of more complex clauses and sentences. These in turn are indicators of more carefully described details and thus semantic highlighting. As expected, division 8 possesses the largest number of prepositions. Its tally of 31 prepositions is 41 percent higher than that of division 6, which has the next highest total.

Like prepositions, adverbs play the role of modifiers, creating a more complex clause or sentence. Three different adverb words are employed in Genesis 1:1–2:3, *kēn, hinnēh,* and *mᵉʾōd.* These are present in six different textual divisions. Only two of these sections, divisions 5 and 8, have more than one adverb; and of these two, division 8 has the most, with 3. What's more, only division 8 contains all 3 of the adverb words.

*Analysis of semantic aspects of the text*

By studying the distribution of words belonging to different semantic categories, we may gain a more well-defined profile of the author-intended significance of each of the divisions. The next portion of the study examines the
lexical distribution associated with selected semantic categories and draws
conclusions based on the evidence.

*Deity references*

Within the culture out of which the written account of the seven days of
creation came, perhaps the most important class of lexical materials was the
one that included nouns referencing the Israelite deity and his supernatural
and physical manifestations. Israel's God was considered the most important
being in the universe; thus his mention in any portion of a narrative automatically made that section of a text stand out. Since 9 of the 10 divisions
in Genesis 1:1–2:3 mention *ᵉlōhîm* (only division 9 lacks this), the dominant
section would be the one that has the largest number of references. The single
lemma present in Genesis 1:1–2:3 belonging to this class is *ᵉlōhîm*. The word
occurs 35 times and is distributed throughout the divisions as indicated in
the data table.

As one might expect, division 8 predominates in this all-important semantic
category, possessing 10 occurrences (about 29 percent) of the usages of the
generic term for deity. This total is exactly twice the count found in the highest of the other divisions. Completely apart from other considerations, the
concentration of this one lemma encourages the conclusion that the author
was attempting to guide the reader's attention primarily to this section of text.

*Verbs connoting domination or control*

As indicated in the data table, four verbal items within the story lexicon express
actional domination: *kābaš* ("to make subservient"), *mālē'* ("to fill"), *māšal*
("to rule"), and *rādâ* ("to rule").

In keeping with the pattern observed elsewhere, division 8 tops the domination category. Four of the 6 uses of words fitting this semantic category
are present in this portion of the story. The clustering of these words in the
account of the sixth day of creation helps to produce the sense within the
reader that this portion of the story is more important than others, even
though the author never explicitly states this is so.

*Verbs connoting creativity, fertility, and procreativity*

Another semantic class that has particular significance in any culture is that
containing creativity, fertility, and procreativity words. In a story that deals with

the creation of life, it is not surprising that a comparatively large number of such words would be present. The six words included in this category are: *bārā'* ("to create"), *zāra'* (hiphil stem, "to produce seed"), *yāṣā'* (hiphil stem, "to bring forth"), *'āśâ* ("to make"), *pārâ* ("to be fruitful"), and *rābâ* ("to become numerous"). The data table presents the distribution of this semantic word category by textual division. Evidence presented in the data table suggests that division 8 is also the textual region of greatest creative focus. This zone also contains fully half of the usages of *bārā'*, the word exclusively relating to divine creative activity.

## Non-verb words connoting superior degree

Apart from deity reference nouns, 4 words that possess the connotation of totality or superior degree are present in the story of the seven days of creation. The words that fit this category are *gādōl* ("great"), *kōl* ("all"), *mᵉ'ōd* ("very"), and *memšelet* ("ruler").

Of the 23 occurrences of words of this category, 13 (57 percent) of them were present in division 8. The practical effect of creating this distributional imbalance is conveyance of the concept that 1:24–31 is unusually significant.

## Non-verbs possessing negative or subordinative connotations

The employment of words with negative or subordinative connotations serves as an effective means by which an author can control theme production in a text, since such words tend subtly to subdue an audience's emotional response to the textual units in which they are found. I understand 7 of the 117 elements of the story lexicon to belong to the general category termed "negative or subordinative." These 7 words are: *bōhû* ("emptiness"), *ḥōšek* ("darkness"), *laylâ* ("night"), *qāṭōn* ("small"), *tᵉhôm* ("primeval ocean"), *tōhû* ("wasteland"), and *tannîn* ("sea monster"). The distribution of each of this word group is indicated in the data table. The reader will note that three of the seven "day" episodes (divisions 3, 6, 7) contain at least one negative or subordinative word. Excluded from this short list is division 8, day six.

One can infer from this observation that the creator of this text was making a deliberate and skillful attempt to avoid casting a semantic shadow on division 8. When combined with the previously established evidence, the absence of "shadow words" in division 8 serves as a corroborative indicator of the author's intention to identify this region as the thematic center of the text.

## Resulting theme focus

From the study of lexical distribution presented above, the unavoidable conclusion is that the stretch of text in Genesis 1:24–31 was encoded by the author as the center of interest. According to the assumptions of discourse criticism this section will contain the thematically central materials of the story.

A content study of division 8 suggests that the following ideas are central within the story:

- God caused the earth to create all sorts of land animals.
- God created humanity, male and female, in his image.
- God blessed humanity and commissioned them to take charge over all his earthly creations.
- God commanded all persons and animals to be herbivorous.
- God evaluated the totality of his creative work as very good.

Are some of these ideas more central to the episode—and therefore to the work as a whole—than others? Undoubtedly. If so, can a study of lexical distribution provide more definitive answers to the question of overall theme than this? Intuitively, I would answer the question in the affirmative.

After dividing the episode into smaller units, a lexical-distribution analysis could be performed on the subunits. In the case of 1:24–31, this might involve separating events directly associated with the creation of land animals (vv. 24–25) from those associated with humanity's creation and commissioning (vv. 26–30) and God's evaluation of his creative efforts (v. 31).

A lexical-distribution analysis performed on these three subsections would clearly reveal that verses 26–30 were most significantly highlighted. Evidence for this is found, for example, in the fact that this subzone of division 8 contains 102 of the division's 149 words, 6 of its 10 deity references, 20 of its 30 verbs, and all of its imperative verbs and domination nouns. The interpretive criteria associated with discourse criticism suggests unambiguously that the text's author intended the creation of humanity in God's image and the divine commissioning/blessing of humanity to be the most significant events in creation.

For this study to be complete, Genesis 1:1–2:3 would also need to be studied as a component in its larger contexts. The story is in at least three higher-level units of material: the Torah, the Hebrew Bible, and the Christian Bible. Only when its contribution to each of these overarching literary contexts is fully examined is a textlinguistic study of the story of the seven days of creation complete. Of course, such a study is beyond the purview of this limited work.

## Conclusions, with Implications for Biblical Studies

The preceding study has provided evidence that discreet distribution of vocabulary, word types, and verb forms within a narrative is a device by which theme is produced in text. To be sure, word distribution is only one means among many by which an author is able to control the focus of an audience's thought processes. Through the use of this and other normally subliminal devices in the communication process, the creator of a text is able with demonstrable success to cause the audience to replicate his or her own ideas—that is, substantially to rethink the thoughts of the author.

Responsible textual interpretation requires that readers find and follow author-supplied guide stones in their quest for a text's meaning. Recognizing the existence of subtle word-level theme-production devices is an essential step in understanding how effective authors guide readers in their interaction with text. Successful authors throughout history—the biblical writers among them—have reduced the subjective element in textual interpretation by discreetly distributing a variety of word-level markers within a text. Careful use of word-level distribution analysis, as well as other methodologies based on the assumptions of discourse linguistics, promises to bring about a greater understanding and appreciation of the mystery that is God's Word in human words.

# 9

# THE CULTURE OF PROPHECY
# AND WRITING
# IN THE ANCIENT NEAR EAST

## JOHN W. HILBER

✺

## Introduction

The 1980s witnessed a paradigm shift in many facets of Old Testament studies, and research into the prophets and their writings proved no exception.
One of the best-known signals of change was Auld's 1983 essay "Prophets
through the Looking Glass," applauded in a response paper by Robert Carroll,
"Poets Not Prophets: A Response to 'Prophets through the Looking Glass.'"[1]
Auld argued that diachronic changes in the terminology for prophetic functionaries, coupled with evidence of thorough Deuteronomistic editing in
prophetic books such as Jeremiah, cast doubt on whether the individuals
whose names appear at the head of these books were properly "prophets"
in the first place and whether their original words, uttered in poetic oracles,
can be reliably gleaned from the present form of the text. The implications
of Auld's paper for the authenticity of prophetic speech were clarified by
Carroll's response.

> We will have to rewrite the history and structure of prophecy. The role of the
> redactor's ideology . . . will be seen as having a much more creative and construc-
> tive part to play in the emergence of the traditions than has often been allowed
> in the past. . . . The original poets were free spirits, poets of the imagination,
> denouncing the social structures of their own time but through redactional
> transformation have become conventional "prophets," a fixed form of institu-

---

[1]A. Graeme Auld, "Prophets through the Looking Glass: Between Writings and Moses," *JSOT* 27
(1983): 3–23; Robert Carroll, "Poets Not Prophets: A Response to 'Prophets Through the Looking-
Glass,'" *JSOT* 27 (1983): 25–31. Williamson's cogent rebuttal is rarely acknowledged (H. G. M.
Williamson, "A Response to A. G. Auld," *JSOT* 27 [1983]: 33–39).

tional activity, and thereby made to serve purposes which they themselves might very well have despised (even denounced on occasions)![2]

This position has become an assumed starting point in many discussions[3] and indeed is similar to the view shared by much of European scholarship since the early twentieth century.[4] Along with disconnection of prophetic books from original prophets, new sociological methods have challenged the reliability of traditional historical reconstruction, leading to a search of how new performance contexts (particularly postexilic) changed the words of the original prophets or enlisted their legendary names in new scribal fabrications.[5]

What relationship, if any, do Old Testament prophetic books have to the individual prophets whose messages they purport to preserve? Several issues are relevant to this question: (1) the general credibility of the Old Testament's portrait of prophetic phenomena; (2) the relationship between prophetic speech and writing; (3) the cultural ethos surrounding the transmission of prophetic speech. In spite of numerous publications on this subject, the close connection between prophecy and writing in the ancient Near East still receives insufficient regard. The purpose of this essay is to redress what I perceive to

---

[2]Carroll, "Poets Not Prophets: A Response to 'Prophets Through the Looking-Glass,'" 27–28. See Auld's affirmation ("Prophets Through the Looking Glass: A Response to Robert Carroll and Hugh Williamson," 41).

[3]E.g., Ferdinand E. Deist, "The Prophets: Are We Heading for a Paradigm Switch?," in *Prophet und Prophetenbuch: Festschrift für Otto Kaiser zum 65. Geburtstag*, ed. V. Fritz and K.-F. Pohlmann, BZAW 185 (Berlin: de Gruyter, 1989), 1–18; Robert R. Wilson, "Current Issues in the Study of Old Testament Prophecy," in *Inspired Speech: Prophecy in the Ancient Near East (Essays in Honour of Herbert B. Huffmon)*, ed. John Kaltner and Louis Stulman, JSOTSup 378 (London: T&T Clark, 2004), 40–41.

[4]Examples cited by Hans M. Barstad, "No Prophets? Recent Developments in Biblical Research and Ancient Near Eastern Prophecy," *JSOT* 57 (1993): 39–43; Robert P. Gordon, "Where Have All the Prophets Gone? The 'Disappearing' Israelite Prophet Against the Background of Ancient Near Eastern Prophecy," *BBR* 5 (1995): 69–70; and Jean-Georges Heintz, "La 'fin' des prophètes bibliques? Nouvelles théories et documents sémitiques anciens," in *Oracles et prophéties dans l'antiquité: Actes du colloque de Strasbourg 15–17 Juin 1995*, ed. Jean-Georges Heintz, Travaux du Centre de Recherche sur le Proche-Orient et la Grèce Antiques 15 (Paris: Universite des Sciences Humaines de Strasbourg, 1997), 195–96.

[5]Deist, "The Prophets: Are We Heading for a Paradigm Switch?" E.g., the institution of prophecy is a scribal creation (Philip R. Davies, "'Pen of iron, point of diamond' [Jer. 17:1]: Prophecy as Writing," in *Writings and Speech in Israelite and Ancient Near Eastern Prophecy*, ed. Ehud Ben Zvi, Michael H. Floyd, and Christopher R. Matthews, SBLSymS 10 [Atlanta: Society of Biblical Literature, 2000], 65–81). Biblical prophets are fictive, literary constructs (Ernst Axel Knauf, "Prophets That Never Were," in *Gott und Mensch im Dialog: Festschrift für Otto Kaiser zum 80. Geburtstag*, ed. Markus Witte, BZAW 345/1 [Berlin: de Gruyter, 2004], 451–56). Even if texts once existed that recorded preexilic prophecy, their contribution became lost in a new matrix of postexilic literature (Ehud Ben Zvi, "The Concept of Prophetic Books and Its Historical Setting," in *The Production of Prophecy: Constructing Prophecy and Prophets in Yehud*, ed. Diana V. Edelman and Ehud Ben Zvi [London: Equinox, 2009], 73–95).

be an imbalance in the way the evidence is commonly interpreted, building upon earlier efforts in this regard.[6]

## Prophetic Phenomena

Throughout the twentieth century, it was customary in Old Testament scholarship to distinguish biblical prophets from their Canaanite and Mesopotamian counterparts by contrasting the superior nature of the biblical prophets and the repugnant excesses of pagan ecstatics. The reality is more complex. We now possess approximately 150 individual texts containing prophetic speech or describing prophetism from Ur, Mari, Babylon, Eshnunna, Biblos, Hatti, Ugarit, Emar, Assyria, Amman, Hamath, Deir 'Alla, and Egypt, spanning from the late third millennium down to the third century BC.[7] In the light of fuller publication of texts, features of prophetism that used to set the biblical prophets apart have been identified among non-Israelite prophets. In 2004, Wilson posed the question currently being asked by many: "To what extent can the distinctive character and theological or ethical value of Israelite prophecy still be maintained when there is accumulating evidence to suggest that Israel's prophets were not all that different from similar figures attested in surrounding cultures?"[8] Much could be said outside the scope of this essay regarding theological and ethical differences, but Gordon's conclusion offers a fair assessment: "In the end the difference between Israelite prophecy and the rest may simply have to be expressed in terms of its conception of its God."[9]

The following survey itemizes the most striking similarities:[10]

---

[6]See Alan R. Millard, "La prophétie et l'écriture: Israël, Aram, Assyrie," *RHR* 202 (1985): 125–45; Barstad, "No Prophets? Recent Developments"; and Gordon, "Where Have All the Prophets Gone?"

[7]For convenient access to almost all sources with commentary, see Martti Nissinen, C. L. Seow, and Robert K. Ritner, *Prophets and Prophecy in the Ancient Near East*, SBLWAW 12 (Atlanta: Society of Biblical Literature, 2003). Specific citations below are by pages; larger passages are by text numbers, the latter indicated by "no(s)."

[8]Wilson, "Current Issues," 39.

[9]Gordon, "Where Have All the Prophets Gone?," 86. Huffmon reminds us that general comparisons often mask important nuances (Herbert B. Huffmon, "A Company of Prophets: Mari, Assyria, Israel," in *Prophecy in Its Ancient Near Eastern Context: Mesopotamian, Biblical, and Arabian Perspectives*, ed. Martti Nissinen, SBLSymS 13 [Atlanta: Society of Biblical Literature, 2000], 47–48, 70); a concern with which Gordon would no doubt agree.

[10]The comparisons from Mari are largely dependent on Robert P. Gordon, "From Mari to Moses: Prophecy at Mari and in Ancient Israel," in *Of Prophets' Visions and the Wisdom of Sages: Essays in Honour of R. Norman Whybray on his Seventieth Birthday*, ed. Heather A. McKay and David J. A. Clines, JSOTSup 162 (Sheffield: JSOT, 1993), 63–79; Gordon, "Where Have All the Prophets Gone?" For Neo-Assyrian prophecy, see Martti Nissinen, "Die Relevanz der neuassyrischen Prophetie für die alttestamentliche Forschung," in *Mesopotamica, Ugaritica, Biblica: Festschrift für Kurt Bergerhof zur Vollendung seines 70. Lebensjahres am 7. Mai, 1992*, ed. Manfred Dietrich and Oswald Loretz, AOAT 232 (Kevelaer: Butzon and Bercker, 1993), 217–58; Martti Nissinen,

JOHN W. HILBER

1. *Ecstatic Behavior* (Num. 11:25–29; 1 Sam. 10:5–13 with 19:18–24; Jer. 29:26?; Byblos [Wenamon]; Ugarit [RS 25.460]; Mesopotamia [*muḫḫu*, ARM 26.214, 222 for verbal form])

2. *Access to Divine Council* (1 Kings 22:19; Isaiah 6; Jer. 23:22; ARM 26.196, 208; Deir 'Alla Plaster; SAA 9.9 [indirectly]; SAA 12.69)

3. *Groups of Prophets* (1 Sam. 10:5–13; 1 Kings 20:35; 22:6; 2 Kings 2:3, 7; 4:38; 6:1; ARM 26.216 [*nābû*]; ARM 27.32)

4. *Prophecy and Dreams* (Joel 2:28; ARM 26.227, 237, 234; Assurbanipal Prism B v 49; Archive of Hor no. 23)

5. *Symbolic Acts* (Isaiah 20; Jer. 13:1–11; 19; 32:6–15; Ezek. 4; ARM 26.206)

6. *Music and Prophecy* (1 Sam. 10:5–13; 2 Kings 3:15; Ritual Text of Ishtar A. 3165 ii 17–21 and A. 1249)

7. *Prophetic "Burden"* (Isa. 21:3; Jer. 23:9; Hab. 3:16; ARM 26.234; Deir 'Alla Plaster)

8. *Response to Inquiry or Lament* (1 Kings 22:5–12; 2 Kings 3:11–12; 2 Chronicles 20; Psalms 12; 60; Isaiah 37–38; ARM 26.207, 212, 216; Hittite plague prayers; Zakkur stele; Assurbanipal Prism B v 46–49; SAA 3.13, 31; SAA 9.1.8; SAA 10.294)

9. *Divine Letters* (Jer. 29:1–32; 36:1–8; 51:59–64; ARM 26.194; FLP 1674 and 2064; SAA 3.47)

10. *Speech Forms* (messenger formulas; "fear not"; self-reference of deity; salvation oracle forms [e.g., speeches of SAA 9 with Isaiah 40–48; Psalm 110]; imagery)

11. *Prophets and Scribes* (Jer. 36:4; ARM 26.414; redacted oracle collections in SAA 9)

12. *Gifts and Royal Support* (1 Kings 14:3; 2 Kings 8:8–9; court prophets Nathan and Isaiah; ARM 9.22; 21.333; 26.199, 206; SAA 10.109)

13. *Promise and Fulfillment* (Deut. 18:21–22; Isa. 41:21–29; 42:9; 48:12–16; Jer. 32:6–8; Ezek. 33:33; SAA 9.1.1 i 15–17; 9.1.4 ii 37; 9.1.10 vi 3–12; 9.2.2 i 17; cf. ARM 26.199)

14. *Prophetic Conflict and True/False Prophecy* (1 Kings 22; Jeremiah 23; 28; SAA 16.60, 61; cf. ARM 26.199, where prophet confirms prophet)

15. *Public Proclamations* (1 Kings 13:1–3; Jer. 7:1–2; Ezek. 14:1–5; Amos 7:10–13; ARM 26.206, 208, 371; SAA 9.3.2; SAA 10.352)

16. *Cultic Admonitions* (Mal. 1:6–14; Psalm 50; ARM 26.206, 215, 220, 221; SAA 9.2.3 ii 24–27; 9.3.5 iii 26–27; SAA 13.144)

17. *Call to Piety* (Mic. 6:8; Zeph. 2:3; SAA 9.1.4 ii 28–29; 9.2.3 ii 17–27; 9.2.6 iv 8)

18. *Royal Admonition* (1 Kings 14:7–16; Amos 7:7; Zeph. 1:8; Mari A.1121+; A.1968; ARM 26.194, 199; cf. SAA 2.6 §10 lines 16–17)

---

"The Socioreligious Role of the Neo-Assyrian Prophets," in Nissinen, *Prophecy in Its Ancient Near Eastern Context*, 89–114; and John W. Hilber, *Cultic Prophecy in the Psalms*, BZAW 352 (Berlin: de Gruyter, 2005), 40–75, 219–21.

19. *Kingship Ideology and Royal Covenants* (2 Sam. 7; 1 Kings 1 [cf. 2 Kings 11]; Psalms 2; 89; 110; 132; Mari A.1121+; A.1968; SAA 9.3)

20. *Social Admonition* (Isa. 1:17; Amos 5:15; Mari A.1121+ A.2731; A.1968; ARM 26.194 [edict of restoration], 206?, 232)[11]

The prophetic portrait from the Old Testament coheres with prophetic phenomena across the ancient Near East, including Neo-Assyrian sources from precisely the time of the classical prophets. This demonstrates historical plausibility in the Old Testament witness to preexilic prophecy.[12]

## Prophecy and Writing

The writing of oral proclamations was common in the ancient Near East, whether the announcement of a legal contract in a city gate or the publication of the affairs of state; and prophecy shared in this practice,[13] along with most other forms of divination (e.g., extispicy, omens, dreams).[14] The royal archives from Mari and Nineveh in particular reveal something of the process whereby oral prophecy came into writing. Also relevant to this discussion are divine letters and the preservation of royal cultic prophecy in Egypt, particularly because some prophecy did not necessarily originate orally but may have been a written form of revelation that was subsequently performed orally. This has important implications for how we view the generation of some Old Testament prophetic writings.[15]

### Prophecy in Correspondence
### Mari

Letters and other administrative documents from the eighteenth-century BC royal archive at Mari disclose much about prophecy in early Mesopotamia.[16]

[11]See Martti Nissinen, "Das kritische Potential in der altorientalischen Prophetie," in *Propheten in Mari, Assyrien und Israel*, ed. Matthias Köckert and Martti Nissinen, FRLANT 201 (Göttingen: Vandenhoeck & Ruprecht, 2003), 1–32.

[12]Gordon, "From Mari to Moses," 79; Gordon, "Where Have All the Prophets Gone?," 85–86, whose conclusions are now strengthened by Neo-Assyrian sources.

[13]Alan R. Millard, "Oral Proclamation and Written Record: Spreading and Preserving Information in Ancient Israel," in *Michael: Historical, Epigraphical and Biblical Studies in Honor of Prof. Michael Heltzer*, ed. Avishur Yitzhak and Robert Deutsch (Tel Aviv-Jaffa: Archaeological Center Publications, 1999), 237–41.

[14]Millard, "La prophétie et l'écriture: Israël, Aram, Assyrie," 129–31.

[15]The following adapts Nissinen's organization by genre (Martti Nissinen, "Spoken, Written, Quoted, and Invented: Orality and Writtenness in Ancient Near Eastern Prophecy," in Ben Zvi, Floyd, and Matthews, *Writings and Speech*, 235–71).

[16]For an overview, see Huffmon, "A Company of Prophets: Mari, Assyria, Israel," 49–56; Karel van der Toorn, "From Oral to the Written: The Case of Old Babylonian Prophecy," in Ben Zvi, Floyd, and Matthews, *Writings and Speech*, 219–34; Dominique Charpin, "Prophètes et rois dans le Proche-Orient

Revelations came to variously titled functionaries by an intuitive cognitive process,[17] sometimes in a dream[18] or a vision (e.g., ARM 26.227, 229, 233, 235, 236, 237, 238), in conjunction with sacrifice (e.g., ARM 26.209, 215), or even induced by drink (e.g., ARM 26.207, 212). Prophecy often originated in temples (e.g., ARM 26.214, 215, 219, 236), although other private contexts and open-air proclamations are noted in some correspondence (ARM 26.206, 208, 212, 371). Subject matter addressed cultic and judicial duties of the king (e.g., A. 1121 + A. 2731; ARM 26.232), as well as political affairs (e.g., ARM 26.199, 214). Whatever the context, local officials were under obligation to take note of divine messages that were relevant to royal affairs (e.g., A. 1121 + A. 2731 [lines 34–45]; ARM 26.196 [lines 5–12]; cf. ARM 26.235 [lines 16–20]). So, when a prophet spoke concerning the king or responded to a royal inquiry, the responsible temple and administrative officials or a member of the royal family passed on the message.[19] The correspondent carefully indicated the circumstances in which the prophecy originated, identifying as well some important details about the prophet and in some cases significant background regarding previous oracles or letters regarding the same affair.[20] Sometimes, a piece of hair or garment from the prophet was sent in order to validate his or her veracity by means of divination (e.g., A. 1968; ARM 26.198, 200, 229, 239 [dreams]; but contrast 233).[21] Millard stresses that the messages were put into writing within days of being spoken (ARM 26.210, 213, 220, 221 [cf. 221bis]).[22] This urgency underscores the importance that officials and the king attached to prophetic revelations.

How accurately did these letters preserve the words of the original prophecy? Durand's assessment is that prophetic words were transmitted with essentially no change, with accuracy sometimes assured by witnesses (e.g.,

---

Amorrite," in *Prophètes et rois: Bible et Proche-Orient*, ed. André Lemaire, Lectio divina hors série (Paris: Les éditions du Cerf, 2001), 21–53; Nissinen, Seow, and Ritner, *Prophets and Prophecy in the Ancient Near East*, 6–7, 13–17.

[17]For a definition, see Manfred Weippert, "Aspekte israelitischer Prophetie im Lichte verwandter Erscheinungen des Alten Orients," in *Ad bene et fideliter seminandum: Festgabe für Karlheinz Deller zum 21. Februar 1987*, ed. Gerlinde Mauer and Ursula Magen, AOAT 220 (Kevelaer: Butzon and Bercker, 1988), 289–90; and Martti Nissinen, "What Is Prophecy? An Ancient Near Eastern Perspective," in Kaltner and Stulman, *Inspired Speech*, 20–21.

[18]Because dreams came to prophetic functionaries and constituted a message for a third party, it is reasonable to classify these reports in Mari letters with prophecy (cf. Martti Nissinen, *References to Prophecy in Neo-Assyrian Sources*, SAAS 7 [Helsinki: University of Helsinki Press, 1998], 8).

[19]Van der Toorn, "From Oral to the Written," 225–26. For the sometimes complex path, see Nissinen, "Spoken, Written, Quoted, and Invented," 256–57.

[20]Simon B. Parker, "Official Attitudes toward Prophecy at Mari and in Israel," *VT* 43 (1993): 52–56.

[21]Jean-Marie Durand, *Archives épistolaires de Mari I/1*, ARM 26 (Paris: Éditions recherche sur les civilisations, 1988), 40–41.

[22]Millard, "La prophétie et l'écriture: Israël, Aram, Assyrie," 137.

A. 1121 + A. 2731; ARM 26.414).[23] Similarly, Millard argues that writing was important in order to *prevent* alteration, which more easily occurs during oral transmission.[24] Other scholars stress that the writers of the letters adapted and altered prophetic citations for their own interests. The oft-cited example (table 3) involves three different letters that presumably report the same prophecy (ARM 26.197, 199, and 202).[25]

**Table 3. Comparison of three reports of the same prophecy**

| Inib-šina (197) | Sammetar (199) | Kanisan/Kibri-Dagan (202) |
|---|---|---|
| *qammatum* of Dagan of Terqa | *qammatum* of Dagan of Terqa | *muḫḫum* of Dagan |
| "The peacemaking of the man of Ešnunna is false: beneath straw water runs! I will gather him into the net that I knot. I will destroy his city and I will ruin his wealth, which comes from time immemorial."[1] | "Beneath straw water runs. They keep on sending to you messages of friendship, they even send their gods [to you], but in their hearts they are planning something else. The king should not take an oath without consulting God." | "Beneath straw water runs. The god of my lord has come! He has delivered his enemies in his hands." |
| [Advice:] "This is what she said to me. Now, protect yourself! Without consulting an oracle do not enter the city!" | [Advice:] "The report of that words that she spoke to me I have hereby sent to my lord. Let my lord consider the matter and act in accordance with his great majesty." | [Advice:] "This is what Kibri-Dagan wrote to me. My lord should not be negligent in letting oracles be delivered for his own good." |

1. Translations throughout are from Nissinen, Seow, and Ritner, *Prophets and Prophecy in the Ancient Near East*. Cf. Sasson, "Water beneath Straw," 606.

The interrelation is recognized by the common citation of the proverb "beneath straw water runs," as well as the mention in ARM 26.197 and 199 of the same prophetess, the *qammatum* of Dagan of Terqa, and the same recipient of an oracle, Inib-šina.[26] Because the words that accompany the proverb differ in each of the three cases, Parker concludes that "the writers

---

[23]Durand, *Archives épistolaires de Mari I/1*, 382–83.

[24]Millard, "La prophétie et l'écriture: Israël, Aram, Assyrie," 143–45. Cf. Charpin, "Prophètes et rois dans le Proche-Orient Amorrite," 31. Possibly, the witnesses were unaware of the contents and only assured sealing and delivery of the message (van der Toorn, "From Oral to the Written," 226–27, 229). Nevertheless, the motive remains to guard the transmission process.

[25]Parker challenges both Durand and Millard, in part on the basis of this example (Parker, "Official Attitudes toward Prophecy at Mari and in Israel," 57, 62 n. 26). Cf. Jack M. Sasson, "Water beneath Straw: Adventures of a Prophetic Phrase in the Mari Archives," in *Solving Riddles and Untying Knots: Biblical, Epigraphic, and Semitic Studies in Honor of Jonas C. Greenfield*, ed. Ziony Zevit, Seymour Gitin, and Michael Sokoloff (Winona Lake, IN: Eisenbrauns, 1995), 607; van der Toorn, "From Oral to the Written," 229–33; Nissinen, "Spoken, Written, Quoted, and Invented," 257–58; and Nissinen, Seow, and Ritner, *Prophets and Prophecy in the Ancient Near East*, 15.

[26]The title of the functionary in ARM 26.197 and 199 is *qammatum*, whereas it is *muḫḫum* in 202 (Nissinen, Seow, and Ritner, *Prophets and Prophecy in the Ancient Near East*, 35 n. a). Parker suggests it is a different prophet "addressing the same situation" (Parker, "Official Attitudes toward Prophecy at Mari and in Israel," 57). The difference in gender supports separate identities for the two rather than different terminology being applied to the same intermediary.

might exercise considerable freedom in shaping [the original oracle]."[27] Sasson argues that the reports mirrored the anxieties of the sender, and therefore people "did not need to be as faithful to *an orally delivered statement* as to a written one" (italics his).[28] Van der Toorn also cites this example as evidence that "the Babylonians attached no particular importance to the *ipsissima verba* of the prophets."[29] However, the prophet cited in ARM 26.202 is different from the prophetess in ARM 26.197 and 199 (an observation recognized by Parker; see note 28). Therefore ARM 26.202 should not be expected to match the wording, except perhaps in the use of the proverb, which could be due to borrowing between the two intermediaries.[30] In addition, the report in ARM 26.202 remarks that the prophet had spoken considerably more words. If this is true for the *muḫḫum* in ARM 26.202, we might expect the same for the oracle(s) from the *qammatum* in 197 and 199. Thus, the prophetic messages were more extensive overall and the words cited in the letters represent only a portion of what was said. This does not mean, as Parker states in the case of ARM 26.202, that "successive communications have reduced it to its mere essence";[31] only that the writer was selective.[32] Another observation is that the performance of the oracle witnessed by Sammetar (ARM 26.199) preceded the subsequent performance by the same prophetess in the presence of Inib-šina (ARM 26.197): "Then she delivered her instructions in the temple of Belet-ekallim to the high priestess Inib-šina" (ARM 26.199, lines 52b–54). Therefore, we do not know to what extent the difference in wording between ARM 26.197 and 199 could be due to the different performances by the prophetess herself. Exact wording of oral delivery often varies depending on the audience. The reports of the two writers could be excerpts of words spoken by the prophetess in these separate performances.[33] So, either selectivity reflected the sender's concerns or different prophetic performances adapted to the anxieties of the senders (or both).

Two additional observations are in order. First, in the case of ARM 26.197, 199, and 202, the writers *did* differentiate their own advice (introduced by a report formula) from the words of the prophet. Second, their advice

---

[27] Parker, "Official Attitudes toward Prophecy at Mari and in Israel," 60.

[28] Jack M. Sasson, "The Posting of Letters with Divine Messages," in *Florilegium marianum II: Recueil d'études à la mémoire de Maurice Birot*, ed. Dominique Charpin and Jean-Marie Durand, Mémoires de N.A.B.U. 3 (Paris: Société pour l'Étude du Proche-Orient Ancien, 1994), 305.

[29] Van der Toorn, "From Oral to the Written," 232.

[30] Durand (*Archives épistolaires de Mari I/1*, 405) notes that their relationship is unclear.

[31] Parker, "Official Attitudes toward Prophecy at Mari and in Israel," 58.

[32] Cf. n. 65, which cites this possibility for SAA 9.8.

[33] A possibility recognized by Parker, "Official Attitudes toward Prophecy at Mari and in Israel," 60.

was a faithful application of the prophet's message.[34] Even if we assume that they loosely conveyed the *locution* of the prophet, they respected the *illocution* (the context of relevance and the intent, in this case a warning).

Perhaps a better example of paraphrase is ARM 26.207 (lines 40–45), a letter from queen Šibtu. Parker argues that the closing words are Šibtu's "own reiteration of the prophet's message" (just cited in lines 20–34). But before concluding that *all* these closing words are simply a paraphrase of the preceding oracle, it is necessary to observe that there were at least two individuals induced to prophesy. Her closing words could incorporate a citation of words spoken by another prophet in addition to those cited in lines 20–34. In both cases, the expressed subject of the introductory speech formula is plural (*šunūma*); yet it is impossible to disentangle what was spoken by any individual. As in the case of ARM 26.197, 199, and 202, Šibtu may have selected from among several similar declarations. The reference to the king as "my lord" is not necessarily an indication of Šibtu's own words (cf. lines 1 and 18).[35] However, her opening report ("He will be placed under the feet of my lord," lines 12–13) and closing statement ("Before my lord's arrival, his army will be dissipated," line 44) may form an inclusio, each being a summary of the two responses to inquiry. We cannot know with certainty to what extent lines 40–43 might be a paraphrase.

Charpin discusses two texts that are relevant to this question but often overlooked; in both cases the correspondent "insists on the exactitude of the transcription":[36] "I have written according to the words [*ana pî*] that Šelebum spoke to me" (ARM 26.198, line r. 1), and "This is what this woman said, and I have written her words [*awāt pīša*] to my lord" (ARM 26.217, lines 27–28).[37] He suggests that in some circumstances exact wording is necessary, but in others the transcription may not be so literal.[38] The same problem of determining verbal correspondence faces the interpretation of letters citing nonprophetic speech as well (e.g., "This time, I just write to my lord what I heard from the mouth of Yarim-Lim," ARM 26.13, lines 27–29).[39]

---

[34] Parker's conclusion that "in these three letters . . . the three authors give quite different advice concerning the oracles they report" is overstated (ibid., 63).

[35] The diplomatic language of respect allows for use of "my lord" in reference to the king, at times even when reporting words from the mouth of a deity (Nissinen, *References to Prophecy*, 103–4).

[36] Charpin, "Prophètes et rois dans le Proche-Orient Amorrite," 31–32. Mari prophets most likely uttered their oracles in Akkadian rather than Amorite, so issues of translation are probably not a factor in this discussion (ibid., 32–33).

[37] Translation from Nissinen, Seow, and Ritner, *Prophets and Prophecy in the Ancient Near East*, 29, 52. One might compare the formula common in Neo-Assyrian oracles, *ša pî* ("by the mouth of"; SAA 9.1.1 i 28; 9.1.2 ii 9, passim).

[38] Cf. van der Toorn, "From Oral to the Written," 229–30.

[39] Following Charpin's translation (Charpin, "Prophètes et rois dans le Proche-Orient Amorrite," 32).

In summary, one might expect paraphrase in a genre such as a letter (hence, *ipsissima vox*). But the evidence for this is not as manifest as is often asserted. It is likely that writers selected the portions of the oracle they deemed most pertinent and transcribed the prophet's words with relative accuracy. In the case of ARM 26.207, the dividing line between the prophet's words and that of the writer's is not explicitly marked, but this case appears exceptional.[40] *Advice* based on an oracle was distinguished from the words of the prophet. When verbal accuracy was important, transmission was literal. As far as the existing evidence is concerned, the correspondent always respected the illocution of the original oracle, even if paraphrasing. Also, it was important to preserve the identity of the individual prophet responsible for the oracle.

### Nineveh

Similar to Mari, the royal archive at Nineveh (seventh century BC) yields correspondence between royal officials and the king, some of which informed him about astronomical and divinatory revelations from across the empire, including prophecies.[41] The Nineveh correspondence contains less detail than Mari regarding the performance setting for prophecy, but the source of most oracles appears to have been cultic.[42] Not surprisingly, then, some excerpts of prophecy in letters from priests address matters of temple concern (e.g., SAA 13.37, 144). Other citations are from scholars, who use such references to bolster political advice based on other divinatory practices (e.g., SAA 10.111, 352). While there is no comparable custom of testing prophets by divination as at Mari, prophecy in Neo-Assyrian times was evidently still regarded as inferior to the "science" of scholars or to the more objective art of diviners.[43] Unlike the latter, who were highly literate, prophets depended on a scribe for written transmission of their messages.[44] As at Mari, it was the duty of officials to report any forms of revelation that pertain to the king or his affairs.[45]

---

[40]For the exceptional circumstances, see Parker, "Official Attitudes toward Prophecy at Mari and in Israel," 62 n. 25.

[41]For an overview, see Nissinen, *References to Prophecy*; Huffmon, "A Company of Prophets: Mari, Assyria, Israel," 57–63; Nissinen, "The Socioreligious Role of the Neo-Assyrian Prophets"; Nissinen, Seow, and Ritner, *Prophets and Prophecy in the Ancient Near East*, 133–36.

[42]Nissinen, "The Socioreligious Role of the Neo-Assyrian Prophets," 98–101; Hilber, *Cultic Prophecy in the Psalms*, 53–61; John W. Hilber, "Cultic Prophecy in Assyria and in the Psalms," *JAOS* 127 (2007): 29–40.

[43]Nissinen, *References to Prophecy*, 90–91, 94; Nissinen, "The Socioreligious Role of the Neo-Assyrian Prophets," 108–9.

[44]Nissinen, "Spoken, Written, Quoted, and Invented," 245.

[45]SAA 2.6 §10; Nissinen, *References to Prophecy*, 156–62, cf. 116–18; Beate Pongratz-Leisten, *Herrschaftswissen in Mesopotamien: Formen der Kommunikation zwischen Gott und König im 2. und 1. Jahrtausend v. Chr.*, SAAS 10 (Helsinki: University of Helsinki Press, 1999), 307; Nissinen, "Spoken, Written, Quoted, and Invented," 240 n. 24.

Some correspondence appears to cite prophecy closely, if not verbatim. For example, a report concerning the substitute-king ritual preserves the correct, first-person to second-person address of prophetic speech even though the writer is narrating the events in third person: "You will take over the kingship!" . . . "I have revealed the thieving polecat of my lord and placed it in your hands" (SAA 10.352, lines 25-r. 4; see also SAA 13.37, lines 10-r. 9, and 144, lines r. 7–11).[46] The citation in SAA 13.139 is more extensive and stylistically matches oracles recorded directly (cf. SAA 9.1.1, 4; 9.2.3, 5).[47]

On the other hand, Nissinen notes examples in which the writer might have drawn loosely on the general tenor of one or more prophecies as a basis for advice to the king (e.g., SAA 10.284, perhaps alluding to SAA 9.2.4 ii 29–33; also SAA 10.111 r. 23–26).[48] He correctly observes that the writer is more concerned with application of these prophetic words to the situation at hand than he is with anchoring the speech in its original performance setting.

A series of communications from one Assyrian official, Nabû-reḫtu-uṣur, to Esarhaddon illustrates the full range of citation technique. He reports a seditious prophecy against Esarhaddon: "This is the word of Nusku [abat nušku ši]: The kingship is for Saši! I will destroy the name and seed of Sennacherib!" (SAA 16.59, lines r. 4–5). The use of an introductory speech formula, followed by direct speech, suggests a carefully chosen excerpt from an oral performance. Nissinen stresses the paraphrastic style used by the same official in a subsequent, related letter, when Nabû-reḫtu-uṣur uses the formula, "This is the word of Mullissu" (dabābu anniu ša Mullissu) to close paragraphs in which he loosely draws from prophetic tradition (SAA 16.60 [CT 53 17:1–9]; cf. lines SAA 16.61 lines 8–9). Furthermore, he actually adapts prophetic words for his own: "Have no fear; Bel, Nabû and Mullissu are standing [with you]" (SAA 16.60 [CT 53.17: r. 14–15]).[49]

These examples confirm conclusions already summarized for Mari; there is a continuum of transcription practice from literal to paraphrase. In each case, however, the illocution, if not the actual wording, of the message is faithfully transmitted. While there are examples of paraphrase,

---

[46]As noted above (see n. 36), the use of "my lord" in the second part of the oracle is possibly a diplomatic idiom. Nissinen opines that these messages were transmitted "without necessarily being verbatim quotations" but "probably repeat their substance correctly" (Nissinen, "Spoken, Written, Quoted, and Invented," 261).

[47]Nissinen comments that this letter incorporates the pattern of an oracle report but that it "is the only one of its kind and does not warrant far-reaching conclusions" (Martti Nissinen, "How Prophecy Became Literature," SJOT 19 [2005]: 169). However, with a sample of only a handful of letters, this example is significant.

[48]Nissinen, "Spoken, Written, Quoted, and Invented," 262–63. Cf. Nissinen, References to Prophecy, 104; cf. Pierre Villard, "Les prophéties à l'époque Néo-Assyrienne," in Lemaire, Prophètes et rois, 76.

[49]Nissinen, References to Prophecy, 152–53.

writers could, and perhaps normally did, cite prophetic speech close to the original wording.

## Lachish Ostraca

Reference to a warning in a letter from an unnamed prophet in Lachish Ostracon 3 indicates two things: (1) the gist of such prophetic messages were in public circulation outside the circles of elite society, snippets of which were cited in correspondence;[50] (2) prophets contemporary with Jeremiah wrote or utilized scribes for correspondence.[51] That prophecy finds a place in ordinary military correspondence supports the possibility that it was also integrated into other official texts such as royal histories.[52]

## Literary Citation of Prophecy

Genres of a more literary nature also cite prophecy. Nissinen draws attention to one reference in a Mari document, the Epic of Zimri-Lim, in which an oracle of victory from a prophet is cited as impetus for marching to war.[53] The degree to which this preserves the exact words of an earlier oracle or only echoes the substance of prophetic performance is impossible to determine. The Egyptian story of Wenamon is perhaps even more complicated in this regard.[54]

Assyrian royal inscriptions make reference to prophetic activity and in several cases preserve oracular speech.[55] Nissinen cites evidence that these inscriptions—"whether accurate quotations or free inventions—may also go back to written reports to which the scribes had easy access."[56] But why would scribes need to resort to "invention" at all if authentic oracles were available to quote. In a similar manner, the Zakkur stele and the Amman Citadel inscription have every appearance of authentic prophecy spoken in the historical situation that these steles commemorate.[57]

Two liturgical texts, the Marduk Ordeal (SAA 3.34/35) and the Dialogue Between Assurbanipal and Nabû (SAA 3.13), likely preserve prophetic words

---

[50]Nissinen, Seow, and Ritner, *Prophets and Prophecy in the Ancient Near East*, 213.

[51]Karel van der Toorn, *Scribal Culture and the Making of the Hebrew Bible* (Cambridge: Harvard University Press, 2007), 181.

[52]André Lemaire, "Prophètes et rois dans les inscriptions ouest-sémitiques," in Lemaire, *Prophètes et rois*, 114–15.

[53]Nissinen, "Spoken, Written, Quoted, and Invented," 263.

[54]Ibid., 264.

[55]Nissinen, *References to Prophecy*, 14–61.

[56]Nissinen, "Spoken, Written, Quoted, and Invented," 265–68.

[57]For texts, see Nissinen, Seow, and Ritner, *Prophets and Prophecy in the Ancient Near East*, nos. 136–37.

actually spoken in ritual. While the oracle excerpt in SAA 3.34/35 is brief, it illustrates the role of prophetic functionaries in worship and represents their oral performance. Kingship renewal rituals of the Akitu festival also illustrate prophecy "frozen" for liturgical performance.[58] The "dialogue" in SAA 3.13 presents a temple ritual in which the king laments before the deity and receives oracular response. It shares many affinities with an actual archived oracle, SAA 9.9.[59] Parpola has observed that both share the same scribal hand and likely emerged from the same historical context.[60] Pongratz-Leisten suggests that the text might be fictive;[61] however, comparison with oracle SAA 9.9 supports authenticity. As with correspondence, literary texts exhibit a range of citation techniques, but any evidence of free invention remains to be seen.

## Oracle Reports and Collections

The royal archive of Nineveh also contained reports and collections of prophetic oracles.[62] Unlike the genres discussed above, which cite prophecy as *one part* of a text with broader purposes, the design of oracular reports was to record and preserve prophetic speech directly, offering close access to the oral performance of prophets.[63] The use of the quotation particle, *mā*, in these texts indicates that they were written by scribes reporting the words of the prophets, not written by the prophets themselves.[64] Nissinen argues that even with faithful copying, once prophecy is put into writing by scribes, it is subject to literary refinement, in terms of both style and interpretation.[65] But it is important to observe that the only evidence for scribal work is the conventional layout to which these reports conformed. The language remains pure Neo-Assyrian, the oral dialect of the prophetesses,[66] not standard Babylonian customarily used in scribal composition and copying.[67] In spite of the elevated

---

[58]Karel van der Toorn, "L'oracle de victoire comme expression prophétique au Proche-Orient ancien," *RB* 94 (1987): 93. For text, see Nissinen, Seow, and Ritner, *Prophets and Prophecy in the Ancient Near East*, no. 133.

[59]Hilber, *Cultic Prophecy in the Psalms*, 70–74.

[60]Simo Parpola, *Assyrian Prophecies*, SAA 9 (Helsinki: University of Helsinki Press, 1997), lxxi.

[61]Pongratz-Leisten, *Herrschaftswissen*, 273 n. 37, 274.

[62]For text and introduction, see Parpola, *Assyrian Prophecies*, and Nissinen, Seow, and Ritner, *Prophets and Prophecy in the Ancient Near East*, 97–101.

[63]Nissinen, "Spoken, Written, Quoted, and Invented," 244.

[64]Parpola, *Assyrian Prophecies*, lv. It is possible that lines 2–4 of SAA 9.8 are descriptive comments by the scribe (Villard, "Les prophéties à l'époque Néo-Assyrienne," 76–77; cf. Nissinen, Seow, and Ritner, *Prophets and Prophecy in the Ancient Near East*, 129 nn. b and c).

[65]Nissinen, "Spoken, Written, Quoted, and Invented," 241, 244. Cf. Pongratz-Leisten, *Herrschaftswissen*, 267.

[66]Parpola, *Assyrian Prophecies*, lxvii.

[67]Villard, "Les prophéties à l'époque Néo-Assyrienne," 75.

semi-poetic style, nothing suggests that the scribe did anything but record closely the words of the oracle.[68] Parpola states, "They were written down from oral performance and apparently not subjected to any substantial editing."[69]

All of the oracles pertain to the king and his affairs, most often promising deliverance from enemies or consolidation of his kingdom, generically a "proclamation of victory";[70] but in a few instances the prophets chided the king for neglect of cultic duties. While the oracles do not share any common form-critical structure, they often exhibit elements that correspond formally with biblical prophecy (e.g., introductory speech formula ["The word of DN"]; self-identification formula ["I am DN"]; reassurance formula ["fear not"]; patterns of announced intervention and result).[71] In each case where damage to the tablet did not obliterate the information, the name of the prophet(ess), city of origin, and in one instance exact date of the oracle are recorded in a colophon.

In order to appreciate the contribution of these texts, it is helpful to understand two different types of cuneiform tablets used by Assyrian scribes.[72] The first was a rectangular, horizontal format (2:1 ratio of width to height, often palm sized) used for immediate and temporary recording of memos and reports. The second was a rectangular, vertical format (1:2 or 2:3 ratio of width to height, size varying), written with multiple columns, used for permanent archive of texts such as treaties and royal decrees. Parpola indicates that in some instances temporary report tablets might have been copied onto archival tablets before being destroyed.[73] Of the 11 prophetic tablets, 4 are single reports in the horizontal format (SAA 9.5–8) and 5 are vertical archive tablets (SAA 9.1–4, 9); two severely damaged tables (SAA 9.10–11) are likely

[68] Nissinen acknowledges that sophisticated rhetoric need not be beyond the competence of the prophetesses (Nissinen, "Spoken, Written, Quoted, and Invented," 244). Cf. Nissinen, "The Socioreligious Role of the Neo-Assyrian Prophets," 97–98. None of the evidence offered by de Jong for scribal reworking of several oracles militates against this (Matthijs J. de Jong, *Isaiah among the Ancient Near Eastern Prophets: A Comparative Study of the Earliest Stages of the Isaiah Tradition and the Neo-Assyrian Prophecies*, VTSup 117 [Leiden: Brill, 2007], 404–12). Coming to my attention too late to incorporate into the content of this essay, but raising many pertinent questions, some of which I have addressed above, is Nissinen, "The Historical Dilemma of Biblical Prophetic Studies," in *Prophecy in the Book of Jeremiah*, ed. Hans M. Barstad and Reinhard G. Kratz, BZAW 388 (Berlin: de Gruyter, 2009), 103–20.
[69] Parpola, *Assyrian Prophecies*, lxvii. Nissinen reasonably suggests that because of space limitations, the oracles may have been abbreviated (Nissinen, "How Prophecy Became Literature," 165).
[70] Manfred Weippert, "Assyrische Prophetien der Zeit Asarhaddons und Assurbanipals," in *Assyrian Royal Inscriptions: New Horizons in Literary, Ideological and Historical Analysis*, ed. F. M. Fales, Orientis Antiqui Colectio 18 (Rome: Istituto per L'Orient, 1981), 90–92.
[71] Cf. Parpola, *Assyrian Prophecies*, lxiv–lxvii.
[72] Ibid., liii–lv. Cf. Karen Radner, "The Relation Between Format and Content of Neo-Assyrian Texts," in *Nineveh, 612 BC: The Glory and Fall of the Assyrian Empire*, ed. Raija Mattila (Helsinki: University of Helsinki Press, 1995), 63–78.
[73] Parpola, *Assyrian Prophecies*, liii.

archival.[74] What is particularly important is that three of the well-preserved, archive tablets (SAA 9.1–3) contain *collections* of between 5 and 10 individual oracles.[75] Even though the origin of the individual oracles in these collections varies as to prophet(ess), sometimes location, and presumably date, the selection process was not random.[76] Parpola notes that they are products of the same scribal hand;[77] and he has correlated the three oracle collections to three phases in Esarhaddon's rise to power following the assassination of his father, Sennacherib.[78] Parpola proposes that a prophet may even have performed the recitation of the oracles in SAA 9.3 during the coronation.[79] Thus, the oracles were organized into archival tablets according to chronological and thematic considerations.[80]

One can only speculate about possible further development of these collections, had another generation flourished at Nineveh predisposed to transmit prophecy.[81] But the Nineveh tablets provide a model of the process from oral performance to written prophecy in a culture contemporary with the classical period of biblical prophecy. Van Seters comments, "The oral utterance of an oracle that is immediately written down and that soon becomes part of a collection of oracles, as we seem to have reflected in Isaiah and Jeremiah, has nothing inherently improbable about it."[82] He goes on to draw an analogy between the organization of the Assyrian oracles around a crucial period in royal history to oracles of Isaiah being organized around the Syro-Ephraimite war or Jeremiah's collections pertaining to the final days of Judah. Van Seters favors further scribal expansion of biblical collections into literary prophetic works in later periods.[83] Whether this was necessarily the case is discussed below. The significance here is that prophetic oracles were inscribed soon after oral delivery, were given shape as collections within a decade of recording,[84]

---

[74]Ibid., liii, lxi–lxii.

[75]One of the archive tablets is too fragmentary to know the original number of oracles in the collection (SAA 9.4) and one contains a single oracle (SAA 9.9). Nissinen ("Spoken, Written, Quoted, and Invented," 248–49) discusses the possibility that SAA 9.7 and 9.8 may contain more than one oracle, even though recorded in report format.

[76]Collection SAA 9.3 names only one prophet in the colophon, perhaps the sole source of all oracles in this collection.

[77]Parpola, *Assyrian Prophecies*, lv.

[78]Ibid., lxviii–lxx.

[79]Ibid., lxiv.

[80]Nissinen, "Spoken, Written, Quoted, and Invented," 250–53; Nissinen, "How Prophecy Became Literature," 165.

[81]Nissinen, "Spoken, Written, Quoted, and Invented," 254.

[82]John Van Seters, "Prophetic Orality in the Context of the Ancient Near East: A Response to Culley, Crenshaw and Davies," in Ben Zvi, Floyd, and Matthews, *Writings and Speech*, 86.

[83]Ibid., 88; Nissinen, "How Prophecy Became Literature," 165–66.

[84]Parpola, *Assyrian Prophecies*, lxix–lxx; cf. Nissinen, "How Prophecy Became Literature," 165–66.

and remained associated with the person of the prophet who actually spoke the oracles.

In addition to the Nineveh archive, a textual discovery on the east side of the Jordan Valley provides evidence of written prophecy from West Semitic sources that are geographically proximate and contemporary with the period of preexilic biblical prophecy.[85] The Deir 'Alla plaster texts, dating to the early eighth century BC, preserve a vision of global destruction. The opening line refers to a "Book [spr] of Balaam, son of Beor" and contains narrative passages contextualizing the reception of the visions. This interlacing of oracular visions with narrative prose suggests to Nissinen a scribal editing process parallel to biblical prophetic books, where final editors accessed written prophetic sources.[86] The plaster text is a copy from a scroll, and so the composition of the original was anterior to the early eighth-century date of the Deir 'Alla inscription.[87] The original literary piece, then, was composed not many miles away from Jerusalem and at a time earlier than that purported for the biblical prophetic books. Taken together, the Deir 'Alla plaster and Nineveh collections offer models whereby one can envision the writing and collection of biblical prophetic material in the historical period during which these works attest to their own origin.

## Divine Letters

Written correspondence between a king and a deity (sent in either direction) is known from Old Babylonian and Neo-Assyrian times.[88] Of particular relevance here are letters from deities to kings.[89] The form of some divine letters

---

[85] For text and introduction, see Nissinen, Seow, and Ritner, *Prophets and Prophecy in the Ancient Near East*, no. 138.

[86] Nissinen, "How Prophecy Became Literature," 164.

[87] Alan R. Millard, "Epigraphic Notes, Aramaic and Hebrew," *PEQ* 110 (1978): 25; Millard, "In Praise of Ancient Scribes," *BA* 45 (1982): 149; Jo Ann Hackett, "Response to Baruch Levine and André Lemaire," in *The Balaam Text from Deir 'Alla Re-evaluated: Proceedings of the International Symposium Held at Leiden 21–24 August 1989*, ed. J. Hoftijzer and G. van der Kooij (Leiden: Brill, 1991), 80–81, esp. n. 10; Manfred Weippert, "The Balaam Text from Deir 'Allā and the Study of the Old Testament," in *The Balaam Text from Deir 'Alla Re-evaluated*, 176–78; André Lemaire, "Le inscriptions sur plâtre de Deir 'Alla et leur signification historique et culturelle," in *The Balaam Text from Deir 'Alla Re-evaluated*, 45; Lemaire, "Oracles, politique et littérature dans les royaumes Araméens et Transjordaniens (IXe–VIIIe s. av. n.è.)," in Heintz, *Oracles et prophéties dans l'antiquité*, 190–91.

[88] R. Borger, "Gottesbrief," in *RlA*, 3:575–76.

[89] Pongratz-Leisten (*Herrschaftswissen*, 207–9) uses the term "Exchange of Letters" for royal requests presented to the deity to which the deity responds either through the (written) mediation of a prophet (e.g., ARM 26.194) or in a letter addressed directly to the king (e.g., ARM 26.192–93, and FLP 1674). She restricts the term "Divine Letter" to a genre of Neo-Assyrian literature in which the deity responds to a royal campaign report (e.g., SAA 3.41–46). This is generally helpful, but perhaps overly refined. First, there is no indication that ARM 26.194 is a reply to royal inquiry, and one letter of the Neo-Assyrian corpus (SAA 3.47) does not conform to the genre of

consists of a repeat of the contents of a campaign report from the king, with the deity's affirmation in response (e.g., SAA 3.41). They give the impression of *verbatim* quotation of the king's words back to him.[90] One letter of this group ends with a promise of future support (SAA 3.44, lines r. 26–29). Even though a written composition incorporating the citation of royal reports, this divine response could be understood as prophetic words spoken from the temple of the deity where the king's report was read.[91]

Other divine letters appear indistinguishable from oral prophecy. From the Old Babylonian period, Mari letter ARM 26.194 originates from a prophet who sends a letter of divine speech directly to the king with the assistance of a scribe (ARM 26.414, lines 31–32).[92] Van der Toorn opines that since ancient scribes often acted as editors, we cannot accept this letter, without qualification, as the *ipsissima verba* of the prophet.[93] This generalization begs the question for a *prophetic* genre; why regard the scribe's work as anything but a close transcription of the prophet's speech, especially since the prophet was already anxious about accurate delivery of the message?[94]

Mari letter ARM 26.192 presents the divine messages of three different deities addressing Zimri-Lim.[95] In this regard, it resembles the Neo-Assyrian prophetic oracle SAA 9.1.4. Apart from the epistolary formula, "Speak to Zimri-Lim, thus DN" (*ana* PN *qibima umma* DN), it resembles other prophetic oracles.

---

other divine letters with which it is grouped; rather it appears stylistically more akin to an oracle (ibid., 232). De Jong correctly refers to SAA 3.44–47 as "compositions of divine words" (de Jong, *Isaiah among the Ancient Near Eastern Prophets*, 413 n. 218). However, his designation "literary derivative" of prophecy (ibid., 419–20) draws an unwarranted distinction between the prophet and compositional origin, since these texts were regarded by the recipients as forms of divine speech. In addition, the presence or absence of an intermediary beside the scribe is uncertain for ARM 26.192–93, and FLP 1674.

[90]Alasdair Livingstone, *Court Poetry and Literary Miscellanea*, SAA 3 (Helsinki: University of Helsinki Press, 1989), xxx.

[91]Cf. Pongratz-Leisten, *Herrschaftswissen*, 269. The future promise is a feature of oracles that distinguishes them from "divine letters" that contain narrative of a royal report (ibid., 270–72). The boundaries are blurred even further by SAA 9.3.3, which is the only oracle with past report of the deity's actions, and therefore might be a portion of a "divine letter" incorporated into an oracle collection (ibid., 272; Villard, "Les prophéties à l'époque Néo-Assyrienne," 80). However, concern about past actions is not foreign to oracles (cf. SAA 9.1.1, 9.1.4, 9.1.10).

[92]Durand, *Archives épistolaires de Mari I/1*, 391; Charpin, "Prophètes et rois dans le Proche-Orient Amorrite," 31.

[93]Van der Toorn, "From Oral to the Written," 229.

[94]This is true whether the word *naṣrum* (line 31) is understood in the sense of "competent" (i.e., able to convey prophetic diction, cf. Durand, *Archives épistolaires de Mari I/1*, 391 n. 80) or "discreet" (i.e., trustworthy regarding confidentiality; cf. Nissinen, Seow, and Ritner, *Prophets and Prophecy in the Ancient Near East*, 75 n. d).

[95]Durand, *Archives épistolaires de Mari I/1*, 413–14.

Another Old Babylonian example (FLP 1674) derives from the temple archive at Ishchali.[96] After extensive literary analysis, Ellis recognizes the possibility that this letter is a record of oral communication. However, she concludes that the "distinct literary flavor . . . and underlying reflexes in the omen literature" suggest that it is probably the work of a scholar (diviner)— perhaps oral discourse polished into its present form.[97] Moran takes exception. He notes the absence of the epistolary form ("to PN" [*ana* PN]), which suggests direct prophetic address, not a scribal letter; and he argues that the style better reflects oral simplicity, even more so than ARM 26.194, which both he and Ellis regard as an *ad lib* composition.[98] So *if* edited, it remains close to the original prophetic performance. In any event, in the estimate of both scholars, FLP 1674 presents itself as direct divine speech to the king (however mediated). It was believed to be authentic prophecy by the intermediary and the king, even if originating from the stylus of a diviner, whom we might then consider to be a "writing prophet."

A Neo-Assyrian example is SAA 3.47, which lacks any trace of response to a royal report (i.e., echoing back to the king the wording of his report). Rather, the text opens with a report of prophetic call to deliver a message: "The great lord, the king of the gods, Ninurta, has sent [*me*]: Say to the prince . . . thus speaks Ninurta" (lines 1–5).

Except for the epistolary formula used in all but one case, these examples of divine communication are indistinguishable in style from prophetic speech. *If* a divine letter originated from oral dictation, there is no way to ascertain the degree to which, *if any*, the letter was elevated in style by a scribe. With the exception of ARM 26.194, there is no indication of a human intermediary between the deity and the scribe, so the original compositions could have been written. Nevertheless, the original recipient, and presumably the author, conceived of this as legitimate, inspired speech.[99] Bifurcation between prophet and scribe is, in these cases, an unnecessary distinction. Perhaps a literate priest composed an oracle in written form. The implications for biblical

---

[96]Maria de Jong Ellis, "The Goddess Kititum Speaks to King Ibalpiel: Oracle Texts from Ishchali," *Mari* 5 (1987): 235–66. A second oracular letter from this archive is too fragmentary for consideration here.
[97]Ibid. In a later publication, Ellis suggests more firmly that the oracle resulted from divinatory activity (Maria de Jong Ellis, "Observations on Mesopotamian Oracles and Prophetic Texts: Literary and Historiographical Considerations," *JCS* 41 [1989]: 139).
[98]William L. Moran, "An Ancient Prophetic Oracle," in *Biblische Theologie und gesellschaftlicher Wandel (Festschrift N. Lohfink)*, ed. George Braulik, Walter Groß, and Sean McEvenue (Freiburg: Herder, 1993), 252–59.
[99]Sharon R. Keller, "Written Communication Between the Human and Divine Spheres in Mesopotamia and Israel," in *The Biblical Canon in Comparative Perspective: Scripture in Context IV*, ed. Bernard F. Batto, William W. Hallo, and K. Lawson Younger Jr., Ancient Near Eastern Texts and Studies 11 (Lewiston: Edwin Mellen, 1991), 302, 304.

prophecy are not generally explored, but Keller has noted biblical indications that written communication between humans and Yahweh was recognized in Israel even as in Mesopotamia.[100] Charpin concludes that divine letters were "an integral part of the dossier of prophecy."[101] Further support for "written prophecy" comes from the Egyptian royal cult.

*Egyptian Royal Cult*

A consensus prevails that prophecy, in the sense of divine-messenger speech, did not exist in Egypt.[102] The Egyptian texts that are usually considered, which contain both foretelling and social criticism, are classified as a subspecies of wisdom literature (e.g., Prophecies of Neferti), not derived from divine-messenger speech.[103] While the assessment of these texts is correct, a class of Egyptian texts has been overlooked in previous discussions on Egyptian prophecy. Numerous royal inscriptions record first-person divine speech that was framed with introductory speech formulas and was delivered to the king in a cultic setting.

Some of the better examples are as follows:[104] Hatshepsut's and Horemheb's coronation rituals set the pattern for succeeding kings from the New Kingdom onward. Both sources record divine speeches to the king, but Hatshepsut's inscription contains a particularly enlightening report of the proceedings: the ritual priests "proclaimed her royal names, for the god caused that it should be in their hearts to make her names according to the form with which he had made them before."[105] Even if fictive in the case of Hatshepsut's unorthodox ascension, this report probably corresponds with actual custom in order to portray a credible coronation. Horemheb's reliefs describe the god coming

---

[100]Ibid.

[101]Charpin, "Prophètes et rois dans le Proche-Orient Amorrite," 24.

[102]E.g., Siegfried Herrmann, "Prophetie in Israel und Ägypten: Recht und Grenze eines Vergleichs," in *Congress Volume Bonn, 1962*, VTSup 9 (Leiden: Brill, 1963), 56–60, 63–64; Robert Schlichting, "Prophetie," in *LÄ*, 4:1122; Hans Bonnet, "Prophezeiung," in *RÄR*, 608–9; Bernd Ulrich Schipper, "'Apokalyptik,' 'Messianismus,' 'Prophetie'—Eine Begriffsbestimung," in *Apokalyptik und Ägypten: Eine kritische Analyse der relevanten Texte aus dem griechish-römischen Ägypten*, ed. Andreas Blasius and Bernd Ulrich Schipper, OLA 107 (Leuven: Peeters, 2002), 38.

[103]Nili Shupak, "Egyptian 'Prophecy' and Biblical Prophecy: Did the Phenomenon of Prophecy, in the Biblical Sense, Exist in Ancient Egypt?," *JEOL* 31 (1989–1990): 5–40; Nili Shupak, "The Egyptian 'Prophecy'—A Reconsideration," in *Von reichlich ägyptischem Verstande: Festschrift für Waltraud Guglielmi zum 65. Geburtstag*, ed. Hans-W. Fischer-Elfert and Karol Zibelius-Chen (Wiesbaden: Harrassowitz, 2006), 133–44.

[104]For a more thorough discussion, see John W. Hilber, "Prophetic Speech in the Egyptian Royal Cult," in *On Stone and Scroll: Essays in Honour of Graham Ivor Davies*, ed. James Aitken, Katharine Dell, and Brian Mastin, BZAW 420 (Berlin: de Gruyter, 2011), 39–53.

[105]James Henry Breasted, *ARE*, 2:§§229–30, 239.

forth from the temple to meet him and declaring his divine sonship.[106] Texts
accompanying the representation of Tutankhamen's Opet festival (later
usurped by Horemheb) set divine address to the king in the context of reliefs
depicting ritual procession, presentation of offerings, dancing, and records of
human speeches and songs celebrating the event.[107] Perhaps the best examples
of royal cultic prophecy are in temple dedication inscriptions of Thutmosis III
and Amenophis III, featuring triumph hymns spoken by Amun to the king,
some of which were preserved at the "Station of the King" in the temple
where the king stood for cultic ritual.[108] Offering scenes accompanying these
texts and internal references in Thutmosis III's poem of visits to the temple
also suggest a live performance.[109] These texts were adapted for the next five
hundred years in royal reliefs depicting sword conferral by the god to the king
and ritual killing of prisoners in cultic context.[110] Therefore, it seems likely
that priests functioned prophetically in the royal cult of Egypt. No care was
given to preserve the name(s) of the functionaries; but this is not surprising
in view of the exclusive place of the Egyptian king in all relief texts and art.[111]

The length, literary artistry, and repeated use of these divine speeches might
suggest scribal composition; however, one must be careful not to set prophet
and scribe in mutually exclusive roles. The priests in Egypt who would have
functioned in the prophetic role were highly literate, and scribal activity in
the "House of Life" was considered "inspired."[112] Indeed, written communication in general was composed for oral performance, which in the Egyptian
context extended to royal inscriptions.[113] Thus, some Egyptian reliefs citing
divine speeches to the king could have been construed by the original audience as "prophetic," whether delivered through oral prophetic performance
or simply read aloud by a priest in the cult in the manner of a divine letter.

---

[106]William J. Murnane, *Texts from the Amarna Period in Egypt*, SBLWAW 5 (Atlanta: Scholars Press, 1995), §§106–7A.

[107]Barbara Cumming and Benedict G. Davies, *Egyptian Historical Records of the Later Eighteenth Dynasty* (Warminster, UK: Aris & Phillips, 1982–1985), fasc. 6, no. 775. For iconography and texts, see Walter Wreszinski, *Atlas zur Altaegyptischen Kulturgeschichte—Teil 2* (Leipzig: Hinrichs, 1935), folios 189–202.

[108]K. A. Kitchen, *Poetry of Ancient Egypt*, Documenta Mundi: Aegyptiaca 1 (Jonsered: Paul Åströms, 1999), §§28–29.

[109]Adolf Erman, *The Ancient Egyptians: A Sourcebook of Their Writings*, trans. Aylward M. Black-man (Gloucester, MA: Peter Smith, 1978), 254 nn. 2 and 4, 256 n. 1.

[110]K. A. Kitchen and G. A. Gaballa, "Ramesside Varia II," *ZÄS* 96 (1969): 23–28.

[111]Barry J. Kemp, *Ancient Egypt: Anatomy of a Civilization* (London: Routledge, 1991), 190.

[112]Alan Gardiner, "The House of Life," *JEA* 24 (1938): 168.

[113]Christopher J. Eyre, "Is Egyptian Historical Literature 'Historical' or 'Literary'?," in *Ancient Egyp-tian Literature: History and Forms*, ed. Antonio Loprieno, Probleme der Ägyptologie 10 (Leiden: Brill, 1996), 420–29. Cf. Donald B. Redford, "Scribe and Speaker," in Ben Zvi, Floyd, and Matthews, *Writings and Speech*, 161–63, 186–88.

The simplest solution is that these were prophetic speeches, composed in advance for liturgical performance.

So "prophecy" in Egypt or Mesopotamia could originate in written form as well as oral.[114] This supports the observation of Floyd, that composition, transmission, and performance of biblical prophecy were all variations of orality so that scribe and prophet might converge.[115]

### Summary

Ancient Near Eastern societies held the divine word in high regard and carefully transmitted prophetic speech in a variety of written genres. While one does not *necessarily* expect letters and literary texts to preserve oral prophecy with word-for-word accuracy, the case for "loose" transmission—especially that we have no confidence in having the actual words of the prophet—is often overstated for these genres. Correspondents and scribes transmitted oracles in letters and literary texts with relative accuracy. Oracle reports and collections demonstrate that direct recording of oral prophecy was common at least in seventh-century Assyria, the time of classical biblical prophecy. The Deir 'Alla texts offer one instance of this for the region of ancient Judah even *before* the phenomenon of written prophecy claimed by the Old Testament. Furthermore, gathering oracles according to chronological or thematic criteria, such as one finds in sections of Old Testament prophetic books, was also practiced in Assyria. The more extensive complexity of Old Testament prophetic books distinguishes them from Neo-Assyrian oracle collections; but the origin of component blocks of text is illustrated by the Assyrian data. In both letters and oracle reports, social conventions insisted on careful preservation of the link between the oracle and the personal identity of the prophet. Divine letters and Egyptian cultic texts suggest that prophecy could originate in writing for subsequent oral performance.

## Social Contexts for Prophetic Scrolls

Were there social contexts in preexilic Israel with both the capacity and disposition to produce prophetic texts and, in addition, to generate the more

---

[114]This differs from a model of anonymous scribes continuing a type of divination on the literary level in postexilic Yehud (so Martti Nissinen, "The Dubious Image of Prophecy," in *Prophets, Prophecy, and Prophetic Texts in Second Temple Judaism*, ed. Michael H. Floyd and Robert D. Haak, OTS 427 [London: T&T Clark, 2006], 26–41; cf. Nissinen, "Inspired Speech," 29–31); rather, these are socially recognized mediators of the divine word, i.e., prophets.

[115]Michael H. Floyd, "'Write the Revelation!' (Hab 2:2): Re-imagining the Cultural History of Prophecy," in Ben Zvi, Floyd, and Matthews, *Writings and Speech*, 103–43.

complex prophetic *literature* found in the Old Testament? Space allows only
a trace of the outline that such a discussion could take.

There is considerable evidence for the presence of an established scribal
class in the later monarchy, which was the setting for the origin of written
prophecy.[116] At times, institutional support could account for its sponsorship. Schniedewind suggests that the demise of the northern kingdom and
subsequent need by Hezekiah to integrate refugees into the south catalyzed
the generation of prophetic texts relevant to the Assyrian crisis.[117] Carr argues
that education and texts served to shape the values of individuals, primarily
the elite leadership of society. But enculturation would trickle down the social
pyramid to a broader cross section of society through oral performance of
texts and instruction.[118] When institutions were opposed to a prophet, writing
of prophetic speech could still come from the support of individual scribes
(e.g., Baruch assisting Jeremiah). Indeed, scribal education and practice took
place not only in royal and temple contexts but also in the independent, professional practice of individual scribes.[119] The disastrous events surrounding
the Assyrian and Babylonian exiles vindicated the message of prophets who
predicted these desperate times, and preservation of their messages provided
theological contextualization of the events. Thus, prophecy also served the
needs of future generations,[120] a function parallel to Neo-Assyrian oracle collections.[121] This portrait is hardly new, but its credibility is supported by what
is known about prophecy and writing outside preexilic Israel.

What accounts for the development of complex prophetic *literature*? If Israel
was capable of generating *any* literature, then the uniquely formed prophetic
books are not in principle outside the capacity of the culture. Considering
the long service of many prophets (decades in some cases), it is not inherently improbable that their oracles were collected and edited into sophisticated, lengthier form under the supervision of the prophets themselves (or

---

[116]William M. Schniedewind, *How the Bible Became a Book* (Cambridge: Cambridge University Press,
2004), 40–45; David M. Carr, *Writing on the Tablet of the Heart: Origins of Scripture and Literature*
(Oxford: Oxford University Press, 2005), 113–15, 131, 164–65; Richard S. Hess, "Questions of Reading and Writing in Ancient Israel," *BBR* 19 (2009): 1–9.

[117]Schniedewind, *How the Bible Became a Book*, 64, 84–90. For temple sponsorship, see van der Toorn,
*Scribal Culture*, 87–88, 183–84. Nissinen, "How Prophecy Became Literature," 156–57, proposes that
the Babylonian debacle was the catalyst for the first prophetic books, but there is no reason it should
not be the crisis facing Hezekiah.

[118]Carr, *Writing on the Tablet of the Heart*, 287–88.

[119]Ibid. Attested in Mesopotamia (Laurie E. Pearce, "The Scribes and Scholars of Ancient Mesopotamia," *CANE*, 4:2273) but not clearly so in Egypt (Edward F. Wente, "The Scribes of Ancient
Egypt," *CANE*, 4:2217).

[120]Ronald E. Clements, "The Prophet as an Author: The Case of the Isaiah Memoir," in Ben Zvi,
Floyd, and Matthews, *Writings and Speech*, 101.

[121]Pongratz-Leisten, *Herrschaftswissen*, 285, 315.

perhaps in the generation of their disciples [e.g., Isa. 8:16; Jer. 36:2]).[122] It is unnecessary to postulate, as does Floyd for example, that prophetic activity "involved writing in limited ways" and only later, in the exilic or postexilic periods, took a literary form.[123] As noted above, there was impetus as early as Hezekiah's time for such literature. While evidence exists for the role of scribes in adapting oral and written tradition for the creation of *new epic or mythic literature* (e.g., Gilgamesh, *Enuma Elish*), this evidence does not extend to prophecy. It is doubtful that scribes freely fabricated any message of prophecy.[124] Similarly, authorship appears relatively unimportant for many genres of text,[125] but prophecy was an exception.[126] Ancient culture respected the connection between prophets and the texts that bear their names.

## Conclusion

The notion that prophetic books are "scribal artifacts" represents only half of the story. Scribes worked in concert with prophets and authentic prophetic tradition, whether oral or written. Nothing indicates that a scribe would substantially alter, let alone invent, prophetic messages. The Neo-Assyrian collections in particular point to the careful preservation of oral prophetic speech, and divine letters and the Egyptian royal cult illustrate prophecy originating in written form. Thus, evidence supports a model wherein preexilic Israel recorded and arranged prophetic messages into literature.

---

[122] See Carr, *Writing on the Tablet of the Heart*, 59–60, 144–46, and van der Toorn, *Scribal Culture*, 184–88. Both Carr and van der Toorn propose significant supplements to the prophecies of Jeremiah and Isaiah by scribal followers. However, discussion of JerMT and JerLXX needs to consider that Jeremiah maintained correspondence with the exiles and addressed his message to them specifically. For Isaiah, see the essay by Richard Schultz in this volume.

[123] Michael H. Floyd, "The Production of Prophetic Books in the Early Second Temple Period," in Floyd and Haak, *Prophets, Prophecy, and Prophetic Texts in Second Temple Judaism*, 277.

[124] Literary-predictive texts (e.g., Marduk Prophecy; The Prophecies of Neferti) are a genre of historiography or wisdom distinct from prophecy (Ellis, "Observations on Mesopotamian Oracles and Prophetic Texts," 146–48; Shupak, "Egyptian 'Prophecy' and Biblical Prophecy," 28; cf. Nissinen, Seow, and Ritner, *Prophets and Prophecy in the Ancient Near East*, 9). This is the fundamental weakness of the proposal by de Jong to compare Mesopotamian literary-predictive texts with literary development in Isaiah (de Jong, *Isaiah among the Ancient Near Eastern Prophets*, esp. 433), or the similar comparison by Weeks of the Egyptian Neferti with Old Testament prophetic literature (Stuart Weeks, "Predictive and Prophetic Literature: Can Neferti Help Us Read the Bible?," in *Prophecy and the Prophets in Ancient Israel*, ed. John Day, OTS 531 [London, New York: T&T Clark, 2010], 25–46).

[125] Schniedewind, *How the Bible Became a Book*, 7; van der Toorn, *Scribal Culture*, 27–49.

[126] Van der Toorn, *Scribal Culture*, 48. He suggests that the unusual attribution of authorship in the Song of Erra might be due to its claim to prophetic-like origin (ibid., 42). Several other nonprophetic texts claim inspired authorship but remain anonymous (Benjamin R. Foster, "On Authorship in Akkadian Literature," *AION* 51 [1991]: 17–32). The Egyptian royal prophecies are anonymous, but this is consistent with the eclipse of human functionaries in royal texts other than the king.

# 10

# ISAIAH, ISAIAHS, AND CURRENT SCHOLARSHIP

## RICHARD L. SCHULTZ[1]

In his 1996 survey article "The Book of Isaiah in Recent Study," Marvin Tate acknowledges that the "one-prophet interpretation" of Isaiah is "still alive in current study,"[2] although it is unclear from his comments whether he is happy to acknowledge this. In a similar review essay published in 2009, Hugh Williamson merely concedes that this "position is still defended from time to time."[3]

What is new in recent years is that a more overt effort is being made *within* evangelical circles to persuade conservative scholars to abandon the one-prophet interpretation. Typical of this is the essay by John Halsey Wood published in *JETS* in 2005.[4] Wood seeks to place Oswald T. Allis, along with his vigorous defense of "single early authorship of the book of Isaiah, . . . in his historical moment," as well as to expose "his methodological inconsistencies" by comparing his treatment of Isaiah with his approach to the Mosaic authorship of the Pentateuch.[5] Wood's critique of Allis can be formulated

---

[1] I addressed similar issues in my essay, "How Many Isaiahs Were There and What Does It Matter? Prophetic Inspiration in Recent Evangelical Scholarship," in *Scripture in the Evangelical Tradition: Tradition, Authority, and Hermeneutics*, ed. V. Bacote, L. Miguelez, and D. Okholm (Downers Grove, IL: InterVarsity, 2004), 150–70, which the reader is encouraged to consult. For the most part, I will not repeat in this essay material covered there, but will focus instead on responding to several evangelical treatments of Isaiah that have been published since I wrote that essay.

[2] M. E. Tate, "The Book of Isaiah in Recent Study," in *Forming Prophetic Literature: Essays on Isaiah and the Twelve*, ed. J. W. Watts and P. R. House (Sheffield: Sheffield Academic, 1996), 26. He cites and summarizes the then recently published commentaries of John Oswalt and J. A. Motyer as evidence.

[3] H. G. M. Williamson, "Recent Issues in the Study of Isaiah," in *Interpreting Isaiah: Issues and Approaches*, ed. D. G. Firth and H. G. M. Williamson (Downers Grove, IL: InterVarsity, 2009), 21.

[4] J. H. Wood, "Oswald T. Allis and the Question of Isaianic Authorship," *JETS* 48 (2005): 249–61. Wood focuses on Allis's brief study *The Unity of Isaiah: A Study in Prophecy* (Philadelphia: Presbyterian and Reformed, 1950).

[5] Wood, "Oswald T. Allis," 249.

as three questions. First of all, since Allis was willing to affirm only the "substantial" or "essential," rather than complete, Mosaic authorship of the Pentateuch despite the New Testament ascriptions of these books to Moses, why was he unwilling to make the same concession regarding the book of Isaiah? Second, why was Allis willing to allow for Moses's utilization of written sources, for example, in composing the early Genesis accounts, without being open to "the possibility of redaction and compilation in prophetic literature"? Here Wood speculates that "probably he [i.e., Allis] felt this would ultimately destroy the validity of prediction."[6] Third, how could Allis claim that Deuteronomy 18 prophesies a "great succession of prophetic voices"[7] culminating in Jesus Christ, while never suggesting a similar interpretation of the Suffering Servant in Isaiah 53?

How are we to account for these "inconsistencies"? In Wood's opinion, Allis's approach resulted from his involvement in the "fundamentalist-modernist controversy." Within that highly charged intellectual-religious context, Allis presumably felt that more was at stake in defending "prophetic prediction" (and consequently the Isaianic authorship of the entire book of Isaiah) than in defending the exclusive Mosaic authorship of the Pentateuch. Wood decries Allis's resultant "inability, or at least unwillingness, to recognize the subtle differences between various critical positions"[8] and his tendency to attribute the critical position to a fundamental rejection of "supernaturalism," whereas the real issue is not whether prophets *could* predict the distant future but whether they, in fact, *would*.[9] According to Wood, the words of Allis's "Isaiah" (at least in chaps. 40ff.) would have been largely insignificant for the prophet's own generation. Allis was also inclined by "the realist-empirical atmosphere at Princeton" to assume (unnecessarily) that prophetic prediction must be "objective, non-metaphorical, and well-defined."[10] Although Wood's essay has an explicitly historical focus, his sustained critique of Allis and more positive reference to Herman Ridderbos (who attributes Isaiah 40–66 primarily to the *disciples* of Isaiah) suggest that his larger (but unstated) purpose is to move conservative scholars who hold to a similarly "wooden" view of prophecy to adopt a more nuanced and defensible position.

Are Allis's view of the prophetic ministry of Isaiah as passé and his treatment of the canonical book of Isaiah as inconsistent as Wood alleges? In my opinion, Wood fails to acknowledge the significant genre differences between

---

[6]Ibid., 257–58.
[7]Ibid., 259, quoting Allis, *God Spake by Moses* (Philadelphia: Presbyterian and Reformed, 1951), 145.
[8]Wood, "Oswald T. Allis," 260.
[9]Ibid.
[10]Ibid., 260–61.

the Pentateuch and the Latter Prophets when accusing Allis of methodological inconsistency.

It is not clear that the ascription of the Pentateuch to Moses or the book of Isaiah to the eighth-century prophet by various New Testament authors requires us to affirm more than "substantial" or "essential" authorship, thereby excluding either the use of *earlier* materials or the addition of *later* explanatory comments or narrative material (e.g., the account of Moses's death). Moreover, in the case of the Pentateuch (and especially in the case of Genesis), it makes good sense that an inspired author such as Moses would make ample use of earlier written source materials, for example, extensive patriarchal narratives. And given the predominantly narrative form of the Pentateuch, it is not surprising to find numerous examples of brief editorial updates for the benefit of later readers, such as the anachronistic mention of Dan in Genesis 14:14.[11] In the case of the prophet Isaiah, however, there is less reason to assume that he had substantial earlier materials to draw on, other than the oracles of his prophetic contemporaries[12] or, possibly, historiographic accounts.[13] More plausible is the (often-made) suggestion that prophetic oracles were editorially updated to indicate how various prophecies were (or were not) fulfilled in the course of Israelite history. For example, Hermann Barth identifies a "Josianic" redactional layer within Isaiah 1–39, which, in his interpretation, clarifies how earlier anti-Assyrian oracles played out in the late seventh century.[14] Yet such "updating," regardless of how minimal or extensive, is quite different from the typical critical claim that less than half of the canonical book of Isaiah originated in the eighth century.

It is mere speculation to claim that Allis was driven by a desire to preserve prophetic "prediction" in treating the composition of Isaiah more strictly than the Pentateuch. Allis's perspective on the much-discussed Cyrus prophecy in Isaiah 44–45, however, is clear since he notes "how greatly the *situation*

---

[11]Duane Garrett offers a thorough discussion of this possibility in *Rethinking Genesis: The Sources and Authorship of the First Book of the Pentateuch* (Grand Rapids: Baker, 1991). See also P. J. Wiseman, *Ancient Records and the Structure of Genesis: A Case for Literary Unity* (Nashville: Nelson, 1985), who views the individual *toledoth* sections as written sources that a later author could utilize. For an example of a recent evangelical analysis of the Pentateuch that affirms both an essential Mosaic authorship *and* extensive late redactional additions, see J. H. Sailhamer, *The Meaning of the Pentateuch: Revelation, Composition and Interpretation* (Downers Grove, IL: InterVarsity, 2009).
[12]See, for example, G. Stansell, *Micah and Isaiah: A Form and Tradition Historical Comparison*, SBLDS 85 (Atlanta: Scholars Press, 1988).
[13]The origin of Isaiah 36–39 (and verses like Isa. 7:1) continues to be debated. Christopher Seitz, however, argues, *contra* Bernhard Duhm, that Isaiah 36–38 belongs to "the Isaiah tradition" rather than originating with the Deuteronomic History. C. R. Seitz, *Zion's Final Destiny: The Development of the Book of Isaiah: A Reassessment of Isaiah 36–39* (Minneapolis: Fortress, 1991), 146–48, 189–91.
[14]H. Barth, *Die Jesaja-Worte in der Josiazeit*, WMANT 48 (Neukirchen-Vluyn: Neukirchener, 1977), 203–75.

which the critics assign to this prophecy reduces its *scope* by eliminating almost completely the predictive element from it."[15] In other words, most proponents of the Second Isaiah hypothesis date Isaiah 40–55 to the 540s, when Cyrus's dramatic military victories made the fall of Babylon to him *inevitable*, and thus there was no need for a divinely inspired prophet to announce it. Furthermore, some scholars deny that Deutero-Isaiah was in any sense "predicting" the events surrounding Cyrus's rise to international prominence. Klaus Baltzer, for example, dates Isaiah 40–55 to "sometime between 450 and 400 B.C.E.," that is, a century later than Cyrus's reign.[16] The approach of Goldingay and Payne to Isaiah 44–45 is more cautious. After considering (and rejecting) the possibility that Cyrus's edict predates Isaiah 44–45 (in other words, that Isaiah 44–45 postdates the fall of Babylon), they affirm rather that the prophet is offering "guidance on the significance of events, before and as they unfold."[17] The prophet's primary contribution then is not in announcing what the Persian monarch is about to do but rather in announcing that he is, in fact, *Yahweh's* anointed agent on the world scene. In the process, however, the claim of Isaiah 44:26 that Yahweh "carries out the words of his servants and *fulfills the predictions of his messengers*, who says of Jerusalem, 'It shall be inhabited' . . ."[18] fades into the background. In this respect, Allis's defense of prophetic "prediction" (here in the prophecies of Isaiah of Jerusalem) is analogous to his defense of the Mosaic origin of Pentateuchal law.[19] As one who upholds the authority of God's Word, Allis is loath to surrender either explicit claim of the text.

Wood's final critique is that Allis treats Deuteronomy 18:15 differently (i.e., inconsistently) from Isaiah 52:13–53:12. The context of Deuteronomy 18 indicates that Moses may well have the rise of the prophetic institution

---

[15]Allis, *The Unity of Isaiah*, 60. Here one should also note that the word *prediction* has come to have a narrow, even technical, use within conservative apologetics. John Walton objects to the common understanding of this term in two respects: (1) The prophets themselves did not predict; they simply announced what God told them. (2) Divine prediction is meaningless (i.e., it is without risk of nonfulfillment) when God is the final cause of all that happens. Instead, Walton prefers to think of prophecy as God's "syllabus" presenting his future plans and intentions. This perspective could also accommodate conditional prophecy. See A. E. Hill and J. H. Walton, *A Survey of the Old Testament* (Grand Rapids: Zondervan, 2009), 511–15.

[16]K. Baltzer, *Deutero-Isaiah: A Commentary on Isaiah 40–55*, Hermeneia (Minneapolis: Augsburg Fortress, 2001), 30–32. German scholars today generally posit a smaller Deutero-Isaianic core, as well as several later redactional layers stemming from the early postexilic period. See the summary comments by Williamson, "Recent Issues in the Study of Isaiah," 35–37.

[17]J. Goldingay and D. Payne, *A Critical and Exegetical Commentary on Isaiah 40–55*, ICC (London: T&T Clark, 2006), 2:18.

[18]Unless otherwise noted, Scripture quotations in this chapter are from the New International Version, 1984 edition.

[19]See O. T. Allis, *The Old Testament: Its Claims and Critics* (Nutley, NJ: Presbyterian and Reformed, 1972), 20–23.

(rather than a single future prophet) in mind to counter—or offer a divinely approved alternative to—all illegitimate sources of "supra-human" guidance (vv. 9–12, 14a, 20–22). This need will presumably continue as long as Israel resides in the Promised Land (vv. 13, 14b–19). Stephen's speech in Acts 3, in which he cites Deuteronomy 18 (Acts 3:22–23) before referring to "all the prophets from Samuel on" (Acts 3:24), confirms this understanding. What is *not* clear from the context is that a messianic prophet is ultimately in view here.[20] In the case of Isaiah 52–53, to the contrary, the extensive, strikingly detailed portrait of the servant's suffering and exaltation makes it highly unlikely that a *succession* of "suffering servants" is in view here.[21]

A more systematic attack against traditional views regarding Isaiah is mounted by Kenton Sparks in his 2008 monograph *God's Word in Human Words*. Its subtitle, *An Evangelical Appropriation of Critical Biblical Scholarship*, expresses both his personal stance regarding the "assured results of biblical criticism" and his agenda.[22] He presents the "Problem of Isaiah" in his lengthy chapter 3 ("The Problem of Biblical Criticism: A Survey of the Flashpoints"), which summarizes the "critical consensus."[23] If "the critical consensus on the Bible is essentially correct and reasonably justified,"[24] as Sparks believes, then this presents a significant "problem" for those holding a traditional viewpoint on the divine inspiration of individual biblical books and its implications for historical reliability, theological consistency, compositional unity, and authorship claims. Expressed differently, the claimed "divine origin" of the Bible in no way mitigates the effect of its human authors' and intended readers' limitations of knowledge and perspective.[25]

Sparks's brief summary of the "problem of Isaiah" mostly follows familiar lines while also containing an unmistakable apologetic for historical-critical scholarship.[26] A point-by-point response to Sparks's critical assessment of

---

[20]See Daniel Block's nonmessianic interpretation of Deut. 18:15, "My Servant David: Ancient Israel's Vision of the Messiah," in *Israel's Messiah in the Bible and the Dead Sea Scrolls*, ed. R. S. Hess and M. D. Carroll R. (Grand Rapids: Baker, 2003), 28–32.

[21]I will respond to several additional issues raised in Wood's essay in the course of discussing Sparks's exposition of the "problem of Isaiah."

[22]K. L. Sparks, *God's Word in Human Words: An Evangelical Appropriation of Critical Biblical Scholarship* (Grand Rapids: Baker Academic, 2008).

[23]Ibid., 73–132.

[24]Ibid., 76.

[25]Ibid., 77.

[26]One of Sparks's favorite rhetorical strategies is to note the names of "evangelical" scholars who hold similar views, implying thereby that (1) the objective evidence is compelling, (2) the theological implications are unproblematic, and (3) any evangelical who disagrees with such an overwhelming consensus is simply ignoring or denying the truth. See, for example, Sparks, *God's Word in Human Words*, 148 ("most biblical scholars, including even many evangelical scholars"), 149 ("even evangelicals like . . .").

Isaiah can serve as a helpful—though by no means exhaustive—introduction to the issue of Isaiah and "Isaiahs" in current scholarship.

First of all, according to Sparks, modern scholars are "not entirely antagonistic to traditional views of the book of Isaiah" since they recognize a degree of "editorial unity" in the canonical form of the book, noting, for example, the recurrence of the divine designation "Holy One of Israel" throughout the book.[27] This claim by Sparks is misleading, since the traditional view that Isaiah of Jerusalem is the primary author or source of the canonical book is uniformly rejected by contemporary critical scholars, with some essentially reducing the eighth-century prophet's contribution to chapters 7–8 and 28–31.[28] Those still holding to the traditional view are subjected to denigrating comments, such as Tate's reference to Motyer's "shopworn appeals to verbal inspiration."[29] Recognizing "editorial unity" in some vague sense hardly represents a move toward the traditional viewpoint since some scholars locate the final editor as late as the third century BC.[30] The phrase "the Holy One of Israel," which occurs twelve times in chapters 1–39, thirteen times in 40–66, and only six times elsewhere in the Hebrew Bible, is cited as evidence both of the book's *authorial* unity and of its *editorial* unity, depending on the scholar's viewpoint. In the latter case, it is accounted for either as Second and Third Isaiah's reuse of their prophetic "master's" favorite designation for God or as an editor's conscious imitation of proto-Isaianic style, in either case in order to give the impression of theological continuity over the centuries.[31] As Longman and Dillard have noted, not without irony, many "arguments from conservatives for unity of authorship based on common themes and vocabulary have now in large part been taken over and pressed into service as arguments for a redactional unity in the book."[32]

---

[27] Sparks, *God's Word in Human Words*, 105.

[28] Matthijs J. de Jong, *Isaiah among the Ancient Near Eastern Prophets: A Comparative Study of the Earliest Stages of the Isaiah Tradition and the Neo-Assyrian Prophecies*, VTSup 117 (Leiden: Brill, 2007), 465, attributes only ninety-five verses to Isaiah of Jerusalem, or, more precisely, "to prophetic activity in the eighth century."

[29] Tate, "Book of Isaiah," 27.

[30] See, for example, Judith Gärtner, *Jesaja 66 und Sacharja 14 als Summe der Prophetie: Eine traditions- und redaktionsgeschichtliche Untersuchung zum Abschluss des Jesaja- und des Zwölfprophetenbuches*, WMANT 114 (Neukirchen-Vluyn: Neukirchener, 2006), 4, who builds on the redactional work of Odil Hannes Steck.

[31] See, for example, E. J. Young, *An Introduction to the Old Testament*, rev. ed. (Grand Rapids: Eerdmans, 1964), 210; R. Rendtorff, *Das Alte Testament: Eine Einführung*, 2nd ed. (Neukirchen-Vluyn: Neukirchener, 1985), 210–11.

[32] T. Longman III and R. B. Dillard, *An Introduction to the Old Testament*, 2nd ed. (Grand Rapids: Zondervan, 2006), 309.

Second, according to Sparks, Isaiah 1–39 generally presupposes an eighth-century (i.e., Assyrian era) Judahite audience,[33] while 40–55 presupposes that the Babylonian exile is drawing to a close. This is a primary claim of the historical-critical Second Isaiah theory, but Sparks's point here presupposes a monolithic critical viewpoint and compelling evidence in support of it. It is without dispute that Isaiah 40–55, at least in part, addresses an exilic audience, but it is unclear that one can date all of the content contained in these chapters to the final years of the exile. The chronological progression within Isaiah 1–39 clearly suggests that chapters 40ff. address those in exile. The book's initial verse ties the prophet's ministry to "the reigns of Uzziah, Jotham, Ahaz and Hezekiah, kings of Judah," during which the northern kingdom was conquered and its leading citizens exiled by the Assyrians, and, under Sennacherib, much of the southern kingdom suffered the same fate.[34] In other words, the majority of Isaiah's fellow countrymen were *already* in exile in his day and could appropriately be addressed as such in his oracles recorded in chapters 40ff. Moreover, Gary Smith has argued recently that Isaiah 40:12–44:23 are better understood as describing the progress of the Assyrian army under Sennacherib in Isaiah's day than as depicting the later Persian army under Cyrus.[35] One should not expect Smith's "new" interpretation (in part, already suggested by Calvin) to persuade many proponents of the Second Isaiah theory who are convinced that the mention of Cyrus in Isaiah 44:28–45:1 compels one to hold to an exilic setting for all of chapters 40–55. And finally, some of the individual verses in this section of Isaiah do not easily fit into the late exilic period. For example, the wording of Isaiah 43:28,

וַאֲחַלֵּל שָׂרֵי קֹדֶשׁ וְאֶתְּנָה לַחֵרֶם יַעֲקֹב וְיִשְׂרָאֵל לְגִדּוּפִים

though somewhat difficult to translate, appears to refer to a *future*, not a *past*, destruction of the temple ("So I will pollute the princes of the sanctuary, And I will consign Jacob to the ban and Israel to revilement," NASB). Whybray responds to this problem as follows: "The two verbs . . . have a

---

[33] Although Sparks does not explain his qualification "generally presupposes," he is compelled to make it since most historical-critical scholars find much material in Isaiah 1–39 that they consider to be later than the eighth century.

[34] See 2 Kings 18:13. In the Assyrian annals, Sennacherib claims to have conquered 46 "fortified walled cities" in Judah and deported 200,150 of its citizens. "Sennacherib's Siege of Jerusalem (2.119B)," in *Monumental Inscriptions from the Biblical World*, vol. 2 of *The Context of Scripture*, ed. W. W. Hallo, trans. M. Cohen (Leiden: Brill, 2000), 303.

[35] G. V. Smith, *Isaiah 40–66*, NAC 15B (Nashville: B&H, 2009), 103–5, 175–88.

future sense as pointed by the Massoretes, but should certainly be pointed as waw-consecutives, giving them a past sense."[36]

Third, according to Sparks, if one holds to the traditional view of Isaiah, chapters 40–55 contain "astonishingly detailed predictions about the end of the Jewish exile two centuries later," rounding up from the more accurate figure of 150, which he gives elsewhere. Although those critical scholars who "do not believe in miraculous prophecies" of necessity date these to the sixth century, they do not all view these as "pseudoprophecies" (or *ex eventu* = "after the fact").[37] For Sparks, these "constitute genuine prophecies written *to* the exiles that predicted their deliverance."[38] Most notable is the announcement of the Persian king Cyrus as God's designated agent of deliverance—his *messiah*—in Isaiah 45, a chapter that, in Sparks's interpretation, reflects Jewish resistance to this divine plan (although the reason for this alleged resistance remains unclear). Sparks contends that this declaration could not have been directed to an eighth-century audience, "who could not have made heads or tales [*sic*] out of Isaiah's rhetoric."[39]

Here again, Sparks overstates the situation with regard to Isaiah 40–55. As Brevard Childs has noted, "only scattered vestiges" of the original historical context remain in these chapters and "no concrete historical situations are addressed." Even in the case of Cyrus, such references are "minimal. Cyrus has become such a theological projection, an instrument in the hand of God, that his role blurs into the description of Abraham."[40] Furthermore, as cited above, Gary Smith claims that the poetic descriptions of the "one from the east" (41:2) in 40:12–44:23 do not actually correspond to Cyrus's military actions as reported in extrabiblical texts.

Sparks's claim that the Cyrus prophecy would have made no sense to an eighth-century audience is a common one.[41] John Goldingay states it even

---

[36]R. N. Whybray, *Isaiah 40–66*, NCB (London: Marshall, Morgan & Scott, 1975), 93. The same Hebrew verb חלל also occurs with קדש in Zeph. 3:4 and Mal. 2:11.

[37]Sparks, *God's Word in Human Words*, 105.

[38]Ibid., 106. Sparks does not consider the claim of *ex eventu* prophecies within the Hebrew Bible to be problematic for an evangelical (see ibid., 223–24). It is unclear from a reading of Sparks whether he believes in "miraculous prophecies." See the treatment of the nonmiraculous nature of the Cyrus prophecy in the discussion of Allis above.

[39]Ibid., 107.

[40]B. S. Childs, *Introduction to the Old Testament as Scripture* (Philadelphia: Fortress, 1979), 325–26. M. E. Baloyi describes these chapters somewhat differently: "The prophetic vividness in 40–66 confuses the historical and chronological sequence of the passages, hence confusing most scholars regarding the date(s) of the prophecies in 40–66. The tenses of the Hebrew verbs offer no solution." "The Unity of the Book Isaiah: Neglected Evidence [Re-]considered," *OTE* 20 (2007): 110.

[41]See, for example, Whybray, *Second Isaiah*, OTG (Sheffield: JSOT, 1983), 4, who claims that "the content of the prophet's message from start to finish is quite inappropriate to the circumstances of the eighth century B.C."

more pointedly, invoking the evangelical doctrine of Scripture: "What would God be doing giving Isaiah in the eighth century words to write down that were addressed to people two centuries later?"[42] Most of Isaiah 40–55 (for example, chaps. 40–43), however, has no clear links to the sixth century. Moreover, using such a hermeneutic could effectively eliminate any genuine messianic or eschatological prophecy, since it could be seen as either irrelevant or opaque to the original audience. The fact that most scholars conclude that the returnees did not experience the glorious return promised by the prophet in Isaiah 40–55 and thus remained *de facto* in a state of "exile"[43] suggests that the late-exilic audience could not truly comprehend these prophetic promises either. In the book of Isaiah, Carroll notes, "far too many themes and topoi are interwoven together to allow for a single integrated, consistent account of diaspora discourses and restoration expectations to be constructed by modern [or presumably by *ancient*] readers."[44]

Fourth, according to Sparks, the existence of the unknown author dubbed Deutero-Isaiah is supported by the nonmention of the prophet Isaiah in Isaiah 40–55 (or 40–66, for that matter), after mention of him *sixteen* times in 1–39. This is a very odd argument, often reinforced by the claim that Isaiah 40 contains Deutero-Isaiah's "call narrative," paralleling Isaiah 6.[45] The distribution of the name Isaiah is anything but uniform, being confined to three "titles" introducing revelatory content (i.e., what Isaiah saw—with Heb. חָזָה; 1:1; 2:1; 13:1) and three sections in which Isaiah participates in the narrated events (7:3; 20:2–3; 37:2, 5, 6, 21; 38:1, 4, 21; 39:3, 5, 8).[46] Is this a sufficient number of occurrences to claim chapters 1–39 for the eighth-century prophet, even though Isaiah's name does not appear once in chapters 21–35, a section that is nearly as long as those chapters attributed to Second Isaiah and longer than Third Isaiah?[47] Furthermore, the absence of an author's name in Isaiah

---

[42] J. Goldingay, "What Are the Characteristics of Evangelical Study of the Old Testament?," *EvQ* 73, no. 2 (2001): 105.

[43] See R. E. Watts, "Consolation or Confrontation? Isaiah 40–55 and the Delay of the New Exodus," *TynBul* 41 (1990): 31–59; and the essays in J. M. Scott, ed., *Exile: Old Testament, Jewish, and Christian Conceptions*, JSJSup 56 (Leiden: Brill, 1997).

[44] R. P. Carroll, "Deportation and Diasporic Discourses in the Prophetic Literature," in Scott, *Exile*, 75.

[45] The identification of Isa. 40:1–11 as a "call narrative" is widespread in critical scholarship but unconvincing and may reflect an effort to compensate for the absence of a named prophet or title at the beginning of chaps. 40–66. For a helpful analysis of Isa. 40:1–11 and the "headings" in the book of Isaiah on the basis of communication theory, see A. L. H. M. van Wieringen, "Isaiah's Roles: The Unity of a Bible Book from the Perspective of the Sender-Role," in *One Text, A Thousand Methods*, ed. P. C. Counet and U. Berges, Biblical Interpretation 71 (Leiden: Brill, 2005), 115–24. The striking fact that Isa. 1:1 relates the entire "vision" (= the canonical book?) to Isaiah of Jerusalem's half century of public ministry is a textual datum that is difficult to harmonize with any view of multiple "Isaiahs."

[46] Isaiah 40–66 contains no titles or narratives, in which a reference to Isaiah might be expected.

[47] There are 295 verses in chaps. 21–35, 333 in chaps. 40–55, and 192 in chaps. 55–66. It is interesting to note that the name Babylon occurs nine times in chaps. 1–39 but only four times in chaps. 40–55.

40–66 does not provide a solid basis for positing the existence of an exilic prophetic author. After surveying a century of German scholarship on the issue, Ulrich Berges concludes:

> One cannot admit that the text is [merely] redactional because it is important, and thus one fabricates the prophetic figure "Deutero-Isaiah." But precisely the fact that we do not know the author by name indicates that a compiler or editor (*ein Bearbeiter oder Redaktor*) is at work here. Genuine prophetic figures did not remain anonymous; the great compilers of biblical books did—and this for good reasons.[48]

Fifth, according to Sparks, the fact that Jeremiah never cites the prophecies of Isaiah 40–55 regarding the Babylonian exile and subsequent deliverance through Cyrus also suggests that Jeremiah's copy of the book of Isaiah did not yet contain these chapters and thus that they must not have been authored in the eighth century. Yet the argument from silence is tenuous. Scholars have still not offered a satisfying explanation for the surprising observation that King Josiah is never directly addressed or spoken about in the book of Jeremiah. Nor do we know why contemporary prophets, such as Hosea, Amos, Isaiah, and Micah, never refer to each other, although there are some indications of the mutual influence of their messages.[49] As for the speculative claim that Jeremiah's copy of the book of Isaiah did not contain Isaiah 40–55, one must note that there have been extensive studies of the relationship between Jeremiah and Second Isaiah by scholars such as Werner Tannert, Shalom Paul, Patricia (Tull) Willey, and Benjamin Sommer.[50] Although these scholars uniformly conclude that Deutero-Isaiah is borrowing from Jeremiah and not vice versa, one gets the impression that they had concluded that Jeremiah preceded Deutero-Isaiah on the basis of the historical-critical consensus *prior to* undertaking their detailed analyses and comparisons. They do not offer any compelling evidence from the examined verbal parallels and allusions that these examples could not have resulted instead from Jeremiah's borrowing

[48]U. Berges, "Das Jesajabuch als Jesajas Buch: Zu neuesten Entwicklungen in der Prophetenforschung," *TRev* 104 (2008): 8, my translation. According to Wilhelm Caspari, "the personal Deutero-Isaiah was [merely] a house plant on the scholars' desk." *Lieder und Gottessprüche der Rückwanderer: Jesaja 40–55*, BZAW 65 (Giessen: A. Töpelmann, 1934), 244, my translation.
[49]See, for example, the monograph of Stansell cited in n. 12.
[50]W. Tannert, "Jeremia und Deuterojesaja: Eine Untersuchung zur Frage ihres literarischen und theologischen Zusammenhanges" (PhD diss., Leipzig, 1956), summarized in *TLZ* 83 (1958): 725–26; S. M. Paul, "Literary and Ideological Echoes of Jeremiah in Deutero-Isaiah," in *Proceedings of the Fifth World Congress of Jewish Studies (1969)* (Jerusalem: World Union of Jewish Studies, 1972), 102–20; P. T. Willey, *Remember the Former Things: The Recollection of Previous Texts in Second Isaiah*, SBLDS 161 (Atlanta: Scholars Press, 1997); B. D. Sommer, *A Prophet Reads Scripture: Allusion in Isaiah 40–66*, The Contraversions Series (Stanford: Stanford University Press, 1998).

from the book of Isaiah.[51] In any case, if one is inclined to date Isaiah 40–55 earlier (as I am)—or the final redaction of the book of Jeremiah later (as some commentators do)[52]—Sparks's claim is clearly false.

Sixth, Sparks also affirms the critical dating of Isaiah 56–66 in the postexilic period on the basis of internal evidence, although acknowledging that this theory is less certain than the Deutero-Isaiah hypothesis. This evidence includes the following observations:

- Israel is described in Deutero-Isaiah as "innocent and redeemed" (40:1–2) but in Trito-Isaiah as "guilty and idolatrous" (chaps. 57–59; 65:1–16).
- Trito-Isaiah "talks frequently about" rebuilding Jerusalem and restoring its temple and cult.
- "Chapters 56–66 come after and are different from Deutero-Isaiah."[53]

Sparks's characterization of Israel in Isaiah 40–55 is overly selective and one-sided; God's people or individuals within Israel are also addressed or described within these chapters as "rebels" (46:8), "stubborn-hearted . . . far from righteousness" (46:12), taking oaths "but not in truth or righteousness" (48:1), "stubborn" (48:4), and "wicked" and "evil man" (55:7). Sparks's reference to idolatry in chapters 56–66 is even more problematic. As has often been pointed out, there is little evidence (for example, from the postexilic historical books and Minor Prophets) that this particular sin was a significant problem among those who returned to the land of Israel from Babylon. Rather, Harrison claims that

with the exception of the description of Babylonian idolatry in Isaiah 47:13, all other references to such practices in chapters 40–66 are specifically to the preexilic Canaanite variety mentioned in Isaiah 1:13, 29; 2:8ff.; 8:19; and elsewhere. Such allusions in the later chapters include 40:19; 41:7, 29; 42:17; 44:9ff., 25; 45:15ff.; 46:6f.; 48:5; 57:5; 63:3ff.; 66:3, 17.[54]

---

[51]See the discussion in R. L. Schultz, *The Search for Quotation: Verbal Parallels in the Prophets*, JSOTSup 180 (Sheffield: JSOT, 1999), 34–42.

[52]See, for example, R. P. Carroll, *Jeremiah*, OTL (London: SCM, 1986), 65–82.

[53]Sparks, *God's Word in Human Words*, 108.

[54]R. K. Harrison, *Introduction to the Old Testament* (Grand Rapids: Eerdmans, 1969), 779. This leads Claus Westermann, *Isaiah 40–66: A Commentary*, trans. D. M. G. Stalker, OTL (Philadelphia: Westminster, 1977), 319–22, to conclude that 57:1–2 and 57:3–6 are, in fact, "pre-exilic prophetic oracles of judgment" that were taken over by Trito-Isaiah. Watts, however, understands this as a description of the "prevalent paganism" in postexilic Palestine *prior to* the reforming work of Ezra and Nehemiah (*Isaiah 34–66*, WBC 25 [Waco: Word, 1987], 256). For Joseph Blenkinsopp, *Isaiah 56–66*, AB 19B (New York: Doubleday, 2003), 164, the allusions to "mortuary cults" in Isa. 57:3–13 and 65:3–4 offer sufficient evidence that these activities "continued on into the early Persian period at least," despite the fact that other sources limit them to the monarchical period.

Furthermore, there are few (or no) references in Isaiah 56–66 to the restoration of the temple or cult. Seitz describes Third Isaiah as "bereft of concrete historical indicators" and suggests that

> if chaps. 56–66 are read more narrowly in the context of the book of Isaiah, as against their putative diachronic neighbors Haggai, Zechariah, Malachi, and Ezra-Nehemiah, a very different picture of the role of the temple emerges; for nowhere in Isaiah is the destruction of the temple explicitly related. . . . In other words, the fall of the temple and its restoration, as such, are not meaningful literary, historical, or theological indexes in Isaiah.[55]

These and other considerations lead Seitz to join a significant and growing group of scholars who question the purported Babylonian provenance of Second Isaiah, the sharp break between chapters 55 and 56, and the very existence of Third Isaiah.[56]

Finally, Sparks concludes, "A sober and serious reading of Isaiah will easily suggest to readers that large portions of this prophetic collection were not written by an eighth-century prophet whose name was Isaiah."[57] This historical-critical, surprisingly matter of fact claim reminds me of the similar claim by John Barton that the Pentateuch, and in fact much of the Old Testament, is "unreadable."[58] Is one then forced to conclude that the vast majority of members of the believing Jewish and Christian communities during the past two millennia and even many today have failed to read Isaiah in a "sober and serious" manner because of carelessness, ignorance, or dishonesty?

It is remarkable to witness the claimed analytical acumen of modern scholars with regard to what could or could not be authored (or rather prophesied) by an individual prophet in a specific time and place. For example, Ronald Clements analyzes the following brief text from Isaiah 2 as follows:

> [10] Go into the rocks, hide in the ground from dread of the LORD and the splendor of his majesty! . . . [12] The LORD Almighty has a day in store for all the proud

[55] C. R. Seitz, "Isaiah, Book of (Third Isaiah)," in *The Anchor Bible Dictionary*, ed. D. N. Freedman (New York: Doubleday, 1992), 3:502–3.

[56] Ibid., 3:503, 506. The most persistent defender of the Palestinian location of "Second Isaiah" is Hans M. Barstad. See especially his monograph *The Babylonian Captivity of the Book of Isaiah: "Exilic" Judah and the Provenance of Isaiah 40–55* (Oslo: Instituttet for sammenlignende kulturforskning, 1997).

[57] Sparks, *God's Word in Human Words*, 108.

[58] More specifically, he refers to scholars "noticing that the text actually cannot *be* understood as it stands" with the slight qualification that "presumably there was *some* period in the life of ancient Israel when this strange compendium of narrative, law, poetry and exhortation was felt to be a coherent whole—to be, in our terminology, 'readable.'" J. Barton, *Reading the Old Testament: Method in Biblical Study*, 2nd ed. (Louisville: Westminster John Knox, 1996), 24, 27.

and lofty, for all that is exalted (and they will be humbled), [13] for all the cedars of Lebanon, tall and lofty, and all the oaks of Bashan, [14] for all the towering mountains and all the high hills, [15] for every lofty tower and every fortified wall, [16] for every trading ship and every stately vessel. [17] The arrogance of man will be brought low and the pride of men humbled; the LORD alone will be exalted in that day *[the original Isaianic unit]*.

[6] You have abandoned your people, the house of Jacob. They are full of superstitions from the East; they practice divination like the Philistines and clasp hands with pagans *[the described business deals point to the age of Nehemiah]*.

[7] Their land is full of silver and gold; there is no end to their treasures. Their land is full of horses; there is no end to their chariots. [8a] Their land is full of idols; . . . [9a] So man will be brought low and mankind humbled *[the earliest secondary expansions, perhaps from the same time as v. 6]*.

[8b] they bow down to the work of their hands, to what their fingers have made *[presupposes, i.e., postdates, the anti-idolatry polemic of Isa. 44:9–20]*.

[9b] —do not forgive them *[a later editorial comment]*.

[11] The eyes of the arrogant man will be humbled and the pride of men brought low; the LORD alone will be exalted in that day *[a trivial addition that interrupts the original connection between vv. 10 and 12–17]*.

[18] and the idols will totally disappear *[a prosaic gloss referring to v. 8a]*.

[19] Men will flee to caves in the rocks and to holes in the ground from dread of the LORD and the splendor of his majesty, when he rises to shake the earth *[a further addition reflecting a literal interpretation of v. 10]*.

[20] In that day men will throw away to the rodents and bats their idols of silver and idols of gold, which they made to worship. [21] They will flee to caverns in the rocks and to the overhanging crags from dread of the LORD and the splendor of his majesty, when he rises to shake the earth. [22] Stop trusting in man, who has but a breath in his nostrils. Of what account is he? *[a postexilic addition describing the effects of the day of the LORD]*.[59]

Is this the kind of "sober and serious reading of Isaiah" to which Sparks is referring, a reading that results in an atomistic and theologically arid—and often highly speculative—exegesis? And exactly how many "Isaiahs" does Clements identify in this brief text? It is not surprising that Williamson, in an essay dedicated to Clements, his former professor, exhibits a similar confidence in his ability to date (or arrange in relative chronological order) each occurrence of the Hebrew word for "glory" (כָּבוֹד) in the book of Isaiah, largely on the basis of how a specific prophet or editor uses the "theme" of

---

[59] R. E. Clements, *Isaiah 1–39*, NCB (Grand Rapids: Eerdmans, 1980), 42–46, cf. 40, where he also dates Isa. 2:2–5 to the early fifth century.

glory.[60] He repeatedly identifies "evident allusions back to earlier [Isaianic] texts" when little more than the word *glory* is present in a given text and is able to conclude that 4:5–6; 11:10; and 24:23 all stem from the latest phase in this thematic development within the Isaiah tradition and perhaps represent a "glory" redactional layer.[61]

This type of redactional analysis is, of course, based on a number of presuppositions about Old Testament prophets and prophecy that cannot be proved, or disproved: (1) that a prophet/editor would not use the same concept or theme in more than one way (e.g., both literally and figuratively);[62] (2) that a prophet would not reuse, allude to, or elaborate upon his own (earlier) oracles (i.e., that any such action must be the work of another); and (3) that a prophet would not proclaim anything that was not clearly relevant and perspicuous for his contemporaries (i.e., that any such texts must be dated to a later date when they would be pertinent and clear). Furthermore, since the prophets are uniformly presented in the Bible as divine spokespersons, one is, in effect, presupposing what God could or would communicate to a particular prophet in a particular era.

In the course of carrying out a thorough analysis of the theme of nationalism versus universalism in the book of Isaiah, I discovered that "both 'nationalism' and 'universalistic' emphases are found in all major sections of Isaiah, sometimes even in adjoining texts," with "all of the major perspectives . . . introduced by chapter 27." This makes the kind of redactional analysis that Clements and Williamson offer extremely difficult to carry out on this theme, and any chronological conclusions rather tenuous. In fact, since "this apparent tension is preserved or even highlighted in the book read as a whole,"[63] any attempt at a historical reconstruction may prove to be hermeneutically counterproductive.

The preceding discussion also confirms the aptness of the assertion by Allis, "It should be remembered then, that the basic question raised by the critics is not, how many Isaiahs there were, but whether there were more Isaiahs than the one."[64] This reminds me of a similar assertion by James Kugel regarding the nature of Hebrew parallelism: "Biblical parallelism is of *one* sort . . . or

---

[60]H. G. M. Williamson, "From One Degree of Glory to Another: Themes and Theology in Isaiah," in *In Search of True Wisdom: Essays in Old Testament Interpretation*, ed. E. Ball, JSOTSup 300 (Sheffield: Sheffield Academic, 1999), 174–95. He explains, "From a purely historical perspective we do not have too much difficulty in sorting out the different levels and rearranging them in order of progression" (ibid., 194).

[61]Williamson, "From One Degree of Glory to Another," 188, also 189–95.

[62]This recalls the frequent twentieth-century claim that a prophet could not proclaim both judgment and salvation.

[63]"Nationalism and Universalism in Isaiah," in Firth and Williamson, *Interpreting Isaiah*, 142–43.

[64]Allis, *The Unity of Isaiah*, 43.

a *hundred* sorts; but it is not *three*."[65] In the case of the book of Isaiah, once one abandons the traditional view that Isaiah of Jerusalem was the sole or primary source of the prophecies in the canonical book, there is virtually no limit to the number of potential contributors that scholars can posit. In any case, to speak of just three Isaiahs is clearly anachronistic in light of current scholarship; even Bernhard Duhm, who is credited with establishing the existence of Trito-Isaiah, identified five or more contributors to the book.[66]

In chapter 4, Sparks rejects several "traditional" responses to biblical-critical analyses of Isaiah. First of all, he accuses the Egyptologist Kenneth Kitchen of making "artificial presentations of the evidence" in defending the traditional view of Isaianic authorship.[67] He criticizes Kitchen for not citing (and countering) the kind of "evidence" that Sparks has cited in the preceding chapter. But one could likewise criticize Sparks for not acknowledging the existence of another very specific prophecy naming a future divine agent more than three centuries in advance, that is, Josiah in 1 Kings 13:1–3.[68] Nor does he mention Isaiah's specific prophecy of the Babylonian exile in 39:5–7, nearly a century before this took place, potentially also entailing the Babylonians' prior defeat of the Assyrians. This text offers a striking parallel with the prophecy of the Babylonian defeat by Cyrus the Persian, though this "prophecy" is, of course, discounted by critical scholars. Clements concludes, for example, that the narrative of Isaiah 39 "was written after 598, but before 587" (i.e., prior to the purported exilic origin of Isaiah 40–55), draining it of any "predictive" import.[69] The chronological inversion of Isaiah 38–39 and 36–37, coupled with the "Babylon exile" prophecy in 39:5–7, has led John Walton to suggest, against this view, that this inversion came from Isaiah and only makes sense if Isaiah 40 directly followed Isaiah 39 whenever Isaiah 36–39 was added to the book.[70]

Sparks also criticizes Kitchen for downplaying the clear implications of Isaiah 48:20a:

---

[65] J. L. Kugel, *The Idea of Biblical Poetry: Parallelism and Its History* (New Haven, CT: Yale University Press, 1981), 58, my emphasis.

[66] B. Duhm, *Das Buch Jesaia, übersetzt und erklärt*, 4th ed., HKAT 3/1 (Göttingen: Vandenhoeck & Ruprecht, 1922).

[67] Sparks, *God's Word in Human Words*, 147–49, in reference to K. A. Kitchen, *On the Reliability of the Old Testament* (Grand Rapids: Eerdmans, 2003), 378–80.

[68] Of course this text is uniformly rejected by historical-critical scholars as an *ex eventu* prophecy.

[69] Clements, *Isaiah 1–39*, 294.

[70] J. H. Walton, "New Observations on the Date of Isaiah," *JETS* 28 (1985): 129–32. Walton's theory is supported and further developed by Eddy Lanz, *Jesaja 36–39 und ihre Bedeutung für die Komposition des Jesajabuches* (Gummersbach: Kopie & Druck R. Klein, 2002). Walton argues further that, since Kings took over this inversion from Isaiah, Isaiah 40ff. must already have been a part of the book of Isaiah when Kings was written. Some scholars, however, would date the addition of chaps. 36–39 to the growing book of Isaiah much later.

> Leave Babylon,
>> flee from the Babylonians!
> Announce this with shouts of joy
>> and proclaim it.

Here it should be noted that the speaker does not appear to be located in Babylon (cf. 52:11). Moreover, it is not clear that every prophetic imperative necessarily calls for an action that must take place immediately rather than one that is recommended as being appropriate at some point in the future. Compare, for example, the following:

> Go into the rocks,
>> hide in the ground
> from dread of the Lord
>> and the splendor of his majesty! (2:10)

> Look upon Zion, the city of our festivals;
>> your eyes will see Jerusalem,
>> a peaceful abode, a tent that will not be moved. (33:20a)

> Look in the scroll of the Lord and read. (34:16a)

> Strengthen the feeble hands,
>> steady the knees that give way. (35:3)

Kitchen's greatest fault, however, is in claiming that the name of Cyrus the Persian may not have been so irrelevant or "nonsensical"[71] to Isaiah's audience as is commonly claimed, since two additional "Cyruses" are known from ancient records: Cyrus I (early sixth century) and Kurash (who ruled in Parsua in 646, around half a century after Isaiah's day). Accordingly, Kitchen suggests that there may have been even earlier, currently undocumented "Cyruses" that Isaiah's audience may have heard of.[72] Sparks dismisses Kitchen's suggestion as based on "no evidence whatsoever," downplays the centrality of the Cyrus prophecy for the Second Isaiah theory, and denigrates the erudition displayed in Kitchen's 600-page apologetic *magnum opus* by citing only this one specific example before accusing him of employing a flawed strategy.[73] To my knowledge, no one has previously pointed to the existence of earlier "Cyruses"; in light of the incomplete nature of the ancient documents that have been discovered and translated, Kitchen's suggestion could one day be validated.

---

[71] This is Sparks's characterization, *God's Word in Human Words*, 148.
[72] Kitchen, *On the Reliability of the Old Testament*, 380.
[73] Sparks, *God's Word in Human Words*, 149.

Second, Sparks accuses me of making "a selective and specious use of modern scholarship that *seems* to support the traditional, evangelical cause."[74] In his opinion, scholars like me are so desperate to find any arguments "in modern scholarship" that support our indefensible traditional convictions that we "inevitably misrepresent it"—not deliberately but unconsciously.[75] In my opinion, however, Sparks makes a misleading use of my essay in seeking support for his criticism of conservative evangelical scholarship. He incorrectly suggests that I cite the growing scholarship in support of the "one book" of Isaiah to reinforce my "one author" viewpoint. On the one hand, he fails to note, however, that I summarize

> "non-evangelical developments in contemporary Old Testament studies" solely to make the ironic observation that "while critical scholars are moving in a more conservative direction [i.e., toward affirming "the basic unity of the canonical book"], there is also a growing trend among evangelicals [like Sparks] . . . to embrace views regarding Isaiah that some critical scholars are discarding."[76]

On the other hand, Sparks seems to be denying the very nature of the biblical-critical enterprise, in which a succession of scholars carefully analyze a particular biblical text in an effort to determine its original meaning and, in many cases, its compositional history. The data that they discover are capable of generating more than one explanatory hypothesis. Just because Williamson concludes that the verbal parallels that he identifies within First and Second Isaiah reflect both authorial *imitations* and editorial *insertions*,[77] that does not mean that another scholar cannot examine the same verbal parallels and draw other conclusions. The history of biblical study is marked by an ongoing revision and replacement of various explanatory theories, often owing to new approaches to the same observed textual phenomena.

---

[74]Ibid., 153, referring to my essay "How Many Isaiahs Were There and What Does It Matter?" cited in n. 1.

[75]Sparks, *God's Word in Human Words*, 155.

[76]Schultz, "How Many Isaiahs," 154–55. For example, at a time when some critical scholars are questioning the very existence of a Third Isaiah, Jacob Stromberg (who could be classified as an evangelical on the basis of his participation in the Tyndale Fellowship's OT Study Group) posits multiple redactional layers within Third Isaiah, which, in turn, draws on Second Isaiah (J. Stromberg, "An Inner-Isaianic Reading of Isaiah 61:1–3," in Firth and Williamson, *Interpreting Isaiah*, 269–71; and *Isaiah After Exile: The Author of Third Isaiah as Reader and Redactor of the Book*, Oxford Theological Monographs [Oxford: Oxford University Press, 2010], building on the work of P. A. Smith, *Rhetoric and Redaction in Trito-Isaiah: The Structure, Growth and Authorship of Isaiah 56–66*, VTSup 62 [Leiden: Brill, 1995]).

[77]H. G. M. Williamson, *The Book Called Isaiah: Deutero-Isaiah's Role in Composition and Redaction* (Oxford: Clarendon, 1994).

Third, citing the purported affirmation by Jesus and the New Testament authors that Isaiah authored the book of Isaiah, Sparks accuses conservative evangelicals of inappropriately "critiquing biblical criticism with the biblical 'testimony.'" For Sparks, Jesus's statements regarding authorship simply reflect "the everyday assumptions of a pious, first-century Jew"—that is, "human and finite."[78] Thus he views the weight of scholarly evidence "against the traditional authorial attributions in the Old Testament" as so heavy that he would rather question traditional evangelical christology than turn his back on the "assured results" of historical criticism. Whether Sparks is correct in questioning the objective truthfulness of Jesus's (and the inspired New Testament authors') statements about Old Testament authorship, it is problematic to base such a conclusion on the "assured results" of biblical criticism.

Finally, Sparks accuses Dillard and Longman of dishonestly "pleading ignorance and obfuscating the issues"[79] when they "seem to imply—but never express explicitly—that they believe the second half of Isaiah was written during or after the exile." In fact, Sparks goes on to suggest that these coauthors "would be quite comfortable if most or all of the standard critical conclusions turned out to be right."[80] It seems, however, that the approach of Dillard and Longman reflects warranted scholarly caution in addressing critical issues and appropriate Christian reverence in interpreting God's Word. Since we know so little regarding precisely how and what God communicated to his prophetic spokespersons and regarding the process through which the individual Old Testament books reached their final forms, scholarly dogmatism is out of place. Sparks is remarkably skeptical concerning the apparent claims of the biblical authors, while remarkably confident in the findings of finite human scholars. We will never be able to prove through scholarly analyses whether the prophet Isaiah could or could not have addressed an exilic audience. But, as I noted in my earlier essay on Isaiah, more is at stake here than

---

[78]Sparks, *God's Word in Human Words*, 164–65. The most recent and thorough assessment of the biblical and extrabiblical evidence related to the authorship of Isaiah is G. K. Beale, *The Erosion of Inerrancy in Evangelicalism: Responding to New Challenges to Biblical Authority* (Wheaton, IL: Crossway, 2009), 124–46. I will not repeat his data or conclusions here.

[79]Sparks, *God's Word in Human Words*, 165–68, referring to Dillard and Longman, *An Introduction to the Old Testament* (Grand Rapids: Zondervan, 1994), 275.

[80]Sparks, *God's Word in Human Words*, 166–67. On the basis of personal conversations with Tremper Longman, as well as many of his publications, I consider this claim to be patently untrue. For example, he defends the traditional dating of Daniel in his commentary *Daniel*, NIVAC (Grand Rapids: Zondervan, 1999), 21–24, despite respectfully presenting the "late date" viewpoint. Sparks proceeds in a rather surprising manner to list several possible contributing factors to the faulty "strategy" represented by conservative evangelicals like Dillard and Longman: theological immaturity, an overly pastoral focus, a "desire to sell books to conservative readers," a self-protective impulse (i.e., seeking to retain their teaching posts at conservative institutions), and poor training and a general lack of knowledge regarding contemporary critical scholarship (*God's Word in Human Words*, 167–68).

simply the choice of whether to adopt the position held by most "respectable" scholars—issues such as the inspiration, validation, and authority of biblical prophecy.[81] The prophet Isaiah offers some helpful guidance for those seeking to practice "believing criticism":[82] "Consult God's instruction and the testimony of warning. If anyone does not speak according to this word, they have no light of dawn" (Isa. 8:20, TNIV).

[81]Schultz, "How Many Isaiahs," 158–70. Sparks has little to say about these topics in his monograph.
[82]I would understand this expression differently from Sparks (*God's Word in Human Words*, 20), emphasizing *believing* rather than *criticism*.

# 11

# DANIEL IN BABYLON

## *An Accurate Record?*

### ALAN R. MILLARD

The book of Daniel tells of events that took place in Babylon in the sixth century BC and forecasts events that should take place during the following four hundred years. Those forecasts give such detail and concur with known history to such an extent that almost all commentators deduce that the book could only have been composed in the second century BC. At the same time, many today ascribe the narratives of affairs in Babylon to a slightly earlier date, accepting that they preserve memories of the Babylonian court. Despite the recovery of thousands of documents from Babylon, including royal inscriptions and chronicles, and extensive reports by Greek writers, notably Herodotus and Xenophon, knowledge of the period is very partial, so the information any ancient writing offers about it deserves to be assessed carefully.

Numerous questions arise concerning the Daniel narratives, and only some can be explored in this essay. Discussions of others can be found in the commentaries and additional studies.[1]

## The Date of Daniel's Exile

In the summer of 605 BC the Babylonian army, commanded by the crown prince Nebuchadnezzar, defeated Egypt's forces at Carchemish and pursued their remnants as far as Hamath. Nebuchadnezzar then took control of

---

[1]Besides the major commentaries by John J. Collins (Minneapolis: Fortress, 1993) and John Goldingay (Dallas: Word, 1989), see the essays in *The Book of Daniel: Composition and Reception*, ed. John J. Collins and Peter W. Flint (Leiden: Brill, 2001), and, in favor of the accuracy of the narratives, Alan R. Millard, "Daniel 1–6 and History," *EvQ* 49, no. 2 (977): 67–73; Terence C. Mitchell, "Achaemenid History and the Book of Daniel," in *Mesopotamia and Iran in the Persian Period: Conquest and Imperialism 539–331 BC*, ed. John Curtis (London: The British Museum Press, 1997), 68–78; Thomas E. Gaston, *Historical Issues in the Book of Daniel* (Oxford: TaanathShiloh, 2009).

the whole region of Hamath, but his father, Nabopolassar, died on August 15–16, so Nebuchadnezzar sped home to be acclaimed king on September 6–7. Thereafter he returned to the Levant, cementing his victory and taking booty until January-February 604.

Jeremiah refers to the Battle of Carchemish, dating it to the fourth year of Jehoiakim of Judah (46:1), a year that he elsewhere equates with Nebuchadnezzar's first year (25:1). The second book of Kings (24:1) simply reports that Jehoiakim submitted to Nebuchadnezzar during his reign, without giving a specific date. As "Jehoiakim became his vassal for three years,"[2] then rebelled, and as that rebellion is unlikely to have occurred before the Babylonian army withdrew in 601, after an inconclusive battle with Egypt, the submission can be placed in 605 or 604. The statement in Daniel 1:1, that Nebuchadnezzar besieged Jerusalem in Jehoiakim's third year, is commonly treated as an error or confusion, because that year would have run from March-April 606 to March-April 605, and there is no likelihood of any Babylonian activity so far south as Judah before the Battle of Carchemish, when the whole area was subject to Egypt. Before dismissing the statement as uncorroborated and thus unacceptable as a historical record, however, we should make every effort to discover if it could be correct. There are two aspects to explore: first, the date; second, Babylonian strategy.

### The Date

The kings of Judah, like the kings of Babylon, counted the first year of their rule from the New Year's Day after their accession, the period of their reign before that being their accession year; so the last year of king A would be termed the accession year of king B, whose first year would commence with the next New Year's Day. That made 609 BC Josiah's last year and 608 Jehoiakim's first (the "accession year" system). Earlier, in Israel, as in Egypt, the year in which a king came to the throne was reckoned his first year, overlapping with the last year of his predecessor (the "non–accession year" system). Thus the last year of king A might also be the first year of king B, making 609 Josiah's last and Jehoiakim's first.

The situation is complicated because there were also two ways of calculating the year. The spring New Year began in the month of Nisan (March-April); the autumn New Year began in the month Tishri (September-October). The book of Jeremiah uses the spring New Year, and the books of Kings use the

---

[2]With few exceptions reflecting the author's preferences, unless otherwise indicated, Scripture quotations in this chapter are from *The Holy Bible, New International Version*®, NIV® Copyright © 1973, 1978, 1984, 2011 by Biblica, Inc. Used by permission. All rights reserved worldwide.

autumn New Year, as appears from Jeremiah's dating Jehoiachin's capture in Nebuchadnezzar's seventh year, and Kings' in his eighth (Jer. 52:28; 2 Kings 24:12). Now the spring New Year would mean Jehoiakim's first year covered 609 to March-April 608 on the non–accession year system, his second 608–607, his third 607–606, and his fourth 606–605; on the accession year system his first year ran from March-April 608 to March-April 607, his second 607–606, and his third 606 to March-April 605. Thus any advance by Nebuchadnezzar against Jerusalem after the Battle of Carchemish would have fallen in Jehoiakim's fourth year (cf. Jer. 46:2). Equally, an autumn New Year would mean Jehoiakim's first year could have fallen in 610–609 or 609–608, for we do not know exactly when he acceded, bringing his third year to 608–607 or 607–606, and his fourth to 607–606 or 606–605, on the non–accession year system. However, on the accession year system and with an autumnal New Year, his first year would run from September-October 608 to September-October 607, his second 607–606, his third September-October 606 to September-October 605. This last would just accommodate the statement of Daniel 1:1 in chronological terms. If the autumn New Year and the accession year dating are not acceptable, then there is probably no alternative to assuming an error in the figure of this verse. Yet the fact that it is possible to reckon the date as 605 BC belies the claim that "the very first statement in chapter 1 can be shown to be inaccurate."[3]

## Babylonian Strategy

The absence of any record of a siege of Jerusalem by Babylonian forces in this year is not a strong argument against its happening. There would be a few weeks after the Battle of Carchemish in which a Babylonian force might threaten Jerusalem and take hostages. Whether Nebuchadnezzar or his generals led the force, it could still be attributed to the king.[4] Taking hostages from rulers previously subject to the defeated Pharaoh would be a means of

---

[3]Norman W. Porteous, *Daniel, A Commentary*, OTL (London: SCM, 1965), 25f.

[4]Assyrian reports attribute to some kings campaigns led by their generals, who were, of course, the kings' agents. In the twenty-seventh to thirty-first years of his reign, Shalmaneser III sent his turtan, Dayyan-Ashur, to command his armies in campaigns against Urartu, Hattina, and other places, and he openly states that in his "annals." What is particularly significant is the continuation of the narratives. Although he said, "I remained in Calah, I dispatched Dayyan-Ashur, . . . he approached city X," he continued, "I marched against Y, I destroyed their cities," and "Dayyan-Ashur advanced against B, he crossed the river C . . . the Urartian enemy heard of it and advanced against me. I fought with him, I defeated him." This fluctuation of persons could be attributed to scribal carelessness; since most of the "annals" are written in the first person, the scribe may have slipped unconsciously into the normal style. However, these passages may be understood in the light of the master-agent relationship. The king could claim that anything his general did was effectively his action—and, of course, he could disclaim anything that did not satisfy him. The situation is no different from my sending you a letter in which I say, 'I wrote to you two months ago,' when, in fact, a secretary wrote the letter at

trying to ensure they did not resume their loyalty to him. In the following years Nebuchadnezzar returned regularly to the Levant; in his first year local kings, probably including Jehoiakim, formally became his subjects, and he took their tribute. The town of Ashkelon had not submitted, so was captured, looted, and sacked. That is the only town named in the surviving lines of the Babylonian Chronicle covering the four years when the king campaigned in the Levant ("Hatti"). Nebuchadnezzar now held the entire region, restricting Egypt to her own land (cf. 2 Kings 24:7).[5]

## The Madness of Nebuchadnezzar

Nebuchadnezzar ruled for forty-three years, from 605 until 562. He left numerous inscriptions vaunting his piety and building works, but few giving information about other aspects of his reign. Clay tablets bearing extracts from the Babylonian Chronicle tell of military activities in his early years, to 594–593, but no Babylonian Chronicle texts survive to cover the rest of his career, and other documents mention little. A small fragment referring to his thirty-seventh year (568–567) may tell of an attack on Egypt.[6] Part of a clay prism lists various persons in Nebuchadnezzar's circle, and fragments of administrative tablets found in the Southern Palace in Babylon include issues of rations to hostages and foreigners there, among them Jehoiachin, king of Judah.[7] The splendor visible in the ruins of Nebuchadnezzar's Babylon shows that he had reason to be proud of his work on its defensive walls, gates, temples, and palaces.

The almost complete silence of Babylonian records about Nebuchadnezzar's activities for thirty years of his kingship allows the assumption that the events of Daniel 2–4 may be placed in that period. Of course, that is reminiscent of a "god of the gaps" approach. Yet it should not be ignored. That a king might suffer illness, physical or mental, is to be expected, especially one who was middle-aged or older; Nebuchadnezzar was no child at the Battle of Carchemish in 605 and reigned for forty-three years. In societies that believed illness was imposed by the gods, a sick king would not necessarily be deposed;

my request. For the texts, see A. Kirk Grayson, *Assyrian Rulers of the Early First Millennium BC II (858–745 BC)*, RIMA 3 (Toronto: University of Toronto Press, 1996), 69–71.
[5]The Babylonian Chronicle tablets give the only information in cuneiform about Nebuchadnezzar's campaigns, see Jean-Jacques Glassner, *Mesopotamian Chronicles*, SBLWAW 19 (Atlanta: Society of Biblical Literature, 2004), 228–31.
[6]A. Leo Oppenheim, in *Ancient Near Eastern Texts Relating to the Bible*, 3rd ed., ed. James B. Pritchard (Princeton: Princeton University Press, 1969), 308 (hereafter *ANET*); note that much more of the text is missing than Oppenheim's translation indicates; see Terence C. Mitchell, "Where Was Putu-Iaman?," *Proceedings of the Seminar for Arabian Studies* 22 (1992): 69–80.
[7]Oppenheim, in *ANET*, 307–8.

nor would he in societies that could diagnose the illness (cf. Uzziah of Judah, 2 Kings 15:5–6, or George III of Britain).[8] Some incomplete lines on a fragment of a cuneiform tablet describe Nebuchadnezzar's pondering and, so far as can be understood, changing his mind, but so much of the text is missing that no conclusions can be based upon it.[9] Vague allusions in Greek writings might indicate knowledge of the king's suffering, the clearest being Josephus's citation of Berossus, a Babylonian who wrote about his country's history in Greek early in the third century BC. After relating Nebuchadnezzar's victory over Egypt and accession to the throne, Berossus tells of his falling ill after beginning his building work, then dying.[10] Interestingly, Berossus reports no other activities by the king.

Most often compared with Daniel's narrative is the Aramaic "Prayer of Nabonidus," preserved in four fragments found among the Dead Sea Scrolls.[11] Nabonidus (written *nbny*), king of Babylon, living in Teima, by decree of the Most High God, was afflicted with horrid boils for seven years and "banished far [from men]." He prayed to God, and a Jewish exorcist forgave him and told him to issue a proclamation in honor of the Most High God. The fragments do not relate directly to the account of Daniel 4, but common opinion holds that "there is every reason to believe" it "preserves a more primitive form" of that and is the product of oral traditions and folkloristic elements merging the figures of Nebuchadnezzar and Nabonidus. In both, the Babylonian king is the speaker, suffers God's punishment for seven years, prays and is relieved, and then is advised by a Jewish expert to honor God.[12] Among noticeable differences are the circumstances: Teima as against Babylon, the illness—boils, or some other debilitating illness that did not result in animal-like behavior—as opposed to Nebuchadnezzar's madness,[13] and Nabonidus's not being

---

[8]The Babylonian Chronicle reports that a king of Elam was paralyzed at the beginning of a year and died only at the end of that year (see Glassner, *Mesopotamian Chronicles*, 198–99, lines 19–27).
[9]A. Kirk Grayson, *Babylonian Historical-Literary Texts* (Toronto: Toronto University Press, 1975), 87–91; Donald J. Wiseman, *Nebuchadrezzar and Babylon*, The Schweich Lectures 1983 (London: The British Academy, 1985), 102–3.
[10]Stanley M. Burstein, *The Babyloniaca of Berossus*, Sources and Monographs, Sources from the Ancient Near East 1/5 (Malibu: Undena, 1978), 28.
[11]John J. Collins, "4Q Prayer of Nabonidus," in *Qumran Cave 4, XVII: Parabiblical Texts, Part 3*, ed. James C. VanderKam (Oxford: Clarendon, 1996), 83–93; Florentino García Martinez, *The Dead Sea Scrolls Translated: The Qumran Texts in English*, trans. Wilfred G. E. Watson (Leiden: Brill, 1994), 289.
[12]See Frank M. Cross, *The Ancient Library of Qumran and Modern Biblical Studies* (New York: Doubleday, 1961), 166–68; Ronald H. Sack, "Nabonidus," in *Anchor Bible Dictionary*, ed. D. N. Freedman, vol. 4 (New York: Doubleday, 1992), 973–76, see 976a; Esther Eshel, "Possible Sources of the Book of Daniel," in Collins and Flint, *The Book of Daniel*, 387–94; see 387–88.
[13]The restoration of line 3 of the prayer to read "I came to be like [the beasts]" offered by Frank M. Cross, "Fragments of the Prayer of Nabonidus," *IEJ* 34 (1984): 260–64, followed by Wiseman, *Nebuchadrezzar*, 103, is no longer supported; see Peter W. Flint, "The Daniel Tradition at Qumran," in Collins and Flint, *The Book of Daniel*, 329–67, esp. 332–36, with 336 note to line 3.

portrayed as boasting about his building works. A case has been made for the dependence of the prayer upon the book of Daniel.[14] The prayer is only one composition found at Qumran that concerns Daniel, the others being even more fragmentary and, where their sense can be followed, referring to the exile by Nebuchadnezzar as God's punishment.[15]

## The Chaldeans

Use of *Chaldean* for a special class of learned men in Daniel is an "undoubted anachronism" for the time of Nebuchadnezzar.[16] The word in Daniel 5:30, "Belshazzar the Chaldean king," and in 9:1, "the realm of the Chaldeans," has an ethnic connotation, and that may be true of the phrase "the letters and language of the Chaldeans" in 1:4. Every other occurrence in Daniel carries the specialized sense of a category among the wise men, sometimes standing for the whole body (cf. 2:2, 4, 10, etc.). The same restricted meaning occurs in Herodotus, *Histories* 1.181f., where the Chaldeans are priests of Bel. This limited meaning, it is argued, could have developed only after the Chaldeans had ceased to have any significance as a people or a power, that is, when the Persian Empire was fully established. Admittedly, the ethnic use did continue to be current for a long while, preserved in the Old Testament writings and used by historians such as Strabo at the end of the first century BC. Were Chaldean a normal gentilic in sixth-century-BC Babylonia, attested in contemporary documents, with no trace of the specialized use, *Daniel's* mode of employing it might be considered anachronistic. But beside the fact that there is no evidence for Chaldean as a professional name in Babylonian texts, we should note the complete absence of the word as an ethnic term from the royal inscriptions of Nebuchadnezzar, his father, and his successors. In Assyrian records of the eighth and seventh centuries it is used as the overall name for a group of tribes often mentioned separately. In this situation it is as improper to label the professional sense of Chaldean a sixth-century usage as it is to call it an anachronism.

A possible analogy can be found among the Medes. According to Herodotus, there was a group of six tribes (*Histories* 1.101). One of the tribes was called the Magi. Now the Magi are well known as religious functionaries in the Persian Empire and as the eponyms of all magicians. Their early history is obscure. R. N. Frye wrote, "One may tentatively suggest that the Magi were a

---

[14]A. Steinmann, "The Chicken and the Egg: A New Proposal for the Relationship between the 'Prayer of Nabonidus' and the 'Book of Daniel,'" *RevQ* 20 (2002): 557–70.

[15]See Martinez, *The Dead Sea Scrolls Translated*, 288–89, and Flint, "The Daniel Tradition at Qumran," 329–67, esp. 332–36.

[16]Porteous, *Daniel*, 28, following the majority of commentators.

'tribe' of the Medes who exercised sacerdotal functions. During the supremacy of the Medes they expanded over the Median empire as a priesthood since the priestly trade was kept, so to speak, 'in the family.'"[17] Perhaps something similar was true of the Chaldeans. *Chaldean* has passed into English from Greek and Latin, the Greek being a correct transliteration of the Babylonian *\*kaldāyu*. In Hebrew the form differs: *kaśdim*. The variation is explicable in the light of historical development within Babylonian and Assyrian. From the mid-second millennium BC onward the combination of sibilant + dental was often written as *1* + dental, revealing a phonetic shift probably universal in the spoken language, though concealed by scribal conservatism in many of the texts that survive.[18] This shift accounts well for the difference between the Akkadian and Greek forms and the Hebrew, which was unaffected by it, deriving from the Chaldeans themselves or from a time before the shift had occurred. Again, to view "Chaldean" as "taken from the Greek rendering of the Hebrew *kaśdim* and corresponding more accurately to the original *kaldu*" appears unjust to the Hebrew-Aramaic text of *Daniel*.[19]

## Belshazzar

### Belshazzar, King of Babylon?

Nebuchadnezzar's son Awel-Marduk became king in 562 and was assassinated after two years, although not until after he had taken Jehoiachin out of prison to eat at his table (2 Kings 25:27–30). The assassin was one of Nebuchadnezzar's generals, probably a son-in-law, Nergal-sharezer, who had been involved in the capture of Jerusalem (Jer. 39:3), but he reigned for only four years (560–556), and then his son for less than a year (Labashi-Marduk, 556). Another of Nebuchadnezzar's officials, Nabonidus, took the throne. He was the last king of Babylon, reigning from 556 until 539. He did not support the god of Babylon, Marduk, in the traditional way, but was devoted to the worship of Sin, the god of the moon. Three years after he became king, he took an army and marched through Transjordan and into Arabia where he lived for ten years at Teima. Arabian tribes were devoted to the moon god, and that may have been one reason for this strange move; there may have been mercantile, political, and strategic reasons too. While Nabonidus was

---

[17]Richard N. Frye, *The Heritage of Persia* (London: Weidenfeld and Nicholson, 1962), 76.
[18]See W. von Soden, *Grundriss der Akkadischen Grammatik*, AnOr 47 (Rome: Pontifical Biblical Institute, 1969), §30g; W. F. Leemans, *Ex Oriente Lux* 10 (1945–1948): 437; Harry W. F. Saggs, "Ur of the Chaldees: A Problem of Identification," *Iraq* 22 (1960): 200–209, here 206 n. 39.
[19]Porteous, *Daniel*, 28.

in Arabia, his son ruled Babylon.[20] That son was Belshazzar. Until 1854 only the book of Daniel and writings derived from it named Belshazzar as a ruler of Babylon. His name is absent from the lists of kings of Babylon preserved correctly in the Greek sources, Berossus, and the Ptolemaic canon.[21] Herodotus and Xenophon report the fall of Babylon to Cyrus during a festival without naming Babylon's king, while Xenophon also fails to name the king who was killed (*Histories* 1.191; *Cyropaedia* 7.5.15). Berossus states that Cyrus captured Nabonidus and exiled him to Carmania (Kirman).[22]

In 1854 four small clay cylinders were dug from the ruins of the temple tower (ziggurat) of the moon god at Ur; more copies were found during Iraqi restoration work on the ziggurat in the 1960s. They carry a prayer by Nabonidus, who had repaired the tower in honor of his god. As well as praying for himself, Nabonidus prayed for the health of his son, the crown prince Belshazzar. Other Babylonian tablets discovered since then show that he was active in business and in state affairs. Some documents record oaths sworn in the names of gods, of Nabonidus, king of Babylon, and of Belshazzar, the crown prince, a formulation unknown in earlier reigns.[23] While his father was in Teima from 553, the Babylonian Chronicle states, "The crown prince, his officers and his troops stayed in" Babylonia.[24] After the Persian conquest, someone wrote a poem denigrating Nabonidus and praising Cyrus. One passage tells that Nabonidus gave command of the army to the crown prince and "entrusted the kingship to him."[25] Belshazzar was effectively king during his father's absence, although he did not bear the title *king* according to any Babylonian source, and, notably, no documents are dated by years of his reign. Therefore H. H. Rowley asserted that the failure of any of these texts to give Belshazzar the title *king* and the absence of any other evidence for his reigning as monarch proved that the author of Daniel was in error. E. J. Young countered that Daniel is not an official document written by Babylonian scribes, and so it could represent an effective situation rather than a state position; Belshazzar was *de facto* king, although not *de jure* king.[26] An older inscription offers support for that position. The statue of a ruler of Gozan

---

[20]For the person and reign of Nabonidus, see Paul Alain Beaulieu, *The Reign of Nabonidus, King of Babylon, 556–539 B.C.* (New Haven, CT: Yale University Press, 1989).
[21]Burstein, *The Babyloniaca of Berossus*, 28, 38.
[22]Ibid., 28.
[23]The material was collected by Raymond P. Dougherty, *Nabonidus and Belshazzar*, YOSR 15 (New Haven, CT: Yale University Press, 1929), and expanded by Beaulieu, *The Reign of Nabonidus*.
[24]Glassner, *Mesopotamian Chronicles*, 234–37.
[25]Oppenheim, in *ANET*, 313. For Nabonidus's period in Arabia, see Wilfred G. Lambert in *Proceedings of the Fifth Seminar for Arabian Studies* (London: Society for Arabian Studies, 1972): 53–64.
[26]Harold H. Rowley, *JTS* 32 (1930): 12–31; Edward J. Young, *A Commentary on Daniel* (Grand Rapids: Eerdmans, 1949; repr., London: Banner of Truth, 1972), 115ff.

(now Tell Halaf in Syria) in the ninth century BC bears two inscriptions, the first in Assyrian, and the second in Aramaic and largely a translation of the former. The text is the ruler's dedication of his statue to his god with prayers for his well-being and curses on anyone who should deface it. In the Assyrian text the ruler bears the title *governor* (*šākin māti*), as a vassal of the Assyrian emperor, while in the Aramaic text his title is *king* (*mlk*), as ruler of Gozan. Each title is appropriate to its audience.[27] Somewhat similar may be the rank of the thirty-two kings who accompanied Ben-Hadad to attack Samaria (1 Kings 20:1, 12, 16). In Babylonian a king who rules other kings is distinguished by the adjective *great* (*rabû*).

### Belshazzar's Ancestry

While cuneiform texts plainly name Nabonidus as the father of Belshazzar, Daniel 5:11 and 18 give that place to Nebuchadnezzar. Of course, *father* may stand for grandfather or for a more remote ancestor in Semitic languages, but it is objected that Nabonidus was not a descendant of Nebuchadnezzar; in fact he was a usurper who took the throne from Labashi-Marduk, son of Neriglissar, who was a grandson of Nebuchadnezzar if, as appears likely, Neriglissar had married Nebuchadnezzar's daughter Kashshaya. There are hints that Nabonidus also held high office in Nebuchadnezzar's reign; the inscription honoring his mother, who lived for 104 years, claims that she forwarded his career in the courts of Nebuchadnezzar and Neriglissar, without specifying any office.[28] It is suggested that Nabonidus, too, may have been married to a daughter of Nebuchadnezzar, putting him in as good a place to take the throne as Neriglissar. Then the mother of Belshazzar would have been a daughter of Nebuchadnezzar. Had that been the case, Nabonidus's mother might have mentioned it when she boasted of placing her son to a high position in the Babylonian court. But this remains speculation unless more evidence becomes available.[29]

### The Third Place in the Realm

In Daniel 5, Belshazzar promises to reward Daniel with the third position in the kingdom if he can interpret the writing on the wall. As previous writers have noted, Belshazzar could not give Daniel the second place because he occupied it, his father holding the first place, as king.

---

[27] Alan R. Millard and Pierre Bordreuil, "A Statue from Syria with Assyrian and Aramaic Inscriptions," *BA* 45 (1982): 135–41, here 139. Note also the claim of a governor to the role of king in the eighth century BC in K. Lawson Younger, "Ninurta-kudurrī-uṣur—the Suḫu Annals," in *The Context of Scripture*, vol. 2, ed. William W. Hallo and K. Lawson Younger (Leiden: Brill, 2000), 279.

[28] Oppenheim, in *ANET*, 560–62.

[29] See Wiseman, *Nebuchadrezzar*, 8–12.

## The Third Year of Belshazzar

Commentators have been at a loss to account for the date of Daniel 8:1, "In the third year of King Belshazzar's reign." If taken at its face value, the year would be 550–549, reckoning from the fourth year of Nabonidus, when he "entrusted the kingship" to his son. That was the year in which Cyrus of Persia finally overcame his nominal suzerain, Astyages the Mede, and established the joint state of the Medes and Persians.[30] That is to say, the events of the vision were beginning at the time they were revealed; the higher horn of the ram (i.e., Persia) was now rising above the other (Media).

## Belshazzar's Feast and Death

The lines of the Nabonidus Chronicle that relate the fall of Babylon to Cyrus tell of fighting and slaughter at Opis (which lay east of the Tigris and north of Babylon), then claim that "the town of Sippar was taken without a battle. Nabonidus fled . . . Ugbaru, governor of Gutium and the army of Cyrus entered Babylon without a battle. Afterwards, when Nabonidus retreated, he was seized in Babylon" (iii.12'–16'). The "Cyrus Cylinder," Herodotus (*Histories* 1.188–91), and Xenophon (*Cyropaedia* 7.5) also assert that there was no battle at Babylon.[31] Although Beaulieu maintained that the accounts of the city being taken by surprise while a festival was in progress (Herodotus, *Histories* 1.191; Xenophon, *Cyropaedia* 7.5; Daniel 5) "can hardly be harmonized with cuneiform evidence," he noted the date of the capture was the day before a festival might have been held and that Xenophon tells how Gobryas, having been alienated by a king of Babylon, joined Cyrus and, entering Babylon first with Cyrus's troops, killed the "unrighteous" king there (*Cyropaedia* 7.20–32). Xenophon's account agrees well with the Nabonidus Chronicle about the lack of fighting, with Herodotus and the book of Daniel about the feast, and with Daniel about the death of the king. In claiming a peaceful occupation, both the chronicle and the Cyrus Cylinder may be presenting Persian propaganda, the view that the Persians took the city because it was the will of its god, Marduk. If some leading Babylonians were killed in the palace, that was not a matter of concern to their authors, since the chronicle had already told of the most important fact, the capture of King Nabonidus. (It should be noted that all the Babylonian chronicle texts are extracts from longer compositions and should not be treated as comprehensive or complete records of any event; they were made for purposes no longer understood.)

---

[30]Noted by Sidney Smith, *Isaiah Chapters XL–LV. The Schweich Lectures 1940* (London: The British Academy, 1944), 125 n. 41; Brian E. Colless, "Cyrus the Persian as Darius the Mede in the Book of Daniel," *JSOT* 56 (1992): 123.

[31]Beaulieu, *The Reign of Nabonidus*, 224–26.

## The Medes

The book of Daniel names the Medes as a power following the Babylonian kingdom and connected with the Persian. The passages are these:

> That very night Belshazzar, king of the Babylonians, was slain, and Darius the Mede took over the kingdom, at the age of sixty-two. (Dan. 5:30–31)

> In the first year of Darius son of Xerxes (a Mede by descent), who was made ruler over the Babylonian kingdom . . . (9:1; cf. 11:1)

> The two-horned ram . . . represents the kings of Media and Persia. (8:20)

> . . . the laws of the Medes and Persians. (6:8, 12, 15)

Whether there was ever a Median Empire that intervened between the Babylonian and the Persian and who Darius the Mede might be are questions that have been endlessly debated. They should be considered separately.

### The Kingdom of the Medes

Assyrian kings fought against the Medes in Iran from the ninth century BC onward, taking control of some of their territory where deported Israelites were settled (2 Kings 17:6; 18:11). Esarhaddon made treaties with some of their rulers in 672, but under King Cyaxares the Medes joined with the Babylonian king Nabopolassar to conquer Assyria in 612, and Berossus reports that Nebuchadnezzar was married to a daughter of the Median king.[32] The political situation changed over the next fifty years, for Nabonidus names Medes, with Egypt and Arabs, as enemies who sought friendly relations with him.[33] The prophets Isaiah (13:17; 21:2 with Elam) and Jeremiah (51:11, 28) forecast the fall of Babylon at the hands of the Medes, Jeremiah including them, with Elam, among the nations whom the Lord would punish (25:25). It is noteworthy that, although Elam is mentioned beside the Medes, there is no hint in those texts of a Persian power. The Chronicle of Nabonidus reports that, in the king's sixth year (550), Cyrus, king of Anshan, conquered Astyages, capturing Ecbatana, the Median capital, and in the king's ninth year (547), Cyrus, now titled king of Persia, attacked Urartu.[34] The impact of the Medes

---

[32]Burstein, *The Babyloniaca of Berossus*, 25.
[33]*ANET*, 126.
[34]Glassner, *Mesopotamian Chronicles*, 234–37. The name of the place attacked has usually been reconstructed as Lydia—only part of the first sign remains—but reexamination of the tablet shows Urartu is more likely (Joachim Oelsner, "Review," *Archiv für Orientforschung* 46/47 [1999/2000]: 373–80, see 378; and Robert Rollinger," The Western Expansion of the 'Median' Empire: A Re-examination,"

on the Greeks is evident in writers, such as Thucydides, calling "the Median War" the war with the Persians and treating various Persian styles as Median, the term *Persian* gradually becoming dominant from the middle of the fifth century BC.[35] As the Medes spread toward western Anatolia, they would be the first Iranian people Greeks living there met, and so it can be understood that they would call all similar people by the same name,[36] just as Europeans call "Chinese" all the people who call themselves "Han" because the Ch'in were the most westerly. Biblical sources display the same pattern as the Greek: the book of Daniel, relating events of the sixth century, echoes the previous dominance of the Medes in the phrase "Medes and Persians," whereas in the book of Esther, reflecting the mid-fifth-century, Persian power is well established, and so the order becomes "Persians and Medes" (see Esther 1:3, 14, 18, 19), except for the history of the rulers, which remains "The annals of the kings of Media and Persia" (10:2).

The Medes clearly made their mark on the ancient Near East. How do they fit in the book of Daniel?

Nebuchadnezzar's dream of the composite statue foretold a lesser kingdom following his own, then a third that would "rule over the whole earth," to be replaced by the iron power with internal division (Dan. 2:36–43, quote from 39). If we take the last to be Alexander the Great's kingdom, the third becomes the Persian, and the second the Median. The same pattern appears in Daniel's dream of four beasts, which are explained as four unnamed kingdoms (7:17). In Daniel's vision of a ram and a goat in chapter 8 the interpretation is specific: "The two-horned ram . . . represents the kings of Media and Persia. The shaggy goat is the king of Greece" (vv. 20–21). Accordingly, commentators have assumed a rigid sequence of kingdoms. However, if the sequence lies in terms of power, the Babylonian and Median can be seen to overlap, and the Persian to arise from the Median—reflecting well the political developments of the sixth century BC. The final phrase in the description of the third beast, "it was given authority to rule" (7:6), may indicate a difference from its predecessor.

As noted, Isaiah and Jeremiah forecast the downfall of Babylon at the hands of the Medes, and so some contend that the author of Daniel had to invent a Median rule and insert it into the narrative to show those prophecies as fulfilled. All are agreed there was a Median kingdom during the first

in *Continuity of Empire (?): Assyria, Media, Persia*, ed. Giovanni B. Lanfranchi, Michael Roaf, and Robert Rollinger [Padova: S.a.r.g.o.n., 2003]: 289–320, here 315–16 n. 128).

[35]David Graf, "Medism: The Origin and Significance of the Term," *Journal of Hellenic Studies* 104 (1984): 15–30.

[36]Cf. Christopher J. Tuplin, "Xenophon in Media," in Lanfranchi, Roaf, and Rollinger, *Continuity of Empire (?)*, 351–89, here 353.

half of the sixth century BC, as the Nabonidus Chronicle and other sources mentioned above demonstrate. (The term *empire* is misleading; the Aramaic of Daniel has simply "kingdom.") The Medes, it seems, were several tribes who might unite for particular purposes under one king, although Jeremiah speaks of the "kings of the Medes" (51:11, 28), and Median strength is apparent in the alliance with the Babylonians to overthrow Assyria, in the threat Nabonidus felt they presented, and in his apparent account of its collapse: "(Marduk) raised up Cyrus, king of Anshan [i.e., Persia], his young servant who scattered the vast (army of the) Medes with his small forces and captured Astyages, king of the Medes."[37]

### The Problem of Darius the Mede

The conqueror of Babylon was Cyrus the Persian. Some years before, in 550–549, he had taken control of the Medes and then the kingdom of Lydia in western Turkey. Now with Babylon and her empire, he ruled all of the Near East; his son Cambyses, who is not mentioned in Scripture, conquered Egypt. Daniel 5:31 states that Belshazzar was killed "and Darius the Mede took over the kingdom, at the age of sixty-two." Here is a major puzzle; there is no doubt from other sources that it was Cyrus who took the crown of Babylon from Nabonidus and his son. Who was Darius the Mede? Some have tried to identify Darius with one of Cyrus's officers, Gubaru, while many scholars say that the author, eager to show that the prophecies were fulfilled and needing to name a king, made a mistake or simply used a known Persian royal name for his fictitious figure, attributing some of the actions of Darius I to him.[38] The question, could there have been a Darius the Mede? remains open.

The neatest clue toward solving the problem was offered in 1957 by D. J. Wiseman, who compared Daniel 6:28, "So Daniel prospered during the reign of Darius and the reign of Cyrus the Persian," with 1 Chronicles 5:26, "And the God of Israel stirred up the spirit of Pul king of Assyria, and the spirit of Tiglathpilneser king of Assyria" (KJV, cf. ASV).[39] Now it is certain that those two names, Pul and Tiglath-pileser, refer to the same man; he ruled as king of Assyria and became king of Babylon by conquest. The Hebrew conjunc-

---

[37]See Beaulieu, *The Reign of Nabonidus*, 107–9; Mario Liverani, "The Rise and Fall of Media," in Lanfranchi, Roaf, and Rollinger, *Continuity of Empire (?)*, 1–12.

[38]Harold H. Rowley, *Darius the Mede and the Four World Empires in the Book of Daniel* (Cardiff: University of Wales Press, 1935), is the classic treatment; John C. Whitcomb, *Darius the Mede: A Study in Historical Identification* (Grand Rapids: Eerdmans, 1959), presents the case for Darius being Gubaru.

[39]"Darius the Mede," *Christianity Today* 2, no. 4 (1957): 7–10; "Some Historical Problems in the Book of Daniel," in Donald J. Wiseman et al., *Notes on Some Problems in the Book of Daniel* (London: Tyndale, 1956), 9–16, expanded by James M. Bulman, "The Identification of Darius the Mede," *WTJ* 35 (1973): 247–67.

tion rendered "and" in older translations of the Bible can also mean "that is to say" or "even." Therefore, 1 Chronicles 5:26 should be translated, "So the God of Israel stirred up the spirit of Pul, king of Assyria, that is to say, the spirit of Tiglath-pileser, king of Assyria" (see RSV and later versions). In past decades it could be stated, "There is no evidence that 'Pulu' was ever used as a contemporary name for the king" because the name was found only in a later copy of a Babylonian king list, in the Bible, and in Greek sources.[40] Therefore the biblical statement might not reflect a custom of Tiglath-pileser's time. Recently a Phoenician inscription from his reign has been deciphered that refers to him four times by this name (*p'l*).[41] By this interpretation, in Aramaic as in Hebrew, Cyrus and Darius are the same king. The use of two names for the same man has been noted as a feature of the book of Daniel.[42] Cyrus may have been his name as king of Persia, and Darius his name as king of the Medes, although the book of Daniel never gives him the title "king of the Medes." Darius was possibly a "throne name," even though it is Persian,[43] for later Persian kings certainly assumed throne names on their accession, for example, Artaxerxes I and II: Arses; Darius II: Ochus, Umasu or Umakuš, Old Persian Va(h)uš or Vauka.[44] That Cyrus had Median ancestry is asserted by Greek sources. Herodotus explains that he was a mule—his father a Persian, his mother a Median princess, daughter of Astyages (*Histories* 1.91; cf. Xenophon, *Cyropaedia* 1.2.1)—and he also reports that a queen of the Massagetae, east of the Caspian Sea, addressed Cyrus as "King of the Medes" (*Histories* 1.206). In Daniel 9:1 Darius is called "son of Xerxes, by birth a Mede." The father of Cyrus was Cambyses, the name also borne by the son who succeeded Cyrus, so if Cyrus is identical with Darius, "son" here can only mean "descendant," but no earlier Xerxes is attested. Cyrus took Babylon when he was about sixty-one years old, the age Daniel 5:31 gives

---

[40] John A. Brinkman, *A Political History of Post-Kassite Babylonia 1158–722 B.C.* (Rome: Pontifical Biblical Institute, 1968), 61–62, 240 n. 1544, 243 n. 1560.

[41] Stephen A. Kaufman, "The Phoenician Inscription of the Incirli Trilingual: A Tentative Reconstruction and Translation," *Maarav* 14, no. 2 (2007): 7–26, here 18.

[42] Colless, "Cyrus the Persian," 113–18.

[43] Note that the name of a Median ruler at the end of the eighth century BC was Darî, apparently a shortened form of a name; see A. Fuchs and R. Schmitt in *The Prosopography of the Neo-Assyrian Empire*, ed. Karen Radner (Helsinki: Neo-Assyrian Text Corpus Project, 1999), 379b.

[44] Frye, *The Heritage of Persia*, 87, states that Cambyses and Cyrus could be personal names or throne names, "but one problem is that neither the name Cyrus nor Cambyses can be adequately explained as one or the other, and we really do not know." See also Pierre Briant, *From Cyrus to Alexander: A History of the Persian Empire*, trans. Peter T. Daniels (Winona Lake, IN: Eisenbrauns, 2002), 570, 588, 591, 615, 664 (cf. 1003), 772, 777 (cf. 1033). On the name Darius, see Rudiger Schmitt, "The Name of Darius," *Acta Iranica* 30 (1990): 194–99, but Manfred Mayrhofer, *Iranisches Personennamenbuch*, 1.2, *Die altpersischen Namen* (Vienna: Österreichischen Akademie der Wissenschaften, 1979), 18, states that it was hardly a throne name for Darius I.

for Darius at that moment is "about sixty-two." Other parallels between the actions of Cyrus and "Darius the Mede" have been proposed.[45] Alas, the Medes did not leave written records that might prove or disprove this idea.

## The 120 Satraps

An objection is raised against Daniel 6:1, "It pleased Darius to appoint 120 satraps to rule throughout the kingdom," because Herodotus states that Darius I created "twenty provincial governorships called satrapies" (*Histories* 3.89). "Satrap" is certainly an Iranian word, apparently of Median origin,[46] denoting the highest subordinates of the king, who controlled the provinces of his empire. When Babylonian and Aramaic texts refer to those governors, however, they use the word *pīḫatu*, taken as a loanword in Aramaic, *pḥh*, which has a wider range of meaning, embracing controllers of the vast territory of Babylonia and Transeuphratene (*ebir nāri*) and of small regions such as Judah or Samaria.[47] The possibility may be envisaged, therefore, that the term could be applied more widely than Herodotus's report about the reign of Darius I implies.

## The Languages

Since S. R. Driver declared, "The *Persian* words presuppose a period after the Persian empire had been well established: the Greek words *demand*, the Hebrew supports, and the Aramaic *permits*, a date *after the conquest of Palestine by Alexander the Great* (B.C. 332),"[48] discoveries of Aramaic documents from the Persian Empire, discoveries of cuneiform texts revealing the presence of Greeks in Nebuchadnezzar's Babylon, and new light on the history of the Hebrew language provided by the Dead Sea Scrolls have changed the situation markedly.

---

[45]Bulman, "Identification of Darius the Mede," 259–64, though not all proposals he advanced are convincing; Colless, "Cyrus the Persian," 115–18, 132–24.

[46]Rudiger Schnitt, "Die Sprache der Meder—eine grosse Unbekannte," in *Continuity of Empire (?)*, 23–36, here 35.

[47]See *The Assyrian Dictionary*, vol. 12, P (Chicago: The Oriental Institute, 2005), 366b; Thierry Petit, "L'évolution sémantique des termes hébreux et araméens *pḥh* et *sgn* et accadiens *pīḫatu* et *šaknu*," *JBL* 107 (1988): 53–67; Matthew W. Stolper, "The Governor of Babylon and Across-the-River in 486 B.C.," *JNES* 48 (1989): 283–305. Briant, *From Cyrus to Alexander*, 712, notes the use of "satrap" in an Aramaic inscription "may indicate that the person . . . held some sort of official position in the region"; Amélie Kuhrt, *The Ancient Near East c. 3000–330 BC* (London: Routledge, 1995), 689, wrote, "The terminology is not always precise: the word can be used of less powerful governors, and Greek writers even apply it on occasion to any officers surrounding the king."

[48]Samuel R. Driver, *An Introduction to the Literature of the Old Testament*, 9th ed. (Edinburgh: T&T Clark, 1913), 508.

When Nebuchadnezzar commanded his experts to explain his dream, they spoke to him in Aramaic, which is the language of all the narrative from that point (Dan. 2:4) until the end of chapter 7. While thousands of cuneiform tablets and scores of royal inscriptions from the days of Nebuchadnezzar and his successors prove the continuing life of Babylonian, "Aramaic had probably become the dominant vernacular."[49] Normally, Aramaic would have been written on parchment, or on wax-covered wooden tablets, which do not survive in the damp Babylonian soil to reveal the extent of its use. One hundred or so clay tablets carry cursive Aramaic notes scratched or written in ink to identify their cuneiform texts, and one of three lines is entirely in Aramaic.[50] A more formal use of Aramaic is evident from stamped bricks. Thousands of bricks in the buildings at Babylonian sites are stamped in cuneiform with the names and titles of Neo-Babylonian kings, following a long-standing Mesopotamian custom, and at Babylon a small proportion is stamped with Aramaic letters. The first examples of these were found in the eighteenth century, but only in 2010 was a comprehensive catalog and study of them produced.[51] The Aramaic stamps are additional to the royal stamps. The purpose of these imprints is uncertain; perhaps they identify the brickworks where they were made. Some give personal names, none royal; some give one or two letters, and others have pictorial designs; but their position on officially marked bricks and their formal or "monumental" script attest an authority behind them. Beside them, another discovery displays the official use of Aramaic: the imprint of a large seal bearing the name of a son of Nebuchadnezzar in cuneiform and in Aramaic.[52] The style of the Aramaic in the book of Daniel is now widely agreed to belong to the Persian period.[53] The Greek words in chapter 3, which are all names of musical instruments, became more accept-

---

[49]Paul-Alain Beaulieu, "Official and Vernacular Languages: The Shifting Sands of Imperial and Cultural Identities in First-Millennium B.C. Mesopotamia," in *Margins of Writing, Origins of Cultures*, ed. Seth L. Sanders, Oriental Institute Seminars 2 (Chicago: Oriental Institute, 2006), 187–216, here 194.
[50]Ran Zadok, "The Representation of Foreigners in Neo- and Late-Babylonian Legal Documents (Eighth through Second Centuries B.C.E.)," in *Judah and the Judeans in the Neo-Babylonian Period*, ed. Oded Lipschits and Joseph Blenkinsopp (Winona Lake, IN: Eisenbrauns, 2003), 471–589, esp. 558–78; Christa Müller-Kessler, "Eine aramäische 'Visitenkarte': Eine spätbabylonische Tontafel aus Babylon," *MDOG* 130 (1998): 189–95.
[51]Benjamin Sass and Joachim Marzahn, *Aramaic and Figural Stamp Impressions on Bricks of the Sixth Century B.C. from Babylon*, Ausgrabungen in Babylon 10, WVDOG 127 (Wiesbaden: Harrassowitz, 2010); see my review in *Journal of the American Oriental Society*, 131, no. 3 (2011).
[52]To be published by Kathleen Abraham.
[53]K. A. Kitchen, "The Aramaic of Daniel," in Wiseman et al., *Notes on Some Problems*, 31–79; Eduard Yechezkel Kutscher, "Aramaic," in *Current Trends in Linguistics*, vol. 6, ed. T. A. Seboek (The Hague: Mouton, 1970), 400–403; Michael Sokoloff, *The Targum of Job from Qumran Cave XI* (Ramat Gan: Bar-Ilan University Press,1974), 9 n. 1; Margaretha L. Folmer, *The Aramaic Language in the Achaemenid Period: A Study in Linguistic Variation* (Leuven: Peeters, 1995), 753–55.

able in a sixth-century setting with the publication of lists of rations issued to people kept in the palace of Nebuchadnezzar. Beside Jehoiachin, king of Judah, there were other people from the Levant and Anatolia, including Greeks.[54] A few further attestations of Greeks living, even owning property, in Babylonia have been traced in legal texts.[55]

The history of biblical Hebrew has come under renewed study, especially in the light of the Dead Sea Scrolls, and the differences appearing between the books are no longer viewed as so clearly marking distinct periods. While the Hebrew of Daniel might support a second-century date, it could equally support an earlier date.[56] The presence of Persian words in a Hebrew (and Aramaic) book written in the Persian period is unexceptionable.

## Conclusion

The book of Daniel correctly reflects the building works of Nebuchadnezzar, in common with Herodotus and other Greek writers, and the use of Aramaic in the Babylonian court, also, no doubt, a widely known fact. Unlike every other known ancient author writing about the fall of Babylon, Daniel preserves the name of Belshazzar, son of the last king of Babylon, according to cuneiform texts. Xenophon is in partial agreement with Daniel, giving an account of a banquet and a king slaughtered (*Cyropaedia* 7.5.15, 21, 25–30). Daniel has Cyrus as king of Persia (10:1) ruling Babylon, in agreement with 2 Chronicles 36:22–23; Ezra 1:1, 7, 8; 2:7; 4:3, 5; 5:13–14, 17; 6:3, 14; and Greek writers and cuneiform tablets. In those respects its narrative may be counted as a reliable record.

In the matter of the Medes and Darius there can be less certainty. The expression "Medes and Persians" may point to the historical priority of Median power to Persian and to a period prior to that of the book of Esther, when the phrase is inverted—"Persians and Medes," as Greek sources also attest. As to Darius the Mede, to dismiss him as a fictional figure, as a composite

---

[54]Ernst F. Weidner, "Jojachin, König von Juda, in Babylonischen Keilschrifttexten," in *Mélanges Syriens Offerts à Monsieur René Dussaud*, vol. 2, Bibliothèque Archéologique et Historique 30 (Paris: Geuthner, 1939), 923–35; Oppenheim, in *ANET*, 308; Terence C. Mitchell, "The Music of the Old Testament Reconsidered," *PEQ* 124 (1992): 124–43, esp. 134–40.

[55]François Joannès, "Diversité ethnique et culturelle en Babylonie récente," and Robert Rollinger and Wouter F. M. Henkelman, "New Observations on 'Greeks' in the Achaemenid Empire according to the Cuneiform Texts from Babylonia and Persepolis," in *Organisation des pouvoirs et contacts culturels dans les pays de l'empire achéménide*, ed. Pierre Briant and Michel Chauveau, *Persika* 14 (Paris: De Boccard, 2009), 217–36, 331–52.

[56]See the discussions in *Biblical Hebrew: Studies in Chronology and Typology*, ed. Ian Young, JSOTSup 369 (London: T&T Clark, 2003), and *Linguistic Dating of Biblical Texts*, ed. Ian Young and Robert Rezetko, 2 vols. (London: Equinox, 2008).

of memories about Persian rulers, or as a simple error is to risk discarding a notice that may be correct. Repeatedly, lone references in ancient writings that scholars have treated as suspect or unfounded have proved to be correct, as the case of Belshazzar illustrates, or that of Sargon II of Assyria, known only from Isaiah 20:1 until his cuneiform inscriptions were deciphered in the mid-nineteenth century.[57] The accuracy of the book of Daniel on such matters contrasts with such Hellenistic compositions as Judith and Tobit.[58]

The parallels between Cyrus and Darius in Daniel strengthen the argument for their identity, but the complete lack of Median documents and the very restricted contemporary records from the Persian court preclude further investigation of, for example, "the laws of the Medes and Persians." Darius I is often held to have drawn up a code of laws, but only in Egypt is he known to have ordered a collection of old precedents to be made.[59] The hypothesis that identifies Cyrus with Darius has been decried as "difficult to falsify" because it cannot be demonstrated or disproved. Yet the proposed alternatives fall into the same category with arguments based upon the supposition that Darius I was the model for "Darius the Mede" in that certain characteristics "could . . . be taken from him," which are also beyond demonstration.[60]

Every ancient document that survives deserves to be examined critically to discover how well or poorly it reflects the era it describes. The book of Daniel has suffered at the hands of scholars who, having assumed "Darius the Mede" is erroneous, have failed to give due attention to the possibility that other statements—and even that one—might be accurate. Now that there is adequate evidence to prove the accuracy of some and circumstantial evidence to allow others, there should be greater willingness to view the book's reports positively. Kenton Sparks's observation that "the need for . . . a critical perspective should be obvious: just because some human view or theory about the Bible has been believed, or is believed, does not ensure its correctness"[61] requires the rider: "nor its error."

---

[57] Steven W. Holladay, "The Quest for Sargon, Pul, and Tiglath-pileser in the Nineteenth Century," in *Mesopotamia and the Bible: Comparative Explorations*, ed. Mark W. Chavalas and K. Lawson Younger, JSOTSup 341 (London: Sheffield Academic, 2002), 68–87, esp. 68–71.

[58] Alan Millard, "Judith, Tobit, Ahiqar and History," in *New Heaven and New Earth: Prophecy and the Millennium: Essays in Honour of Anthony Gelston*, ed. P. J. Harland and C. T. R. Hayward, VTSup 77 (Leiden: Brill, 1999), 195–203. Note also Wilfred G. Lambert's characterization in *The Background of Jewish Apocalyptic* (London: Athlone, 1978), 15: "the mish-mash of spurious items about Babylon that are characteristic of Greek Hellenistic literature."

[59] Briant, *From Cyrus to Alexander*, 474, 510–11, 956–57.

[60] Lester L. Grabbe, "Another Look at the Gestalt of 'Darius the Mede,'" *CBQ* 50 (1988): 198–213.

[61] Kenton L. Sparks, *God's Word in Human Words* (Grand Rapids: Baker Academic, 2008), 57.

# 12

# A CRITICAL-REALISTIC READING OF THE PSALM TITLES

## *Authenticity, Inspiration, and Evangelicals*

## WILLEM A. VANGEMEREN

## AND

## JASON STANGHELLE[1]

꧁

For the everyday reader, the psalm titles provide avenues for linking psalms to stories or characters in the Bible. For scholars, the psalm titles raise a number of questions pertaining to their authority and inspiration. After providing a preliminary orientation to the issue by surveying several approaches and the manuscript evidence, we will explore the usefulness of Paul Hiebert's critical realism in constructing an evangelical approach to psalm titles.

Scholars have wrestled with the connection between the psalm titles and the psalms. On the one hand, critical scholars dismiss them all too readily, and, on the other hand, evangelicals at times have argued for their belonging to the original composition. In his *Introduction to the Old Testament as Scripture of the Church*, Childs observes that by 1850 the connection between the headings and the psalms was "almost universally abandoned."[2] He laments "the rupture within the traditional Jewish-Christian understanding of the Psalter" resulting from sociological approaches to the Psalter.[3] He feels so strongly that Gunkel's approach cut off the Psalms from earlier interpreters that he

---

[1]We are grateful for the helpful suggestions made by Andrew Abernethy.
[2]Brevard S. Childs, *Introduction to the Old Testament as Scripture of the Church* (Philadelphia: Fortress, 1979), 509.
[3]Ibid., 510.

observes, "With one stroke [of the pen] Gunkel appeared to have rendered all pre-critical exegesis of the Psalter invalid."[4]

In this chapter we shall review a number of approaches to the titles by looking at (1) evangelical approaches, (2) the complexity of the recent text-critical evidence, (3) the canonization, authority, and authenticity of the book of Psalms, (4) a critical-realistic reading and its application to the Psalter, and (5) a canonical and associative reading of the titles.

## Evangelical Approaches to the Titles

More than sixty years ago Edward J. Young, a conservative Old Testament scholar at Westminster Theological Seminary, published a major introduction to the Old Testament that served several generations of evangelicals.[5] In it Young rejects the critical attitude to the Old Testament that denies David's contribution to the Psalter, but he is also critical of rabbinic traditions that make statements like the following: "David wrote the book of psalms . . . with the help of ten elders . . . and Heman and Jeduthun, and Asaph, and the three sons of Korah."[6] In Young's sober judgment the Talmud claims too much in attributing all the psalms to David. It lacks "historical foundation"[7] because many psalms were composed after David and during the exile.

Young concludes that at least some of the Davidic psalms were written by David on the ground that there is a presumption for such a claim in the titles. He meets the critical rejection of David's penning some of the psalms with counterarguments[8] citing historical allusions to David's life, his musical fame, his poetic imagination, his deep religious commitment, and his rich experience.[9] Further, he accepts the New Testament claims of Davidic authorship as "infallible expression[s]."[10] He accepts Psalm 2 (without a title in the Masoretic Text) to be Davidic because Peter attributes it to him in Acts 4:25. In comparison with the claims of Baba Bathra, Young concludes modestly, "David did, therefore, compose some of the Psalms. Of that there can be no doubt."[11] He cites favorably Ecclesiasticus 47:8, where sacred songs and liturgy are associated with David, as they are also in the postexilic books

---

[4]Ibid., 510.
[5]See Edward J. Young, *Introduction to the Old Testament* (Grand Rapids: Eerdmans, 1949). References will be made to the 1965 retypeset edition.
[6]Ibid., 297. This quotation comes from Baba Bathra 14b.
[7]Ibid.
[8]Ibid., 304.
[9]Ibid., 298–300.
[10]Ibid., 298.
[11]Ibid.

of Chronicles, Ezra, and Nehemiah.[12] He admits that lĕdāwîd (lit. "to or concerning David") "need not necessarily refer to authorship."[13] Yet he concludes that the phrase is "clearly intended to indicate authorship by David" in the psalms alluding to an episode in David's life (Psalms 3; 7; 18; 30; 34; 51; 52; 54; 56; 57; 59; 60; 63; 142).[14] He extrapolates that other psalms with lĕdāwîd are Davidic as well. He concludes that "unless the testimony of the title is actually contrary to the contents of the Psalm the title may be regarded as trustworthy."[15] Though he evidently knows the differences in the textual witnesses as to the number of the superscriptions in the MT, LXX, and Vulgate, he accepts the MT. He ably responds to historical and text-critical issues, explaining objections that have been raised, such as the use of *king* in Davidic psalms, references to the temple, Aramaisms, and the identity of the enemies in the psalms ascribed to David.[16]

Young admits that the connections between the titles and the text may not always be helpful, but he turns the argument around by asking why the superscriptions would have to be later than the composition of the psalms? Young even suggests that 2 Samuel could well be "dependent upon the Psalms and their titles."[17]

In summary, Young takes the New Testament witness, the reliability of the titles, and the correspondence between the titles and the contents of the psalms as evidence for the authenticity of the superscriptions. He affirms the reliability of the headings in the face of the critics, while recognizing alternative interpretations. In a footnote he seems to qualify his position: "It is possible that in some cases the title may mean merely 'belonging to David' and thus indicate that the Psalm in question is Davidic in character, or is like David's Psalm."[18]

Some thirty years later Dillard and Longman, two Westminster Seminary graduates and onetime professors of Old Testament at Westminster, also wrote *An Introduction to the Old Testament*.[19] They summarize Young as saying that "the psalm titles are not authentic but rather reflect early reliable tradition";[20] Young may admit their not being original, but he certainly

---

[12]Ibid.
[13]Ibid., 298.
[14]Ibid.
[15]Ibid., 301, 304.
[16]Ibid., 302–4.
[17]Ibid., 301.
[18]Ibid., 298.
[19]Raymond B. Dillard and Tremper Longman III, *An Introduction to the Old Testament* (Grand Rapids: Zondervan, 1994).
[20]Ibid., 214.

would treat the titles as authentic in some sense. He takes the Psalter to be "basically Davidic."[21]

In 1991 Bruce Waltke, while teaching at Westminster Theological Seminary, raised the question of postscripts.[22] The idea goes back one hundred years to J. W. Thirtle,[23] whose contribution considered the superscript and postscript in Habakkuk 3:1, 19 as a way of encountering the function of the titles in the Psalms. Waltke marshals impressive evidence from the ancient Near East (colophons), Qumran (Psalm 145), and the LXX (Psalms 104–6; 111–17) and explains many features of the titles. Among others, he suggests that the superscript gives details on the composition, and the postscript helps identify the nature of the presentation. The evidence of his impressive article has not garnered a following, though it cannot be ignored.

Dale Brueggemann, at least, has picked it up as an interpretive possibility, writing, "All in all, these arguments make a case for suggesting that everything up to the note of literary genre and authorship may be postscript of the previous psalm."[24] Following Waltke, he proceeds by dividing the title information as follows: "Postscripts: Performance Directions" and "Superscripts: Composition."[25] Regrettably, Brueggemann does not assess the method critically. He does raise a question on the meaning of the *lamedh* before personal names (*lĕdāwîd*), whether it signifies that the poem belongs to a cycle or series, but sides with Waltke and O'Connor's judgment that it represents the *lamedh auctoris* (authorship).[26] When faced with the syntactic regularity in psalms each of which includes a note linking the psalm to an episode in David's life, he wonders whether this reveals an editorial hand or a "reliable tradition."[27]

In his more recent contribution to *NIDOTTE*, Waltke bypasses the issue of superscripts and postscripts. He strongly advocates the historical context for interpreting the Psalms.[28] Waltke, like Childs, argues for an integration

---

[21] Young, *Introduction to the Old Testament*, 300. Dillard and Longman view the titles as an "early reliable tradition concerning the authorship and setting of the psalms." They are not original or canonical (Dillard and Longman, *Introduction to the Old Testament*, 214; see also 216).

[22] Bruce Waltke, "Superscripts, Postscripts, or Both," *JBL* 110 (1991): 538–96.

[23] J. W. Thirtle, *The Titles of the Psalms: Their Nature and Meaning* (London: Frowde, 1904).

[24] D. A. Brueggemann, "Psalms 4: Titles," in *Dictionary of the Old Testament: Wisdom, Poetry and Writings*, ed. Peter Enns and Tremper Longman III (Downers Grove, IL: InterVarsity, 2008), 615–21.

[25] Ibid., 615–20.

[26] Ibid., 619. See also Bruce K. Waltke and M. O'Connor, *An Introduction to Hebrew Syntax* (Winona Lake, IN: Eisenbrauns, 1990), 206.

[27] Ibid.

[28] See Waltke, "Psalms: Theology of," in *NIDOTTE*, 4:1100–4. Childs adds: "By placing a Psalm within the setting of a particular historical incident in the life of David, the reader suddenly was given access to previously unknown information. David's inner life was now unlocked to the reader, who was allowed to hear his intimate thoughts and reflections." Brevard S. Childs, "Psalm Titles and Midrashic Exegesis," *JSS* 16 (Autumn 1971): 149.

of superscript and text, suggesting a richer interpretation of the Davidic psalms: "It allows the reader to hear the most intimate thoughts of Israel's greatest king."[29]

## Textual History of the Psalm Titles

The diversity of opinions concerning the titles in both critical and evangelical scholarship springs out of the complicated textual history of the Psalter. The discovery of the Qumran Psalms material only increased the complexity of the picture. In order to assess critically the evidence, we will review the current scholarly discussion and then examine foundational epistemological presuppositions about the evidence.

The MT, the LXX, and manuscripts from Qumran each represent different textual histories of psalm titles. The MT of the Psalms has been the *textus receptus* for centuries. The superscriptions of the MT are a significant part of the tradition, as well as the numbering and number of the psalms. It has been known that the Septuagintal (LXX) numbering and titles vary from those of the MT. In the MT Psalter one finds 117 titles (out of 150), and 73 psalms are connected with David. The LXX expands the Davidic titles by 14 (Psalms 33; 43; 71; 91; 93–99; 104; 137; and 151 if it is considered "supernumerary").[30] While these differences between the MT and the LXX are apparent, the manuscripts at Qumran contribute greatly to an understanding of the development of psalm titles.

The Qumran evidence demonstrates the importance of the Psalter within the desert community. Some 40 manuscripts have been found with as many as 126 out of the 150 canonical psalms and 16 fragments of noncanonical psalms.[31] In addition to the variation in contents, the order of the psalms suggests that the order and contents in the last two books (Psalms 90–150) reveal greater fluidity.[32] Several text types coexisted: the MT, the LXX, and the Qumran Cave 11.[33] Both the LXX and Cave 11 text types place their hope on a Davidic king who will bring deliverance to his people. The MT, rather, places the focus on Yahweh's universal kingship (Psalms 145–50).

The evidence of 11QPs[a] aids in the reconstruction of the formation of the Psalter. Since Sanders's 1965 publication of 11QPs[a] in *Discoveries in the Judean Desert of Jordan,* volume 4, *The Psalms Scroll of Qumrân Cave 11,*

---

[29]Waltke, "Psalms: Theology of," *NIDOTTE,* 4:1104.
[30]Brueggemann, "Psalms 4: Titles," 614.
[31]See Dwight D. Swanson, "Qumran and the Psalms," in *Interpreting the Psalms,* ed. David Firth and Philip S. Johnston (Downers Grove, IL: InterVarsity, 2005), 254–57.
[32]Ibid., 258.
[33]Ibid.

several questions have been raised about its role in the canonical development
of the Psalter. Sanders argued that 11QPs[a] represents a separate canonical text
tradition that was authoritative but not closed.[34] Several years later, P. Flint
advanced Sanders claims that 11QPs[a] represents a unique canonical collection
in what he termed the "Qumran Psalms Hypothesis."[35] Flint argued that the
editing and use of titles in the collection are similar to practices seen in the
MT.[36] Further he noted that most arguments against the canonical status of
11QPs[a] presuppose a preexisting MT order from which the Qumran community deviated for liturgical purposes. There is no clear evidence that the
MT order was universally accepted by the Jews as early as the second century
BC.[37] There is also no textual evidence at Qumran that "clearly confirms the
longer order of the received MT against 11QPs[a]."[38] The dominance of this
arrangement at Qumran, the similarity of the use of titles to books 4 and 5,
and the Davidic emphasis throughout all the Qumran Psalm manuscripts point
to an independent edition of the Psalter within which "the 11QPs[a]-Psalter is
the foremost representative of the Book of Psalms in the Dead Sea Scrolls."[39]
Both 11QPs[a] and the noncanonical psalms at Qumran exhibit a tendency
toward attributing the entire Psalter to David.[40]

Hope in the Davidic dynasty is stronger in the Qumran textual witness than
in the MT. The editorial postscript in the MT after Psalm 72 closes the collection of Psalms 1–72 on a high note of the royal role of the Davidic dynasty.
The Psalms scroll at 11QPs[a] also adds a postscript to Psalm 145, suggesting
a similarly important closure of the Davidic psalm.[41]

According to Wilson,

> The 11QPs[a] Psalter is structured in such a way that "hopes are focused on the
> 'horn' whom Yhwh will raise out of Jesse in response to his people's wise and

---

[34]For a review of Sanders's extensive work on the Qumran psalms scrolls, see G. H. Wilson, *The
Editing of the Hebrew Psalter* (Chico, CA: Scholars Press, 1985), 70–73.

[35]Peter W. Flint, "The Book of Psalms in Light of the Dead Sea Scrolls," *VT* 48 (1999): 459.

[36]"Wilson's analysis shows that this collection was organized in accordance with principles similar
to those found in Books IV and V in the MT-150 Psalter. Such organization is most evident in the
juxtaposition of superscripts and postscripts which highlight different kinds of groupings in 11QPsa."
Ibid., 466.

[37]Ibid., 468.

[38]Ibid., 469.

[39]Ibid.

[40]See Eileen M. Schuller, *Non-Canonical Psalms from Qumran: A Pseudepigraphic Collection* (Atlanta:
Scholars Press, 1986).

[41]Wilson observes, "Here, however, the psalm and its postscript follow a major grouping of halelu-yah
and hodu compositions (Psalms 135; 136; Catena) that also have a concluding function in the masoretic
Psalter. It seems best to conclude that these halelu-yah and hodu psalms and the postscript of Psalm
145 all participate in closing the preceding segment of the scroll." G. H. Wilson, "The Qumran Scroll
Psalms Scroll (11QPsa) and the Canonical Psalter: Comparison of Editorial Shaping," *CBQ* (1997): 464.

diligent obedience to Torah. In the masoretic Psalter, though the place of Torah is acknowledged (Psalms 1; 19; 119) and David is honored, trust in the power of human kings and kingship is ultimately given up, and hopes rest solely on Yhwh, who rules forever, and who alone is able to save."[42]

This shift toward a Davidic Psalter is also attested by changes in the ascriptions of authorship. The MT and LXX attribute Psalm 82 to Asaph, while Qumran attributes it to David. The difference between the LXX and 11QPs[a] superscripts to Psalm 151 reflects unique changes. The LXX ascription reads, "This is a self-written [*idiographos*] Psalm of David and supernumerary, when he fought Goliath in single combat"; 11QPs[a] simply says, "A Hallelujah of David the Son of Jesse." Sanders observes that the LXX attestation of *idiographos* may indicate some doubt about the authenticity of the superscript, while no such doubt was at Qumran.[43] Psalm 151 formed a theological conclusion to the Qumran collection rather than a supernumerary "add-on" to the LXX Psalter. The shift in the title from the LXX fits the theological purposes of the Qumran community, focusing upon the Davidic agent. The noncanonical prose composition, *David's Compositions*, found toward the end of 11QPs[a], describes David as a musical composer and as "a ḥakham, a wise man, comparable to Ben Sira."[44] *David's Compositions* states that David wrote 3,600 psalms and 450 songs.

The evidence of Qumran, the LXX, and the MT points to fluidity in the development of the Psalter. The arrangement and use of the titles were part of a larger historical process. The titles play an integral role in shaping the overall character and theme of the Psalter.[45] This historical process would eventually end in the closing of the canonical Psalter. Swanson's helpful review of Wilson's extensive evidence concludes with a note on the provenance of the MT: "The manuscript evidence reveals increasingly alignment with the MT from the middle of the first century, and with the later scrolls (late first and second centuries) from Masada (MasPs[a]) and Nahal Hever."[46] It is probable that the MT text type of the Psalms became accepted after the fall of Jerusalem and the collapse of the hopes of people in a Davidic messiah by some Jewish communities.

---

[42]Ibid., 464.
[43]See J. A. Sanders, *Discoveries in the Judaean Desert of Jordan*, vol. 4, *The Psalms Scroll of Qumrân Cave 11* (Oxford: Oxford University Press, 1965), 58.
[44]Ibid., 92.
[45]For the development of the titles in the MT tradition, see Wilson, *The Editing of the Hebrew Psalter*.
[46]Swanson, "Qumran and the Psalms," 259.

## The Question of Canon

This brief review of the textual evidence demonstrates the difficulty in deter-mining the historical origin and authenticity of the titles. However, a review of the facts alone is not sufficient to give an adequate account of the titles. Having reviewed the evidence we must now critically evaluate common assumptions about this data and its importance. The debate on this issue has often been reduced to the sole issue of authenticity. Were the psalms written by the attrib-uted authors or not? This single view tends to ignore the multifaceted nature of the problem. Additionally, this approach conflates the separate issues of authenticity and authority.

The development of the canon was a historical process. For some biblical books several different Hebrew texts existed that were regarded as authori-tative among different Jewish communities. There appear to have been two different Hebrew versions of Jeremiah, different recensions of the Pentateuch, and several different Psalters. The development of the canon was anything but a simple "committee decision"[47] at a particular point in time. The titles are but one dimension of a long and intricate historical process.

To assess the role of the titles within the canon, a clarification of terms is necessary. Wilson distinguishes carefully between the terms *canonicity*, *authority*, and *priority*.[48] In regards to canonicity he makes three observations. First, canonicity does not necessarily mean closed. "A 'closed list of books' is not . . . simply a 'canon,' but a 'closed canon.'"[49] There was a long period of time where the canon was open-ended, but still functioned authoritatively for the Jewish communities. Second, "'fixation of form' does not *necessarily* imply 'canonical.'"[50] Third, "canonicity can only be satisfactorily determined by statements to the affirmative or contrary of that view."[51]

On authority Wilson observes the important point that lack of inclusion in a closed canon does not necessarily imply lack of authority.[52] He points out that the early church fathers viewed many of the apocryphal writings as Scripture.[53] They had scriptural authority even though the books were not canonical. The final distinction Wilson makes is that "'priority' of a collec-

---

[47] Wilson, *The Editing of the Hebrew Psalter*, 89. For further reading, see Eugene Ulrich, *The Dead Sea Scrolls and the Origins of the Bible*, Studies in the Dead Sea Scrolls and Related Literature (Grand Rapids: Eerdmans, 1999), and Craig A. Evans and Emanuel Tov, eds., *Exploring the Origins of the Bible: Canon Formation in Historical, Literary, and Theological Perspective* (Grand Rapids Baker, 2008).
[48] Wilson, *The Editing of the Hebrew Psalter*, 88–92.
[49] Ibid., 89.
[50] Ibid.
[51] Ibid.
[52] Ibid., 89–90.
[53] Ibid.

tion does not preclude the 'authority' of another, dependent collection."[54] He points to the differences between Kings and Chronicles as an example. These canonical works represent different arrangements of related material.

Wilson's categories are applicable to the titles. If the titles are later additions, this does not necessarily rule out their canonical status or negate their authority. The titles may not be original, but may still be canonical and authoritative. Their authority need not be ruled out if the titles are later additions and not authentic to the author. Because the canonical book of Psalms was open for a long period of time, we must take into consideration the process of development as well as the final canonical form. To further understand the concept of authenticity we turn to some underlying epistemological assumptions.

## Critical Realism and the Titles

### Paul Hiebert and Critical Realism

The question of canon proposed above demonstrates the importance of examining underlying assumptions about the evidence of the Psalter. Being a critical scholar, regardless of theological predisposition, means not just assessing the evidence, but also examining implicit assumptions about the evidence. In what follows we propose that there are new and critically valid ways to understand the titles. We will critically assess unhelpful ways of understanding the titles and propose a new critical-realistic approach based on the epistemology of Paul Hiebert.

Hiebert, a missiologist and anthropologist, spent much of his life studying epistemological issues related to culture. He develops his epistemological position of critical realism in many works, but systematically in *Missiological Implications of Epistemological Shifts* (1999). Hiebert claims that there is objective *realia* independent of human observation (*realism*) that can be appropriated subjectively through human perception (*critical*). He writes, "It [the *realia*] affirms the presence of objective truth but recognizes that this is subjectively apprehended."[55]

Hiebert contrasts critical realism with positivism and instrumentalism. Positivism, which grew out of the empirical success of modern science, argues that there is an external *realia* that can be objectively known and apprehended. Positivism argues that all reality could be explained through science and empirical observation. Hiebert argues against this approach to knowledge because it separates the evaluative and affective aspects of knowledge from

[54]Ibid., 90.
[55]Paul G. Hiebert, *Missiological Implications of Epistemological Shifts* (Harrisburg, PA: Trinity Press International, 1999), 69.

the cognitive.[56] In short, positivism is reductionistic in its view of knowledge. On the other side of positivism is what Hiebert calls instrumentalism or pragmatism.[57] Instrumentalism argues that there is an external reality, "but that it sees our knowledge of it mainly as a cultural creation."[58] Because reality cannot be known objectively, what matters is how knowledge is used (instrumentalism). For Hiebert, instrumentalism went too far in abandoning any epistemological connection to *realia*.[59]

Critical realism offers a middle ground that prevents the reductionistic view of knowledge in positivism, but also argues for an external *realia* that can be apprehended to a certain degree of reliability. Hiebert defines critical realism.

> Critical realism does not claim pure objectivity for human knowledge. In fact, it argues that total objectivity, if that could be achieved, would not be knowledge, for knowledge is more than factual information. It is used by people to live their lives. Knowledge in critical realism is the correspondence between our mental maps and the real world; it is objective reality subjectively known and appropriated in human lives.[60]

At the heart of epistemology is how an individual or society categorizes the world. Hiebert, who studied physics and math before turning to anthropology, employed mathematical research on set theory to explain the epistemological importance of categories in knowledge.[61] He differentiates between intrinsic and extrinsic sets. Intrinsic sets are sets based on quantifiable, objective data: sex (male/female), age, career, and so forth. Extrinsic sets focus upon relational logic. A person is known not by the intrinsic categories such as material possessions or a PhD, but as "the wife of Peter, the daughter of John and Mary, and the mother of Sarah."[62]

Hiebert developed several different kinds of sets out of this typology: bounded, fuzzy, and centered sets.[63] He argued that Western culture (influenced by positivism) views the world in intrinsic bounded sets. Bounded sets are characterized by tight definitions, black or white perspectives, yes or no answers. This approach to knowledge prioritizes the intrinsic nature of an object and its objective status. Fuzzy sets are another kind of intrinsic set.

---

[56]For Hiebert's critique of positivism, see ibid., 29–35.
[57]See ibid., 36–67.
[58]Ibid., 38.
[59]For Hiebert's critique of instrumentalism, see ibid., 63–67.
[60]Ibid., 74.
[61]See Paul G. Hiebert, *Transforming Worldviews: An Anthropological Understanding of How People Change* (Grand Rapids: Baker Academic, 2008), 33–46.
[62]Ibid., 35.
[63]Ibid., 36.

Instead of clear categories, there is ambiguity between the boundaries in fuzzy sets. Fuzzy sets are characterized by yes, no, or maybe answers; unclear boundaries; and an absence of black or white categories. An example Hiebert uses is the difference between the music of one culture and that of another.[64] Western music divides the octave into seven clearly distinct notes (a bounded set). Indian music divides the octave into a myriad of incremental microtones (a fuzzy set).

The final typology, the centered set, is based upon extrinsic relational logic. In this typology a clearly defined center remains, but the inclusion of variables within the set is based upon their relationship to the center. Inclusion in the set is based upon an object's extrinsic connection to the center.

## Set Theory and the Titles

The application of a centered set to the psalm titles and canonical development offers new possibilities. The question of authenticity has often been posed as a bounded-set problem: either the superscripts are canonical or they are not. This is a bounded-set approach similar to approaches taken to a closed canon discussed above. An alternative approach based on a fuzzy-set logic is to treat the titles as authentic without critically evaluating the evidence. In this view we may doubt the validity of some of the titles, but they are collectively treated as authored by David. There is a blurring between the categories of authentic and nonauthentic titles. Additionally, both of these approaches argue only from intrinsic categories and do not employ extrinsic logic. This fuzzy-set view takes a pragmatic view of the titles. Because the community or canon uses the titles as if they are authentic, then they are treated as genuinely Davidic. The question of the historicity of the titles is left unanswered. How they are used (instrumentalism) is what matters. Neither of these approaches is satisfactory. The bounded-set approach, with its strict categories, ignores the historical development of the Psalter. It imposes categories upon the text that do not give an adequate account for everything that is going on in the canon. The fuzzy-set approach, on the other hand, ignores the critical textual evidence.

In place of these two views we propose a critical-realistic examination of the titles based on a centered-set approach. This approach will evaluate critically the evidence while not reducing the issue to merely intrinsic, bounded-set categories. A critical-realistic centered-set approach offers a way forward to explore different ways the titles can be understood to be both authentic and authoritative.

---

[64]Ibid., 33–34.

### A Critical-Realistic Assessment of the Authenticity of the Superscripts in the Psalter

To test the value of a critical-realistic centered-set approach, we will survey the work of several scholars and explain how a critical-realistic centered-set approach can help move beyond the current discussion on authenticity. Dillard and Longman define *authenticity* as "titles written by the inspired author of the psalm at approximately the same time that the psalm was written."[65] After some discussion they aver that the titles are not authentic, that is, not "original or canonical."[66] Instead they maintain that the titles follow "an early reliable tradition."[67]

Dillard and Longman make a distinction between the positions of E. J. Young and Derek Kidner. According to them, Kidner represents the most conservative position—"the titles are original and infallible"—unlike Young's position that the titles "are not authentic but reflect an early reliable tradition."[68] Young's argument is more nuanced than Dillard and Longman suggest, but so also is that of Kidner. He represents a long-standing tradition according to which the titles are authoritative and important for the interpretation of the psalms. He admits that the titles were added by later editors and are, therefore, not original.[69] Anticipating Waltke, Kidner is open to the possibility that some of the titles are in fact colophons.[70] He, as many others, accepts the New Testament evidence where reference of authorship of a psalm is important in accepting the titles. But he also remains open to further evidence: "But as we have no direct way in which these comments came into being, it should perhaps be left an open question, whether some are the product of comparing scripture with scripture, and others the product of historical records."[71] In the end, he holds to the reliability of the titles.

Dale Brueggemann argues for the authenticity of the titles from the ancient Near Eastern context of the king being recognized as patron of the cult. On the basis of evidence from the Old Testament and the Second Temple writings as to David's fame as a "poet-singer," he concludes that the MT titles are

---

[65] Dillard and Longman, *Introduction to the Old Testament*, 214.

[66] Ibid., 215.

[67] Ibid.

[68] Ibid., 214. We do not recall Kidner's usage of the term *infallible*. He holds to the truthfulness of the titles, but is open to consider interpretive possibilities (see Derek Kidner, *Psalm 1–72*, Tyndale Old Testament Commentaries [London: Inter-Varsity, 1973], 45–46; see below).

[69] Kidner, *Psalm 1–72*, 33. Truthfulness is an expression of trustworthiness. The titles are subject to interpretation.

[70] Ibid., 33.

[71] Ibid., 46. Though he has in view the titles with references to David's experiences, his final comment reveals his concern for the psalm titles.

authentic.[72] He clinches his argument by reference to the New Testament where Jesus and the apostles argue from the authenticity of the Davidic authorship of several psalms.[73] However, these examples do not justify the authenticity of all titles. At the most one could agree with Brueggemann that some psalms are genuinely Davidic, but the claim that all psalm titles are authentic has not been argued or advanced. Further, his supposition that the MT is preferable because Greek translators had difficulty in translating technical terms avers too much.[74] At best it may argue in favor of the antiquity, but not the authenticity, of the titles. Finally, Brueggemann ignores the knotty problem of the text types.

What exactly is authenticity? As we have seen, evangelicals are ambivalent on the usage. A differentiation may be made between the *vox* and the *verba* of the person mentioned in the title. For example, evangelicals assume the essential Mosaic authorship of the Pentateuch, while allowing for significant additions (post-Mosaica). Daniel Block argues that the book of Deuteronomy represents the authentic voice of Moses and that someone else put the book together: "We can only speculate when the individual speeches of Moses were combined, arranged, and linked with their present narrative stitching."[75] Block is content to hear the "voice" of Moses in Deuteronomy, while he also supports the book's claims (4:2) that nothing was to be added or taken from the book.[76] What is authentic in this case? Is it the canonical form or the very words of Moses? Block concludes in favor of both. The canonical form contains the speeches of Moses that were put together by "a prophet." He writes:

> The book of Deuteronomy is unequivocal in declaring that Moses' voice is to be heard in the speeches of the book. It is equally clear in its assertion of Mosaic involvement in the transcription of at least one of those speeches. If one can accept these basic facts and acknowledge that the person responsible for producing the book of Deuteronomy was a prophet "like unto Moses," then later Israelites who spoke of the "Book of the Torah of Moses," accurately recalled the source and authority of the book of Deuteronomy.[77]

The *vox* and *verba* distinction is one also familiar to the study of the Gospels. Many scholars have long argued that the Gospels faithfully represent

[72]Brueggemann, "Psalms 4: Titles," 614–15.
[73]Ibid.
[74]Ibid., 615.
[75]Daniel I. Block, "Deuteronomy, Book of," in *Dictionary for Theological Interpretation of the Bible*, ed. Kevin Vanhoozer and Daniel Treier (Grand Rapids: Baker Academic, 2005), 167–68; see also his "Recovering the Voice of Moses: The Genesis of Deuteronomy," *JETS* 44 (2001): 193–212.
[76]Block, "Deuteronomy," 169–70.
[77]Block, "Recovering the Voice of Moses," 207.

the *vox* (the authentic voice) of Jesus rather than the *ipsissima verba* (the exact words) of Jesus. Jesus may not have spoken exactly the words quoted in the text, but the argument is that he spoke along their lines. The practice of editing historical material in such fashion is well documented in both ancient Near Eastern and Greco-Roman writings.

These solutions to critical issues, used by evangelical scholars, demonstrate the plausibility of a similar critical-realistic approach to the titles. In both of these cases authority is about not merely the *intrinsic* nature of the text but also its *extrinsic* relationship to the central authoritative person (i.e., Moses or Jesus). In other words texts are authoritative not just because of what they say, but also because of their relationship to the locus of authority. A bounded-set approach looks only at the intrinsic *verba*, while a centered-set approach looks at both the *verba* of the text (what it is saying) and the extrinsic relationship to the clear center, the *vox* (the source of authority).

## A Canonical and Associative Reading: The Place of David in Samuel and the Psalms

The titles allow authentic "associative" readings between the historical David and the David of the Psalter. A number of scholars have proposed similar approaches, which we shall review below. However, there has not been a critical explanation for the validity of associative reasoning. The benefit of the critical-realistic approach is that it gives an epistemological basis from which to argue for the validity of associative readings. Associative readings are based on extrinsic logic, the logic of the centered set. After reviewing the scholarly discussion, we illustrate how an associative reading between Samuel and the Psalms may work.

Dale Brueggemann's response to issues raised by critical students of the Psalms helpfully summarizes the nature of evangelical answers. We shall look at the issues and then raise the realistic question of whether the response is adequate given the evidence. First, he tackles the question of whether David could compose psalms during his flight from Saul (Psalms 18; 52; 53; 59), especially when he was hiding in a cave (Psalms 57; 142). From the analogy of the poetry produced by soldiers fighting in the trenches during World War I, he suggests that David could have written psalms. The analogy is helpful, but does not raise the deeper question of whether the biblical record speaks of David composing poetry during Saul's pursuit of him. Nor does it satisfy the question of whether David is the composer of all the psalms attributed to him. What we know is that David played the harp (1 Sam. 16:18, 23; 18:10; 19:9) and that praise is associated with him in his experiences of Yahweh's deliverance

(2 Samuel 22//Psalm 18). But most of the Davidic psalms are laments. Where does one find David lamenting in the Former Prophets[78] or in Chronicles?

Next Brueggemann considers several historical issues arising from a comparison of parallel accounts and from the state of the Hebrew language. The mention of David being taken by the people of Gath (Psalm 56) appears to be a variation of the account in 1 Samuel 21:12–23:1. The use of late Aramaisms may raise the question of dating, but can be readily explained by evidence in the use of loanwords in the ancient Near East. Further, in the process of copying a text, scribes occasionally updated the language. We agree with Brueggemann's conclusion that "the titles were authentic canonical editorial activity," but we need to explore what is meant by "canonical editorial activity."[79]

A conservative approach to the titles affirms that it is likely that David is the author of some psalms. Evangelicals are aware of the critical objections to the titles, the problems of interpreting the titles, and the textual issues. Their main dispute with the negative critical assessment of the titles comes from the biblical traditions of David as "the sweet singer." While we are sympathetic to the traditional view, we question the definitive conclusion drawn from the evidence that "therefore, while the titles are not canonical, they may be reliable" and that they are not to be used in the interpretation of "individual psalms."[80] What then is the purpose of the titles when they do not contribute to the interpretation of individual psalms or to reading the Psalter in the context of Scripture?[81]

We hold that the key lies in what Brueggemann calls the "canonical editorial activity."[82] The name of David was readily associated with praise and with the temple. By reading the prophetical writings (the books of Samuel and Kings) in association with the book of Psalms, the reader recovers aspects of an "authentic canonical editorial activity" within the Old Testament.[83]

First, David is "Israel's beloved singer" (2 Sam. 23:1, NIV MARGIN).[84] His name is connected with a song (2 Samuel 22) and with a poetic oracle

---

[78]The dirge in 2 Sam. 1:18–27 is a form of lament, but its close connection with the historical circumstance of the death of Saul and Jonathan is unlike the lament psalms that have a historical reference in the title, while the content of the poem lacks any historical specificity.

[79]Brueggemann, "Psalms 4: Titles," 614.

[80]Ibid.

[81]For an attempt at reading the individual psalms in relation to each other, see Willem A. VanGemeren, "Psalms," EBC 5 (Grand Rapids: Zondervan, 2008), 34–40. See also my "Retrospective and Prospective Considerations for Entering the Textual World of the Psalms: Literary Analysis" (paper presented at the annual meeting for the Evangelical Theological Society, New Orleans, 2009).

[82]Brueggemann, "Psalms 4: Titles," 614.

[83]Ibid.

[84]Some read the expression as "protector of Israel"; see A. A. Anderson, 2 Samuel, WBC 11 (Dallas: Word, 1989), 266–68.

(2 Sam. 23:1–7). These poetic expressions form part of an appendix (chaps. 20–24) whose purpose is to shape the reader's understanding of the books of Samuel. Childs calls it "a hermeneutical guide for understanding the books of Samuel."[85] The appendix reconnects David with Saul: the godly David who justly brought closure to the famine resulting from the blood-stained record of Saul's reign (21:1–14) and who was delivered by the Lord from Saul and the enemies (21:15–22:20). David praises the Lord for his victories, for Yahweh's grace, for David's growth in righteousness, and for the privilege of serving as the anointed king (22:21–51). The mention of Saul in chapters 21–22 takes on a symbolic significance in both chapters. The vindictive Saul stands in contrast to the righteous David. Both Saul and David are larger than life. Saul stands for evil, adversity, and enmity. David stands for righteousness, suffering, and deliverance. Both characters affirm the faithfulness of God, who punishes and rewards, who judges and delivers. The song in praise for Yahweh's deliverance "from the hand of Saul"[86] (22:1) ties the two books of Samuel together. The main characters are Samuel, Saul, and David. Saul's character and accomplishments are set aside because of a character flaw. David's sins and character flaws are forgiven because of Yahweh's grace to him. The David of 2 Samuel 21–23 takes on heroic and saintly proportions even though the book portrays David as responsible for his suffering and concludes with a David responsible for bringing about a plague that killed seventy thousand Israelites (2 Samuel 24).

The song also associates the Davidic narrative with the Psalter, particularly with its parallel in Psalm 18 and with four psalms that mention Saul in the headings (Psalms 52; 53; 57; 59).[87] The parallel Psalm 18, a hymn of praise, is flanked by a lament psalm (Psalm 17), a hymn of praise (thanksgiving, 19:1–6), and a wisdom psalm (19:7–14). In Psalm 18 we meet a David who is rejoicing in God's goodness and redemption. But in an associative reading with Psalm 17, we also meet a David familiar with grief and suffering and longing for redemption. An associative reading connects the "righteous" David with the sinful David (see Psalms 25; 41). The David of Samuel and of the Psalms, while at times idealized, is a man familiar with both innocent and deserved suffering. David is familiar with guilt and with the consequences of sin.

The Saul in the psalm titles is larger than in David's experiences recorded in Samuel. As in 2 Samuel 23:1, Saul stands for the enemies at large, and David becomes symbolic of adversity and suffering. The association between the books of Samuel and Psalms forges an associative reading so as to present

[85] Childs, *Introduction to the Old Testament as Scripture*, 274.
[86] Some have revocalized "Saul" to "Sheol."
[87] See B. S. Childs, "Psalm Titles and Midrashic Exegesis," 137–50.

David's anguish and suffering as God's school of discipleship. David is a star pupil who invites people into his way of life, into his inner thought, and into his communion with God. While David's anguish is anchored in the experiences of Saul's betrayal and vindictiveness, his suffering continues during his kingship (Absalom's rebellion, Psalm 3). The David of the Psalms is largely known for his lament in which he pours out his soul, demonstrates his confidence in Yahweh, longs for redemption, experiences deliverance, and praises God. However, despite David's songs of thanksgiving, we largely remember a lamenting David from the Psalter. Further, he invites his readers to join him in the "fellowship of his suffering" by modeling a wise response to adversity and by instructing them.

Second, David is also to be remembered as a sage who was specially anointed to teach Israel through his songs.

> The oracle of David son of Jesse,
>> the oracle of the man exalted by the Most High,
> the man anointed by the God of Jacob,
>> Israel's singer of songs. (2 Sam 23:1, NIV)

A. A. Anderson considers David's oracle (2 Sam. 23:1–7) to be "a very brief theological evaluation of David's reign in general."[88] David's self-assessment of his role as a messianic agent reveals his commitment to establish a just rule in Israel and gives support to the hope that the Davidic covenant will endure (23:3–5).[89] On the one hand, David's self-knowledge and his confidence in Yahweh's plans, purposes, and promises open up the psalmist's private prayers for all to read and internalize. The pursuit of a lifestyle of integrity marks the Davidic psalms (Psalms 7; 19; 25; 26; 41; 101; cf. 78:72), as does the contrast between the wicked and the righteous, the wise and the fools. David is one of the major persons associated with the Psalms (73 out of 150 psalms). He is a teacher and a model of righteousness, even after having sinned and confessed his sin.[90] Two of the major themes of the Psalter also occur in 2 Samuel 23:1–7, namely, wisdom (justice) and the hope in the Davidic agency.[91] Rendtorff's

---

[88] Anderson, *2 Samuel*, 268.
[89] Childs, *Introduction to the Old Testament as Scripture*, 275.
[90] See my article "David: Model and Teacher of Wisdom" (forthcoming).
[91] These two themes are heightened in 11QPs according to Gerald Wilson. He comments, "In light of growing evidence of the significant roles given to psalms influenced by wisdom in the editorial framework of the masoretic Psalter [16], the appearance of so many 'new' wisdom compositions in 11QPsa is striking confirmation of the continued importance of sapiential compositions in giving shape to collections of psalms even at a late date. Equally striking is the Davidic emphasis associated with these psalms." ("The Qumran Psalms Scroll (11Qps[a]) and the Canonical Psalter: Comparison

study of "David in the Psalms" is helpful in a brief assessment of the evidence. He concludes that

> only in a minority of the psalms is the "historical" David portrayed as king. In a number of other psalms the name David represents the royal dynasty, and even later kings can be identified or identify themselves with this name. . . . This shows that even in those psalms in which the name David stands for the ruling king, it is not the image of the ruling and victorious one that is in the foreground, but that of the righteous one who serves and helps his people.[92]

Third, the account of David's failure, God's judgment, and David's sacrifice and purchase of the site of the future temple connects David with the temple. The mention of the temple in Davidic psalms appears to be anachronistic—for example:

> But I, by your great mercy,
>     will come into your house;
> in reverence will I bow down
>     toward your holy temple. (5:7, NIV; cf. Psalm 132)

David had planned for the construction of the temple, but how could he have entered the temple? The usual response is of a linguistic nature: the word *house* can designate the tabernacle (Josh. 6:24; cf. 1 Sam. 1:9). But there was no tabernacle at David's time, and whatever structure the ark was in was not called tabernacle, house, or sanctuary in 1, 2 Samuel. The postexilic book of Chronicles does indeed use the expression "house of the LORD" (1 Chron. 6:31, but see 17:5–6).[93] David is to be remembered as the patron of the temple (see Psalm 132). He still dwells in the house of the Lord (Ps. 23:6) and remains concerned with the purity and the holiness of those who approach the temple through Psalms 15 and 24.

The Samuel appendix gives a canonical and hermeneutical understanding of David's walk with Yahweh, accomplishments, wisdom, hope, and failure, as well as of Yahweh's faithfulness, promise, judgment, and deliverance. David is both a righteous man and a sinner. He praises Yahweh and reflects on his own life and on Yahweh's promises. The idealization of David is qualified by

---

of Editorial Shaping," *CBQ* 59 [1997]: 454). He treats two additional themes, "an awareness of human sin and weakness, and the contrasted theme of Yhwh's powerful trustworthiness to save" (ibid.).

[92] R. Rendtorff, "David in the Psalms," in *The Book of Psalms: Composition and Reception*, ed. Peter W. Flint and Patrick D. Miller, VTSup 96 (Leiden: Brill, 2005), 64.

[93] The association between David's house and the temple is developed in the *midrash*. See John Goldingay, *Psalms*, vol. 1, *Psalms 1–41*, Baker Commentary on the Old Testament Wisdom and Psalms (Grand Rapids: Baker, 2006), 425.

the accounts of his failures and needs. In the end, he is a model of the Davidic agency, a persona, a patron of the temple, a teacher of Israel, and a prophet. He is larger than life. The David of the Psalter is also idealized, as he is in Chronicles. The intent is not deceptive. Idealization fits within the genre of writing in the ancient Near East. The editors of the Psalter and their forebears associated psalms with David in order to honor his name in perpetuity. More than that, they encourage the reading of Scripture in association with Scripture (i.e., Psalms with 1, 2 Samuel, and 1, 2 Samuel with Psalms). They success-fully create the persona of David, whose voice, if not his words, is heard in the Davidic psalms. Similarly, the two psalms associated with Solomon evoke the image of Solomon as searching and praying for wisdom (Psalms 72; 127) and as the "builder" of the temple (Psalm 127). The psalms connected with the Korahites and Asaphites further the connection with the temple, in that these guilds were known as worship leaders at the temple (2 Chron. 20:19; 35:15). Finally, the psalm connected with Moses ties the drama of redemp-tion together: Moses, David, and Solomon; the tabernacle and the temple; the transgenerational importance of wisdom and the abiding significance of divine revelation (Moses and David).

Forty years ago B. S. Childs argued for the titles representing what he called midrashic exegesis. By this he meant an attempt at integrating the Psalms with "a narrative setting," allowing for "information of author and setting."[94] Child's assessment of the evidence is that the process of ascribing authorship to psalms "was already at work toward the end of the Old Testament period in the formation of the psalm titles."[95] This practice increased in the LXX, Syriac, Qumran, and rabbinic writings. But the evidence points to the likelihood of the practice within the Old Testament period itself. Childs gives a rough approxi-mation that the titles within the MT probably emerged between the time of the Chroniclers and 11QPs$^a$, "where the technique had been fully developed."[96]

He argues that these titles were not merely pseudonymous ascriptions. The titles were part of a self-generating process from the text that sought to under-stand and give fuller life to the interpretation of the text. This is not "post-biblical 'Jewish Distortion' but part of the biblical tradition itself."[97]

We prefer not to use the expression "midrashic exegesis," but would argue for a "canonical editorial activity," much on the order of the division of the five

---

[94]See Childs, "Psalm Titles and Midrashic Exegesis," 142. His approach is significantly different from Sigmund Mowinckel's approach to the psalm titles and to his usage of the term "late midrashic additions" (Sigmund Mowinckel, *The Psalms in Israel's Worship*, trans. D. R. Ap-Thomas [Nashville: Abingdon Press, 1967], 2:100–101; see Childs, "Psalm Titles and Midrashic Exegesis," 137).
[95]Ibid., 143.
[96]Ibid., 148.
[97]Ibid.

books of psalms, the doxological conclusions, and the associations between psalms in their canonical contexts. The titles gain their authority by being centered on the text and pointing us back to the Davidic *vox* prominent within the text.

From a critical-realistic perspective the titles are authentic, not because the titles are original or because the psalms were written by David, but because of their relationship to the Davidic *vox*. From a centered-set perspective the titles have authority owing to their relationship to the texts. They arise out of the sacred text and are part of the historical development of the canon.

Like the voice of Jesus in the Gospels and that of Moses in the Pentateuch, we hear the voice of David in the Psalter. The titles are authentic in the sense that they were part of a historical process of editing that led to its final canonical shape. As such they have great authority in helping us to interpret the Psalter, and they form the canonical function of pointing us back to the Davidic persona within the Psalter. This is the theology of analogy by which we are invited to read, interpret, and live the psalms in our own day, just as the editors of the Psalms did in their own day.[98]

## Conclusion: Communal Hermeneutics

Having applied Hiebert's epistemological framework to the issue of the titles, we close with a final thought from his work. Integral to Hiebert's critical realism is the idea of a hermeneutical community. He writes, "Critical realists argue that community investigation is an essential part of the hermeneutical process of searching for truth, and that far from undermining the process, it is a powerful corrective against the subjective biases of individual scholars."[99] This is not an instrumentalist view of knowledge, because "a critical realist approach to theology must begin with scripture."[100] The hermeneutical community also does not arrive at truth by simple "majority vote."[101] Rather, within this community specialists have a vital role to play in a community's understanding of truth.[102] It is a robust community seeking truth, with "specialists in biblical exegesis, specialists in systematic and biblical theology, homileticians, and lay church members acting as a single community."[103]

---

[98]Goldingay favors a theology of imagination: "It may be a helpful exercise in imagination (or it may not—not everyone likes stained glass)." *Psalms 1–41*, 30; see 28–30.

[99]Hiebert, *Missiological Implications*, 94.

[100]Ibid., 101.

[101]Ibid., 102.

[102]Ibid.

[103]Ibid., 102–3.

A critical-realistic approach to the titles keeps open the possibility of further evidence that may alter the preliminary conclusions. It is open to interpretive possibilities suggested by the believing community. This approach is more than "believing criticism," Kenton L. Sparks's proposal for holding together the trustworthiness of the Bible and of scholarship. Sparks defines believing criticism as follows: "I have suggested *believing criticism* as another way to construe the situation, which is able at the same time to trust the Bible as our authority and to admit and even to appreciate the insights of biblical scholarship."[104] Unlike Sparks's believing criticism, which separates the scholars from the believing community,[105] a critical-realistic approach opens up a robust discussion among evangelicals (scholars, pastors, and fellow pilgrims). Unlike Sparks's approach, which looks at the critical community for approval, critical realism is an attempt at interpreting Scripture with Scripture. It is open to all the evidence and is content in leaving questions and issues for resolution in due time.[106] Unlike believing criticism that is critical of leaders in the believing community, we deeply appreciate stalwart defenders of Scripture (Young, Kidner, Waltke) against critical attempts to force their hegemony. They wrestled with the evidence and did not succumb to the sirens of the critical community. Their eyes were on Scripture and on the believing community. Their scholarship embraced the reality of Scripture and allowed that reality to shape their lives and teaching for the good of the community.

---

[104]Kenton L. Sparks, *God's Word in Human Words: An Evangelical Appropriation of Critical Biblical Scholarship* (Grand Rapids: Baker Academic, 2008), 357–58.
[105]Ibid., 358–62.
[106]See Peter Enns, "Continuing the Conversation: Learning to Listen," in *Inspiration and Incarnation: Evangelicals and the Problem of the Old Testament* (Grand Rapids: Baker Academic, 2005), 171–73.

# 13

# THE OLD TESTAMENT
# AS CULTURAL MEMORY

## JENS BRUUN KOFOED

※

## Introduction

"Memories are not flies in amber," Ann Rigney reminds us in an article on the way in which literary texts can function as a social framework for memory.[1] Rigney thereby points out two important realizations in the overlapping fields of history, sociology, anthropology, and psychology that have recently made their headway into biblical studies. First, it has become increasingly clear that historiography—or history "proper"—written by professional historians is far from the only "symbolic form in which a society takes account for its past."[2] This "accounting for," Rigney writes, "takes place not only through historiography, but also through a wide range of other activities: commemorative ceremonies, museum visits, apologies on behalf of states, meetings or reenactment societies, watching historical films and reading historical fiction, family gatherings and genealogical research."[3] Second, it has been realized that just as individual memory is a social phenomenon in which the individual introduces an order and a structure into its neural content that are socially or externally conditioned, so too, the society's accounting for its past is not just the totality of what has been said, written, and stored, but an "ongoing elaboration of a collective relationship to the past through the mediation of discourse."[4] It is, in other words, a continuous reconstruction, reconfiguration, and re-presentation of memories that for some reason or other are found meaningful and important enough to keep alive by a given society. And since

---

[1] Ann Rigney, "Portable Monuments: Literature, Cultural Memory, and the Case of Jeanie Deans," *Poetics Today* 25, no. 2 (2004): 367.
[2] Johan Huizinga, *Cultuurhistorische verkenningen* (Haarlem: H. D. Tjeenk Willink en Zoon, 1929), 166.
[3] Rigney, "Portable Monuments," 363.
[4] Ibid., 368.

there is no such thing as a culturally monolithic society, cultural memory is the result of an ongoing negotiation or struggle between competing individual and collective memories, which involves amnesia, distortion, perspectivation, and recall. It is a shared cultural memory that overcomes the differences between individuals and groups in the society until it too becomes unstable because of challenges from new counter-memories, and a new compromise is needed in order to create a new shared memory that holds the group or nation together. Such "cultural memorization," according to Mieke Bal, is to be seen as

> an activity occurring in the present, in which the past is continuously modified and re-described even as it continues to shape the future: The memorial presence of the past takes many forms and serves many purposes, ranging from conscious recall to unreflected re-emergence, from nostalgic longing for what is lost to polemical use of the past to shape the present.[5]

Cultural memory, therefore, "is always a reflection of its present interests, needs, and current levels of experience. The latter determine both the way a society deals with the past and the forms that a given memorial culture takes, which itself is subject to historical change."[6]

Instead of relegating all other forms of remembrance and recollections of the past to the category of "improper history," the groundbreaking works of the French historians Maurice Halbwachs[7] and Marc Bloch on collective memory, together with the German art historian Aby Warburg's use of the term *social memory* to analyze artworks as repositories of history, have received renewed attention in cultural studies, especially in the works of Jan and Aleida Assmann. It was Jan Assmann who suggested the concept of "das Kulturelle Gedächtnis"—"cultural memory"—as a conceptual tool for understanding how not only historiography but a variety of other memorial forms contribute to what another French historian, Lucien Fevre, has called the social function of history, that is, the way we organize the past in accordance with the needs of the present.[8] In order to differentiate types of collective memory, Assmann

---

[5]Mieke Bal, "Introduction," in *Acts of Memory: Cultural Recall in the Present*, ed. Mieke Bal, Jonathan Crew, and Leo Spitzer (Hanover, NH: University Press of New England, 1999), vii; Astrid Erll and Ansgar Nünning, "Where Literature and Memory Meet: Towards a Systematic Approach to the Concepts of Memory Used in Literary Studies," in *Literature, Literary History, and Cultural Memory*, ed. Herbert Grabes, Yearbook of Research in English and American Literature 21 (Tübingen: Gunter Narr, 2005), 262.
[6]Erll and Nünning, "Where Literature and Memory Meet," 262.
[7]Maurice Halbwachs, *On Collective Memory* (Chicago: University of Chicago Press, 1992).
[8]Jan Assmann, *Moses the Egyptian: The Memory of Egypt in Western Monotheism* (Cambridge, MA: Harvard University Press, 1997); Assmann, *Das kulturelle Gedächtnis: Schrift, Erinnerung und Identität in frühen Hochkulturen* (Munich: Beck, 1999).

introduced a distinction between the so-called *communicative* memory and *cultural* memory. Communicative memory, according to Assmann, is shared and conveyed within a "memory community" (a social group defined by common memories) in personal interaction through the means of verbal communication over a time span of only eighty to a hundred years. The participation in this memory that the individual shares with his contemporaries is unstructured, according to Assmann, because everybody can join the personal interaction, that is, the communication, and thereby shape the communicative memory. Because the participation is unstructured, this memory has the character of a private interpretation of a community's own past; it is a group's unofficial "everyday memory." The cultural memory, on the other hand, is characterized by a more differentiated form of participation: not all members of a given memory community can influence the memory to the same extent, because the power to interpret and define the past is unevenly spread within the collective. The cultural memory is a group's official memory and is intrinsically related to power and tradition. Since tradition is the central category of this memory—instead of communication for the communicative memory—it covers a much longer period of time. The cultural memory also serves as a "memory reservoir," containing several collective memories and identities. Assmann defines the "cultural texts" of this "memory reservoir" as all sign complexes, that is, not just texts, but also dances, rites, symbols, and the rest, that possess a particular normative and formative authority in the establishment of meaning and identity. Cultural texts lay claim to an authority that embraces society as a whole; they determine its identity and coherence. They structure the world of meaning in which society makes itself understood, and also the sense of unity, belonging, and individuality that can be handed down through the generations, thus enabling a society to reproduce itself as a recognizable group.[9]

Proceeding from the basic insight that the past is not a given, but must instead be continually reconstructed and re-presented, Astrid Erll points to the logical conclusion of the developments within cultural theory that "the useless opposition of history vs. memory in favor of a notion of different modes of remembering in culture" must be dissolved. "There are different modes of remembering identical past events . . . . Seen in this way, history is but yet another mode of cultural memory, and historiography its specific medium."[10]

---

[9] Jan Assmann, *Religion and Cultural Memory: Ten Studies* (Stanford, CA: Stanford University Press, 2006), 123–24.

[10] Astrid Erll and Ansgar Nünning, eds., *Cultural Memory Studies: An International and Interdisciplinary Handbook* (Berlin: de Gruyter, 2008), 7.

It is this "dissolving" of the dichotomy between "proper" and "improper" history into the concept of cultural memory that has become a significant subject in biblical studies in recent years. Biblical scholars such as Joseph Blenkinsopp,[11] Marc Brettler,[12] Ronald Hendel,[13] Mark Smith,[14] and, most recently, Philip Davies,[15] have sought to demonstrate that the Old Testament contains both the collective memory and amnesia of ancient Israel, and that "cultural memory" therefore is the best conceptual tool for analyzing the so-called historical books in the Old Testament. Davies and Hendel say:

> Cultural memory provides a better conceptual tool than history, myth, or tradition for classifying the biblical narratives about the past because it better reflects the ways in which the past was understood and utilized in ancient societies. Regarding the Biblical narratives as a Judean collection of cultural memories, integrated into continuous accounts, enables the historian to understand better the problems that they raise for conventional historical reconstruction but also sheds more light on the history behind these memories and their literary production.[16]

> According to an old tradition preserved in the Palestinian Targums, the Hebrew Bible is "the Book of Memories." . . . The sacred past that is recalled in this book serves as a model and wellspring for the present. "Remember the ancient days," Moses counsels the Israelites in the Song of Moses (Deut 32:7), for the present is rooted in the constitutive events of the past. The remembered past is the material with which biblical Israel constructed its identity as a people, a religion, and a culture.[17]

In my *Text and History* from 2005 I argued that the generic categorization of the biblical texts along the historiography-antiquarianism continuum is

---

[11]Joseph Blenkinsopp, "Memory, Tradition, and the Construction of the Past in Ancient Israel," *Biblical Theology Bulletin* 27 (1997): 76–82.

[12]Marc Zvi Brettler, "Memory in Ancient Israel," in *Memory and History in Christianity and Judaism*, ed. M. Signer (Notre Dame, IN: University of Notre Dame Press, 2001), 1–17; Brettler, *The Creation of History in Ancient Israel* (London: Routledge, 2003).

[13]Ronald Hendel, "The Exodus in Biblical Memory," *JBL* 120, no. 4 (2001): 601–22; Hendel, *Remembering Abraham: Culture, Memory, and History in the Hebrew Bible* (New York: Oxford University Press, 2005).

[14]Mark Smith, "Remembering God: Collective Memory in Israelite Religion," *CBQ* 64 (2002): 631–51; Smith, *The Memoirs of God: History, Memory, and the Experience of the Divine* (Minneapolis: Augsburg Fortress, 2004).

[15]Philip R. Davies, *Memories of Ancient Israel: An Introduction to Biblical History—Ancient and Modern* (Louisville, KY: Westminster John Knox, 2008).

[16]Ibid., 122.

[17]Hendel, *Remembering Abraham*, ix.

highly problematic.[18] The histories of Herodotus and Thucydides may be the yardstick for measuring what can and cannot be dubbed historiography, and the label *antiquarianism* may be the best fit for the historical texts of the Old Testament among conventional Greco-Roman genre designations. Since none of these genre descriptions does justice to the particular configuration of literary devices and historical intent in the Old Testament, I expressed my hopes that future research would develop a generic taxonomy that is able to describe the literary, social, and cultural strategies for recollection of the past in the Old Testament[19] without squeezing them into Greco-Roman generic taxonomy. The concept of cultural memory may very well fill this taxonomic gap, and though more formally based subgenres as antiquarianism and historiography are still useful to describe certain *literary* modes of remembering, I believe the above-mentioned dynamics of cultural memory is the best description of how the societies of ancient Israel constructed, deconstructed, and reconstructed their past.

## History and Mnemohistory

In the introduction to Maurice Halbwachs's *On Collective Memory*, the translator, Lewis A. Coser, points out that, in order to understand Halbwachs's concept of collective memory, it is crucial to distinguish between history and mnemohistory.[20] Whereas historians are interested in providing a true or at least plausible reconstruction of the past, the mnemohistorian is concerned not with the past as such, but only with the past as it is remembered. The same distinction is maintained by Jan Assmann, who, in *Moses the Egyptian*, is not interested in whether Moses ever existed, but in how the *figure* Moses fared diachronically in the cultural memory over the centuries: "I shall not even ask the question—let alone, answer it—whether Moses was an Egyptian, or a Hebrew, or a Midianite. This question concerns the historical Moses and thus pertains to history. I am concerned with Moses as a figure of memory."[21] "Mnemohistory," Assmann argues, "is reception theory applied to history," and the "proper way of dealing with the working of cultural memory is mnemohistory."[22]

The distinction between history and mnemohistory is not as easy to maintain as it seems, however, since the professional historian, at one and the same

---

[18] Jens Bruun Kofoed, *Text and History: Historiography and the Study of the Biblical Text* (Winona Lake, IN: Eisenbrauns, 2005).
[19] Ibid., 247.
[20] Halbwachs, *On Collective Memory*, 21–28.
[21] Assmann, *Moses the Egyptian*, 11.
[22] Ibid., 9, 14.

time, uses the various *lieux de mémoire*[23] as sources for his reconstruction of the past and—on the basis of this "history"—contributes to the ongoing transmission and change of the cultural memory attached to the very same "sites of memory." It is this reconstruction of the society's past that explains the need for a renegotiation of the existing cultural memory, and it is this reconstruction that, in due course, becomes the yardstick against which the cultural memory's historical reliability, validity, and persuasiveness are measured.

"Mnemohistory," Assmann argues, "analyzes the importance which a present ascribes to the past," and in contrast to historical positivism, Assmann continues, "mnemohistory consists in analyzing the mythical elements in tradition and discovering their hidden agenda."[24] Now, Assmann defines myth very broadly by saying that "history turns into myth as soon as it is remembered, narrated, and used, that is, woven into the fabric of the present," and insists that these "mythical qualities of history have nothing to do with its truth values."[25] This may be true in the radical postmodern sense of the concepts of history, myth, and truth, but hardly in the real world, where both the *lieux de mémoire* and the historical anchoring of memory that sparked the tradition do make a difference in everyday discourse. An obvious example is the use of the past in the present dispute over land rights between Israelis and Palestinians. In the recent article "Invention, Memory, and the Place," Edward Said argues, "By inventing an ancient Israeli kingdom that displaced Canaanite Palestinian history, modern scholars have made it nearly impossible for present-day Palestinians to say that their claims to Palestine have any long-term historical validity."[26] The argument is based on Keith Whitelam's (de)construction of the conventional reconstruction of ancient Israel's history, which, in the optic of Said, demonstrates how modern Zionism as "a purposeful political movement could invent a serviceable past that became a crucial aspect of Israel's modern collective memory," and that the mayor of Jerusalem, when he "a few years ago proclaimed that the city represented

---

[23] I.e., "realms" or "sites of memory," a key concept in cultural-memory studies coined by the French historian Pierre Nora, designating "any significant entity, whether material or nonmaterial in nature, which by dint of human will or the work of time has become a symbolic element of the memorial heritage of any community (in this case, the French community). In other words, sites of memory are "where [cultural] memory crystallizes and secretes itself" (Nora, *Realms of Memory: The Construction of the French Past*, 3 vols., trans. A. Goldhammer, ed. L. D. Kritzman [New York: Columbia University Press, 1997], 7). These include (1) places such as archives, museums, cathedrals, palaces, cemeteries, and memorials; (2) concepts and practices such as commemorations, generations, mottos, and all rituals; (3) objects such as inherited property, commemorative monuments, manuals, emblems, basic texts, and symbols.

[24] Assmann, *Moses the Egyptian*, 10.

[25] Ibid., 14.

[26] Edward Said, "Invention, Memory, and Place," *Critical Inquiry* 26, no. 2 (2000): 187.

3,000 years of unbroken Jewish dominance," was "mobilizing an invented story for the political purposes of a modern state still trying to dispossess native Palestinians who are now seen as barely tolerated aliens."[27] Now, there can be no doubt that a certain (biblical) construction of ancient Israel's history is crucial to "Zionist ideology," and that the same construction is used for political purposes by the modern state of Israel. It is also a matter of fact that the far more complex, pluricultural identity of Iron Age Palestine to a large extent is downplayed, suppressed, or silenced in the narratives of the Old Testament. And my point is *not* to support, substantiate, and legitimize a certain religious, ideological, or politically one-sided reconstruction of ancient Israel's history, but to point out how the appeal to *wie es eigentlich gewesen*— "what essentially happened"—is crucial to both parties in the dispute. If the biblical narratives about a united monarchy under David and Solomon in the tenth century BC are an invention by later authors, the Israeli's claim for land obviously loses an important chunk of its long-term validity. Correspondingly, if the Palestinian side is able to demonstrate how "the history of ancient Palestine was gradually replaced by a largely fabricated image of ancient Israel, a political entity that in reality played only a small role in the area of geographical Palestine," and that "ancient Palestine was the home of many diverse peoples and histories," and that this more complex and rich history has been silenced for modern religious, ideological, and political purposes,[28] their claim for the land must be considered as valid long-term as the Israeli's.

The epistemic dichotomy between "in reality" and "fabricated" obviously plays a crucial role in the argument. The question is, therefore, whether it is possible for cultural-memory studies to analyze "the mythical elements in tradition" and discover "their hidden agenda," as Assmann argues, without discussing the historical intentionality and reliability of the narratives of the Old Testament in order to determine whether they should be used as reliable primary sources for the history of ancient Israel/Palestine. I think not, and we will return to this below. First, however, a number of related methodological problems must be addressed.

## Circular Reasoning

First, in the attempt to interpret the cultural memory that developed over the centuries about ancient Israel, we easily fall prey to the logical fallacy of circular reasoning, as the influence of the history of reception on the mnemohistorian often subconsciously blinds him to what has been forgotten and

---

[27] Ibid.
[28] Ibid., 186.

lures him to find what he is looking for in the primary sources. This is precisely what Alon Confino has in mind, when, in discussing Henry Rousso's book *The Vichy Syndrome*, he warns the mnemohistorian against reading into the evidence of reception what he has already learned from other sources.

> When historians attempt to interpret evidence of memory from a representation of the past, the risk of a circular argumentation through "cultural" reading is high. The overall consequence is an arbitrary interpretation: a conception of the meaning of Vichy memory was formed before exploring the reception of the memory.[29]

The solution is not, Confino argues, to isolate the evolution of the narratives from their reception history so that "the evolution of memory stands like a foundation story against which reception is measured." This would be "an artificial separation," Confino continues, "for the meaning of memory's evolution commingles with, and is dependent on, the story of its reception."[30] "The solution to these questions, in terms of narrative and method lies," Confino concludes, "in writing the history of memory's construction as commingling with that of memory's contestation," and in realizing that

> historical actors participate in various processes at the same time, that they simultaneously represent, receive, and contest memory. To accept that none of these processes has primacy and yet to understand the meaning of memory, we need to understand all of them as intertwined—memory as a whole that is bigger than the sum of its parts.[31]

When we apply this caveat to the mnemohistory of ancient Israel, two important points become clear. First, the shared memory of ancient Israel's history as we have it in, for example, the books of Kings, is *not* a foundational story against which the various receptions of it in the books of Chronicles, the books of Maccabees, and the works of Josephus should be measured. It is already itself a result of the above-mentioned negotiation between memories and countermemories. It is this complex relationship between these parallel histories that Hendel has in mind when he argues:

> In the Hebrew Bible, interpretation and revision are joined to textual bricolage. For example, the book of Chronicles revises the presentation of the past in the books of Samuel and Kings by recombining and interpreting these texts to

---

[29] Alon Confino, "Collective Memory and Cultural History: Problems of Method," *The American Historical Review* 102, no. 5 (1997): 1397.
[30] Ibid.
[31] Ibid., 1398–99.

bring them into line with current understandings—embellishing events that are important, omitting episodes that are irrelevant or problematic, and harmonizing divergent presentations in the source texts. Yet even as it revises the older representations of the past, Chronicles also seems to presume the existence and authority of these source texts. It positions itself as a guide or commentary on earlier histories, even as it revises those histories in its own text. The later text does not displace the earlier but rather sets itself over it as an exegetical frame, bringing the older text into focus. . . . The prior versions are not repudiated but are corrected, curtailed, revised, or supplemented, as warranted by the historical horizons and certainties of the biblical writer, including the writer's literary practices and theological motivations. The operative criteria are not truth versus fiction but rather interpretation and revision. To borrow Meir Sternberg's terms, biblical historiography moves between the truth and the whole truth. History carries the authority of sacred tradition. But tradition can be—and must be—revised in order to retain its truth.[32]

The book of Chronicles should, therefore, be understood not as a completely separate counter-memory in relation to the books of Samuel and Kings, but as the result of a new negotiation between the existing—and still authoritative—shared memory, on the one hand, and, on the other, new contestations of it in postexilic Yehud. It is a negotiation that again became contested in the Maccabean period, thus sparking off yet another representation of Israel's history in the books of Maccabees. Furthermore, since the extant version of the book of Kings reflects the selected and agreed-on representation of the past of *exilic* Israel, the exilic period must also be the *terminus a quo* for studies in ancient Israel's cultural memory. The book of Kings is still a source for the *history* of the preexilic period, but we simply don't know what the *cultural memory* of the past looked like prior to the exilic period, and therefore we cannot paint a picture of the negotiating process of competing memories leading to the creation and acceptance of the so-called Deuteronomistic History as a unifying image of the past. This makes the *postexilic* biblical texts, not least the books of Chronicles, the first interesting case study in ancient Israel's cultural memory, since it is possible to some extent to paint a picture of the societal changes in postexilic Yehud that created a need for a different reconstruction and representation of Israel's past.

Second, the caveat mentioned above reminds us that "the risk of a circular argumentation through 'cultural' reading is high" indeed when it comes to the modern mnemohistorian, since there is a considerable temporal and cultural gap between the latter and the context in which the primary sources were produced—a risk that has materialized itself in the description of the

---

[32]Hendel, *Remembering Abraham*, 97–98.

relationship between memory and reality in the recent volumes by Brettler, Hendel, Smith, and Davies. A lucid example is found in Davies's recent volume, where he attempts to posit the existence of a repressed Benjaminite history that has been replaced by the canonical Judean one. In a recent review Paul Evans hits the nail on the head when he notes that

> given that Davies consistently displays tremendous skepticism toward the histo-
> ricity of virtually any biblical source, it appears somewhat strange when he uses
> the same sources to reconstruct his Benjaminite history. If the sources are late
> and unreliable, how can one use the same source to reconstruct a new picture?[33]

And when we read the volumes of Brettler, Hendel, Smith, and Davies, it becomes obvious that their use of "cultural memory" as a conceptual tool for describing the mnemohistory of ancient Israel is mostly old wine in new bottles, since they clearly use conventional source criticism and redaction criti- cism to reconstruct the "real history," which method therefore "reads into the evidence of reception what [they have] already learned from other sources," namely, the nonextant, hypothetical, and reconstructed sources. Brettler, in his commentary on the book of Judges, opens his concluding chapter by stating that a paradigm shift has occurred in biblical studies "away from a simplistic model of the Bible as history," and that "much more attention has been given to the period that various sources derive from."[34] Brettler nonetheless bases his answer to the question, "What background may we propose that will make the Book of Judges in its entirety fall into place?"[35] on the existence of a Deuteronomistic History created in the seventh or sixth century BC, with later, post-Deuteronomistic revisions.[36] The same is true of Hendel's attempt to demonstrate that, in 1 Kings 1–2, "we approach two King Solomons—one historical and the other discursive—who are not wholly separable";[37] and of Smith, when he argues that "in ancient Israel, collective memory was expressed in family settings and at royal and nonroyal sanctuaries," and that this expres- sion "involved shifts of submersion and displacement as well as points of crystallization in Israelite history and memory, eventuating in the influential

[33]Paul S. Evans, "Review of Philip R. Davies, *The Origins of Biblical Israel*," *JHS* 9 (2009).
[34]Marc Zvi Brettler, *The Book of Judges* (Oxford: Routledge, 2002), 103; Brettler, *The Creation of History in Ancient Israel*, 1–7.
[35]Brettler, *The Book of Judges*, 102.
[36]Ibid., 109–16.
[37]Ronald Hendel, "The Archaeology of Memory: King Solomon, Chronology, and Biblical Interpre- tation," in *Confronting the Past: Archaeological and Historical Essays on Ancient Israel in Honor of William G. Dever*, ed. Seymor Gitin, J. Edward Wright, and J. P. Dessel (Winona Lake, IN: Eisen- brauns, 2006), 228.

priestly worldview evident in the Pentateuch and in a Deuteronomistic perspective shaping the Deuteronomistic History."[38]

The fact that biblical scholars like Brettler, Hendel, Smith, and Davies use
conventional source criticism and redaction criticism to reconstruct the "real
history" against which the extant text is analyzed as cultural memory is rather
curious, since most of them recognize that though there are some analogues
between cultural-memory studies and biblical form criticism, there are also
important differences. On the one hand, Hendel, for example, states that

> this type of inquiry [mnemohistory] has some analogues in the "history of
> religions" school of Hermann Gunkel and Hugo Gressman, particularly in its
> focus on the products of tradition and not primarily on the reconstruction of
> critical history. Moreover, like much of Gunkel's work, it seeks to locate the
> discursive setting of such traditions, their *Sitze im Leben*, in order to explore
> the social and institutional structure in which they circulate.[39]

On the other hand, he is also well aware that mnemohistory is not *just* form
criticism *redivivus*.

> This kind of inquiry also takes its bearings from the *Annales* school of histori-
> ography, which emphasizes the social contexts and functions of history. Lucien
> Febvre stated that "organizing the past in accordance with the needs of the pres-
> ent, that is what one could call the social function of history." Mnemohistory
> is concerned with the social function of history in this sense.[40]

Brettler shows the same awareness in the conclusion to his commentary on
Judges.[41] And from New Testament studies we may mention Kirk and Thatcher,
who write on the Jesus tradition as social memory, that, "consistent with the
form-critical model, social memory theory views present social realities as
decisive factors in the constant rearticulation of a community's salient past,
and it contends that the past is never objectified apart from the frameworks
for memory supplied by present circumstances."[42] While Hendel, Brettler, and
Smith seem to be stuck in conventional source criticism and maintain the idea
that it is possible to reconstruct the *Sitze im Leben* from the very same text

---

[38]Smith, "Remembering God," 2.
[39]Hendel, "The Exodus in Biblical Memory," 603.
[40]Ibid.; Holly Hearon, "The Construction of Social Memory in Biblical Interpretation," *Encounter* 67, no. 4 (2006): 348.
[41]Brettler, *The Book of Judges*, 103–4.
[42]Alan Kirk and Tom Thatcher, "Jesus Traditions as Social Memory," in *Memory, Tradition, and Text: Uses of the Past in Early Christianity*, ed. Alan Kirk and Tom Thatcher (Leiden: Brill, 2005), 32.

whose cultural memory we aim to analyze, Kirk and Thatcher are much more aware of the complex relationship between the tradition and its mnemohistory.

> But social memory theory departs significantly from the form-critical legacy by refusing to authorize any sharp distinction between memory and tradition. Memory is not equivalent to the individual faculty of recall, and the transmission of memories is not an isolated sharing of data between individuals. Instead, cultivation of memory takes place within a number of settings of community life and, correspondingly, across a broad range of memorializing practices. . . . From this perspective, "tradition" and "memory" are not elements of the Gospels that can be pried apart through application of particular criteria. Rather, tradition is the indissoluble, irreducibly complex artifact of the continual negotiation and semantic interpenetration of present social realities and memorialized pasts. . . . Applied to the problem of the Gospel tradition processes, this approach argues that Jesus was represented through multiple acts of remembering that semantically fused the present situations of the respective communities with their memory of the past as worked out in commemorative practices, with neither factor swallowed up by, or made epiphenomenal of, the other.[43]

It is precisely the same problem the American sociologist Barry Schwartz addresses when he criticizes conventional Bultmannian form criticism for asserting what it seeks to demonstrate.

> "In seeking to bring unity and order to the heterogeneity of the first thirty years," Robert Wilken asserts, Luke "interpreted the material he had inherited to fit into his scheme." Perhaps so, but since no one knows who wrote Luke, Wilken can present no evidence on the author's motives, let alone refute an alternate hypothesis: that the material Luke's author inherited *changed* his scheme.[44]

Great caution must be observed, therefore, if we seek to describe the mnemohistorical development from the event to later recollections and remembering of it. Without sources that are contemporary with and a description of the initial stages of a given cultural memory, it is impossible to demonstrate what has changed and what has not.

The above-mentioned scholars stand, of course, in a long and well-established tradition of historical-critical research, and the point is not to question the possibility or validity of their readings, but to expose these historical-critical presuppositions as a "cultural reading" and to question whether their combination of conventional source and redactional criticism

---

[43]Ibid., 32–33; Hearon, "The Construction of Social Memory in Biblical Interpretation," 348.
[44]Barry Schwartz, "Christian Origins: Historical Truth and Social Memory," in Kirk and Thatcher, *Memory, Tradition, and Text*, 48.

is compatible with the concept of cultural memory as it is defined and used as a conceptual tool in cultural studies in general.

## Text and Context

Another methodological issue Confino mentions has to do with the tendency to isolate memories instead of placing them in relation to one another and to society as a whole.

> I would like to view memory as an outcome of the relationship between a distinct representation of the past and the full spectrum of symbolic representations available in a given culture. This view posits the study of memory as the relationship between the whole and its component parts, seeing society as a global entity—social, symbolic, political—where different memories interact.[45]

In order for us to understand ancient Israel's cultural memory, the *text*, for example, the book of Kings, cannot be isolated from the *context*, in this case the exilic society that received and accepted it as an image of the past that united the various groups and gave them an experience of a shared destiny. Confino argues:

> The crucial issue in the history of memory is not how a past is represented but why it was received or rejected. For every society sets up images of the past. Yet to make a difference in a society, it is not enough for a certain past to be selected. It must steer emotions, motivate people to act, be received; in short, it must become a socio-cultural mode of action.[46]

In order to understand why precisely *this* text was selected, we need to understand which questions it answered better than other texts. In other words, only by understanding the exilic society as a whole will we be able to understand why the book of Kings came to be the selected, agreed-on, and transmitted cultural memory. Only in light of the societal changes that took place in the transition from exile to homecoming does it become clear why certain memories were silenced while others came to the fore and were given a new, privileged status in the agreed-on image of the past as evidenced in the book of Chronicles (and other postexilic historical narratives). The fact that the Old Testament contains *both* histories—i.e., both the so-called Deuteronomistic History and the books of Chronicles—demonstrates that a significant number of people—or a number of significant people—deemed

---

[45]Confino, "Collective Memory and Cultural History," 1391.
[46]Ibid., 1390.

both versions important enough to keep them alive, and that the contestation of the existing construction of ancient Israel's history in the book of Kings was not necessarily a contestation of the historical reliability of the former, but a contestation of its particular configuration of memories. The cultural memory of the book of Kings was, as mentioned above, not replaced by but supplemented with the books of Chronicles.

## History from Above

A third methodological problem Confino mentions is the tendency to sacrifice the social and cultural aspects of cultural memory by sanctifying the political. Confino argues:

> One unfortunate side effect of treating memory as a symptom of politics is the lack of explorations of power in areas that are not politically evident. Consequently, a search for memory traces is made mostly among visible places and familiar names, where memory construction is explicit and its meaning palpably manipulated, while in fact we should look for memory where it is implied rather than said, blurred rather than clear, in the realm of collective mentality.[47]

Political memory is by nature a memory created from above, and if such a memory is studied in isolation from larger patterns of historical mentality in the society, it cannot be considered a study of *collective* memory proper. As the book of Kings, for example, may be described as precisely such an immediately visible memory from above, we need to look for the more invisible expressions of a memory from below before we can paint a picture of the *collective* memory of ancient exilic Israel.

Where does all this take us? First, if the cultural or official memory attested in the parallel histories of the Old Testament must be understood as a "memory from above," the authors will most likely have tried to blur or silence competing memories "from below," and we can thus only with great caution use the biblical text in our reconstruction of these larger patterns of exilic Israel's historical mentality. Forgetting, as mentioned above, is an intrinsic part of the evolution of cultural memory, and identifying the forgotten is therefore an important part of mnemohistory. Susan Rasmussen writes on the uses of memory:

> Forgetting, or at least modifying, the intentions of memorials, monuments and exhibits is as much a part of memory-making as remembering. Anti-memory may serve ends of the nation-building regime, of the state in the making, or

---

[47]Ibid., 1394–95.

it may become the defensive or subversive drive of subalterns asserting selves against the state or its dominant elites. . . . To forget becomes as powerfully meaningful and contested as to remember.[48]

Comparing, for example, the books of Kings and Chronicles makes it possible to identify some of this "forgetting" and "modifying." But if we are to paint a broader, more nuanced, or more representative picture of how ancient Israelites understood themselves, the extrabiblical sources—texts and artifacts—are indispensable, since the gaps in the extant biblical texts—the forgetting and suppression of memories—can be filled out only by the "extra" information from these sources.

## Cultural Memory and the Actual Past

It was argued above that without sources contemporary with the initial stages of a given cultural memory, it is impossible to demonstrate what has changed and what has not in the course of mnemohistory. It is important to realize, however, that this is true for the study of cultural memory, that is, *mnemohistory*, but not necessarily for the study of the past *referred to* in later sources, that is, the actual past or history. Peter Burke writes on history as social memory:

> Historians are concerned, or at any rate need to be concerned, with memory from two different points of view. In the first place, they need to study memory as a historical *source*, to produce a critique of the reliability of reminiscence on the lines of the traditional critique of historical documents. . . . In the second place, historians are concerned, or should be concerned, with memory as a historical phenomenon; with what might be called the social history of remembering. Given the fact that the social memory, like the individual memory, is selective, we need to identify the principles of selection and to note how they vary from place to place or from one group to another and how they change over time. Memories are malleable, and we need to understand how they are shaped and by whom.[49]

When the author of Chronicles suppresses the memory of David's affair with Bathsheba, the aim of the *mnemohistorian* is to expose the author's selective strategy and describe the needs and interests in the time of the author that made such amnesia or "anti-remembering" convenient. The *mnemohistorian*, in other words, is concerned with how David as a figure of memory fared diachronically in the cultural memory over the centuries. Whether he

---

[48]Susan Rasmussen, "The Uses of Memory," *Culture and Psychology* 8, no. 1 (2002): 122.
[49]Peter Burke, "History as Social Memory," in *Memory: History, Culture and the Mind*, ed. Thomas Butler (Oxford: Basil Blackwell, 1989), 99–100.

existed or not is a question that must be answered by the *historian* subjecting the literary sources to the conventional heuristic and source-critical analysis. And the mere fact that Chronicles are the product of the author's subjective selection of memories and that his narrative has been cast into a certain mode of emplotment, does not mean that it is also fictitious. In *Text and History* I argued on the basis of Ricoeur that there is no equation between literary device or narrative, on the one hand, and fiction, on the other—only tendentiousness: (historical) narrative tends to draw the reader into a literary world without any necessary referents in the real world.[50] Whatever literary devices it contains, it may or may not refer to real events in time. "To my mind," Ricoeur argues,

> the reply cannot be found at the level of the literary representation where the gap between fiction and reality is bridged by the very devices of representation, either narrative, rhetorical, or fictional; the solution resides at the two previous stages of the historiographical process, at the level of explanation and beyond it at that of documentary evidence.[51]

Speaking on the discipline of historiography as "a paradigmatic case of human science, which extends between the two poles of science and arts," Ricoeur points out three distinct phases in the process of history writing: the documentary phase, the explanatory or comprehensive phrase, and the literary phase. The initial stage is dubbed "documentary" because it is from written documents or "testimonies" that the historiographer takes his departure. It is such trusted testimonies that, according to Ricoeur, constitute the basic scientific component of truth claims raised by historical knowledge. The next step is the explanatory phase, in which questions about causes and reasons are asked. In the final, literary, phase the trusted, "raw" material of the first phase is given order on the basis of the explanation of the second phase, in a literary representation, the narrative or historical discourse.[52]

It is not surprising, therefore, that one of the more general critiques of Halbwachs is directed toward this problem. Schwartz is representative when he writes:

> Halbwachs's greatest failure is his inability to see commemoration as anything more than an elaborate delusion. . . . Halbwachs advances a pejorative concep-

---

[50]Kofoed, *Text and History*, 201ff.
[51]Paul Ricoeur, "Humanities between Science and Art" (address at the opening ceremony for the "Humanities at the Turn of the Millennium" conference, University of Aarhus, Denmark, June 4, 1999, accessed November 4, 2010, http://www.hum.au.dk/ckulturf/pages/publications/pr/hbsa.htm.
[52]Kofoed, *Text and History*, 202.

tion of collective memory, one that distrusts and works to undermine established beliefs. He assumes that memory, as opposed to history, is inauthentic, manipulative, shady, sometimes to be overcome rather than accepted in its own right. That commemoration is a selective celebration rather than an inferior version of history escapes Halbwachs.[53]

Yael Zerubavel, in the same vein, criticizes Halbwachs for exaggerating collective memory's adaptability to the present and for insisting on the opposition of memory to history. Instead Zerubavel suggests that

> collective memory is not an entirely fluid knowledge nor is it totally detached from historical memory. . . . Collective memory continuously negotiates between available historical records and current social and political agendas. And in the process of referring back to these records, it shifts its interpretation, selectively emphasizing, suppressing, and elaborating different aspects of that record.[54]

In this process, according to Zerubavel, memory is not only tied to history but also constrained by historical reconstructions of the past.

The above-mentioned observation by Ricoeur is important, since it locates these constraints "at the level of explanation and beyond it at that of documentary evidence," and it is noteworthy that a number of mnemohistorians refer precisely to the level of explanation as decisive for understanding the relation between cultural memory and the actual past. Reliability in orally transmitted memories, Jan Vansina maintains, cannot be rejected *a priori*, because certain kinds of oral transmission—owing to their genre and performative setting—tend to be more stable and to preserve reliable historical information better than others: "Factual traditions or accounts are transmitted differently—with more regard to faithful reproduction of content—than are fictional narratives such as tales, proverbs, or sayings. The criterion hinges on the notion of truth, which varies from one culture to another and which must be studied."[55] Worldview matters, Jan Assmann argues in a similar way: "Along with a particular worldview, cultural memory disseminates and reproduces a consciousness of unity, particularity, and a sense of belonging among the members of a group."[56]

---

[53]Schwartz, "Christian Origins," 49–50; Burke, "History as Social Memory," 89ff.

[54]Yael Zerubavel, *Recovered Roots: Collective Memory and the Making of Israeli National Tradition* (Chicago: University of Chicago Press, 1995), 5.

[55]Jan Vansina, *Oral Tradition: A Study in Historical Methodology* (Chicago: Aldine, 1965), 111; Kofoed, *Text and History*, 64.

[56]Jan Assmann, *Religion and Cultural Memory*, 38; cf. also Jens Brockmeier, "Remembering and Forgetting: Narrative as Cultural Memory," *Culture and Psychology* 8, no. 1 (2002): 15–43, on the relationship between mnemonic processes and the discursive contexts.

If "the notion of truth" and "a particular worldview" are so important for understanding the relationship between the cultural memory and the actual past of a given group, how should we describe the dynamics of historical consciousness in cultural memory? This is precisely the question Peter Burke and Steven Knapp seek to answer.

> Why is there such a sharp contrast in attitudes to the past in different cultures? It is often said that history is written by victors. It might also be said that history is forgotten by the victors. They can afford to forget, while the losers are unable to accept what happened and are condemned to brood over it, relive it, and reflect how different it might have been. Another explanation might be given in terms of cultural roots. When you have them you can afford to take them for granted but when you lose them you search for them. The Irish and Poles have been uprooted, their countries partitioned; it is no wonder they seem obsessed by their past.[57]

> Why aren't narratives of events in our actual past simply replaceable by other narratives that meet our criteria of symbolic relevant? They are incapable of satisfying our curiosity about our own origins; they fail to provide *explanations* of how we got where we are. When it comes to explanation, in contrast to analogy, the lines of force that matter are indeed those that run from past to present, and that do so following a particular and irreplaceable causal chain. . . . For if the past is merely a source of analogies, particular past events may provide models for present action but are in principle expendable; they can all be replaced by analogies borrowed from other traditions or from fiction.[58]

Whether the cultural memory contained in the historical narratives of the Old Testament also should be given credit as reliable historical sources for the events they purport to describe depends, in other words, on the authors' worldview(s) and notion(s) of truth, as well as the degree of uprootedness and need for explanation of origins in the authors' memory community.

It is clear from these references that Davies is mistaken, therefore, when he argues that historical reliability was of no concern to the authors of the biblical narratives and therefore must be described as an obsession of the modern(istic) historian.[59] And it stands in stark contrast to mainstream approaches in cultural-memory theory when he argues that "the point is not that cultural memory has no true recollection, but that true recollection is not intrinsic to its mechanism or its purpose; equally important are inventing and forgetting."[60]

---

[57]Burke, "History as Social Memory," 106.
[58]Steven Knapp, "Collective Memory and the Actual Past," *Representations* 26 (1989): 131.
[59]Davies, *Memories of Ancient Israel*, 142.
[60]Ibid., 112.

Brettler is only slightly more optimistic. On the one hand, he admits that "even though the terms 'fiction' and 'non-fiction' did not exist in ancient Israel, the ancient Israelites could clearly think in these terms." On the other hand, he argues that no biblical text may be determined to be reliable on the basis of internal biblical evidence alone.

> This principle, which is too often ignored, sounds dogmatic, but is in line with general historiographical methods, which often demand more than one piece of *independent* evidence before reconstructing an event. When reconstructing Biblical history, I call this "the Deuteronomy 17.6 principle of reconstructing history," in line with "A person shall be put to death only on the testimony of two or more witnesses; he must not be put to death on the testimony of a single witness."[61]

However agreed-on this historical methodology may seem in Davies's optic and Brettler's presentation, it is not beyond dispute among professional historians. I have argued elsewhere *in extenso* that the rules of evidence underlying Davies's work—including the definitions of primary and secondary sources—are not those that the world of secular historians requires, and that we should approach the biblical testimonies precisely the same way we approach testimonies in general, namely, with an epistemologically open mind, trusting them *unless* we are compelled to do otherwise.[62]

Brettler's use of "the Deuteronomy 17.6 principle" may therefore very well be described as an epistemological "own goal." Instead of using the principle in reverse by arguing that the information provided by the Old Testament must be put to "source-critical" death unless we can provide two or more witnesses that *confirm* the information, the above-mentioned epistemological openness requires that we use the principle *as it stands* so that a piece of biblical information "shall be put to death" only on the testimony of two or more witnesses. In other words, unless we are compelled by other internal or external testimonies, the biblical account should be given the benefit of doubt. Such an epistemological openness drastically changes the picture. If the historical information in, for example, the book of Kings proves reliable wherever it can be checked against independent sources, then it is very likely that it has got things right where we presently cannot check the information against independent sources.

---

[61] Marc Zvi Brettler, "Method in the Application in Biblical Source Material to Historical Writing (with Particular Reference to Ninth Century BCE)," in *Understanding the History of Ancient Israel*, ed. H. G. M. Williamson (Oxford: Oxford University Press, 2007), 309, 315.
[62] Kofoed, *Text and History*, 39ff.

It is true, as Davies argues, that "accepting that cultural memory—like personal memory—not only recalls the past but also forgets and invents it severs the notion of a necessary link between historical event and narrative account."[63] The link is indeed not *necessary* (just as it is unnecessary between historical event and any other narrative account). But it is a non sequitur that it *precludes* such a link and that the only sensible strategy is to focus "on the purpose for which the past is recalled, forgotten, or created rather than on its historical reliability" in order for mnemohistory to provide "a means whereby these memories can be treated as an important part of the cultural history of ancient Israel and Judah." If historical intent is an integral part of the authorial intent, as it demonstrably is in the book of Kings, our understanding of it as "cultural memory" has consequences not only for the definition of "cultural memory" but, importantly, also for its reception history.

## Conclusion

From the discussion above we can now conclude that some of the problems that haunted earlier discussions have indeed survived the reconceptualization in cultural-memory studies. In addition, the renewed focus on collective memory in social memory studies has generated its own discussion on similar issues of the relationship between cultural memory and the actual past. The concept of cultural memory, nevertheless, still seems to be the best description currently available of how the societies of ancient Israel constructed, deconstructed, and reconstructed their past, since it is able to weave together a number of interrelated forces in the complex dynamics of how societies remember their past. The concept of *lieux de mémoire* makes clear that literary texts interacted with a great variety of other cultural texts or modes of remembering—not least that of ritual and commemoration—in the official memory of postexilic Yehud as a reflection of its present interests, needs, and levels of experience. As official memory the texts furthermore functioned as a "memory reservoir" containing several collective memories and identities ready for use whenever present needs called for a reconfiguration of stored memories into a new shared memory. Though a sense of uprootedness along with a need for explanation of origins in all likelihood was a major impetus for the writing and collection of historical narratives in the exilic and postexilic communities, the dynamics of cultural memory remind us that they, too, are creations of *both* remembering *and* anti-remembering, and that we must read the texts in the light of all other contemporary cultural texts in order to secure the counter-memories in a more nuanced description of the various

---

[63]Davies, *Memories of Ancient Israel*, 122.

memory communities within the society as a whole. The distinction between history and mnemohistory makes it clear, finally, that while the mnemohistorian is allowed to bypass the question of historical reliability and focus on the history of *memory*, the texts are of great importance for the historian as sources for the history of ancient Israel. Memories may not be flies in amber, but we still have the flies to catch!

# Part 3

# THE NEW TESTAMENT AND ISSUES OF HISTORY, AUTHENTICITY, AND AUTHORITY

# 14

# GOD'S WORD IN HUMAN WORDS

## Form-Critical Reflections

### ROBERT W. YARBROUGH

❊

### The Reality of Literary Forms

From the 1920s to the 1950s, an approach to the Gospels called "form criticism" (German *Formgeschichte*) enjoyed considerable popularity in scholarly circles. The method had been pioneered earlier in Old Testament studies by H. Gunkel and J. Wellhausen. By the 1920s, it was being adapted for use on New Testament sources by German scholars such as K. L. Schmidt, M. Albertz, M. Dibelius, and R. Bultmann. Eventually English scholars including V. Taylor and R. H. Lightfoot took up the method, albeit with generally less radical premises and results.

Working hypotheses of form-critical practitioners typically included the following: (1) Teachings by and about Jesus were transmitted orally for several generations before being written down. (2) These units of oral tradition circulated in fragmentary and independent form. (3) These units circulated much like the stories that came to make up the folk literature of various European locales as these literatures took shape in the Middle Ages and early modern period. It was widely recognized that folk literature gets shaped, embellished, and generally transformed in the process of retelling and reuse. (4) New Testament accounts of Jesus are generally not reliable reports of "what happened" but rather embellished stories that require sometimes radical reconstruction. Only in this way can accretions and other extraneous additions be stripped away, allowing access to something closer to the underlying truth of early Christian representations regarding what Jesus may have said and done.

Given these hypotheses, scholars embarked on a threefold mission: (1) to classify the various units of teaching or narrative in the Gospels according to their "form" (hence "form criticism"), (2) to imagine the life setting (*Sitz im Leben*) that may have given rise to a unit's shape or substance in the early church's telling and retelling, and (3) to reconstruct the presumed history of the various units and forms as they circulated through the years and decades.

No single list of the "forms" found in Gospel writings came to enjoy universal assent. But the following six were frequently proposed: (1) individual sayings, like Jesus's "I am" sayings or apocalyptic statements; (2) pronouncement stories (also called paradigms or apophthegms), which were accounts that lead up to a climactic declaration; (3) parables; (4) speeches, like the Sermon on the Mount; (5) miracle stories, like Jesus's healings or nature miracles; and (6) legends or myths, like the account of Jesus's birth replete with wise men and angels (Luke 2:1–20).

By the 1950s form criticism found a rival in what was called redaction criticism. The two approaches flourished parallel to each other for some years. But by the 1960s Gospels studies sought to move beyond older methods. Societal upheaval in much of the West supported this trend. By around 1980 the so-called New Perspective on Paul and the third quest for (or of) the historical Jesus attracted much attention. In Gospels studies a literary approach gained momentum. Today form criticism is less a frontline tool for Gospels research than a fondly remembered chapter in the history of twentieth-century Gospels research. In Richard Burridge's recent survey of research into the Gospels (which he takes to be primarily biographical in form), form criticism (which rejected any biographical quality to the Gospels) receives a scant two paragraphs.[1]

Form criticism did call attention to the important point that the Gospels comprise units of expression that may be sorted into discernible categories. Admittedly, form critics approached Gospel sources with premises and convictions that created blind spots in their observation. Limitations to the method as typically practiced[2] amounted to built-in obsolescence that would eventually doom it to irrelevancy in the estimation of most Gospels interpreters today. But to study works from the form-critical era is to be reminded that literary subunits—even in sacred sources—can be grouped and analyzed according to the type of discourse they enshrine and the clues to cultural surroundings they may yield. How much truer this is of a work like Kenton Sparks's volume, which is a focal point of discussion in this book.

---

[1] Burridge, "Gospels," *The Oxford Handbook of Biblical Studies*, ed. J. W. Rogerson and J. M. Lieu (Oxford: University Press, 2006), 432–44; on form criticism, see p. 434.
[2] Note the six criticisms listed by E. Schnabel, "Form- und Gattungsanalyse," in *Das Studium des Neuen Testaments*, vol. 1, *Eine Einführung in die Methoden der Exegese*, ed. H.-W. Neudorfer and E. Schnabel (Wuppertal: R. Brockhaus; Giessen: Brunnen, 1999), 283–84.

## Shift Stories: Not a One-Way Street

*God's Word in Human Words*[3] (hereafter *GWHW*) could be and has been viewed in various lights.[4] A. Boulet applauds the book and finds himself "in full agreement with Sparks that evangelicals shirk the difficult questions when it comes to biblical criticism and revert to fideism, hiding their heads in the sand of the 'essentially divine' origin of Scripture."[5] That is to say, for Boulet the book is a successful indictment of the failed pretentions of evangelical biblical scholarship and the untenability of its high view of Scripture. Borrowing a page from the form critic's playbook, we might coin the term *shift story* as a formal classification for describing Sparks's volume. Formerly, Sparks's view of Scripture was like that of evangelicals he now criticizes. But a decisive shift occurred for Sparks at age twenty-seven.[6] He realized at that time in graduate school under John Van Seters's teaching at the University of North Carolina that Van Seters was right about the origins of the Pentateuch, while evangelicals like Kenneth Kitchen were by comparison arguing that the earth is flat.[7] This led to a memorable component of Sparks's book: the claim to have uncovered betrayal of scholarly ideals among evangelical scholars with whom he once identified, and now to be setting forth a better way, one consistent with the approaches of certain North American universities (like his alma mater, the University of North Carolina), which provide training superior to that available from Jewish institutions and European universities.[8] In terms of literary form, Sparks's volume is a shift story explaining and justifying his "new generation" reading of the Bible, over against that of "old-school evangelicals."[9]

In assessing Sparks's claims, we should note that other scholars have taken a course quite the opposite of his when it comes to choosing between the results of biblical criticism, on the one hand, and the high view of Scripture upheld by Christian scholars over the centuries, on the other. Let us survey two examples.

The first is the story of a Jewish scholar, much of whose training was in Germany. (Sparks's high regard for the outlook he associates with certain

---

[3]Sparks, *God's Word in Human Words: An Evangelical Appropriation of Critical Biblical Scholarship* (Grand Rapids: Baker Academic, 2008).

[4]I reviewed Sparks's book along with three others in "The Embattled Bible: Four More Books," *Themelios* 34, no. 1 (April 2009): 6–25. I will try to avoid repeating in this chapter what I have written by way of summary and analysis in my earlier review.

[5]Review of *GWHW*, *Review of Biblical Literature* 01/2009, accessed September 9, 2010, http://www .bookreviews.org/pdf/6514_7393.pdf.

[6]Ibid., 11.

[7]Ibid., 12.

[8]Cf. Ibid., 168.

[9]Ibid., 12–13.

American degrees should not make us despair of uncovering intelligence and academic rigor elsewhere on earth, too.) Heinz Cassirer (1903–1979) is one of those people about whom one wonders, *How did he ever come to make a profession of personal faith in Jesus?* His family was of European Jewish descent, from the part of Germany that is now in Poland. By the late nineteenth century, the family grew so secular that they abolished circumcision of their newborn boys. Heinz grew up in Germany, the son of perhaps the world's foremost Kant scholar of the age, Ernst Cassirer (1874–1945).[10]

Ronald Weitzman wrote of Heinz, "His Kantian upbringing made him scorn the idea that any kind of 'supernatural' help could be called on to assist a human being in solving a moral predicament."[11] Heinz Cassirer lived a thoroughly naturalistic existence, with no interest whatsoever in religion. He found it expedient to flee Germany after Hitler came to power in 1933. He later learned of many relatives dead in the Reich's death camps.[12]

Heinz ended up lecturing in Oxford and then Glasgow. He had attained recognition as an authority on Aristotle while still a young man in Germany.[13] At the University of Glasgow he taught philosophy for over a quarter century. He published commentaries on two of Kant's critiques. He translated various Greek sources in addition to his studies on Aristotle. This is hardly a man to suspect of mean intellectual endowment.

Quite remarkably, as we survey his life as a whole, we note among his last published works a translation (into English) of the Greek New Testament, a feat he accomplished in just thirteen months (July 1972–August 1973).[14] In addition, there is the intriguingly titled *Grace and Law: St. Paul, Kant, and the Hebrew Prophets*.[15] These works confirm his personal acceptance of the gospel call to faith in Jesus as Messiah and personal Savior.

What explains his move from secular Jew to baptized Christian? At about age fifty Cassirer conceived an interest in religion for the first time in his life. He was convinced that Kant was the greatest ethical analyst of all time. Kant brilliantly limned the scale and pathos of the human ethical dilemma, but he offered no compelling or even sufficient solution to the problem. The accomplished Greek scholar Cassirer, having read (he said) pretty much the

---

[10] Among the many works of Ernst Cassirer, perhaps most notable is *The Philosophy of Symbolic Forms* (1923–1929; ET 1953–1957).

[11] See preface to H. W. Cassirer, *God's New Covenant: A New Testament Translation* (Grand Rapids: Eerdmans, 1989), xi.

[12] According to http://www.genealogy.metastudies.net/ZDocs/Stories/stories02_2.html, accessed October 13, 2010.

[13] L. W. Wood, *Theology as History and Hermeneutics* (Louisville: Emeth, 2005), 238.

[14] Published posthumously (like the work in the next note) as *God's New Covenant* (see n. 11 above).

[15] Grand Rapids: Eerdmans, 1988.

whole of the Western philosophical corpus, picked up the Greek writings of another brilliant Jewish thinker. We know this thinker as the author of letters with titles like Romans, Galatians, and 1 Timothy. What happened when Cassirer encountered Paul and his epochal claims? Cassirer "experienced a collapse, a total inward paralysis," says Weitzman.[16]

For the second time in his life Cassirer felt he had encountered a thinker who truly saw into the depths of our inner dilemma: we know the ought, but we do not and we cannot do all that we ought (cf. Romans 7). But unlike Kant, Paul offered a remedy. Paul pointed to another Jewish man, a first-century Galilean no less, yet someone more than just a man. For the first time in his life, Cassirer began to feel the promise and hope of Christian salvation. In 1955, Cassirer was baptized into the Anglican Church. After twenty-five more years of study, he produced his remarkable New Testament translation. In Wood's words, "Cassirer was summoned to the reality of faith by listening to the testimony of Paul."[17]

Sparks's book is a form of expression that hallows certain judgments of reason as deployed by a university subindustry that has come to be called "historical-critical" interpretation. His book constitutes an apology for these judgments impressive in its scope and claims. But other scholars have moved in the opposite direction. While Sparks calls for a loosening of the constraints of biblical authority in favor of the authority of an ill-defined and shifting coterie of scholars who are badly divided among themselves in many respects, Cassirer may be regarded as realizing that "the personal and religious issues of life are not finally resolved by rational criteria, as important as reason is. . . . In setting aside the modernist pretensions of reason, [Cassirer] heard the word of God that came through the testimony of Paul."[18] In my view we could even say that Cassirer came to regard Paul's writings as what a fellow apostle termed them, "the Scriptures"[19] affirmed by Hebrews, Jews, and eventually the church as divinely given and normative in their entirety. Sparks shifts from a high view of Scripture's veracity to a reduced one, Cassirer from a nonexistent or disdainful view to one that evidently captured his whole soul and mind.

Cassirer's story has points of contact with the pilgrimage of Eta Linnemann, who died in May 2009 at the age of eighty-two. Though she was a student of Rudolf Bultmann (1884–1976) and an internationally recognized Gospels scholar,[20] in the late 1970s Linnemann's life as a university professor fell into

---

[16]Preface to *God's New Covenant*, xii.
[17]Wood, *Theology as History and Hermeneutics*, 240.
[18]Ibid.
[19]See 2 Pet. 3:16. Peter places Paul's letters on the same level as the Old Testament.
[20]See Linnemann, *Gleichnisse Jesu. Einführung und Auslegung* (Göttingen: Vandenhoeck & Ruprecht, 1961; ET 1966), which was followed by *Studien zur Passionsgeschichte* (Göttingen: Vandenhoeck & Ruprecht, 1970).

crisis. She began to doubt the validity of her antisupernaturalist animus against Scripture's message, against its redemptive claims, and against the trustworthiness of the canonical Gospels. Emerging from her crisis she renounced her lifelong professional and personal commitment to what she called "historical-critical theology." In its place she developed an understanding of Scripture as completely free of error. Summarizing her view, an obituary in Germany aptly quoted her as saying, "It is not dangerous to take the inerrant [*irrtumsfrei*] Scriptures with utmost literal seriousness; what is dangerous is not to."[21] In a number of works[22] she tested the claims of historical-critical views that she had been taught as a student and then as a professor had inflicted on hapless university undergraduates in an attempt to disabuse them of their Christian faith in Jesus and the Bible, the better to equip them for service in enlightened post-Christian German society.[23] The outcome and theme of her scholarship (and missionary service, in Indonesia and elsewhere) for nearly three decades after her conversion were that Scripture is entirely reliable; the shifting and often conflicting claims of scholars who largely reject Scripture's saving message, and certainly reject the historic understanding of its full trustworthiness, are what deserve careful scrutiny and often robust doubt.

Analysis of her early postconversion books and their reception is available elsewhere.[24] In academic mode, whether lecturing or in writing, Linnemann tended toward overstatement and polemics. It is as if a couple of decades of vehement rejection of the Gospels' trustworthiness created a corresponding zeal for their defense once she rejected the "critical" paradigm she embraced in Bultmann's heyday and under the spell of her identity as one of his students. Her scholarly pro-Bible writings are not a model of balanced scholarship, cautious investigation, and measured, gracious interaction with those she viewed as soft on the question of the Bible's accuracy.

Still, like Cassirer, Linnemann illustrates the Sparks phenomenon, albeit running the other direction—Sparks distancing himself from an earlier high view of Scripture, Linnemann embracing with gusto an understanding of

---

[21] Http://www.idea.de/nachrichten/detailartikel/archive/2009/mai/artikel/theologieprofessorin-eta -linnemann-gestorben.html?tx_ttnews%5Bday%5D=15&cHash=fd6d416326, accessed October 13, 2010.

[22] In English one may consult the following by Linnemann: *Historical Criticism of the Bible: Methodology or Ideology* (Grand Rapids: Kregel, 2001); *Is There a Synoptic Problem? Rethinking the Literary Dependence of the First Three Gospels* (Grand Rapids: Baker, 1992); *Biblical Criticism on Trial: How Scientific Is Scientific Theology* (Grand Rapids: Kregel, 2001).

[23] This account of her understanding of her mission as a New Testament professor who taught education majors at the University of Brunswick (Braunschweig) was shared with me by Linnemann on several occasions in personal conversation.

[24] See my essay "Eta Linnemann: Friend or Foe of Scholarship?," in *The Jesus Crisis: The Inroads of Historical Criticism into Evangelical Scholarship*, ed. R. L. Thomas and F. David Farnell (Grand Rapids: Kregel, 1998), 158–84.

the Bible embarrassing at times in its confidence and aggressiveness (and lamentable in its willingness to impute bad faith and judgment even to other evangelical scholars—a significant point of contact with Sparks[25]). From the writings of both Cassirer and Linnemann we can distill shift stories urging onlookers (tacitly in Cassirer's case) to more reverence and attentiveness toward Scripture and its message. From Sparks we get a shift story too, just one giving less credence to Scripture rather than more.

If time sufficed, more such stories could be told. Timothy Larsen has written of influential Victorians who, like Sparks, at some point found reason to embrace a more secular regard for claims made by Scripture and the Christian tradition.[26] But in time these individuals—William Hone, Frederic Young, Thomas Cooper, John Henry Gordon, Joseph Barker, John Bebbington, and George Sexton—reconverted to the faith they had earlier doubted. Larsen's point is that, contrary to the historiography that sees nineteenth-century England as increasingly awash in religious doubt, there were plenty of thinkers who became skeptical of such skepticism. As a result, they returned to at least a strong semblance of their earlier confession of Christian faith. It must not be supposed that the direction for which Sparks has opted is the only one possible for scholars or other public figures. One lacuna in *GWHW* is Sparks's failure to account for why many of the people he criticizes embrace a high view of Scripture: not because of unthinking traditionalism or partisan loyalty, but because their own research, life experience, and other factors have convinced them that biblical inerrancy has at least as much to say for it as the -isms (e.g., Sparks's historical criticism) that serve as platforms for casting doubt on claims found in God's written word.

## *Sitz im Leben*: The Struggle and Sacrifice of Faith

One reviewer of *GWHW* projects that "this book will probably have its greatest effect on undergraduates who are not well acquainted with the old debates and critical stances represented here."[27] Another reviewer thinks that *GWHW* is "likely to define the debate about the Bible among evangelicals for the foreseeable future. No seminary professor and student can afford to neglect this book."[28] This is a book of perceived import and influence. Because it is a

---

[25]One review of *GWHW* notes, "In the final chapter there is some slightly unnerving speculation about fundamentalists not possessing 'psychological wholeness.' Even [James] Barr [in *Fundamentalism*] didn't go quite that far, I think." See R. S. Briggs, *EvQ* 81, no. 2 (2009): 164.

[26]*Crisis of Doubt: Honest Faith in Nineteenth-Century England* (New York: Oxford University Press, 2006).

[27]S. Baugh, http://www.reformation21.org/shelf-life/review-gods-word-in-human-words.php, accessed October 14, 2010.

[28]K. T. Bauder, *RelSRev* 35, no. 2 (2009): 125.

shift story (see previous section), it is worth pondering the milieu in which it appears. In that milieu Sparks's move from greater affirmation of Scripture's truthfulness to lesser is hardly newsworthy. In fact it would be fair to say it is commonplace. Just as people with little or no confidence in Christian Scripture and its message (cf. Cassirer and Linnemann above) reverse their course, people with a great confidence (like Sparks in former times) find themselves in doubt.

This is highlighted in the transcript of a round-table interview conducted by Hershel Shanks on November 19, 2006.[29] Bart Ehrman, William Dever, James Strange, and Lawrence Schiffman gathered to discuss personal faith, scholarship, and the interplay of the two in their thought and lives. The result is a reminder of two things: (1) Sparks is not alone or unique in downgrading biblical authority in favor of an academic enterprise that accords cognitive privilege primarily to itself; (2) the academic enterprise may pose a greater threat to historic Christian faith than Sparks's book acknowledges.

First, regarding the rejection of biblical authority by academics, Ehrman and Dever anticipate and outrun Sparks in his proposal that evangelicals lighten their grip on adherence to all that the Bible states and teaches, favoring instead the conclusions of experts who have decided that the Bible is not to be trusted at any number of key points. Ehrman's case is well known. As a youth he affirmed (some version of) Christian faith. It must not have been very well informed—he was not aware, for example, of what footnotes in most Bibles produced in North America have made clear for decades: there are textual ambiguities owing to the nature of textual transmission in antiquity. Ehrman had a notion of textual purity and uniformity that was Qur'anic in its strictness and ahistoricity. When he attended graduate school, his faith in the pristine Bible of his youthful understanding collapsed. With this he moved to become "a fairly mainline liberal Protestant Christian."[30] The coup de grâce to historic Christian belief came while he was teaching a class at Rutgers University on the problem of suffering. He realized that different books of the Bible say different things.

> This made me think more deeply about my own understanding of why there's suffering in the world. Finally, because I became dissatisfied with all the conventional answers, I decided I couldn't believe in a God who was in any way

---

[29] Transcript published as "Losing Faith: Who Did and Who Didn't. How Scholarship Affects Scholars," *BAR* 33, no. 2 (2007): 50–57.
[30] Ibid., 51.

intervening in this world, given the state of things. So that's when I ended up losing my faith.[31]

So Sparks's pilgrimage to a lesser confidence is not exactly front-page news in its novelty. One might even term it banal: people of former strict versions of belief publishing books that challenge historic Christian faith, in part or in toto, are pretty standard book-marketing fare.[32] Or, as Hannah Faith Notes has written about evangelical women at the present time, "Some of us find our Christian faith growing stronger as the years pass, while others of us find ourselves drifting away from the churches in which we were raised."[33]

William Dever's story has a similar ending, though the path was different from Ehrman's. Dever's father, he says, was "a fire-breathing fundamentalist" preacher. Dever was ordained at age seventeen. He pastored for thirteen years; it appears that it was income from this activity that helped see him through his years of graduate school. During his theological training he was gripped by G. W. Wright's book *God Who Acts.* A statement in that book turned Dever's life around by setting him up for a great fall: "In Biblical faith . . . everything depends upon whether the original events actually happened."[34]

When he attended Harvard to study under Wright, he was taught and accepted that many events reported in the Bible did not happen. This set off a sequence of events for Dever, leading to reduction, then loss, then repudiation of Christian faith. When Hershel Shanks asks, "Well, then your scholarship did destroy your faith?" Dever replies, "Absolutely." In connection with working in Israel and marrying a Jewish wife, Dever embraced a faith so skeptical that fellow panel member Schiffman (who is Jewish) challenges the irreligiousness that Dever espouses: when Dever avers that he converted to Judaism "precisely because you don't have to be religious to be a Jew," Schiffman disagrees. There is little panel response to Dever's final statement

---

[31]Ibid., 52. This contrasts sharply with the conviction of another person (albeit not a professor) who has struggled with actual personal calamity (paralysis from the neck down in 1967 as a teenager, now breast cancer), not just the intellectual challenge posed by accounting for it in a world where a putatively good God is sovereign. See Susan Olasky, "In the Thick of It," *World,* October 23, 2010, accessed October 27, 2010, http://www.worldmag.com/articles/17198, with reference to Joni Eareckson Tada, *A Place of Healing: Wrestling with the Mysteries of Suffering, Pain, and God's Sovereignty* (Colorado Springs: David C. Cook, 2010).

[32]See, e.g., D. Barker, *Godless: How an Evangelical Preacher Became One of America's Leading Atheists* (Berkeley, CA: Ulysses, 2008); J. Loftus, *Why I Became an Atheist: A Former Preacher Rejects Christianity* (Amherst, NY: Prometheus, 2008); Loftus, ed., *The Christian Delusion: Why Faith Fails* (Amherst, NY: Prometheus, 2010).

[33]Hannah Faith Notes, ed., *Jesus Girls: True Tales of Growing Up Female and Evangelical* (Eugene, OR: Cascade, 2009), xiv.

[34]"Losing Faith," 54.

that he survived the death of his son five years previous only because he had ceased believing in God by that point.[35]

Ehrman's and Dever's respective stories are different from Sparks's in degree—he retains a robust faith confession (to this point) by comparison. But they are similar in kind and in tone, as Sparks voices the same unhappiness with a high view of Scripture that these older scholars arrived at long ago. It is all, in fact, a quite familiar progression.

Overall, Sparks's book urges a "believing criticism" on the reader (*GWHW*, 20, 133–34, 322, 356–58). There is little if any acknowledgment of the numerous instances (as with Ehrman and Dever) where the enterprise of a certain kind of approach to the Bible has overwhelmed any ability or even will to accept its saving message any longer. Dever seems almost to revel in this. When Strange comments that he sees God in things that Dever does not, Dever replies, "I'm glad you do [see God.] I just don't need to do that. Religion doesn't do anything for me and it hasn't for a long time, and I've decided I don't need its excess baggage."[36] Ehrman's interjection in the interview at this point may seem surprising: "I have a different view. I would actually like to believe."[37] This (wistful?) admission prompts Dever to reverse course: "I would too. I wish it were true. I really do."[38] The poignancy of the outcome of Ehrman's and Dever's pilgrimage, in which "criticism" has seemingly put an end to any prospect of "believing," should not be overlooked.

The academic enterprise in its frequent post- if not anti-confessional dress may represent a greater threat to historic Christian faith than Sparks's book indicates. It is not only a question of whether faith survives—it frequently does not. Also at stake is the shape and substance of that faith. This is underscored by James Strange's responses in the Hershel Shanks interview under consideration here. Strange gets credit as the Christian on the panel who retains faith. But it would be hard to convict it of being recognizably *Christian* faith by historic standards. His "faith is not based on anything like a propositional argument" or even testable assertions. It has no relation to his academic work with its religious connections. His "faith is based on [his] own experience" and leaves him "not really much interested" in God's attributes or anything else of a propositional nature.[39] Nor in doctrinal teachings: faith is "certainly not just a set of beliefs."[40] Doubtless that is true; but the question remains whether *any* classic beliefs or creedal affirmations remain essential to the

---

[35] Ibid., 54–56.
[36] Ibid., 57.
[37] Ibid.
[38] Ibid.
[39] Ibid., 52.
[40] Ibid., 57.

religion Strange espouses—except maybe that personal faith is pure experience with no necessary cognitive or propositional substance.

Take the resurrection. When in the course of the interview Bart Ehrman objects to Strange that Christian faith "has always been grounded in certain historical claims," like Jesus's bodily resurrection from the dead, Strange replies, "I don't believe *that*" (his emphasis). He takes the resurrection instead as "sort of a metaphor." He concludes that he is "not in any position to check" early Christian historical claims "or even decide on their plausibility." Strange's self-assessment of this seeming agnosticism is, "I guess I just don't worry about it."[41]

In the previous section we talked about shift stories, accounts of scholars moving away or toward classic Christian faith. Cassirer and Linnemann moved toward it, while Sparks with *GWHW* has moved toward a faith less constrained by historic Christian conviction and more constrained by certain scholars of post-Enlightenment orientation whom he has come to respect, admire, and follow.

In this section, the point of summarizing the interview of Ehrman, Strange, Dever, and Schiffman has been to place Sparks's shift story into its *Sitz im Leben*. We live in an age where biblical scholars routinely dismiss and even disdain the gospel message historically associated with Christian Scripture. As Ehrman helpfully clarifies, Jesus either "was raised from the dead or he rotted in his grave,"[42] and Ehrman has staked his (non-) faith on the latter. Even Strange, who qualifies as a man of faith and "a Baptist minister," rejects Jesus's bodily resurrection and faith as defined by propositions and doctrines.[43] In such a *Sitz im Leben*, while we should not be dismissive of the scholarly proposals in Sparks's book that merit pondering, neither should it be thought innovative, progressive, or attractively risqué that an "evangelical" Bible teacher turns on forebears, peers, and elders in the guild and takes a sizable step toward the embrace of a contrasting set of authority figures at the point of one of Christianity's foundational teachings: the doctrine of Scripture.

## Evangelical Disenchantment as Community Phenomenon

In form-critical theory, at the heart of Gospel origins was the community. The Gospels are not individual compilations but the result and reflection of community needs and convictions as these gradually assumed written shape for transmission to posterity.

---

[41]Ibid., 53.
[42]Ibid.
[43]Ibid., 52.

*GWHW* is in part an apology for the community of "critical" scholars to be given more authority in affirming or denying what Christians can accept as true in Scripture. A few reminders about the historical origins and convictions of this community should be borne in mind.

A recent magisterial volume on the history of New Testament scholarship documents one of the realizations that undergirds *GWHW*: few of the leading scholars of modern times have upheld a high view of Scripture.[44] While many of these scholars were sons of the manse, the list of those who grew up in pastors' homes and then turned against Christian teaching, sometimes in drastic ways, includes A. Ritschl (1822–1889), H. Holtzmann (1832–1910), and Adolf von Harnack (1851–1930). In various manners, these scholars exerted an influence on New Testament interpretation that was dominant throughout the twentieth century and persists up till now. In Baird's judgment, Holtzmann "articulated an emerging critical consensus" by means of scholarship weighed down with "a complexity that contributes to the scholarly captivity of the Bible."[45] Harnack similarly exhibits "dedication to meticulous criticism" in such a way that not Scripture's claims or message but, in the end, his own "religious piety prevails: his Jesus is the simple Jesus; his religion is ethics; his God is created in his own image."[46] No wonder Harnack's pastor-father agonized over young Adolf's drift and told him that in his opinion, his son's view of the resurrection made him "no longer a Christian theologian."[47]

The history of Christianity is in key respects the history of great thinkers and writers whom we rightly call "scholars." When the church abdicates its call to rigorous thought, to "criticism" in that sense, it abdicates one of its own high and holy callings. But the "historical" methods (often grounded in covert theological convictions) of Protestant scholars since the Enlightenment, who have set the tone and made the rules for the "criticism" Sparks commends, emanate from a community that has overall rendered a negative verdict on the truth of the Christian message of salvation through the saving death and resurrection of the incarnate Son of God. In the wake of pioneering "liberal" hermeneutics advanced by Ritschl, Holtzmann, and Harnack, subsequent generations of "scholars" raised in parsonages cast increasingly grave aspersions on Scripture as supportive of historic Christian faith.

W. Wrede (1859–1906), a student of both Harnack and Ritschl, helped usher in a "criticism" that Baird treats under the heading of "the return

---

[44]See William Baird, *History of New Testament Research*, vol. 2, *From Jonathan Edwards to Rudolf Bultmann* (Minneapolis: Fortress, 2003).
[45]Ibid., 121.
[46]Ibid., 135.
[47]Ibid., 123.

of skepticism."[48] Wrede disallowed all (Christian) theological convictions in "scholarly" reading of Scripture; there is nothing divine or transcendent whatsoever in or behind the New Testament writings. Consistent with this, Wrede flatly rejected Jesus's messiahship.

J. Wellhausen (1844–1918), whose Old Testament reconstruction is praised alongside that of W. M. L. de Wette by Sparks (*GWHW*, 93 n. 28), had the integrity to say, "It strikes me as a lie . . . that I should be educating ministers of an Evangelical Church to which in my heart I do not belong."[49] Later he turned his talents to works of New Testament scholarship. Like Wrede a pastor's son, Wellhausen merits inclusion under Baird's "return of skepticism" rubric. Wellhausen's work is characterized by an "antidogmatic, antiecclesiastical bias . . . fostered by his liberalism."[50] We should recognize here that "liberalism" is not a slur or even value judgment: it is simply a descriptive term for a conceptualization of the "Christian" faith that gained currency in nineteenth-century Europe with the help of "historical criticism" and that became the dominant conviction of "mainline" Western Christianity in the twentieth century, with that conviction maintaining influence (though hardly its former monopolistic dominance) to the current time. In the "liberal" conception, pre-Enlightenment Christian confession—the faith professed in the Apostles' or Nicene Creed, for example—is intellectually untenable. It therefore must be abandoned and Christian language reinvested with meanings amenable to post-Enlightenment conviction as defined, typically, by liberal academicians.

In most "evangelical" understanding, thoroughgoing "liberal" conviction has placed itself outside the pale of Christian belief.[51] It therefore seems curious, if not hazardous, for *GWHW* to affirm so earnestly the virtue of "critical" scholarship without some corresponding recognition of the theological convictions that are undeniable and inseparable components of typical "critical" approaches to Scripture and its interpretation.

Baird's study shows that in the course of time the march of pastors' sons who turn away from or severely qualify the substance of Christian faith includes A. Schweitzer (1875–1965), W. Boussett (1865–1920), M. Dibelius (1883–1947), R. Bultmann (1884–1976), B. Bacon (1860–1932), and M. Goguel (1880–1955). Space does not permit tracing the devolution of creedal conviction across the hundreds of publications that these intellectual leaders produced. In every case there would be complex issues to consider. Schweitzer deserves credit for

---

[48]Ibid., chap. 4 (137–73).

[49]Ibid., 151. Here "Evangelical Church" refers to the *Evangelische Kirche in Deutschland*, or the German Protestant Church. Lutheran churches in North America are descendants of the state "Protestant" churches in Germany and Scandinavia.

[50]Ibid., 156.

[51]Classically expressed by J. G. Machen, *Christianity and Liberalism* (Grand Rapids: Eerdmans, 1946).

his astonishing range of achievement, not only in biblical studies but also in music, medicine, and humanitarian self-sacrifice. Bultmann's brilliance was more focused in expression but hardly less influential in its effect on how the New Testament came to be read worldwide in the second half of the twentieth century. His father was a liberal pastor, so Bultmann came by those views honestly, but his mother preserved biblical and creedal conviction and did not approve of her son's direction.[52] No scholar's theological pilgrimage should be thought simple or unilinear in its background or gradual unfolding.

What unites the "critical" thinkers above is an approach to Scripture that agrees that historic Christian understanding of it has been substantially qualified and indeed largely falsified by "historical criticism." Bultmann made a point of this already as a student: while at university in Berlin, he complained in a letter about dogmatics lectures from Julius Kaftan: "What rubbish is contained in terms like 'revelation,' 'Trinity,' 'miracle,' 'God's attributes'—it's appalling!"[53] As Sparks in *GWHW* urges us to be more open to "critical" insights and reconstruction, the impression is given that "evangelical" reading has been indebted to outmoded conviction, ignorance, and other lamentable factors. There is no need to deny that this has too often been the case. But it would be equally unscholarly to be unaware that the community of "critical" scholars has produced a genre of writings no less dependent on outmoded conviction and ignorance, whether unwitting or willful, along with (at times) open hostility to Christian belief. It is arguable that there has been at least as much arbitrary and unsupportable "scholarship" produced by "critical" thinkers in the thralldom of once-chic "liberal" beliefs as by the "evangelical" community from whose convictions on Scripture Sparks wishes to distance himself. We therefore do well to exercise caution in supposing that a "believing criticism" as such will do much more for us than adulterate the "believing" that is necessary to keep discerning, rigorous thought from devolving into apostasy.

*GWHW* and its proposals may also be viewed in the light of another community disenchanted with historic Christian belief: that of evangelical faith in its more popular expression. David Hempton has dedicated a monograph to this phenomenon: *Evangelical Disenchantment: Nine Portraits of Faith and Doubt*.[54] If the survey of post-Enlightenment sons of pastors (above) documents existence of a skeptical "critical" community at the academic and technical level about which *GWHW* has too little to say, Hempton reminds us of another kind of disaffection. This is disaffection with and exodus from

---

[52]See Konrad Hammann, *Rudolf Bultmann—Eine Biographie* (Tübingen: Mohr Siebeck, 2009), 4–11.
[53]Ibid., 23.
[54]New Haven, CT: Yale University Press, 2008.

evangelical conviction that is always part of evangelical community life. For some in every generation, it seems, the entrance to evangelical conviction turns out to be a revolving door.

The nineteenth- and twentieth-century figures Hempton treats are George Eliot (= Mary Anne Evans; 1819–1880); Francis W. Newman (1805–1897); Theodore Dwight Weld (1803–1895); the trio of Sarah Grimké (1792–1873), Elizabeth Cady Stanton (1815–1902), and Frances Willard (1839–1898); Vincent van Gogh (1853–1890); Edmund Gosse (1849–1928); and James Baldwin (1924–1987). These leading lights in various fields constitute a group of luminaries "who once embraced a version of evangelical Protestantism" but who "subsequently repudiated that tradition for something else."[55] Hempton adds that their "stories are part of that tradition—not shameful aberrations from it—and they deserve to be told."[56]

Will a historian a century from now look back on the early twenty-first century and write about Kenton Sparks and *GWHW* as part of a similar movement? Certainly at this point the answer would be no: Sparks is not leaving evangelicalism but calling for its reform through revision of its approach to Scripture. But since historically its view of Scripture has been a defining plank in the evangelical platform,[57] and since *GWHW* is calling for substantial (and all-too-familiar) alteration of this plank, it is not justified at this point to rule out the possibility. Seen in historical light, *GWHW* deserves to be viewed in parallel with works or convictional moves of Hempton's nine figures who found it infeasible to continue to locate themselves within the fold—or stifling confines, as it turned out—of evangelical conviction about the Bible and its truly holy status. If *GWHW* fails to preserve the impression that canonical Scripture, in the end, merits a more reverent approach than "historical criticism" tends to support and encourage, it is easy to imagine Sparks's more critical proposals as turning out to support a more negative verdict on Scripture's veracity than a positive one.

## Conclusion

This essay began by noting that the four Gospels of Holy Scripture can be analyzed by means of a "form criticism" that identifies generic likeness between various Gospel subunits. We observed that *GWHW* likewise falls into a discernible literary form. Taken as a whole, *GWHW* is a shift story, furnishing justification for how a "new generation" wishes to understand Scripture with

---

[55]Ibid., 198.
[56]Ibid.
[57]Ibid., 5.

much more input from "historical criticism" and less from the convictions held by "old-line evangelicals."

While Sparks's shift is a familiar story, we noted in the second section above that scholars like H. Cassirer and E. Linnemann are examples of thinkers moving in the opposite direction. They turned away from forms of the "critical" thinking that Sparks values so highly and affirmed instead the authority of Scripture—or perhaps rather, in Cassirer's case, knowledge of the God who gave it through faith in Jesus—over the deployment of reason that is perhaps most characteristic of "historical criticism" in its dominant historical manifestations.

In our third section, attention to an interview by Herschel Shanks of leading biblical scholars Bart Ehrman, William Dever, James Strange, and Lawrence Schiffman documented the deleterious effects that may well attend "critical" reading of Scripture. Among those interviewed, whose status as "critical" scholars cannot be gainsaid, scarcely any trace of historic Christian faith remains. (It should be noted that Schiffman's Jewish convictions have not been damaged by his scholarly activity or convictions.) The argument was not that critical thought requires sacrifice of Christian faith. But in ways that *GWHW* hardly acknowledges, that has often been its outcome, as the interview plainly demonstrated.

In the fourth section we viewed *GHWH* in communal light. The "critical" community that established and upholds the "criticism" toward which Sparks urges greater openness has little to no record of fostering or aiding Christian belief. In fact leading practitioners in the history of criticism have generally won their renown through renunciation of the "evangelical" convictions that Sparks wishes to retain. This is true even (especially?) when these scholars' fathers were pastors, a curious fact that probably bears more research than it has heretofore received.

At the more popular level, too, Sparks's move from more to less aggressive affirmation of Scripture's full trustworthiness can be viewed in community perspective. Hempton's *Evangelical Disenchantment* is a helpful analytic tool for constructive thinking about what may be going on in the case of scholars today who are working to separate themselves from the convictions of their forebears that they used to affirm but can no longer support.

Hempton ends by observing that the evangelical tradition "is now one of the largest and fastest growing faith traditions in the world."[58] This could be put more strongly: "The greatest surge in the history of Christianity occurred in Africa over the past one hundred years, and indeed continues its breathtaking

---

[58]Ibid., 198.

trajectory into the twenty-first century."[59] Explosive growth has been discernible in other regions of the world, as well—but not in the postcritical West. The form that worldwide Christian growth has taken seems rather squarely in line with the fully accurate Bible of "the old evangelicals" that Sparks has now left behind.[60] Whether *GWHW*, Sparks, and the "new generation" he claims to represent are part of a dying "critical" order or of a rising confessional one lies enshrouded in the future.

---

[59] Jonathan J. Bonk, "Ecclesiastical Cartography and the Invisible Continent," *International Bulletin of Missionary Research* 28, no. 4 (2004): 154.
[60] Cf., e.g., Philip Jenkins, *The New Faces of Christianity: Believing the Bible in the Global South* (Oxford: Oxford University Press, 2006).

# 15

# A CONSTRUCTIVE TRADITIONAL RESPONSE TO NEW TESTAMENT CRITICISM

## CRAIG L. BLOMBERG

The Synoptic Gospels clearly depict Jesus's last meal with his disciples as a Passover meal (Mark 14:12 and pars.). One common reading of John's Gospel finds the Fourth Evangelist relocating this meal to the day *before* the main Jewish Passover meal that traditionally inaugurated the week-long Festival of the Unleavened Bread (see esp. John 13:1; 18:28; 19:14a). John is then said to have changed the day on which Jesus was crucified so that it coincided with the time (the sixth hour, or noon) of the slaughtering of the lambs in the temple precincts in preparation for the main evening Passover meal (19:14b). On this view, John has thus also changed the time of day of the crucifixion from Mark's third hour or 9:00 a.m. (Mark 15:25) because he wants to portray Jesus as the sacrificial Lamb. Theological affirmation thus trumps historical accuracy.[1]

A variety of alternatives compete in the scholarly literature. Perhaps, like the Essenes, Jesus was following a different liturgical calendar. Maybe, because he knew he would not live long enough, he simply celebrated his last meal with his disciples as if it were Passover, one night earlier than he otherwise would have. Or perhaps a closer analysis of the key texts might disclose that John is *not* claiming Jesus was crucified just before the start of the festival after all.[2] In a book on the historical reliability of the Gospels in general,

---

[1]See, e.g., Raymond E. Brown, *The Gospel according to John XIII–XXI* (Garden City, NY: Doubleday, 1970), 555–56, 846, 895–96; C. K. Barrett, *The Gospel according to St. John*, 2nd ed. (London: SPCK; Philadelphia: Westminster, 1978), 48–51; Maurice Casey, *Is John's Gospel True?* (London: Routledge, 1996), 18–25.

[2]For a good survey of the various theories, see I. Howard Marshall, *Last Supper and Lord's Supper* (Exeter: Paternoster; Grand Rapids: Eerdmans, 1980; repr., Vancouver: Regent College, 2006), 71–75.

and in another one just on the trustworthiness of John, I have opted for and
defended the last of these options.[3]

In an important recent book, Kenton Sparks rejects many examples of what
he calls "'traditional' responses to biblical criticism." Most of his illustrations
come from Old Testament scholarship; the harmonization of John and the
Synoptics on the Last Supper that I support forms his most detailed example
from the New Testament. In every case, Sparks argues that evangelicals should
adopt what he calls the "standard, critical" approaches, labeling these the
"'constructive' responses to biblical criticism."[4]

Not only does Sparks argue for different responses, but throughout his
book he uses impassioned language, especially related to authors' motives,
that goes well beyond what any historian can ever know and that shows that
he is particularly exercised on this topic. In just the three pages in which he
rejects my views, for example, Sparks asks, "Why did John go *out of his way*
to dissociate Jesus's final meal from the Passover?" He states that I fail to
explain "why John would . . . *push so very hard* to associate the crucifixion
with the Passover, juxtaposing it *in blatant fashion* with the correct day and
time of the slaying of the Passover lambs." He points out what he calls "one
of the *most glaring* problems" of my thesis. He considers my approach to be
"based *largely on conjecture* and with *so many dangling* questions." He again
insists that "John's Gospel *is everywhere at pains to insure* that [Jesus's last
meal] is not [the Passover]." Finally, Sparks quotes E. J. Young's wise words
against proposing strained and forced harmonizations rather than admitting
we have no solutions to problems. Sparks concludes:

> I cannot but agree with Young's sentiment. Harmonizations so historically
> and rationally *strained* as those offered by . . . Blomberg cannot pass as *serious*
> scholarly readings of the biblical text, mainly because the authors present their
> *very improbable* reconstructions as if they are likely or even highly probable.[5]

Sparks is scarcely alone among recent writers who want to retain the label
*evangelical*, or who are at least open to doing so, but who think evangelicals should embrace considerably more of the perspectives of more liberal
scholarship with respect to issues of the authorship, historicity, composition,

---

[3]Craig L. Blomberg, *The Historical Reliability of the Gospels*, 2nd ed. (Downers Grove, IL: Inter-
Varsity, 2007), 221–25; Blomberg, *The Historical Reliability of John's Gospel* (Downers Grove, IL:
InterVarsity, 2001), 187–88, 237–39, 246–47; esp. following D. A. Carson, *The Gospel according to
John* (Leicester: Inter-Varsity; Grand Rapids: Eerdmans, 1991), 455–58.
[4]Kenton L. Sparks, *God's Word in Human Words: An Evangelical Appropriation of Critical Biblical
Scholarship* (Grand Rapids: Baker Academic, 2008), esp. 133–203.
[5]Ibid., 162–64. All italics in this paragraph are mine, to highlight Sparks's exaggerated, emotive
language.

canonization, and theological diversity of the biblical books.[6] Typically, the doctrine of inerrancy is one of the first theologoumena to be challenged by these writers. They argue that it *a priori* restricts scholars who affirm it from concluding whatever their research determines to be most probable, allowing them only a small window of acceptable results without landing them in trouble with the societies to which they belong or the institutions that employ them. Carlos Bovell warns younger evangelicals not to tie much, if any, of their biblical scholarship to the doctrine of inerrancy, because it doesn't settle intractable exegetical problems anyway (like the complementarian-egalitarian debate) and because it can create an "all-or-nothing" mentality, so that if one clear error in Scripture emerges, the only alternative left is to slide down the "slippery slope" into unbelief.[7]

Bart Ehrman's reflections on his spiritual pilgrimage offer a case in point. Ehrman describes how he began his studies as a conservative evangelical committed to inerrancy. In a paper for his doctoral program at Princeton he tried to solve the apparent contradiction of the Mark 2:26 reference to Abiathar, when the proper Old Testament character was Ahimelech. But when a professor asked why Ehrman didn't just accept that Mark had made a mistake, the floodgates opened.[8] Today, Ehrman is a self-described agnostic with a large part of his professional career devoted to countering evangelical beliefs. Ironically, Ehrman apparently skipped over all kinds of intermediate, Christian options that are neither evangelical (or at least not inerrantist) nor agnostic but still widely held in diverse Christian traditions.[9]

In New Testament studies, the issues most commonly cited as areas where evangelicals should accept more of the critical consensus are (1) the impossibility of harmonizing the Synoptic Gospels one with another; (2) the frequent "contradictions" between John and the Synoptics, with the Fourth Gospel much less historically reliable; (3) the less trustworthy nature of Acts compared with the letters of Paul; (4) the unknown authorship of the four Gospels; (5) the deutero-Pauline nature of 2 Thessalonians, Colossians, Ephesians, and

---

[6]See, e.g., Peter Enns, *Inspiration and Incarnation: Evangelicals and the Problem of the Old Testament* (Grand Rapids: Baker Academic, 2005); N. T. Wright, *The Last Word: Beyond the Bible Wars to a New Understanding of the Authority of Scripture* (London: SPCK; San Francisco: Harper San Francisco, 2005); and Craig D. Allert, *A High View of Scripture? The Authority of the Bible and the Formation of the New Testament Canon* (Grand Rapids: Baker, 2007).

[7]Carlos Bovell, *Inerrancy and the Spiritual Formation of Younger Evangelicals* (Eugene, OR: Wipf & Stock, 2007).

[8]Bart D. Ehrman, *Misquoting Jesus: The Story Behind Who Changed the Bible and Why?* (San Francisco: Harper San Francisco, 2005), 8–10.

[9]The edited collection of essays by William P. Brown, *Engaging Biblical Authority: Perspectives on the Bible as Scripture* (Louisville: Westminster John Knox, 2007), represents a concise, clear, recent collection of such options.

the Pastoral Epistles; (6) the pseudonymity of James, 1 and 2 Peter, and Jude and the unlikelihood that John who was the son of Zebedee wrote 1–3 John and Revelation; (7) the composite nature of some of the epistles, particularly 2 Corinthians and Philippians; (8) the lack of detailed theological unity among the various New Testament writers and books; (9) the presence of myth and legend in accounts of supposedly supernatural events; (10) the uses of the Old Testament by New Testament writers that fly in the face of sound hermeneutics; and (11) the inadequate criteria employed in the canonization of the New Testament.[10] Adoption of any or all of these or similar perspectives requires the evangelical to replace inerrancy with neoorthodoxy, *Heilsgeschichte*, biblical theology, narrative theology, canonical criticism, and/ or the Bible as authoritative tradition.[11]

While all eleven of these flash points can trigger impassioned defenses of more traditional approaches, followed by shrill attacks on those who would attempt such defenses, none seems to generate as much emotion and rhetorical hyperbole as the debate over harmonization. Gerald Borchert, writing in the very conservative New American Commentary series, declares in his remarks on John 2:13–22 that "the familiar argument of two [temple] cleansings is a historiographic monstrosity that has no basis in the texts of the Gospel. *There is only one cleansing of the temple in each Gospel.*"[12] Robert H. Gundry, author of a recent collection of essays aptly entitled *The Old Is Better: New Testament Essays in Support of Traditional Interpretations*,[13] in his review of the new edition of my *Historical Reliability of the Gospels*, devotes nine of his fourteen paragraphs to just two of my nine chapters—those on harmonization. In most cases Gundry wishes I would have adopted a different approach to the seeming contradictions among the four Gospels, admitting inaccuracies in the text and identifying theological reasons why the Gospel writers introduced the tensions that they did.[14]

Gundry, of course, is no stranger to such controversy. In 1982, he published a detailed redaction-critical commentary on Matthew, in which he accounted for most all of the differences between Matthew and its two main written sources, Mark and Q, by means of unhistorical, often midrashic embellish-

---

[10]For representative viewpoints from a range of perspectives on any of these issues, see a thorough New Testament introduction. Particularly helpful now, not least because it does not take sides, is Mark A. Powell, *Introducing the New Testament: A Historical, Literary, and Theological Survey* (Grand Rapids: Baker, 2009).

[11]Sparks, *God's Word in Human Words*, 171–203.

[12]Gerald L. Borchert, *John 1–11* (Nashville: Broadman & Holman, 1996), 160, his emphasis.

[13]Tübingen: Mohr Siebeck, 2005.

[14]Robert H. Gundry, "Review of Craig L. Blomberg, *The Historical Reliability of the Gospels*, 2nd ed.," *RBL*, September, 8, 2010, accessed September 30, 2010, http://www.bookreviews.org/bookdetail .asp?TitleId=7602&CodePage=2029,7602.

ment. But Gundry also argued that Matthew's audience would have known his sources well enough to recognize what he was doing (just as Jewish readers understood, say, Jubilees' treatment of Genesis) and therefore would not misinterpret him. For Gundry, inerrancy would be called into question only if Matthew were making truth claims that were in fact false. But if Matthew were employing a different style, form, or genre of writing that was not making truth claims about what happened historically when he added to his sources, then he could not be charged with falsifying the truth. Preachers throughout church history have similarly added speculative detail, local color, possible historical reconstruction, and theological commentary to their retelling of biblical stories. As long as their audiences know the text of Scripture well enough to distinguish between the Bible and the preacher's additions, they typically recognize what the preacher is doing and do not impugn his or her trustworthiness.[15]

A substantial majority of the voting members of the Evangelical Theological Society present at the business meeting of its annual conference in 1983 disagreed that Gundry's views were indeed consistent with inerrancy, at that time the sole tenet in the society's doctrinal statement, and requested his resignation from the organization. I voted with the minority. Following the papers and writings of my own professors from seminary, especially D. A. Carson and Douglas Moo, I believed Gundry *had* shown how his view could be consistent with inerrancy, even though I did not find his actual approach to Matthew convincing. In other words, the issue was a hermeneutical one, not a theological one.[16] The trustees of Westmont College, where Gundry taught, agreed, and he continued his illustrious teaching and writing career there until his retirement.

In some extremely conservative Christian scholarly circles, even the views of mainstream inerrantists are considered "diabolical"! In one of the most imbalanced and inaccurate publications to appear from a mainstream evangelical publishing house in recent decades, Robert L. Thomas and F. David Farnell, of the Master's Seminary in Southern California, coedited and contributed to a collection of essays entitled *The Jesus Crisis: The Inroads of Historical Criticism into Evangelical Scholarship.*[17] Most of the contributors consider all forms of what they label *historical criticism* off-limits for the

---

[15]Robert H. Gundry, *Matthew: A Commentary on His Literary and Theological Art* (Grand Rapids: Eerdmans, 1982). A second edition was retitled *Matthew: A Commentary on His Handbook for a Mixed Church under Persecution* (Grand Rapids: Eerdmans, 1994) and included responses to the published criticism of his first edition.

[16]See esp. Douglas J. Moo, "Matthew and Midrash: An Evaluation of R. H. Gundry's Approach," *JETS* 26 (1983): 31–39; and D. A. Carson, "Gundry on Matthew: A Critical Review," *TJ* 3 (1982): 71–91.

[17]Grand Rapids: Kregel, 1998.

evangelical, including any theory of literary dependence among the Gospels, any appropriation of form criticism or redaction criticism, or any form of harmonization that is not "additive"—that is, solving the problem of two seemingly different accounts of the same event by saying that they happened twice. Staunch inerrantist writers such as Carson, Moo, Darrell Bock, Grant Osborne, and I are maligned at least as much as the classic German founders of some of these disciplines such as Rudolf Bultmann and Martin Dibelius.

Here is how Thomas phrases things in the epilogue to his volume:

> This must be one of the greatest mysteries of this century! How can those who profess to believe in the inerrancy of the Bible openly advocate a methodology—actually an *ideology*—that is so blatantly contrary to historical accuracy in Synoptic Gospel texts? This defies rational explanation. The situation is reminiscent of the predicament that arose in the first-century Colossian church to whom Paul wrote, "Beware lest there should be anyone who leads you captive through philosophy and vain deceit according to the tradition of men, according to the rudiments of the world and not according to Christ" (Col. 2:8). A present-day ideological system has a stranglehold on evangelical New Testament scholarship that is choking to death what is supposed be [*sic*] the bastion of truth. Yet few recognize the satanic blindness that is contributing to the deterioration of the gospel records.[18]

Inerrantists who recognize that historical criticism makes a lot of legitimate contributions to scholarship that do not impugn the trustworthiness of the text but who reject those approaches that do so impugn it are thus "damned if they do and damned if they don't." Thomas actually lumps my approach together with Gundry's,[19] while Gundry, in his review of my work, focuses almost all his attention on the handful of places where Thomas would approve of my harmonizations. Sparks and Bovell would argue that I have barely begun to embrace the critical consensus and should move a lot further to the "left"; Thomas and Farnell accuse me of having already fully capitulated to it so that I should move a lot further to the "right."

---

[18]Robert L. Thomas, "Epilogue," in *The Jesus Crisis: The Inroads of Historical Criticism into Evangelical Scholarship*, ed. R. L. Thomas and F. David Farnell (Grand Rapids: Kregel, 1998), 380.

[19]In addition to unnecessarily inflated and condemnatory rhetoric, the volume is filled with egregious misrepresentations. E.g., Robert L. Thomas and F. David Farnell ("The Synoptic Gospels in the Ancient Church," in ibid., 83 n. 159) "cite" me together with Gundry because we allegedly "accept the existence of 'outright discrepancies' in the Gospels" (ibid., 66), citing my essay, "The Legitimacy and Limits of Harmonization," in *Hermeneutics, Authority, and Canon*, ed. D. A. Carson and John D. Woodbridge (Grand Rapids: Baker, 1984; Grand Rapids: Zondervan, 1986; Eugene, OR: Wipf & Stock, 2005). They cite p. 145 of the Baker edition, wrongly attributing it to 1995. But what I actually refer to there are "apparent discrepancies," in the contexts of suggesting solutions to them!

What, then, is the proper approach to the thorny debates over biblical authorship, historicity, use of critical tools, harmonization of parallel passages, theological diversity, and the like? Though not a panacea for every conceivable debate, much more sensitive reflection over the implications of the various literary and rhetorical genres in the Bible would seem an important first step that is not taken often enough. The framers of the Chicago Statement on Biblical Inerrancy recognized this. Particularly crucial for them was the second paragraph of Article XIII.

> We deny that it is proper to evaluate Scripture according to standards of truth and error that are alien to its usage or purpose. We further deny that inerrancy is negated by Biblical phenomena such as a lack of modern technical precision, irregularities of grammar or spelling, observational descriptions of nature, the reporting of falsehoods, the use of hyperbole and round numbers, the topical arrangement of material, variant selections of material in parallel accounts, or the use of free citations.[20]

In more recent years, the application of speech-act theory to biblical interpretation has taught many scholars to recognize not merely the locution of a text or discourse (the meaning of the words in their rhetorical or literary context) but its illocutionary force (what authors do by saying something—e.g., commissioning, warning, lamenting, etc.) and its perlocutionary effects (what the utterance accomplishes with its audience—e.g., shocking, convincing, offending, etc.) as well.[21] Or to sum much of this up more concisely, the inerrancy of the Scriptures should refer to their complete truthfulness "in everything that they affirm."[22] But in some contexts it may take some careful hermeneutical discernment to determine just what a text is or is not affirming. Style, figures of speech, species of rhetoric and literary form and genre all go a long way toward disclosing those affirmations.[23]

Take pseudonymity, for example. Two different scholars may come to the identical conclusion concerning a given epistle, namely, that it was not written by the person whose name appears in its opening greeting. Yet the routes by

---

[20]"The Chicago Statement on Biblical Inerrancy," in *Inerrancy*, ed. Norman L. Geisler (Grand Rapids: Zondervan, 1979), 496.

[21]Kevin J. Vanhoozer, *Is There a Meaning in This Text? The Bible, the Reader, and the Morality of Literary Knowledge* (Grand Rapids: Zondervan, 1998), 209.

[22]Still very useful is the definition by Paul D. Feinberg ("The Meaning of Inerrancy," in Geisler, *Inerrancy*, 294): "Inerrancy means that when all facts are known, the Scriptures in their original autographs and properly interpreted will be shown to be wholly true *in everything that they affirm*, whether that has to do with doctrine or morality or with the social, physical, or life sciences" (my emphasis).

[23]See further William W. Klein, Craig L. Blomberg, and Robert L. Hubbard Jr., *Introduction to Biblical Interpretation*, 2nd ed. (Nashville: Nelson, 2004), 323–448.

which those scholars arrive at that conclusion may diametrically oppose each other. A *methodology* consistent with evangelical convictions might argue that there was an accepted literary convention that allowed a follower, say, of Paul, in the generation after his martyrdom, to write a letter in Paul's name to one of the churches that had come under his sphere of influence. The church would have recognized that it could not have come from the apostle they knew had died two or three decades earlier, and they would have realized that the true author was writing thoughts indebted to the earlier teaching of Paul. In a world without footnotes or bibliographies, this was one way of giving credit where credit was due. Modesty prevented the real author from using his own name, so he wrote in ways he could easily have envisioned Paul writing were the apostle still alive. *Whether or not this is what actually happened*, such a hypothesis is thoroughly consistent with a high view of Scripture and an inerrant Bible. We simply have to recognize what is and is not being claimed by the use of the name "Paul" in that given letter.[24]

Another way of concluding that an epistle is pseudonymous is to envision a process by which an unknown Christian of the second or third generation of Christianity wanted to foist his letter off on an unsuspecting church audience as truly apostolic and inspired. Without the legitimate credentials to gain such respect, the author deliberately sets out to deceive his readers by doing his best to imitate the style and contents of a genuinely Pauline epistle.[25] Now we have a proposal about an author's motives and methods that does not seem at all ethically congruent with an evangelical Christian mindset and must be rejected as incompatible with inerrancy.

Note carefully my distinctions between methods and conclusions. It is not the conclusion one comes to on the issue that determines whether one can still fairly claim to be evangelical, or even inerrantist, but *how* one arrives at that conclusion. A commentator could easily decide that Paul did in fact write Romans but so disagree with his theology in the letter that it would make no sense to label his or her views as evangelical. But if another commentator argued that the Ephesians would have recognized a letter sent to them in the

---

[24]See esp. David G. Meade, *Pseudonymity and Canon: An Investigation into the Relationship of Authorship and Authority in Jewish and Early Christian Tradition* (Tübingen: Mohr, 1986; Grand Rapids: Eerdmans, 1987). Acknowledging that we cannot find actual examples of this process *in early Christian circles for works accepted into the New Testament canon*, I. H. Marshall, with Philip H. Towner (*A Critical and Exegetical Commentary on the Pastoral Epistles* [Edinburgh: T&T Clark, 1999]), nevertheless believes this is what happened with the Pastorals. Recognizing the unparalleled nature of this practice, Marshall coins a new word for it—"allonymity." The true author is thus using the name of another (Gk. ἄλλος) person but is not thinking of it as a false (Gk. ψευδής) attribution of authorship.

[25]A classic example, also with respect to the Pastoral Epistles, is Lewis R. Donelson, *Pseudepigraphy and Ethical Argument in the Pastoral Epistles* (Tübingen: Mohr, 1986).

90s alleged to be by Paul as the sincere, even inspired reflections of one of Paul's close followers, writing his understanding of God's word in the tradition of Paul's theology to the churches in Ephesus, there is no necessary contradiction with inerrancy. In other words, the way for scholarship to proceed with such varying theories is actually to evaluate their respective merits. Can other examples of "benign" pseudonymity be demonstrated in the ancient Mediterranean world? How close are such examples in date and location to the setting of a biblical epistle suspected of being pseudonymous? How much do the various letters resemble each other with respect to a wider variety of features of genre or form? One's acceptance or rejection of the overall theory of authorship should then depend on the answers to these kinds of questions, not on some *a priori* determination that pseudonymity is in every instance compatible or incompatible with evangelicalism.[26]

The same is true with assessments of historical reliability more broadly. How loosely may someone's words be paraphrased before one may fairly be accused of misrepresenting the original author or speaker? The answer to that question will vary from one context to the next and will depend on the cultural standards of the setting in which the paraphrase was first composed. Even the longest speeches or sermons in the Gospels and Acts seem far too short to reflect everything of what Jesus or one of the early Christians actually spoke in the given contexts. To borrow Darrell Bock's language, we must surely see them as offering the "gist" of much longer and more detailed addresses.[27] But that observation in itself has no necessary bearing on how accurate they are. One could use the same number of words as an original discourse and completely misrepresent it, just as one can drastically abbreviate a speaker's words and faithfully represent them.

Indeed, there are parallels to all eleven categories of debates itemized above. Is it compatible with a high view of Scripture to hypothesize that early Christian scribes may have combined two or more letters or letter fragments of Paul on the same scroll to create what was subsequently copied as one document, which we know as 2 Corinthians? If one can find examples of others doing that in Paul's world without any deception and, in fact, for

---

[26] Two excellent, full-length studies of the topic are Jeremy Duff, "A Reconsideration of Pseudepigraphy in Early Christianity" (DPhil thesis, Oxford University, 1998); and Terry L. Wilder, *Pseudonymity, the New Testament, and Deception* (Lanham, MA: University Press of America, 2004). In German, cf. esp. Armin D. Baum, *Pseudepigraphie und literarische Fälschung im frühen Christentum* (Tübingen: Mohr, 2001).

[27] Darrell L. Bock, "The Words of Jesus in the Gospels: Live, Jive, or Memorex?," in *Jesus under Fire: Modern Scholarship Reinvents the Historical Jesus*, ed. Michael J. Wilkins and J. P. Moreland (Grand Rapids: Zondervan, 1995), 73–99.

good reason, then the answer should surely be yes.[28] Did it actually happen
that way? The cases of those who suggest that it did would then have to be
evaluated on their own merits and accepted or rejected accordingly.[29] Was the
process of canonization messy and fraught with ambiguity in places? God's
Spirit regularly works through the messy, ambiguous circumstances of life.
Such a proposal shouldn't inherently cause anyone alarm.[30] What were the
specific circumstances of New Testament canonization? That is a separate
question; different proposals have to be assessed according to the persuasiveness of the evidence put forward.[31] Might some passages in the Gospels and
Acts traditionally thought of as historical actually be mythical or legendary?
I see no way to exclude a positive answer *a priori*. The questions would be
whether any given proposal to that effect demonstrated the existence of an
accepted literary form likely known to the Evangelists' audiences, established
as a legitimate device for communicating theological truth through historical
fiction.[32] In each case it is not the proposal itself that should be off limits for
the evangelical. The important question is whether any given proposal has
actually made its case. The ultraconservative critics need to embrace the first
of these principles; those who want to push evangelicals to adopt more of the
"critical consensus" need to embrace the second.

What, then, shall we say about the lightning rod of harmonization? Can
the conclusion that John relocated the Last Supper to the night before the
first, main Passover meal be consistent with inerrancy? Is it even what a close
reading of the text of John, completely apart from the Synoptics, most naturally suggests? Is the notion that John does *not* claim that Jesus was crucified
while the Passover lambs were being slaughtered in the temple some desperate
expedient of harmonizing that flies in the face of all the evidence, appealed

---

[28]E.g., in four instances ancient compilers of Cicero's letters created multiple-letter collections in a
single manuscript, in the chronological order of the letters. See Thomas Schmeller, "Die Cicerobriefe
und die Frage nach der Einheitlichkeit des 2. Korintherbriefs," *ZNW* 95 (2004): 181–208.

[29]Of many suggested options, maybe the best is that Paul dictated the letter over a period of time,
so that chaps. 10–13 were written in the same letter, but only after fresh news of new trouble in
Corinth had arrived after Paul had completed chaps. 1–9. See esp. Ralph P. Martin, *2 Corinthians*
(Waco, TX: Word, 1986), xlvii–li.

[30]As, e.g., in Lee M. McDonald, *The Biblical Canon: Its Origin, Transmission, and Authority*
(Peabody, MA: Hendrickson, 2007).

[31]Perhaps the best book-length overview, at least for New Testament material, remains F. F. Bruce,
*The Canon of Scripture* (Downers Grove, IL: InterVarsity, 1988).

[32]It is often not noticed that the so-called miracle of the fish with a coin in its mouth (Matt. 17:27)
is not even a narrative; it is merely a command from Jesus to Peter to go to the lake and catch such a
fish. We don't even know whether Peter obeyed the command. Here is a good reminder to pay careful
attention to literary form. See further Craig L. Blomberg, "The New Testament Miracles and Higher
Criticism: Climbing Up the Slippery Slope," *JETS* 27 (1984): 425–38.

to only by those blinded by some obfuscating presupposition of inerrancy? Let us return to the last half of John once again.

John 13:1 is loosely connected to what immediately follows, functioning more like a headline over much or all of the last main section of the Gospel (chaps. 13–20).[33] The entire Passion Narrative will disclose how Jesus loved his disciples "fully" and/or "to the end." Numerous translations or editions of the Greek New Testament put either a subparagraph or full paragraph break after this verse.[34] It was before the Passover Festival when Jesus knew his hour had come, as already indicated in 12:23.

Imagine if I were to write about a comparable treasured annual American festival, Thanksgiving, that for many people leads to a four-day weekend of festive eating but with Thursday dinner being the most significant meal that kicks off the celebration: "Now before the Thanksgiving Feast, my grandmother, knowing that her days were numbered, decided to go all out for her family and shower her love on us." Then imagine that, after a pause, my narrative continued, "When dinner time came . . ." Without reference to any other meals anywhere in the context, would any American reader think of any dinner other than the eagerly expected Thanksgiving dinner? One would surmise that the great love my grandmother had decided to display had to do with making a lavish Thanksgiving dinner, and that now that dinner was beginning.

Surely the same is true for the dinner of John 13:2, after the reference to the Passover in verse 1.[35] And if some listeners did begin to wonder whether this was some earlier meal before the start of the festival itself, even if they had never heard the story exactly as in the Synoptics, previous accounts of the events of Jesus's last night on earth were as deeply embedded in the orally transmitted Gospel tradition as accounts of any other part of the life of Christ. For example, well before any written Gospel was compiled, Paul describes Jesus's institution of the "Lord's Supper" in 1 Corinthians 11:23–26, in wording closely reminiscent of the synoptic accounts, especially Luke's (Matt. 26:26–29; Mark 14:22–25; Luke 22:14–20).[36] By the time John

[33]Herman N. Ridderbos, *The Gospel according to John: A Theological Commentary* (Grand Rapids: Eerdmans, 1997): 452.

[34]The 4th edition of the UBS Greek New Testament notes in its discourse segmentation apparatus at John 13:1 that the Nestle-Aland Greek text puts a subparagraph break after this verse, and that the TEV, NIV, NJB, NEB, La Nouvelle Version Segond Revisée, La Bible en Français Courant, and La Biblia Versión Popular all put a full paragraph break after it.

[35]Cf. Karl T. Kleinknecht, "Johannes 13, die Synoptiker und die 'Methode' der johanneischen Evangelienüberlieferung," *ZTK* 82 (1985): 370–71; J. Ramsey Michaels, *John: A Good News Commentary* (New York: Harper & Row, 1983), 230; Gary M. Burge, *John* (Grand Rapids: Zondervan, 2000), 365–67.

[36]For a careful comparison of the accounts and discussion of their similarities and differences, see Marshall, *Last Supper and Lord's Supper*, 50–76.

observes that at the meal in John 13 Jesus foretells both his betrayal by Judas (John 13:21–30; pars. Matt. 26:20–25; Mark 14:17–21; Luke 22:21–23) and his denial by Peter (John 13:36–38; pars. Matt. 26:31–35; Mark 14:27–31; Luke 22:31–34), his audiences would recognize that, though much of the other information he chooses to include and omit differs from the Synoptics, John *is* describing the same meal that the synoptic writers unequivocally identify as the Passover meal (Mark 14:12, 16 and pars.).[37]

Incidental confirmation of this conclusion comes from John 13:29. When Judas left the meal, some of the other disciples "thought Jesus was telling him to buy what was needed for the festival, or to give something to the poor" (NIV). It was on the first night of Passover Week that shops would have been open late in case people ran out of provisions, not the night before Passover. It was that same night when beggars stood by the gates of Jerusalem and it was considered meritorious to give them alms, not the night before. If John really were going so "out of his way to dissociate Jesus' final meal from the Passover," as Sparks alleges, all these details would become inexplicable.[38] It is simply false to claim with Sparks that John "is everywhere at pains to insure" that Jesus's final meal is not the Passover meal (recall above, 346).

Why, then, does John 18:28 depict the Jewish leaders the next morning remaining outside Pilate's palace to avoid the ritual impurity that would prevent them from being "able to eat the Passover" (NIV)? Again, it is Sparks's reconstruction that is historically garbled. This kind of ritual impurity lasted only for a day; ceremonial washings could then render one ritually pure again. The Jewish leaders could not have been worried about the upcoming evening meal, because the new Jewish day began at dusk, and their period of uncleanness would have ceased. But they would have been concerned about being able to participate in the midday meal, the *hagigah*, the late morning or early afternoon after the feast had begun.[39] This, too, was an important part of

---

[37]Ironically, it is Cullen I. K. Story ("The Bearing of Old Testament Terminology on the Johannine Chronology of the Final Passover of Jesus," *NovT* 31 [1989]: 317), the very Princeton Seminary professor to whom Ehrman attributes the comment on his paper asking why he didn't just admit that Mark made a mistake in Mark 2:26 (see above, 347), who writes of John 13: "The presence of Judas, Jesus' prediction of his betrayal, Judas' departure from the table (implicit in the Synoptics, explicit in John), the affirmation by Peter of unswerving loyalty to Jesus, and Jesus' prediction of his denial: all of these circumstances together form solid lines of connection between the meal in John 13 and the Synoptic account of the holy supper."
[38]For documentation and elaboration, see Joachim Jeremias, *The Eucharistic Words of Jesus* (London: SCM; New York: Scribner's, 1966), 54, 82. Cf. Carson, *The Gospel according to John*, 471; Colin G. Kruse, *The Gospel according to John* (Leicester: Inter-Varsity; Grand Rapids: Eerdmans, 2003), 290.
[39]For documentation and elaboration, see Barry D. Smith, "The Chronology of the Last Supper," *WTJ* 53 (1991): 29–45. Cf. Andreas Köstenberger, *John* (Grand Rapids: Baker, 2004), 524; Burge, *John*, 499. A more severe form of uncleanness could have been incurred that would have left them ritually impure for a week (Gerald L. Borchert, *John 12–21* [Nashville: Broadman & Holman, 2002],

the celebration, as were all the meals throughout the week-long festival. So important were these meals that an entire Mishnaic tractate (*Moed Katan*) is devoted to the laws surrounding them and analogous feasts (the "mid-festival" days, as they were called).

Yet surely, the counterargument would reply, John 19:14 settles the matter. That same morning of what we today call Good Friday is explicitly stated as "the day of Preparation of the Passover." If that is the best translation in this context of the Greek παρασκευὴ τοῦ πάσχα, then every previous exegetical decision made on this passage has been wrong, *not because we have been trying to harmonize John with the Synoptics*, but within our reading of the narrative of John in its own context. Then it is John who will have sent out confusing signals pointing in different directions rather than uniformly having crafted his narrative to differ from the Synoptics.

But it is hard to believe that John 19:14 claims that it is the day before the Passover began. The word παρασκευή appears four other times in the New Testament, all in the context of this specific day. In both 19:31 and 42, John clarifies that it was the day of preparation *for the Sabbath*, that is, Friday, the day before Saturday. Mark 15:42 and Matthew 27:62, the only other verses in which this word appears, confirm this usage. This was the most common day of preparation for ancient Jews, occurring weekly, rather than annually like the day of preparation for the Passover. Intriguingly, *in Greek*, no doubt because of the centuries of Christian influence, to this day the word for Friday is παρασκευή. Παρασκευὴ τοῦ πάσχα, in 19:14, must therefore mean the day of preparation (for the Sabbath) *during the Passover Festival*.[40] Compare the rendering of the NIV of this verse: "It was the day of Preparation of Passover Week," or even more clearly in God's Word to the Nations (GWN): "on the Friday of the Passover Festival." The New Century Version (NCV) likewise reads "on Preparation Day of Passover week," even while most translations leave the text ambiguous, and possibly even misleading, by not adding any explanatory words.

Finally, we must address the last half of John 19:14—"it was about noon" (ὥρα ἦν ὡς ἕκτη), literally, "it was about the sixth hour." Assuming, as is probable, that John was following the Jewish method of reckoning hours from an average time for dawn, or 6:00 a.m., this brings us to approximately noon.[41] Given the sundial as the most precise timekeeping device of the day,

238), but if that is what the Jewish leaders feared, then they would not have been ready for an evening meal even a day and a half later.

[40]Ridderbos (*The Gospel according to John*, 456), in fact, observes that the expression παρασκευὴ τοῦ πάσχα, meaning "the day of Preparation for the Passover," is nowhere else attested.

[41]Older commentators sometimes suggested that John was following the Roman method of reckoning hours from midnight on, but a three-hour discrepancy with Mark still remains—just involving

and given the frequent division of each day and each night into fourths, as in the standard four watches of the night, it is possible that the "about" intends to signal no more precise a period of time than sometime between 10:30 a.m. and 1:30 p.m. Given that Roman procurators liked to start their work very early in the morning and work only a few hours on many days, if this time is not very close to noon, it is more likely earlier than later.[42] Even the long-distinguished Harvard professor Henry J. Cadbury, speaking of expressions of time in the Gospels, opined, "It seems to me more likely that in spite of the opportunity offered by an hourly nomenclature the ancients found that for many purposes the simpler three-hour interval was sufficiently definite."[43]

Does the sixth hour also have symbolic significance for John? Some references to time in John's Gospel do; some do not. Each has to be examined individually. It is true that John alone among New Testament writers refers to Jesus as the "lamb of God." But this expression appears only twice in his Gospel, with both instances occurring in the first chapter, on the lips of John the Baptist (1:29, 36), a long way from the Passion Narrative. It can hardly be called a major emphasis in this Gospel. To be sure, the unqualified expression "Lamb" occurs thirty-one times in Revelation, but John's readers will not have read this book yet. Indeed, the only two references to *Passover* lambs anywhere in the Gospels come in Mark and Luke (Mark 14:12; Luke 22:7), not in John. And the three times in Scripture that *Christ* is explicitly likened to the Passover lamb are in other authors as well (Acts 8:32; 1 Cor. 5:7; 1 Pet. 1:19). If one also observes that the Greek term for "lamb" in the two Johannine uses of "lamb of God" is ἀμνός, not ἀρνίον, as in all the

---

different hours—and John's use of specifically numbered hours elsewhere in his Gospel does not makes as good sense on the Roman system as on the Jewish system.

[42] See esp. Johnny V. Miller, "The Time of the Crucifixion," *JETS* 26 (1983): 157–66. Cf. also William M. Ramsay, "About the Sixth Hour," *Expositor* 7, 4th series (1893): 216–23; and Carson, *The Gospel according to John*, 604–5; Leon Morris, *The Gospel according to John*, 2nd ed. (Grand Rapids: Eerdmans, 1995), 708; Darrel L. Bock, *Jesus according to Scripture* (Grand Rapids: Baker; Leicester: Apollos, 2002), 534.

[43] Henry J. Cadbury, "Some Lukan Expressions of Time (Lexical Notes on Luke-Acts VII)," *JBL* 82 (1963): 278. Borchert himself (*John 12–21*, 258) notes that he has observed "this same phenomenon as a missionary among people who do not wear watches and for whom a designated meeting time of 10:00 a.m. means some time in the middle of the day, and it can actually take place not in the morning but in the early afternoon." For a survey of all the main solutions to this problem proposed throughout church history, see Johannes Karavidopoulos, "L'heure de la crucifixion de Jésus selon Jean et les Synoptiques: Mc 15.25 par rapport à Jn 19,14–16," in *John and the Synoptics*, ed. Albert Denaux (Leuven: Leuven University Press, 1992), 608–13. Sparks wonders what would happen if my particular solution to the apparent contradiction were found inadequate (*God's Word in Human Words*, 163). Put simply, one would need to evaluate the merits of all the other suggested solutions.

other New Testament occurrences, even John's later use of the concept in Revelation seems less significant.[44]

About this point, then, it becomes important to ask, just where exactly *does* John "push so very hard to associate the crucifixion with the Passover, juxtaposing it in blatant fashion with the correct day and time of the slaying of the Passover lambs" (recall above, 346)? The total amount of evidence for this blatant, hard push boils down to one solitary datum, the time of day mentioned. And lest John's largely Gentile-Christian readership not happen to know the fine points of the timing of the slaughter of the lambs in a Jewish ritual, John gives not a word of explanation to help them out. If that is the meaning of the reference to the sixth hour, they must intuit it entirely on their own. Is it really such a stretch to suggest that John, the one Gospel writer to include far more chronology, chronological sequence, and apparent chronological accuracy than any of the other three, tells us that Pilate judged Jesus worthy of death and handed him over to be crucified at about noon because it was in fact roughly midday when those events actually happened?[45]

If Mark says it was the third hour (9:00 a.m.) when they crucified him, is it really a "glaring problem" based "largely on conjecture" with so many "dangling questions" to observe that, of the twenty-three specific references to an hour of the day modified by an ordinal number in the New Testament, twenty of them refer to the third, sixth, or ninth hours? Two other references—to the seventh and tenth hours—appear only in John, without obvious symbolism (4:52; 1:39), and the remaining reference—to the eleventh hour (Matt. 20:9)—is in a parable where a time very close to the end of the day is required by the context. Robert Stein rightly observes:

> This raises the question of how a person might refer to an event taking place between 9 a.m. and noon. It would probably be described as either the "third" hour or the "sixth" hour (Stein 1990: 66–69). Some have suggested that John would have preferred the latter designation because of his particular reckon-

---

[44]Even Mark A. Matson ("The Historical Plausibility of John's Passion Dating," in *John, Jesus, and History*, 2 vols., ed. Paul N. Anderson, Felix Just, and Tom Thatcher [Atlanta: Society of Biblical Literature, 2009], 2:308), who is one of those rare scholars who finds a contradiction between the Fourth Gospel and the Synoptics on the day of Christ's crucifixion while supporting the historicity of John over against the Synoptics, does not use John 19:14 or lamb-of-God theology to support his case. He observes, "It seems likely that if John were focusing on Jesus as a paschal sacrifice, he would underline or highlight the similarities with the Passover, especially since John is at such variance with the Synoptic tradition." Matson concludes, "But what is remarkable is that John has only these two time markers early in the narrative [John 18:28; 19:14], and then makes no specific reference to the time of Jesus' death. Again, the internal structure of John's account shows little apologetic interest in linking this Passover to Jesus' death; or, if such an apologetic interest is there, John is astonishingly subtle in his presentation."

[45]Cf. also Köstenberger, *John*, 538; Carson, *The Gospel according to John*, 605.

ing of the Passover (see the introduction to 14:12–31), for at noon the Passover lambs were slain (Gundry 1993: 957; Evans 2001: 503). But could John have expected his readers to understand this? If he had to explain to them that Jews have no dealings with Samaritans (4:9), that the Jews have certain burial customs (19:40), that the word "Messiah" means "Christ" (1:41; 4:25), that "Rabbi" means "Teacher" (1:38), that "Siloam" means "Sent" (9:7), and so on, it is very unlikely that they would have known that on the sixth hour of the day before the Passover, the Passover lambs were slain, and that this coincided exactly with when Jesus was crucified. Furthermore, the sixth-hour designation in John 19:14 is associated not with the time of Jesus' crucifixion but with the verdict at his trial before Pilate. If we recognize the general preference of the third or sixth hour to designate a period between 9 a.m. and noon and the lack of precision in telling time in the first century (Miller 1983), the two different time designations do not present an insurmountable problem.[46]

Sparks's language in rejecting this harmonization seems at the very least to be an example of rhetorical overkill!

In the case of pseudonymity, I envisaged a scenario in which the "critical consensus" approach could, in my opinion, be consistent with inerrancy. The potential fluidity in the meaning of attaching a name to a document where one expects its author's identity to appear is what allowed me to envisage that scenario. Partial parallels appear today when an author's name appears on a book jacket and title page, but if we keep reading in the front matter we discover that the book was edited, completed, and published posthumously or was told to a ghostwriter. We normally recognize such conventions as other than duplicitous. But when Sparks insists that John has gone out of his way to tell us that Jesus was crucified during a certain twenty-four-hour period of time in order to exploit the symbolism that alone attached to that period of time, when in fact Jesus was crucified during a different twenty-four-hour period of time, and that the language used by John in its historical and literary contexts unambiguously referred to those day-long periods of time, I do not see how John can be spared the charge of both error and duplicity. All anyone with access to the synoptic tradition would have had to do was to reply, "I'm sorry, John, but Jesus can't be the Lamb of God based upon your claim in your Passion Narrative, because that is not when he was crucified."[47]

---

[46]Robert H. Stein, *Mark* (Grand Rapids: Baker, 2008), 713.

[47]And it is increasingly widely being accepted that John, while not necessarily literarily dependent on the Synoptics, knew substantial amounts of their content, as did his readers. See esp. Richard Bauckham, "John for Readers of Mark," in *The Gospels for All Christians: Rethinking the Gospel Audiences*, ed. Richard Bauckham (Grand Rapids: Eerdmans, 1998), 147–71; more cautiously, Edward W. Klink III, *The Sheep of the Fold: The Audience and Origin of the Gospel of John* (Cambridge: Cambridge University Press, 2007), 157–81.

In the example of the one versus two temple cleansings, the data are a bit different. Here John's Gospel breaks from its heretofore uninterrupted pattern of referring to new pericopae as occurring "on the next day" or "on the third day" (John 1:29, 35, 43; 2:1). John 2:13, literally translated, yields simply, "And the Passover of the Jews was near, and Jesus went up to Jerusalem." The next new pericope, containing the dialogue between John and Nicodemus, is introduced with similar vagueness: "Now there was a man of the Pharisees, Nicodemus by name, a ruler of the Jews. This one came to him by night and said . . ."[48] It is perfectly conceivable that John has thematically transposed the temple incident to the beginning of his Gospel because of its programmatic significance—for Jesus's signs, Jesus as the new Temple, the polarization of the crowds, various levels of belief in response to signs, and so on.[49] No necessary chronological contradiction appears because the text makes no explicit claim as to when this event took place.

On the other hand, I remain intrigued by the unusually precise reference to forty-six years since Herod began to have the temple rebuilt (John 2:20). Unless it has actually been at least forty-eight years since the start of the rebuilding of the temple when the unnamed Jews spoke these words, it cannot be any later than AD 28, two years too early for the temple cleansing in the last week of Jesus's life, even on the earlier of the two options for dating the crucifixion (30 and 33).[50] Nor does forty-six appear to be a round number or an approximation, or to have any symbolic significance. The Jewish leaders could have erred in their calculation, and John could have accurately reported their errant statement, but how likely is this here? Heavily desirous of a finally and fully rebuilt temple, the temple leaders—of all people—most likely kept an accurate count of how long they had been waiting.

The synoptic account seems less detachable from its context. And while none of its details necessarily contradicts those in John,[51] there are enough that differ to make one wonder whether John intends to narrate a different

---

[48] Andreas Köstenberger (*A Theology of John's Gospel and Letters* [Grand Rapids: Zondervan, 2009], 193 n. 44) is thus unnecessarily cautious when he declares, "I remain to be persuaded, however, that this is a legitimate option for evangelicals with an inerrant view of Scripture."

[49] See esp. R. T. France, "Chronological Aspects of 'Gospel Harmony,'" *VE* 16 (1986): 40–43; Michaels, *John*, 50; Craig S. Keener, *The Gospel of John: A Commentary*, 2 vols. (Peabody, MA: Hendrickson, 2003), 1:519.

[50] James F. McGrath, "'Destroy This Temple': Issues of History in John 2:13–22," in Anderson, Just, and Thatcher, *John, Jesus, and History*, 2:40; Francis J. Moloney, "The Fourth Gospel and the Jesus of History," *NTS* 46 (2000): 55.

[51] See Paul Trudinger, "The Cleansing of the Temple: St John's Independent, Subtle Reflections," *ExpTim* 108 (1997): 329–30.

temple incident.[52] Is this really a "historiographical monstrosity"? Randy Richards has suggested a very plausible scenario on the basis of the ancient Mediterranean dynamics of honor and shame whereby two similar but separate incidents might well have framed Jesus's career: the first one discrediting him in the eyes of the temple leaders but the second one demonstrating him to be dangerous and to be done away with from their perspective.[53] I don't know for sure whether Richards's interpretation is correct, but I see nothing monstrous about it.

As for Borchert's point that no Gospel presents more than one temple cleansing, are we thereby establishing a historiographical criterion that when two Gospels each have partially similar incidents appearing once and once only in their narratives, even if in entirely different contexts, we may *never* assume that more than one such episode occurred? By this logic, the curing of the paralyzed man in Mark 2:1–12 in Capernaum must be a variant of the curing of the paralyzed man in Jerusalem in John 5:1–15, since each of these two Gospels narrates only one miraculous cure of a paralyzed man. By this logic, the healings of the blind beggar in Luke 18:35–43 and of the man born blind in John 9:1–12 must be variants of the same event, since each of these two Gospels likewise narrates only one healing of a blind man. By this logic, the resurrection of Lazarus in John 11 and of Jairus's daughter in Mark 5 must be variants of the same event, since each of these two Gospels narrates only one resurrection performed by Jesus. Yet Borchert does not opt for any of these three conclusions.[54] That he doesn't suggests that *his* historiographical criterion is overly restrictive.

What about the vexed problem of Abiathar in Mark 2:26? Even if we had no other record of this incident from David's day, we might suspect that Mark meant something other than simply "when Abiathar was high priest." The Greek expression is ἐπὶ Ἀβιαθὰρ ἀρχιερέως. The preposition ἐπί occurs seventy-one times in Mark but only once elsewhere with a proper noun, and then its object is in the accusative case, not the genitive as it is here (Mark 15:22). There the personal noun is a place name (Golgotha) so that it makes sense to say that they brought Jesus ἐπί ("to") that location. Twenty-one of the seventy-one occurrences are with the genitive, sixteen clearly referring to places (earth, sea, desert, street, rooftops), so that it makes sense to think of something happening "to," "onto," or "upon" those locations. Twice the

---

[52]This appears to have been the standard view of the early church, and one can still find it frequently proposed well into the twentieth century, even if it is only rarely defended today.

[53]E. Randolph Richards, "An Honor/Shame Argument for Two Temple Clearings," *TJ* 29 (2008): 19–43.

[54]Borchert, *John 1–11*, 229, 310–12, 349.

idiom ἐπὶ ἀληθείας appears ("upon a truth," i.e., "truly"), and once people are brought "to" or "before" governors and kings (Mark 13:9). None of these uses helps at all in understanding ἐπὶ Ἀβιαθάρ as an adverbial modifier of David's *entering* into God's house in 2:26. The latest edition of Bauer's lexicon gives nine columns of uses, subuses, and examples of possible meanings of ἐπί, and not until the eighteenth and final use do we come to "marker of temporal associations, *in the time of, at, on, for*."[55] Yet even "in the time of Abiathar, the high priest" is not quite the same as "when Abiathar was high priest." The expression could theoretically mean during the lifetime of Abiathar, who was one of Israel's high priests.

But we have skipped one other use of ἐπί plus the genitive in Mark. Mark 12:26 reads, "But concerning the dead that are raised, have you never read in the book of Moses ἐπὶ τοῦ βάτου how God said to him . . . ?" "Upon the bush"? "In the time of the bush"? "To, toward, upon, in, or at the bush"? Almost all the major English translations render this "in the passage about the bush." Now we have an option that makes sense for 2:26 as well: "in the passage about Abiathar." But how long was a passage? Ancient Jews regularly read aloud portions of their Scripture in weekly synagogue services of sufficient length to read through the Torah every year and the rest of the "Old Testament" (the *haftarah*) in three years. This regularly meant multiple chapters of each per week. Each segment was given a name based on some prominent element within it, though in most cases we have lost the actual names utilized.[56] Abiathar was a more prominent and influential individual than Ahimelech, so even before we consult the narrative of 1 Samuel 21:1–6 and discover that Ahimelech was the actual priest who interacted with David in those verses, we might suspect that Mark's quotation of Jesus using the unusual Greek construction that he does meant something other than that he was merely reproducing a factual error on Christ's part. After all, as free as the Gospel writers were to modify or omit embarrassing material in other places, including modifying Old Testament quotations, surely Mark would have taken pains not to let an expression stand that he understood to be a historical mistake on his Lord's part. Perhaps matters would have been different if "Abiathar" had appeared simply in Mark's narrative material. That neither Matthew's nor Luke's parallel "corrects" Mark's narrative by inserting the name Ahimelech, but simply rewords the account so that no priest's name is mentioned, suggests they realized that something other than just a factual

---

[55]BDAG, 363–67.
[56]See, e.g., Michael D. Goulder, *Midrash and Lection in Matthew* (London: SPCK, 1974; Eugene, OR: Wipf & Stock, 2004).

364 CRAIG L. BLOMBERG

mistake had occurred, but that because misunderstanding could arise, they just omitted the phrase.[57]

Perhaps this is not the best explanation of Mark 2:26, though it seems to me the best of those I have read or considered. Perhaps in places in my larger works on the Gospels where I have adopted one kind of explanation of apparent historical discrepancies, a different approach is needed instead. My point here is merely to suggest that there are good exegetical reasons for seriously considering the kinds of interpretations I have adopted, whether or not one presupposes the inerrancy, inspiration, or even just the general trustworthiness of the text. Such presuppositions, over one's scholarly career, may turn into what can be thought of as functional nonnegotiables, overturnable only by a Kuhnian revolution in one's thinking.[58] But if they are not simply prejudices, they must be overturnable given sufficient evidence. On the other hand, when one has examined a large number of the apparent contradictions in Scripture and time and again discovered plausible solutions—at times even more than one plausible solution—it is only natural to reach a point where one gives the text the benefit of the doubt on the rare occasions of confronting seemingly more intractable problems.[59] These are the kinds of replies that are important to give to a professor who asks a student, whether Bart Ehrman or anyone else, "Why not just admit that Mark [or any other scriptural author] made an error?"

May evangelicals, as a result, proceed further into the twenty-first century with the confidence that the vast majority of the most problematic issues in scriptural interpretation that lead some to abandon inerrancy have been resolved, some many times over throughout the history of the church, and that the remaining handful of problems have received at least *plausible* solutions, so that, *contra* Sparks, Gundry, Bovell, and others, we need not adopt more radical approaches that former generations of our scholarly forebears in no way countenanced. On the other hand, let those on the "far right" neither anathematize those who do explore and defend new options nor immediately seek to ban them from organizations or institutions to which they belong. If new proposals (or at least proposals that are new for otherwise evangelical scholars) cannot withstand scholarly rigor, then let their refutations proceed

---

[57]For many of the points in this line of reasoning, see John W. Wenham, "Mark 2:26," *JTS* 1 (1950): 156. Cf. also James R. Edwards, *The Gospel according to Mark* (Grand Rapids: Eerdmans; Leicester: Apollos, 2002), 95 n. 42; and Ben Witherington III, *The Gospel of Mark: A Socio-Rhetorical Commentary* (Grand Rapids: Eerdmans, 2001), 130.

[58]Cf. D. A. Carson, *The Gagging of God: Christianity Confronts Pluralism* (Grand Rapids: Zondervan, 1996), 88–90.

[59]Cf. I. Howard Marshall, *Luke: Historian and Theologian*, 3rd ed. (Exeter: Paternoster; Downers Grove, IL: InterVarsity, 1988), esp. 53–76.

at that level, with convincing scholarship, rather than with the kind of cen-
sorship that makes one wonder whether those who object have no persuasive
reply and so have to resort simply to demonizing and/or silencing the voices
with which they disagree. If evangelical scholarship proceeded in this more
measured fashion, neither inherently favoring nor inherently resisting "critical"
conclusions, whether or not they form a consensus, then it might fairly be
said to be both traditional *and* constructive.[60]

---

[60] A reasonably good model on this topic is Ben Witherington III, *The Living Word of God: Rethinking the Theology of the Bible* (Waco, TX: Baylor University Press, 2007). A bit more on the traditional side, but very well articulated, is Timothy Ward, *Words of Life: Scripture as the Living and Active Word of God* (Downers Grove, IL: InterVarsity, 2009). More mixed in nature, as is often the case with anthologies, but with more chapters seemingly "pushing boundaries" than not, is *Evangelicals and Scripture: Tradition, Authority, and Hermeneutics*, ed. Vincent Bacote, Laura C. Miguélez, and Dennis L. Okholm (Downers Grove, IL: InterVarsity. 2004).

# 16

# PRECISION AND ACCURACY

*Making Distinctions in the Cultural Context*
*That Give Us Pause in Pitting the Gospels*
*against Each Other*

## DARRELL L. BOCK

※

Several years ago in explaining the historical orientation of the Scriptures, I made a point about the level of precision found in the utterances of Jesus and other speakers in the Gospels.[1] I argued there that all that was required in these utterances, even in thinking about inerrancy, was the voice of Jesus (*ipsissima vox*), not always his exact words (*ipsissima verba*).[2] I made the argument by showing numerous parallel passages where variation took place. I now wish to extend those observations to other elements of the Gospels. One of the ways God accommodated himself within the inspiration of these documents was to allow the authors to express themselves in the manner they were accustomed to speaking. What should we expect from the Gospels in terms of their genre, event telling, use of the Old Testament, descriptions, chronology, and geography? Should we distinguish between precision and accuracy? Is the standard of accuracy one that leads us into trusting the core of the accounts they present?

The reason this discussion is so important is that some challenge teaching on the inspiration of Scripture in terms of fidelity, infallibility, or, especially, inerrancy, as if what is required for such a connection is a level of significant precision in the accounts. They read the Gospels to pit them against each

---

[1]See my "The Words of Jesus in the Gospels: Live, Jive, or Memorex?," in *Jesus under Fire: Modern Scholarship Reinvents the Historical Jesus*, ed. Michael Wilkens and J. P. Moreland (Grand Rapids: Zondervan 1996), 73–99.

[2]Paul Feinberg had made this point with less detail in "The Meaning of Inerrancy," in *Inerrancy*, ed. Norman L. Geisler (Grand Rapids: Zondervan, 1980), 265–304. What is significant about this volume is that it sought to explain the Chicago Statement on Inerrancy.

other in what I like to call a "divide and conquer" strategy. The implicit
assumption is that one Gospel writer says something different to challenge
what another Gospel writer has said. Yet these Gospel texts show a literary
and historical flexibility that some suggest belies such an adversarial understanding. In addition, the way ancients saw history and related events with
variation tells us that we should be slow to make the assumption of a contrary
stance behind differences in detail. Our simple question is whether the texts
and their details warrant such a skeptical reading of the relationship between
these texts. We are considering whether an author's expression and intention
permit a distinction between precision and accuracy when compared with
accounts from another author.

## Ancient Biography

When we think about the Gospels, there sometimes is debate about the genre
of this material. There was a time when this material was considered unique
in its literary orientation. However, recently a consensus has emerged that the
Gospels are a form of ancient *bios*.[3] This is not the same as modern biography,
in which issues of personality and psychological description often dominate.
In ancient biography actions and sayings are the focus of the portrayal. The
timing of events is of less concern than the fact that they happened. Sometimes
figures from distinct periods can be juxtaposed in ways that compare how they
acted.[4] The model of the figure that explains his greatness and presents him as
one worthy of imitation stands at the core of such a presentation. The central
figure in a *bios* often is inspiring. The presentation of Jesus in the Gospels fits
this general goal. Who the person was emerges from the portrait. It is seen as
more central and more interesting than personal details about the figure in
question. To assess what we have in the Gospels we need to appreciate what
we are being given. This genre background is our starting point.

## Testimony in Event Telling: Variation and Core Consistency

If anything shows how variation of detail can work while keeping the gist
of the story the same, it is the threefold telling of the story of Saul's (Paul's)
conversion on the road to Damascus in Acts (Acts 9, 22, 26). What makes this
such an appropriate example is that it clearly involves multiple versions of the
same scene. It also involves the same author. This kind of variation indicates

---

[3]Richard Burridge, *What Are the Gospels? A Comparison with Greco-Roman Biography* (Cambridge:
Cambridge University Press, 1992).
[4]One thinks here of the comparisons between great Greek and Roman figures that Plutarch's *Lives*
was responsible for presenting.

how a basically oral ancient culture told and retold stories. A comparison makes for some interesting observations.

In the third telling, in Acts 26, we get no mention of Paul's blindness or of Ananias, who is a key figure in earlier versions. If we had this account alone and took the method of some critics, we might argue, coming across one of the earlier versions somewhere else, that Ananias was a church creation of some kind. Other parts of the story are completely consistent. Jesus accuses Saul of having persecuted him when he attacked the church. The scene impresses upon Paul that Jesus has been raised. It details the account of the Lord's direct revelatory appearing, about which Paul tells us so little in Galatians 1. This third telling illustrates something we should never forget. Luke illustrates that New Testament authors do not write in a vacuum of information. There is an oral tradition circulating in the churches. Basic stories and events may well have been known. What additional tellings supplied were additional perspective and detail. These tellings are selective, as we can see in this case, where the same writer telling the same story nevertheless tells it with some variation. He does not do so to suggest that one version is better or more accurate than another. He does it to enhance what may already be known about core events. Each telling is designed to add perspective and angles to what may already be known in brief. The Gospels are likely meant to work this way if one recalls that oral versions of what Jesus taught and did likely circulated before these Gospels were written.

Comparing the accounts through what is said in Acts 22 is also interesting. The appearance began with a great heavenly light at about noon (26:13). Acts 22:11 speaks of the blindness that emerged in the day, a possible allusion to Deuteronomy 28:28–29 and a sign that disobedience is now being addressed. No time for the appearance is given in Acts 9, so this is a new detail in verse 6. In addition, the reference to the greatness of the light intensifies the account of Acts 9. Here we learn that the light was brighter than the midday sun. This was no dream or vision. A different term to describe the "glory" (*doxēs*) of the risen Jesus is used in Acts 9:3 (*phōs*, "light"). The reference to glory or light explains the source of Paul's blindness as an external, not an internal, event.

Much of Acts 22:6–11 repeats 9:3–8. With Saul prostrate on the ground, a voice asked why Saul persecuted him. This led to the disclosure that the heavenly voice addressing Saul belonged to "Jesus of Nazareth, whom you are persecuting." The addition of a reference to Nazareth intensifies the remark by highlighting Jesus's earthly roots. Those present at the incident on the Damascus road saw a light but heard no voice, a probable reference to not comprehending rather than not hearing the voice, since 9:7 indicates that a voice, or at least sound, was heard. Wallace notes that an alleged distinction in meaning based on a difference in case for *phōnē* ("voice," here accusative but genitive in 9:7) does not work because there are too many exceptions to the rule (Matt. 2:9; Acts 3:23; Matt. 13:19; Acts 5:24, to name but a few).[5] It is overinterpretation to suggest that Acts 9:7 says that they did not see the light whereas here it says they did. After all, we have the same author for both accounts. All that is said here is that they did not see anyone. For those with Saul, there was neither an appearance nor a revelation. The point is that the others knew something happened and that Saul did not have a merely inner, psychological experience. Those with Paul, however, did not know exactly what took place. Saul responded with a question about what he should do. This adds to what Acts 9 relates. In addressing Jesus as Lord, he was indicating his respect for Jesus; here he was not concerned with how his Jewish audience would take this, since in this context its meaning is ambiguous as an address of respect to a superior. Jesus told Saul what would happen. In Damascus Saul would hear about what he stood appointed (*tetaktai*) to do. The perfect-tense verb indicates that Paul was part of an established divine plan. In the later account at 26:16, Saul was given a commission at this point. Next Paul related that he was blind from the brightness of the glory of the light. This refers to the brightness of the Shekinah (2 Cor. 4:4–6). Those who were with him led Saul to Damascus. This is another intensified description, as Acts 9 implies but does not directly state that brightness was the cause of Saul's blindness. Paul then speaks about the role of Ananias (9:13–14), a devout man according to the law and well spoken of by the Jews. He was the one through whom the Lord restored his sight. It may well be that the mention of Ananias the believer here is why the high priest Ananias is not named earlier, so that no confusion would result. The note about Ananias's character shows that others who respected the law were responsive to Jesus. In 9:10 Ananias is described as a believer. Acts 22 lacks any mention of a vision to Ananias. So the Acts 22 version has many differences in detail from Acts 9. This is an example of variation in event telling in the ancient world.

Such a comparison of readings advises us to be careful in how we fill in gaps when accounts differ. We should be especially hesitant to pit accounts against each other. One version will inevitably be more precise than another at points, but that does not mean either account is wrong. One can be accurate without being precise.

---

[5]Daniel Wallace, *Greek Grammar Beyond the Basics: An Exegetical Syntax of the New Testament* (Grand Rapids: Zondervan, 1996), 133–34.

## Sayings Variation: *Ipsissima Verba* and *Vox* in Parallel Versions

I have fully developed the category of variation between parallel versions in an essay noted earlier. I will summarize here. If we consider differences in wording at John's baptism of Jesus or in Peter's confession at Caesarea Philippi or in the words at the Last Supper, we can see the same principle of variation and gist. I select three examples involving three different speakers to show that the issue is not who is speaking. We are dealing with a kind of convention. Did the voice at the baptism speak directly to Jesus or more generally about him ("this is my beloved Son" versus "you are my beloved Son")? One of the writers is likely giving the significance of what took place (probably Matthew with his "this"). Did Peter speak of Jesus as Son of God, as only Matthew 16:16 notes, or is the core confession that Jesus is the Christ, as all three versions suggest? The Christ confession is likely key, and "Son of God" may go back to Peter or may reflect the force of that christological confession, since the King is Son. Did Jesus speak explicitly of the new covenant (Luke 22:20) or only of a covenant established by his death (Matt. 26:28)?

Either way the provision of the forgiveness of sins points to the new covenant. If Matthew omitted the reference to the new covenant, he is less precise but still accurate. If "new" is an explanation added by Luke, then the evangelist makes explicit what is implicit. Either way, each is accurate, even if one version is the more precise. Ironically, the precision may go both ways! It may be more precise historically that Jesus alluded only indirectly to the new covenant in his exact words, but it may be more precise theologically for the reference to the new covenant to be identified explicitly because it was implied. This shows how complex writing a Gospel that sought to explain Jesus was.

## "Updated" Sayings: A Possible Example from the Olivet Discourse

Another example comes to us from the beginning of the Olivet Discourse. Many who are familiar with this passage know that there is debate about how much of the text applies to AD 70 and how much is relevant to the return of Jesus. Part of the debate surfaces as a result of how the discourse begins. Mark 13:4 states the opening query this way: "Tell us, when will these things be, and what will be the sign when all these things are about to be accomplished?" Luke 21:7 has, "Teacher, when will these things be, and what will be the sign when these things are about to take place?" As we can see, Mark and Luke are very close, asking essentially the same question. Compare this with Matthew 24:3, which reads, "Tell us, when will these things be, and what

will be the sign of your coming and of the end of the age?" One can see how
Matthew's question is much more focused on the end and the return. But
there is another issue here. How could the disciples have asked about Jesus's
coming if they were not yet grasping the resurrection?

There are two ways to think about this question. One is that Jesus's description of the destruction of the temple led the disciples to think Jesus was
discussing the end. That is quite possible, since Jerusalem was at the center
of Second Temple hope, as a reading of *Psalms of Solomon* 17–18 shows.
In that text, Messiah will purge Jerusalem when he vindicates the saints and
brings righteousness. However, even when read in this light, it seems likely
that a reader of Matthew's Gospel would be thinking of the second coming
or return of Jesus, something the disciples did not yet have a category for
as a matter of their faith. So the second option is that Matthew has simply
updated the force of the question, introducing the idea of the end as the topic
Jesus implied by his remark about the temple.

Either option is possible. The point I am raising is that something is going on
between the versions in Mark and Luke in comparison to Matthew. Matthew
24:3 seems to me to be a good example of a summarized saying. In effect,
Matthew has taken the question as it was in Mark and Luke and has presented
what the disciples essentially were asking, even if they did not appreciate all
the implications in the question at the time. This is true about the wording of
Matthew's question no matter which option we take for explaining the difference in wording. Whether the disciples say the end is in view or Matthew is
drawing that out as inherent in the question asked, the point is that Matthew
has made the focus of the question clearer than the more ambiguous way it
is asked in Mark and Luke.[6]

There is an irony in this way of thinking about this text. In one sense,
Mark and Luke may be giving us the more precise wording of the question.
However, Matthew may actually be giving us the more precise force and point
of the question, now paraphrased in light of a fuller understanding of what
Jesus's career was to look like. So here the difference between accuracy and
precision depends on whether we focus on the wording or on the actual force
of the question. In the end, both wordings are important and accurate, just
in distinct ways.

---

[6]One could perhaps suggest that Matthew has merely selected an additional thing said at the time
versus Mark's and Luke's opening question, but the historical tension remains whether the disciples
asked this explicitly or Matthew has paraphrased the question's force from Mark and Luke. The key
here is recognizing that a "second" coming was not yet in the disciples' frame of reference.

## Use of Old Testament in New Testament

Another example where some see errors but where we need to exercise more care about describing what is really taking place involves the use of the Old Testament in the New. It is well known that numerous uses of the Old Testament in the New have variations of wording from the Hebrew text, often in the direction of the LXX, a natural move in that the Greek version fits the language of the materials being written. These examples can be traced in detail by examining the volume edited by Greg Beale and Donald Carson, *Commentary on the New Testament Use of the Old Testament*.[7] I want to highlight one often brought forward in this discussion, the use of Malachi 3:1 in Mark 1:2–3. It is often claimed that what Mark introduces as from Isaiah is in fact a fused citation, in part from Malachi and also from Isaiah 40, and so Mark has been sloppy and made an error. This claim misses what is taking place in the text. The fused citation, which we do have here, uses a technique known as *gezerah shewa*, where two passages are linked because they share a word. In Greek, the link is the term *hodon* ("way"), which reflects a Hebrew *derek*. However, there also is a *gezerah shewa* with the exposition that follows in Mark 1:4. The expression "in the wilderness" (*en tē erēmō*) is both in the Isaiah citation and in Mark's exposition. What this means is that Mark is expounding only the portion of the citation from Isaiah.[8] This means that by highlighting the introductory phrase as he does, he is accurately reflecting his exposition. There is no error. Mark is precise in pointing to the part of the citation that interests him most.

## Issues of Story-Telling Choices

Details in parallel accounts often raise questions within the Gospels. I select a few key examples here for attention, while noting that the question of what each detail addresses may affect how the detail is judged.

### The Healing of the Centurion's Son

Two accounts that are clearly parallel and that have a major difference involve the healing of the centurion's son in Capernaum. Describing the same event, Matthew 8:5–13 follows the Sermon on the Mount, and Luke 7:1–10 follows the Sermon on the Plain. Matthew has the centurion speaking to Jesus directly, while Luke has Jewish emissaries speaking to Jesus, and the centurion never talks directly with Jesus. So what is taking place here?

---

[7] Grand Rapids: Baker Academic, 2007.
[8] Note how this explanation adds more detail to the possibilities noted by Rikk E. Watts, "Mark," in Beale and Carson, *Commentary on the New Testament Use of the Old Testament*, 114.

Two things are happening at once. The cultural context of the sent emissary (*shaliach*) and literary compression are both in play. Matthew often compresses accounts. For example, his telling of the healing of Jairus's daughter is more compact, as is his telling of the triumphal entry (see, e.g., Matt. 9:18–26; 21:18–19 and parallels: Luke 8:49; Mark 11:20–21).[9] Luke, given his concern for Jew-Gentile relations, offers more detail by noting the representatives. When the *shaliach*, as an emissary, spoke on behalf of someone, it was as good as that person speaking. Jesus said as much of his disciples when he said that to accept the disciples was to accept him (John 13:20; also 2 Kings 19:20–34). A modern analogy would be how a press secretary speaks for the White House and the president. So Luke gives us the detail of the event, and Matthew simplifies its telling by compressing things literarily. Each account is accurate, but Luke's is more precise.

### Abiathar

Another text often brought forward as a problem is the reference to Abiathar as high priest when David took the showbread in Mark 2:26. This detail presented enough of a problem that the other Gospels omit it, and no obvious solution is present. However, two suggestions have been made. One is that the reference is to the section of Scripture in which Abiathar is the key high priest (recalling that chapters and verses were added later), and thus this identifies the general location of the passage. This view, while subtle in assuming a kind of literary shorthand, is plausible. Another option is to argue that the Greek reflects an Aramaic idiom meaning "in the time of Abiathar the high priest," so the point is not that Abiathar was the high priest when this took place but that he was alive at the time. This has been proposed by Maurice Casey.[10] He notes that some manuscripts have an additional article, *tou*, before the reference to the high priest and may reflect this idiom (A, C, Θ, family 13). In this case, the detail points to either a literary or an idiomatic expression and is not an error.

### Chronology of the Resurrection Appearance in John

Another issue that some raise is how the resurrection account in John differs from accounts in the Synoptics. A key figure, Mary Magdalene, leads those who inform the disciples of the empty tomb in the Synoptics after being told Jesus was raised. Luke 24:4 and John 23:13 have this announcement begin with two angels, Matthew 28:5 speaks about an angel, and Mark 16:5 has

---

[9]Only his citing of Zechariah makes the entry account appear as long.
[10]*Aramaic Sources of Mark's Gospel*, SNTSMS 102 (Cambridge: Cambridge University Press, 1998), 151–52.

a young man tell them. Yet in John Mary is perplexed and does not know where the body is until Jesus appears to her, a scene described after John and Peter have run to the tomb. These differences suggest several versions of these events. More than one tradition is at work here.

The opening of the appearance accounts with women is important since in that culture women could not be witnesses. Josephus, in *Antiquities* 4.19, speaks of not allowing women to be witnesses because of the temerity of their sex. In the Mishnah, an oath of testimony applies to men but not women (*m. Shevu'ot* 4:1; *m. Rosh HaShanah* 1:8). The later Talmud speaks of a woman as disqualified from bringing evidence (*b. Bava Qamma* 88a). This important cultural background implies that one would not invent a story to teach a controversial belief like the resurrection and use women to be the lead witnesses; they must have actually been there at the event.

So what is one to make of these differences? My own understanding is that part of the issue is resolved by seeing that John's telling begins with how John and Peter experienced the event. John has Mary begin her report even though John and Peter do not wait for her to tell her whole story but run to check the empty tomb. Then John tells in detail what Mary experienced. John's mention that the women did not know where the body was placed is where their report to him begins, but the report did not get as far as the messenger's announcement of Jesus's resurrection before Peter and John departed to see what had taken place. This is all collapsed in the Synoptics into the women's report to the group about the announcement of an empty tomb. John often supplements the Synoptics with fresh details that overlap the accounts of the other evangelists. Likewise here, literary arrangement and choices are the keys to differences in sequencing.

### Filling in Gaps: The Sayings on the Cross in Luke and Mark

Another difference tied to Jesus's death involves what he said from the cross. This issue has been highlighted by Bart Ehrman in his work *Jesus Interrupted* and even appeared in Amazon's promotional video for his book. Ehrman argues that in Mark 15:34, when Jesus cries out, "My God, my God, why have you forsaken me," using Psalm 22, we have an agonizing Jesus going to his death, while in Luke 23:46 we have Jesus calmly uttering a statement of trust from Psalm 31:5. Ehrman sees two different Jesuses portrayed here, one struggling in the midst of suffering and the other confident. We are to choose between the two.

Ehrman fails to indicate to his readers the significance of several key facts pertaining to this example: (1) Most scholars agree that Luke used Mark. On this, Ehrman and I concur, but he does not apply Luke's use of Mark to the sayings on the cross. I will show why that is important below. (2) Mark speaks of a second cry from the cross in his account, but does not give its content. (3) Jesus in Mark (and in the Mark that Luke works with) is predicting his death and choosing to face his death long before the pain of the cross. Jesus knows what he is facing and goes there following God's will. Predictions of this show up as early as Mark 8. (4) In fact, Jesus, in Mark 14:62, supplies the very testimony against himself at the Jewish trial scene that leads into his crucifixion, hardly the act of a completely despairing man. I make this last point because Ehrman denies that the citation of Psalm 22:1 may point to the whole psalm, which ends with a word of trust. This example of reading both the psalm and Mark reflects the very flat, excessively literal fundamentalist way of handling the text Ehrman often criticizes others for using. In the midst of discussing Luke, Ehrman claims that Luke has no substitution of sin in Jesus's theology, ignoring the explicit statement in Acts 20:28 (remember, we are discussing Luke's theology as the basis for his changes in Mark). Another feature of Ehrman's approach is that he consistently appeals to what are possible readings of texts in combination while chiding those who combine texts differently and more harmoniously. It is significant to recall that we are speaking of Gospel writers who respected each other enough to be using each other's material.

I would claim three things from this example: (1) Luke does highlight Jesus's control of the situation to a degree that Mark does not (so Ehrman and I agree on this point). However, conservatives have affirmed the different emphases between Gospel writers for years (I even wrote a book that worked through this called *Jesus according to Scripture*), and numerous commentaries by scholars (not all conservative) could see such differences without going on to create the theological distance Ehrman does between Mark and Luke. (2) Luke, knowing of the second cry in Mark, supplies what else Jesus said in a process, not unlike a lawyer or an investigator following up on such a detail. Now, we could debate whether Luke made up the second saying (as I suspect Ehrman might argue) or whether he had access to sources (as I am inclined to think), but my point is that one can easily read Luke as supplementing Mark here, not completely rejecting Mark's portrait of Jesus. Luke could do so while omitting reference to Psalm 22:1 because its content was already known from Mark. It is important to note that Luke's placement of this utterance comes at the spot where the second cry comes in Mark. (3) The theologies are not as diverse as Ehrman claims. Rather what we have are complementary emphases. Mark shows Jesus going triumphantly to his death while genuinely and fully suffering as an example to us. (If Jesus is as despairing as Ehrman suggests, then Jesus ceases to be the example Mark sets forth.) Luke shows Jesus in control, which other passages in Mark also indicate. Jesus spent several hours on the cross. Differing time frames in terms of when actions are being described contribute to the impression of a difference here. However, the result is not really as distinct as Ehrman contends. Mark notes the cry of suffering made, while Luke shows Jesus trusting later in the sequence. One need not choose between the portraits. Each account is accurate, and both together give us more detail than either by itself.

## Issues of Description

### Mark and Hand Washing

Understanding rhetoric can be important in dealing with the text. In Mark 7:3–5, the Gospel states that the "Pharisees and all the Jews do not eat unless they wash their hands properly, holding to the tradition of the elders, and when they come from the market place, they do not eat unless they wash. And there are many other traditions that they observe, such as the washing of cups and pots and copper vessels" (vv. 3–4). Now, many accuse Mark of being inaccurate here because he refers to all Jews. But we are simply dealing with rhetorical hyperbole. "All" is a way of saying most Jews. Mark's point is that the question about the disciples' failure to wash is motivated by the fact that Jews normally do wash, out of concern for purity. Interestingly, it was long thought that such observance was more prevalent in Judea than in Galilee, to the north. However, recent archaeological work in Galilee shows that numerous stone vessels have been found in various communities (Sepphoris, Jotapata, Gamala) pointing to a popular concern to keep, at least to some degree, this practice.[11] In light of this widespread Jewish practice, the disciples' unwashed hands gave pause to observers. This is all that Mark intends. His use of language is not uncommon. In Romans Paul speaks of all Israel being saved where he means not every single Israelite, but the vast majority in contrast to the current remnant of believers (Rom. 11:26).

### Luke's Census

The discussion of a census in Luke 2:1–2 is one of the most difficult problems in the Gospels, since Luke attaches the census to Quirinius (AD 6), who ruled almost a decade after Jesus was born (on the assumption that Jesus's birth was near the time of Herod the Great's death in 4 BC). Herod's death is tied to an

---

[11] See the discussion by Sean Freyne, "Archaeology and the Historical Jesus," in *Jesus and Archaeology*, ed. James H. Charlesworth (Grand Rapids: Eerdmans, 2006), 75–77. Also at the possible site of Cana, in the same volume, Urban C. von Wahlde, "Archaeology and John's Gospel," 540 n. 40.

eclipse, which allows us to date it fairly precisely in ancient terms (Josephus, *Antiquities* 17.167). I have discussed this census issue at length elsewhere.[12] I summarize here.

Once again we meet the use of hyperbole when Luke says that Augustus undertook a worldwide census. We have evidence that Augustus undertook to register the empire regions over a long period of time.[13] This description is collapsed into the claim of an empire-wide registration. Josephus tells us of the innovation of this census in the time of Quirinius, an act that caused riots (*Antiquities* 17.342–44, 355; 18.1–10). Various approaches to this passage see its remarks as accurate. Some appeal to a grammatical solution so that Luke merely claims the census began before Quirinius was governor. This is possible, though reading the Greek this way is not the normal way to render the sequence. Second, some suggest that Quirinius was not governor at the time but oversaw the census in question (much as we might speak of a "president" even in reference to a time before he assumed that title). The problem with this explanation is that the timing of the census still seems too early. A third option is to note that the collection and administration of the census took several years and was finalized under Quirinius. His name thus became tied to its direct collection of taxes, which is what made it controversial. After all, things did not move as fast in the ancient world as they do in ours.

Though these options do not yield a clear favorite, they suggest that it is premature to declare "error" in this example.

## Issues of Chronology and Geography

### Transfiguration

The transfiguration is not a difficult example, but it illustrates the sense of chronology that the ancients had. In Mark 9:1–2, the timing of the transfiguration is placed at six days after Jesus's teaching that some would not die before they see the kingdom. In Luke 9:28, this event appears after "about eight days." What is interesting about this difference is that Luke is usually seen as being written with a prior knowledge of Mark. So the less specific timing appears in the later version of the account. Did Luke follow a different tradition on the timing? No one knows. Again the difference is that one rendering is more precise than the other, but neither is inaccurate, since one

---

[12]*Luke 1:1–9:50*, BECNT (Grand Rapids: Baker, 1994), 903–9.
[13]Egypt was even on a fourteen-year cycle and other censuses beyond these three took place in the empire throughout the century, suggesting that this process took time to implement (D. J. Hayles, "The Roman Census and Jesus' Birth; Was Luke Correct? Part 1," *BurH* 9 [1973]: 113–32, esp. 120–29, and "Part 2," *BurH* 10 [1974]: 16–31).

is an approximation. Nothing in the difference changes the core story about Jesus's revealing his glory to some of the disciples.

### Last Supper and Crucifixion

One of the more famous and most discussed differences in chronology deals with the timing of the Last Supper and the crucifixion. In Mark 14:12 we are told that the supper took place on the first day of unleavened bread, when they sacrificed the Passover lamb (also Luke 22:15 goes in this direction, referring to this Passover). Part of what is taking place is that the Passover (Nisan 14) and unleavened bread (Nisan 15 and the following week) were celebrated one right after the other, so that both names became attached to the feast (Josephus, *Jewish War* 5.99, speaks of the feast of unleavened bread on Nisan 14). The very way in which these dates and feasts are handled shows that proximate dating could be used. The problem is that John 19:14 and 31 have Jesus crucified on the Passover preparation day, which appears to be a day after the meal portrayed in the Synoptics as the Passover meal.[14] This is a complex problem, as a detailed study by Howard Marshall shows.[15]

Several proposals deal with the difference without seeing an error. Some posit the use of two calendars or of differences in the reckoning of a day, with each Gospel writer selecting a different reckoning.[16] This is possible, but there is no clear evidence for a difference in calendar at this point in Second Temple history (though we do have some evidence for it later in certain cases); nor is it clear that the evangelists reckoned days differently, although they could have done so.[17] So this two-calendar solution may explain the difference, but it is not clearly demonstrable. Others argue that the Synoptics are correct, and that the day of preparation in John 19 refers not to the Passover day but to the sacrifice of the Sabbath of Passover week (which was the next day with a Friday crucifixion).[18] Again this option is possible, but it is not the most natural reading of the text. Others, favoring John's chronology but accepting the synoptic sense of the meal, suggest that the meal has a Passover feel to it or was presented like a Passover even though it was not technically a Passover

---

[14]V. 14 is explicit in mentioning the Passover preparation day, while v. 31 speaks only of the day of preparation.

[15]I. Howard Marshall, "The Last Supper," in *Key Events in the Life of the Historical Jesus*, ed. Darrell L. Bock and Robert L. Webb, WUNT 247 (Tübingen: Mohr Siebeck, 2009), 481–588, esp. 549–60.

[16]Harold Hoehner, "Chronology," in *Dictionary of Jesus and the Gospels*, 120–21; David Instone-Brewer, "Jesus' Last Passover: The Synoptics and John," *ExpTim* 112 (2001): 122–23.

[17]M *Zebaḥ* 1:3 seems to suggest a debate about when to sacrifice all of these lambs and allows for an early start. Technically the early offerings were called peace offerings, but they were tied to the Passover as well. Instone-Brewer, "Jesus' Last Passover," notes this issue.

[18]Joachim Jeremias, *The Eucharistic Words of Jesus*, trans. Norman Perrin, NTL (London: SCM, 1966), 81–82.

meal offered on the official day.[19] Once again, this is feasible, but there is no direct evidence for this practice.

Where does this leave us? Two approaches may work. The early sacrifice may explain what is taking place, or John's preparation may refer to the Sabbath preparation. If the latter is the point, then Jesus is crucified in the midst of the Passover season, not on the day of Passover, and the meal was a Passover meal, just as the Synoptics present it. This can work in the sense that the entire period is associated with the Passover. A modern analogy would be that people celebrate Christmas office parties on many days other than Christmas. Such associations are popular in orientation and not technical. Thus Jesus is crucified in the midst of the Passover season, with his death connected to a Passover meal, and he is seen as crucified with a Passover significance. It may be that rather than trying to work out all the technical details, we are better off to regard the season as appealed to in a popular ancient manner and the association made that way. It may be that one of these options or a combination of them offers a solution even though demonstrating that is difficult. A less technical approach allows for a distinction between accuracy and precision in what is a popular reckoning of a generalized ancient chronology.

### An Example in Geography: Gerasene or Gadarene

Competing references to the Gadarenes and the Gerasenes raise questions about which text is the superior reading in each case and then about the resultant meaning. The textual evidence I have treated in full elsewhere.[20] In summary, Gadara is the locale noted in Matthew 8:28, while Gerasa looks slightly more likely in Mark 5:1. The Lucan testimony is more complicated, but appears to agree with Mark. Where ℵ* and B line up with *Gadara*, the same plus D read *Gerasa* in Mark, and the same with p[75] read *Gerasa* in Luke 8:26.[21] It is important to appreciate that Gadara is the administrative center in the region opposite the Galilee, while Gerasa is another well-known locale in the area. The problem is the locale of Gerasa (modern Jerash in Jordan). It is more than twenty miles southeast of the Sea of Galilee in the Decapolis, too far away to be the scene of the swine running into the sea. So some argue that there is an error of location in either the Gerasa or the Gadara reference.

---

[19]Scot McKnight, *Jesus and His Death* (Waco, TX: Baylor University Press, 2005), 271–73.
[20]Bock, *Luke 1:1–9:50*, 782–84.
[21]ℵ, B, and D are key early (fourth-century) manuscripts for the Gospels of Matthew, Mark, and Luke. ℵ* reflects the original hand of the manuscript, as ℵ also appears with corrections by a later scribe that give a different reading. We do not know the date of the later hand. So ℵ* and B have one location (Gadara) in Matthew, but read Geresa in Mark and Luke. The Lucan manuscript p75 is also early, coming from the third century.

Now, some manuscripts ($\aleph^a$ for example) and Origen speak of the locale as Gergesa, also known as Kursi, situated right next to the sea. If this is the locale intended, there is no issue. The testimony for this location, however, is late.

Let us assume that the reading is distributed in a manner whereby Gadara and Gerasa are present in the different versions. What is happening? We do not know for sure, but one option is that the man was from one locale and the healing took place in a locale tied to that region, since we know that the man had left his home to roam in the countryside. Remember the references are regional, since the texts speak of the country of the locale (Matt. 8:28; Mark 5:1; Luke 8:26). So the authors or their tradition may have selected different names for the same regional locale. This is no different than identifying where you are from in terms of a well-known city in your general vicinity rather than the exact but lesser-known town. It is analogous to someone telling you that an event took place in Dallas–Fort Worth when it occurred in Denton, Texas. One is a better-known locale than the other, and yet the smaller city is thirty miles from Dallas while still in the region of the event. We commonly do this sort of thing when we are not sure someone will be able to place the lesser-known locale. Measured against intent and a popular manner of communicating, one reference may be slightly less precise, but regionally accurate and even more informative. The Gerasa reference is more informative in showing the association of the man with the Decapolis and not just with Galilee.

## Summary: Harmonizing or Playing the Gospels against Each Other

We have considered a whole series of examples in a variety of areas. The same distinction between accuracy and precision comes up again and again. Many examples fit into an ancient, popular way of communicating in which general accuracy is actually preferable to precision. When parallel accounts are compared, one version is more precise. However, this does not mean the other version is in error. The author has intended a more generalized description, and the text should be evaluated and appreciated that way.

# 17

# PAUL, TIMOTHY, AND TITUS

*The Assumption of a Pseudonymous Author
and of Pseudonymous Recipients in the Light
of Literary, Theological, and Historical Evidence*

## ECKHARD J. SCHNABEL

Despite the pressure of majority opinion, the assumption of the pseudonymity of the letters to Timothy and Titus (called Pastoral Epistles) has weaker support than the assumption of authenticity. Literary, theological, and historical evidence supports Pauline authorship, particularly when the three letters are evaluated separately rather than as a corpus. The largely accepted notion that pseudonymous writing was an acceptable literary practice in antiquity—for example when the teaching or the authority of a school head was confirmed and defended by a later follower—proves to be incorrect. Writings that appeared under a pseudonymous name were not accepted as classic or authoritative texts but rejected as forgeries. The authorship of the letters to Timothy and Titus has significant consequences for their status in the New Testament canon as the church's Scripture.

## The Power of Majorities

Majority positions can be a powerful reality, especially if a hypothesis is deemed to have been verified and thus is thought worthy of acceptance as true. The view that the New Testament letters to Timothy and to Titus have been written not by Paul but by a later writer who uses "Paul" as a pseudonym, first suggested in the nineteenth century by the German critics J. E. C. Schmidt, F. D. E. Schleiermacher, J. G. Eichhorn, and F. C. Baur,[1]

---

[1] Johann E. C. Schmidt, *Historisch-Kritische Einleitung ins Neue Testament*, 2 vols. (Gießen: Töpelmann, 1804–1805); Friedrich Daniel E. Schleiermacher, *Werke* (Berlin: Reimer, 1834–1856); Schleiermacher, *Über den sogenannten ersten Brief des Paulus an den Timotheos* (Berlin:

and "proven" in the nearly three hundred pages of introduction of H. J. Holtzmann's commentary on the Pastoral Epistles,[2] has become a majority view in academic study and exerts as such a powerful influence. This can be seen in the stance of authors who note that some (conservatives) continue to argue against pseudonymity but then point out that "the consensus of New Testament historical scholarship is against authenticity."[3] Some scholars, mostly in Germany, regard the discussion as "closed" and the attempt to argue for authenticity as a "rearguard action" that evidently is not worthy of considered discussion.[4] Luke Timothy Johnson is correct when he states that "little real discussion of the issue of authenticity still occurs." He reminds his readers that the current academic consensus "resulted as much from social dynamics as from the independent assessment of the evidence by each individual scholar."[5]

The power of the academic consensus is seen in authors who review with consistent fairness the arguments for and against the authenticity of the Pastoral Epistles and who are not convinced by the arguments adduced against their authenticity, but who cannot bring themselves to accept their authenticity. One example is the treatment of the Pastoral Epistles in *An Introduction to the New Testament,* by David deSilva, who prefaces his discussion with the statement that "the Pauline authorship of these letters is widely rejected in favor of pseudonymity" while only a minority—albeit a "respected" one— "still argues for their authenticity."[6] After an extensive presentation of the evidence and the arguments, deSilva does not want to make up his mind: he holds that there is "enough doubt to prevent us from blithely assuming Pauline authorship," and he believes that "it is presumptuous to discount the

Realschulbuchhandlung, 1807), in Schleiermacher, *Werke,* 2:223–24; Johann Gottfried Eichhorn, *Einleitung in das Neue Testament,* 5 vols. (Leipzig: Weidmann, 1804–1812), 3/1:315–28; Ferdinand Christian Baur, *Die sogenannten Pastoralbriefe des Apostels Paulus aufs neue kritisch untersucht* (Stuttgart: Cotta, 1835).

[2]Heinrich J. Holtzmann, *Die Pastoralbriefe kritisch und exegetisch bearbeitet* (Leipzig: Engelmann, 1880), 1–282. Jürgen Roloff, *Der erste Brief an Timotheus,* EKK 15 (Zürich: Benzinger; Neukirchen-Vluyn: Neukirchner, 1988), 24, is impressed with Holtzmann's ability to "destroy" the arguments of the proponents of the authenticity of the Pastoral Epistles and to prove "in a convincing manner" the "impossibility of Pauline authorship of these letters."

[3]Frances Margaret Young, *The Theology of the Pastoral Letters,* New Testament Theology (Cambridge: Cambridge University Press, 1994), 23 n. 40.

[4]Annette Merz, *Die fiktive Selbstauslegung des Paulus: Intertextuelle Studien zur Intention und Rezeption der Pastoralbriefe,* NTOA 52 (Göttingen: Vandenhoeck & Ruprecht, 2004), 72; she mentions English and American authors who still argue for authenticity, and she voices surprise that "even" the commentary on the letters to Timothy that appeared in the Anchor Bible series subscribes to Pauline authorship.

[5]Luke T. Johnson, *The First and Second Letters to Timothy,* AB 35A (New York: Doubleday, 2001), 55.

[6]David A. deSilva, *An Introduction to the New Testament: Contexts, Methods and Ministry Formation* (Downers Grove, IL: InterVarsity, 2004), 733; the following quotations are from 747–48.

possibility that Paul did write these letters in some sense," suggesting that "students of these letters should investigate the evidence more fully." While it is always wise counsel to continue to investigate the evidence and weigh the arguments, a "skyhook solution" that suspends a verdict on the available evidence is hardly satisfying.

The attempt of some scholars to appear evenhanded is less than convincing. In their work *Introducing the New Testament: Its Literature and Theology*, Paul Achtemeier, Joel Green, and Marianne Meye Thompson rehearse the arguments that scholars cite for a pseudonymous author of the Pastoral Epistles, but not the arguments for Pauline authorship.[7] Such a procedure characterizes many critics who reject the authenticity of the Pastoral Epistles without giving the proponents of authenticity a fair hearing.[8] When Achtemeier, Green, and Thompson suggest that "perhaps the author of the Pastorals was a student of Paul or a member of his circle," they agree with the many who "deem it unlikely that the apostle wrote these three letters." But they fail to inform their readers that the verdict of many is not merely "unlikely" but impossible. The qualifier "certainty in this matter is simply not available" is curious in the context of their suggestion that the Pastorals were written "probably [in] the last third of the first century, after the death of Paul." If certainty is not available, then speculation about the date and context of the composition of these letters is moot. Since the authors venture suggestions about the author, date, and context of the Pastorals in a post-Pauline setting, they evidently side with the "many" who reject Pauline authorship. The fact that they do not describe potential contexts in a Pauline setting suggests that their statement that certainty about authorship is not possible is a tactical maneuver rather than the informed commitment to a scholarly position that informs the presentation of the evidence.

The stakes are high. Some have suggested that the anonymous author of the Pastoral Epistles employed pseudonymity as an accepted literary device that was not meant to deceive anyone: the author's readers recognized his decision to write under the assumed name of Paul as a way of affirming and emphasizing the significance of Pauline tradition.[9] Jürgen Roloff rejects

---

[7]Paul J. Achtemeier, Joel B. Green, and Marianne Meye Thompson, *Introducing the New Testament: Its Literature and Theology* (Grand Rapids: Eerdmans, 2001), 461–634; quotations in this paragraph are from 463–64.

[8]Examples are the commentaries of Roloff, *Der erste Brief an Timotheus*, 23–39; Alfons Weiser, *Der zweite Brief an Timotheus*, EKK 16/1 (Zürich: Benzinger; Neukirchen-Vluyn: Neukirchner, 2003), 51–63.

[9]This is the main thesis of David G. Meade, *Pseudonymity and Canon: An Investigation into the Relationship of Authorship and Authority in Jewish and Earliest Christian Tradition*, WUNT 39 (Tübingen: Mohr Siebeck, 1986).

this suggestion as a trivialization (*Verharmlosung*) that is not justified by any evidence.[10] Wolfgang Schenk demands the "de-canonization" of the Pastoral Epistles as inevitable.[11] Authors who retain a commitment to the church and to the concept of canon plead with their readers not to draw radical conclusions from the inauthentic character of the Pastoral Epistles. DeSilva argues that "inquiries into their authorship have no bearing on their status as sacred Scripture, for the church determined these *texts* to have been inspired."[12] Achtemeier, Green, and Thompson argue that

> it is simply not true, as one scholar has argued, that our judgment of their value depends on whether the person who wrote them was Paul or a disciple of Paul. These letters have been treasured by the worldwide Christian community for almost 2000 years and have proved of value regardless of their author.[13]

The options are the following. (1) The Pastoral Epistles were written by the apostle Paul to his coworkers Timothy and Titus, as asserted in 1 Timothy 1:1; 2 Timothy 1:1; and Titus 1:1. (2) The Pastoral Epistles were written in the name of Paul by a later Christian author who assumed that the identification of Paul as author would be recognized by his Christian readers as an act of respect and reverence for the great apostle. (3) The Pastoral Epistles were written by a later Christian author who deliberately misled his Christian readers about the authorship of these letters in order to have them accepted as authoritative. In the following discussion we will survey the linguistic, theological, and historical arguments that are central for the authenticity, or pseudonymity, of the Pastoral Epistles. We will conclude with a discussion of the consequences if these three letters are deemed to be pseudonymous.

## Literary Arguments

Under the factors that are relevant for authorship, the language and style of the Pastoral Epistles figure prominently. First, it is argued that the vocabulary

---

[10]Roloff, *Der erste Brief an Timotheus*, 37.

[11]Wolfgang Schenk, "Die Briefe an Timotheus I und II und an Titus (Pastoralbriefe) in der neueren Forschung (1945–1985)," *ANRW*, 2.25.4 (1987), 3404–38, 3428 n. 93.

[12]DeSilva, *An Introduction to the New Testament*, 736; similarly ibid., 748.

[13]Achtemeier, Green, and Thompson, *Introducing the New Testament*, 461. They neither identify the "one scholar" in the quotation nor inform their readers that there is more than one scholar who argues that pseudonymous writings do not deserve to be in the canon; cf. Stanley E. Porter, "Pauline Authorship and the Pastoral Epistles: Implications for Canon," *BBR* 5 (1995): 105–23; Porter, "Pauline Authorship and the Pastoral Epistles: A Response to R. W. Wall's Response," *BBR* 6 (1996): 133–38. Note the comment of Earle E. Ellis, *The Making of the New Testament Documents* (1999; repr., Leiden: Brill, 2002), 294 n. 306, on 2 Peter, whose Petrine authorship is disputed: "I was prepared, if need be, to live with a 26-book, New Testament canon since, if Peter is not the author, the book is clearly a blatant and pretentious forgery."

is different from that in Paul's letters: there is a higher frequency of words that otherwise do not occur in the New Testament; many conjunctions and particles that characterize Paul's letters are absent.[14] Second, the style of Greek is said to be different, considering matters such as the length of sentences and the positioning of words.[15] Third, the manner of argumentation is judged to be different from Paul's letters; for example, the author uses doctrinal material to confirm ethical exhortations whereas Paul is said to proceed from theological explication to ethical application.[16]

While many scholars take these arguments to be decisive in proving that the Pastoral Epistles cannot have been written by Paul,[17] others have remained unconvinced that the criterion of style presents a problem for Pauline authorship. The following arguments are important.[18]

First, the Pastoral Epistles are too small for (stylo)statistical analysis, which according to linguistic experts requires texts with at least 10,000 words.[19] The Pastoral Epistles together have only 3,488 words, which makes statistical analysis a problematic proposition.[20] Also, the fact that the vocabulary of the ten undisputed Pauline letters (2,301 words) is only a fraction of the total number of words in ancient Greek—the standard dictionary of classical Greek edited by H. G. Liddell, R. Scott, and H. S. Jones[21] has approximately

---

[14]Main studies in English include Percy Neale Harrison, *The Problem of the Pastoral Epistles* (Oxford: Oxford University Press, 1921); Kenneth Grayston and Gustav Herdan, "The Authorship of the Pastorals in the Light of Linguistic Statistics," *NTS* 6 (1959): 1–15.

[15]Cf. David L. Mealand, "Positional Stylometry Reassessed: Testing a Seven Epistle Theory of Pauline Authorship," *NTS* 35 (1989): 266–86; Kenneth J. Neumann, *The Authenticity of the Pauline Epistles in the Light of Stylostatistical Analysis*, SBLDS 120 (Atlanta: Scholars Press, 1990).

[16]Cf. Benjamin Fiore, *The Function of Personal Example in the Socratic and Pastoral Epistles*, AnBib 105 (Rome: Biblical Institute, 1986); Lewis R. Donelson, *Pseudepigraphy and Ethical Argument in the Pastoral Epistles*, HUT 22 (Tübingen: Mohr Siebeck, 1986).

[17]Cf. Roloff, *Der erste Brief an Timotheus*, 30.

[18]Cf. William D. Mounce, *Pastoral Epistles*, WBC 46 (Nashville: Nelson, 2000), xcix–cxviii; Johnson, *First and Second Letters to Timothy*, 58–63, 68–72; D. A. Carson and Douglas J. Moo, *An Introduction to the New Testament*, 2nd ed. (Grand Rapids: Zondervan, 2005), 555–61; Philip H. Towner, *The Letters to Timothy and Titus*, NICNT (Grand Rapids: Eerdmans, 2006), 23–25; Ben Witherington, *Letters and Homilies for Hellenized Christians*, vol. 1, *A Socio-Rhetorical Commentary on Titus, 1–2 Timothy and 1–3 John* (Downers Grove, IL: InterVarsity Academic, 2006), 54–62. For a survey of linguistic-statistical studies on the *Corpus Paulinum*, see Neumann, *The Authenticity of the Pauline Epistles*; Matthew Brook O'Donnell, "Linguistic Fingerprints or Style by Numbers? The Use of Statistics in the Discussion of Authorship of New Testament Documents," in *Linguistics and the New Testament: Critical Junctures*, ed. S. E. Porter and D. A. Carson, JSNTSup 168 (Sheffield: Sheffield Academic, 1999), 206–62.

[19]Cf. David Crystal, *The Cambridge Encyclopedia of Language* (Cambridge: Cambridge University Press, 1987), 69.

[20]Romans, Paul's longest letter, contains 7,114 words. Paul's letters without the Pastoral Epistles have 23,867 words.

[21]Henry George Liddell, Robert Scott, and Henry Stuart Jones, *A Greek-English Lexicon*, 9th ed. with revised supplement (Oxford: Clarendon, 1996).

125,000 headwords or lemmata (excluding numerals and proper names)—makes conclusions based on the nonoccurrence of words futile. Paul certainly had a much larger active vocabulary than is present in his letters.[22] Statistical-attribution analyses of Shakespeare's writings and texts where Shakespearean authorship has been disputed have not yielded a consensus.[23]

Second, the analysis of vocabulary is distorted if it is carried out on the three Pastoral Epistles as a group and on the undisputed Pauline Epistles as a group. Since the authenticity of each letter should be determined individually and not as part of an assumed corpus, the problem of statistical analysis is even more pronounced: 1 Timothy has 1,591 words, 2 Timothy 1,238 words, and Titus 659 words.[24] If we apply the method of Grayston and Herdan to Romans 1:1–9:17, a passage equal in length to 1 Timothy, the statistical analysis of 1 Timothy compares favorably with this passage from Romans.[25] If 2 Timothy is compared with the undisputed Pauline Epistles, the differences are not as great. For a majority of the distinctive words in each of the Pastoral Epistles, one can find synonyms within the accepted letters of Paul; for example, in the case of Titus, for more than 70 out of 83 distinctive words, synonyms within the rest of Paul's letters can be found.[26]

---

[22] Cf. Mounce, *Pastoral Epistles*, xcvi; he points out that of the 2,301 words of the undisputed Pauline letters, 969 words occur only once (42 percent), while of the 5,434 different words in the Greek New Testament, 1,947 occur only once (36 percent), and he asks, "If we have so little of Paul's writing that fewer than half the words occur only once, what is the possibility of doing reliable statistical work?"

[23] There continue to be disagreements concerning *1 Henry VI*, *Arden of Faversham*, and the Hand-D addition to *Sir Thomas More*; see Ward E. Y. Elliott and Robert J. Valenza, "Oxford by the Numbers: What Are the Odds that the Earl of Oxford could have written Shakespeare's Poems and Plays?" *Tennessee Law Review* 72 (2004): 323–453; Elliott and Valenza, "Two Tough Nuts to Crack: Did Shakespeare Write the 'Shakespeare' Portions of Sir Thomas More and Edward III?" *Literary and Linguistic Computing* 25 (2010): 67–83, 165–77; Hugh Craig and Arthur F. Kinney, *Shakespeare, Computers, and the Mystery of Authorship* (New York: Cambridge University Press, 2009). Lukas Erne, in a review of Craig and Kinney, concludes that "in situations where the acknowledged experts disagree, a possibility that should not be discarded is that the truth about a compositional process which took place four centuries ago is simply too complex to be recovered" (*Times Literary Supplement*, June 4, 2010, 11).

[24] Thomas A. Robinson, "Grayston and Herdan's 'C' Quantity Formula and the Authorship of the Pastoral Epistles," *NTS* 30 (1984): 282–88, here 286, argues that if we apply the statistical method of Grayston and Herdan (see n. 14 above) to each of these three letters individually, this yields numbers comparable to those of Paul's undisputed letters. This is incorrect: there can be no doubt that "the semantic inventory of the Pastoral Epistles features a much higher percentage of distinctive words than the rest of the Pauline letters" (Armin D. Baum, "Semantic Variation within the *Corpus Paulinum*: Linguistic Considerations Concerning the Richer Vocabulary of the Pastoral Epistles," *TynBul* 59 [2008]: 271–92, 277). The distinctive semantic inventory of each of the Pastoral Epistles (1 Timothy, 9 percent; 2 Timothy, 8 percent; Titus, 8 percent) is two to three times as high as the distinctive semantic inventory of Pauline letters of similar length (Colossians, 4 percent; 1 Thessalonians, 3 percent; 2 Thessalonians, 3 percent) (ibid., 278).

[25] Anthony E. Bird, "The Authorship of the Pastoral Epistles: Quantifying Literary Style," *RTR* 56 (1997): 118–37, here 128.

[26] Baum, "Semantic Variation," 279–85 (with an extensive word list). He concludes that "one may thin out the comparatively rich vocabulary of the Pastoral Epistles with little effort so that it correlates in

Third, the difference in distinctive subject matter accounts for vocabulary clusters with unusual words in all Pauline letters. Vocabulary that is generally acknowledged as "characteristically Pauline" occurs in a very erratic manner throughout Paul's letters. For example, the term "righteousness" (Gk. *dikaiosynē*) occurs twelve times in Romans, seven times in 2 Corinthians, five times in Galatians, three times each in Ephesians, Philippians, and 2 Timothy, and once in 1 Corinthians, 1 Timothy, and Titus, and is missing from Colossians, Philemon, 1 Thessalonians, and 2 Thessalonians; the term "law" (Gk. *nomos*) occurs seventy-two times in Romans, thirty-one times in Galatians, eight times in 1 Corinthians, three times in Philippians, twice in 2 Timothy, and once in Ephesians, and is absent from 2 Corinthians, Colossians, Philemon, 1 Thessalonians, 2 Thessalonians, and 2 Timothy.

Fourth, the notion that an author has a consistent style is a romantic notion of the modern Western world. In the Greco-Roman world, the rhetorical ideal was *prosōpopoiia* (writing in character or personification). In his treatise on the curriculum for prose composition taught in the *gymnasia*, Aelius Theon describes *prosōpopoiia* as

> the introduction of a person to whom words are attributed that are suitable to the speaker and have an indisputable application to the subject discussed; for examples, What words would a man say to his wife when leaving on a journey? Or a general to his soldiers in time of danger? . . . Under this genus of exercise fall the species of consolations and exhortation and letter writing. First of all, then, one should have in mind what the personality of the speaker is like, and to whom the speech is addressed. . . . Different ways of speaking belong to different ages of life, not the same to an older man and a younger one; the speech of a younger man will be mingled with simplicity and modesty, that of an older man with knowledge and experience. . . . What is said is also affected by the places and occasions when it is said. . . . And surely each subject has its appropriate form of expression.[27]

It is the occasion that determines the style adopted.[28]

Fifth, the dialogical style of Romans, 1 Corinthians, and Galatians owes at least some of its characteristics to the use of the diatribe mode rather than to

---

its type-token-ratio to the other ten Paulines" (ibid., 287).

[27]Aelius Theon, *Progymnasmata* 8.115–16 (George A. Kennedy, *Progymnasmata: Greek Textbooks of Prose Composition and Rhetoric*, Writings from the Greco-Roman World 10 [Atlanta: Society of Biblical Literature, 2003], 47–48).

[28]David Wheatley writes in a review of *Letters of Louis MacNeice*, ed. J. Allison (London: Faber, 2010), that "there is hardly a great writer in his or her letters who does not have a repertoire of styles and registers from which to choose, depending on the correspondent and the occasion" (*Times Literary Supplement*, July 16, 2010, 5).

Paul's personal "style" of writing; if the Pastoral Epistles are compared with Philippians or 1 Thessalonians, the differences are not as pronounced. And the "biblical style" of the Pauline letters acknowledged to be genuine may be due to the frequent quotations of and allusions to Old Testament texts, which are less frequent in the Pastoral Epistles, a fact that may help explain the "Greek" sensibilities of the latter; also, Paul's "biblical idiom" is stronger in Romans and Galatians than in Philippians.

Sixth, Paul's letters quote from the Old Testament and use early Christian traditions such as confessional formulas and liturgical traditions. Both Old Testament quotations and early Christian traditions affect the language of Paul's letters.

Seventh, discussing the question in terms of Pauline or non-Pauline authorship often does not take into account indications that the process of composition seems to have been complex. Paul dictated some of his letters,[29] which opens the possibility that his amanuenses (secretaries) had some part in the formulation of the text. Paul mentions "cosponsors" in many of his letters,[30] a fact that may or may not indicate the cooperation of other persons in the composition of Paul's letters.

Eighth, the difference in vocabulary and style between the accepted letters of Paul and the Pastoral Epistles can be explained with the difference between (conceptual) orality and (conceptual) writing. In the former, parentheses (insertions that interrupt the construction of the sentence) and instances of anacoluthon (inadequate sentence structure) are common; in the latter they are much less common. While parenthesis and anacolutha are regular features of the style of the accepted letters of Paul, this irregular and wooden sentence structure is rare in the Pastoral Epistles. This means that the Pastoral Epistles are closer to (conceptual) writing than the accepted Pauline letters, which means that "their author has expressed himself more carefully and probably had more time at his disposal than the author (or the authors) of the other ten Paulines."[31]

Ninth, the earliest church fathers, who never doubted the Pauline authorship of the Pastoral Epistles,[32] were native speakers of Greek whose sense of

---

[29]Rom. 16:22; 1 Cor. 16:21; Col. 4:18; 2 Thess. 3:17; cf. Gal. 6:11.

[30]1 Cor. 1:1 (Sosthenes); 2 Cor. 1:1 (Timothy); Phil. 1:1 (Timothy); Col. 1:1 (Timothy); Philem. 1 (Timothy); 1 Thess. 1:1 (Silas and Timothy); 2 Thess. 1:1 (Silas and Timothy). Only Romans, Ephesians, and the three Pastoral Epistles mention Paul alone as writer of the letter.

[31]Baum, "Semantic Variation," 290, who refers to Marius Reiser, "Paulus als Stilist," *SEÅ* 66 (2001): 151–65, who asserts with regard to the style of the ten accepted letters of Paul: he "wrote down something that no one before him had ever wanted to write down: . . . spoken language of a competent speaker with the typical characteristics of spontaneous speech."

[32]Polycarp (ca. AD 110–135) and *1 Clement* in all probability knew and used the letters to Timothy and Titus, Irenaeus (ca. AD 120–200) attributes 1 Timothy to "the apostle," and Clement of Alexandria

"style" was surely on a par with that of modern scholars, who learn Greek in artificial classroom settings as teenagers or later in life and who never attain the fluency of a native speaker—they only read Greek, but do not speak or write Greek. The certainty of the latter concerning the Greek style of New Testament documents is more impressive in its audacity than convincing in its cogency.

In sum, the degree of difference between the style of the Pastoral Epistles and the Pauline letters generally accepted as authentic is a matter of judgment. The language of the Pastoral Epistles, despite some distinctive characteristics, renders Pauline authorship neither impossible nor implausible.

## Theological Arguments

Scholars who think that the Pastoral Epistles were written by an author other than Paul argue that the theology of these three letters is different from the undisputed Pauline epistles: they do not contain genuine Pauline theology; rather, they convey Pauline tradition.[33] The following arguments are relevant.

First, differences in theological assertion or emphasis are not sufficient to call into question Pauline authorship: we should not assume that the ten undisputed letters contain the entire scope and all the emphases of Paul's theological thinking. If we assume a (relatively slow) rate of reading 150 words per minute, it would take only three hours to read the 27,300 words of text that we have in the New Testament (the figure includes the disputed and the undisputed letters of Paul). If Acts 20:7, 11 is any indication, there were occasions when Paul spoke for a much longer period with Christian believers. When Luke notes that Paul taught the word of God in Corinth for a year and six months (Acts 18:11), it would be preposterous to assume that Paul taught the same three-hour curriculum over and over again. There are numerous topics that Paul touches on in his letters but does not elaborate in

---

(ca. AD 150–211) cites the three letters. For a full discussion of the evidence, see Johnson, *First and Second Letters to Timothy*, 20–26; I. Howard Marshall, *The Pastoral Epistles*, ICC (Edinburgh: T&T Clark, 1999), 2–8; Towner, *Letters to Timothy and Titus*, 4–6, who concludes that "the indicators confirm that the three letters were known and used—as Pauline writings—prior to the time of Polycarp (110–135; possibly by the time of *1 Clement*) and consistently afterward through the early centuries of the church."

[33] Cf. Peter Trummer, *Die Paulustradition der Pastoralbriefe*, BBET 8 (Frankfurt/Bern: Lang, 1978); Michael Wolter, *Die Pastoralbriefe als Paulustradition*, FRLANT 146 (Göttingen: Vandenhoeck & Ruprecht, 1988); Mark Harding, *Tradition and Rhetoric in the Pastoral Epistles*, Studies in Biblical Literature 3 (New York: Lang, 1998); Merz, *Die fiktive Selbstauslegung des Paulus*; James W. Aageson, *Paul, the Pastoral Epistles, and the Early Church* (Peabody, MA: Hendrickson, 2007). For a different assessment, see Mark M. Yarbrough, *Paul's Utilization of Preformed Traditions in 1 Timothy: An Evaluation of the Apostle's Literary, Rhetorical, and Theological Tactics*, Library of New Testament Studies (London: T&T Clark, 2009).

detail, such as the concept of the kingdom of God,[34] God's judgment,[35] and Jesus's second coming.[36] These and other topics would have been explained by Paul on some occasions succinctly, on other occasions in great detail. The absence of Pauline theological themes from the Pastoral Epistles (e.g., the cross, the Holy Spirit, the flesh/spirit dichotomy) does not prove inauthenticity. There is no reason why Paul should mention the whole range of basic theological topics in all of his letters, particularly in letters to coworkers who know his theology.[37] It is only if it could be shown that the theology of the Pastoral Epistles *contradicts* Paul's undisputed letters that we would have a serious problem.

Second, some alleged contradictions between theological statements in the Pastoral Epistles and in the undisputed letters of Paul can be plausibly explained as variation and development of Pauline statements. For example, it is claimed that "faith" in the Pastoral Epistles is not a gift from God, as in the undisputed Pauline letters, but "a deposit to which nothing can be added."[38] This understanding of faith as "object" of belief is not much different from several references to faith in Paul's letters (Rom. 1:8; 2 Cor. 13:5; Gal. 1:23; Phil. 1:27; Col. 2:7). Similarly, it is claimed that "righteousness" in the Pastoral Epistles is not a gift from God but a Christian virtue. A. T. Hanson finds it "hard to imagine a more un-Pauline phrase than 'training in righteousness'" (commenting on 2 Tim. 3:16).[39] However, for Paul "righteousness" is not *only* a gift but also a responsibility that Christian believers exhibit in their everyday living.[40] L. T. Johnson sees in the use of the term "righteousness" in 2 Timothy 3:16 obvious Pauline resonances, "here considered primarily in moral terms."[41] The exhortation that Christians live "quiet and peaceful lives" (1 Tim. 2:2) is neither bourgeois ethics nor un-Pauline advice, as some allege, but in agreement with Romans 12:18 ("If possible, so far as it depends upon you, live peaceably with all") and 2 Thessalonians 3:12 ("Now such persons

[34] Note the brief, unexplained references in Rom. 14:17; 1 Cor. 4:20; 6:9–10; 15:24, 50; Gal. 5:21; Eph. 5:5; Col. 1:13; 4:11; 1 Thess. 2:12; 2 Thess. 1:5; 2 Tim. 4:1, 18.
[35] See Rom. 2:1–5; 3:6; 5:16; 11:33; 13:2; 14:10; and brief references in other letters.
[36] See 1 Thess. 1:9–10; 4:13–5:11, and references to the "day of the Lord" (1 Thess. 5:2; 2 Thess. 2:2), "day of the Lord Jesus (Christ)" (1 Cor. 1:8; 5:5; 2 Cor. 1:14; Phil. 1:6, 10; 2:16), and other passages.
[37] See Mounce, *Pastoral Epistles*, lxxxix–xci.
[38] Martin Dibelius and Hans Conzelmann, *The Pastoral Epistles*, Hermeneia (Philadelphia: Fortress, 1972), 13.
[39] Anthony T. Hanson, *The Pastoral Epistles*, NCB (London: Marshall, Morgan & Scott, 1982), 152.
[40] Mounce, *Pastoral Epistles*, xcii, with reference to Gordon D. Fee, *The First Epistle to the Corinthians*, NICNT (Grand Rapids: Eerdmans, 1987), 143, on comments on 1 Cor. 3:14–15.
[41] Johnson, *First and Second Letters to Timothy*, 421.

we command and exhort in the Lord Jesus Christ to do their work in quiet-
ness and to earn their own living").[42]

Third, the pseudonymous origin of the Pastoral Epistles is linked with the
argument that the author presumes a gospel tradition that is fixed as "sound
teaching," described as "the faith," and promulgated as "the truth" (1 Tim.
1:10, 19; 3:9, 13; 4:1, 6; 6:3, 10; 2 Tim. 1:13; 4:3; Titus 1:9, 13; 2:1), reflecting
a third- or fourth-generation situation in which the concern had shifted from
the lively and creative development of theological ideas to a fixed body of
beliefs that was passed on to the next generation. However, this concern for the
truth of the gospel that must be maintained is also seen in Paul's undisputed
letters. In Galatians 1:6–9 Paul pronounces a curse on anyone who teaches
"a different gospel." In Romans 16:17 Paul tells Christians to avoid "those
who create dissensions and difficulties, in opposition to the doctrine which
you have been taught." In 1 Corinthians 11:2 Paul commends the Corinthian
believers because they "maintain the traditions" that he has "delivered" to
them (see also 1 Cor. 15:1–3; 2 Thess. 2:15). In 1 Corinthians 4:17 he speaks of
Timothy as his trusted coworker, his "beloved and faithful child in the Lord"
whom he sent to Corinth "to remind you of my ways in Christ, as I teach
them everywhere in every church" (NRSV). Timothy's role here is no different
from his and Titus's role in the Pastoral Epistles.

Fourth, it is indeed true that both God and Jesus Christ are called "savior"
(sōtēr) in the Pastoral Epistles (God: 1 Tim. 1:1; 2:3; 4:10; Titus 1:3; 2:10,
13; 3:4; Christ: 2 Tim. 1:10; Titus 1:4; 3:6). Taken together, this seems to
highlight a theological theme of the Pastoral Epistles not found in Paul's letters. However, if we evaluate the Pastoral Epistles independently, a different
picture emerges. In 2 Timothy the title "savior" is used only with reference
to Jesus Christ (2 Tim. 1:10). In 1 Timothy, the title is used only for God
(1 Tim. 1:1; 2:3; 4:10). Significant is Titus, particularly since God and Christ
are designated as "savior" in close proximity (Titus 1:3, 4; 3:4, 6), which has
the dramatic effect of identifying God and Christ as both sharing this title.
While "epiphany" (epiphaneia) language (1 Tim. 6:14; 2 Tim. 1:10; 4:1, 8;
Titus 2:13) is distinctive to the Pastoral Epistles, it does not express a concept
that was foreign to Paul. P. H. Towner notes that

> with the epiphany language and category, God's story is retold in Hellenistic
> christological dress in a way that forces a rethinking of common categories.
> . . . "Epiphany" called to mind power and divine intervention (in secular Greek
> thought, in Hellenistic Judaism, and in the Roman Empire). But in the epiphany

---

[42]Unless otherwise indicated, these and subsequent Scripture quotations in this chapter are the
author's translations or adaptations of existing versions.

of Jesus Christ, divine power and presence are disguised in human weakness, suffering, and death (cf. 2 Corinthians 12).[43]

Fifth, the term "piety" or "godliness" (*eusebeia*) occurs in the Pastoral Epistles (1 Tim. 2:2; 3:16; 4:7, 8; 6:3, 5, 6, 11; 2 Tim. 3:5; Titus 1:1) but not in the undisputed Pauline letters.[44] This does not mean, however, that the former present a different view of the Christian life than the latter. In Hellenistic Judaism, the term *piety* was used "to describe a life lived in response to God's covenant lovingkindness," which means that "there is no reason to think it is at odds with Pauline theology."[45] The use of the term in the Septuagint (cf. Prov. 1:7; Isa. 11:2; 33:6) and in Hellenistic Judaism combined the notions of the knowledge of God, fear of the Lord, and the appropriate behavioral response (to God and to the law). This renders superfluous interpretations of *eusebeia* in the Pastoral Epistles in the sense of a nontheological morality for a church that was understood as an institution[46] or in the sense of a bourgeois morality that was more interested in peaceful coexistence with the world than in Jesus Christ's return.[47] Paul most likely uses *eusebeia* not because the term is used by the opponents he attacks in the Pastoral Epistles. Rather, since *eusebeia* "defines genuine Christian existence as the ongoing interplay of faith in Christ (= knowledge of God) and the manner of conduct issuing from that relationship," Paul uses the term in order to present "contemporary culture with the challenge that this highly prized Hellenistic cardinal virtue is truly attainable only in Christ."[48]

Sixth, the description of the church as "the household of God" and as "the pillar and foundation of the truth" (1 Tim. 3:15) is regarded as distinct from Paul's theology.[49] We note, however, that Paul does use the language of household and household management (1 Cor. 4:1; Gal. 6:10; Eph. 2:19). And the reference to "foundation" is used by Paul as well (1 Cor. 3:11; Eph. 2:20). The statement in 1 Timothy 3:15 is "a new configuration, with new

[43] Towner, *Letters to Timothy and Titus*, 62.

[44] Cf. Donelson, *Pseudepigraphy*, who argues that the author fictionalized Pauline history and Pauline thought providing a "moderate, authoritarian, and ethical rendition of Paul" (200).

[45] Towner, *Letters to Timothy and Titus*, 57, who asserts, "We may ask why Paul chose such a distinctively Greek way of articulating this aspect of his message, but the difference between this expression and that of Phil 4:8–9 is only one of degree; the thought is continuous" (ibid.). The answer may be the use of the term *eusebeia* in connection with the cult of Artemis in Ephesus (ibid., 172).

[46] Holtzmann, *Pastoralbriefe*, 176–79.

[47] Dibelius and Conzelmann, *Pastoral Epistles*, 39.

[48] Towner, *Letters to Timothy and Titus*, 174; see 171–74 for a critique of Holtzmann and Dibelius/Conzelmann concerning the term *eusebeia*.

[49] Cf. Margaret Y. MacDonald, *The Pauline Churches: A Socio-Historical Study of Institutionalization in the Pauline and Deutero-Pauline Writings*, SNTSMS 60 (Cambridge: Cambridge University Press, 1988).

language for a completely different situation (that of heresy) in which Paul employs the architectural language to underscore the church's responsibility to guard the gospel and proclaim it."[50] The suggestion that the emphasis on permanence, strength, and immovability is at odds with Paul's primary concern for the growth of the church (1 Cor. 3:6–7; Eph. 4:15–16; Col. 2:19) and for the presence of the Spirit in the church (1 Cor. 3:16; 2 Cor. 6:16) is unwarranted: Paul is clearly concerned for the permanence of the church (Rom. 8:31–39).

Seventh, scholars who doubt that Paul wrote the Pastoral Epistles point to the mode of argumentation: the author attacks the opponents and relies on institutional offices, while Paul argues theologically.[51] This argument misses the fact that Paul sometimes attacks opponents as well (Rom. 2:8; 1 Cor. 16:22; Gal. 1:8–9; Phil. 3:18–19; 2 Thess. 3:6, 14), using terms like "dogs" (Phil. 3:2), that he can appeal to his teaching as refutation of opposing views without explanation (Rom. 16:17; Gal. 1:8–9; 2 Thess. 3:6), and that he writes to coworkers who would not need fuller explanations of the heretics' views.[52]

In sum, the willingness to deem the Pastoral Epistles as inauthentic on the basis of an enumeration of theological differences alone is a serious methodological flaw. Any undisputed Pauline letter could be assessed as "non-Pauline" if the dissimilarity with Paul's letters is stressed and the similarities with Paul's letters are downplayed or ignored. The question of why Paul did not use the more overtly Hellenistic modes of expression (e.g., *epiphaneia* language) in his earlier letters[53] can be answered with reference to the addressees (coworkers as individuals, not churches) and the subject matter (local opponents in Ephesus). Paul's language and theological focus seems to have determined the role of epiphany language

in the Imperial and (in the case of the Artemis cult in Ephesus) local discourses. The strategy is that of hijacking or "co-opting," and Paul can be seen to engage the culture at various levels by such a use of the language of current cultural

[50]Towner, *Letters to Timothy and Titus*, 275; for the following comment, see 275–76.
[51]Cf. Norbert Brox, *Die Pastoralbriefe* (1969; repr., RNT, Regensburg: Pustet, 1989), 39–42.
[52]Mounce, *Pastoral Epistles*, xcvii, who further suggests that the lack of content and coherence of the "Ephesian error" made it impossible for Paul to provide a more systematic evaluation of the heresy.
[53]Marshall, *Pastoral Epistles*, 78, who allows that one can indeed argue that "there is nothing here that Paul himself could not have done with his broad background in both Palestinian and Hellenistic Judaism" (ibid.). Marshall himself is convinced neither by the arguments for authenticity nor by the arguments for fictional pseudonymity; he thinks that "allonymity" is a better term than *pseudepigraphy* or *pseudonymity* to explain the style and the theology of the Pastoral Epistles: a disciple of Paul edited notes of the deceased apostle, or he continued to write as he thought Paul would have done, without the intention of deceiving his readers (ibid., 83–84).

fixtures/institutions that carried significant political/economic/religious freight in the dominant discourse of the empire.[54]

## Historical Arguments

Critics who reject the authenticity of the letters to Timothy and Titus as genuinely Pauline argue that these letters cannot be located in the history and the geography of Paul's ministry.[55] This means that not only the stated author (Paul) is pseudonymous; the addressees named as Timothy and Titus are pseudonymous as well. The following considerations are important.

First, pseudonymous letters are confronted with the problem that specific details included in the text are potentially very easily detected as fictitious by the actual audience. For pseudonymity to "work," both the "I" (the author) and the "you" (the audience) need to be pseudonymous; otherwise the audience recognizes the document as a forgery. There is no unambiguously pseudonymous letter in which the supposed addressees and the real readers are identical.[56] R. J. Bauckham asserts that "if a pseudepigraphal writer wished to address his own contemporaries under cover of the supposed addressees of a pseudepigraphal letter, then *either* he had to keep his content very general" or "he had to make clear that the situation of the supposed addressees was comparable to that of the real readers."[57] One way to bridge the gap between the supposed (fictitious) addressees and the real readers was to address supposed addressees as predecessors of the real readers who find themselves in a situation that has not changed much from the time of the real addressees. Applied to the letters to Timothy and Titus, this would mean that the pseudonymous writer addresses his contemporary audience (the real readers) by asking them to identify with the churches in which Timothy and Titus worked, so that the remarks relevant to the situation of the supposed churches of Timothy and Titus are relevant to the situation of the real churches who read the fictitious letters. Since the Pastoral Epistles do show some interest in historical scene setting (see e.g., 2 Tim. 2:17–18), this is not a decisive characteristic of the letters. At the same time, if the pseudepigraphical assumption is taken seriously,

---

[54]Towner, *Letters to Timothy and Titus*, 417; see 37–50 for a discussion of the historical-cultural context and the opposition that the letters to Timothy and Titus address.

[55]Cf. Ernest F. Scott, *The Pastoral Epistles* (1936; repr., Moffat New Testament Commentary, New York: n.p., 1952), xvi–xvii ("That Paul cannot have been the author is most clearly apparent when we examine the historical framework of the letters" ); Roloff, *Der erste Brief an Timotheus*, 26–27.

[56]Richard J. Bauckham, "Pseudo-Apostolic Letters," *JBL* 107 (1988): 469–94, here 475: "The readers of a pseudepigraphal letter cannot read it as though they were being directly addressed either by the supposed author or by the real author (except in the special cases to be noted later); they must read it as a letter written to other people, in the past."

[57]Ibid., 478.

which presupposes that the situation that Paul (the supposed author) foresees after his death is the situation of the real readers (of the "real" author), we have to reckon with the possibility "that at the real time of writing, the time Paul foresees, Timothy was still alive."[58]

Second, some scholars integrate the letters to Timothy and Titus in the framework of Paul's ministry provided by the book of Acts, working with the (generally acknowledged) assumption that Luke does not provide a complete picture of Paul's travels. J. A. T. Robinson dates 1 Timothy to the time of Paul's Ephesian ministry between 1 Corinthians and 2 Corinthians, the letter to Titus to Paul's last journey from Achaia/Macedonia back to Jerusalem, and 2 Timothy to Paul's imprisonment in Caesarea.[59] S. de Lestapis suggests that the letters to Titus and 1 Timothy were written when Paul visited Philippi during his last journey to Jerusalem (Acts 20:30), and that Paul wrote 2 Timothy from his Roman imprisonment.[60] J. van Bruggen suggests that 1 Timothy was written during Paul's Ephesian ministry, as was the letter to Titus (assuming a gap between Acts 19:20 and 19:21, a year-long interval during which Paul was away from Ephesus, traveling to Corinth and back to Ephesus), while 2 Timothy was written during the time of Paul's imprisonment in Rome.[61] L. T. Johnson emphasizes the selective nature of the material in the book of Acts and suggests tentatively that 1 Timothy and Titus were written after the conclusion of Paul's Ephesian ministry (during Paul's work indicated in Acts 20:1–2), and that 2 Timothy comes from Paul's Roman imprisonment.[62]

Third, some scholars connect the letters to Timothy and Titus with the time after Paul's release from his first imprisonment at the end of the two years in Rome (Acts 28:30).[63] This solution has the advantage of providing the time needed for Paul to engage in the travels indicated in the letters to

---

[58] Ibid., 494. Bauckham reckons with the possibility that "the Pastorals were written after Paul's death but within Timothy's lifetime, then most probably they were written by Timothy himself" (ibid.).

[59] J. A. T. Robinson, *Redating the New Testament* (Philadelphia: Westminster, 1976), 67–85. Cf. Bo Reicke, "Chronologie der Pastoralbriefe," *TLZ* 101 (1976): 81–94.

[60] S. de Lestapis, *L'énigme des pastorales de saint Paul* (Paris: Gabalda, 1976), 167–77.

[61] Jakob van Bruggen, *Die geschichtliche Einordnung der Pastoralbriefe* (Wuppertal: Brockhaus, 1981).

[62] Johnson, *First and Second Letters to Timothy*, 61–62. He points out that Luke "describes" eight of the twelve years between AD 50–62 in four lines: Paul worked for eighteen months in Corinth (Acts 18:11), over two years in Ephesus (Acts 19:10), two years in Caesarea (Acts 24:27), and two years in Rome (Acts 28:30). Cf. Towner, *Letters to Timothy and Titus*, 14, 22, 83–86.

[63] Joseph B. Lightfoot, *Biblical Essays*, 2nd ed. (London: MacMillan, 1904), 421–37; Ceslas Spicq, *Les Épîtres pastorales*, 4th ed., Éditions Bibliques (Paris: Gabalda, 1969), 140–41; Michael Prior, *Paul the Letter-Writer and the Second Letter to Timothy*, JSNTSup 23 (Sheffield: JSOT, 1989), 73–84, 90; Jerome Murphy-O'Connor, *Paul: A Critical Life* (Oxford: Oxford University Press, 1996), 359–60; D. Guthrie, "Pastoral Epistles," in *New Bible Commentary: 21st Century Edition*, 4th ed., ed. D. A. Carson et al. (Downers Grove, IL: InterVarsity, 1994), lxxxv–lxxxvi; George W. Knight, *The Pastoral Epistles*, NIGTC (Grand Rapids: Eerdmans, 1992), 17–20.

Timothy and Titus, but it depends on the plausibility of Paul's release from his (first) Roman imprisonment and the assumption of a second imprisonment (indicated by 2 Timothy). Early Christian texts suggest that Paul was indeed released from his imprisonment in Rome, described in Acts 28:15–31, and reached Spain, which was Paul's plan according to Romans 15:24. According to *1 Clement* 5:7, Paul "came to the limits of the West," which suggests Spain.[64] The *Muratori Canon* includes the comment that Paul "from the city (of Rome) proceeded to Spain" (line 39). In the apocryphal *Acts of Peter* (ca. AD 180–190), Paul is sent by the Lord as "a physician to the Spaniards" (par. 1). If Paul was indeed released from his imprisonment in Rome and reached Spain,[65] to be imprisoned in Rome for a second time a few years later, this does not prove that the letters to Timothy and Titus were written between his first and second imprisonment in Rome, although that becomes a possibility.

In sum, there are several possibilities of connecting the letters to Timothy and Titus with Paul's travels. While the proposed historical reconstructions must remain hypothetical, they are not less than the alleged fictional situations of a pseudonymous author and the anonymous churches to whom the three letters were written.

## Pseudonymity and its Consequences

Critics who assume that the named author of the Pastoral Epistles is fictional generally assume that the named recipients are fictional and that the personal information included in the letters is fictional. This raises the question of whether the false teachers could be fictional as well. Some have taken this position. C. K. Barrett writes, "Judaism, legalism, mythology, and gnosis are lumped together in a way that suggests rather that the author was concerned to omit no heresy he had heard of than that he wished, or was able,

---

[64]*First Clement* is usually dated to AD 96, but a pre-70 date is not impossible. Clement's statement in 5:7 cannot be dismissed as an interpretation of Rom. 15:25: if Clement were depending entirely on Paul's letter to the Romans, he would presumably not speak in general terms of the "limits of the West" that Paul reached but would use the word "Spain" to describe Paul's mission to the West. See Hermut Löhr, "Zur Paulus-Notiz in 1 Clem 5.5–7," in *Das Ende des Paulus: Historische, theologische und literaturgeschichtliche Aspekte*, ed. F. W. Horn, BZNW 106 (Berlin: de Gruyter, 2001), 197–213.
[65]Accepted also by Colin J. Hemer, *The Book of Acts in the Setting of Hellenistic History*, ed. C. H. Gempf (1989; repr., WUNT 49, Tübingen: Mohr Siebeck, 2001), 390–404; Earle E. Ellis, "'The End of the Earth' (Acts 1:8)," *BBR* 1 (1991): 123–32; Löhr, "Paulus-Notiz," 207–12; as possibility cf. Martin Hengel and Anna Maria Schwemer, *Paul Between Damascus and Antioch: The Unknown Years* (London: SCM; Louisville: Westminster John Knox, 1997), 476 n. 1373; Bernd Wander, "Warum wollte Paulus nach Spanien? Ein forschungs- und motivgeschichtlicher Überblick," in Horn, *Das Ende des Paulus*, 175–95.

to analyse, sub-divide and classify."[66] More often the heresy that the author attacks is regarded as real by authors who assume pseudonymity of author and recipients. Most biblical scholars who hold this position defend the legitimacy of writing a pseudonymous text. It is argued that pseudonymity was a widespread and accepted literary practice in antiquity.[67] Jewish, Greek, and Roman authors often ascribed a text to an acknowledged authority, particularly in the context of school traditions where students and followers wrote in the name of the master who needed to be defended against (later) attacks and misinterpretations.[68] Some argue that neither the notion of intellectual property nor a "copyright mentality" existed in antiquity.[69] It is argued that false authorship attributions were not meant to deceive: they were a transparent literary fiction and were recognized as such. Others explain pseudonymous authorship attributions in the context of charismatic traditions,[70] as ecstatically inspired identifications,[71] or as actualization and confirmation of apostolic tradition.[72] The following considerations are important.

First, pseudonymous attribution of authorship was not an accepted practice in antiquity, despite claims to the contrary. The numerous terms for literary forgery[73] indicate that this matter was seriously discussed. Both Greeks and Romans demonstrate a clear interest in the preservation of the authenticity of their "classical" texts from the past.[74] Sometimes stychometric techniques

---

[66]C. K. Barrett, "Pauline Controversies in the Post-Pauline Period [1974]," in *On Paul: Essays on His Life, Work and Influence in the Early Church* (London: T&T Clark, 2003), 155–77, 171.

[67]Meade, *Pseudonymity and Canon*, 4–15; Petr Pokorny, "Das theologische Problem der neutestamentlichen Pseudepigraphie," *EvT* 44 (1984): 486–96; Pokorny, "Pseudepigraphie I. Altes und Neues Testament," *TRE*, 27 (1997), 644–55.

[68]Cf. Norbert Brox, *Falsche Verfasserangaben: Zur Erklärung der frühchristlichen Pseudepigraphie*, SBS 79 (Stuttgart: Katholisches Bibelwerk, 1975), 5–6.

[69]Cf. Martin Hengel, "Anonymität, Pseudepigraphie und 'Literarische Fälschung' in der jüdisch-hellenistischen Literatur [1972]," in *Judaica et Hellenistica: Kleine Schriften I*, WUNT 90 (Tübingen: Mohr Siebeck, 1996), 196–251.

[70]Cf. Kurt Aland, "Das Problem der Anonymität und Pseudonymität in der christlichen Literatur der ersten beiden Jahrhunderte," in *Studien zur Überlieferung des Neuen Testaments und seines Textes*, ANTF 2 (Berlin: de Gruyter, 1967), 24–34.

[71]Cf. Frederick Torm, "Die Psychologie der Pseudonymität im Hinblick auf die Literatur des Urchristentums," in *Pseudepigraphie in der heidnischen und jüdisch-christlichen Antike*, ed. N. Brox, WdF 484 (Darmstadt: Wissenschaftliche Buchgesellschaft, 1977), 149–53; Josef A. Sint, *Pseudonymität im Altertum: Ihre Formen und ihre Gründe*, Commentationes Aenipontanae 15 (Innsbruck: Wagner, 1960); Wolfgang Speyer, "Echte religiöse Pseudepigraphie," in *Pseudepigrapha I: Pseudopythagorica—Lettres de Platon—Littérature pseudépigraphique juive*, Fondation Hardt, Entretiens sur l'antiquité classique 18 (Vandoeuvres-Genève: Fondation Hardt, 1972), 333–66.

[72]Cf. Horst R. Balz, "Anonymität und Pseudepigraphie im Urchristentum," *ZTK* 66 (1969): 403–36; this is the main thesis of Meade, *Pseudonymity and Canon*, passim.

[73]Greek terms include *kibdeleuein, notheuein, paracharattein, plattein, radiourgein*; relevant Latin terms are *adulerare, confingere, falsare, supponere*.

[74]Wolfgang Speyer, *Die literarische Fälschung im heidnischen und christlichen Altertum: Ein Versuch ihrer Deutung*, Handbuch der klassischen Altertumswissenschaft 1/2 (Munich: Beck, 1971), 88–93,

were used to guarantee authenticity.[75] Philosophers, historians, and grammarians since Herodotus were engaged in a determined critical discussion of the authenticity of historical and literary works with the goal of controlling and condemning the practice of pseudepigraphy. Criteria used to determine the authenticity of texts included comparison of style, analysis of vocabulary, examination of doctrine (e.g., in philosophical texts), and chronological discussions (to detect anachronisms). Pseudonymous claims of authorship, if discovered, were criticized and rejected. The notion that there was no "copyright mentality," while perhaps correct if understood in a financial sense, must be rejected. Both Hellenistic and Jewish culture knew what "intellectual property" was. This is confirmed by passages such as 2 Thessalonians 2:1–2:

> We beg you, brothers and sisters, not to be quickly shaken in mind or alarmed, either by spirit or by word or by letter, as though from us, to the effect that the day of the Lord is already here (NRSV);

and Revelation 22:18–19:

> I warn everyone who hears the words of the prophecy of this book: if anyone adds to them, God will add to that person the plagues described in this book; if anyone takes away from the words of the book of this prophecy, God will take away that person's share in the tree of life and in the holy city, which are described in this book (NRSV).[76]

There is no unambiguous evidence that Jews accepted a text whose pseudonymous attribution to a particular author was recognized as false.[77] If a text that claimed philosophical or religious authority was recognized by Greek or Roman critics as a literary forgery, that is, as a text with a pseudonymous author, it was rejected.[78] The same is true for later Christian authors: "No writing known as pseudepigraphical was ever accepted as authoritative in the early church."[79] The rejection of pseudepigraphical writings as noncanonical in the early church "resulted from the basic agreement with Jewish convictions

---

112–28, 243–44.

[75]Josephus's *Antiquitates* end with the comment that the twenty volumes of the work have sixty thousand lines.

[76]Cf. Brox, *Falsche Verfasserangaben*, 69–70.

[77]Ibid., 41–45; Donelson, *Pseudepigraphy*, 10–11.

[78]Speyer, *Literarische Fälschung*, 112–27; Brox, *Falsche Verfasserangaben*, 71–80.

[79]Donelson, *Pseudepigraphy*, 11–12, with reference to James S. Candlish, "On the Moral Character of Pseudonymous Books," *The Expositor* 4 (1891): 91–107, 262–79, here 103. Cf. Speyer, *Literarische Fälschung*, 179–209; Brox, *Falsche Verfasserangaben*, 71–81; Armin D. Baum, *Pseudepigraphie und literarische Fälschung im frühen Christentum*, WUNT 2/138 (Tübingen: Mohr Siebeck, 2001), 99–125, with evidence from Serapion of Antioch (in Eusebius, *Hist. eccl.* 6.12.2–6), Tertullian (*Bapt.* 17.4–5),

that God does not lie, that holy scriptures are God's Word, and that therefore holy scriptures cannot contain any lies."[80]

Second, the category of *inspiration* cannot explain early Jewish (or Christian) pseudonymity. Authors of apocalyptic texts who wrote under the pseudonym of Enoch, Moses, Ezra, Baruch, Solomon, or the patriarchs were inspired not by these "school heads" of the past but by angels; a revelation from the archangel Michael cannot explain why Moses or Enoch is used as the name of the author. And why would they not write in their own names, as Isaiah, Jeremiah, or Ezekiel did? In New Testament writings that are deemed to be pseudonymous, the concept of inspiration is not referred to in a context in which the author would explain his procedure, message, or authority. Also, if divine inspiration is the cause of pseudonymity, then Paul, who wrote to the Roman and Corinthian Christians, would have to be regarded as less conscious of being inspired by the Spirit since he was willing to write under his own name.

Third, the suggestion that the postapostolic period was a time of perplexity and helplessness because the promised return of Jesus (*parousia*) had not happened, explaining the need for apostolic authority, is not convincing. Jesus, Paul, and John speak not only of an imminent return of Jesus but also of a period between his first and second comings whose length was unknown. There is no evidence that the alleged "problem of the delayed parousia" was a problem for Christians in the late first or early second century. The continued missionary growth of the church in the second century disproves the assumption of a perplexed and helpless church. Christian leaders such as Clement, Ignatius, Polycarp, and Papias had no qualms at all writing under their own names.

Fourth, the suggestion that false author names are not deceptive since the motivation for pseudonymity was the faithful transmission of apostolic tradition or a concern for apostolic authority is unconvincing. Concerns for the fidelity of Christian tradition, for the affirmation of authoritative tradition, and for the truth of the gospel are motivation not for pseudonymous author attributions but for faithfulness in naming the author of a text. Affirmation of authoritative apostolic tradition is hardly credible when it is linked with a fictitious author and fictitious recipients. The suggestion to speak of "decep-

---

Julius Africanus (*Ep. Orig.* 2), Origen (*Ep. Afric.* 15), Eusebius of Caesarea (*Hist. eccl.* 25.1–7), Augustine (*Civ.* 18.38), and Jerome (*Prol. Sal.*).

[80] Baum, *Pseudepigraphie*, 195, summarizing 125–40. The authors of early Christian pseudepigrapha such as the *Apostolic Constitutions*, the *Pseudo-Clementines*, and the *Third Letter to the Corinthians* justified their literary forgeries by "claiming the right to extend the use of a positively motivated 'lie of necessity' into the realm of religion instead of limiting such a lie to the secular realm" (ibid., 195, summarizing 164–77).

tion" rather than forgery, the latter being morally problematic,[81] is artificial: deception is hardly morally superior to forgery. Both primary sources and indirect evidence show that pseudepigraphical statements of authorship were regarded as attempts to deceive.[82] The Roman author Vitruvius (ca. 80–10 BC) writes in the introduction to the seventh volume of his work *De architectura*:

> It was a wise and useful provision of the ancients to transmit their thoughts to posterity by recording them in treatises, so that they should not be lost. . . . So, while they deserve our thanks, those, on the contrary, deserve our reproaches, who steal the writings of such men and publish them as their own; and those also, who depend in their writings, not on their own ideas, but who enviously do wrong to the works of others and boast of it, deserve not merely to be blamed, but to be sentenced to actual punishment for their wicked course of life. With the ancients, however, it is said that such things did not pass without pretty strict chastisement. What the results of their judgments were, it may not be out of place to set forth as they are transmitted to us. (Preface 1, 3)[83]

Fifth, the opinion that the pseudonymous character of the letters to Timothy and Titus does not call into question their canonicity is based on the suggestion that the early church did not regard pseudepigraphical writings to be forgeries. The historical evidence of the second and third centuries does not bear this out. The early church rejected writings as noncanonical whose authorship was pseudonymous.

In the light of this evidence, there are only three options. A first option suggests that we abandon the view of the early church concerning divine revelation and the canon, which insisted on the normativity of entire writings (not just ideas) that were regarded as authentic texts of the apostolic authors, and replace it with the concept of a "canon within the canon."[84] This solution leads to subjective views of what belongs to this normative canon within the biblical canon since there are no objective and generally recognized criteria for what is "in" and what can be excluded. The second option is to recognize the seriousness of the fact that the Pastoral Epistles are forgeries and to

---

[81]Meade, *Pseudonymity and Canon*, 2, 120–21, 197–99. He asserts that "when we examine the issue of 'deception' in literary propagation, it is with the understanding that the word is not used in its modern configuration, and applies only to the first level, that of literary origins" (197). For a critique of Meade, see Eckhard J. Schnabel, "Der biblische Kanon und das Phänomen der Pseudonymität," *JETh* 3 (1989): 59–96.

[82]Baum, *Pseudepigraphie*, 32–99. The only exception is Salvian of Marseille (AD 400–480).

[83]Morris H. Morgan, *Vitruvius: The Ten Books on Architecture*, LCL (Cambridge: Harvard University Press, 1914).

[84]Thus Werner Georg Kümmel, "Notwendigkeit und Grenzen des neutestamentlichen Kanons [1950]," in *Heilsgeschehen und Geschichte. Gesammelte Aufsätze*, 2 vols., ed. E. Grässer (Marburg: Elwert, 1965–1978), 230–59.

exclude them from the canon of authoritative Scripture.[85] Scholars who have abandoned the concept of a normative canon of Holy Scripture altogether find this an easy solution, although this consequence is seldom drawn from the (assumed) pseudonymous character of the Pastoral Epistles. It would "simply" mean that churches should publish revised Bible editions from which pseudonymous writings are omitted. Finally, for scholars and Christians who accept the biblical writings as Scripture, the weight of tradition that includes the Pastoral Epistles in the New Testament canon seems to prevent the suggestion that these letters should be excluded on the basis of the assumption that the early church failed to see their pseudonymous character. This third option prompts us to take seriously the early church's acceptance of the letters to Timothy and Titus as authentic letters of Paul and to reevaluate the arguments for pseudonymity and against authenticity. As the evidence that has been surveyed demonstrates, there are good reasons to accept the Pauline authorship of these three letters.

---

[85]Schenk, "Briefe an Timotheus I und II und an Titus," 3428 n. 93.

# 18

# SAINT PAUL ON CYPRUS

## *The Transformation of an Apostle*

## THOMAS W. DAVIS[1]

The cool evening breeze provides a welcome respite from the warmth of the day. The two travelers look warily around the crowded atrium, unsure of what to do and where to be. All of the elite of the community are there, and the two latecomers are ill at ease. The official who has delivered the invitation has made it quite clear that their attendance is strongly requested. "We are but simple Jewish merchants," protests the spokesman for the pair; "we do not dine with governors." The Roman official is unperturbed. "The proconsul is an intelligent man and wishes to engage you in conversation. He enjoys having philosophical discussions after eating." After a disquieting pause he adds flatly, "He expects your attendance."

## The Pauline Comfort Zone

### Introduction

"The two of them, sent on their way by the Holy Spirit, went down [from Antioch] to Seleucia and sailed from there to Cyprus" (Acts 13:4);[2] so the Acts of the Apostles records the beginning of the most important missionary trip in the history of the Christian church. The first missionary journey of the apostle Paul from Antioch to the island of Cyprus led to a revolutionary change in the Christian message. At Antioch, Paul of Tarsus had been within

---

[1]Thomas W. Davis conducted extensive research on the archaeology of Cyprus during his tenure as director of the Cyprus American Archaeological Research Institute. He took up his position on the faculty of Southwestern Baptist Theological Seminary for the fall term of 2011. He is director of excavations at Kourion.
[2]Scripture quotations in this chapter are from the New International Version, 1984 edition.

his comfort zone, a world that he knew intimately. It was a mercantile world, a Hellenistic world, and a Jewish Christian world. On Cyprus, specifically in Paphos, he was forced to enter a new reality outside his immediate experience: a political world, a patrician world, and a pagan Roman world. I believe this challenged his understanding of his calling, which changed profoundly the way he continued his missionary endeavors.

### The Comfort Zone

At the beginning of the Cyprus narrative Paul is in what I describe as his "comfort zone"—the urban world of the eastern Roman Empire. Paul is an urban man.[3] After his conversion on the road to Damascus, Paul spends fourteen years in Syria, Cilicia, and Arabia. After visiting Jerusalem at least once, he bases himself in Tarsus (Acts 11:25). He reflects an urban self-understanding when he tells the arresting Roman in Acts 22 that he is from "Tarsus in Cilicia," no ordinary city. Paul has a typical Hellenized self-identity, which is city based. He has the urban pride of the Hellenistic world, where one's city is more important than one's province or kingdom. He divides the world into city, wilderness, and sea in 2 Corinthians 11:26. Throughout his career Paul travels through the wilderness and on the sea, but makes his home in cities. The churches he plants are urban associations, and he illustrates his lessons with images of urban life.

Paul is a business man, by profession a *skēnopoios*, a tentmaker or, more generally, a leather worker. According to Acts 18, Paul works his trade while living in Corinth. In a speech recorded in Acts 20, Paul reminds the elders of the church in Ephesus of his business acumen: "You yourselves know that these hands of mine have supplied my own needs and the needs of my companions" (Acts 20:34). In his own writings, Paul complains that it seems that only he and his colleague Barnabas have had to work for a living (1 Cor. 9:6)! Paul is in his comfort zone in the shop and the street market.

It is par excellence, for Paul, a Jewish world, or at least a Jewish-Christian world. His Jewish *ethnos* is a core element of his identity.[4] In 2 Corinthians he states what he calls "a little . . . foolishness" (2 Cor. 11:1) in the defense of his mission, laying out his strong Jewish roots against challenges: "Are they Hebrews? So am I. Are they Israelites? So am I. Are they Abraham's descendents? So am I" (11:22). In Galatians 1:14 Paul speaks of his zeal for "the traditions of my fathers." After his conversion he remains a syna-

---

[3] Wayne Meeks, *The First Urban Christians: The Social World of the Apostle Paul* (New Haven, CT: Yale University Press, 1983).

[4] F. F. Bruce, *Paul: Apostle of the Heart Set Free* (Grand Rapids: Eerdmans, 1977). Bruce remains my guide to all things Pauline.

gogue attendee. He is among Greek "God-fearers" in Antioch and feels called to reach out and welcome them, but it is still a Jewish world he inhabits comfortably.

## Antioch

Antioch-on-the-Orontes, one of the great cities of the ancient world, becomes the "home church" for Paul for his first missionary journeys and is the heartland of the comfort zone for Paul. Located on the Orontes River near its mouth, Antioch was a nexus point for the trade routes from Mesopotamia and the north-south coastal road along the Mediterranean. One of Alexander's generals, Seleucus I, founded the city in 300 BC and named it after his father, Antiochus. Seleucus had a conscious policy of urbanization in upper Syria to create a counterweight to the ancient Mesopotamian cities; the result was the restoration of the Bronze and Iron Age patterns of urbanism.[5] Warwick Ball suggests that the location was too strategic not to be occupied before the Macedonian foundation and that the evidence for previous settlements is obscured by the massive occupational debris beneath the modern city.[6] The Romans gained control over the city in 64 BC when they annexed the remains of the Seleucid kingdom.

The excavations in the 1930s revealed little about Roman Antioch, owing to the eleven meters of accumulated debris and the high water table of the Orontes River.[7] However, the basic layout of the city is known. The walls were pierced by at least four gates with five bridges across the Orontes River. The main street, crossing the city from the Aleppo Gate to the Daphne Gate, measured approximately two Roman miles in length with several strata of repaving. It was thirty-six meters wide, with colonnades on each side and probably roofing over the main carriageway. The main street was almost certainly the major market of the city, with the broad avenue lined with market stalls. *Tetrapyla* marked the major intersections, and a statue of Tiberius brooded over the main crossroads.[8] The slopes above the Orontes River held the wealthier private quarter, placed to catch the breeze and with better views.[9]

---

[5]Henri Seyrig, "Séleucus I et la fondation de la monarchie syrienne, " *Syria* 47 (1970): 290–311.
[6]Warwick Ball, *Rome in the East: The Transformation of an Empire* (London: Routledge, 2001), 157.
[7]Richard Stillwell, ed., *Antioch on the Orontes III: The Excavations of 1937–1939* (Princeton: Princeton University Press, 1941), 7. The Antioch excavations were a classic example of colonialist treatment of archaeological heritage. The international consortia of museum and universities sponsoring the excavation removed half of the recovered mosaics (more than three hundred) to their respective museums.
[8]Ball, *Rome in the East*, 155.
[9]Christine Kondoleon, ed., *Antioch: The Lost Ancient City* (Princeton: Princeton University Press, 2000).

The Roman presence in Antioch was formal and official, reflecting the strategic importance of Antioch and Syria.[10] The Romans appointed governors who were politically reliable, and under the Principate, a procurator was paired with them and both resided at Antioch. Owing to the proximity of Parthia, the Roman army assigned to Syria was the largest in the east, with four legions and twenty thousand auxiliaries.[11] Because of the size of the army, the imperial governors had to be politically reliable, members of the aristocracy of the Principate. As part of his strategy of indirect rule, Augustus created a web of *clientalia* in the cities of the eastern empire. This helped thwart any possible tendencies to independence in the urbanized upper class.[12] These co-opted elites dominated the mercantile and social life of the city.

Beneath the "superficial veneer" of Roman rule, Antioch was a multiethnic city.[13] Aramaic would have been the dominant language in the Syrian countryside, with the use of Greek widespread in the urban population. There was a substantial Jewish population in Antioch with its own archon.[14] Paul would have been able to blend in among his co-religionists. Seleucus I Nicator gave Jewish mercenaries the same rights as Greeks and Macedonians to settle in Antioch when it was founded. Jews lived in the southeastern quarter inside the walls of Tiberius but outside the early walls of Seleucus. Antioch's proximity to Palestine and its economic and political importance made it an attractive place of settlement for Jews. Local and ethnically related cults were important factors for maintaining personal identity in a minority situation in the ancient world, and the Roman Empire in particular witnessed this phenomenon. Synagogues fulfilled the same function for the Jewish Diaspora community. No direct archaeological evidence of a synagogue in Antioch has been recovered, but textual references document synagogues within the city and in the suburb of Daphne in the Roman period. According to one recent scholar, Antiochene Jewish life was "a rare historical example of Jews fully integrated into the life of a city while maintaining their own ancestral traditions."[15]

Antioch's prime mercantile location at a nexus of trade routes was an obvious advantage for Paul. The raw material for his tents would have been easily obtainable from the eastern steppe lands that have supported nomadic

[10]Glanville Downey, *A History of Antioch in Syria from Seleucus to the Arab Conquest* (Princeton: Princeton University Press, 1961).
[11]Alan Bowman, Edward Champlin, and Andrew Lintott, *The Augustan Empire*, 2nd ed., CAH 10 (Cambridge: Cambridge University Press, 1996), 714.
[12]Meeks, *First Urban Christians*, 12.
[13]Ball, *Rome in the East*, 157.
[14]Wayne Meeks and Robert Wilken, *Jews and Christians in Antioch in the First Four Centuries of the Common Era* (Ann Arbor, MI: Society of Biblical Literature, 1978), 1.
[15]Bernadette Brooten, "The Jews of Ancient Antioch," in Kondoleon, *Antioch*, 29–38.

herders from the Neolithic period onward, and the passing trade caravans would have been a likely market for Paul's products. He probably rented a spot on one of the colonnaded markets in Antioch. Colonnaded streets were a dominant feature in eastern Roman urbanism. They functioned as market centers, replacing the typical western-style *agora*.[16]

From a base here, Paul could easily have traveled throughout Syria and along the Levantine coast, trading and making contacts. Antioch and Tarsus lay within the same market region being directly linked by road and by sea routes, so this was a familiar world for Paul. He had probably already established a network of clients while he was based in Tarsus, which could easily have included contacts in Antioch. The wealthy Jewish community would have provided a strong potential market for Paul, easily accessible given his shared cultural identity. The presence of a Roman army base in the city also provided another potential local market for Paul's leather goods and tents.

Seleucia was the main port for Antioch. The Roman port was artificially created north of the mouth of the Orontes because of the silting from the river; eventually this also silted up. Limited archaeological investigation in the late 1930s revealed the remains of a theater and some houses. Scattered remnants of the port installations were also identified.[17]

### The Cyprus Connection in the Antioch Church

In Acts 11 Luke recounts the scattering of the believers after the stoning of Stephen: "Some of them, however, men from Cyprus and Cyrene, went to Antioch and began to speak to Greeks also, telling them the good news about the Lord Jesus" (Acts 11:20). Later, Luke records the names of five of the leaders of the church in Antioch, and the mention of Barnabas from Cyprus speaks to the continued influence and presence of Cypriot Christians. From the text, we must assume that the missionaries from Cyprus were Jews, like Barnabas, who is first mentioned in Acts 4. The Jerusalem church hears about this new church in Antioch (Luke shows the ability of people and news to travel easily), and shrewdly sends a Cypriot Jewish Christian, Barnabas, to find out what is happening. The relatively easy success of the missionaries in Antioch is a product of the shared cultural milieu between the Syrian city dwellers and the Cypriots. As a Cypriot, Barnabas would not be perceived as a threat by either the new converts or the missionaries and would be able more easily to gain their confidence.

Barnabas brings Paul of Tarsus to Antioch, where he will begin his publicly visible ministry. We do not know how long Paul was in Tarsus before Barnabas

---

[16]Ball, *Rome in the East*, 262.

[17]Stillwell, *Antioch on the Orontes III*.

sought him out, but the Lukan chronology implies at least a decade. These are silent years with no mention of any ministry in either the Acts or Paul's letters, except a simple mention in Galatians 1:22, where Paul speaks of time spent in Syria and Cilicia. Of crucial importance is what is not said by either Luke or Paul: neither Luke in Acts nor Paul in his letters makes any mention of Gentile mission work that Paul might have undertaken during this period. His proselytizing appears to have been confined to the Jewish community of Damascus and possibly Arabia. If he did reach out to Gentiles in Arabia, Cilicia, and Damascus, the results have gone unrecorded.

It is probably Barnabas who persuades the Antioch church that Cyprus should be the first "foreign" mission field for the fledgling congregation. Perhaps it is a way for the Antioch believers to partially repay the debt they owe to their spiritual midwives from Cyprus who have brought them into the new faith. It is also a safe choice, since some of the congregation probably has family ties and commercial links. Salamis, Barnabas's home city, is only a day's sail from the port of Antioch at Seleucia. "After all," the church leadership may have reasoned, "if the people of Antioch responded to the gospel as presented by Cypriots, then the Cypriots should respond to a mission led by one of their own."

## Paul on Cyprus: Out of the Comfort Zone

### The Cypriot Context

Cyprus is the third largest island in the Mediterranean Sea, measuring approximately 225 kilometers east-west by 95 kilometers north-south. Located in the northeast corner of the Mediterranean, approximately 70 kilometers south of Turkey and 120 kilometers west of Syria, Cyprus is enveloped by Asia Minor and the Levantine coast. Fernand Braudel's concept of *le long durée*, "a history in slow motion from which permanent values can be detected" is a valuable tool for envisioning the Cyprus Paul and Barnabas encountered.[18] These "permanent values" are critical to understanding the island's cultural identity. Such permanent values include its island identity, its strategic location, and its abundant natural resources. Throughout its history, Cyprus's island identity provided a protective shell around Cyprus's cultural identity. As an island, Cyprus forced invasions and colonization attempts to be episodic in nature, resulting in a millennia-long process of cultural negotiation between indigenous populations and newcomers, which produced acculturation rather than annihilation. In his perceptive study of Cypriot prehistory, A. Bernard

---

[18]Fernand Braudel, *The Mediterranean in the Age of Philip II*, vol. I (New York: Harper & Row, 1972), 23.

Knapp emphasizes the fluctuating degree of "openness or boundedness" on Cyprus.[19]

*Ptolemaic Rule*

Whenever dominance over the eastern Mediterranean was contested between rival powers, the control of Cyprus became a strategic necessity for the competing states. Following the death of Alexander the Great, Cyprus became a prize of war for the successor states, eventually coming under the full control of the Ptolemaic state of Egypt when the last local dynasts were suppressed. During the next two hundred years, the dynastic struggles of the Egyptian ruling house caused Cyprus to have periodic episodes of nearly independent rule under a claimant or exiled claimant to the Egyptian throne. The military ruled the island in the person of a high-ranking *stratēgos* and a mercenary garrison protected the island.[20]

Cyprus was an economic prize in the fourth century BC as well. The 2006 discovery of a mid-fourth-century-BC shipwreck off of the south coast at Mazatos underlines the maritime importance of the island, which had been first established archaeologically by the discovery of the Kyrenia ship in the late 1960s.[21] The Mazatos wreck appears to have carried mostly Aegean wine and may have been heading for one of the southern ports, such as Amathus or Kourion. The Kyrenia ship, which sank in the first quarter of the third century BC, likewise carried Aegean wine, but also Cypriot almonds, and was probably headed for the Syrian coast.

Nea Paphos ("Paphos" in common parlance in the first century), founded on the southwest coast at the end of the fourth century BC, became the Ptolemaic capital because of its naval advantages.[22] The remains of Roman Paphos mostly obscure the Ptolemaic city, with the exception of the necropolis called the "Tombs of the Kings" (actually of the societal elites of Paphos), a late fourth-century-BC pebble mosaic depicting Scylla, an appropriate theme for a naval-oriented city, and newly discovered frescoes from a third-century-BC

[19]A. Bernard Knapp, *Prehistoric and Protohistoric Cyprus: Identity, Insularity, and Connectivity* (Oxford: Oxford University Press, 2008), 23.

[20]Veronica Tatton-Brown, "The Hellenistic Period," in *Footprints in Cyprus*, ed. David Hunt (London: Trigraph, 1990), 98–109.

[21]Michael Katzev, "The Kyrenia Shipwreck," *Expedition* 11, no. 2 (1969): 54–59; Stella Demesticha, "The 4th-Century BC Mazatos Shipwreck, Cyprus: A Preliminary Report," *International Journal of Nautical Archaeology* (2010): 1–21. The final report on the excavation and conservation of the Kyrenia ship currently is being completed by Katzev's widow, Susan Katzev, and the architect of the excavation, Helena Wylde Swiny. I was privileged to be on board the University of Cyprus dive boat for a morning during the Mazatos-shipwreck 2010 field season.

[22]Danielle Parks, "The Roman Coinage of Cyprus," *The Numismatic Report* 34–35 (2003–2004): 1–316.

house, which are evidence of the rich lifestyle of the elites of the province.[23] The new city was a product of imperial power, following the pattern established by Alexander. The establishment of Paphos was a direct challenge to the primacy of Salamis as the leading Cypriot city. Geography dictated the Ptolemaic choice. Salamis harbor was silting up and lay too close to the Syrian coast, whereas Paphos could be reached from Alexandria in a direct sail that avoided Seleucid territory. The establishment of Nea Paphos, prevented the great pan-Cypriot sanctuary of Paphian Aphrodite, located at Palaipaphos, approximately sixteen kilometers east of the newly established capital, from exercising its traditional political role in the region.[24]

Jody Gordon has applied postcolonial theory to the Ptolemaic and Roman empires on Cyprus.[25] His examination of the material expression of imperial ideology emphasizes the ruling powers' attempts to seduce Cyprus into becoming a compliant province, where the negotiation of cultural identity eventually produced a politically unified province masking internal complexity. By the first century BC, Ptolemaic rule was well established and Cyprus did not have an independent voice in the civil wars of the last century of the Roman Republic.

Rome first annexed Cyprus in 58 BC, joining it to Cilicia. Cicero was the most famous early governor of the joint province. However, Julius Caesar returned Cyprus to Ptolemaic rule in the person of his mistress, Cleopatra VII. This gift was confirmed in 36 BC by Mark Anthony. Cyprus returned to Roman rule after the battle of Actium in 31 BC.

Current excavations on Yeronisos Island, a small islet off the west coast of Cyprus, illuminate the last days of Ptolemaic rule under Cleopatra. On Yeronisos, Joan Breton Connelly has excavated the fragmentary remains of a late Hellenistic-style temple.[26] She hypothesizes that the temple was associated with boys' rites of passage, in light of the recovery of small limestone amulets normally depicted on "temple boy" sculptures from the Hellenistic world. She persuasively argues that the temple was dedicated to Cleopatra, the New Isis, and her son by Julius Caesar, Caesarion, the New Horus, marking his passage to adulthood. This would be in keeping with the Ptolemaic tradition

---

[23] Claire Balandier, personal communication 2010.

[24] Jolanta Mlynarczyk, *Nea Paphos III, Nea Paphos in the Hellenistic Period* (Warsaw: The Polish Center of Mediterranean Archaeology of the Polish Academy of Sciences, 1990).

[25] Jody Gordon, "Why Empires Matter: A Postcolonial Archaeology of Cultural Identity in Hellenistic and Roman Cyprus" (paper presented at the Cyprus American Archaeological Research Institute, Nicosia, Cyprus, 2010). This forms part of his dissertation to be submitted to the Department of Classics of the University of Cincinnati.

[26] Joan Breton Connelly, "Twilight of the Ptolemies: Egyptian Presence on Late Hellenistic Yeronisos," in *Egypt and Cyprus in Antiquity*, ed. D. Michaelides, V. Kassianidou, and R. S. Merrillees (Oxford: Oxbow Books, 2010), 194–209.

of a royal cult, first established on Cyprus when Arsinoe Philadelphus, the wife of Ptolemy II was deified on her death.

## Roman Rule

Augustus separated Cyprus from Egypt and made it a senatorial province, governed by a proconsul. By the beginning of the first century AD, Cyprus was already becoming a political backwater in the Roman Empire. The ancient sources are largely silent about the island during the Roman period. In Mitford's words, "In 22 BC Cyprus entered upon more than three centuries of tranquil obscurity."[27] Inscriptions and coins together record only forty-eight proconsuls from 22 BC to AD 293, less than a sixth of the total. The proconsul served for only a one-year term; Mitford points out that this short period of office prevented corruption. In consequence, Cyprus probably was not seen as an attractive posting for a young Roman aristocrat who needed to line his pockets to advance his political career; we know of only six governors who went on to become consuls. Proconsuls had quaestors to assist them in public finance; the proconsul would normally have an advisory council and could summon locals for help. Cyprus was divided into four administrative districts.

Augustan coinage for Cyprus reflects a conscious attempt to integrate Cyprus into the empire. One Cypriot Roman coin uses a portrait bust of Augustus that echoes strongly back to the coinage of Julius Caesar.[28] This may have been a deliberate attempt to highlight Octavian's Caesarian heritage, designed to appeal to supporters of the defeated Ptolemaic monarchy. In the political hagiography of the Ptolemaic kingdom, Caesar was a "good Roman" who supported their queen and fathered their last king.

Despite political obscurity, Cyprus retained economic importance. Dimitrios Michaelides has emphasized the importance of Cyprus's economic role and the outsized contribution the island made to the Roman economy.[29] His survey of the economic role of Cyprus highlights the amount of perishable items Cyprus may have exported, evidence that has not survived in the archaeological record. The island continued to be a major source of copper; Augustus supplied King Herod with 150 talents in annual revenues from half of the mines and allowed the king to directly manage the other half.[30] There is no evidence of any imperial estates on Cyprus, but centuriation (laying out of

---

[27]T. B. Mitford, "Roman Cyprus," in *ANRW*, 2.7.2, 1285–1388, esp. 1295.
[28]Parks, "Roman Coinage of Cyprus"; Gordon, "Why Empires Matter," suggests the resemblance of the Augustus bust on the obverse of the coin to the iconography of Julius Caesar.
[29]Demetrios Michaelides, "The Economy of Cyprus during the Hellenistic and Roman Periods," in *The Development of the Cypriot Economy from the Prehistoric Period to the Present Day*, ed. V. Karageorghis and D. Michaelides (Nicosia: Bank of Cyprus, 1996), 139–52.
[30]Josephus, *Antiquities* 16.128.

agricultural field strips by imperial surveyors) near Salamis might indicate the reallocation of land confiscated from Ptolemaic elites.[31]

Urban life flourished in the Roman period on Cyprus. There is a great deal of archaeological and inscriptional evidence for extensive building in the first century AD in the Cypriot urban centers of Paphos, Salamis, Kourion, Amathus, and Soloi. New temples, baths and aqueducts, public spaces, and markets were constructed. It is fair to say that Cyprus circa AD 50 was an urban world. Following the dictates of its island identity, the large urban centers of Cyprus lay on the coast. This coastal orientation was strengthened on Cyprus by the security situation under the *Pax Romana*, and would continue until the seventh century AD.

The Cypriot cities in the Roman period lacked the usual sense of strong local identity that most cities in the eastern empire evidenced. Cyprus did not have many urban dedications that exalted the city; for the most part, the inscriptions were dedicated to the imperial family on behalf of an individual, or the community, the *koinon kyprion*. A sign of the diminished role of urban identity is that in the reign of Claudius, the *koinon kyprion* was made responsible for minting the coins of Cyprus rather than individual cities.[32]

Religiously, Cyprus maintained its public attachment to the traditional male and female deities of Cyprus, with roots far back into prehistory. The Romans knew them as Aphrodite, Zeus, and Apollo. It is no surprise that the earliest segment of the Roman road system to be completed was the segment joining the temple of Apollo Hylates at Kourion with the temple of Aphrodite at Palaipaphos.[33] The Aphrodite sanctuary, founded in the Late Bronze Age, remained a major pilgrimage shrine under both Ptolemaic and Roman rule. The Romans continued the Ptolemaic policy of a ruler cult. As a Julian, Augustus was able to follow his adopted father, Julius Caesar, and claim descent from Venus, that is, Aphrodite. The great temple of Palaipaphos, with its claim to be the birthplace of the goddess, was an obvious candidate to become the "national" shrine of Roman Cyprus.

## Salamis

The site of Salamis has been excavated since the late nineteenth century, mainly by a major French mission, the British colonial authorities, and Dr. Vassos Karageorghis on behalf of the Department of Antiquities of the Republic of Cyprus. The *coup d'etat* against Cypriot President Makarios in July 1974

---

[31]Mitford, "Roman Cyprus," 1296 n. 30.
[32]Parks, "Roman Coinage of Cyprus."
[33]T. Bekker-Nielson, *The Roads of Ancient Cyprus* (Copenhagen: University of Copenhagen, 2004), 108.

led to the invasion and occupation of northern Cyprus, including the site of
Salamis, by the Turkish army. Since that date, no internationally condoned
archaeological excavations have been undertaken in the areas outside the
direct control of the Republic of Cyprus. Turkish Republic archaeologists and
Turkish Cypriot scholars have undertaken some excavation and survey work
in the north of Cyprus, but these are not published internationally and have
been condemned by UNESCO and the international community.

Salamis was excavated in the classical tradition of large-scale exposures
with a focus on public space, the setting for the political and social elites of
the ancient world. The primary aims of such excavations were chronology
building to elucidate political history, and the recovery of works of art and
ancient inscriptions. This reflected the desires of the Western (European and
American) intelligentsia and the membership of the funding societies, including societal elites linked to the museum community.

Salamis was founded after the abandonment of the Bronze Age entrepôt of
Enkomi around 1050 BC.[34] A powerful city-state in the Iron Age, Salamis was
heavily involved in the Persian wars for control of the island. Blessed with a
rich agricultural hinterland and a prime location along the shore facing the
markets of Syria, Salamis was the dominant city politically, culturally, and
economically before the time of Alexander.

Salamis was still in the comfort zone for Paul. First-century Salamis contained all the urban amenities characteristic of a successful and prosperous
eastern Roman city. It had grown organically, rather than as a product of imperial fiat. Travelers entering the city from the harbor would pass through a major
bath-gymnasium complex graced with fine statuary and elegant frescoes. Paul
and Barnabas would then have encountered a magnificent theater with a seat-
ing capacity of fifteen thousand. Other excavated urban public spaces include
the Hellenistic agora, still functioning in the Roman period, and the famous
temple of Zeus Olympios, also founded in the Hellenistic period. The line
of the classical/Hellenistic city wall, probably still functional in the Roman
period, has been identified. Recent excavations by the University of Ankara
have identified a major urban thoroughfare, lined with shops, reflecting the
eastern Roman commercial pattern.[35] A population estimate based on the
aqueduct capacity suggests a first-century population of around 120,000.[36]
All of this would have been familiar and comfortable territory for Paul.

---

[34] Vassos Karageorghis, *Salamis in Cyprus: Homeric, Hellenistic and Roman* (London: Thames &
Hudson, 1969).

[35] This information is from personal visits to the site.

[36] George F. Hill, *A History of Cyprus*, vol. 1 (Cambridge: Cambridge University Press, 1940), 42.

None of the excavation teams have yet focused on the domestic space of Salamis. We have no sense of the cityscape, how its visible amenities were linked, or what the arrangement of the neighborhoods was. Understandably, we lack any evidence of a synagogue, although Salamis had a very large Jewish population, who were encouraged to settle there under the Ptolemies. Acts 13:5 emphasizes the large Jewish population in the city when it reports that Paul and Barnabas proclaimed their message in the "Jewish synagogues" (plural). The late fourth-century basilica of St. Epiphanius, was built within a domestic quarter after a major earthquake in AD 342 severely damaged the city. In light of the placement of early Byzantine churches in urban neighborhoods in the Levantine mainland, one would normally argue that the neighborhood of the basilica of St. Epiphanius was likely to be Jewish and may have had a synagogue as a near neighbor.[37] However, the total destruction of the Cypriot Jewish community in the Diaspora revolt of AD 117 eliminates this line of research for understanding the Jewish neighborhoods of Salamis. Barnabas was a native of Salamis, and his purported tomb outside the city is now a major pilgrimage site on the island. Paul and Barnabas were almost certainly hosted by his family, but we cannot yet provide the proper domestic backdrop for this visit.

## Paphos

The book of Acts records that Paul and Barnabas traveled "through the whole island" (Acts 13:6) until they arrived in Paphos. The Roman road system on Cyprus was not completed until sometime in the early fourth century AD, but some sections were already in place by the Pauline visit.[38] The first segment completed under Augustus linked the temple of Apollo at Kourion and the temple of Aphrodite at Palaipaphos.[39] This had a strategic value, linking the political capital with the prime religious sanctuary of the island. A Roman governor would want quick access to the temple leadership and more importantly, to the treasury. Undoubtedly the Roman roads followed Ptolemaic and older tracks where available. David Gill points out that Luke's phraseology implies a land journey without using the more efficient coastal shipping.[40] We do not know how long the passage across Cyprus took Paul and Barnabas. A direct journey from Salamis to Paphos, stopping only at night, would have taken about seven days. Since the missionaries had already spent some time in Salamis speaking in a number of synagogues, it is more likely that they did

---

[37]Eric Meyers, "Early Judaism and Christianity in the Light of Archaeology," *BA* 51, no. 2 (1988): 69–79.
[38]Bekker-Nielsen, *Roads of Ancient Cyprus.*
[39]T. B. Mitford, "Three Milestones of Western Cyprus," *AJA* 70 (1966): 89–99.
[40]David W. J. Gill, "Paul's Travels Through Cyprus (Acts 13:4–12)," *TynBul* 46, no. 2 (1995): 219–28.

not feel time constraints. If it was a more leisurely passage, then a two-wheel vehicle was the likeliest form of transport for two commercial travelers such as Paul and Barnabas.[41] This cart could carry their trade goods, that is, tents. We know Paul worked during his future mission journeys; there was no reason why Barnabas and Paul could not have teamed up here to do business as well since it appears they had the time.

They almost certainly passed along the southern coastal road as this was a major track linking the coastal cities and the best way by foot to Paphos. The fourth/fifth-century text entitled *Acts of Barnabas* records a journey of Mark and Barnabas that supposedly retraced the original route of Paul and Barnabas. In this text they pass along the coastal road, seeing both the temple of Apollo at Kourion and the temple of Aphrodite at Palaipaphos. Although the coastal road was present in the first century AD, the itinerary of the *Acts of Barnabas* reflects the mature Roman road system of Late Antiquity. This text is more likely a product of the campaign of the institutionalized Cypriot Church to gain autocephalous status.[42]

The Cypriot journey of the apostle ended at Paphos, the capital of the Roman province. The city had been severely damaged in an earthquake, leading Augustus to intervene and help repair the city. In gratitude, the city was renamed Sebaste. Later Claudius would name the city Sebaste Claudia Flavia.[43]

The site of Paphos has been investigated since the 1960s by the Cyprus Department of Antiquities and a number of foreign missions. The discovery of the first urban house with intact mosaics was as a result of a chance discovery during construction activity in 1962.[44] Since then, it has become clear that magnificent floor mosaics were common among the elite houses of Paphos.

The Roman city Paul entered is hard to envision and its remains are almost completely obscured by the monumental public buildings and magnificent urban villas of the second and third centuries AD. The city was walled and was laid out on a grid system with well-defined commercial and residential quarters. It was graced with an excellent harbor, which gave a strong impetus to trade.[45] The main civic theater, recently uncovered near the Kourion gate, seated 8,500. The magnificent House of Theseus is considered to be the resi-

---

[41] Bekker-Nielsen, *Roads of Ancient Cyprus*, 72–74.
[42] Thomas W. Davis, "Earthquakes and the Crises of Faith: Social Transformation in Late Antique Cyprus," *BurH* 46 (2010): 3–14.
[43] Mitford, "Roman Cyprus," 1310.
[44] Mlynarczyk, *Nea Paphos III*.
[45] John R. Leonard and Robert L. Holfelder, "Paphos Harbor, Past and Present: The 1991–1992 Underwater Survey" (report of the Department of Antiquities, Cyprus, 1993), 365–79.

dence of the Roman governor.[46] It is the largest residence known from Roman Cyprus, measuring at 120 × 80 meters, with more than a hundred rooms. It is thought to date to the third century AD and continues to be occupied after a series of earthquakes in the fourth century severely damaged the city, leading to the provincial government being moved to Salamis. Fragmentary evidence of a previous structure on the site may be all that remains of the governor's residence at the time of the Pauline visit. It is certainly possible that Sergius Paulus occupied another residence, which has not been located.

## The Encounter: Out of the Comfort Zone

The main focus of the account in Acts of the Cyprus mission is the encounter in Paphos between Paul and the Roman governor, Sergius Paulus.[47] Luke sees this as a seminal event, changing Paul's name and, in essence, his ministry. Although the change of name has been subjected to extensive speculation in biblical scholarship,[48] the impact on the ministry of Paul has been almost ignored. There seemed to be no rationale for a change in Paul's thinking at this time. The image of a province unified by Augustan *Romanitas*, such as in Mitford's magisterial survey of Roman Cyprus, has provided the cultural backdrop for scholarly analysis of the Pauline encounter. This homogenization of Roman Cyprus has obscured any suggestion of a new environment or new pressures that might have produced a Cypriot impact on Pauline theology.

### A Cultural Divide

An examination of recent scholarship on Roman Cyprus suggests that the province was not as unified in the first century as previously thought. The elite of Paphos appear to have embraced elements of a separate cultural identity from the rest of Cyprus. New studies indicate an east/west economic divide in Roman Cyprus between Paphos and the eastern two-thirds of the island. Anthi Kaldelis's doctoral study of Roman trade amphorae found on Cyprus indicates the complex interchange network Cyprus took part in.[49] Kaldelis's analysis shows that Amathus and Salamis traded heavily with Antioch, Cilicia,

---

[46] This is not yet well published. The most accessible discussion is by W. A. Daszewski, *Guide to the Paphos Mosaics* (Nicosia: Bank of Cyprus, 1988), 52–63.

[47] The three possible inscriptions that may attest to his governorship are well summarized by Alanna Nobbs, "Cyprus," in *The Book of Acts in Its First-Century Setting*, vol. 2, *The Graeco-Roman Setting*, ed. David W. J. Gill and Conrad Gempf (Grand Rapids: Eerdmans 1994), 279–90. The Roman Tiber inscription is the most likely.

[48] This goes all the way back to Jerome and Augustine. A good summary of the discussion of Paul's name is by C. J. Hemer, "The Name of Paul," *TynBul* 36 (1985): 179–83.

[49] Anthi Kaldelis, *Roman Amphorae from Cyprus: Integrating Trade and Exchange in the Mediterranean* (PhD thesis, University College London, 2008).

and the Levant, while Paphos looked strongly west with a high percentage of imports from Italy and Rome itself; this is particularly strong in the first century. The evidence presented by John Lund in his studies of Roman fine ware suggests a similar division.[50] The Paphos region was the production center for Cypriot Sigillata fine ware, while Eastern Sigillata ware produced in Syria dominate the fine ware sub-assemblages of Salamis and Amathus.

Roman coinage under the Julio-Claudians also hints at an east/west social/cultural divide that the first-century Romans were aware of. Under Augustus, the primary mint appears to have been in the provincial capital of Nea Paphos, and the coins seem to have been widely circulated. Gordon points out that the iconography and legends were presumably selected by Roman officials and mint officials and thus can be read to illustrate their goals for and attitude about Cyprus and Cypriots.[51] On this evidence, Rome was aware of a provincial divide between east and west. A series of coins produced under Augustus has two distinct reverse images: the temple of Aphrodite at Palaipaphos and the temple of Zeus at Salamis, built under imperial patronage of the Ptolemies.

The concurrent issuing of a "Salamis" coin may have been an attempt to acknowledge or recognize a religious divide in the province. The Palaipaphos temple image was meant to address the local elite in the Paphos area, while the statue of Zeus reverse was intended to appease Salaminians, thus placating both segments of the island.[52]

Paphos appears to be a particularly "Roman" district. Elsewhere in the eastern empire, depictions of temples housing the imperial cult are common on contemporary coin issues. On the basis of this, and the obvious "family" links of the Julians to Aphrodite, many scholars have suggested that the imperial ritual may have been somehow blended with the island's primary cult to Aphrodite.[53]

The east/west dichotomy is also hinted at by Parks in her discussion of the second use of the Aphrodite temple/Zeus Salaminos on coin issues by Drusus Minor.[54] Drusus, Tiberius's son, actually combined both images on one coin, further encouraging a unified province. Parks states that both images may have been used "to keep the people of each city happy." Barnabas seems to show evidence of the Cypriot cultural divide in his life as Luke depicts it in Acts. Barnabas, like

[50] John Lund, "On the Circulation of Goods in Hellenistic and Early Roman Cyprus: The Ceramic Evidence," in *Panayia Ematousa II: Political, Cultural, Ethnic and Social Relations in Cyprus: Approaches to Regional Studies*, ed. L. Wreidt Sorensen and K. Winther Jacobsen (Athens: Danish Institute of Athens, 2006), 31–49.

[51] Gordon, "Why Empires Matter."

[52] Ibid.

[53] Mitford, "Roman Cyprus."

[54] Parks, "The Roman Coinage of Cyprus," 68.

Salamis itself, has an eastern orientation. He is at home in Jerusalem, Antioch, and eastern Cyprus, but when the story shifts to Paphos, Paul becomes the spokesman and leader. Luke portrays Paul as more open to the cultural challenge of the pagan Roman world than Barnabas, who appears out of his depth. This could also be evidence of a subtle anti-Roman bias in Barnabas, perhaps because he was from Salamis, the quintessential Hellenistic city of Cyprus. Fergus Millar notes the value of the New Testament writings for their insight into the negotiation of identity between subject and ruler in the Roman Empire, and Paul and Barnabas may epitomize this negotiation in a Cypriot context.[55]

## The Encounter

Paul and Barnabas are invited by the governor to discuss their beliefs in Acts 13:7. This is the first record of a conversation between Paul and a high Roman official, certainly not a comfortable moment at this point in the apostle's life. Although dating after the Pauline visit, the House of Theseus does provide us with an idea of how the Roman governors wanted to display themselves and how a visitor would have been forcibly reminded of Roman power and authority. The visitors atrium was provided with benches and was dominated by a statue of a nude Venus armed with a bow. It has been suggested that this statue may also represent Roma, combining the main goddess of Cyprus with the titular goddess of the empire.[56]

It is most likely that Paul and Barnabas are invited to be part of the after-dinner "entertainment" at a banquet given by the governor. Philosophical readings and discussions would be a normal part of the evening at the home of an "intelligent man"—one who was educated, spoke Greek, was interested in philosophical questions, and therefore was open to a new faith. The inclusion of the Jewish magician Bar-Jesus makes it almost a certainty that this was more of a social occasion than an official meeting held during office hours. The rival philosophers would be pitted against one another for the enjoyment of the dinner guests and, in the governor's case, out of an honest interest in the subject. If this is a correct interpretation of the setting for the conversation, then this is also the first time Paul has been invited to a pagan Gentile's house for dinner; another experience outside of his "comfort zone."

A recent study of Roman Cypriot magic texts from the site of Amathus makes clear that Luke's account of the contest between Bar-Jesus and Paul accurately reflects a Cypriot milieu.[57] Cypriot magic was often employed to

---

[55] Fergus Millar, *The Roman Empire and Its Neighbors*, 2nd ed. (London: Duckworth, 1991), 81.
[56] Gordon, "Why Empires Matter."
[57] Andrew T. Wilburn, "*Materia Magica*: The Archaeology of Magic in Roman Egypt, Cyprus and Spain" (PhD diss., University of Michigan, 2005).

prevent someone from speaking, and blindness could be used as a preventative measure in these cases; in the Acts account, Bar-Jesus is trying to prevent Paul from speaking to the governor about the faith; so in typical Lukan irony, the magician is struck down by the very weapon he was probably trying to use against Paul. After some discussion, Sergius Paulus "believes," but he is not baptized (Acts 13:12). It is likely that he has had a personal conversion, making Jesus his personal deity, while still maintaining the religious aspects of his public role as governor.

### The Impact on Paul

When Paul entered Paphos he crossed an economic, social, and political boundary that divided the province into an eastern-oriented zone and a western-oriented zone. It is now reasonable to propose that in Paphos, Paul left behind the economic, social, and religious comfort zone in which he had spent his entire Christian ministry. Therefore, when Paul met the governor, it is certainly possible that he was for the first time forced to confront new possibilities in his Christian mission. The positive results of his encounter with the governor, in contrast to the apparent failure of the synagogue mission within the Pauline comfort zone in Salamis, may provide the catalyst for a fundamental change in the Pauline ministry: Paul now embraces the truly pagan world as his mission field. In Pisidian Antioch he first goes to the synagogue, where he preaches his "classic" outreach sermon to the Diaspora Jews. Luke records that when his sermon is challenged by some of the Jews, Paul responds, "We now turn to the Gentiles" (Acts 13:46).

Paul's retelling of his conversion in the Acts accounts (Acts 22 and 26) makes his call to Gentile ministry to be contemporaneous with his conversion.[58] This is the central message of the vision Paul had in the temple during his first visit to Jerusalem. However, he may have been resisting this call until he saw the work of the Holy Spirit in Paphos. The first letter Paul writes to the churches he may have visited on this trip, Galatians, shows his embrace of the call and is a defense of his Gentile ministry. Paul in his own letters defines his own ministry as "Gentile" in aim from the very beginning. It is possible that Paul is indulging in a little hindsight here, reading his growing understanding of his true calling back into his original conversion and the beginnings of his ministry.

Luke consistently has Paul first reaching out to Jews, and only after he has been rejected does he reach out to Gentiles. In Luke's report of Paul's defense before Agrippa, he quotes the apostle: "First to those in Damascus, then to those in Jerusalem and in all Judea and to the Gentiles also" (Acts 26:20).

---

[58]Bruce, Paul, 87.

Notice the separation of the dwellers in Damascus and Jerusalem from the Gentiles. The implication is that he has reached out to his fellow Jews as well as to Gentiles.

This cultural shock of Paphos also eliminates much of the perceived "tension" between Luke's record of Paul's practice of first seeking out a Jewish audience and Paul's self-proclaimed call to the Gentiles. It also may be a semantic difference between Luke and Paul. Luke may think of real "Gentile" ministry as outreach to untouched pagans. It is possible, however, that Paul's initial "Gentile" outreach was confined to the already acclimatized Gentiles (in religious terms), who have already been attracted to Judaism—the so-called "God-fearers" who would have been most easily encountered in the synagogue.[59] Paul may also be referring to Diaspora Jews who have shed their religious identity and Hellenized. A recent sociological study of the early church concludes that Diaspora Jews were the overwhelming majority of converts in the first centuries of the faith.[60] In this scenario, Luke is accurate in that Paul first targeted the synagogue, and Paul is correct in that he specifically targeted the "Gentile" Hellenized secular Jews and the Greek converts to Judaism.

## Lukan Accuracy

Current archaeological evidence demonstrates that Luke's understanding of mid-first-century Cyprus is accurate and nuanced. The cultural shock Paul experienced in Paphos provides the unexplained justification for the change in Paul's theology. The east/west cultural divide that Paul encountered in Roman Cyprus was strongest in the first half of the first century, exactly when Luke places Paul on Cyprus. Archaeological evidence for the east/west cultural divide after the mid-first century lessens, particularly in the numismatic evidence. Following the reign of Claudius, Cypriot coinage minted on the island is labeled as the product of the koinon Kyprion and indicates that the elites of the Cypriot cities are presenting a unified message, acting in concert with Rome.

The vibrant mid-first-century Jewish community with strong ties to Judea depicted by Luke also is supported by the evidence of Cypriot coinage. Judean coins on Cyprus are "quite common" during the Julio-Claudian period, but almost disappear at the time of Vespasian.[61] By the early second century Judean imports completely disappear from the archaeological record and

[59]Irina Levenskaya, The Book of Acts in Its First Century Setting, vol. 5, Diaspora Setting (Grand Rapids: Eerdmans, 1996).

[60]Rodney Stark, Cities of God (New York: Harper Collins, 2006).

[61]Parks, "The Roman Coinage of Cyprus," 142.

are replaced by Roman imperial coins minted in the west.[62] This is stark evidence of the complete destruction of the local Jewish community in the Diaspora revolt of AD 117. Although John Dominic Crossan and Jonathan Reed, in a recent study of Paul, recognize that Luke may include "correct details, accurate places and even travel sequences," they conclude negatively: "Luke's Acts were written in the 80s or 90s, several decades after Paul's time and Luke gives him an overall interpretation from within his geographical situation, historical understanding and theological vision."[63] The picture of mid-first-century Cyprus derived from the archaeological data challenges this confident assertion and strongly improves the case for the book of Acts to be an accurate reflection of a mid-first-century milieu. When measured by the current state of archaeological understanding, Luke's account of Paul's Cyprus visit reflects a cultural geography that can be found only during the mid-first century.

This new understanding of mid-first-century Cyprus also provides a psychologically clear justification for Paul's radical theological vision of the Gentile ministry. When Paul returns to Antioch from his Cypriot mission, he has been transformed, the gospel message has been transformed, and as a result, the "followers of this Way" (Acts 22:4) will be transformed. "On arriving there, they gathered the church together and reported all that God had done through them and how he opened the door of faith to the Gentiles" (Acts 14:27). The invitation to Jews to accept the Messiah of God has become an open door to the entire pagan world, and a Jewish messianic sect will become the Christian church. The crucible for all of these changes is Cyprus.

---

[62]Ibid., 167.

[63]John Dominic Crossan and Jonathan L. Reed, *In Search of Paul: How Jesus' Apostle Opposed Rome's Empire with God's Kingdom* (London: Society for Promoting Christian Knowledge, 2005). With unconscious irony they precede the sentence quoted above with the phrase "Put positively."

❈ Part 4

# THE OLD TESTAMENT
# AND ARCHAEOLOGY

# 19

# ENTER JOSHUA

## The "Mother of Current Debates" in Biblical Archaeology

## JOHN M. MONSON

❧

## Introduction

The God of the Bible acts in time and space. But readers of Scripture are far removed from the times and places of events that the Bible records. Modern readers, like previous generations of scholars in both the church and the academy, seek to harmonize these two statements with the philosophical and theological thinking of their day. They rely in large part upon historical criticism, a scientific method committed to determining the historicity and original meaning of the text. Over the past century this method brought not only a range of helpful tools for the study of the Bible but also challenges to more traditional views of Scripture. Decades of rising skepticism toward the Bible in both intellectual circles and the culture at large yielded a "hermeneutic of suspicion" that is the norm today.[1] The God of the Bible, it is argued, if he exists at all, is attested just as powerfully—or more so—in theological constructs and personal experience as he is in ancient texts, rife with potential inconsistencies and contradictions.

Many contemporary readers of the Bible therefore face an apparent obstacle around which they must navigate: How do we understand the truth claims of Scripture in light of the historical-critical method and empirical evidence from archaeology and ancient sources? Some evangelical academics confront the issue head on and in public. Others ignore it altogether in their professional work but maintain a private faith. Most recently, "progressive evangelicals"

---

[1] P. Ricoeur, "Biblical Hermeneutics," *Semia* 4 (1975): 27–48; Jon Levenson, "The Bible: Unexamined Commitments of Criticism," *First Things* 30 (1993): 24–33.

are calling upon scholars of traditional and biblically conservative views to embrace more intentionally the historical-critical method, as well as some of its more radical presuppositions. There is underway a migration of some evangelicals toward positions that challenge the Bible as a consistently reliable historical document. Some even give tacit approval to the "minimalist" approaches concerning biblical persons and events.[2] This is occurring at the very time that the exponential increase in textual and archaeological data from the ancient Near East is only just beginning to have a voice in biblical and theological studies at large.

In ancient Near Eastern studies and archaeology the landscape is also changing.[3] From the perspective of the text today one can see the Bible's connection to ancient Near Eastern thought and modes of expression more clearly than ever before.[4] From the perspective of archaeology, the increasing use of technology, widespread surveys, and ongoing excavation continues to yield spectacular and sometimes surprising results. Some of these finds shed new light on biblical characters or episodes that in previous years were discounted altogether.[5] The combined use of linguistic, geographical, and archaeological data—what I call "contextual criticism"—makes it possible to situate the biblical record more confidently within its own spatial, temporal, and cultural setting than ever before.[6]

In light of these issues it seems fitting to revisit briefly Israel's entry into Canaan since it lies at the intersection of the Bible, history, archaeology, and theology—adding the necessary component of geography. This "mother of

---

[2]Kenton L. Sparks, *God's Word in Human Words: An Evangelical Appropriation of Critical Biblical Scholarship* (Grand Rapids: Baker Academic, 2008), 356; Peter Enns, *Inspiration and Incarnation: Evangelicals and the Problem of the Old Testament* (Grand Rapids: Baker Academic, 2005).

[3]Good methods and sober expectations characterize the new generation of archaeologists, religious and secular, and there is gradually more willingness to invoke anthropology and history in tandem. See the new book *Historical Biblical Archaeology and the Future: The New Pragmatism*, ed. Thomas Levy (New York: Equinox, 2010).

[4]K. Lawson Younger, *Ancient Conquest Accounts: A Study in Ancient Near Eastern and Biblical History Writing* (Sheffield: JSOT, 1990); John H. Walton, *Ancient Near Eastern Thought and the Old Testament: Introducing the Conceptual World of the Hebrew Bible* (Grand Rapids: Baker Academic, 2006); Kenton L. Sparks, *Ancient Texts for the Study Of the Hebrew Bible: A Guide to the Background Literature* (Peabody, MA: Hendrickson, 2005).

[5]Note most recently the Davidic era fort at Qeiyafa, the Iron Age mines in Transjordan, and the compelling parallels to Solomon's temple: Yosef Garfinkel and Saar Ganor, *Khirbet Qeiyafa*, vol. 1, *Excavation Report 2007–2008* (Jerusalem: Israel Exploration Society, 2009); Erez Ben-Yosef et al., "The Beginning of Iron Age Copper Production in the Southern Levant: New Evidence from Khirbat al-Jariya, Faynan, Jordan," *Antiquity* 84 (2010): 724–46; John Monson, "The Temples of 'Ain Dara and Jerusalem," in *Text, Artifact, and Image: Revealing Ancient Israelite Religion*, ed. G. Beckman and T. Lewis (Providence, RI: Brown University Judaic Studies, 2006).

[6]John Monson, "Original Context as a Framework for Biblical Interpretation," in *Ancient Israel: Ancient Kingdom or Late Invention?*, ed. Daniel I. Block (Nashville: B&H, 2008).

all biblical archaeology debates" has a scholarly literature too vast and issues too numerous to receive even a cursory survey here. It may, however, serve as a touchstone for friendly discussion with those who would attenuate the historicity of the Old Testament and in its place elevate scholarly consensus, theological reflection, and select doctrines.

## The Background of the Debate

The so-called "conquest" and settlement of Israel are tied to the history of two major disciplines. The textual issues are governed by the history of biblical studies, whereas the archaeological issues reflect the history of biblical archaeology. Both trajectories are relevant to critical scholarship and evangelical understanding of Scripture in the twenty-first century.[7] Beginning in the eighteenth and nineteenth centuries, exploration and nascent archaeological inquiry brought greater appreciation of the Bible's geographical and cultural setting, even as the biblical text came under the increasingly hostile scrutiny of biblical criticism.[8] It was only natural that some scholars of Judeo-Christian background sought to harness the burgeoning discoveries of the Near East in defense of a literal reading of the Bible.[9]

When in the 1930s a dominant scholar like W. F. Albright came to favor an archaeology-based historical reconstruction of the Bible over the more radical forms of source criticism, many came to trust his judgment on issues of biblical history.[10] Among other things, Albright and his student G. E. Wright argued that already in their day excavations yielded sufficient evidence to posit a focused, widespread, and destructive Israelite conquest of Canaan.[11] On the positive side, Albright grounded biblical study in science and history by making evident the Bible's setting within the geography of the Holy Land,

---

[7] K. A. Kitchen, *On the Reliability of the Old Testament* (Grand Rapids: Eerdmans, 2003); D. Merling, "The Relationship between Archaeology and the Bible: Expectations and Reality," in *The Future of Biblical Archaeology*, ed. James K. Hoffmeier and Alan R. Millard (Grand Rapids: Eerdmans, 2004), 29–42; Richard Hess, "Early Israel in Canaan: A Survey of Recent Evidence and Interpretations," *PEQ* 195 (1993): 125–42; Younger, *Ancient Conquest Accounts*.

[8] See especially Thomas W. Davis, *Shifting Sands: The Rise and Fall of Biblical Archaeology* (Oxford: Oxford University Press, 2004); Edward Robinson, *Biblical Researches in Palestine, Mount Sinai and Arabia Petræa: A Journal of Travels in the Year 1838* (repr., Ann Arbor: University of Michigan Library, 2006; Iain Provan, V. Philips Long, and Tremper Longman III, *A Biblical History of Israel* (Louisville: Westminster John Knox, 2003), 3–35. Some of these debates culminated in the fundamentalist-modernist controversy (V. Philips Long, *The Art of Biblical History*, Foundations of Contemporary Interpretation 5 (Grand Rapids: Zondervan, 1994), 120–68.

[9] Davis, *Shifting Sands*, 228.

[10] W. F. Albright, *Archaeology of Palestine and the Bible* (New York: Revell, 1932).

[11] This dominant view is expressed forcefully and documented well by J. P. Free and G. E. Wright. See Free, *Archaeology and Bible History*, 5th ed. (Wheaton, IL: Scripture Press, 1956), 124–37; and Wright, "Epic of Conquest," *BA* 3 (1940): 25–40.

its connection to ancient Near Eastern texts, and its rootedness in ancient cultural realities. On the negative side, he described a unified conquest that was more dramatic than even the Bible's description, and he attributed to the Israelites the last destruction phases of Canaanite cities. When it became clear that the destruction and decline of Late Bronze Age cities occurred later than the commonly accepted thirteenth-century-BC date of Joshua, the conclusion followed that this evidence could not be attributed to Israel's entry into Canaan. Moreover, excavations at Jericho and Ai, two cities that Joshua burned with fire, did not yield what was felt to be the necessary evidence of a Late Bronze Age destruction.[12] Thus Albright's famous overreach of biblical archaeology, which was itself a reaction to radical biblical criticism, ironically led to an abandonment of the Joshua narrative as holding any historical value. This clouds the conquest debate to this day.

Subsequent syntheses were also reflective of larger trends in science, social studies, and biblical studies.[13] The "peaceful infiltration" model of Alt envisioned peoples from various locations and backgrounds, including mainly pastoralists, coalescing in the highlands of Canaan around a deity named Yahweh.[14] Among them were tribal elements from Transjordan, Canaan, and Egypt. The conquest narratives of Joshua were regarded as later etiological stories composed during the Israelite monarchy. Just as Albright saw the text of Joshua through the lens of Late Bronze Age destructions in Canaan, so Alt projected the ideas of nomad-farmer coexistence and Greek tribal confederacy onto the emergence of Israel. In both cases a governing model overcame the selectivity and ambiguity of the textual and archaeological data but did so at the cost of creating oversimplified reconstructions.

During the past several decades the conquest debate has been recast within the larger rubric of the findings from archaeological surveys that revealed changes in settlement patterns and culture during the late second millennium BC. This transition from thirteenth-century-BC Late Bronze Age urban city-states to twelfth-century-BC villages on the so-called highland frontier

---

[12]Josh. 6:24; 8:19, 28; 11:11–13; Carl Rasmussen, "Conquest, Infiltration, Revolt, or Resettlement? What Really Happened During the Exodus–Judges Period?," in *Giving the Sense: Understanding and Using the Old Testament Historical Books* (Grand Rapids: Kregel, 2003), 138–59.

[13]Patrick Mazani, "The Appearance of Israel in Canaan in Recent Scholarship," in *Critical Issues in Early Israelite History*, ed. Richard S. Hess, Gerald A. Klingbeil, and Paul J. Ray Jr., BBRSup 3 (Winona Lake, IN: Eisenbrauns, 2008), 95–110; K. Lawson Younger, "Early Israel in Recent Scholarship," in *The Face of Old Testament Studies: A Survey of Contemporary Approaches*, ed. David W. Baker and Bill T. Arnold (Grand Rapids: Baker, 1999), 176–206.

[14]A. Alt, "The Settlement of the Israelites in Palestine," in *Essays in Old Testament History and Religion* (Oxford: Blackwell, 1966), 133–69.

seemed to correlate quite well with the local emergence of Israel, however that emergence might be conceived.[15]

Within this broad framework a good number of interpretations were proposed, most of them appealing to sociological and anthropological models. Among them was the peasant-revolt hypothesis, which saw the Israelites as nothing more than Canaanites who rebelled against their overlords.[16] Israel Finkelstein interpreted the cultural change as part of a long-term ebb and flow between pastoralists and a sedentary population in Palestine.[17] Yet another proposal explained Israel's emergence as a ruralization process whereby populations who left the collapsing city-states of Late Bronze Age Canaan built nested housing compounds and villages in the adjacent highlands (Stager, Dever). A more radical (so-called minimalist) view held by scholars such as Thompson saw the demographic changes as a purely local development unrelated to the origins of Israel since they considered Joshua and the majority of the Old Testament to be merely a late fiction.[18]

In sum, the textual aspect of the conquest debate for the most part has become simply a reflection of trends in biblical criticism. For the past few decades all but the most conservative biblical scholars have considered the Joshua account to be historically unreliable.[19] Archaeology, once thought to support the biblical text, has since Albright's day come to be seen as a negative reality check to biblical claims. Archaeology has been given a privileged role of proving or—through assumed lack of evidence—denying the biblical record. Yet archaeological surveys and excavations—past and present—reveal

---

[15]The villages include, among other new features, houses with four rooms, pillars, and storage silos within small compounds that form a rural culture sharply contrasted with the lowland cities of Late Bronze Canaan. There is, however, also considerable evidence for cultural continuity. See L. Stager, "Forging an Identity: The Emergence of Ancient Israel," in *The Oxford History of the Biblical World*, ed. Michael Coogan (New York: Oxford, 1998), 123–76, and recent summaries in Hess, Klingbeil, and Ray, *Critical Issues in Early Israelite History*. Also, William Dever, "Cultural Continuity, Ethnicity in the Archaeological Record, and the Question of Israelite Origins," *ErIsr* 24 (1993): 22*–33*; asterisks indicate pagination of the English-language section.

[16]Norman Gottwald, *The Tribes of Yahweh: A Sociology of the Religion of Liberated Israel, 1250–1050 B.C.E.* (Maryknoll, NY: Orbis, 1979).

[17]*The Archaeology of the Israelite Settlement* (Jerusalem: Israel Exploration Society, 1988).

[18]Thomas L. Thompson, *The Mythic Past: Biblical Archaeology and Myth of Israel* (London: Basic Books, 1999), 200–228; Niels P. Lemche, *Early Israel: Anthropological and Historical Studies on the Israelite Society before the Monarchy* (Leiden: Brill, 1985).

[19]Max Miller, "Archaeology and the Israelite Conquest of Canaan: Some Methodological Observations," *PEQ* 109 (1977): 87–93; William Dever, *What Did the Biblical Writers Know and When Did They Know It? What Archaeology Can Tell Us About the Reality of Ancient Israel* (Grand Rapids: Eerdmans, 2002), 97–158. In fact, today the battle has shifted to David and Solomon, whose historicity is the subject of spirited debate: Israel Finkelstein and Niel Silberman, *David and Solomon: In Search of the Bible's Sacred Kings and the Roots of the Western Tradition* (New York: Free Press, 2007), 261–85.

a complex picture that requires interpretation if it is to be connected to the Bible. It is clear that there emerged a new phenomenon in the highlands of Palestine during the end of the Late Bronze Age in the latter part of the second millennium BC—and this too requires an explanation. There are hypotheses that rely solely upon local revolt, collapse of larger cities, or the ebb and flow of settlement patterns between pastoralists, city dwellers, and farmers, but none of these explanations is entirely satisfying. Stager is certainly correct when he writes, "It is in this broader framework that we must try to locate the more specific causes that led to the emergence of Israel."[20] When one tries to isolate those specific causes, however, both the archaeological record and the biblical account suggest that Israel's entry into Canaan involved several processes rather than a singular event.[21]

## Back to Basics

So much has been written about the so-called "Israelite conquest of Canaan" that it can be a challenge merely to isolate and address the main issues of the debate.[22] Generally speaking, in most contemporary biblical scholarship the text is treated as a tendentious, unreliable reflection on the past. In contrast, archaeological findings are held up as the scientific arbiter. Geography, which features so prominently in the Joshua narrative, is seldom addressed and, if so, only in a cursory manner. The following observations on the text, archaeology, and geography of the conquest narratives are offered not as a summary or update but rather as a selective demonstration that the biblical account of Israel's entry into Canaan should be accepted as a legitimate historical source.[23] The purpose is not to "prove the Bible" per se but rather to make note of the compelling reasons why one should engage rather than dismiss these relevant biblical texts.

---

[20] Stager, "Forging an Identity," 142.

[21] "We should speak of an Israelite *entry* into Canaan, and settlement: *neither* only a conquest (although raids and attacks were made), *nor* simply an infiltration (although some tribes moved in alongside the Canaanites), *nor* just re-formation of local Canaanites into a new society 'Israel' (although others, as at Shechem, may have joined the Hebrew nucleus; cf. Gibeon). But the elements of several processes can be seen in the biblical narratives." Kenneth Kitchen, *On the Reliability of the Old Testament* (Grand Rapids: Eerdmans, 2003), 190.

[22] James K. Hoffmeier, *Israel in Egypt* (Oxford: Oxford University Press, 1996), 3–51, offers an excellent summary. See also the thoughtful update of Gordon McConville and Stephen Williams, *Joshua*, Two Horizons Old Testament Commentary (Grand Rapids: Eerdmans, 2010).

[23] Geography is given the most attention here because, unlike the textual and archaeological components of the conquest debate, it has received very little attention even though it can provide some of the most compelling material for historical issues related to the conquest.

## The Book of Joshua as Ancient Near Eastern Text

The book of Joshua is a highly structured narrative account replete with advanced literary techniques and "complex macro-structures."[24] It is thought to be part of the so-called Deuteronomic History (commonly understood as Deuteronomy—2 Kings) and may reflect the concerns of that work, among them the question of what went wrong with the Israelite monarchies and perhaps why Ephraim and the northern kingdom fell away. But that is another story. The form and content of Joshua, as well as the events that it describes (replete with battles, destructions, and geographical descriptions), are reminiscent of the late second millennium BC, as Younger has shown.[25] These include especially the conquest accounts of chapters 9–12 but also the boundary lists of Joshua 13–19, as well as onomastic evidence, and the use of hyperbole.[26] The latter feature exists in numerous military accounts of the ancient Near East, and it lends further support for tracing part of its content to the late second millennium BC.[27] The key lesson here is that in light of parallel accounts from the ancient Near East there is little justification for dismissing the biblical conquest episodes on account of the miracles, deity, and hyperbole incorporated in the text. These are recognizable and unexceptional features of Near Eastern texts ancient and modern.[28]

A further textual challenge to the authenticity and relevance of the Joshua conquest accounts is the relationship of these passages to the first chapter of the book of Judges. Although many scholars see a contradiction between the claims of success in the Joshua narrative and the partial settlement described in Judges 1, there is precedent in Assyrian texts and elsewhere for conquest

---

[24]L. Younger, "The Rhetorical Structuring of the Joshua Narratives," in Hess, Klingbeil, and Ray, *Critical Issues in Early Israelite History*, 3–32.

[25]Younger, *Ancient Conquest Accounts*; Richard Hess, *Joshua*, Tyndale Old Testament Commentaries (Downers Grove, IL: InterVarsity, 1996), 35; Gordon McConville, "*Joshua*," in *The Oxford Bible Commentary*, ed. J. Barton and J. Muddiman (Oxford: Oxford University Press, 2001), 159.

[26]R. Hess, "Asking Historical Questions of Joshua 13–19: Recent Discussion Concerning the Date of the Boundary Lists," *Faith, Tradition, and History: Old Testament Historiography in Its Near Eastern Context*, ed. A. R. Millard, J. Hoffmeier, and D. Baker (Winona Lake, IN: Eisenbrauns, 1994), 165–80; Hess, "Fallacies in the Study of Early Israel: An Onomastic Perspective," *TynBul* 45 (1994): 338–54.

[27]Younger, *Ancient Conquest Accounts*, 208–37. There are those who vociferously disagree, but seldom do they offer conclusive evidence for their own positions. Nadav Na'aman, for example, draws close parallels between the Joshua accounts and Israelite battles of the Assyrian and later periods. "The entire concept of an invasion and conquest of the high lands in the 13th–12th centuries is alien to historical reality." See Nadav Na'aman, "The 'Conquest of Canaan' in Joshua and in History," in *From Nomadism to Monarchy: Archaeological and Historical Aspects of Early Israel*, ed. N. Na'aman and I. Finkelstein (Jerusalem: Israel Exploration Society, 1990), 250, 284–347.

[28]See, for example, R. Patai, *The Arab Mind* (New York: Hatherleigh), 43–78.

## Table 4. Sites attacked but not occupied by Israel

| © Biblical Background, Inc. www.bibback.com | לְקַח take | לָכַד sieze | נכה smite | שָׂרִיד survive | חרם wipe out | שָׁמַד destroy | שָׂרַף burn | יָרַשׁ possess | בנה build | יָשַׁב settle |
|---|---|---|---|---|---|---|---|---|---|---|
| **EDOM** | | | | | | | | | | |
| **MOAB** | | | | | | | | | | |
| **HESHBON** Jahaz Jazer King Sihon | | | | | | | | | | |
| **EDREI** Ashtaroth King Og of Bashan | | | | | | | | | | |
| **GILEAD** | | | | | | | | | | |
| Summary | | | | | | | | | | |
| **JERICHO** | | | | | | | | | | |
| **AI** | | | | | | | | | | |
| **(SHECHEM)** | | | | | | | | | | |
| **GIBEON** | | | | | | | | | | |
| **MAKKEDAH** | | | | | | | | | | |
| **LIBNAH** | | | | | | | | | | |
| **LACHISH** | | | | | | | | | | |
| **King of Gezer** | | | | | | | | | | |
| **EGLON** | | | | | | | | | | |
| **HEBRON** | | | | | | | | | | |
| **DEBIR** | | | | | | | | | | |
| Summary | | | | | | | | | | |
| **MEROM** | | | | | | | | | | |
| **HAZOR** | | | | | | | | | | |
| Tell Cities | | | | | | | | | | |
| Summary | | | | | | | | | | |

(Transjordan labels left side for Heshbon/Edrei group; Cisjordan labels for Jericho through Hazor group.)

accounts to describe "two aspects of one process."[29] Moreover, the book of Joshua itself records that Israel did not settle the entire land.[30]

There is yet another textual aspect to the Joshua conquest narratives that needs to be addressed, and that is the vocabulary used when Israel captured enemy cities. As noted above, one of the complicating factors in understanding the so-called Israelite conquest is the commonly held belief that the Israelites entered rapidly into Cisjordan (the land west of the Jordan River), destroyed

---

[29]L. Younger "Judges 1 in Its Near Eastern Literary Context," in Millard, Hoffmeier, and Baker, *Faith, Tradition, and History*, 207–28.
[30]Josh. 13:1–7, 29–31; 17:5–6, 11–18.

the majority of Canaanite cities, possessed the cities, built or rebuilt them, and settled down in place of the former population.[31] This view, however, is derived from a misunderstanding of the vocabulary associated with city assaults in Joshua 6–11, for which one can consult table 4. Whereas cities in Transjordan are "possessed" and "settled," all but three of the cities in Cisjordan are "taken," "seized," "wiped out," or such, but they were not "burned with fire" (שׂרף באשׁ). The reports of battles in the book of Joshua make no claim that these cities were possessed upon Israel's entry into Canaan! This fact is paramount to the "conquest" debate! In light of the vocabulary, Joshua's campaigns in Cisjordan may well have been only raids or responses to those who resisted Israel's growing presence (such as the king of Jerusalem and his allies). The modern reader must adjust his or her expectations of the text and let it speak for itself.[32]

> When Joshua is viewed as a piece of Near Eastern military writing, and its literary character is properly understood, the idea of a group of tribes coming to Canaan, using some military force, partially taking a number of cities and areas over a period of some years, destroying (burning) just three cities, and coexisting alongside the Canaanites and other ethnic groups for a period of time before the beginnings of monarchy, does not require blind faith.[33]

### Archaeology's Changing Role

Archaeology is a relatively young field of study, and its relationship to other disciplines is still very much in flux.[34] As noted above, the twentieth century began with very favorable (though sometimes overstated) interconnections being made between archaeology and the Bible. The conquest narrative played a central role in this synergy of disciplines. By the end of the century, however, critical views of Scripture combined with vast amounts of new material and textual evidence gave rise to new skepticism about the integration of material finds and biblical texts. The Late Bronze–Iron Age I transition, for example, proved to be much more intricate than previously thought. And yet, running throughout the history of biblical archaeology is an especially strong interest in the book of Joshua. As David Merling writes, "No other biblical book has been so thoroughly reviewed by the archaeological community as Joshua.

---

[31] Had this happened, one would expect this fact to be reflected overtly in the book of Joshua—without clear statements to the contrary, as we stated above.

[32] In contrast to these "eyewitness accounts," the summary reports and boundary lists in Joshua may well have been written later as a frame to the actual battle accounts (e.g., Josh. 11:16; 15–19).

[33] Hoffmeier, *Israel in Egypt*, 43–44.

[34] A. Burke, "The Archaeology of the Levant in America," in Levy, *Historical Biblical Archaeology and the Future*, 82–87.

The reason for this interest is that no other book of the Bible appears to be as susceptible to archaeological investigation as the book of Joshua."[35]

Most of the debate centers on the three aforementioned cities that, according to the conquest narrative in the book of Joshua, the Israelites "burned . . . with fire"—Hazor, Jericho, and Ai.[36] The Israelites "seized" or "smote" other cities, but the text does not say they burnt them with fire. Moreover, since most Late Bronze Age sites suffered multiple destructions, in most cases it is not possible to associate a single destruction layer with the Israelites.

## Hazor

Hazor's archaeological excavations have yielded Late Bronze Age finds that correlate with the book of Joshua very well. The site has destruction layers that fit both the early and late dates of the exodus/conquest, but because Hazor suffered a particularly massive conflagration in the thirteenth century BC, Ben-Tor contends that the Israelites were most likely the people who ransacked this large city, the "head of all those kingdoms." He reaches this conclusion through a process of elimination.[37]

## Jericho

Unlike Hazor, Jericho and Ai are sites that are more challenging to harmonize with the biblical account of Israel's entry into Canaan because of apparent incongruities between the archaeological finds and the claims in the book of Joshua that they were "burned with fire." Jericho was the first place that Joshua destroyed in Canaan (Josh. 6:21, 24). Its Late Bronze Age remains have been discussed so extensively elsewhere that for the current purposes we need only quote Amihai Mazar.

> At Jericho, no remains of the Late Bronze fortifications were found; this was taken as evidence against the historical value of the narrative in the Book of Joshua. The finds at Jericho, however, show that there was a settlement there during the Late Bronze Age, though most of its remains were eroded or removed by human activity. Perhaps, as at other sites, the massive Middle Bronze fortifications were reutilized in the Late Bronze Age. The Late Bronze Age settlement at Jericho was followed by an occupation gap in Iron Age I. Thus, in the case

[35]"The Book of Joshua, Part I—Its Evaluation and Evidence," AUSS 39 (2001): 61–72.
[36]Josh. 6:24; 11:11; see also 8:28.
[37]Canaanites, it is argued, would not deface their own deities; the Egyptians would not destroy a friendly city; and the Philistines could not have been responsible for the destruction because they had yet to arrive in the Levant (A. Ben-Tor, "The Fall of Canaanite Hazor—the 'Who' and 'When' Questions," in Mediterranean Peoples in Transition: Thirteenth to Early Tenth Centuries BCE, ed. S. Gitin, A. Mazar, and E. Stern (Jerusalem: Israel Exploration Society, 1998), 456–67.

of Jericho, the archaeological data cannot serve as decisive evidence to deny a historical nucleus in the Book of Joshua concerning the conquest of this city.[38]

Beyond this summary two points must also be noted. First, the presence of tombs nearby confirms that there was a settlement during the period of the Israelite conquest, however small it may have been. Second, whatever walls did exist were constructed atop those of the substantial Middle Bronze Age city structures. When one considers the arid climate of the Jericho region and the intense, sporadic downpours in winter, together with the ban that Joshua placed on the city, the likely erosion of most Late Bronze Age structures atop the ancient mound makes perfect sense.[39]

## Ai

Ai, the third city to be "burned with fire," offers even more of a challenge than Jericho. Here also we can rely upon Mazar, but with several caveats to be addressed below. He writes:

> A long gap in occupation followed the large Early Bronze Age city at ʿAi until a small village was established there during the Israelite settlement in the twelfth and eleventh centuries B.C.E. This lack of any Late Bronze Canaanite city at the site or in the vicinity contradicts the narrative in Joshua 8 and shows that it was not based on historical reality despite its topographical and tactical plausibility. The ʿAi story can only be explained as being of etiological nature, created at a time when there was an Israelite settlement on the site—which was the case in the period of the Judges.[40]

The apparent gap in occupation at the time of the Israelite entry to Canaan requires comment because the excavations at Ai were extensive, so one would expect to find at least a trace of the Late Bronze city if indeed it was occupied in that period. Numerous explanations have been proposed, but thus far none fully accounts for the specific description of a king and a gate at Ai in Joshua's day. The strongest proposals are (1) that the city of the period was located down the slope underneath the Arab village of Deir Dibwan and (2) that Ai is located at Khirbet Maqatir, a small site excavated by Bryant Wood.[41] Richard Hess has put forth perfectly viable responses to some of the

---

[38]A. Mazar, *Archaeology of the Land of the Bible* (New York: Doubleday, 1990), 331.
[39]*The New Encyclopedia of Archaeological Excavations in the Holy Land*, ed. E. Stern, 4 vols. (Jerusalem: Israel Exploration Society and Carta, 1993), 2:679–81.
[40]Mazar, *Archaeology of the Land of the Bible*, 331–32.
[41]In response to the first proposal, one would expect to find traces of Late Bronze Age pottery near the modern village, but none has been found. The second proposal is very intriguing (Bryant Wood, "Khirbet el-Maqatir, 2000," *IEJ* 51 [2001]: 246–52). But Khirbet Maqatir is very small, and its limited

problems associated with Ai. The term "king" (מלך) can designate not only a conventional king but also a regional officer. Moreover, "wall" (חומה) is a lexeme used for a variety of entities in settlements large and small.[42]

As the quest for biblical Ai continues, simpler solutions should not be rejected out of hand.[43] For all we know, the place was nothing more than a small squatter's settlement in the vicinity of the imposing ruins of the mighty Early Bronze Age city of the third millennium BC. Such a seemingly simplistic proposal would account for the "king" (מלך), "gate" (שער), and burning in the biblical account, as well as the words of the Israelite spies concerning the site and its environs: "they are few" (Josh. 7:3). The question of Ai is addressed again in the case study offered below.

*Summary of Archaeology*
In dealing with the archaeology of Israel's entry to Canaan one must first place it within the context of the demographic and cultural changes of the Late Bronze–Iron Age I transition. Second, it is crucial to let the text of Joshua speak for itself—and especially the vocabulary concerning Joshua's assault on the cities of Canaan. Problems arise when one discipline or another—whether linguistic study, archaeology, or theology—is allowed to put a straightjacket on the others. Third, the geographical descriptions must be taken seriously and brought into the discussion. Most prior discussions of the topic ignore this component altogether. Finally, archaeological finds must not be treated as a set of objective scientific controls or a "final answer" in the matter.[44]

This last point is crucial, particularly with regard to the three (and there are only three) cities Joshua burned with fire but did not "seize" or "wipe out." For too long archaeologists, biblical scholars, and also people of faith (!) have not adequately taken into account a wide range of relevant studies and possible reconstructions that are available. David Merling writes:

---

pottery is contemporary with an early date of the exodus and Israelite entrance into Canaan. Most scholars posit a late date to the exodus (thirteenth century BC), but for many legitimate reasons, biblical and contextual, an early date of the fourteenth century BC should by no means be ruled out.
[42]Richard Hess, "The Jericho and Ai of the Book of Joshua," in Hess, Klingbeil, and Ray, *Critical Issues in Early Israelite History*, 33–46. In this piece Hess also evaluates most reconstructions offered to date.
[43]In Josh. 7:5 and 8:29 the term *gate*, in Hebrew שער, is an expression that can mean an opening or an architectural entrance. It may well be that in this case the "gate" is nothing more than the narrow ridge by which one ascends to Bethel and the central highland plateau. This is discussed in the case study below. Of course there is no proof of this, but neither can it be ruled out. It is also noteworthy that there are sixteen occurrences of the word *gate* in Hebrew in which it means "dwelling," sometimes metaphorically (e.g., Deut. 5:15; Ps. 100:4). See A. Even-Shoshan, *A New Concordance of the Bible* (Jerusalem: Kiryat Sepher 1981), 1195–97.
[44]Fredric R. Brandfon, "The Limits of Evidence: Archaeology and Objectivity," *Maarav* 4 (1987): 5–43.

The idea that archaeology is the verifier of ancient literary works has been accepted at face value, and evidence to the contrary is not easily accepted. When the nonevidence is used as data and is assumed within a theory, it becomes destructive because theorists are then obligated to fight for the validity of the nonevidence as though it had an existence.[45]

In fact, most positions that dismiss the book of Joshua's relevance to the archaeological realities of the Late Bronze Age are built upon the "fallacy of the negative proof," which is in effect to say, "If we have not found it, then we know with certainty that it does not exist."[46]

While I disagree with those who believe that the Bible and archaeology offer different kinds of information that for the most part cannot be compared, I am much more optimistic. It is true that archaeological evidence is scattered, random, and incomplete, just as the Bible's record is selective, ancient, and theologically oriented. Any attempt to relate these two sets of information is fraught with challenges—and this is especially so in the case of Israel's entry into Canaan. There are perceived contradictions between text and archaeology but also reasonable congruencies. Every proposal in fact is constrained by limited data and unlimited theories. The debate can become toxic when matters of faith and unbelief are raised. Sadly, there are bitter polemics and "fundamentalists" on all sides of this debate!

But when text and archaeology are brought into a more fluid exchange based upon probabilities and broader patterns of corroboration, a wider, potentially more fruitful range of possibilities presents itself. The challenge is first to interpret the biblical text on its own terms and with its own set of disciplines. In like manner, it is advisable first to study the complicated picture derived from archaeology according to its own interpretive processes before bringing the two into dialogue. In my own view the nexus between physical and linguistic forms of human expression is one of the most promising areas of biblical archaeology. And it can be applied with equal effectiveness to artifacts and historical problems.[47]

In the case of Israel's entry into Canaan, if one paints with broader strokes and looks for general patterns of correspondence, then it is possible to propose historical reconstructions based not upon airtight "proof" but upon

---

[45]Merling, "Book of Joshua," 72. In that piece Merling discusses several of the most important studies of the conquest narratives.

[46]Merling discusses the implications of this statement in ibid., 65, where he also quotes Fischer: "This occurs whenever a historian declares that there is no evidence that X is the case, and then proceeds to affirm or assume that not-X is the case." David Hackett Fischer, *Historians' Fallacies: Toward a Logic of Historical Thought* (New York: Harper & Row, 1970), 47.

[47]John Monson, "The Temple of Solomon and the Temple of 'Ain Dara, Syria," *Qadmoniot* 29 (1996): 33–38 (Hebrew).

cumulative evidence and probabilities, that is to say, "what is most likely and logical, given available data."[48] When dealing with ancient texts and artifacts, the latter model is no less compelling than the former.

In light of these observations I would suggest that the text of Joshua fits in well linguistically, stylistically, and in terms of its content with the literature of the late second millennium BC, even if it is framed within a larger, later historical work (as noted above). The book of Joshua's account of the Israelite entry into Canaan does overlap with archaeology, albeit in broad strokes. Jericho and Ai are not unsolvable challenges, and they can be harmonized with the biblical text without improperly imposing text or archaeology one upon the other. The larger historical and archaeological context fits very well. And the geographical rootedness of the text points to a real story in a real place. The polemic of the past decade is unnecessary.

### Arrival of the Israelites: Geography's Unique Contribution

To this point we have attempted to define textual and archaeological issues that relate to what has been termed the "Israelite conquest of Canaan." It is now possible to address geography, a discipline that is often overlooked but in our view is the most useful resource for studying Israel's entry into Canaan. The first task is to place Joshua's major recorded campaigns within the greater land. Next, we will turn to that part of the land in which Joshua's campaigns to Ai took place, the region that lies between Jericho in the Rift Valley and Bethel in Cisjordan's central hill country.

Events recorded in the book of Joshua include detailed descriptions of regions and terrain that match very precisely the geographical realities of Canaan as a whole and lend credibility to the battle accounts. The Israelite arrival in Transjordan flows logically through known regions. In the area of Medeba and Heshbon instructions are given about settlements and territory, including such graphic terms such as "from the 'lip' of the Arnon" (Deut. 3:16), the precipitous edge of the great Arnon canyon, "to the 'hand' of the Jabbok" (Deut. 2:37), the upper tributaries of the Jabbok, which come together like a "hand at the wrist" at the site of Rabbah (modern Amman).[49] The biblical narrative carefully sets Israel's arrival within the actual geographical context of Transjordan that includes a narrow strip of habitable land in Moab and

---

[48]I continue to be intrigued by V. P. Long's analogy of a painting versus a portrait, and the reasonableness of cumulative but partial information lending credibility to a text (Long, *The Art of Biblical History*, 106–7, 222–23).

[49]Josh. 12:2–3. For this translation and a full discussion of these verses and the general region, see J. M. Monson and S. P. Lancaster, *Geobasics Study Guide: Central Arena*, part 2 (Rockford, IL: Biblical Backgrounds, 2010): 94–100, http://www.bibback.com.

Edom (adjacent to the vast Arabian plateau), known uplifted parts of Gilead, and specific battlegrounds around Medeba and Edrei.[50]

Once the Israelites entered the land, even more detail is recorded in the book of Joshua. Organizational plans on the Plains of Moab across from Jericho, the crossing of the Jordan and the defeat of Jericho (the backdoor into Canaan), and even the high country behind Jericho as a hiding place for the spies after they left Rahab at Jericho all seem to suggest that the writer is relying on some type of eyewitness account.[51] The geographical data recorded in the campaigns that follow the fall of Jericho in the region of Ai are so specific that they are presented in a case study below.[52]

The next account of geography in the book of Joshua concerns the battle for the strategic plateau that surrounds Gibeon in the central hill country. While it is not possible to know from which "Gilgal" Joshua's forces came,[53] the overall strategy is clear. The ruse of the Gibeonites had left the inhabitants of the plateau in league with Joshua and effectively in control of the local north-south highway through the hill country, as well as direct connections to the east and to the west. The king of Jerusalem and his allies in the southern hill country and the Shephelah in the west organized a defense in the all-important plateau around Gibeon. These kings had all become vulnerable now and could not tolerate this new threat. In response, Joshua raided cities and regions that had confronted Gibeon and in this manner secured the plateau. Remarkably, every geographical aspect of this campaign—from the ascent of Beth-Horon to "turning back to Debir"—fits the geography of the regions in which the events transpired.[54] The later covenant renewal at Shechem points to the fact that the writer of the book of Joshua recognized the importance of this area and accurately situated these events there.[55]

---

[50]For example, the multitude of biblical references about Bashan suggest that the King of Og at Edrei was an actual figure and that the Israelites sought to expand into parts of his fertile territory that lay beyond the sterile plains of Lower Gilead. These events are covered generally in Num. 21:13–22:1; 32; 33:45–49; Deut. 2:16–3:17; and Josh. 13:7–33.

[51]Joshua 1–6.

[52]Josh. 7:1–8:29.

[53]The Gilgal near Jericho or the Gilgal deep in the hill country of Ephraim near Shiloh?

[54]Joshua 9–10. The strategy followed here reflects the one used after Joshua's day, right down to the invasion of the Romans and the British General Allenby in World War I. The most effective way to occupy the land is to "divide and conquer" by securing this strategic region, which James Monson and his students call the "Central Benjamin Plateau." This plateau is a geographical saddle in the heart of the central hill country, which ultimately was allotted to the tribe of Benjamin and remained a constant battlefield in Israel's history, as reflected in Jacob's "blessing" on Benjamin (Gen. 49:27). For a detailed discussion, see J. Monson, *The Land Between* (Rockford, IL: Biblical Backgrounds, 1996): 171–74.

[55]Josh. 8:30–35; cf. Deut. 11:26–32:27; Josh. 24:1–28. Related events are too numerous to reference here, but they include the hegemony of Labayu in the Amarna Age, as well as events in 1–2 Kings and the Gospels.

The text of Joshua next skips forward to the northern campaign of Merom in the heart of Upper Galilee, which must have taken place sometime later, after the Israelites settled this area. Here again, geography underlies the events and helps to clarify them. The trade route from Gilead in Transjordan ran through the land of Geshur, Hazor, and Kedesh and across the watershed of Upper Galilee before making its way to Tyre on an island just off the mainland of the Mediterranean. Control of this route was crucial for the economies of both Tyre and Hazor.[56] But it was particularly difficult since it passed near remote regions that were vulnerable to attack. Egyptian military activity in the Late Bronze Age highlights the nature of this region, and a letter from the Amarna Age relates tensions between Hazor and Tyre over control of this road between them.[57] Joshua and all his militia with him "came and fell upon them" as they encamped in the valleys along "the waters of Merom" at the foot of steep slopes. The two viable paths of retreat described after the attack, one to the northwest, the other to the northeast, fit precisely the terrain of the area.[58]

In sum, the geographical setting is a vital resource for understanding Israel's entry into Canaan. The locales that are incorporated in the narrative—be they large regions, settlements, or minute geographical features—are recorded with such frequency and specificity that they give the accounts a strong sense of authenticity. One must ask why such details would be recounted were the story merely etiological or contrived. The cumulative effect of geographical indicators becomes even more dramatic when one considers the meticulous report of Joshua's campaign at Ai.

## A Case Study: Joshua's Campaigns in the Region of Ai

Joshua's campaigns in the region of Ai present a challenge to the modern reader because of the seeming disconnect between the biblical account and the results of archaeological inquiry. The following case study is intended to demonstrate that the geography of this specific region is the key to interpreting this biblical episode and that it provides the integrative "glue" for understanding both this biblical text and the corresponding archaeological record. When textual and archaeological data are analyzed in tandem and anchored to the

---

[56] John Monson, "Overlooking a Coveted Commercial Corridor: The Land of Geshur to Tyre via Hazor" (paper presented to the American Schools of Oriental Research, Atlanta, 2010).

[57] Within this region Israelite settlement and expansion in the adjacent highlands appear to have posed a threat to the king of Hazor, who gathered his allies for war at a central position adjacent to Israelite territory in Upper Galilee. See el-Amarna letter 148:41–47, in *The Amarna Letters*, ed. and trans. William L. Moran (Baltimore, MD: John Hopkins University Press, 1987).

[58] Josh. 11:1–15.

geographical setting, a better understanding of Joshua's two campaigns into the central hill country is the result (Joshua 7–8).

### "The Ruin"

The term *Ai* means "a heap of ruins." In the Hebrew of Joshua 7–8, however, it most often occurs with the definite article to yield הָעַי, (*hāʿay*). Therefore the best way to appreciate the present name of this site is to treat it as a proper noun and translate it as "The Ruin," which is the actual meaning of the expression in the Joshua narrative.[59] The site dominates the entire area in which these campaigns took place. A large Early Bronze Age city arose here centuries before Abraham entered the land, and already in his day the 27.5 acre site had become heaped-up ruins descending eastward from a rocky summit to a small plain on which the Arab village of Deir Dibwan is located today. Whereas most large ancient cities in the land have preserved some form of toponym (place name) over the millennia, The Ruin has not. Perhaps this is because, as noted above, the site was unoccupied from 2400 BC (over a millennium before Joshua) until the late thirteenth century BC (at least a century after the time of Joshua), and then only for a brief time.[60]

The implications of the proper name The Ruin are often ignored or dismissed in discussions about Joshua's two campaigns into the central highlands of Canaan.[61] Some maintain that the name was transferred to a different site somewhere in the area and that such a site could have been a functioning city in the days of Joshua. One wonders, however, what self-respecting community, especially in the honor/shame-based culture of the Near East, would call its city The Ruin! And yet the name persists in the Bible. Whoever recorded this story likely considered the site to be deserted as far back as the days of Abraham.[62] A straightforward and more logical way to account for this odd name with its definite article is to understand that it was an actual ruined site rather than a built-up urban center. Indeed, The Ruin was (and is today) a landmark throughout the entire region and would have served as a natural

---

[59] The definite article differentiates the word from common nouns. See the masters thesis of my student Jonathan Colby, "Grammatical Geography: An Analysis of Toponyms with the Definite Article in the Historical Books of the Hebrew Bible" (Trinity Evangelical Divinity School, 2011), 84, 114, 139. James Monson coined the expression "The Ruin" in the 1970s during one of many research walks through the region. Robert Boling, who participated on one of the walks, later adopted the expression (R. G. Boling and G. E. Wright, *Joshua*, AB [Garden City, NY: Doubleday, 1982], 216).

[60] To date, no Middle or Late Bronze Age remains have been found at Ai. In this respect it is similar to such sites as Arad in the Negev and Jarmuth in the Shephelah. However, the names of Arad and Jarmuth are preserved in Arabic toponyms, while the name of Ai is not. See Stern, *The New Encyclopedia*, 1:44–45.

[61] Joshua 7–8.

[62] Cf. Gen. 12:8 and 13:3.

gathering point for local inhabitants. An encampment or meeting place called The Ruin may well have existed below the impressive remains of this ancient site. The obvious location of such a place would be within today's Arab village of Deir Dibwan, perhaps at the very center of the village where a mosque now stands (see map 1). By this line of thinking the so-called "king of The Ruin" may well have been a local chieftain (or "sheikh"). Given The Ruin's landmark status and its prominent position on the main route from Jericho into the country's central highlands, the term "The Ruin" can be applied to the immediate vicinity that it dominates, an area we call "the region of Ai."[63]

### The Region of Ai (Map 1)

The region of Ai is a relatively low area (a slight geological syncline) situated between the uplifted hill country to the west (a major geological anticline) and a slight geological uplift to the east, above the eroded chalk wilderness (see map 2). The area is relatively flat in comparison to surrounding canyons and scarps, but seen from the air (or with the aid of Google Earth) it appears as a broad, somewhat level and cultivated region. Since biblical Hebrew has no specific lexeme for such a geographical feature, the biblical author employed a simple term "the valley," העמק, which significantly is also a Hebrew noun with a definite article (Josh. 8:13). "The Valley," therefore, is an identifiable subregion within the region of Ai.

The main road from Jericho climbs through the wilderness to reach The Valley and from The Ruin ascends directly to Bethel, only two kilometers (1.2 miles). Thus the historical developments in the region of Ai, The Ruin, and the city of Bethel were closely intertwined. The Ruin and Bethel were in such proximity that it appears only one of them could be an urban center at any given time. Bethel seems to have flourished in the Middle and Late Bronze Age,[64] during which time The Ruin was maintained as a meager outpost or an encampment on the road to Jericho. The words of Joshua's spies concerning those who were living at that time in the region of Ai echo this reality: "for they are but few."[65]

---

[63]Situated atop tilted beds of limestone, the summit of The Ruin offers a commanding view of the entire eastern horizon. The region of Ai quickly drops off into the chalk wilderness, beyond which one has a stunning view of the Rift Valley, the Dead Sea, and the scarps of Gilead, Moab, and Edom rising in the distance. I have visited the site and region of Ai on numerous occasions and have carefully examined the entire area surrounding the region of Ai (some three hundred square kilometers). On one such visit a United States special forces trainer accompanied me and concluded with vigor that Joshua's strategy as recorded in the biblical account perfectly fits this terrain and represents a cohesive battle plan for any army, ancient or modern.

[64]For the archaeology of Bethel, see Stern, The New Encyclopedia, 1:192–94.

[65]Josh. 7:3 (RSV).

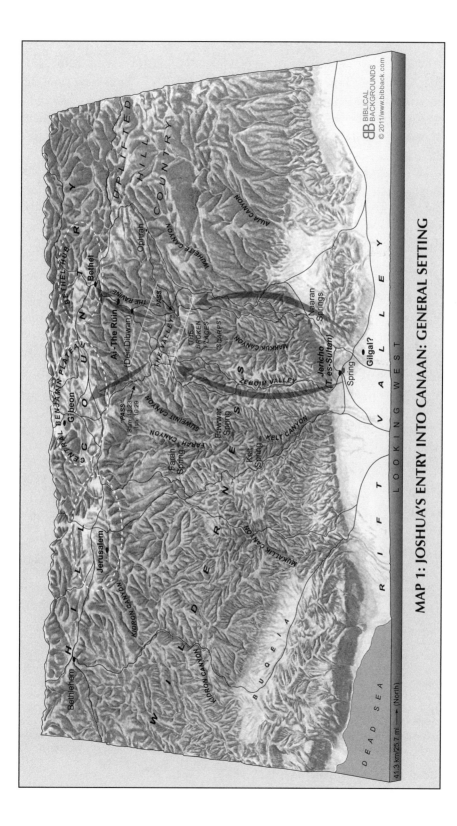

MAP 1: JOSHUA'S ENTRY INTO CANAAN: GENERAL SETTING

The strategic importance of the region of Ai cannot be overestimated. Not only was it the all-important springboard for any invader coming from the east and eyeing the nearby pivotal site of Bethel, but it was also the key to the strategic highland region called the Central Benjamin Plateau (see map 1). One reached this plateau via what the Bible calls "a pass" (מעבר).[66] It is clear that anyone invading the hill country from Jericho first had to secure routes within the region of Ai, and in the case of Joshua, specifically the ridge route ascending to Bethel. Control of The Valley beneath The Ruin was an absolute prerequisite to taking Bethel or the Central Benjamin Plateau. This geographical setting is fundamental to understanding Joshua's initial campaigns into the central hill country.[67]

### Joshua's First Campaign (Map 2)

The narrative of Joshua's first campaign to the region of Ai is short but highlights this region's geographical setting. The spies returned with a report that accords very well with the scenario described above. Because there were few people living in the area, there was no need for a large Israelite force to make the arduous climb from Gilgal through the wilderness to the region of Ai. It is important to note that the spies did not describe a bustling city, a powerful king, or strong fortifications. Their report seems to describe a small outpost or a group of local herdsmen and regional farmers. Their opinion was that only a small force, a few "squads," would be required to secure the region of Ai.[68] In all likelihood fewer than fifty men climbed the steep scarps to the wilderness and entered the region of Ai to assault the area's inhabitants. They were met by a small but determined force, which had superior knowledge of the terrain (Josh. 7:4). Caught off guard and cut off from the route by which

---

[66] This pass played a key role in Joshua's subsequent assault on the highlands through the territory of Benjamin (Josh. 10:9) and appears in other biblical texts as well (1 Sam. 13:23; Isa. 10:29). A second pass within this flatter synclinal area leads north.

[67] It also explains why the king of Jerusalem attempted to secure control of the Central Benjamin Plateau after the people of Gibeon (the chief city of that plateau) allied themselves with Joshua (Josh. 10:1–5). Centuries later Isaiah 10:28–32 made the importance of this region crystal clear as it highlighted the strategic nature of the region of Ai (Aiath). A powerful geographical sequence by the prophet describes an attack (imaginary or real) that began in the region of Ai, secured the Central Benjamin Plateau, and dissected the central hill country in two before easily descending upon Jerusalem. In AD 69–70 the Romans employed the same strategy in their campaign against Jerusalem, as did the Israeli army during the 1967 war.

[68] The Hebrew term אלף has various meanings, including "clan," but in this military context it may be translated "squad," or a small group of what one might call "special forces." See Even-Shoshan, A New Concordance of the Bible, 78–79. Contemporary soldiers who train such groups claim that the most efficient number for such a group is somewhere from twelve to fifteen troops. Fewer than twelve may not be enough to accomplish the task, while more than fifteen or twenty loses flexibility. "Troop" rather than "thousand" is the preferred translation of אלף, as Richard Hess has shown ("The Jericho and Ai of the Book of Joshua," 41–42).

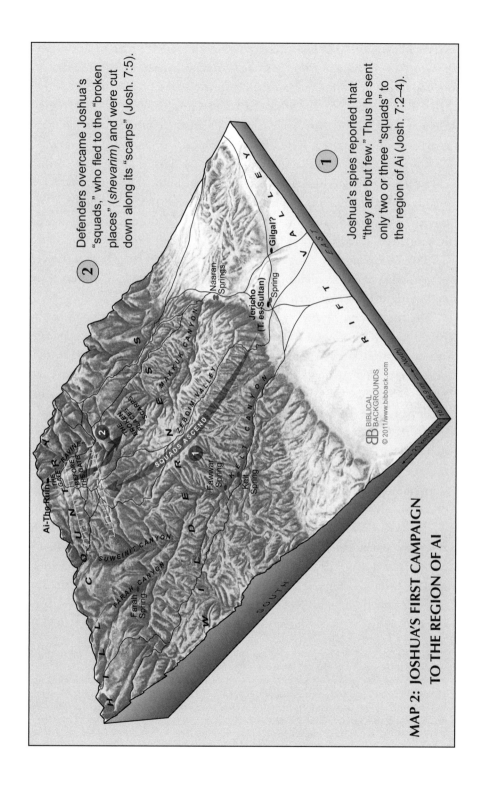

**1** Joshua's spies reported that "they are but few." Thus he sent only two or three "squads" to the region of Ai (Josh. 7:2–4).

**2** Defenders overcame Joshua's "squads," who fled to the "broken places" (*shevarim*) and were cut down along its "scarps" (Josh. 7:5).

BIBLICAL BACKGROUNDS
© 2011/www.bibback.com

**MAP 2: JOSHUA'S FIRST CAMPAIGN TO THE REGION OF AI**

they had ascended, the Israelites "took flight before the men of Ai . . . who chased them from before the 'gate' as far as the 'shebarim'" (Josh. 7:5).

Given the preceding analysis the Hebrew text here is best understood as referring to geographical features that figure prominently in the story. The Hebrew term שער, or "gate," typically denotes an architectural unit, but it can also have other meanings, including geographical features.[69] The ancient ruins of Ai stood precisely as a sentinel on the narrow ridge—a "gate" (!)—which led to the key site of Bethel, the all-important hub of this part of the hill country.[70] The inhabitants of Bethel were well aware that they could not lose the region of Ai to the enemy, for their city could be the next domino to fall. In short, both the Israelite invaders and the author of the story considered The Ruin to be literally *a natural "gate" from the region of Ai to the narrow ridge leading directly to Bethel*. Beyond that "gate" the highland regions north and south of Bethel would lie open to the invader.

The second important Hebrew term used to describe the flight of the Israelite squads in Joshua 7:5 is "the shebarim," in Hebrew, השברים, which is sometimes translated as "quarries."[71] However, this word also takes the definite article, which strongly suggests that it refers not to a random quarry but rather to a distinct, well-known feature (as is the case for the natural "gate" described above). When one explores this area extensively by foot, the meaning of the term becomes quite clear. Three kilometers (1.8 miles) directly east of The Ruin, The Valley gives way to "the Broken Places," which is the literal meaning of "the shebarim." This region is totally hidden from view until one suddenly reaches a point where rugged beds of limestone plunge precipitously into the arid chalk wilderness and the deep Makkuk Canyon. The tragedy described in Joshua 7:5 occurred in these Broken Places. Here those few defenders of the region of Ai, well acquainted with this difficult terrain, cut down thirty-six Israelites; only a few survivors made their way back to Joshua's camp.[72] Pinpointing such a small and obscure geographical area not only illuminates Joshua's initial campaign but also lends stark realism and credibility to the larger account.

---

[69]Even-Shoshan, *A New Concordance of the Bible*, 1195. See by way of analogy 1 Sam. 17:52, in which both "the gates of Gath" and "Shaaraim" ("two gates") may well denote geographical features.

[70]Bethel's prominent position is not only attested in the days of Abraham, the judges, Samuel, Jeroboam I, and the remaining centuries of the monarchy, but the first-century-AD historian Josephus tells us that in the First Revolt the Romans fought their way to Bethel and established a garrison there before moving south to Jerusalem (*Jewish War* 4:551/ix.9).

[71]This is a very strained and unlikely translation. See Even-Shoshan, *A New Concordance of the Bible*, 1197.

[72]This was indeed a tragedy for Joshua's approximately forty-five troops ("two or three squads").

## Joshua's Second Campaign (Map 3)

Joshua's second campaign to the region of Ai had to be foolproof, and this would require a much more substantial force. Defenders from Bethel had already arrived at the The Ruin to defend this natural gateway ("the gate") to their city. The Israelites had to be stopped here since, if the region of Ai fell, everyone knew that Bethel would be next and the central hill country would be open to the Israelites (Josh. 8:13). A sophisticated, well-orchestrated battle ensued in which Joshua exploited every geographic feature of the region and planned every detail, down to the maneuverability of his forces and the time of day to attack.

He first divided his forces into two groups and sent his main army by night into the hill country to set up camp on a mountain slope northeast of The Ruin.[73] They would be in place at the crack of dawn to surprise the defenders, who in turn would focus their attention on that same Israelite camp to the northeast. This particular chain of events could only occur in this region's unique terrain, all of which is carefully noted in the Bible. A deep "ravine" (Heb. גיא)[74] separated the Israelites from their adversaries, such that Joshua's main army was effectively "north" of that canyon, while the defenders were to the south.[75] The defenders could watch the movement of the Israelites, but there was no way they could reach them without circumventing the canyon via a narrow pass some distance away.[76] Meanwhile Joshua secretly sent a small ambush force to make its way to a series of gullies behind the enemy and out of sight. Once positioned, Joshua's ambush was within easy striking distance of the enemy's encampment.[77]

At this point in the battle account the writer provides a key detail: "That night Joshua positioned himself 'within the valley'" (בתוך העמק, Josh. 8:13). If this expression is understood to be The Valley discussed above, then Joshua's position can be identified clearly as a small hill just south of the modern village of Deir Dibwan, a place from which one has an unhindered view of the

---

[73] Josh. 8:3. The interpretation of "squad" again brings the number of this main force to some 450 troops rather than thirty thousand.

[74] Josh. 8:11. There is a distinct difference between a גיא and an עמק in Hebrew. The former is a restricted narrowing passage such as one would find at the base of a canyon or a narrowing between two more open areas, while the later portrays a lower and often broader area surrounded by higher ground, which in English is a "valley."

[75] The details being discussed are found in Josh. 8:9–14. Biblical directions do not follow traditional absolute compass directions but rather are "functional" directions, i.e., directions from the reference point of terrain. The main Israelite force need not have been due north of the ruin of Ai, nor did Joshua's ambush need to be due west of the enemy. This "functional" approach is clearly illustrated later in the description of the location of Shiloh in Judg. 21:19.

[76] Some scarps along this canyon drop over 150 meters/500 feet in the midst of adjacent higher hilltops.

[77] The ambush numbered some seventy-five troops (not five thousand), small enough to be concealed in the nearby gullies but large enough to constitute a crack fighting force (Josh. 8:14).

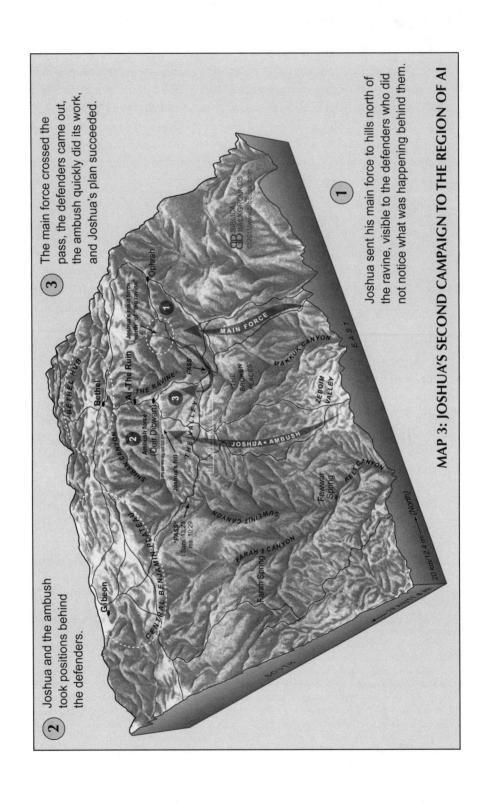

**1** Joshua sent his main force to hills north of the ravine, visible to the defenders who did not notice what was happening behind them.

**2** Joshua and the ambush took positions behind the defenders.

**3** The main force crossed the pass, the defenders came out, the ambush quickly did its work, and Joshua's plan succeeded.

MAP 3: JOSHUA'S SECOND CAMPAIGN TO THE REGION OF AI

entire area. From this hill "within the valley" Joshua could direct the battle, since he had visual contact with both his ambush team and his main force, and he could also see The Ruin, the enemy's camp, and their movements. For its part the enemy remained fixed on the main Israelite camp to the northeast, located on the hills beyond the deep canyon. The strategy and events leading to the actual confrontation—and the battle itself—all fit precisely the geography of the region of Ai.

The ruse that Joshua had planned was working. Within the enemy camp at the foot of The Ruin, all who had come to defend the region thought that they had the advantage because Joshua's main force would have to descend from its elevated position to the north, make its way across a pass some 40 meters/130 feet deep in order to circumvent much deeper ravines and then regroup before it could mount its attack. Moreover, the invaders would have to ascend a steep ridge to meet their enemy descending from higher ground. Obviously, this was no surprise attack but rather a clear diversionary tactic.

At the sight of movement in Joshua's main force, the defenders left their camp below The Ruin and moved to higher ground from whence they could descend quickly down the ridge to engage Joshua's main force, which had been instructed to feign retreat. From his vantage point Joshua gave a signal with his javelin, and the ambush force went into action.[78] It quickly reached the abandoned camp,[79] set it on fire for a signal to Joshua and his main force, and then hastened to the battle below. The defenders were emboldened by the Israelite retreat toward the same Broken Places to which they had chased Joshua's squads of the first, failed campaign (!), but once the ambush force appeared on higher ground behind them and they saw the smoke of their camp rising in the distance, they knew there was no hope. Within this carefully orchestrated sequence Joshua had signaled his main force to halt their retreat and to counterattack. This left the defenders caught between the two Israelite forces. Joshua had directed each move of this campaign, and his ruse had worked. The region of Ai was now in Israelite hands. Such a detailed battle sequence seems far too intricate and extensive to be considered a late

---

[78] Josh. 8:18.

[79] My earlier use of "few" in the region of Ai comes from Josh. 7:3, but here in Josh. 8:17 we are told specifically that "not a man was left in Ai or Bethel who did not go out after Israel. They left the city open and pursued Israel." This strongly suggests that the encampment was not a "city" as we understand that term, but was rather a gathering place for all of the defenders, both from the region of Ai and from Bethel. One must understand the language of Josh. 8:28–29 in light of the entire story and its setting. The "king of Ai" was the leader of the locals, and the "gate of the city" was the entrance to some type of settlement or camp, perhaps now beneath the modern village of Deir Dibwan.

etiological story invented to explain to later Israelites the origin of the heaped-up ruins from the Early Bronze Age city.[80]

## The Two Campaigns: Conclusions

This case study of Joshua's two campaigns to the region of Ai allows the Bible to speak through the land—and the land to speak through the Bible. The detailed descriptions argue against the idea that the story was manufactured or that its origins can be dated to the first millennium BC.[81] To the contrary, the text of Joshua and its ancient Near Eastern literary setting both showcase the geography and give the sense of a very ancient and authentic battle plan. Why would the Joshua conquest accounts offer such specific and verifiable geographical data were they not reflective of actual historical events? While many other models have been offered—etiological arguments, dating the story to the days of Hezekiah in the late eighth century BC, claiming that the absence of Late Bronze Age ruins at The Ruin discredits the entire account, or simply dismissing it outright as fiction—these invariably introduce more speculation and forced readings than does a plain reading of the text informed first by geography, then by ancient Near Eastern context, and finally by archaeological evidence or the lack thereof.

In sum, it is clear that when geographical analysis is added to the study of Israel's entry into Canaan, and when archaeological data (which remains partial and inconsistent) is prevented from being the final arbiter of all things historical, the most plausible and understandable reconstruction is that the biblical text reflects actual events of the Israelite arrival in Late Bronze Age Canaan. The burden of proof lies with those who would deconstruct these stories or find some alternate explanation for this expansive, geographically focused account.

## The "Conquest of Canaan," Historical Criticism, and "Progressive Evangelicals"

Israel's entry into Canaan is the "mother of all biblical archaeology debates" because it is a pivotal event in Israel's history for which there exists a great deal of background material. Over time, this colorful biblical episode came

---

[80]The "large heap/circle of stones" made an impressive memorial of the event, covering the dead leader. But it certainly did not cover the 27.5 acres of the Early Bronze Age city, as some imply. Such a memorial would have brought home dramatically the fact that, like that of The Ruin nearby, so was the demise of the local chieftain and perhaps the nearby city of Bethel (though it does not feature in this account but only in Judg. 1:22–26). If so, then the second campaign climaxes with a dramatic punch line.
[81]This is true regardless of what date one might assign to the summary passages of Joshua (e.g., 11:21–12:24).

to be understood as a complete and concentrated "Israelite conquest" despite the fact that the Bible does not make this claim. This exaggerated view lies at the heart of longstanding debates over the historicity of the Bible. When archaeological discoveries did not align with this larger-than-life reconstruction, the biblical narrative itself was called into question. In this study we have employed a range of disciplines in order to bring these biblical events back to biblical size. In response to the title of this volume we assert that historical matters indeed matter to faith.

At the beginning of this essay I posed a question: "How do we understand the truth claims of Scripture in light of the historical-critical method and empirical evidence from archaeology and ancient sources?" For people of faith this is a serious question, especially those involved in ministry and academics. Throughout the history of the church every generation has had to interact with the prevailing winds of philosophy, culture, and science. In this era of globalization, modernism and the reaction to it, and the exponential increase in every kind of data, Christian scholars of the Bible do not have the option of being insular. Nor should they feel the need to be defensive. Thankfully, there is a long and distinguished list of evangelical scholars who have made good-faith efforts to work through these issues.

Most recently, Peter Enns and Kenton Sparks have contributed thoughtful and penetrating books that address the question posed above. In *Inspiration and Incarnation*, Enns follows the analogy of the incarnation in order to address the human dimension of Scripture that so often challenges Christian readers. Essentially, "we are to think of the Bible in the same way that Christians think about Jesus."[82] The Bible, he contends, was not an "abstract, otherworldly book, dropped out of heaven."[83] With this in mind, it is understandable—though unfortunate—that in his advocacy for the "incarnational analogy" Enns places most of his emphasis upon the human dimension of Scripture. Some parts of the book have also sparked considerable debate. For example, he allows for the Bible's direct borrowing from ancient cultures: "God *transformed* the ancient myths so that Israel's story would come to focus on its God, the real one."[84] Ultimately, he suggests, the Bible, like the incarnation, "can never be fully understood."[85]

Kenton Sparks's book *God's Word in Human Words* is an invitation to "believing criticism," which represents a rigorous, good-faith effort to embrace

---

[82]Enns, *Inspiration and Incarnation*, 17.
[83]Ibid.
[84]Ibid., 54. It is unclear to me whether Enns understands the God of Scripture and history to be present in the ancient Near Eastern myths before he transformed them, or whether both the original ancient Near Eastern myths and their biblical versions are entirely ahistorical.
[85]Ibid., 168.

historical criticism without also jettisoning the essentials of the Christian faith. In the book Sparks personally navigates this tightrope with a sophisticated engagement of hermeneutical and critical issues, as well as earnest affirmations of orthodox Christian tradition. In the end, however, historical-critical positions appear to win the day on most issues, except those few that, in keeping with (presumably Roman) Catholic tradition, must be considered historical if one is to maintain the validity of the Christian faith.[86] Thus, events like the virgin birth and the resurrection may not pass the test of historical inquiry, but they are nevertheless "theologically reasonable and necessary."[87] Sparks writes:

> Although some and perhaps many of Scripture's narratives are not strictly historical in all respects, there are narratives in Scripture—some of them about miracles—whose historicity is essential to the validity and cogency of the creedal faith. Consequently, in any given case, our judgments on the Bible's historicity will have to weigh not only the relevant contextual evidence but also the philosophical and theological evidence, including especially the theological traditions of the church. One consequence of this approach is that we will sometimes accept the historicity of an event even when it does not pass our everyday litmus tests for history.[88]

He does not spell out how the creeds or a Christ-focused hermeneutic might adjudicate the historical reliability of events recorded in Scripture, much less how they or he might determine a hierarchy of their relative necessity for the Christian faith. If, for example, our belief in the historicity of the exodus must depend upon the "necessity of faith" rather than conventional historical evidence, as Sparks suggests, how is one to decide which parts of the Bible fall under that category and which do not?[89] Is it a creed or a tradition? Or is it the logic and reason of the individual that will determine the historical reliability and relative theological importance of a biblical text and the content it communicates?[90]

At this juncture we may return yet again to the question posed at the beginning of the current essay. Both Enns and Sparks point out that we are "inescapably creatures of time and space" and that when approaching the Bible we have no "absolute point of reference" outside our own cultural context.[91]

---

[86] Sparks, *God's Word in Human Words*, 320.
[87] Ibid.
[88] Ibid., 322.
[89] Ibid., 100.
[90] Perhaps N. T. Wright's version of "critical realism" is a helpful alternative (N. T. Wright, *The New Testament and the People of God* [Minneapolis: Fortress, 1992], 35).
[91] Enns, *Inspiration and Incarnation*, 169.

I agree up to a point, but if this is so, should we still not make every effort and use every available resource for the purpose of entering into the time and space—"the real world"—of the biblical authors and the people and things about which they wrote? Anyone who has climbed up the imposing Assyrian siege ramp still visible today at ancient Lachish and stood in the throne room of Sennacherib at the British Museum cannot help but read Isaiah and 2 Kings with an understanding that is quite removed from one's own life circumstances. While I applaud Enns for urging us to place Scripture in its time and place, that endeavor involves a much larger enterprise than comparative analysis of ancient Near Eastern texts. Enns and Sparks are calling us to recognize more fully the human dimension of Scripture at the very moment in history when profound new discoveries are being made that have a direct bearing upon our understanding of Scripture and *its* time and space. Much of this new information lends general support to the picture painted by the Bible as a whole.

In my own view, now is certainly not the time (nor, for that matter, is it ever appropriate) to dismiss biblical texts or events that on the surface do not seem to hold up before the rigors of historical criticism. Rather than navigate around the challenges by downplaying selectively the historicity of biblical events, we should examine with renewed vigor the hard issues because doing so is timely, given the burgeoning body of information available today from the ancient Near East—be it linguistic, cultural, or geographical!

Furthermore, a serious engagement of Scripture's original context must not be hamstrung by a narrow understanding of apostolic hermeneutics. Far from "not engaging the Old Testament in an effort to remain consistent with the original context and intention of the Old Testament author,"[92] Paul the Jew was steeped in the Old Testament, not only from "Christ down," so to speak, but also from "Abraham up." In my own view, Paul and Isaiah are kindred spirits, conversation partners, one might say; Romans and Isaiah go hand in hand. The exodus and the Passover were not mere allegories or theological constructs for the apostolic church, and they should not be so for us today. "For we did not follow cleverly devised myths when we made known to you the power and coming of our Lord Jesus Christ, but we were eyewitnesses of his majesty" (1 Pet. 1:16).

Israel's entry into Canaan also relates to these questions and has a role to play in addressing them. How might we approach that particular question in light of ancient Near Eastern studies, on the one hand, and the hermeneutics of "progressive evangelicals," on the other? Sparks makes a passing comment on this biblical episode after suggesting that "theological sifting" is necessary

---

[92]Ibid., 116.

when jarring passages such as the genocide of the Canaanites do not sit well with the Bible's other theological priorities.

> So there *is* something of genuine theological value in the Old Testament conquest account, even if we embrace not the whole text but only aspects of it. Now this modern reading of the Old Testament is by no means an allegory, but its exegetical result is precisely like that of an allegory. Certain dimensions of the text are preserved, while others are set aside.[93]

My view, in contrast, is that we must not take such license with the biblical text. For all its complexity and color the biblical account of Israel's entry into Canaan, when it is placed within its literary, cultural, and geographical context, is more reasonable as a second-millennium historical event than any of the alternatives proposed to date. The Bible's account of Joshua's entry into the land is far more compelling and in line with available evidence than are the stale verdicts of historical criticism. It is not a matter of "proving the Bible" or defending traditional views in knee-jerk fashion. At issue is the degree of openness to reasonable reconstructions even if they challenge the "orthodoxy" of modern criticism that is largely negative toward the historicity of the biblical text. *Cumulative evidence that yields strong probabilities in favor of the biblical text is far more convincing than nonevidence.*

In this context it may be helpful to note N. T. Wright's assertion that despite all the challenges to understanding the events of the first Easter, the prospect that the resurrection stories are "late inventions" is not the best historical explanation. Rather, it is "enormously more probable at the level of sheer history" that the tomb of Christ was empty and that he rose from the dead.[94] If one accepts Wright's statement despite the fact that most of the nonbiblical "evidence" is circumstantial, why would one at the same time dismiss Joshua's entry into Canaan with its abundance of direct and circumstantial data?

The Bible is indeed both human and divine. Despite our best attempts to understand and interpret it, Scripture is, after all, the living word of God that records the Lord's intervention and redemptive work in human history. As believers we must embrace it. "For since, in the wisdom of God, the world did not know God through wisdom, it pleased God through the folly of what we preach to save those who believe" (1 Cor. 1:21).

King Solomon of Israel, in his own time and space, also knew something about these matters. When he became king, he asked for wisdom. In building the temple he borrowed selectively from the common stock of ancient Near

[93]Sparks, *God's Word in Human Words*, 326.
[94]N. T. Wright, *The Resurrection of the Son of God* (Minneapolis: Fortress, 2003), 10, 687–96, 736–38.

Eastern culture. But when he also embraced the mindset and religion of his neighbors, he lost his way and never recovered (1 Kings 11:11). May it never be that evangelical scholars of the Bible follow Solomon's tragic path.

In conclusion, Joshua too has something to teach us. A powerful message is embedded within the specific events and historical annals in the book of Joshua. From the opening of the book ("Be strong and courageous!" Josh. 1:9), to its close ("Choose this day whom you will serve!" Josh. 24:15), Joshua ben-Nun remained faithful to his God even as others fell away—from the Israelite entry into Canaan through reaffirming Abraham's and Moses's fidelity on the slopes of Mount Ebal just above Shechem. Over a millennium later, another Joshua walked through this same region. He too remained faithful. If we dismiss the real Joshua ben-Nun and his times, what is to stop us from dismissing the later Joshua, Jesus of Nazareth?

# 20

# YAHWEH'S "WIFE" AND BELIEF
# IN ONE GOD IN
# THE OLD TESTAMENT

## RICHARD S. HESS

The question of belief in one God in ancient Israel has focused the study of the religion of that culture in recent decades. In some ways this area of study has its roots in the Reformation and the centuries that followed, when attempts were made to distinguish what was appropriate to a study of religion. Thus Johann P. Gabler's famous inaugural lecture at the University of Altdorf in 1787 is often used as the starting point for the distinction between the study of biblical theology and that which is traditionally referred to as systematic theology in Protestant Christianity. However, this lecture was equally important for establishing the distinction between theology and religion, as it would come to be known. For Gabler (who refers to Tittmann's work five years earlier),

> religion is passed on by the doctrine in the Scriptures, teaching what each Christian ought to know and believe and do in order to secure happiness in this life and in the life to come. Religion then, is everyday, transparently clear knowledge; but theology is subtle, learned knowledge, surrounded by a retinue of many disciplines, and by the same token derived not only from the sacred Scripture but also from elsewhere, especially from the domain of philosophy and history.[1]

This distinction appears to separate the more cerebral elements of theory and philosophy into theology, while preserving what is universally accessible

---

[1] Johann P. Gabler, "An Oration on the Proper Distinction between Biblical and Dogmatic Theology and the Specific Objections of Each," in Ben C. Ollenburger, ed., *Old Testament Theology: Flowering and Future*, trans. John Sandys-Wunsch and Laurence Eldredge, rev. ed., Sources for Biblical and Theological Study 1 (Winona Lake, IN: Eisenbrauns, 2004), 500.

to all who wish "to know and believe and do" in terms of day-to-day living. It is this latter understanding of religion that has been applied and remains a key element of the Israelite religion as it is studied in the present day. Specifically, much of the discussion of religion concerns practices and activities, as well as the ideas that may or may not lie behind them.[2]

From this perspective there is a wealth of evidence for religion in ancient Israel, that is, the era between Israel's early appearance in the land ca. 1200 BC (as attested by the mention of Israel as a people group for the first time on the Merneptah stele) and the termination of the Judean monarchy in 587/586 BC. There is a wealth of related data from the material culture, the epigraphic materials preserved, and the Bible itself.

It is not surprising that the results of decades of study of this material, both in its publication and in analysis by hundreds of scholars, should result in what is now generally accepted as a diversity of religious expressions in ancient Israel. So understood, there was a diversity of religions there as well.

However, beyond this there is much disagreement in the interpretation of the results. For most of its history the study of Israelite religion has been largely the province of professional scholars who based their results on a critical interpretation of the Old Testament or Hebrew Bible. This was evident in the nineteenth century, when arguably the most important work produced in Old Testament higher criticism was that of the German scholar Julius Wellhausen. In1878 he published the work translated into English as *Prolegomena to the History of Ancient Israel*.[3] This included three major parts—"History of the Ordinances of Worship," "History of Tradition," and "Israel and Judaism"—the third of which examined the evolution of Israelite religion into what became known as Judaism. This work has had an effect on the interpretation of the Pentateuch and the whole Bible up to the present day. While it deals with a variety of subjects, its emphasis remains with the question of Israelite religion.

Later studies, in the twentieth century, built upon the assumptions of Wellhausen, as well as scholars of tradition history, such as Albrecht Alt and Martin Noth, to recreate Israelite religion.[4] In North America their work

---

[2]See, for example, the definition of Ziony Zevit, *The Religions of Ancient Israel: A Synthesis of Parallactic Approaches* (New York: Continuum, 2001), 15, 24–27, which includes an emphasis of a phenomenological method that seeks to interpret what can be observed.

[3]Julius Wellhausen, *Prolegomena to the History of Ancient Israel*, trans. J. Sutherland Black and Allan Menzies (repr., Gloucester: Peter Smith, 1973).

[4]See, e.g., Albrecht Alt, *Essays on Old Testament History and Religion*, trans. R. A. Wilson (Sheffield: Sheffield Academic, 1989); Martin Noth, *A History of Pentateuchal Traditions* (Englewood Cliffs, NJ: Princeton University Press, 1972).

was supplemented by that of William F. Albright and his students.[5] All these studies tended to follow the critical interpretation of the Old Testament and to use archaeological and extrabiblical textual discoveries to supplement this research. The effect was to create a dichotomy in which Israel was either worshipping Yahweh alone or involved in worshipping Baal, Asherah, and other deities of Canaan. Thus Georg Fohrer's study represents the view that the worship of Yahweh in ancient Israel during the monarchy could be found either with those who worshipped only this deity or with those who saw Yahweh as the chief national God, and other deities clearly subordinate to him as part of a pantheon.[6] At the other end of the critical spectrum, Yehezkel Kaufmann saw a dramatic opposition between worship of Yahweh and that of multiple deities.[7]

Various factors brought this general consensus to an end. Arguably the single most significant was the discovery of clear inscriptions in northeast Sinai at an ancient caravansary known as Kuntillet 'Ajrud. These inscriptions included several examples in which people were blessed "to Yahweh and his Asherah."[8] For the first time evidence was presented that was outside the spectrum of evidence as found in the Bible. In the biblical text Yahweh always stood alone. He may have been worshipped along with some other deities, but the latter were always in a clearly subordinate relationship.

Here for the first time was evidence from early in the eighth century BC, during a period that the Bible recognizes as a one of general prosperity for the northern kingdom of Israel (under Jeroboam II) and for the southern kingdom of Judah (under Uzziah), that Israelites worshipped a goddess alongside Yahweh. In many ways this provided impetus for new dimensions in the study of religion. Were scholars becoming interested in family religion? This gave new direction for interpretations of the religion of the family or household, one that could include goddess worship alongside the chief deity.[9] Was there a new direction in feminist and womanist religion in

---

[5]See, e.g., William F. Albright, *From the Stone Age to Christianity: Monotheism and the Historical Process* (Garden City, NY: Doubleday, 1957); *Ancient Israelite Religion: Essays in Honor of Frank Moore Cross*, ed. P. D. Miller Jr., P. D. Hanson, and S. D. McBride (Philadelphia: Fortress, 1987).

[6]Georg Fohrer, *History of Israelite Religion*, trans. David E. Green (Nashville: Abingdon, 1972).

[7]The translation and epitome of the five-volume work originally published in Hebrew is Yehezkel Kaufmann, *The Religion of Israel: From Its Beginnings to the Babylonian Exile*, trans. Moshe Greenberg (New York: Schocken, 1972).

[8]Hebrew *lyhwh wl'srth*. Yahweh was further identified as Yahweh of Teman or Yahweh of Samaria. See Z. Meshel, *Kuntillet 'Ajrud: A Religious Centre from the Time of the Judean Monarchy on the Border of Sinai* (Jerusalem: Israel Museum, 1978).

[9]See, e.g., Karel van der Toorn, *Family Religion in Babylonia, Syria and Israel: Continuity and Change in the Forms of Religious Life*, Studies in the History and Culture of the Ancient Near East 7 (Leiden: Brill, 1996).

ancient Israel? This provided the possibility of identifying female figurines and other cultic materials as evidence of an alternative religion for women who were excluded from the cult of Israel by an all-male priesthood.[10] Did one find female personifications of wisdom and other elements in the biblical texts? This allowed scholars to trace those appearances back to a female deity, effaced in the victory of monotheism but still to be found in the traces that remained there.[11]

In some ways, however, there was an even more important ramification for the critical study of the Hebrew Bible and the development of Israelite religion. The Bible bore no explicit testimony to the presence of this relationship between Yahweh and a goddess. Some, it is true, argued that the term for Asherah that appeared on these inscriptions did not refer to the goddess commonly identified throughout the ancient West Semitic world. Instead, the Asherah was a cultic image that symbolized Yahweh or someone or something other than a goddess.[12] However, the dominant interpretation that developed and has remained is that we have here an indication of the goddess Asherah who serves as the partner of Yahweh in these blessings. This also provided the basis for the recognition of an identical blessing at Khirbet el-Qôm in southern Judah from about the same time.[13] Furthermore, neutron-activation analysis has established that the jars on which some of these inscriptions appeared had their origin in Jerusalem, as did similar jars from Arad and Beersheba, also places with cult centers in southern Judah.[14] The transportation of a commodity, such as grain or oil, from Jerusalem to the cult center at Kuntillet 'Ajrud, like Arad and Beersheba, implies some sort of Judean control. Thus these inscriptions contain sentiments that would have been tolerated, if not promoted, by the political powers in Jerusalem at the time of their composition.

What is unusual about all this is that it is nowhere mentioned in the Bible. This then is the important point that lies behind many of the sentiments expressed by scholars working in this field from the 1970s onward. The Bible does not reveal a full or complete picture of Israelite religion during the monarchy. This led many scholars to deconstruct the biblical text and to argue that

---

[10]See, e.g., William G. Dever, *Did God Have a Wife? Archaeology and Folk Religion in Ancient Israel* (Grand Rapids: Eerdmans, 2005).

[11]Judith M. Hadley, *The Cult of Asherah in Ancient Israel and Judah: Evidence for a Hebrew Goddess*, University of Cambridge Oriental Publications 57 (Cambridge: Cambridge University Press, 2000).

[12]See, e.g., André Lemaire, "Who or What Was Yahweh's Asherah?," *BAR* 10, no. 6 (Nov.–Dec. 1984): 42–51.

[13]Ziony Zevit, "The Khirbet el-Qôm Inscription Mentioning a Goddess," *BASOR* 255 (1984): 33–41; William G. Dever, "Asherah, Consort of Yahweh? New Evidence from Kuntillet 'Ajrud," *BASOR* 255 (1984): 21–37.

[14]Zevit, *The Religions of Ancient Israel*, 379.

many of its descriptions of the earlier periods were unreliable. There were those who sought a wholesale rejection of any historical information in the Old Testament; but these theories have been challenged and are no longer accepted by many scholars.[15] Nevertheless, a strong suspicion remains that the historical claims of earliest Israel are not reliable and that the religious and theological descriptions of many or all of the Israelites before the exile are distorted by later writers.

The result has been a reexamination of the biblical text coupled with the assumption that the belief in a single deity should not be presumed or accepted before the late monarchy or even before the exile. Thus Rainer Albertz has argued that monotheism, or at least belief that Israelites had only one God that they should worship, is the product of Deuteronomist writers and editors under King Josiah in the late seventh century.[16] They sought to merge the official religion of the king and state, which accepted only one God, Yahweh, with their family and personal piety, which accepted many deities and worshipped ancestors. The result was the worship of a single God under royal control.[17] For Philip Davies, however, there was no cult centralization in preexilic Jerusalem. Yahweh was a national and dynastic God in Jerusalem and the "God of Israel" in the northern state of Samaria; but the ideal of the unified worship of a single deity is a fiction coming from a period after the monarchy.[18] Thomas Römer connects the emergence of monotheism with Second Isaiah. Unlike some, he does not see Second Isaiah as the highest expression of a preexistent belief in one God. Rather, it is the first expression of monotheism and serves the ideological purpose of arguing the power of Yahweh, despite the destruction of his temple and city, to recreate Israel in a

---

[15]For some challenges, see Philip R. Davies, *In Search of "Ancient Israel,"* JSOTSup 148 (Sheffield: Sheffield Academic, 1992; Niels Peter Lemche, *Prelude to Israel's Past: Background and Beginnings of Israelite History and Identity*, trans. E. F. Maniscalco (Peabody, MA: Hendrickson, 1998); and Thomas L. Thompson, *Early History of the Israelite People: From the Written and Archaeological Sources*, SHANE 4 (Leiden: Brill, 1992). For an example of alternative views that accept some historical value to the biblical traditions, see John Day, ed., *In Search of Pre-Exilic Israel*, JSOTSup 406 (London: T&T Clark, 2004). For a higher view of the historical value of the biblical texts, see V. Philips Long, David W. Baker, and Gordon J. Wenham, eds., *Windows into Old Testament History: Evidence, Argument, and the Crisis of "Biblical Israel"* (Grand Rapids: Eerdmans, 2002); *The Future of Biblical Archaeology: Reassessing Methodologies and Assumptions*, ed. James K. Hoffmeier and Alan Millard (Grand Rapids: Eerdmans, 2004); *Israel: Ancient Kingdom or Late Invention?*, ed. Daniel I. Block, Bryan H. Cribb, and Gregory S. Smith (Nashville: B&H Academic, 2008); and, *Critical Issues in Early Israelite History*, ed. Richard S. Hess, Gerald A. Klingbeil, and Paul J. Ray, BBRSup 3 (Winona Lake, IN: Eisenbrauns, 2008).

[16]Rainer Albertz, "Personal Piety," in *Religious Diversity in Ancient Israel and Judah*, ed. Francesca Stavrakopoulou and John Barton (London: T&T Clark, 2010), 143.

[17]Ibid., 143.

[18]Philip Davies, "Urban Religion and Rural Religion," in Stavrakopoulou and Barton, *Religious Diversity in Ancient Israel and Judah*, 112.

new manner.[19] Herbert Niehr argues for a late and evolutionary development to monotheism. Apparently, the period of the monarchy saw the emergence of Yahweh in Jerusalem as chief over the pantheon. At this time the inscriptions indicate a "poly-Yahwism" in which the Kuntillet ʿAjrud texts speak of Yahweh of Teman and Yahweh of Samaria as different deities. During the Persian period and "even later" the other strata of the pantheon "were gradually discarded" because Yahweh became more powerful. As with Römer, Niehr points to Second Isaiah as the example of monotheism. However, he dates this text as postexilic, later than when Römer would date it.[20]

This brief survey demonstrates two points. First, there is no agreement on exactly when or how belief in a single God emerged in Israel. It is, however, seen as late in the history of the Old Testament, either just before the exile, or during or after the exile. Behind this is the implication that there was no belief in a single God anywhere in Israel before this time. This is an extremely important point because it goes to the heart of the discussion about Yahweh's "wife" and the existence of other deities in the belief systems of ancient Israel. The authors of these theories propound a host of views about the great varieties of religious observances. Some include Yahweh with other deities. Some do not. Some provide gods distinct from Yahweh as the chief deities in Israel. Some simply see Yahweh as an amalgamation of the characteristics and traits of other deities, with nothing distinctive until the late rise of monotheism. The single unacceptable view is that anyone in ancient Israel believed and worshiped a single deity before Josiah or Second Isaiah. The authors cited and other recent scholars do not mention this as a possibility.

The second point is that addressed by John Barton in his conclusion to a book that collects many of the essays cited above. As he notes, the question remains, "How did monotheism ever arise?" His subsequent observations demonstrate that he is concerned with the possibility that some belief in a single God may have occurred earlier.[21]

What hints are there in early material of what would eventually become this innovative and strikingly distinctive religious position? Perhaps a number of the cultures around Israel and Judah were already tending to "monolatry" in early times: certainly each had its chief god, as Israel and Judah had YHWH. But nowhere else did there emerge the insistence that there is only one God (rightly

---

[19]Thomas Römer, *The So-Called Deuteronomistic History: A Sociological, Historical and Literary Introduction* (London: T&T Clark, 2007), 112.
[20]Herbert Niehr, "'Israelite' Religion and 'Canaanite' Religion," in Stavrakopoulou and Barton, *Religious Diversity in Ancient Israel and Judah*, 31.
[21]John Barton, "Reflecting on Religious Diversity," in Stavrakopoulou and Barton, *Religious Diversity in Ancient Israel and Judah*, 192.

spelt with a capital G) who ruled over all nations and must be worshipped in only one, official way.

As one may observe by looking at the studies, a great deal of the details in the arrival of monotheism on ancient Israelite soil depends on the particular scholar and his or her reconstruction of the biblical data. There is no agreement on the dating of any of the texts. Even Second Isaiah, traditionally assigned to the period near the end of the exile (mid-sixth century BC) no longer commands a consensus as to its supposed time of composition.

It is not the purpose of this essay to present evidence for a new scheme of dating the controversial biblical texts. Rather, I will look at the extrabiblical data and consider (1) whether there is evidence from outside the Hebrew Bible that makes belief in a single deity impossible before the end of the seventh century or later, and (2) what evidence may point away from polytheism as being the exclusive religion in ancient Israel (however diverse).

## Was Belief in a Single Deity Impossible before the Time of Josiah?

To anticipate my conclusions regarding the first point, there is no biblical evidence that makes belief in a single deity impossible before the end of the seventh century. It is well known that the precedent of belief in one God was realized in Egypt in the fourteenth century BC by the Pharaoh Akhenaten, who revolted from the traditional polytheism and sought to worship the deified sun disk Aten. Although his attempts to build a new capital at Amarna and to revolutionize the worship and culture of the royal family proved short-lived, he nevertheless demonstrated the theoretical possibility of the belief in a single deity in the ancient Near East more than six hundred years before Josiah. This also predated the thirteenth century BC and the appearance of Israel as a nation in the Bible, as well as its mention in the Merneptah stele.

A corollary to this point is that there is no biblical or extrabiblical text that suggests that no one in ancient Israel believed in a single deity. This may seem obvious to those who have done any studying in the field. However, it needs to be said because the assumption is often made that there was nothing but polytheism in early Israel, and monotheism (understood here has belief in a single deity) emerged late. Now, this would of course be difficult to prove because there remains relatively little written material from the time of the monarchy. In Israel most writing was done on papyrus or animal skin. However, this would have perished in climates where there remains some moisture. Thus longer texts, such as biblical texts, are not preserved in any climate in southern Canaan, except in the extremely dry desert where the Dead Sea Scrolls were found. However, these scrolls date no earlier than the second century BC, with the exception of a palimpsest. This is a papyrus on which something was written from the seventh century BC and then brought to Wadi Murabba'at, where something else was written over the earlier writing many centuries later. The earlier writing may have been a personal letter, but nothing of religious significance for our consideration has been identified.[22]

Beyond this there is little in terms of archaeology that requires that no one believed in a single deity. Of course the presence of images of various deities and even images of Yahweh, if such exist, proves nothing about the belief in a single deity among some in Israel. The Bible attests in the Decalogue that there must be no images of Yahweh (Ex. 20:4–5; Deut. 5:8–9). So one might expect that aniconic representations of Yahweh would not leave much in the way of material evidence. On the other hand, if we found evidence in Jerusalem for two or more temples operating at the same time, we might conclude that this suggests the worship of multiple deities. This occurs, for example, on the acropolis of Ugarit. Of course, even that would not suggest that *no one* in the kingdom worshipped a single deity. It would, however, suggest that the official state religion for some period of time involved the recognition of multiple deities. Even that would be an advance toward the conclusion that there was more than one deity worshipped officially in the capital of ancient Judah. However, we have nothing like this. There is indeed the shrine at Judean Arad that preserves evidence of two incense altars and two standing stones (with possibly a third contemporary with these or from a slightly different time). However, this does not prove the worship of multiple deities and, even if it did, that would not suggest that it was official practice, much less that it was incumbent upon every citizen to worship the multiple deities.

The epigraphic evidence certainly mentions deities other than Yahweh. However, this does not suggest that no one believed in the worship of Yahweh alone. There are plenty of inscriptions that mention Yahweh and no other god. Beside various blessings in the Lachish and especially the Arad ostraca, there are also texts from En Gedi and Khirbet Beit Lei that may mention the worship of Yahweh earlier than the end of the monarchy. In theory, any one of these could have been composed by a worshipper of Yahweh alone. The same is true of the many hundreds of seals, bullae, and other sources for personal names whose only clear divine name element is a form of the name Yahweh. More of this will be discussed in the following section, which considers the evidence for a single deity.

Finally, we may ask what is it that requires belief that Josiah at the end of the seventh century, or Second Isaiah in the middle of the sixth century, or

---

[22]F. W. Dobbs-Allsopp et al., eds., *Hebrew Inscriptions: Texts from the Biblical Period of the Monarchy with Concordance* (New Haven, CT: Yale University Press, 2005), 381–84.

some other later priestly writer would have been the first to introduce a belief in a single deity. For those who opt for Josiah, a connection is normally drawn with the Deuteronomist writers, who saw this as an opportunity to centralize power around the king by focusing on a single sanctuary in Jerusalem worshipping a single deity, Yahweh. This does not, however, make a lot of sense in the light of contemporary political engagement. The greatest powers of the age, such as Assyria, Babylon, and Persia, each gave their rulers great power and created theologies that justified such power. This often exalted the national deity—Ashur, Marduk, or Ahuramazda.[23] However, there is no evidence that any of these imperial theologies excluded the worship of other deities. To the contrary, either they tended to demonstrate how the national god conquered the other deities and thus established sovereignty, just as Assyria or Babylonia did, or they tended to promote the worship of the other deities as a further source of support for the emperor, as with Persia. Why would Josiah want to close the other sanctuaries or "high places," if his goal was centralized power and control? Surely this could have been achieved even more effectively by keeping all those places open and serving his own interests in the promotion of royal policy. Arguably, making everyone come to the temple in Jerusalem to worship Yahweh was a good way to discourage the worship of this single deity, rather than to promote it.

As for the texts commonly ascribed to Second Isaiah, one may or may not assume that this prophet wrote during the middle of the sixth century. Certainly, the message fits with that period, and just as certainly it is a high point in the poetic expression of the worship and praise of Yahweh alone. However, none of this suggests that Second Isaiah introduced the concept of monotheism. Arguably, an already existing belief could have better formed a foundation for the mature and sophisticated literary and theological reflection demonstrated in Isaiah 40–55. Further, one may question the argument that Second Isaiah needed to exalt Yahweh and therefore used monotheism to explain how, despite the destruction of the temple and of Jerusalem, Yahweh was still really in control and powerful enough to bring Israel back from being scattered across the empire. However, groups such as the Neirabians, who returned to their homeland from exile about the same time as the Judeans did, and the Paeonians who were resettled by Darius, did not develop a monotheistic theology to explain their fate and any new opportunities.[24] There is nothing

---

[23] Assyria's treatment of its conquered nations varied according to many factors. See Steven W. Holloway, *Aššur Is King! Aššur Is King! Religion in the Exercise of Power in the Neo-Assyrian Empire*, CHANE 10 (Leiden: Brill, 2002).

[24] See the summary in Kenneth G. Hoglund, *Achaemenid Imperial Administration in Syria-Palestine and the Missions of Ezra and Nehemiah*, SBLDS 125 (Atlanta: Scholars Press, 1992), 20, 27, 238.

in the presentation of these chapters from the Isaiah scroll that claims or can be taken as evidence that they represent the invention of monotheism in Israel.

The third possibility is that monotheism developed in the postexilic period. The priestly theocracy that is credited with ruling much of this time would suggest no reason to innovate such a dramatic new religion. And there is no way that the change from the worship of multiple gods and goddesses to the worship of a single deity can be described as other than a profoundly different religion. One might point to the events in classical Greece and the advent there of philosophers who looked to a single deity. However, these people controlled small schools of disciples at best. They did not rule over a community and enforce a new religion on that group without any trace of resistance in the literature. Further, there is increasing evidence that many of the cultic and legal traditions connected with the priestly establishment were neither innovative in the sixth and fifth centuries nor known in contemporary texts from Babylon or elsewhere. Instead, the closest comparisons are best found in the West Semitic cultures that reach far back into the preexilic period of Israel.[25] If many of the structures and laws have preexilic antecedents, how much more likely does it appear that the belief in one God should not be seen as a late innovation awkwardly superimposed on early precedents (for no clear reason) rather than as something that was already present and well established.

## What Evidence Exists for the Absence of Polytheism among Some Ancient Israelites?

With this observation it is time to turn to the evidence for a diversity of religions in ancient Israel that could include belief in a single deity. A traditional reading of the biblical text argues that such a teaching was foundational and found at the beginning of Israel's existence, seen clearly in the first commandment of the Decalogue (Ex. 20:3; Deut. 5:7) and the confession of the first words of the Shema (Deut. 5:4), not to mention the spirit and teaching of the Law, the Prophets, and many of the other texts of ancient Israel. However, these are the same works that are evaluated as the product of later editors

---

[25]The strongest, longest, and most convincing argument for an Iron Age 2 (eighth/seventh century BC) composition of the major priestly collection, now constituting the book of Leviticus, can be found in the three-volume commentary (over 2,700 pages) of Jacob Milgrom, *Leviticus 1–16: A New Translation and Commentary*, AB 3 (New York: Doubleday, 1991); *Leviticus 17–22: A New Translation and Commentary*, AB 3a (New York: Doubleday, 2000); *Leviticus 23–27: A New Translation and Commentary*, AB 3b (New York: Doubleday, 2000). For a summary of the approach, see R. S. Hess, "A Reassessment of the Priestly Cultic and Legal Texts," *Journal of Law and Religion* 17 (2002): 375–91. For close connections between the Levitical rituals and the Emar rituals, see the summary of these texts and further bibliography in R. S. Hess, *Israelite Religions: An Archaeological and Biblical Survey* (Grand Rapids: Baker, 2007), 112–23.

and pseudonymous authors who wished to lend credibility to their lately developed monotheism by ascribing them to early authorities such as Moses. Rather than reviewing and evaluating the many critical arguments for the dating and editing of this literature, I will here survey some of the most salient extrabiblical evidence for the existence of belief in a single deity, including cult sites, iconography, epigraphy, and personal names.

## Cult Sites

Cult sites do not provide much certainty as to how many deities were worshipped at any site. One method is to count the number of sites, altars, or temples. The earliest sites associated with Israel would be the Ebal site and the bull site east of Dothan. The Ebal site is anomalous and remains difficult to explain. It is a fact that many have seen it as cultic in nature, owing to the distribution of animal bones that correspond to sacrifices in later Israel and owing to the single large structure that resembles an altar in the eyes of many. Ziony Zevit argues for a regional altar and notes its composition of unworked fieldstones, unlike every other altar of Bronze Age and contemporary Canaan.[26] Anson Rainey, however, argues that the presence of inner rooms within the structure and "garbage pits" in the structure cannot support the interpretation of an altar here. He prefers the identification of the site as a farmhouse.[27] The so-called bull site contained the image of a bronze bull, as well as a standing stone within an oval-shaped sacred space marked off by a line of stones.[28] Although it is also dated to the twelfth–eleventh centuries BC, it is difficult to recognize here the expectation of a single deity, unlike what a single altar might suggest on Mount Ebal (if there were an altar there!).

The following centuries saw a shift to urban-centered habitation styles in inland Palestine. With the growth in population and evidence for many cultic centers, there are two that stand out and date from Iron Age II (ca. 1000–586 BC). The first is in the south at the fortress of Arad.[29] In one corner of the fort a sanctuary was constructed. This was an official shrine in Judah as may be indicated by its prominent position in a fortress that, according to the information from the correspondence in the Arad ostraca, as well as names related to the priestly families of the Bible, served the interests of the capital. I have already discussed the niche, often referred to as the Holy of Holies, where the incense altars and standing stones were found. The whole sanctuary was

---

[26] Zevit, *The Religions of Ancient Israel*, 196–201.

[27] Anson F. Rainey, "Notes on Two Archaeological Sites," *ErIsr* 29 (2009): 186*–87*.

[28] Zevit, *The Religions of Ancient Israel*, 180, 250–251; Hess, *Israelite Religions*, 236.

[29] Ze'ev Herzog, *Arad Part 2: The Arad Fortress* (Tel Aviv: Hakkibbutz Hammeuchad, 1997) (Hebrew); Herzog, "The Fortress Mound at Tel Arad: An Interim Report," *TA* 29 (2002): 3–109; Hess, *Israelite Religions*, 303–4.

of three parts, including the niche. In the outer room of the three rooms was
a square altar built entirely of fieldstones. If the Mount Ebal site is an altar,
it represents the only other such altar in the region. Even the incense altars
in the inner room were made of stone that had been shaped and smoothed
artificially. Only this altar was constructed of fieldstones. One cannot draw
certain conclusions about such an artifact. The unhewn stones however are
reminiscent of the desert and of the standing stones, open air sanctuaries,
and other holy sites there. Further, the text of Exodus 20:22–26 requires that
altars to Yahweh be made of this type of construction. The single altar, its
typological comparison with desert shrines and only with desert shrines, and
the Judean connection all suggest that this may have involved the worship
of a single God. When compared with Exodus 20:22–26, as well as both the
biblical and possibly other origins of Yahweh in the desert south of Arad and
into the Sinai, the one altar may signify a single deity who can be reasonably
associated with Yahweh. The much smaller incense altars and standing stones
may or may not signify other deities. The single altar and the niche with the
standing stones and incense altars are as far from each other as possible within
the overall sacred space. Whether this was a sacred space for more than one
religious expression cannot be concluded at this point.

If the sanctuary of Arad provides an example of an official shrine in the
south, the decades of labor by the late Abraham Biran at Tel Dan in the north
have revealed a sanctuary at the center of the site.[30] Its size and importance
best identify it as a temple. At the top of the tell, this site exhibits evidence of
a major open space for what might have been an altar. One horn of that altar
may have been found. If so, it suggests a single large structure that would not
allow room for another altar of comparable size. However, further back and
higher up is a platform with rooms to the side that presumably served as the
most sacred of spaces. In light of 1 Kings 12:28, 32, this has been identified as
the place where the gold calf was exhibited for worship by the northern kingdom of Israel. If so, we again see a single altar, a single image, and evidence
of a single deity. However, the degree of certainty to this reconstruction is
not as high, on the basis of the archaeology alone, as the sanctuary at Arad.

### Iconography

As with the cult sites, there is little evidence for iconography in the period of
Iron Age I, between 1200 and about 1000 BC. In the subsequent period there
is much more evidence. We may consider three examples from this period:
the Taanach cult stand, the Kuntillet 'Ajrud figures, and the Judean pillar

---

[30]Avraham Biran, *Biblical Dan* (Jerusalem: Israel Exploration Society and Hebrew Union College/
Jewish Institute of Religion, 1994); Hess, *Israelite Religions*, 301–3.

figurines. The Taanach cult stand probably dates from the latter part of the tenth century. Taanach was a Canaanite city with evidence of worship of various deities. This cult stand was not the only one found from that period. However, it is the most ornate. The terra-cotta stand, used perhaps for burning incense or for some other part of the cultic activities, has four panels on what must be the front.[31] The first panel at the top portrays a horse or a calf with a winged sun disk over it. Voluted columns appear on either side. The second panel, immediately beneath the top one, displays a tree flanked by an ibex on each side and then two guardian lions facing the front and forming the frame for the image. The third panel has two sphinx or cherubim flanking (just as the two lions above them) an empty space. The fourth panel, at the bottom of the stand, portrays a nude woman facing front with lions on either side, just as in the second panel.

As this is a religious object, it is appropriate to see on these panels images of deities. Thus the fourth panel may represent the chief goddess, perhaps Asherah or Astarte. The second panel, with the tree in the center, may represent the symbol of this goddess. Astarte is explicitly associated with lions at Ugarit; and the tree of life symbolizes the goddess in various contexts. If the second and fourth panels represent the same goddess deity, do the first and third panels represent the same masculine deity? If so, then who is represented by the animal in the first panel? If it is a calf, then this is a perfect match for the calves already mentioned and installed by Jeroboam at Dan and Bethel. If it is a horse, then one is reminded of 2 Kings 23:11, which mentions horses dedicated to the sun in the temple in Jerusalem. Both of these associations would suggest Yahweh or an equivalent deity who brought Israel out of Egypt. The third panel is remarkable as an empty space flanked by a sphinx on each side. It is difficult to imagine more clearly the portrayal of the presence of the unseen deity in the most holy place of the temple, flanked by the cherubim. Here as well we may have a symbol of Yahweh, albeit aniconic.

The evidence from this cult stand does not argue for the worship of Yahweh alone. If the second and fourth panels do represent Yahweh, and not Baal or some other deity, then at most this argues for the high position of Yahweh in the pantheon of the northern kingdom of Israel, and especially in this cult center of the Canaanite city of Taanach.

---

[31]Paul W. Lapp, "The 1968 Excavations at Tell Ta'annek: The New Cultic Stand," *BASOR* 195 (1969): 42–44; Ruth Hestrin, "The Cult Stand from Ta'anach and Its Religious Background," in *Phoenician and the East Mediterranean in the First Millennium B.C.: Proceedings of the Conference Held in Leuven from the 14th to the 16th of November 1985*, ed. E. Lipinski, Studia Phoenicia 5, OLA 22 (Leuven: Peeters, 1987), 61–77; J. Glen Taylor, "The Two Earliest Known Representations of Yahweh," in *Ascribe to the Lord: Biblical and Other Studies in Memory of Peter C. Craigie*, ed. L. Eslinger and G. Taylor, JSOTSup 67 (Sheffield: JSOT, 1988), 557–66; Hess, *Israelite Religions*, 321–24.

The second religious pictorial portrayal is that of three figures found alongside one of the inscriptions already mentioned at Kuntillet ʿAjrud, south of
Judah in the northern Sinai desert.[32] These appear on a potsherd with the
dedication of blessing someone to or for Yahweh of Samaria and Asherah
(or his Asherah). It has been suggested that these figures represent Yahweh
and the goddess Asherah. Often the two standing figures are understood
as this divine couple, while the seated lyre player is entertaining them with
music. Sometimes the lyre player is interpreted as Asherah. However, a closer
examination of the standing figures with their distinctively bovine faces has
led art historians of the period to identify them as Bes figures.[33] Bes was a
deity from Egypt, short of stature and often portrayed in this manner. Bes
figures can be found in abundance, as they were a kind of good-luck charm.
Ziony Zevit has suggested that the Bes figures represented deities such as
Yahweh.[34] However, we lack evidence for this sort of secondary representation
of Yahweh by Bes. The most likely conclusion is that we cannot be certain
of any clear connection between the figures and the written text. Indeed, an
examination of the potsherd demonstrates other drawings and written texts
on the same pieces. These could be images and texts that were not intended
to be related to one another.

A third iconographic representation is found in the Judean pillar-based
figurines. Hundreds of these have been located all around Judah during the
last century and a half of that kingdom's independent existence. Many are
found in domestic dwellings in Jerusalem and throughout Judah, but nowhere
outside the state. Some scholars have seen here the deity Asherah, who is
thought to have provided a cult for women, who were excluded from the male-
dominated temple and priesthood. It would be unusual for images of deities
such as Asherah to be so crudely and cheaply made of clay, as these are. More
likely would be some sort of votive offering or "prayer in clay" to a deity. The
image symbolizes the female Judean in prayer to a god (or goddess, the nature
of the intended deity is not clear from the image itself) for purposes of special
concern, such as a successful conception, pregnancy, and birth of a child.
Or perhaps these are prayerful petitions for lactation (given the pronounced
breasts) and for the nurturing of the baby. Other suggestions are also possible
(good luck charms), but there is no certainty that the images represent a deity.[35]

Thus the images in ancient Israel are difficult to identify. Even when they
appear with writing, as at Kuntillet ʿAjrud, it is not clear that the written

[32]Meshel, *Kuntillet ʿAjrud*; Hess, *Israelite Religions*, 319–21.
[33]P. Beck, "The Drawings from Óorvat Teiman (Kuntillet ʿAjrud)," *TA* 9 (1982): 3–68.
[34]Zevit, *The Religions of Ancient Israel*, 388–89.
[35]Ibid., 267–76; Hess, *Israelite Religions*, 308–11.

text must relate to the pictures. One can suggest that multiple deities were worshipped by some, and one can find evidence of the worship of Yahweh (with the assistance of biblical connections), but little more.

## Epigraphy

Written texts may hold more promise than images for the understanding of beliefs in ancient Israel and any evidence for or against the worship of Yahweh alone. Before the tenth century BC, there is little in the way of inscriptions from Israel, other than a few letters here and there inscribed on some potsherds. An exception is the eleventh-century abecedary from Izbet Sartah, perhaps ancient Ebenezer, and the tenth-century abecedary from Tel Zayit, west and south of Jerusalem. Both of these texts demonstrate an interest in learning to read and write in small villages and towns that were or would become part of Israel and Judah.[36] More significant are the five lines of early Hebrew writing discovered on a potsherd from Tell Qeiyafa, an Israelite fort on the Elah Valley occupied for a short time ca. 1000 BC.[37] This text has not yielded easily to reading and translation. It seems to be more than a list of names, either a letter or some reference to legal matters. The roots for the words *king* and *judge* appear, whether as nouns or verbs.[38] Yahweh, however, is not mentioned.

Indeed, the first mention of Yahweh as a God in Israel appears in the stele of King Mesha of Moab, a land to the east of the Dead Sea in modern Jordan.[39] There in the ninth century BC the foreign king Mesha records how he captured the "altar hearth of Yahweh" from an Israelite town controlled by the dynasty of Omri, father of Ahab. This is the only deity that Mesha associates with Israel in his account of his wars with Israel. Thus in the ninth century BC a neighboring king records only one deity associated with Israel, and that deity is Yahweh. As already mentioned, Israelite and Judean inscriptions from the

---

[36] On the abecedaries, see now P. Kyle McCarter, "Paleographic Notes on the Tel Zayit Abecedary," in *Literate Culture and Tenth-Century Canaan: The Tel Zayit Abecedary*, ed. R. E. Tappy and P. K. McCarter Jr. (Winona Lake, IN: Eisenbrauns, 2008), 45–60. For the question of literacy, see, e.g., R. S. Hess, "Literacy in Iron Age Israel," in Long, Baker, and Wenham, *Windows into Old Testament History*, 82–102; Hess, "Writing about Writing: Abecedaries and Evidence for Literacy in Ancient Israel," *VT* 56 (2006): 342–46; Hess, "Questions of Reading and Writing in Ancient Israel," *BBR* 19 (2009): 1–9; Hess, review of *Literate Culture and Tenth-Century Canaan: The Tel Zayit Abecedary*, ed. by R. E. Tappy and P. K. McCarter Jr., *BBR* 19 (2009): 595–97.

[37] Yosef Garfinkel and Saar Ganor, "Khirbet Qeiyafa in Context," in *Khirbet Qeiyafa*, vol. 1, *Excavation Report 2007–2008*, ed. Y. Garfinkel and S. Ganor (Jerusalem: Israel Exploration Society and Institute of Archaeology of The Hebrew University of Jerusalem, 2009), 3–18.

[38] Haggai Misgav, Yosef Garfinkel, and Saar Ganor, "The Ostracon," in Garfinkel and Ganor, *Khirbet Qeiyafa*, 1:243–57.

[39] For this and the following three paragraphs, see Hess, *Israelite Religions*, 274–90.

ninth and eighth centuries mention Yahweh, Asherah, and Baal. These occur
at the sites of Kuntillet ʿAjrud and Khirbet el-Qôm.

From this same period the inscriptions from Deir ʿAlla, on the east side of
the Jordan River, record the vision of Balaam. He sees the chief god, called
El (a title or a name?) and a divine council composed of the Shaddayin and
gods. The texts are not written in Israelite or Judean Hebrew and may reflect
a religious group distinct to the vicinity of the site.

From ca. 800 BC the Jerusalem pomegranate is best regarded as authentic,
and its text is best translated, "Belonging to the temple of Yahweh, holy to
the priests." From perhaps this same era a seal mentions a certain Miqneyahu,
who is a "servant of Yahweh." No other deities are mentioned on seals from
Israel and Judah. From Ein Gedi ca. 700 BC, Yahweh is described as blessed,
as ruler of the nations, and as "my lord" by the writer. From about the same
time at Khirbet Beit Lei, also in Judah, Yahweh's sovereignty over Jerusalem
and probably Judah is confessed. This text also includes what may be a prayer
for Yahweh's absolution. As already noted, in the final decades of the Judean
monarchy, Yahweh alone is mentioned in formulaic blessings on military correspondence between the leaders of the forts at Arad and Lachish and presumably the capital of Jerusalem. One ostracon at Arad (18) also mentions a
temple of Yahweh.

Thus, despite the mention of other deities sometimes associated with
Yahweh, there is a growing literary tradition that seems to be present as
early as Mesha. This tradition recognizes Yahweh alone as the god of Israel
and Judah. Yahweh is the only one associated with a cult image and temple.
He alone is appealed to for blessing and absolution, and his rulership alone
is confessed over Jerusalem, Judah, and the nations.

### Personal Names

There are more than seventeen hundred personal names that appear on seals,
bullae (seal impressions preserved in clay), and other inscriptions in preexilic
Israel and Judah.[40] Jeffrey Tigay has estimated, at the time of his writing in
1986, that 46 percent included the divine name Yahweh as part of their personal name, 6 percent included ʾl as part of their personal name, less than 1
percent included some other deity in their personal name, and the rest had
names that were not constructed with any explicit divine name.[41] It should
be noted that the name ʾl can refer to the title "god" and thus cannot be used

---

[40]Ibid., 269–74.
[41]Jeffrey H. Tigay, *You Shall Have No Other Gods: Israelite Religion in the Light of Hebrew Inscriptions*, HSS 31 (Atlanta: Scholars Press, 1986).

as evidence for a different deity. The picture from the personal names is that Israel and Judah were overwhelmingly Yahwistic.

There is only one period and place where the possible significant presence of another divine name may appear in the onomastica. That is in the northern kingdom of Israel in the early eighth century. The Samaria ostraca mention several personal names made up of the divine name Baal. Here again it is important to note that this Hebrew term, $b'l$, may refer merely to a title such as "lord" or "master," and not to a separate deity.[42] This is the one and only time that any other possible divine name is so pronounced. Even in this collection of names, however, the name Yahweh is dominant in personal names. Indeed, a study of four collections of personal names, including those from the Samaria ostraca, demonstrates that in every case Yahweh is dominant on an order of nearly 90 percent or more beyond all other divine names of specific gods found in Israelite personal names.[43] In fact, in the latest archives of names, from the months and years immediately preceding the Babylonian destruction of Jerusalem in 587/586 BC, the dominance of Yahweh as a theophoric element in personal names approaches 100 percent.

This is distinctive to Israel and especially to Judah. In no way is it comparable to the profiles of theophoric names from the neighboring lands of Ammon, Moab, Edom, Philistia, or elsewhere.[44] In Ammon, which preserves the largest number of personal names among these states, the chief god, $mlkm$, occurs in only nine out of more than 160 personal names with divine elements.[45] Most names there use the "generic" $'l$ element, but some ten contain other recognizable names of deities. Only among the ancient Israelites was their God Yahweh confessed in the personal names to an extent that approached exclusivity.

Personal names do not "prove" the religion of ancient Israel. However, they remain an important datum and one that demonstrates the unique extent to

---

[42]For a discussion of the different understandings possible for this name element, see Jeremy M. Hutton, "Southern, Northern and Transjordanian Perspectives," in Stavrakopoulou and Barton, *Religious Diversity in Ancient Israel and Judah*, 153–56.

[43]R. S. Hess, "Aspects of Israelite Personal Names and Pre-Exilic Israelite Religion," in *New Seals and Inscriptions, Hebrew, Idumean and Cuneiform*, ed. M. Lubetski, Hebrew Bible Monographs 8 (Sheffield: Sheffield Phoenix, 2007), 301–13.

[44]*Contra* the implication of some statements that assume comparable profiles in ancient Israel and Judah and in these other nations. See, e.g., Albertz, "Personal Piety," 138–41. For more details about the distinctive theology of the confessional names of Israel and Judah in contrast to the surrounding states, see Jeaneane D. Fowler, *Theophoric Personal Names in Ancient Hebrew: A Comparative Study*, JSOTSup 49 (Sheffield: JSOT, 1988).

[45]Kent Jackson, "Ammonite Personal Names in the Context of West Semitic Onomasticon," in *The Word of the Lord Shall Go Forth: Essays in Honor of David Noel Freedman in Celebration of His Sixtieth Birthday*, ed. C. L. Meyers and M. O'Connor (Philadelphia: American Schools of Oriental Research, 1983), 507–21.

which Yahweh alone was confessed and worshipped on a popular level for so much of the attested history of Israel and Judah. Contrary to claims made by some scholars, these results are not comparable with the neighboring states. Instead they represent an explicit testimony to the prominence of the recognition of Yahweh as a special deity in Israel.

## Concluding Remarks

How can we make sense of all this evidence? First, I would reaffirm the earlier observation that there is no evidence that excludes the possibility that Yahweh was worshipped by some in ancient Israel as sole deity. This possibility exists from earliest Israel through to the Babylonian destruction of Jerusalem.

Second, I would affirm that the picture of religious practice in ancient Israel was mixed. The mute testimony of the archaeological sites and the iconographic portrayals do not exclude the possibility that in some times and contexts a single deity was worshipped. This is especially true where there remains a single altar that may suggest worship of a single God. It is not possible to identify this deity with Yahweh, although the iconographic witness and the textual evidence combine to confess an awareness of the prominence of Yahweh in the times and places of these cult centers.

Third, the witness of the inscriptions and especially the personal names suggests that there were multiple views of the divine world in ancient Israel. Clearly there were those who reverenced more than one deity. In their pantheon, Yahweh could and did appear as a major God. However, there also seems to be considerable evidence for groups in Israel, and at times official recognition by outsiders such as Mesha the Moabite, of the worship of only one named deity, Yahweh. If anything, this becomes more pronounced by the end of the Judean monarchy. Nevertheless, just as the Bible witnesses to multiple religions and worship practices right up to the end of the monarchy, so the extrabiblical evidence cannot exclude the possibility that Yahweh was not the only deity worshipped by some, even in the final years of the period under study.

# 21

# NEW EXCAVATIONS AT KHIRBET QEIYAFA AND THE EARLY HISTORY OF JUDAH

## MICHAEL G. HASEL

The kingdom of David and Solomon is pivotal for biblical history. According to the Bible, it is David who defeats the Philistines, bringing under control decades of antagonism and conflict (1 Samuel 17; 19; 23; 2 Samuel 5; 1 Chron. 18:1).[1] It is David who galvanizes the twelve tribes under his monarchy and establishes the capital of Jerusalem (2 Samuel 5), and it is David who composes much of the liturgy of Israelite worship (Psalms 9; 18; 30; 56–57). Finally, it is through the line of Jesse and David that the Messiah is promised to Israel (Isa. 11:1–10; Rev. 22:16).[2] No other person is mentioned more frequently throughout the Old and New Testaments than David, from the earliest references in Samuel to the final chapter of Revelation.[3] His son Solomon builds the temple in Jerusalem, refortifies the cities of Megiddo, Hazor, Gezer, and Jerusalem (1 Kings 9:15), and establishes an extensive trade network, exponentially increasing the wealth of Israel.

---

[1] On the extended life and final demise of the Philistines in the archaeological record, see Seymour Gitin, "Philistia in Transition: The Tenth Century and Beyond," in *Mediterranean Peoples in Transition, in Honor of Trude Dothan*, ed. S. Gitin, A. Mazar, and E. Stern (Jerusalem: Israel Exploration Society, 1998), 162–83; Gitin, "Philistines in the Books of Kings," in *The Books of Kings: Sources, Composition, Historiography and Reception*, ed. André Lemaire and Baruch Halpern (Leiden: Brill, 2010), 308–9.

[2] On the messianic descriptions pertaining to David, see Philip E. Satterthwaite, "David in the Books of Samuel: A Messianic Hope?," in *The Lord's Anointed: Interpretation of Old Testament Messianic Texts*, ed. P. E. Satterthwaite, R. S. Hess, and G. J. Wenham (Grand Rapids: Baker, 1995), 41–65; Daniel I. Block, "Bringing Back David: Ezekiel's Messianic Hope," in *The Lord's Anointed*, 167–88; Block, "My Servant David: Ancient Israel's Vision of the Messiah," in *Israel's Messiah in the Bible and the Dead Sea Scrolls*, ed. Richard S. Hess, R. Carroll, and M. Daniel (Grand Rapids: Baker, 2003), 17–56.

[3] The name David is mentioned 1,087 times: 976 times in the Old Testament and 111 times in the New.

Today the consensus on the biblical and archaeological evidence for the
united monarchy has been challenged in the wake of late-modern and postmodern revisionism.[4] As Gary Knoppers observes in his 1997 article, "Three
decades ago scholars viewed the united monarchy as one of the most secure
periods of historical reconstruction . . . . Virtually all modern historians wrote
histories that included, if not commenced with, the monarchy of David and
Solomon. This is no longer the case."[5]

## Literary Approaches and History

Fourteen years later this epoch seems shrouded in a deepening fog of historical
uncertainty and debate within literary criticism.[6] The wide-ranging theories
for the Davidic narratives spawned through source-, tradition-history-, form-,
and redaction-critical lenses have finally produced such a myriad of hypotheses
that among some, "the number of editors and revisers has proliferated to the
point of absurdity."[7] In the source-critical debates of the earlier twentieth century, Otto Eisefeldt continued to defend the J and E sources of Wellhausen for
Samuel, but added an earlier L source.[8] Hermann Gunkel placed the David
narratives in Solomon's court,[9] followed by Hugo Gressmann, who placed it
back in David's time.[10] Leonard Rost tried to demonstrate a thematic unity in
these narratives and claimed that it was reported by a contemporary eyewitness
early in Solomon's reign.[11] A. Lods promoted the "seer" and "Jabesh" sources,[12]

---

[4]On the presuppositions and established conclusions of the Albright school, see W. F. Albright,
"Was the Age of Solomon Without Monumental Art?" *ErIsr* 5 (Mazar volume) (1958): 1*–9*; G. E.
Wright, *Biblical Archaeology* (Philadelphia: Westminster, 1960), 66–89; and on the apparent demise
of the Albright school, see William G. Dever, "What Remains of the House That Albright Built?,"
*BA* 56 (1993): 25–35.
[5]Gary N. Knoppers, "The Vanishing Solomon: The Disappearance of the United Monarchy from
Recent Histories of Ancient Israel," *JBL* 116 (1997): 19–20.
[6]The various interpretations are thoroughly outlined in John Van Seters, *The Biblical Saga of King
David* (Winona Lake, IN: Eisenbrauns, 2009), 3–52.
[7]Ibid., 32.
[8]Otto Eissfeldt, *Die Komposition der Samuelbücher* (Leipzig: Hinrichs, 1931); Eissfeldt, *The Old
Testament: An Introduction*, trans. P. Ackroyd (New York: Harper & Row, 1965), 271–90.
[9]Hermann Gunkel, "Geschichtsschreibung im A.T.," in *Religion in Geschichte und Gegenwart*, ed.
Hermann Gunkel (Tübingen: Mohr, 1909–1913), 2:1348–54; Gunkel, "Die isrealitsche Literatur," in
*Die orientalische Literaturen*, 2nd ed., ed. P. Hinneberg (Berlin: Teubner, 1925), 53–112.
[10]Hugo Gressmann, "The Oldest History Writing in Israel," in *Narrative and Novella in Samuel:
Studies by Hugo Gressmann and Other Scholars 1906–1923*, ed. David M. Gunn, JSOTSup 116
(Sheffield: Almond, 1991), 9–58.
[11]Leonhard Rost, *Die Überlieferung von der Thronnachfolge Davids*, BWANT 3/6 (Stuttgart: Kohl-
hammer, 1926), 105.
[12]A. Lods, *Israel from Its Beginning to the Middle of the Eighth Century*, trans. S. H. Hooke (New
York: Alfred Knopf, 1948), 358–62.

while A. R. S. Kennedy divided 1 Samuel into four strands.[13] Others based various sources on geographical locales.[14] In the end, Bruce Birch states that "none of the various subdivisions of the material have been able to achieve widespread support."[15] With the DtrH hypothesis of Martin Noth a new direction emerged, yet with increasing complexity and without any clear resolution. Noth, and others who followed, believed that the DtrH incorporated into his work the earlier sources in the seventh century BC. How and when this was done continues to be debated. The Göttingen school now divides the DtrH into the DtrG, DtrP, and DtrN.[16] Frank Moore Cross, P. Kyle McCarter, and others suggest a two-source Dtr[1] and Dtr[2].[17] McCarter also adds a Prophetic History (PH) prior to the DtrH,[18] while Anthony Campbell prefers the term Prophetic Record (PR).[19] Add the new hypothesis of I. Willi-Plein of the DHG (*Davidshausgeschichte*),[20] and it is little wonder that some lament the end of the DtrH altogether.[21] In regards to Samuel, one can readily see that consensus is lacking among scholars on the date of these biblical texts, their compositional history, or the origin of various sources and strands. It is important to remember that these dynamic hypotheses

---

[13] A. R. S. Kennedy, *Samuel*, NCB (New York: Frowde, 1905), 13–20.

[14] A. Weiser, *Samuel: Seine geschichtliche Aufgabe und religiöse Bedeutung* (Göttingen: Vandenhoeck & Ruprecht, 1962), 819–30; H. W. Hertzberg, *I and II Samuel*, trans. J. S. Bowden (Philadelphia: Westminster, 1964); Klaus-Dietrich Schunk, *Benjamin*, BZAW 86 (Berlin: Alfred Töppelmann, 1963).

[15] Bruce Birch, *The Rise of the Israelite Monarchy: The Growth and Development of I Samuel 7–15*, SBLDS 27 (Missoula, MT: Scholars Press, 1976), 3.

[16] T. Veijola, *Die ewige Dynastie: David und die Entstehung seiner Dynastie nach der deuterono-mischen Darstellung*, Suomalaisen Tiedeakatemian Toimituksia Annales Academiae Scientiarum Fennicae Series B 193 (Helsinki: Suomalainen Tiedeakatemia, 1975); Walter Dietrich, *The Early Monarchy in Israel: The Tenth Century B.C.E.*, trans. Joachim Vette, Biblical Encyclopedia 3 (Atlanta: Scholars, 2007), 1–98.

[17] P. K. McCarter, *I Samuel*, AB 8 (Garden City, NY: Doubleday, 1980); McCarter, *II Samuel*, AB 9 (Garden City, NY: Doubleday, 1984).

[18] Followed by Birch, *The Rise of the Israelite Monarchy*, 18, 20–21.

[19] Anthony F. Campbell, *Of Prophets and Kings: A Late Ninth-Century Document (1 Samuel 1–2 Kings 10)*, CBQMS 17 (Washington, DC: Catholic Biblical Association, 1986), 70–71.

[20] I. Willi-Plein, "1 Sam 18–19 und die Davidshausgeschichte," in *David und Saul im Wiederstreit: Diachronie und Synchronie im Wettstreit*, ed. Walter Dietrich, OBO 206 (Freiburg: Academic; Göttingen: Vandenhoeck & Ruprecht, 2004), 138–77; Willi-Plein, "Michal und die Anfänge des Königtums in Israel," in *Congress Volume, Cambridge 1995*, ed. J. A. Emerton, VTSup 66 (Leiden: Brill, 1997), 401–19.

[21] E. Würthwein, "Erwägungen zum sog. deuteronomistischen Geschichtswerk: Eine Skizze," in *Studien zum deuteronomistischen Geschichtswerk*, BZAW 227 (Berlin: de Gruyter, 1994), 1–11; Claus Westermann, *Die Geschichtbücher des Alten Testaments: Gab es ein deuteronomistisches Geschichtswerk?* (Gütersloh: Mohn, 1994); A. Graeme Auld, *Joshua Retold: Synoptic Perspectives* (Edinburgh: T&T Clark, 1998), 120–26; J. R. Linville, *Israel in the Book of Kings: The Past as a Project of Social Identity*, JSOTSup 272 (Sheffield: JSOT, 1998), 46–73; Ernst Axel Knauf, "Does the 'Deuteronomistic Historiography' (DtrH) Exist?" in *Israel Constructs Its History: Deuteronomistic History in Recent Research*, ed. A. de Pury, T. Römer, and J.-D. Macchi, JSOTSup 306 (Sheffield: JSOT, 2000), 388–98.

of the nineteenth century are "constructions of modern scholarship"[22] and that they continue to evolve and change. Recent postmodern revisionism attempts to redate this entire history to the third and second centuries BC and denies the existence of David and Solomon altogether,[23] following the ultimate, logical conclusion in a trajectory that earlier dismissed the patriarchs and the exodus/ conquest accounts.[24] In the end both diachronic and synchronic approaches have struggled to provide an assured *Sitz im Leben* in the ancient world. This has led biblical scholars to turn increasingly to the archaeology of Israel for answers, but this too has led to varying opinions and interpretations.

## The Role of Archaeology and Methodology

In his most recent work, *The Biblical Saga of King David*, John Van Seters sets out to demonstrate that the David story is a late saga with little reference to the tenth century BC. His opening argument is the so-called lack of evidence for the united monarchy in the archaeological record, following exclusively the recent work of the Tel Aviv School and the Low Chronology advocated by Israel Finkelstein and others.[25] Finkelstein and David Ussishkin redate the Solomonic gates of Hazor, Megiddo, and Gezer to the ninth century.[26] What

---

[22]Thomas C. Römer and Marc Z. Brettler, "Deuteronomy and the Case for a Persian Hexateuch," *JBL* 119 (2000): 417.

[23]Philip R. Davies writes, "I doubt whether the term 'Deuteronomistic History' should continue to be used by scholars as if it were a fact instead of a theory" (*In Search of "Ancient Israel,"* JSOTSup 148 [Sheffield: JSOT, 1992], 131); see also Niels-Peter Lemche, "The Old Testament—A Hellenistic Book?," *SJOT* 7 (1993): 163–93; Thomas L. Thompson, *Early History of the Israelite People: From the Written and Archaeological Sources*, SHANE 4 (Leiden: Brill, 1992); and most recently their student Emanuel Pfoh, *The Emergence of Israel in Ancient Palestine* (London: Equinox, 2009), 90–107; see the critique by William G. Dever, *What Did the Biblical Writers Know and When Did They Know It?* (Grand Rapids: Eerdmans, 2001).

[24]Both Thompson and Van Seters, who earlier rejected the patriarchal period, but once accepted the united monarchy, have now come to largely dismiss this history as well (Thomas L. Thompson, *The Historicity of the Patriarchal Narratives* [Berlin: de Gruyter, 1974]; John Van Seters, *Abraham in History and Tradition* [New Haven, CT: Yale University Press, 1975]). See the observations of this trend by Edwin Yamauchi, "The Current State of Old Testament Historiography," in *Faith, Tradition, and History*, ed. A. R. Millard, J. K. Hoffmeier, and D. W. Baker (Winona Lake, IN: Eisenbrauns, 1994), 21–26.

[25]Van Seters, *The Biblical Saga of King David*, 53–73.

[26]Israel Finkelstein, "The Gate of Gezer's Outer Wall," *TA* 8 (1981): 136–45; Finkelstein, "On Archaeological Methods and Historical Considerations: Iron II Gezer and Samaria," *BASOR* 277/278 (1990): 109–30; David Ussishkin, "Was the 'Solomonic' City Gate at Megiddo Built by Solomon?," *BASOR* 239 (1980): 1–18; Ussishkin, "Notes on Megiddo, Gezer, Ashdod, and Tel Batash in the Tenth and Ninth Centuries B.C.," *BASOR* 277/278 (1990): 71–91; see the vigorous responses by Yigael Yadin, "A Rejoinder," *BASOR* 239 (1980): 19–23; William G. Dever, "Late Bronze Age and Solomonic Defenses: New Evidence," *BASOR* 262 (1986): 9–34; Dever, "Of Myths and Methods," *BASOR* 277/278 (1990): 121–30; Randall W. Younker, "A Preliminary Report of the 1990 Season at Tel Gezer: Excavations of the 'Outer Wall' and the 'Solomonic Gateway' (July 2 to August 10, 1990)," *AUSS* 29 (1991): 19–60; Dever, "The Date of the 'Outer Wall' at Gezer," *BASOR* 289 (1993): 33–54.

were once dated to Solomon now become Ahab's building activities. In recent years Finkelstein proposes a down-dating of all material culture by nearly a century through the wholesale reassignment of strata to later periods.[27] On what basis do they suggest their hypothesis? In the recent introduction to their book *David and Solomon*, Finkelstein and Neil Asher Silberman state, "The familiar stories about David and Solomon based on early folk traditions, are the results of extensive reworking and editorial expansion during the four centuries that followed David and Solomon's reigns . . . they contain little reliable history." In the very next paragraph they write:

> The first obvious challenge in assessing the historical reliability of the David and Solomon stories is to determine the precise date of their reigns. This must be based on evidence within the Bible . . . . We must rely—with due caution—on the chronological clues preserved in the Deuteronomistic History.[28]

Finkelstein and Silberman largely base their reconstruction of the reigns of David and Solomon on the selective, subjective choice of which texts *they* decide are historical and which texts are not, with little detail concerning the compositional development of the biblical record. In fact, as Amihai Mazar has pointed out:

> Many of the same scholars who deny the historicity of the United Monarchy do accept the historicity of the Northern Kingdom of Israel ruled by Omri and Ahab in the ninth century . . . . Yet the time lapse between the United Monarchy and the Omride Dynasty is less than a century, while several centuries separate the ninth century from the supposed time when the biblical texts were composed, namely in the seventh century BCE.[29]

Finkelstein responds by saying, "Accepting the historicity of one verse and rejecting another is *exactly* the meaning of two centuries of biblical scholarship."[30] But as summarized above, which part of the last two hundred

---

[27]Israel Finkelstein, "The Archaeology of the United Monarchy: An Alternative View," *Levant* 28 (1996): 177–87.

[28]Finkelstein and Silberman, *David and Solomon: In Search of the Bible's Sacred Kings and the Roots of the Western Tradition* (New York: Free Press, 2006), 17.

[29]Amihai Mazar, "The Search for David and Solomon: An Archaeological Perspective," in *The Quest for the Historical Israel: Debating Archaeology and the History of Early Israel*, ed. Brian B. Schmidt, SBLABS 17 (Atlanta: Society of Biblical Literature, 2007), 118; see also Mazar, "The 1997–1998 Excavations at Tel Rehov: Preliminary Report," *IEJ* (1999): 40 n. 38; Amnon Ben-Tor, "Hazor and the Chronology of the Northern Israel: A Reply to Israel Finkelstein," *BASOR* 317 (2000): 12, 14.

[30]Israel Finkelstein, "A Low Chronology Update: Archaeology, History, and Bible," in *The Bible and Radiocarbon Dating: Archaeology, Text, and Bible*, ed. Thomas E. Levy and Thomas Higham (London: Equinox, 2005), 38.

years of biblical interpretation is Finkelstein choosing? This tautological approach leaves ambiguous the relationship of data and interpretation.[31]

Recognizing the need for sophistication in one's approach to biblical sources, Van Seters, building on the Low Chronology, has written his monumental study "to construct a literary analysis that will more clearly reflect this new understanding of Judah's social history."[32] But this raises the question: Is the new proposed literary analysis based on the archaeological evidence garnered by the Low Chronology, as Van Seters claims? Or is the archaeological data redated to accord with the *Sitz im Leben* and lack of historicity assumed *a priori* for the stories of the biblical narrative? To put it differently, do assumptions about the text drive archaeological interpretation, or does archaeological data determine the date of the texts? This relationship is not altogether clear. Both sides of the debate over the tenth century claim that archaeology is the driving force behind their reconstructions of ancient Israel.[33] But how much of the argument of the Low Chronology is, in the end, based on actual archaeological data? How much is based on existing data simply reinterpreted or even ignored? Finally, how much is based on negative evidence, or the "absence of evidence"?

In this essay I will primarily deal with the negative-evidence argument for the time period of David, since other arguments for the Low Chronology have been addressed elsewhere.[34] I will conclude with the positive evidence

---

[31]Ironically, the accusation of "circular reasoning" is also levied against the mainstream chronology by Israel Finkelstein, "King Solomon's Golden Age: History or Myth?" in Schmidt, *The Quest for the Historical Israel*, 111.

[32]Van Seters, *The Biblical Saga of King David*, 89.

[33]Dever, *What Did the Biblical Writers Know?*, 132; Dever, "Archaeology and the 'Age of Solomon': A Case Study in Archaeology and Historiography," in *The Age of Solomon: Scholarship at the Turn of the Millennium*, ed. Lowell K. Handy (Leiden: Brill, 1997), 251: "I have made no reference to the biblical texts as evidence . . . . My evidence throughout has been archaeological. We *have* an Israelite state in the Iron IIA period." On the other hand, Finkelstein and Silberman state, "In the following chapters we will present archaeological evidence to show that there was no united monarchy of Israel in the way that the Bible describes it" (*David and Solomon*, 22).

[34]See the critiques by A. Mazar, "Iron Age Chronology: A Reply to Finkelstein," *Levant* 29 (1997): 157–67; Ben-Tor, "Hazor and the Chronology," 9–16; Ben-Tor and David Ben-Ami, "Hazor and the Archaeology of the 10th Century B.C.E.," *IEJ* 48 (1998): 1–37; William G. Dever, "Excavating the Bible or Burying It Again?," *BASOR* 322 (2001): 67–77; Dever, "Histories and Non-Histories of Ancient Israel: The Question of the United Monarchy," in *In Search of Pre-Exilic Israel*, ed. John Day (London: T&T Clark, 2004), 65–94; Steven M. Ortiz, "Does the 'Low Chronology' Work? A Case Study of Tell Qasile X, Tel Gezer X, and Lachish V," in *"I Will Speak the Riddle of Ancient Times": Archaeological and Historical Studies in Honor of Amihai Mazar on the Occasion of His Sixtieth Birthday*, ed. A. M. Maeir and P. de Miroschedji (Winona Lake, IN: Eisenbrauns, 2006), 587–611; and most recently the dialogue between Mazar and Finkelstein in Schmidt, *Quest for the Historical Israel*; see also the cogent arguments by Daniel A. Frese and Thomas E. Levy, "The Four Pillars of the Iron Age Low Chronology," in *Historical Biblical Archaeology and the Future: The New Pragmatism*, ed. Thomas E. Levy (London: Equinox, 2010), 187–202.

of new data produced by excavations at a site virtually unknown until four years ago—Khirbet Qeiyafa.

## "Absence of Evidence" Arguments and the Nature of the Archaeological Record

In their recent popular books *The Bible Unearthed* (2001) and *David and Solomon* (2006),[35] Finkelstein and Silberman contend that the history of the united monarchy must be revised because in their assessment there is "not the slightest evidence of any change in the landscape of Judah until the following century. The population remained low and the villages modest and few."[36] There is "no evidence for David's conquests,"[37] "no sign of monumental architecture, or important city in Jerusalem,"[38] "no sign of grand scale building at Megiddo, Hazor, and Gezer,"[39] and "no trace of written documents, inscriptions, or even signs of the kind of widespread literacy that would be necessary for a widespread monarchy."[40] In fact, "there is no sign of extensive literacy or writing in Judah until the end of the eighth century."[41] For Solomon the alleged copper mines at Tell el-Kheleifah "proved to be fantasy," for there was "no evidence for smelting activity at the site."[42] There is "no archaeological evidence whatsoever that the situation of north and south [the divided kingdom] grew out of earlier political unity—particularly one centered in the south."[43] The list goes on.[44]

But, according to Jane M. Cahill, "Theories based on negative evidence should never be preferred to theories based on positive evidence. Stated another way, absence of evidence is not evidence of absence."[45] Historian David Hackett Fischer maintains that such arguments are historical fallacies. "Evidence must always be affirmative. Negative evidence is a contradiction in terms—it is no

---

[35]Finkelstein and Silberman, *David and Solomon* (see n. 28 above); Finkelstein and Silberman, *The Bible Unearthed: Archaeology's New Vision of Ancient Israel and the Origin of Its Sacred Texts* (New York: Free Press, 2001).

[36]Finkelstein and Silberman, *David and Solomon*, 96.

[37]Finkelstein and Silberman, *Bible Unearthed*, 131; Finkelstein and Silberman, *David and Solomon*, 96–97.

[38]Finkelstein and Silberman, *Bible Unearthed*, 131.

[39]Ibid.

[40]Ibid., 142.

[41]Finkelstein and Silberman, *David and Solomon*, 86.

[42]Ibid., 284.

[43]Finkelstein and Silberman, *Bible Unearthed*, 158.

[44]For further assertions and arguments, see Frese and Levy, "The Four Pillars of the Iron Age Low Chronology," 198–99.

[45]Jane M. Cahill, "Jerusalem at the Time of the United Monarchy: The Archaeological Evidence," in *Jerusalem in Bible and Archaeology: The First Temple Period*, ed. Andrew G. Vaughn and Ann E. Killebrew (Atlanta: Society of Biblical Literature, 2003), 73.

evidence at all."[46] There are perhaps five reasons why evidence of this nature is not readily at hand.

First, it must be recognized that the heartland of David and Solomon's kingdom, as described in Samuel and Kings, has been inaccessible to archaeologists for the past half century. The West Bank, with hundreds of sites, remains largely unexcavated, and the results of surveys only provide limited data.[47] Those sites that have been excavated have only been excavated to a limited extent. Jerusalem remains an inhabited city with limited access because of housing, roads, and other structures.[48] It is estimated that nearly half of the Iron Age city is under the Temple Mount and is archaeologically unknown.[49] One might compare similar situations at other ancient cities occupied in modern times, including Damascus, Tyre, and Sidon.[50] After multiple seasons at Gezer in the 1960s and '70s and the renewed excavations in this decade, only about 2 percent of the site has been investigated for Iron IIA material.[51] At Megiddo, more of the site was exposed by the early Chicago excavations, but less than 5 percent of the Iron Age site has been reexcavated by Tel Aviv University.[52]

---

[46]David Hackett Fischer, *Historians' Fallacies: Toward a Logic of Historical Thought* (New York: Harper & Row, 1970), 62.

[47]The results of surveys in this territory are now published by Adam Zertal, *The Manasseh Hill Country Survey*, vol. 1, *The Shechem Syncline*, CHANE 21/1 (Leiden: Brill, 2004); Zertal, *The Manasseh Hill Country Survey*, vol. 2, *The Eastern Valleys and the Fringes of the Desert*, CHANE 21/2 (Leiden: Brill, 2007); earlier surveys from the territory of Ephraim were published by Israel Finkelstein, *The Archaeology of the Israelite Settlement* (Jerusalem: Israel Exploration Society, 1988).

[48]For similar arguments, see Alan Millard, "David and Solomon's Jerusalem: Do the Bible and Archaeology Disagree?," in *Israel: Ancient Kingdom or Late Invention?*, ed. Daniel I. Block, Bryan H. Cribb, and Gregory S. Smith (Nashville: B&H Academic, 2008), 194–98.

[49]Amihai Mazar, "Remarks on Biblical Traditions and Archaeological Evidence Concerning Early Israel," in *Symbiosis, Symbolism, and the Power of the Past: Canaan, Ancient Israel, and Their Neighbors from the Late Bronze Age through Roman Palaestina. Proceedings of the Centennial Symposium W. F. Albright Institute of Archaeological Research and American Schools of Oriental Research, Jerusalem, May 29–May 31, 2000*, ed. W. G. Dever and S. Gitin (Winona Lake, IN: Eisenbrauns, 2003), 91.

[50]Millard, "David and Solomon's Jerusalem," 196–98.

[51]Steven M. Ortiz, personal communication, January 12, 2011; for the Hebrew Union College excavations at Gezer, see the final publications, W. G. Dever, H. D. Lance, and G. E. Wright, *Gezer I: Preliminary Report of the 1964–66 Seasons* (Jerusalem: Hebrew Union College Biblical and Archaeological School, 1970); W. G. Dever et al., *Gezer II: Report of the 1967–70 Seasons in Fields I and II*, ed. W. G. Dever (Jerusalem: Hebrew Union College/Nelson Glueck School of Biblical Archaeology, 1974); Seymour Gitin, *Gezer III: A Ceramic Typology of the Late Iron II, Persian, and Hellenistic Periods at Tell Gezer* (Jerusalem: Hebrew Union College/Nelson Glueck School of Biblical Archaeology, 1990); *Gezer IV: The 1969–71 Seasons in Field VI, the "Acropolis,"* ed. W. G. Dever (Jerusalem: Hebrew Union College/Nelson Glueck School of Biblical Archaeology, 1986).

[52]Israel Finkelstein, David Ussishkin, and Baruch Halpern, eds., *Megiddo III: The 1992–1996 Seasons* (Tel Aviv: Tel Aviv University, Sonia and Marco Nadler Institute of Archaeology, 2000); Finkelstein, Ussishkin, and Halpern, eds., *Megiddo IV: The 1998–2004 Seasons* (Tel Aviv: Tel Aviv University, Sonia and Marco Nadler Institute of Archaeology, 2006); see the recent plan of the area of excavation in Gunner Lehmann and Ann E. Killebrew, "Palace 6000 at Megiddo in Context: Iron Age Central Hall Tetra-Partite Residencies and the *Bīt-Hilāni* Building Tradition in the Southern Levant," *BASOR* 359 (2010): 14, fig. 1.

Second, of those sites that have been excavated, few are fully published. The final Chicago report of the Megiddo excavations pertaining to this crucial period has only now been published after a period of seventy years, and the interpretation of the data seriously undermines the conclusions and recent publications of the Tel Aviv excavations and the Low Chronology.[53] The conclusion that Jerusalem was wholly unoccupied, or at best an impoverished village, ignores the fact that all the major excavators of Jerusalem—Kenyon, Shiloh, and now Eilat Mazar—concluded otherwise.[54] Shiloh insisted that the stone-stepped structure found by Kenyon in the City of David represented monumental architecture and was constructed in the early Iron Age or earlier.[55] In fact "virtually every archaeologist to have excavated in the City of David claims to have found architecture and artifacts dating to these periods."[56] Eilat Mazar, in her current excavations in Jerusalem, has also claimed to have found a monumental building that may have been the palace of David.[57] The data supporting these claims are still being processed and await final publication,[58] yet these claims are already summarily being dismissed by adherents of the Low Chronology as suspect, if not altogether false.[59]

Third, the reason that some data elude the modern investigator is that there is massive destruction of archaeological remains and structures over

---

[53]Timothy P. Harrison, *Megiddo 3: Final Report on the Stratum VI Excavations* (Chicago: Oriental Institute Publications, 2004).

[54]Kathleen Kenyon, *Jerusalem: Excavation 3000 Years of History* (New York: McGraw-Hill, 1967), 31–62; Kenyon, *Digging Up Jerusalem* (London: Ernest Benn, 1974), 98–106; Yigal Shiloh, "The City of David, 1978–1983," in *Biblical Archaeology Today: Proceedings of the International Congress on Biblical Archaeology, Jerusalem April 1984*, ed. Avraham Biran et al. (Jerusalem: Israel Exploration Society, 1985), 453–54.

[55]Cahill, "Jerusalem at the Time of the United Monarchy," 76.

[56]Ibid.; Jane Cahill and David Tarler, "Response to Margreet Steiner—The Jebusite Ramp from Jerusalem: The Evidence from the Macalister, Kenyon, and Shiloh Excavations," in *Biblical Archaeology Today 1990: Proceedings of the Second International Congress on Biblical Archaeology*, ed. Avraham Biran and Joseph Aviram (Jerusalem: Israel Exploration Society, 1993), 625–26; Cahill, "David's Jerusalem: Fiction or Reality, It Is There, The Archaeological Evidence Proves It," *BAR* 24, no. 4 (1998): 34–41; Cahill, "Jerusalem in David and Solomon's Time: There Really Was a Major City in the Tenth Century BCE," *BAR* 30, no. 6 (2004): 20–31, 62–63.

[57]Eilat Mazar, "Did I Find King David's Palace?" *BAR* 32, no. 1 (2006): 16–27, 70; E. Mazar, "The Undiscovered Palace of King David in Jerusalem: A Study in Biblical Archaeology" (Hebrew), in *New Studies in Jerusalem: Proceedings of the Second Conference*, ed. A. Faust (Ramat Gan: Bar-Ilan University, 1996), 9–20.

[58]The major excavators of Jerusalem—Kenyon, Benjamin Mazar, and Nahman Avigad—excavated in Jerusalem toward the ends of their careers and did not live to publish their final reports. Shiloh excavated earlier in his life, but likewise died before final publications were completed. On the issue of posthumous publications, see Jane M. Cahill, "Who Is Responsible for Publishing the Work of a Deceased Archaeologist?," in *Archaeology's Publication Problem*, ed. H. Shanks (Washington, DC: Biblical Archaeology Society, 1999), 2:47–57; and Margreet Steiner, *Excavations by Kathleen M. Kenyon in Jerusalem 1961–1967*, vol. 3, *The Settlement in the Bronze and Iron Ages*, Copenhagen International Series 9 (London: Sheffield Academic, 2001), xv.

[59]Steiner, "The Jebusite Ramp of Jerusalem: The Evidence from the Macalister, Kenyon, and Shiloh Excavations," in Biran and Aviram, *Biblical Archaeology Today 1990*, 585–88.

the centuries. We find what survives and what the ancients did not need and left behind. What evidence of literacy should one expect when parchment and papyrus do not survive in the climate of the central hill country? Millard points out that "of about 120 kings known from a dozen Iron Age states of the Levant, including Israel and Judah, at the most only 20 have left inscriptions that are known today."[60] In some cases materials were carried away by invading armies, destroyed, or reused; there are several ways that cultural and natural formation processes affect material remains.[61] Erosion is also a major factor on hill-country sites.[62] Then the question might also be asked, Would one really expect monumental inscriptions when Egypt was in decline at this time, and Assyria had not even risen to domination in the east?[63]

Fourth, the ancients left us with texts dealing with what *they* were interested in. What external records are we to expect of major campaigns, especially when they experienced defeats? These kinds of admissions are exceedingly rare and in most cases not existent at all among ancient sources.[64] In terms of the archaeological record itself, what kind of evidence for ancient military activity, be they David's or another king's, would exist today? How often do we actually find textual records that can pinpoint the cause of a given archaeological destruction or discontinuity conclusively? What the adherents of the Low Chronology paradigm do is take one destruction, such as that traditionally attributed to Shishak/Sheshonq I, and simply redate it to Hazael,

---

[60]Millard, "David and Solomon's Jerusalem," 198.

[61]See Michael B. Schiffer, *Formation Processes of the Archaeological Record* (Tucson: University of Arizona, 1987).

[62]Cahill, "Jerusalem at the Time of the United Monarchy," 77.

[63]This argument has been made by A. Mazar, "Search for David and Solomon," 134–35; Mazar, "Remarks on Biblical Traditions and Archaeological Evidence Concerning Early Israel," in Dever and Gitin, *Symbiosis, Symbolism, and the Power of the Past*, 90. One major inscription that we do have at Megiddo is the fragment of a stela left by Shishak, king of Egypt, commemorating his campaign, which is also recorded in detail at Karnak. Shishak's Karnak inscription mentions entities in the north and seventy entities in the Negev of Israel. As Mazar has pointed out, "The only plausible explanation for this, must be the existence of a political power in the central hill country that was significant enough in the eyes of the Egyptians to justify such an exceptional route for a campaign" (Mazar, "Search for David and Solomon," 124; Mazar, "Biblical Traditions," 92–93). On the campaign of Shishak/Sheshonq I, see Kenneth A. Kitchen, *The Third Intermediate Period in Egypt (1100–650 BC)*, 2nd ed. (Warminster, UK: Aris & Phillips, 1996); Kitchen, "The Sheshonqs of Egypt and Palestine," *JSOT* 93 (2001): 3–12; Kitchen, "Egyptian Interventions in the Levant in Iron Age II," in Dever and Gitin, *Symbiosis, Symbolism, and the Power of the Past*, 121–27.

[64]Kenneth A. Kitchen, *On the Reliability of the Old Testament* (Grand Rapids: Eerdmans, 2003), 246. The assertion by Kenton L. Sparks that modern scholars do not demand such evidence is altogether false (*God's Word in Human Words* [Grand Rapids: Baker Academic, 2008], 156–57). It is precisely because the external evidence is lacking for an event that it is summarily dismissed. Sparks himself states, "The silence from the Egyptian evidence is therefore an important argument against the historicity of these miracle reports" (p. 157). If anything, the Old Testament account, which includes the defeats as well as the victories of ancient Israel, presents a more balanced history than the nuanced propaganda found in the ancient Near East.

in this way shifting the entire sequence. But by what internal (textual) and external (archaeological) criteria are these decisions made? Are destructions systematically analyzed (in order to ascertain what the specific correlates of destruction are in the archaeological record) to justify this reassignment?[65] Or is the shift simply based on the *a priori* assumption that the architecture could not date to Solomon?

Finally, reports and interpretations of specific sites and their contribution to understanding the history of the region remain tentative and may change with the next season of excavation. The triumphant tone of Philip R. Davies and others[66] who declared that David and his kingdom were mythical in 1992, based on the absence of evidence for his name in the archaeological record, must now be modified by the discovery in 1993–1994 at the site of Tel Dan of an inscription mentioning the "house of David."[67] For these reasons, conclusions based on both the presence and lack of evidence must be tentative and provisional, avoiding sweeping generalizations.

## New Excavations at Khirbet Qeiyafa

In the wake of the debate over David and the early history of Judah, the excavations at Khirbet Qeiyafa, a 2.3 hectare site in the Shephelah located on a ridge overlooking the Elah Valley, have provided surprising results.[68] Although known for over a century,[69] this site was largely overlooked until 2007, when a

---

[65] On the archaeological correlates of destruction in warfare, see Michael G. Hasel, *Domination and Resistance: Egyptian Military Activity in the Southern Levant, 1300–1185 BC*, Probleme der Ägyptologie 11 (Leiden: Brill, 1998), 9–11, 240–56; Hasel, *Military Practice and Polemic: Israel's Laws of Warfare in Near Eastern Perspective* (Berrien Springs, MI: Andrews University Press, 2005); Hasel, "Assyrian Military Practices and Deuteronomy's Laws of Warfare," in *Writing and Reading War: Rhetoric, Gender, and Ethics in Biblical and Modern Contexts*, ed. Brad Kelle and Frank Ames, SBLSymS 42 (Atlanta: Society of Biblical Literature, 2008), 67–81; Hasel, "War, Methods, Tactics, Weapons of (Bronze Age through Persian Period)," in *The New Interpreter's Dictionary of the Bible*, ed. Katherine Doob Sakenfeld (Nashville: Abingdon, 2009), 5:805–10.

[66] Davies declared that "the biblical 'empire' of David and Solomon has not the faintest echo in the archaeological record—as yet" (*In Search of "Ancient Israel,"* 69).

[67] Avraham Biran and Joseph Naveh, "An Aramaic Stele Fragment from Tel Dan," *IEJ* 43 (1993): 81–98; Biran and Naveh, "The Tel Dan Inscription: A New Fragment," *IEJ* 45 (1995): 1–18; for an overview of the interpretations of the Dan inscription, see H. Hagelia, *The Tel Dan Inscription: A Critical Investigation of Recent Research on Its Palaeography and Philology*, Acta Universitates Upsaliensis, Studia Semitica Upsaliensia 22 (Uppsala: Uppsala Universitet, 2006).

[68] The material on Khirbet Qeiyafa has been adopted and updated from Yosef Garfinkel, Saar Ganor, and Michael Hasel, "The Contribution of Khirbet Qeiyafa to Our Understanding of the Iron Age Period," *Strata: Bulletin of the Anglo-Israel Archaeological Society* 28 (2010): 39–54; on the 2009 season, see also Garfinkel et al., "Khirbet Qeiyafa 2009 (Notes and News)," *IEJ* 59 (2009): 214–20.

[69] It was noted in the nineteenth century by Guerin, Condor, and Kitchener, then mostly ignored during the twentieth century until surveyed by Yehuda Dagan. See the discussion in Yosef Garfinkel and Saar Ganor, "Site Location and Setting, and History of Research," in Garfinkel and Ganor, *Khirbet Qeiyafa*, 1:28–32.

short, two-week excavation by the Hebrew University of Jerusalem revealed a massive gate from the early Iron Age.[70] Today, after four seasons of excavation (2007–2010), Khirbet Qeiyafa has come into the center of the debate, providing new data that impinges on our understanding of the early history of Judah in the tenth century BC. About 10 percent of the site has been excavated in five different excavation areas (A–E). Areas B–E are located on the site periphery, adjacent to the massive fortifications. The fortification system includes a casemate city wall with casemates 4 meters wide. The base of the Iron Age city wall is composed of cyclopean stones, some weighing 4–8 tons, while its upper part is built with medium-sized stones. Two identical four-chambered city gates had been uncovered, one in Area B and the other in Area C. Adjacent to the city wall, simple dwellings were constructed, and each building used one casemate as a room. In each of the five excavation areas, complete pottery vessels were found on floors. Intensive activity took place at the site, as indicated by the large quantities of pottery uncovered in each building and unique finds like an ostracon, metal blades, basins, and other household items. The site functioned as a rich urban center. One would expect mention of a town of such importance in the biblical records; indeed, I suggest its identification with Sha'arayim, mentioned twice in the biblical account in association with the late eleventh century BC (1 Sam. 17:52; 1 Chron. 4:31–32).[71] The Iron IIA city came to a sudden end. Its location on the border between Judah and the Philistine kingdom of Gath suggests that it might have been destroyed or abandoned during one of the many military clashes that took place in this area. How does this site contribute to our understanding of the tenth century and the identification and emergence of Judah? Here I mention ten areas.

### Surveys and Reconstructing Settlement Patterns

Khirbet Qeiyafa was surveyed by Yehuda Dagan, who identified, on the basis of pottery collected on the site surface, occupation phases from the Iron I and Iron IIB, but no settlement at all from the Iron IIA.[72] However, the excava-

[70]The Khirbet Qeiyafa Archaeological Project is directed by Yosef Garfinkel and Saar Ganor on behalf of the Hebrew University of Jerusalem. Michael G. Hasel is associate director, with Southern Adventist University as a senior partner. Other participating institutions include Oakland University and Virginia Commonwealth University and volunteers from twenty countries. Sponsors are the Institute of Archaeology, Hebrew University; Institute of Archaeology, Southern Adventist University; National Geographic Society; Foundation Stone; J. B. Silver; Burton and Dorothy Keppler Endowment; ASI International; Donn and Esther Latour; and Doug and Christy Zinke.

[71]For a discussion of these contexts, see Garfinkel and Ganor, "Khirbet Qeiyafa: Sha'arayim," *JHS* 8 (2008): art. 22; David L. Adams, "Between Socoh and Azekah: The Role of the Elah Valley in Biblical History and the Identification of Khirbet Qeiyafa," in Garfinkel and Ganor, *Khirbet Qeiyafa*, 1:47–66.

[72]Yehuda Dagan, "Khirbet Qeiyafa in the Judean Shephelah: Some Considerations," *TA* 36 (2009): 68–81.

tions revealed an opposite picture: no finds at all from the Iron I or Iron IIB, but a massive fortified city from the Iron IIA period.[73] Excavation at Khirbet Qeiyafa indicates that the surveys completely overlooked the large fortified Iron IIA city at the site and that Iron Age pottery collected from the site surface should not be dated by centuries, but only to larger chronological units, such as Late Bronze or Iron Age. A further subdivision is wrong and misleading.

In the extensive surveys conducted in the Judean Shephelah (from Beth Shemesh to Lachish), hardly any sites from the early Iron IIA were noticed.[74] The same picture was reported in various other surveys conducted in the hill country and has thus created a false impression of Judah as an empty land during the tenth and ninth centuries BC and as becoming a full-blown state only in the late eighth century BC.[75] Excavations at Khirbet Qeiyafa demonstrate that the surveys in Judah failed to recognize the early Iron IIA period. The reconstructed settlement patterns predicated on surveys have no solid base.[76] How many more sites have been missed in the heartland of Judah by surveys?

### Fortifications and the Social Organization in the Tenth Century

One main issue in the debate concerning the early Iron Age IIA is whether it was a centralized urban society or an unfortified rural tribal community. Traditional scholarship ascribes the building of fortified cities like Hazor, Megiddo, and Gezer to the time of King Solomon.[77] In the same way, the fortifications of various other sites have been related to the tenth century BC.[78] As stated above, advocates of the Low Chronology, however, date the same building activities to the Omride Dynasty. In this vein Herzog and Singer-Avitz have suggested that the Iron Age IIA should be subdivided into two phases in the south. They place several settlements, namely, Arad XII, Beersheba VII, Lachish V, Tel Batash IV, and Tel Masos II, in the early Iron Age IIA.[79] These are not fortified cities but, rather, enclosures with houses arranged along the

---

[73]Garfinkel and Ganor, *Khirbet Qeiyafa*, vol. 1.

[74]Yehuda Dagan, "Bet Shemesh and Nes Harim Maps, Survey," *Excavations and Surveys in Israel* 13 (1993): 94–95; Dagan, "The Settlement in the Judean Shephela in the Second and First Millennium B.C." (PhD diss., Tel Aviv University, 2000, Hebrew).

[75]"The Judahite hill country was also relatively empty, inhabited by a small number of people who lived in a limited number of villages" (Finkelstein, "The Rise of Jerusalem and Judah: The Missing Link," *Levant* 33 [2001]: 105–15).

[76]See ibid. and Gunner Lehmann, "The United Monarchy in the Countryside: Jerusalem, Judah and the Shephelah during the 10th Century B.C.E.," in Vaughn and Killebrew, *Jerusalem in Bible and Archaeology*, 117–64.

[77]See n. 26 above.

[78]Amihai Mazar, *Archaeology of the Land of the Bible, 10,000 to 586 B.C.E.* (New York: Doubleday, 1990), 380–90.

[79]Z. Herzog and L. Singer-Avitz, "Redefining the Centre: The Emergence of State in Judah," *TA* 31 (2004): 209–44.

periphery of the site. They argue that the first fortified cities were constructed only in the late Iron Age IIA, approximately in the mid-ninth century BC, citing Arad XI, Beersheba VI, and Lachish IV in this context. The pottery assemblage of Khirbet Qeiyafa is similar to the earlier group of sites, however, and it is associated with a fortified city.[80] Khirbet Qeiyafa, with its massive fortification system built with an estimated two hundred thousand tons of stone and with its ceramic assemblage dating to the early Iron IIA, demonstrates that the social organization of early Iron IIA Judah was already that of an urban, centralized society. If this is the case for Khirbet Qeiyafa, then there are also implications for seeing fortified cities later in the tenth century.

## City Planning in the Iron Age

The planning of Khirbet Qeiyafa includes the casemate city wall and a belt of houses abutting the casemates, incorporating them as part of the construction. This is a typical feature of urban planning in Judean cities of the ninth and eighth centuries BC and is known in the cities of Beersheba, Tell Beit Mirsim, Tell en-Nasbeh, and Tel Beth-Shemesh.[81] Khirbet Qeiyafa is the earliest known example of this city plan and indicates that this pattern had already been developed in the very early Iron IIA period.

## The Pottery Repertoire of the Early Iron IIA

Because Khirbet Qeiyafa was abandoned suddenly, large quantities of restorable Iron Age IIA pottery vessels are found on the floors of each excavated room.[82] This rich assemblage is in contrast to the other published assemblages of this period, which usually include a small number of sherds, but not complete vessels, as can be seen in Arad Stratum XII, Beersheba Stratum VII, and Tel Batash Stratum IV. The Khirbet Qeiyafa painted pottery known as "Ashdod Ware" enables us to subdivide this pottery tradition into two groups, earlier (Ashdod I) and later (Ashdod II).[83] This reveals that a one-period site can contribute much more than tell sites to our understanding of a specific short period of time. At the end of the project, when hundreds of restorable vessels will be available, Khirbet Qeiyafa will become a type site for early tenth-century-BC pottery.

---

[80]Hoo-Goo Kang and Y. Garfinkel, "The Early Iron Age IIA Pottery," in Garfinkel and Ganor, *Khirbet Qeiyafa*, 1:119–49.

[81]Yigael Shiloh, "The Four-Room House: Its Situation and Function in the Israelite City," *IEJ* 20 (1970): 180–90; Shiloh, "Elements in the Development of Town Planning in the Israelite City," *IEJ* 28 (1978): 36–51; Ze'ev Herzog, *Archaeology of the City: Urban Planning in Ancient Israel and Its Social Implications* (Tel Aviv: Emery and Claire Yass Archaeology Press, 1997).

[82]Kang and Garfinkel, "Early Iron Age IIA Pottery," 119–49.

[83]Hoo-Goo Kang and Y. Garfinkel, "Ashdod Ware I: Middle Philistine Decorated Ware," in Garfinkel and Ganor, *Khirbet Qeiyafa*, 1:151–60.

## New Radiocarbon Dates for Judah

Adherents of the Low Chronology have claimed strong support from radio-carbon data gathered at several sites in the north.[84] Piasetzky and Finkelstein state: "Absolute dating based on [14]C measurements makes it possible to obtain a conclusive answer to the debate concerning the date of the Iron Age strata in the Levant. The data published so far unambiguously support the Low Chronology and disagree with the High Chronology."[85] Although other dating sequences from Tel Beth Shean and Tel Rehov have been garnered to counter the Low Chronology (and are now seen to support a Modified Conventional Chronology),[86] all the samples in the debate have so far come from the north[87] or from Tel Dor on the coast[88] and not from Judah. Khirbet Qeiyafa, built directly on bedrock, can now provide new dates for comparison. Nowhere in the buildings of this city have we uncovered superimposed floors, walls, or installations, which indicates a rather short existence for Stratum IV. So far six radiocarbon samples have been sent for analysis to Oxford University. All the measurements have been made on short-lived olive pits. The six samples from the same stratum yield a calibrated average of 1021–975 BC (59.2 percent probability) or 1050–971 BC (78.1 percent probability).

Two recently published articles have suggested that Khirbet Qeiyafa belongs in the very late Iron Age I.[89] The combination of both articles leads to the conclusion that the Iron Age I, including occupation at Khirbet Qeiyafa, should end at the third quarter of the tenth century BC. Singer-Avitz writes:

[84]Eli Piasetzky and Israel Finkelstein, "14C Results from Megiddo, Tel Dor, Tel Rohov and Tel Hadar: Where Do They Lead Us?," in Levy and Higham, Bible and Radiocarbon Dating, 294–301; Finkelstein, "High or Low: Megiddo and Tel Rehov," in Levy and Higham, Bible and Radiocarbon Dating, 302–9; Finkelstein and Piasetzky, "Recent Radiocarbon Results and King Solomon," Antiquity 298 (2003): 771–79; Finkelstein and Piasetzky, "Comments on '14C Dates from Tel Rehov: Iron Age Chronology,'" Science 302 (2003): 658b; Finkelstein and Piasetzky, "Wrong and Right, High and Low: 14C Dates from Tel Rehov and Iron Age Chronology," TA 30 (2003): 283–95.

[85]Piasetzky and Finkelstein, "14C Results from Megiddo, Tel Dor, Tel Rohov and Tel Hadar," 300.

[86]A. Mazar and I. Carmi, "Radiocarbon Dates from Iron Age Strata at Tel Beth Shean and Tel Rehov," Radiocarbon 43 (2001): 1333–42; Mazar, "The Debate Over the Chronology of the Iron Age in the Southern Levant," in Levy and Higham, Bible and Radiocarbon Dating, 15–30; Mazar et al., "Ladder of Time at Tel Rehov: Stratigraphy, Archaeological Context, Pottery, and Radiocarbon Dates," in Levy and Higham, Bible and Radiocarbon Dating, 193–255; J. van der Plicht and H. J. Bruins, "Quality Control of Groningen 14C Results from Tel Rehov," in Levy and Higham, Bible and Radiocarbon Dating, 256–70; Bruins, Plicht et al., "The Groningen Radiocarbon Series from Tel Rehov," in Levy and Higham, Bible and Radiocarbon Dating, 271–93.

[87]For Tel Dan, see H. J. Bruins et al., "Iron Age 14C Dates from Tel Dan: A High Chronology," in Levy and Higham, Bible and Radiocarbon Dating, 323–36.

[88]Ayelet Gilboa and Ilan Sharon, "Early Iron Age Radiometric Dates from Tel Dor: Preliminary Implications for Phoenicia and Beyond," Radiocarbon 43 (2001): 1342–52.

[89]L. Singer-Avitz, "The Relative Chronology of Khirbet Qeiyafa," TA 37 (2010): 79–83; Israel Finkelstein and E. Piasetzky, "Khirbet Qeiyafa: Absolute Chronology," TA 37 (2010): 84–88.

Considerable continuity in pottery types makes it difficult to distinguish between the late Iron Age I and the early Iron Age IIA assemblages. Indeed, as is clear from Kang and Garfinkel's comparisons, most vessels of the Khirbet Qeiyafa assemblage are known in both ceramic phases. Dating such an assemblage can therefore be done only according to forms that appeared *exclusively* in one of these ceramic phases.[90]

However, Singer-Avitz does not follow her own criteria on three points: (1) irregular hand burnish on red slip; (2) deep, large, carinated kraters with an everted rim; and (3) an elongated storage jar with a rounded shoulder and a small flat base. These are unique and occur only in Iron IIA.[91]

Finkelstein and Piasetzky accept the radiometric datings of Khirbet Qeiyafa, but do not average them. They argue for a long settlement sequence at the site, a lifespan of ca. 135 years, from ca. 1050 to 915 BC. Their interpretation is not derived from the archaeological data, which indicates a very short occupation, but is aimed at supporting the Low Chronology paradigm. In any case, it is not clear what Finkelstein and Piasetzky would like to achieve by their new interpretation. The main debate regarding the Low Chronology focuses on when the transition to urbanism and state formation took place in Judah and Israel. Had Khirbet Qeiyafa not been abandoned, it would have been a city in the ninth and eighth centuries BC as well. The end of Khirbet Qeiyafa has no bearing on the date of its construction toward the end of the eleventh century BC or early tenth century BC.

## Preparation and Consumption of Food

Khirbet Qeiyafa is different from the nearby Philistine centers of Tel Miqne-Ekron and Tell es-Safi-Gath in two main aspects. First, after 10 percent of the site has been excavated, pig bones continue to be entirely absent at Khirbet Qeiyafa, while they were largely consumed by the Philistine population.[92] At Tel Miqne-Ekron pig bones increase from 14 percent of all faunal remains in Stratum VII, to 17 percent in Stratum VI, and 26 percent in Stratum V,

---

[90]Singer-Avitz, "Relative Chronology," 79.

[91]Y. Garfinkel and Hoo-Goo Kang, "The Relative and Absolute Chronology of Khirbet Qeiyafa: Very Late Iron Age I or Very Early Iron Age IIA?" *IEJ* forthcoming.

[92]Ron Kehati, "The Faunal Assemblage," in Garfinkel and Ganor, *Khirbet Qeiyafa*, 1:201–98; on pig bones at Tel Mqne (Ekron) and Tell es-Safi (Gath), see Justin Lev-Tov, "Pigs, Philistines, and Ancient Animal Economy of Ekron from the Late Bronze Age to the Iron II" (PhD diss., University of Tennessee, Knoxville, 2000); Lev-Tov, "A Preliminary Report on the Late Iron Age Faunal Assemblages from Tell es-Safi/Gath," in *Excavations at Tell es-Safi/Gath*, vol. 1, ed. Aren M. Maeir, Ägypten und Altes Testament (Wiesbaden: Harrassowitz, forthcoming); Brian Hesse and Paula Wapnish, "Can Pig Remains Be Used for Ethnic Diagnosis in the Ancient Near East?," in *Archaeology of Israel: Constructing the Past, Interpreting the Present*, ed. N. A. Silberman and D. B. Small (Sheffield: Sheffield Academic, 1997), 238–70.

indicating that "pork is an important component of the Philistine diet."[93] At Beth Shemesh, another Judean site to the north of Khirbet Qeiyafa, only 0.20 percent of the bones are pig, indicating a differentiation between these sites and neighboring Philistine cities.[94] Second, pottery-baking trays, which were found at Khirbet Qeiyafa, are unknown at Tel Miqne and Tell es-Safi.[95] Archaeological data at Khirbet Qeiyafa demonstrates that two different populations coexisted in the Iron Age Shephelah, and that the Qeiyafa population is clearly not Philistine.

## Household Archaeology

A total of twelve well-preserved dwellings were excavated in Areas B and C. For most of the houses, the entire architecture was preserved, providing a well-defined ground plan for each building. On the floors of each room, various installations, large quantities of pottery, and stone tools were found. The excellent state of preservation gives a vivid picture of how the households were organized. The expedition aims to uncover twenty complete houses along the city wall. Our model for a large horizontal exposure follows the excavations of Ruth Amiran at Early Bronze Age Arad and Yohanan Aharoni in Iron Age IIB Beersheba.[96] The Khirbet Qeiyafa excavations will create a database for household archaeology of an early tenth-century-BC settlement for the first time in the archaeology of the Iron Age.

## Writing in the Tenth Century

The most prominent find from Khirbet Qeiyafa is an ostracon, a text written with ink on a broken pottery sherd.[97] While most texts from this time period

---

[93]Gitin, "Philistines in the Books of Kings," 337; Justin Lev-Tov, "The Faunal Remains: Animal Economy in the Iron Age I," in *Tel Miqne-Ekron Excavations, 1995–1996, Field INE East Slope: Late Bronze Age II–Iron I (Early Philistine Period)*, Tel Miqne-Ekron Final Report Series 8 (Jerusalem: Albright Institute and Hebrew University of Jerusalem, 2006), 211–13.

[94]On the percentage of pig bones at nearby Beth Shemesh, see Shlomo Bunimovitz and Zvi Lederman, "The Archaeology of Border Communities: Renewed Excavations at Tell Beth-Shemesh, Part 1: The Iron Age," *Near Eastern Archaeology* 72 (2009): 123–24.

[95]Kang and Garfinkel, "Early Iron Age IIA Pottery," 127, 131 (fig. 6.13).

[96]Yohanan Aharoni, "The Israelite City," in *Beer-Sheba I*, ed. Y. Aharoni (Tel Aviv: University of Tel Aviv, 1973), 13–18; Ruth Amiran and Ornit Ilan, "The Urban Character and Town Planning of the EB II City: Features and Concepts," in *Early Arad*, vol. 2 (Jerusalem: Israel Museum/Israel Exploration Society, 1996), 140–47.

[97]Official publications include, Haggai Misgav, Yosef Garfinkel, and Saar Ganor, "The Khirbet Qeiyafa Ostracon," in *New Studies in the Archaeology of Jerusalem and Its Region*, ed. D. Amit, G. D. Stiebel, and O. Peleg-Barkat (Jerusalem: Israel Antiquities Authority and the Institute of Archaeology, the Hebrew University of Jerusalem, 2009), 111–23 (Hebrew); Misgav, Garfinkel, and Ganor, "The Ostracon," in Garfinkel and Ganor, *Khirbet Qeiyafa*, 1:243–57; Ada Yardeni, "The Khirbet Qeiyafa Inscription—Response A," in Amit, Stiebel, and Peleg-Barkat, *New Studies in the Archaeology of Jerusalem*, 124–25; Misgav, Garfinkel, and Ganor, "Further Observations on the Ostracon," in Garfinkel

are rather short, the Khirbet Qeiyafa ostracon is a five-line inscription with nearly seventy letters. Many of the inscriptions from this period lack provenance or stratigraphic context,[98] yet the Khirbet Qeiyafa ostracon was found directly on the floor of a house and is securely dated to the early tenth century BC. For these reasons it is of tremendous importance for understanding the development of *both* script and language in the Iron Age.

The script of the ostracon is in the Canaanite tradition (so-called "Proto-Canaanite"). According to the studies of Frank Moore Cross, this script came out of use during the middle of the eleventh century BC, but the Khirbet Qeiyafa ostracon demonstrates that this script was used until the beginning of the tenth century BC. A comparison study of the script on other inscriptions, like the ʿIzbet Sartah ostracon and metal arrowheads, which were traditionally dated to the twelfth–eleventh centuries BC, now enables us to date these items to the late eleventh–early tenth centuries BC. The language of the ostracon is now under dispute. If we accept the reading *'l t's* (אל תעש = "do not do") in the beginning of the first line, then the language is Hebrew. Other possible languages could be Canaanite, Phoenician, Philistine, or an unknown Semitic dialect. According to the expedition interpretation of the site, its location, architecture, and diet, it was part of the kingdom of Judah. Thus, the language is more likely very early Hebrew.

The publication of the ostracon allows scholars from around the world to reexamine it and to improve its reading and meaning. Articles have already been published by Emile Peuch and Gershon Galil,[99] and others have announced that they are currently preparing new publications (Christopher Rollston and André Lemaire). Undoubtedly, the importance of this ostracon will generate dozens of articles in years to come. We can only hope that these studies will contribute to a better understanding of this rather enigmatic text.

As Gary A. Rendsburg has observed, "Taken together, the Tel Zayit abecedary, the Khirbet Qeiyafa inscription and the Gezer calendar demonstrate that writing was well-established in tenth-century Israel—certainly sufficiently so for many of the works later incorporated into the Hebrew Bible to have been

---

and Ganor, *Khirbet Qeiyafa*, 1:259–60; Shmuel Ahituv, "The Khirbet Qeiyafa Inscription—Response C," in Amit, Stiebel, and Peleg-Barkat, *New Studies in the Archaeology of Jerusalem*, 130–32; Aaron Demsky, "The Enigmatic Inscription from Khirbet Qeiyafa—Response B," in Amit, Stiebel, and Peleg-Barkat, *New Studies in the Archaeology of Jerusalem*, 126–29; Greg Bearman and William A. Christens-Barry, "Imaging the Ostracon," in Garfinkel and Ganor, *Khirbet Qeiyafa*, 1:261–69.

[98] For the most recent discussion, see Christopher A. Rollston, *Writing and Literacy in the World of Ancient Israel: Epigraphic Evidence from the Iron Age*, SBLABS 11 (Atlanta: Society of Biblical Literature, 2010).

[99] Emile Peuch, "L'Ostracon de Khirbet Qeyafa et les débuts de la royauté en Israël," *RB* 117 (2010): 162–84; Gershon Galil, "The Hebrew Inscription from Khirbet Qeiyafa/Netaʿim, Script, Language, Literature and History," *UF* 41 (2009): 193–242.

composed at this time."[100] The existence of writing at such an early stage of the Iron Age is significant because it implies that historical data could have been documented and passed on from the early tenth century BC until the biblical narrative was finally formulated. It also indicates that the paucity of evidence for writing is less secure than previously thought.

## Historical Geography: Is Khirbet Qeiyafa Biblical Sha'arayim?

Another aspect relating to Khirbet Qeiyafa is its ancient name. Do we have enough solid data for the complicated task of site identification? Various suggestions had been proposed both in scientific and in popular publications.[101] The current expedition accepted the name Sha'arayim, which appears three times in the biblical tradition. Of these, in two cases it is mentioned in the context of the Elah Valley and in two cases in association with King David. In addition, Khirbet Qeiyafa has two city gates, and the term Sha'arayim means "two gates" in Hebrew.[102]

## The Early Kingdom of Judah

According to the biblical narrative, King David first ruled from Hebron for seven years. Later he conquered Jerusalem and moved there to establish a new capital. The archaeological picture of Jerusalem in the tenth century BC is obscure for the reasons outlined above, and fundamentally different suggestions and interpretations have been raised. Hebron is also a difficult site to excavate, and the few expeditions that worked there did not find any meaningful remains from the early tenth century BC. So far there is no clear published archaeological data regarding the period of King David in the two major cities of his kingdom. The absence of evidence has raised serious questions concerning the nature of the political structure in the tenth century BC. The mainstream view points to a single, powerful, centralized authority in Jerusalem that controlled the entire country,[103] while Finkelstein and others suggest various local, autonomous forms of organization.

---

[100]Gary A. Rendsburg, "Review of Ron E. Tappy and P. Kyle McCarter (eds.), *Literate Culture and Tenth-Century Canaan,*" BASOR 359 (2010): 89.

[101]See the overview and critique of other suggested identifications in Adams, "Between Socoh and Azekah," 47–66.

[102]See the discussion of the term *Sha'araim* by ibid. and in Garfinkel and Ganor, "Khirbet Qeiyafa: Sha'arayim."

[103]For the mainstream view, see in addition to sources listed above, Benjamin Mazar, "The Philistines and the Rise of Israel and Tyre," in *The Early Biblical Period: Historical Studies,* ed. Benjamin Mazar (Jerusalem: Israel Exploration Society), 63–82; A. Mazar, *Archaeology of the Land of the Bible,* 368–402; Daniel M. Master, "State Formation Theory and the Kingdom of Israel," *JNES* 60 (2001): 117–31; Master, "Reconstructing the Tenth Century in Israel," in *100 Years of American Archaeology in the Middle East: Proceedings of the American Schools of Oriental Research Centennial Celebration, Washington DC, April 2000,* ed. Douglas R. Clark and Victor H. Matthews (Boston: American

The Khirbet Qeiyafa excavations have completely altered this situation. Now we have a fortified city in Judah located within a one-day walk from Jerusalem and a one-day walk from Hebron. The distance between these three cities corresponds well to the expected distance between central cities in a kingdom. Khirbet Qeiyafa might have functioned as the third-most important city in the early kingdom of Judah. Its strategic importance is due not only to its relative distance from Jerusalem and Hebron, but also to its location on the border between Judah and Philistia, opposite Tell es-Safi (Gath), a very large Philistine city during this specific period.[104] Khirbet Qeiyafa, with its position on the main road leading from the coastal plain into the hill country, functioned as a "gate city" to the kingdom; a check-point on the western border of Judah. In a similar way, Khirbet ed-Dawwara probably functioned as a border city on the northeastern border of the kingdom in the same period.[105] While Jerusalem and Hebron remain problematic in light of many of the issues discussed above, Khirbet Qeiyafa provides significant data for the early kingdom of Judah.

---

Schools of Oriental Research, 2003), 215–29; Lawrence E. Stager, "The Patrimonial Kingdom of Solomon," in Dever and Gitin, *Symbiosis, Symbolism, and the Power of the Past*, 63–74.

[104] Aren M. Maier and J. Uziel, "A Tale of Two Tells: A Comparative Perspective on Tel Miqne-Ekron and Tell es-Safi/Gath in Light of Recent Archaeological Research," in *"Up to the Gates of Ekron": Essays on the Archaeology and History of the Eastern Mediterranean in Honor of Seymour Gitin*, ed. Amnon Ben-Tor et al. (Jerusalem: Israel Exploration Society, 2007), 29–42.

[105] Israel Finkelstein, "Excavations at Khirbet ed-Dawwara: An Iron Age Site Northeast of Jerusalem," *TA* 17 (1990): 163–208.

# 22

# THE ARCHAEOLOGY OF DAVID AND SOLOMON

*Method or Madness?*

## STEVEN M. ORTIZ

## Introduction

The biblical account of the life of David has always fascinated a wide spectrum of individuals, from biblical scholars to Hollywood producers, artists, and sculptors. The emphasis on the kingdom of David and Solomon has not escaped biblical archaeologists as we have focused our attention on identifying and associating archaeological discoveries with the united monarchy of Israel. Today, several basic questions face the archaeologist studying the united monarchy. Does the archaeological record reflect the existence of a mighty kingdom like that described in the biblical sources? Does the archaeological record reflect the internal development of the kingdom from Saul until the time of Solomon? Can archaeology shed light on the transition from tribal society to a centralized rule of a monarchy? The reality is that the archaeological evidence for the period of the united monarchy is sparse, is often controversial, and provides ambiguous answers to these questions. So much so, that some critics have pointed out that we do not have anything in the archaeological record that can be associated with David or Solomon. Some have concluded that David and Solomon did not exist. Today, there is a small but influential group (the minimalist camp) who claim that there was no state during the tenth century BC.[1] Their conclusion is that the biblical accounts of the united monarchy are fictitious, merely later literary creations of a glori-

---

[1]Philip Davies, *In Search of "Ancient Israel"* (Sheffield: Sheffield Academic, 1992); Giovanni Garbini, *Myth and History in the Bible* (London: Sheffield Academic, 2003); Niels Lemche, *The Israelites in History and Tradition* (London: SPCK, 1998); Thomas Thompson, *The Mythic Past* (London: Basic

fied past to legitimize the Israelite kingdom that did not come into existence until the eighth century BC.

This understanding was challenged with the discovery of the Tel Dan inscription.[2] Minimalists had to backpedal in regard to the historicity of David and Solomon with the discovery, as they had to admit that David was an actual person.[3] The question today is not, has archaeology proved that David and Solomon existed? It is, rather, was there a Jerusalem-based united monarchy, and what was the nature of this kingdom? Was it a large centralized kingdom from northern Syria to the Gulf of Aqaba, or was it a small tribal village controlled by a chiefdom? The answer depends on how you interpret the data.

The question arises as to whether the biblical texts are accurate in their depiction of the united monarchy. Unfortunately archaeology cannot address specific episodes in the life of David (e.g., the battle with Goliath, sooth- ing Saul with a harp, shepherding flocks in Bethlehem). Given the nature of archaeological data there are not many specific events in time that the archaeological record can specifically address. What it can do is determine whether an account has historical plausibility. Hence, when we come to the archaeology of David and Solomon, the most archaeology can do is deter- mine if there was a kingdom during the tenth century BC—more specifically whether there is evidence of centralized authority.

For evangelical scholars, one of the underlying questions is whether the Bible contains authentic history. With the influence of critical scholarship, some evangelicals have opted for a methodology that allows for human error. While they are correct that the biblical text is written in a specific historical context with human authors, some have fully adopted these trends without any critical evaluation of their assumptions. Although trends in literary stud- ies such as intertextuality, processes of later editing, and the like have greatly enhanced our analysis of the biblical text, the underlying assumption that these reflect a "created fictitious history" instead of a "theological interpre- tation of historical events" has become the dominant model. While critical scholarship has been an important correction for literalistic explanations of

---

Books, 1999). For a more balanced approach, see Walter Dietrich, *The Early Monarchy in Israel: The Tenth Century B.C.E.* (Atlanta: Society of Biblical Literature, 2007).

[2] Avraham Biran and Joseph Naveh, "An Aramaic Stele Fragment from Tel Dan," *IEJ* 43 (1993): 81–98; "The Tel Dan Inscription: A New Fragment," *IEJ* 45 (1995): 1–18.

[3] There was a period after the discovery when we saw a flurry of articles, papers, and discussions introducing a new social construct called Beit Daud. Some had even accused the excavator of plant- ing or being fooled by a forgery. (These positions have not been publicly abandoned, but they are no longer prominently proposed.) For an overview and history of the debate, see George Athas, *The Tel Dan Inscription: A Reappraisal and a New Interpretation* (Sheffield: Sheffield Academic, 2003).

the text, the underlying postulate that the Bible was written several hundred years after the events is untenable. It is clear that the text has a long history even before the process of canonization. Nevertheless, the texts reflect such a high degree of correspondence with the archaeological record that several scholars acknowledge that the crystallization of the traditions (whether oral or written accounts) must have happened close to the actual events. This is especially the case with the early monarchy.[4]

Ironically, even though archaeologists claim to have moved away from the biblical text for archaeological interpretation, recent scholarship on the archaeology of David and Solomon has uncritically adopted minimalist biblical trends. The most prominent is the Low Chronology proposal by Israel Finkelstein.[5] Finkelstein does not go as far as denying the existence of David and Solomon, but he proposes that David was merely a sheik of a small tribal society and that the state did not develop until the ninth century. This chapter will be a brief programmatic overview of the issues of the current debate among archaeologists.

## Albright and Yadin

The Albright model has been the dominant paradigm in biblical archaeology. The archaeology of David and Solomon is a central feature of this foundational paradigm. William F. Albright, considered the father of American biblical archaeology, developed the current ceramic stratigraphy of Syro-Palestine. On the basis of his excavations of Tell Beit Mirsim, he associated the sudden appearance of red-slip burnished pottery with the united monarchy.

Yigael Yadin was the Israeli counterpart to Albright. He excavated Hazor and noted that the gate systems at Megiddo and at Hazor were very similar.[6] Recalling the text of 1 Kings 9:17–19 (Solomon's building projects), he associated the gate systems with a common architect, and hence, a central authority. Yadin went back to Megiddo and Hazor and isolated monumental features that he associated with Solomon, notably Palaces 6000 and 1723 at Megiddo. He also went to the old McAllister excavation reports of Gezer and postulated a third Solomonic gate, erroneously identified as a Hellenistic Tower. William G. Dever, who reexcavated Gezer utilizing the newer methods and techniques of the New Archaeology, found that Yadin's intuitions were

---

[4]For an example of this approach, see, Kenneth Kitchen, *On the Reliability of the Old Testament* (Grand Rapids: Eerdmans, 2003); Iain Provan, V. Philips Long, and Tremper Longman III, *A Biblical History of Israel* (Louisville: Westminster John Knox, 2003).
[5]Israel Finkelstein, "The Date of the Settlement of the Philistines in Canaan," *TA* 22 (1995): 213–39.
[6]Yigael Yadin, "Solomon's City Wall and Gate at Gezer, " *IEJ* 8 (1958): 80–86.

correct.[7] Yadin's association of the six-chambered gates of the Iron Age with the Solomonic building projects became the hallmark of the current archaeo-logical position that associates the tenth-century-BC archaeological finds with the united monarchy. Amnon Ben-Tor's recent reinvestigation of the gate, its ceramics, and its stratigraphy aligns with Yadin's earlier conclusions.[8]

## The Myth of Solomon

In the early '90s, a debate over the stratigraphy of the Iron Age appeared in several articles. The debate was initiated with an article by Wightman, who came out proposing a redating of stratigraphy associated with the tenth cen-tury, particularly the Solomonic levels.[9] Wightman based his stratigraphy on the results of Kenyon's excavations. Kenyon challenged Albright's ceramic chronology, dating the appearance of the red-slip burnished pottery to the ninth century BC, and attempted to lower the Megiddo and Hazor stratig-raphy (1957). One of the issues pertinent to the debate was whether sherds within the fill beneath the floor were contemporary with the surface.[10] The Samaria ceramic corpus was recently critiqued and reevaluated by Ron Tappy.[11] Wightman's proposals were never seriously accepted or supported by the archaeological record. In fact, the debate went in another chronological direc-tion, as archaeologists discussed if red-slip burnished pottery first appeared along the coastal plain in the eleventh century BC (Phoenicia and Philistia).[12]

## Low Chronology

This chronological debate came to fruition with Finkelstein's radical proposal, which he termed the Low Chronology. He first defined the Low Chronology in his 1995 article "The Date of the Settlement of the Philistines in Canaan." In this article, he proposed lowering the currently accepted dates of the initial

---

[7]William G. Dever et al., "Further Excavations at Gezer, 1967–71," *BA* 34 (1971): 94–132.

[8]A. Ben-Tor and D. Ben-Ami, "Hazor and the Archaeology of the Tenth Century, *IEJ* 48 (1998): 1–37; Ben-Tor, "Excavating Hazor: Solomon's City Rises from the Ashes, *BAR* 25, no. 2 (1999): 26–37, 60; and Ben-Tor, "Responding to Finkelstein's Addendum (on the Dating of Hazor X–VII)," *TA* 28 (2001): 301–4.

[9]G. J. Wightman, "The Myth of Solomon," *BASOR* 277/278 (1990): 5–22.

[10]The methodological problems associated with dating a surface based on the fills below instead of the debris above were debated in the 1950s by K. Kenyon and G. E. Wright (Kathleen Kenyon, "Megiddo, Hazor, Samaria and Chronology," *BASOR* 4 [1964]: 143–56; G. Ernest Wright, "Israelite Samaria and Iron Age Chronology," *BASOR* 155 [1959]: 13–29).

[11]Ron E. Tappy, *The Archaeology of Israelite Samaria* (Winona Lake, IN: Eisenbrauns, 1992).

[12]For a full discussion, see A. Mazar, *Archaeology of the Land of the Bible 10,000–586 B.C.E.* (New York: Doubleday, 1990); and J. S. Holladay, "The Kingdoms of Israel and Judah: Political and Eco-nomic Centralization in the Iron IIA–B (ca. 1000–750 BC)," in *The Archaeology of Society in the Holy Land*, ed. T. Levy (New York: Facts on File, 1995), 368–98.

Philistine occupation in southern Canaan from the twelfth to the eleventh century BC.[13] He based this proposal on two assumptions. The first assumption is that the Egyptians ruled over the southern coastal plain and the Shephelah (Ashkelon-Lachish line) in the first half of the twelfth century until the middle of the eleventh century. The second assumption is that sites in close proximity to each other must have similar ceramic assemblages. Finkelstein assumed that if the Philistines occupied sites in the southern coastal plain during Iron Age IA (ca. 1200–1150/30 BC), as evidenced by locally made monochrome pottery (Myc IIIC:1b), this pottery should also be found at nearby sites controlled by Egyptians. Since these sites (e.g., Lachish VI and Tel Sera' X) do not have monochrome pottery, the initial Philistine presence must postdate these levels.

The next stage of Finkelstein's Low Chronology proposal came a year later with the publication of his article "The Archaeology of the United Monarchy: An Alternative View."[14] In this study, Finkelstein contends that the current dating of the rise of the Israelite state to the tenth century BC is wrong. Finkelstein's arguments are based on a correlation between the stratigraphy of Megiddo and Jezreel.

The Low Chronology did not go unchallenged. Several articles addressing these issues were produced by Amihai Mazar,[15] Amnon Ben-Tor,[16] Anabel Zarzeki-Peleg,[17] and Nadav Na'aman.[18] Mazar published an immediate response to Finkelstein's article that proposed redating the united monarchy. Mazar concluded that Finkelstein's suggestion to push the date of the monochrome Philistine pottery beyond the end of the Egyptian presence in Canaan is based on a debatable assumption. Mazar also introduced two additional critical variables into the debate: important northern assemblages that contradict the redating and examples in other periods where we have regional patterning.[19] Zarzeki-Peleg also quickly addressed Finkelstein's use of northern assemblages in an article focusing on the Iron Age stratigraphy

---

[13]Proposals to redate Iron Age stratigraphy were already presented in the literature by David Ussishkin, "Levels VII and VI at Tel Lachish and the End of the Late Bronze Age in Canaan," in *Papers in Honour of Olga Tufnell*, ed. J. N. Tubb (London: University College Institute of Archaeology, 1985), 213–30; and Wightman, "The Myth of Solomon."

[14]*Levant* 28 (1996): 177–87.

[15]A. Mazar, "Iron Age Chronology: A Reply to I. Finkelstein," *Levant* 29 (1997): 157–67.

[16]Ben-Tor, "Hazor and the Chronology of Northern Israel: A Reply to Israel Finkelstein," *BASOR* 317 (2000): 9–16; Ben-Tor, "Responding to Finkelstein's Addendum (on the Dating of Hazor X–VII)," 301–4. For a response, see David Ussishkin, "The Credibility of the Tel Jezreel Excavations: A Rejoinder to Amnon Ben-Tor," *TA* 27 (2000): 248–56.

[17]Anabel Zarzeki-Peleg, "Hazor, Jokneam and Megiddo in the Tenth Century B.C.E.," *TA* 24 (1997): 258–88.

[18]N. Na'aman, "The Contribution of the Trojan Grey Ware from Lachish and Tel Miqne-Ekron to the Chronology of the Philistine Monochrome Pottery," *BASOR* 317 (2000): 1–7.

[19]A. Mazar, "Iron Age Chronology," 157–67.

of northern assemblages (e.g., Megiddo, Jokneam, and Hazor).[20] Finkelstein promptly responded to these criticisms, and the debate has not subsided.[21]

The past decade has seen the publication of a flurry of studies by the Low Chronology supporters, with other scholars offering rejoinders.[22] Unfortunately, outsiders, whether popular reporters or biblical scholars, have concluded that the archaeological record is ambiguous or worse; they assume that the Low Chronology has demonstrated the stance of critical biblical scholars. Today the archaeology of David and Solomon remains polarized between Finkelstein's Low Chronology model and advocates of the standard model. Israel Finkelstein and Amihai Mazar have been the key figures in the debate.[23] The issues in the debate coalesce around four variables: (1) paucity of archaeological data dating to the tenth century, (2) Iron Age ceramics and chronology, (3) state development, centralized authority, and whether there was a capital (e.g., archaeology of Jerusalem), and (4) the relation between archaeology and the biblical text.

### The Paucity of Archaeological Data

One of the basic issues prevalent in the archaeological discussion of the united monarchy is the paucity and ambiguity of the data that can be assigned to the monarchy. It is true that there is a lot more material culture for the Iron Age IIB (ninth–eighth centuries BC) than the Iron Age IIA (tenth century). The methodological question is whether this pattern demonstrates that a centralized state did not develop until the eighth century. This was the position taken by D. Jamieson-Drake in his influential book *Scribes and Schools*

---

[20]Zarzeki-Peleg, "Hazor, Jokneam and Megiddo in the Tenth Century B.C.E.," 258–88.

[21]Israel Finkelstein, "Bible Archaeology or Archaeology of Palestine in the Iron Age? A Rejoinder," *Levant* 30 (1998): 167–74; Finkelstein, "Notes on the Stratigraphy and Chronology of Iron Age Ta'anach," *TA* 25 (1998): 208–18; Finkelstein, "Hazor and the North in the Iron Age: A Low Chronology Perspective," *BASOR* 314 (1999): 55–70; A. Ben-Tor, "Hazor and the Chronology of Northern Israel," 9–16; I. Finkelstein, "Hazor XII–XI with an Addendum on Ben-Tor's Dating of Hazor X–VII," *TA* 27 (2000): 231–47.

[22]For a review of the Low Chronology, see Steven Ortiz, "Deconstructing and Reconstructing the United Monarchy: House of David or Tent of David," in *The Future of Biblical Archaeology: Reassessing Methodologies and Assumptions*, ed. James K. Hoffmeier and Alan R. Millard (Grand Rapids: Eerdmans, 2004), 121–47; and Daniel A. Frese and Thomas E. Levy, "The Four Pillars of the Iron Age Low Chronology," in *Historical Biblical Archaeology and the Future: The New Pragmatism*, ed. T. Levy (London: Equinox, 2010), 187–202.

[23]This is not to say that they are the only two scholars debating the issues, but current publications have tended to have each of them make statements regarding the current positions. Israel Finkelstein and Amihai Mazar, *The Quest for the Historical Israel: Debating Archaeology and the History of Early Israel*, ed. Brian B. Schmidt (Atlanta: Society of Biblical Literature, 2007). See also, Finkelstein, "A Great United Monarchy? Archaeological and Historical Perspectives," in *One God–One Cult–One Nation: Archaeological and Biblical Perspectives*, ed. Reinhard G. Kratz and Hermann Spieckermann (Berlin: de Gruyter, 2010), 3–28; and Amihai Mazar, "Archaeology and the Biblical Narrative: The Case of the United Monarchy," in Kratz and Spieckermann, *One God–One Cult–One Nation*, 29–58.

*in Monarchic Judah* (1991). Jamieson-Drake proposed that the explosion of epigraphic finds from the eighth century represents intense scribal activity of a large bureaucracy, which in turn is evidence of a centralized authority. This pattern could indicate that a state did not exist until the eighth century in the southern Levant. Most archaeologists assume that the complexity of settlement patterns and sites determines the nature of a site or period (e.g., small, simple buildings will indicate a village, while large public buildings and evidence of urbanization will indicate a city). While this is normative for most historical reconstructions based on archaeological data, this could also be a fallacious argument. For example, the centralized authority of the United States was more complex with a more elaborate infrastructure in 1960 than in 1800, but it would be foolish to say that it did not become a state until 1960 because the United States had a larger imprint on material-culture remains.

It is accurate to maintain that evidence for centralization such as settlement patterns, site hierarchy, city planning, and urbanization is more abundant and complex in the eighth century BC than the tenth century. This is especially true for Jerusalem.[24] Nevertheless, there is much data to support a major change in the tenth century, which was influential in the shift in periodization between Iron Age I and Iron Age II. This change in the archaeological record is evident to most archaeologists and has become the standard model for the rise of secondary states in the southern Levant.[25] Archaeology had shown that there was a major shift in the archaeological record from villages and towns to cities at the tenth century BC.[26] While this evidence lacks epigraphic references to David or Solomon, it is reasonable to assume that there was some major king or political shift to account for the change.

Ironically, Finkelstein admits that there is ample evidence for a state; the only difference is the dating of these components (e.g., settlement patterns, city planning, pillared buildings, palaces, city fortifications, etc.). He believes that we have misdated the record, and it should move down to the ninth century.[27]

---

[24]There are no substantial tenth-century-BC remains found in any of the excavations, particularly the City of David excavations by Hebrew University. Since Jerusalem was the capital of the monarchy, it is logical to assume that we should find remains of such an important city.

[25]For a detailed analysis, see Mazar, *Archaeology of the Land of the Bible 10,000–586 B.C.E.*; J. Holladay, "The Kingdoms of Israel and Judah: Political and Economic Centralization in the Iron IIA–B (ca. 1000–750 BC)"; G. Barkay, "The Iron Age II–III," in *The Archaeology of Ancient Israel*, ed. Amnon Ben-Tor (New Haven, CT: Yale University Press, 1992), 302–73; Larry Herr, "The Iron Age II Period: Emerging Nations," *BA* 60, no. 3 (1997): 114–83.

[26]See n. 25 above.

[27]Israel Finkelstein, "A Low Chronology Update: Archaeology, History and Bible," in *The Bible and Radiocarbon Dating: Archaeology, Text and Science*, ed. Thomas Levy and Thomas Higham (London: Equinox, 2005), 31–42.

Those who support the conventional Iron Age chronology and those in support of the Low Chronology are in agreement as to the overall interpretation of the archaeological data. Archaeologists agree that the changes in the archaeological record between Iron Age I and Iron Age II demonstrate state development; we disagree on the dating of this transition. Critical biblical scholars assume that the archaeological record is "ambiguous" because of the disagreement. But they miss the nuances of the debate: the issue is not the interpretation of the data, but the dating.

### Iron Age Ceramics and Chronology

At the heart of the Low Chronology proposal lies ceramic analysis. Finkelstein's proposal is to move the standard Iron Age I corpus to the end of the tenth century instead of the beginning. According to this model, the introduction of tenth-century ceramic changes (e.g., the dominance of red-slip burnished pottery) actually occurred in the ninth century.[28]

This proposal was revolutionary and fully welcomed by critical biblical scholars. On this assumption, all the archaeological evidence of centralized authority (e.g., six-chambered gates, pillared buildings, city walls, etc.) originally dated to the tenth century should be redated to the ninth. Evidence for the state now moves to the ninth century. The Iron Age I villages move down to the tenth century. In light of the supposed new evidence, the tenth century looks like a series of small tribal villages and towns that were originally associated with the Israelite settlement period before the united monarchy. For the first time, critical scholars had the "hard, scientific" evidence that archaeology provides. This shift is needed by historical minimalists in order to remove evidence for a state in the tenth century and thus to conclude that David was a fictitious king. Biblical scholars jumped on Finkelstein's Low Chronology bandwagon even though it has not been widely accepted by the broader archaeological community.

One of the main reasons Finkelstein's Low Chronology is not accepted is that its underlying assumptions are not supported by current research in Iron Age ceramic chronology. In the past several decades the field has seen refinements in ceramic seriation, regionalism, and the discernment of sociological factors that have had an impact on ceramic variation. Iron Age ceramic analysis has expanded our understanding and defining of ceramic patterns that reflect homogeneity and of patterns that reflect differences within ceramic horizons that can be attributed to a multitude of variables (e.g., ethnicity, social stratification, regionalism, trade and economic spheres, technological

[28]For a complete analysis, see Ortiz, "Deconstructing and Reconstructing the United Monarchy," 118–35.

and functional attributes, urban vs. rural societies).[29] I have discussed the issues of the ceramic assumptions of the Low Chronology in previous studies.[30] Finkelstein's theory rests on three domains: homogeneity of assemblages, ethnicity (e.g., distribution of Philistine pottery), and a supposed ninth-century gap in the archaeological record.

## Homogeneity of Assemblages

An underlying methodological assumption of the Low Chronology is that sites in close proximity must contain the same material culture. All relative chronology is based on the degree of homogeneity between ceramic assemblages. The principle of homogeneity in ceramic development is the hallmark for dating and comparing various sites and their strata. Recent trends have confirmed that while ceramic change is consistent within ceramic horizons (the principle of homogeneity), these horizons can contain subsets of different ceramic corpuses (e.g., Philistine monochrome pottery is a particular corpus within the Iron Age IA horizon, but it is not necessarily found at all Iron Age IA sites). The ceramic record is more complex than the simplistic equation of using a single type (form, decoration) to determine chronological relationships between ceramic assemblages. There are several regional variations within the Iron Age ceramic horizon. Variables that influence differences in assemblages are geography, ethnicity, function, and settlement hierarchy.

## Ethnicity

It does not surprise archaeologists that Lachish would not contain Philistine pottery even though the site is in close proximity to known Philistine settlements. Many studies have demonstrated that the hallmark Philistine pottery is concentrated only along the southern coastal plain.[31] It is not necessary to

[29]Bryant G. Wood, *The Sociology of Pottery in Ancient Israel: The Ceramic Industry and the Diffusion of Ceramic Style in the Bronze and Iron Ages* (Sheffield: Sheffield Academic, 1990); Ann E. Killebrew, *Biblical Peoples and Ethnicity: An Archaeological Study of Egyptians, Canaanites, Philistines, and Early Israel 1300–1100 B.C.E.* (Atlanta: Society of Biblical Literature, 2005); John S. Holladay Jr., "The Use of Pottery and Other Diagnostic Criteria, from the Solomonic Era to the Divided Kingdom," in *Biblical Archaeology Today 1990*, ed. Avraham Biran and Joseph Aviram (Jerusalem: Israel Exploration Society, 1993), 86–01.
[30]Ortiz, "Deconstructing and Reconstructing the United Monarchy," 118–35; Ortiz, "Does the Low Chronology Work? A Case Study of Tell Qasile X, Tel Gezer X, and Lachish V," in *"I Will Speak the Riddles of Ancient Times": Archaeological and Historical Studies in Honor of Amihai Mazar on the Occasion of His Sixtieth Birthday*, ed. Aren Maeir and Pierre DeMiroschedji (Winona Lake, IN: Eisenbrauns, 2006), 587–611.
[31]Tristan Barako, "The Philistine Settlement as Mercantile Phenomenon?," *AJA* 104 (2000): 513–30; Trude Dothan and Alexander Zukerman, "A Preliminary Study of the Mycenaean IIIC:1 Pottery Assemblages from Tel Miqne-Ekron and Ashdod," *BASOR* 333 (2004): 1–54; Seymour Gitin, "The Philistines: Neighbors of the Canaanites, Phoenicians and Israelites," in *100 Years of American Archaeology in the Middle East: Proceedings of the American Schools of Oriental Research Centennial*

suggest that the complete Iron Age ceramic horizon needs to be redated just because Lachish does not have Philistine monochrome pottery. The absence of monochrome pottery at Lachish VI is due to an established border (whether cultural or political) between the Lachish Valley and the Philistine coast—and not because archaeologists have their stratigraphy confused.[32]

One of the recent developments in Iron Age ceramics since Finkelstein's initial publication is the identification of late Philistine decorated ware (LPDW), formerly called Ashdod ware.[33] This is a later assemblage of fine ware, dating to the tenth and ninth centuries, that was produced probably in Ashdod and Gath. Ironically, this assemblage is not found at Lachish![34] A major problem for the core principles of the proposed Low Chronology is the dilemma caused by Lachish V and IV (tenth and ninth centuries BC respectively), which do not contain LPDW. Assuming the methodology of the original Low Chronology proposal, sites with LPDW would also have to be changed. The problem is that LPDW also does not exist at Lachish III or II (eighth and seventh centuries BC respectively). The methodological flaw in the Low Chronology is that while the principle of homogeneity of ceramics is valid, some assemblages are found only in specific regions; hence the attempted redating of strata because of the lack of Philistine monochrome during Lachish VI (1200–1150 BC) is invalid. As archaeologists continue to conduct research, and new data are produced from current excavations, the data obtained from ceramic studies continue to invalidate the underlying premises of the Low Chronology.[35]

*Ninth-Century Gap*
One of the issues has been the ninth-century pottery. This ceramic horizon has been elusive to biblical archaeologists and difficult to define. One problem is that tenth-century and ninth-century assemblages are very similar. Finkelstein assumed that the Low Chronology proposal would solve this problem (e.g., all the tenth-century sites are really ninth-century sites). Archaeologists debated and offered various schemes for Iron Age stratigraphy. One of the standard references to come under scrutiny has been Shishak's destruction. Several destruction layers in the archaeological record have been attributed to Pharaoh

---

*Celebration, Washington D.C., April, 2000*, ed. Douglas Clark and Victor Matthews (Boston: American Schools of Oriental Research, 2004), 57–83.

[32] Shlomo Bunimovitz and Avraham Faust, "Chronological Separation, Geographical Segregation, or Ethnic Demarcation? Ethnography and Iron Age Low Chronology," *BASOR* 322 (1996): 1–10.

[33] David Ben-Shlomo, Itzhaq Shai, and Aren M. Maeir, "Late Philistine Decorated Ware ("Ashdod Ware"): Typology, Chronology, and Production Centers," *BASOR* 335 (2004): 1–35.

[34] Although the map presented in ibid. includes Lachish, there is no discussion of this pottery found at the site, nor is it reported in any Lachish excavation reports.

[35] This principle of ceramic variation can also be seen in the distribution of Hippo storage jars (Y. Alexander, "The 'Hippo' Jar and Other Storage Jars at Hurvat Rosh Zayit," *TA* 22 [1995]: 77–88).

Shishak (ca. 925 BC), but since the pottery of the tenth and ninth centuries is very similar, perhaps some of these destructions actually belong to the ninth century and are evidence of various Aramean campaigns. Hence the debate shifted to defining absolute dates for the tenth and ninth centuries. Low Chronology proponents used Jezreel as a site that provided absolute dating. Since Jezreel was founded in the ninth century,[36] its ceramic assemblage provides a standard. Low Chronology proponents redated all tenth-century assemblages to the ninth century (since they are similar and the principle of homogeneity helps in dating them). Several attempts to use the Jezreel Enclosure as a solution to the dating problem focused on pottery, historical dead reckoning, and mason's marks. As stated earlier, the debate shifted to northern sites as major projects were in the field (e.g., Megiddo, Beth Shean, and Tel Rehov). The debate continued with those who supported the standard chronology holding ground as archaeologists found it difficult to cram multistrata sites such as Tel Rehov and Hazor into a single century. Most fell back to the position that these sites illustrate the long tradition of typical tenth-century ceramic forms into the ninth century.[37]

*Radiocarbon Dating*

The methodological tenets of the revisionist Low Chronology are not supported by the ceramic record. The debate quickly shifted to the use of radiocarbon dates to provide the answer for the dating of assemblages. Each side readily produced dates that supported the Low Chronology or the standard chronology.[38] This has been an unfortunate diversion as most radiocarbon dates provide a range of one hundred years, thus offering no solution to a chronological debate that spans less than a hundred years! The irony is that the most recent salvo in the debate from the Low Chronology camp has concluded that the best methodological solution to the carbon dating is to use historical dead reckoning to determine absolute dates of the various carbon-14 samples from the southern Levant. Having gone full circle, archaeologists are returning to using biblical texts and Egyptian and Assyrian campaigns to determine the best C-14 dates![39]

---

[36] As pointed out by other archaeologists (e.g., A. Mazar, "Iron Age Chronology," 157–67; Ben-Tor, "Hazor and the Chronology of Northern Israel," 9–16), the critique of dating tenth-century assemblages because of the biblical text also applies to dating Jezreel based on the biblical text!

[37] Finkelstein has admitted that the Low Chronology still remains the minority position ("Radiocarbon Dating the Iron Age in the Levant: A Bayesian Model for Six Ceramic Phases and Six Transitions," *Antiquity* 84 [2010]: 374–85).

[38] Levy and Higham, *The Bible and Radiocarbon Dating.*

[39] Israel Finkelstein and Eli Piasetzky, "Radiocarbon-Dated Destruction Layers: A Skeleton for Iron Age Chronology in the Levant," *Oxford Journal of Archaeology* 28, no. 3 (2009): 255–74; Finkelstein, "Radiocarbon Dating the Iron Age in the Levant," 374–85.

*State Development*

One of the implications of the Low Chronology model for the archaeology of David and Solomon is the interpretation of David as a small-tribal chiefdom. As stated in the introduction, this has been a major factor in the assumption that the biblical texts created a glorified past. The nature of the material culture is a good indicator of the complexity of society. Another objection the Low Chronology advocates raise with regard to the traditional chronology is the lack of tenth-century monumental structures (e.g., fortifications, palaces, temples, public buildings) in Jerusalem. Also, they have pointed out that most evidence for a state dates to the eighth century, and tenth-century remains (even for the standard chronology) are poorer when compared to the later Iron Age IIB.

One of the methodological fallacies is the simplistic approach to state development relying solely on a trait list. Anthropologists, however, have abandoned the outmoded trait-list method for determining levels of cultural and social complexity, adopting instead processual and systemic approaches to defining a state. Several studies and conferences have attempted to address the variables and trajectories of the Davidic and Solomonic state using anthropological models. Recent research has defined mechanisms of state formation such as center periphery, secondary state formation, ethnicity, and tribalism. An example of such systemic model building is Daniel Master's proposal that Weber's patrimonial model is more pertinent to the tenth century BC than are the previous evolutionary typology models.[40] Alexander Joffe has demonstrated that the tenth century in the southern Levant typifies secondary state formation models.[41] Raz Kletter has used state-formation theory to falsify the tenets of the Low Chronology proposal.[42] None of these models has yet been addressed by Finkelstein and his followers; instead they continue to use the antiquated trait-list approach to determine whether there was a tenth-century state in Judah.

In spite of the paucity of archaeological data, the evidence for a state in the tenth century remains strong, such as architectural features that exhibit a central authority, settlement processes (urbanization, regional standardization, population growth, demographic shifts), historical-architectural analogy, and inscriptions. Most of the evidence is based on the use of anthropological models for state formation.

---

[40] Daniel Master, "State Formation Theory and the Kingdom of Israel," *JNES* 60 (2001): 117–31.

[41] Alexander H. Joffe, "The Rise of Secondary States in the Iron Age Levant," *JESHO* 45, no. 4 (2002): 425–67

[42] Raz Kletter, "Low Chronology and United Monarchy: A Methodological Review," *ZDPV* 120 (2004): 13–54.

## Monumental Architecture

Large public works have been typical identifying features of a state-level society. Evidence of monumental architecture dating to the tenth century BC is found throughout ancient Palestine in the form of large public buildings, fortifications, palaces, and monumental ornamentation. Several large public buildings have been found dating to the tenth century. These buildings are usually associated with gate complexes or palaces. They consist of cobbled flagstone surfaces with several rows of pillars supporting a superstructure. They have been interpreted as stables,[43] storehouses,[44] barracks,[45] and marketplaces.[46] The earliest examples are found along the coast in the eleventh century BC (Qasile and Abu Hawam). This structure becomes common during the ninth century BC as they are found at Megiddo, Lachish, Hazor, Tel el Hesi, and at Beersheba. Regardless of the functional interpretation of these structures, they demonstrate a socio-economic behavior (both quality and quantity) that is found only in state-level societies.

In addition to these large public buildings, several palaces have been excavated.[47] At Megiddo, two palaces were excavated that date to the tenth century BC. All the other palaces so far excavated date to the eighth–seventh centuries BC. David Ussishkin has postulated that Solomon's palace and the Megiddo palaces get their designs from the Syrian types commonly referred to as *bit hilani*.[48] They consist of a portico, throne room, and a great hall. This premise has recently been modified as it is clear that the southern Levant has its own tradition of large palace structures. Sharon and Zarzeki-Peleg have defined the palatial architecture of the Iron Age Levant as lateral-access podium structures (LAP).[49] These are associated with other public structures (usually tripartite

---

[43] Y. Yadin, "The Megiddo Stables," in *Magnalia Dei, the Mighty Acts of God: Essays on the Bible and Archaeology in Memory of G. Ernest Wright*, ed. F. M. Cross, W. E. Lemke, and P. D. Miller (Garden City, NY: Doubleday, 1976), 249–52; J. S. Holladay, "The Stables of Ancient Israel," in *The Archaeology of Jordan and Other Studies Presented to Siegfried H. Horn*, ed. L. T. Geraty and L. G. Herr (Berrien Springs, MI: Andrews University Press, 1986), 103–95.

[44] James Pritchard, "The Megiddo Stables: A Re-Assessment," in *Near Eastern Archaeology in the 20th Century: Essays in Honor of Nelson Glueck*, ed. J. A. Sanders (Garden City, NY: Doubleday, 1970), 268–76; Y. Yadin, *Hazor: The Head of All Those Kingdoms*, The Schweich Lectures of the British Academy 1970 (London: Oxford University Press, 1972), 168.

[45] Volkmar Fritz, *The City in Ancient Israel*, Biblical Seminar 29 (Sheffield: Sheffield Academic, 1995), 142.

[46] Larry G. Herr, "Tripartite Pillared Buildings and the Market Place in Iron Age Palestine," *BASOR* 272 (1988): 47–67.

[47] E.g., Megiddo, Samaria, Hazor, Lachish, Ramat Rahel, Jerusalem.

[48] David Ussishkin, "King Solomon's Palace and Building 1723 in Megiddo," *IEJ* 16 (1966): 174–86.

[49] Ilan Sharon and Anabel Zarzeki-Peleg, "Podium Structures with Lateral Access: Authority Ploys in Royal Architecture in the Iron Age Levant," in *Confronting the Past: Archaeological and Historical Essays on Ancient Israel in Honor of William G. Dever*, ed. Seymour Gitin, Edward Wright, and J. P. Dessel (Winona Lake, IN: Eisenbrauns, 2006), 145–67.

buildings) in an enclosure that is set apart in the city. These buildings are smaller than the *bit hilanis* in northern Syria and are usually square, versus the broad-house of the *bit hilani*. Lehmann and Killebrew have followed up on these palaces and have proposed that a better definition is "central hall tetra-partite residencies."[50] While a majority of these structures date to the ninth and eighth centuries BC, it is clear that they represent a local tradition and possibly first appear in the tenth century. The authors do agree that they are part of a central authority and are royal architectural elements.

In addition to monumental buildings, proto-aeolic capitals have also been found throughout ancient Palestine during the Iron Age. Large capitals are evidence of palatial structures and are only found associated with monumental public buildings. Proto-aeolic capitals[51] have been found at Hazor, Megiddo, Samaria, Jerusalem, and Ramat Rahal.[52]

*Settlement Processes*
One diagnostic feature defining the difference between a state and a chiefdom is settlement processes. Analyses of settlement hierarchy, demographics, and settlement distribution can easily determine the nature of any ancient society. Archaeological surveys and excavations have well documented the process of urbanization in the Iron Age in the western highlands. Surveys of the hill country have shown that there were several small villages and towns that dominated the Ephraim and Manasseh hills. Finkelstein has proposed that the urban planning across the span of the Iron Age demonstrates pastoralists settling down into circular settlements, which eventually evolved into the city plan of the Iron Age II.[53] Site hierarchy distributions show that there was a structural imposition across the landscape that can only be attributed to a state level of societal development.

A new type of house, with four rooms, also appears in sites in the hill country, commonly called the "Israelite four-room house" because it appears so frequently in the western highlands.[54] Population estimates for the Iron

[50]Gunnar Lehmann and Ann E. Killebrew, "Palace 6000 at Megiddo in Context: Iron Age Central Hall Tetra-Partite Residencies and the *Bit-Hilani* Building Tradition in the Levant," *BASOR* 359 (2010): 13–33.
[51]A total of thirty-four, to date (Y. Shiloh, *The Proto-Aeolic Capital*, Qedem 11 [Jerusalem: Israel Exploration Society, 1979]).
[52]One has also been found in Jordan at Meeibiyeh, north of Wadi Hassa.
[53]Israel Finkelstein, *The Archaeology of the Israelite Settlement* (Jerusalem: Israel Exploration Society, 1988). See also Zeev Herzog, "Settlement and Fortification Planning in the Iron Age," in *The Architecture of Ancient Israel: From the Prehistoric to the Persian Periods*, ed. Aharon Kempinski and Ronny Reich (Jerusalem: Israel Exploration Society, 1992), 231–74.
[54]Ehud Netzer, "Domestic Architecture in the Iron Age," in Kempinski and Reich, *The Architecture of Ancient Israel*, 193–201.

Age shows a marked demographic shift between the villages of the Iron Age I and the tenth century BC.

The archaeological record indicates that the rise of urbanization occurred from the Iron Age I to the Iron Age II. It is apparent that the archaeological record does not verify any historical person with these new features, but we can conclude that the record does bear evidence for the rise of a state in ancient Israel dated to the transition between the Iron Age I and Iron Age II periods.

*Jerusalem and Solomon's Temple*

Naturally when we discuss the kingdom of David and Solomon, we must address the capital city of Jerusalem. One of the major arguments used by deniers of a Jerusalem-based state for Israel and the united monarchy is the absence of clear tenth-century structures in Jerusalem despite rather thorough excavation there over the decades.[55] Jerusalem, they reason, could not have been a major capital during this period. It is accurate to note that there is little archaeological data identified in Jerusalem from the united monarchy. This presents a major problem for those who hold to the historicity of the Davidic monarchy. The question that must be raised is, what has caused this pattern in the archaeological record? The assumption of critics is that an absence of data indicates that David and Solomon did not exist or that the biblical account distorts the true nature of their kingdom. This interpretation of the archaeological record does not account for the nature of the archaeology of Jerusalem and demonstrates a naive understanding of the problems of Jerusalem.

The archaeology of Iron Age Jerusalem presents several difficulties. First, Jerusalem is a living city. People currently reside on the site of the ancient city, which allows for only selective areas to be excavated. Second, Jerusalem is a sacred city, and the entire temple mount is off-limits to archaeological investigation. Third, the Iron Age (and Bronze Age) city was built on the crest of the eastern hill with the Tyropean Valley to the west and the Kidron Valley to the east. Since the city was rebuilt throughout history in response to continuous destruction and reoccupation on the crest of the hill, the amount of Iron Age occupation that remains *in situ* is minimal. Another factor to consider is that each rebuilding phase destroyed the previous city in order to get to bedrock. The consequence is an extremely complicated stratigraphical problem for the interpretation of the archaeological record.

---

[55]There were three major excavations: City of David by Y. Shiloh, Southern Wall excavations by B. Mazar, and the Jewish Quarter excavations by N. Avigad. All three were sponsored by the Hebrew University of Jerusalem.

Any interpretation of the archaeology of Jerusalem as it relates to David and Solomon must take into account the complexity of Jerusalem archaeology. The so-called problem of Jerusalem is due largely to the lack of preservation of the archaeological record—not that the city did not exist during the tenth century BC. Nevertheless, recent excavations and the results of the City of David excavations now being published by Y. Shiloh's staff are providing much evidence for Jerusalem during the tenth century.[56] Three major architectural features give evidence of large public buildings that can be associated with a centralized authority. The first is the large stepped-stone structure that serves as a support terrace for the "Large Stone Structure" (popularly referred to as the "palace of King David") recently excavated by Eilat Mazar.[57] The third structure is a series of massive buildings and a water system around the Gihon spring that was originally built during the Middle Bronze Age and was used until the Iron Age IIB period. A. Mazar has provided an updated analysis and summary of these developments in Jerusalem archaeology and their implications for reconstructing the capital of Jerusalem.[58] While he notes that the topography does not allow for a large city to be built, these massive structures do suggest that this city was set apart from other contemporary urban centers of the southern Levant.[59]

Associated with the difficulties in the archaeology of Jerusalem is Solomon's temple. Some scholars are quick to point out that there is no archaeological evidence for the temple of Solomon. This is a straw man argument, a naive assumption of the nature of archaeological data. We do not have archaeological evidence of Herod's temple, but no scholar seriously doubts its existence. Even though there is no archaeological evidence for Solomon's temple, a standard methodological approach within material-culture studies—typology and classification—can be used to address the archaeological realia of the description of the temple in the biblical texts.[60]

Archaeologists can look at the evolution and development of temples throughout the ancient Near East and make comparisons between the temple built by Solomon and other cultic structures found in excavations.

---

[56]Eilat Mazar, *The Palace of King David: Excavations at the Summit of the City of David, Preliminary Report of Seasons 2005–2007* (Jerusalem: Shoham Academic Research and Publication, 2009); Jane M. Cahill, "Jerusalem at the Time of the United Monarchy: The Archaeological Evidence," in *Jerusalem in Bible and Archaeology: The First Temple Period*, ed. A. Vaughn and A. Killebrew, SBLSymS 18 (Atlanta: Society of Biblical Literature, 2003), 31–80.

[57]E. Mazar, "Did I Find King David's Palace?," *BAR* 32, no. 1 (2006): 16–27; and E. Mazar, *The Palace of King David*.

[58]A. Mazar, "Archaeology and the Biblical Narrative," 34–49.

[59]Ibid., 34.

[60]See for example John Monson, "The 'Ain Dara Temple: Closest Solomon Parallel," *BAR* 26, no. 3 (2000): 20–35, 67, and his forthcoming book with Oxford University Press.

Several temples have been excavated from the Early Bronze Age to the Roman Period in Syro-Palestine. When one compares these temples, the description of Solomon's temple corresponds with cultic structures of the Iron I–II transition. Temple architecture is one of the best examples we have for the evolution of architectural forms and influences. The tripartite temple has been well established as an early Iron Age form. The religious architecture of the southern Levant has a consistent evolution from the second millennium to the first across many geographical zones. The description of the Jerusalem temple in the biblical text has a *Sitz im Leben* in the Iron Age I–IIA period. Ironically, while there is no archaeological evidence[61] for the temple, using comparative typology based on the archaeology of religious structures of the southern Levant validates the description of the temple found in 2 Kings.

Perhaps the most common comparison has been between Solomon's temple and the Tayanat temple found in Syria.[62] Recently, renewed investigations have found a similar temple at 'Ain Dara, also in northern Syria. The published excavation report of the 'Ain Dara temple shows close parallels to the biblical description of Solomon's temple. Now, just because we find a temple in Syria, that does not prove the existence of Solomon's temple. As the corpus of ancient Near Eastern temples continues to grow, evidence from comparative analysis of temple architecture strongly suggests that the temple of Solomon fits within a tenth-century-BC architectural tradition of tripartite temples.

*Recent Discoveries: Edom and the Elah Valley*
Two recent excavations have made an impact on the discussion concerning state formation in the southern Levant. The first are the excavations at Khirbet en-Nahas in the Feinan region, east of Wadi Arabah in Jordan. These excavations are directed by T. Levy. A large-scale copper mining industry has been discovered. Carbon-14 dates place it in the tenth–ninth centuries. A large citadel and administrative buildings are dated by the excavation team to the tenth century BC.[63] Levy proposes that this site demonstrates that Edom was a centralized polity beginning in the tenth century with an extensive trade network, indicating that the same developments could have been in progress on the west side of the Jordan River.

Khirbet Qeiyafa, two kilometers east of Azekah, north of the Elah Valley, is a single-period fortified settlement dated to the early part of the tenth

---

[61]Some have challenged the historicity of the Bible since there is no evidence for the temple. Ironically, no one questions the existence of the Second Temple even though this temple also lacks an archaeological footprint.

[62]Monson, "The 'Ain Dara Temple," 20–35, 67.

[63]T. Levy et al., "Reassessing the Chronology of Biblical Edom: New Excavations and 14C Dates from Khirbet en-Nahas (Jordan)," *Antiquity* 78 (2004): 865–79.

century BC.[64] This site consists of a town with a massive stone casemate wall and a four-chambered gate. While this is a new project and the results are tentative, there is no doubt that this unknown site has major implications for the debate over state formation in the southern Levant. The nature of the site implies a centralized state in Judah, particularly as it sits on the border between Judah and Philistia. The dating of the site is key because it implies a major political border in the tenth century and possibly even before.[65] (For a detailed treatment of Khirbet Qeiyafa, see chapter 21, by Michael Hasel.)

While both these sites are still being excavated and analyzed, they have already altered the discussion regarding state development in the tenth century.[66] Current archaeological research continues to demonstrate that the traditional model of state formation beginning in the tenth century BC is the most accurate reconstruction of the history and evolution of the state in the southern Levant.

*Summary of State Formation*

Research has started to illustrate that there are a multitude of variables when it comes to defining a state in the Iron Age. Researchers need to define the political and ethnic borders, sociological variables that influence the ceramic patterns—such as ceramic industry, production, and distribution—ethnicity in the archaeological record, and the use of ethnoarchaeological models. The contention that there is no evidence for David and Solomon at Jerusalem is a straw man argument by proponents of the Low Chronology because all the evidence for the state is conveniently moved to the ninth century! As recent excavations are demonstrating, the evidence continues to support a state in the tenth century in the western highlands with a center in Jerusalem. The biblical texts have a tendency to speak in hyperbole regarding the grandeur of Jerusalem, but it is not unusual for a nation to develop high praise for its capital or for biblical prophets to speak metaphorically of Jerusalem. The irony is that it is critical biblical scholars who, insisting on a literalistic reading of the biblical texts, expect to find a large urban center for David's capital

---

[64]Yosef Garfinkel and Saar Ganor, eds. *Khirbet Qeiyafa*, vol. 1, *Excavation Report 2007–2008* (Jerusalem: Israel Exploration Society, 2009).

[65]Not discussed in this essay, but a key site for the nature of the Jerusalem-based state in the tenth century BC, is the site of Beth Shemesh. The new excavations of Khirbet Qeiyafa only strengthen the tenth-century boundary between Judah and Philistia as proposed by the Tel Beth Shemesh excavation project. See Shlomo Bunimovitz and Zvi Lederman, "The Iron Age Fortifications of Tel Beth-Shemesh: A 1990–2000 Perspective," *IEJ* 51 (2001): 121–48.

[66]See discussion in Finkelstein, "A Great United Monarchy," and A. Mazar, "Archaeology and the Biblical Narrative."

rather than a more modest center for a nation in its infancy. More urban development, city planning, and monumental architecture become apparent after a century of centralized authority. This is the pattern that we find in the archaeological record.[67]

### Archaeology and the Biblical Text

The fourth methodological comment concerns the correlation between the archaeological and biblical record. The paradigm of the New Archaeology succeeded in separating the two disciplines of biblical studies and Syro-Palestinian archaeology. On the one hand, this was good because archaeologists work with a different data set than do biblical scholars; on the other hand, it was also unfortunate because now we tend to talk past each other, usually in a polemical manner. This point is pertinent because it frames an important interpretive element of Iron Age archaeology. Would archaeologists reconstruct a unified state in the tenth century if we did not have the biblical text, particularly the narratives of the united monarchy? The question of the historicity of David became moot with the discovery in 1993 of the House of David inscription (e.g., Tel Dan inscription, Aramaic inscription from Tel Dan).

The early days of biblical archaeology found that there was a tendency to force a one-to-one correlation between the archaeological record and the textual record. Earlier scholars were derided as fundamentalist. Those who viewed the biblical text as reflecting historical trajectories were accused of having an agenda and forcing the data into their particular mold. The irony is that method and theory within Syro-Palestinian archaeology has advanced beyond the simple equation of text = artifact. Critics of the state in the tenth century appear to be the ones forcing the data into a particular mold.

Does archaeology conclusively prove David and Solomon existed with a capital in Jerusalem? I would have to say no. If the question is rephrased as to whether there is archaeological evidence for a state in the hill country in the tenth century BC, I would answer in the affirmative. When it comes to research on the Israelite settlement, conquest, and state development, archaeological research illustrates that there are multiple variables to consider. Again, researchers need to define the political and ethnic borders, sociological factors that influence the ceramic patterns, ethnicity in the archaeological record, and the use of ethnoarchaeological models. Recent epigraphic finds, new comparative temples in Syria, renewed evaluation of the data in light of historical processes (e.g., urbanization and sedantarization), and more sophisticated

---

[67]Lehmann and Killebrew, "Palace 6000 at Megiddo in Context," 13–33. Zeev Herzog, "Administrative Structures in the Iron Age," in Kempinski and Reich, *The Architecture of Ancient Israel*, 223–30; Sharon and Zarzeki-Peleg, "Podium Structures with Lateral Access," 145–67.

ceramic analyses demonstrate that a state existed in the hill country in the tenth century BC. Given the epigraphic evidence[68] and the biblical narrative, I believe we can confidently associate this state found in the archaeological record with the Davidic monarchy.

The question archaeologists and biblical historians must address is whether the Low Chronology is supported by the data. Finkelstein's David is reduced to a tribal chief controlling a loose group of tribes. His reconstruction works only if we move the Iron Age ceramic horizon down a century. It is logical to conclude that if we move the villages of the eleventh century BC in the western highlands down to the tenth century, and the archaeological evidence for a state in the tenth century down to the ninth century, David becomes only a tribal king. But before the reconstructions of the Low Chronology can be offered as a viable hypothesis, Finkelstein needs to provide convincing evidence for his redating. It appears that today, when we discuss the archaeology of David and Solomon, we are back at the beginning. It still comes down to the pottery. I propose that recent revisionist approaches to the historicity of the united monarchy are wrong, if not disingenuous, in their historical reconstruction of the tenth century BC.

---

[68]See discussion in Kitchen, *On the Reliability of the Old Testament*, 92–93.

# CONTRIBUTORS

**Richard E. Averbeck** (PhD, Dropsie College/Annenberg Research Institute), Professor of Old Testament and Semitic Languages, Trinity Evangelical Divinity School

**Robert D. Bergen** (PhD, Southwestern Baptist Theological Seminary), Professor of Old Testament and Biblical Languages; Associate Dean of Academic Affairs, Hannibal-LaGrange University

**Craig L. Blomberg** (PhD, Aberdeen University, Scotland), Distinguished Professor of New Testament, Denver Seminary

**Darrell L. Bock** (PhD, Aberdeen University, Scotland), Research Professor of New Testament Studies, Dallas Theological Seminary

**Graham A. Cole** (ThD, Australian College of Theology), Anglican Professor of Divinity, Beeson Theological School

**Robert B. Chisholm Jr.** (PhD, Dallas Theological Seminary), Professor of Old Testament, Dallas Theological Seminary

**Thomas W. Davis** (PhD, University of Arizona), Associate Professor of Archaeology and Biblical Backgrounds, Southwestern Baptist Theological Seminary

**Michael G. Hasel** (PhD, University of Arizona), Professor of Near Eastern Studies and Archaeology, Southern Adventist University

**Michael A. G. Haykin** (PhD, University of Toronto), Professor of Church History and Biblical Spirituality, The Southern Baptist Theological Seminary

**Richard S. Hess** (PhD, Hebrew Union College), Earl S. Kalland Professor of Old Testament and Semitic Languages, Denver Seminary

**John W. Hilber** (PhD, Cambridge University), Associate Professor of Old Testament, Dallas Theological Seminary

**James K. Hoffmeier** (PhD, University of Toronto), Professor of Near Eastern Archaeology and Old Testament, Trinity Evangelical Divinity School

**Jens Bruun Kofoed** (PhD, University of Aarhus), Associate Professor of Old Testament, Copenhagen Lutheran School of Theology

**Dennis R. Magary** (PhD, University of Wisconsin-Madison), Associate Professor of Old Testament and Semitic Languages, Trinity Evangelical Divinity School

**Thomas H. McCall** (PhD, Calvin Theological Seminary), Associate Professor of Biblical and Systematic Theology, Trinity Evangelical Divinity School

**Alan R. Millard** (MPhil, Oxford; MA, University of London), Emeritus Rankin Professor of Hebrew and Semitic Studies, University of Liverpool

**John M. Monson** (PhD, Harvard University), Associate Professor of Old Testament and Semitic Languages, Trinity Evangelical Divinity School

**Steven M. Ortiz** (PhD, University of Arizona), Associate Professor of Archaeology and Biblical Backgrounds, Southwestern Theological Seminary

**Eckhard J. Schnabel** (PhD, Aberdeen University, Scotland), Professor of New Testament, Trinity Evangelical Divinity School

**Richard L. Schultz** (PhD, Yale University), Carl Armerding and Hudson T. Armerding Professor of Biblical Studies/Professor of Old Testament, Wheaton College

**Jason Stanghelle** (PhD candidate, Trinity Evangelical Divinity School)

**Mark D. Thompson** (DPhil, Oxford University), Head of Department of Theology, Philosophy, and Ethics, Moore Theological College, Australia

**Willem A. VanGemeren** (PhD, University of Wisconsin-Madison), Professor of Old Testament, Trinity Evangelical Divinity School

**Robert W. Yarbrough** (PhD, Aberdeen University, Scotland), Professor of New Testament, Covenant Theological Seminary

# GENERAL INDEX

Robinson, J. A. T., 397
Rofé, Alexander, 182
Rogers, Jack, 16, 91
Rollston, Christopher, 494
Roloff, Jürgen, 385
Roman Catholic Church, on inerrancy,
    14–15
Römer, Thomas, 463, 464
Rost, Leonard, 478
Rousso, Henry, 310
Rowley, H. H., 270

Sabbath, 118
*Sachkritik*, 65
Said, Edward, 308
Salamis, 414–16, 418–20, 421
salvation, Irenaeus on, 144
Sanders, J. A., 285–86, 287
Sargon II, 280
Sarna, Nahum M., 166
Sasson, Jack M., 226
satraps, 277
Saul, 191–94
sayings on the cross, 375–77
Schenk, Wolfgang, 386
Schiffman, Lawrence, 334, 335, 337,
    342
Schleiermacher, Friedrich, 58n12, 63,
    383
Schmidt, J. E. C., 383
Schmidt, K. L., 327
Schniedewind, William M., 240
Schwartz, Barry, 314, 318–19
Schweitzer, Albert, 20, 339
Scott, Ernest F., 396n55
Scott, R., 387
Scottish common sense realism, 78
scribal artifacts, 241
scribal class, 240
Scripture. *See* Bible
Second Isaiah. *See* Deutero-Isaiah
Second Temple Judaism, 372
secularism, in biblical scholarship, 154
Seebert, Reinhold, 139
Seitz, Christopher, 245n13, 254
semantic features, 203, 205
Semler, Johann Salomo, 17, 91n60
*sensus divinitatis*, 38
Septuagint, 190–91

Sergius Paulus, 418, 421
settlement processes, 510–11
Sexton, George, 333
Sha'arayim, 495
Shanks, Hershel, 334–36, 342
Sharon, Ilan, 509
Shema, 468
shift stories, 329–33, 341
Shiloh, Y., 485, 511n55, 512
Silberman, Neil Asher, 106, 481,
    482n33, 483
Simon, Richard, 90n60
Singer-Avitz, L., 491–92
*Sitz im Leben*, 328, 337, 480
Ska, Jean-Louis, 159, 165, 167, 168–69
skeptical theism, 54n69
skepticism, of Bible, 13, 155–56
Smith, Gary, 249
Smith, Mark, 306, 312, 313
social memory, 304
Society of Biblical Literature, 111
Socinians, on accommodation, 16–17,
    65–66, 90–91
Solomon, 456–57, 477, 497–500,
    512–13, 515
Sommer, Benjamin, 252
Song of Deborah, 121
Song of Miriam, 121
Song of Moses, 121
source criticism, 33, 107–8, 151, 164–
    67, 181–99, 313–14, 478–79
southern kingdom, 461
Sparks, Kenton, 13–18, 21–23, 41,
    46–51, 52, 76n19, 91, 111, 280,
    356
    on accommodation, 64–66
    on believing criticism, 301, 453–55
    criticism of Alexander, 161, 167,
        169, 181n1
    as disenchanted evangelical, 342–43
    on exodus, 107–9
    on negative evidence, 486n64
    pilgrimage as "shift story," 328, 329,
        331, 333–37
    on problem of Isaiah, 247–60
    rejection of harmonization, 360, 364
    on Septuagint, 190
    on traditional responses to biblical
        criticism, 346
    on Wellhausen, 339

# SCRIPTURE INDEX